Qualitative Research in Social Work

Qualitative Research in Social Work

Second Edition

EDITED BY

ANNE E. FORTUNE
WILLIAM J. REID
ROBERT L. MILLER, JR.

Columbia University Press   New York

Columbia University Press
Publishers Since 1893
New York   Chichester, West Sussex
cup.columbia.edu
Copyright © 2013 Columbia University Press
All rights reserved

Library of Congress Cataloging-in-Publication Data

Qualitative research in social work / edited by Anne E. Fortune, William J. Reid,
Robert L. Miller, Jr. — 2nd ed.
p. cm.
Includes bibliographical references and index.
ISBN 978-0-231-16138-1 (cloth : alk. paper) — ISBN 978-0-231-16139-8 (pbk. : alk. paper) —
ISBN 978-0-231-53544-1 (ebook)
1. Social service—Research—Methodology. 2. Qualitative research.
I. Fortune, Anne E., 1945– II. Reid, William James, 1928– III. Miller, Robert L., Jr.

HV11.Q28 2012
361.3072—dc23

2012036492

c 10 9 8 7 6 5 4 3 2 1
p 10 9 8 7 6 5 4 3 2 1

Cover design: Milenda Nan Ok Lee

References to websites (URLs) were accurate at the time of writing. Neither the author nor
Columbia University Press is responsible for URLs that may have expired or changed since
the manuscript was prepared.

Contents

Contents

Contents

Preface

An increasing problem in many countries is the aging of the population, necessitating family caregiving that may pose serious burdens on the caregiving individuals. How should a researcher approach the burdens and strategies of caregiving? Here are two examples:

EXAMPLE 1:

Lai and Thompson (2011) contacted 340 family members who cared for an elderly person. They conducted a telephone interview with each family member and gave them a structured questionnaire that included measures of caregiving burden, demographics, and social support. They used statistical methods to assess the impact of perceived adequacy of social support on the caregiving burden among male and female caregivers; that is, did caregivers who thought they received more support feel less of a burden? Part of the results of their multiple regressions are included in table 1.

The authors conclude: "Perceived adequacy of social support was the most important correlate of caregiving burden for female caregivers and the second most important correlate of caregiving burden for male caregivers. For both male and female caregivers, the perceived adequacy of

Table 1 Portion of Multiple Regression, Predictors of Caregiving Burden

Variable	Beta	
	Females ($n = 249$)	Males ($n = 91$)
Caregiver age	−0.06	0.10
Caregiver marital status (married)	−0.02	−0.09
Caregiver education	0.17*	0.08
Caregiver self-rated financial adequacy	−0.03	−0.31*
Caregiver being primary caregiver	0.20*	0.26*
Caregiver months of providing care	0.09	0.13
Number of illnesses of care-receiver	0.22*	0.25*
Adequacy of caregiving activity support	−0.24*	−0.39*
Adequacy of financial and material support	−0.19*	−0.07
Adequacy of emotional support	−0.11	0.17
Adjusted R-squared	0.33	0.45

Table adapted from: Lai, D. W. L. and C. Thomson (2011). "The impact of perceived adequacy of social support on caregiving burden of family caregivers." *Families in Society*, 92(1):99–106.

*$p ≤ .05$

social support variables accounted for a larger proportion of the variance of caregiving burden than did the health of the care receivers. (2011:104)."

EXAMPLE 2:

Thornton and Hopp (2011) interviewed seven adult daughters who were caring for their parents with heart failure, using four open-ended questions about the illness, the most challenging thing about caregiving, assistance with caregiving, and what might improve their caregiving. They used a phenomenological approach and several steps of coding to analyze themes (caregiving stress and caregiver coping strategies). Here is part of what they had to say about valuing the caregiver role (a subtheme of caregiver coping strategies):

Several daughters reported receiving recognition from others in their community for their caregiving. This recognition was very important to the caregivers and seemed to help sustain them in their difficult vocation. As one caregiver explained, "There's a lot of people with kids and they be telling her, 'I wish I had your daughter for a daughter,' because I take care of my mother." Valuing the caregiving role, evidenced by reflecting on caregiving qualities, identifying caregiving benefits, and accepting community validation for caregiving, helped the caregivers cope with the stressors of their work (Thornton and Hopp 2011:214).

Although the two examples deal with similar topics, they represent very different approaches to social work research. Example 1 is, of course, a quantitative research study. It relies on standardized questionnaires with the assumption that the questions have the same meaning for everyone, involves a fairly large number of participants, uses statistics to look at the relationship between social support and caregiving burden, and enlists probability to determine the likelihood of a "true" relationship. Example 2 is a qualitative research study. It relies on a set of open-ended stimulus questions, queries a small number of participants but involves in-depth questions about the topic, and determines participants' key themes through the researchers' interpretation using a systematic multi-level coding procedure. Instead of statistics, it uses the participants' own words to illustrate and validate the themes.

Example 1, the quantitative study, can give the relation between social support and caregiving burden for the hypothetical average caregiver. It cannot tell what that support looks like nor how an individual felt if she did or did not get the support she expected. Example 2, the qualitative study, can determine how the women perceived the support, what it meant to them, and in this case, what type of support was useful. In this particular study, however, whether support increased or decreased the caregiver burden cannot be determined.

This book is about qualitative research methodology in social work, example 2. The first edition of Edmund Sherman and William J. Reid's (1994) *Qualitative Research in Social Work* was one of the earliest attempts to present qualitative methods from a social work point of view. At a time of epistemological debates but not much actual research, it included not only methodology but exemplary social work research and commentaries from most of the seminal researchers of the time. It quickly became an essential text for those learning qualitative methodologies.

Qualitative methodology in social work has evolved rapidly since 1994. In 1998, Deborah Padgett completed the first edition of her qualitative text, and in 2008, the second. Ian Shaw and Nick Gould (2001) also published a qualitative textbook. In 2002, Ian Shaw and Roy Ruckdeschel launched the international journal, *Qualitative Social Work: Research and Practice.* Many standard research texts added sections on qualitative methods (see, for example, Grinnell and Unrau 2011 and Rubin and Babbie 2008). Qualitative researchers were accepted at the Society for Social Work Research (SSWR) and developed a robust qualitative working group. Between 1990 and 2007, among peer-reviewed articles included in the database *Social Work Abstracts,* qualitative studies increased four times as rapidly as quantitative studies (still, in 2006/07 there were five times as many quantitative as qualitative studies) (Miller 2008). The National Institutes of Health funded qualitative research proposals in areas such as HIV-AIDS disease, drug abuse, domestic violence, and child welfare. Social work training in qualitative research methods increased at the doctoral level in social work education and through workshops sponsored by organizations such as SSWR, the Institute for the Advancement of Social Work Practice Research (IASWR), and various universities.

This volume, *Qualitative Research in Social Work,* second edition, is an effort to move social work qualitative research to the next level of innovation and relevance—to that of building knowledge about social work. It documents current application of qualitative methodology at many levels of social work practice. It tackles old and new research issues such as quality, ethics, and epistemological stance. It includes the most recent ideas about data collection and analysis and integrates these with examples of knowledge development for social work practice. As an edited book, it includes diverse and authoritative accounts from multiple social work researchers.

Qualitative Research

In introducing this volume, an initial question is: What is qualitative research? Although everyone "understands" qualitative research, there is no simple or easy definition. Deborah Padgett (2004:xvii–xvii) suggests "qualitative studies are arrayed along multiple continua based upon epistemology, methodology, mode of presentation, and audience." In the first of these continua, qualitative research can be understood as an epistemological or paradigmatic stance, a statement of what can be known—constructions of the world—and how it can be known. Such qualitative epistemologies derive from Greek rationalist theory that emphasized reason as the means of knowing (versus experience or empiricism) and rejected the ability of easily mistaken senses/physical experience to provide knowledge (Reamer 1993). Knowledge is thus understood as a social construction—a worldview for groups of people. Since the infusion of critical theories in the 1980s, qualitative research includes specific approaches that view the world from the perspective of particular (usually disadvantaged) groups. These critical theories include feminist, postmodern, poststructural, race theory, queer theory, Third World perspectives, and intersectionality (LeCompte 2002). The commonality among them is the rationalist belief that reality is defined by the perceiver (or community of perceivers), and that human experience should be described from the critical perspective of nondominant groups.

Quantitative epistemologies, by contrast, derive from Greek empiricist theory that the senses provide the basis for understanding knowledge. If you cannot sense it, it is not there; and if it exists, you (and everyone else) must be able to sense it. Such empiricist theory led in social work to Walter Hudson's infamous first axiom of treatment: "if you cannot measure the client's problem, it does not exist"(Hudson 1978:65). Variants of empiricism include logical positivism and postpositivism; they assume that truth is real and can be measured.

Padgett's second continuum—methodology—varies from highly structured to barely structured methods of data collection and analysis. Qualitative research tends to use less structured approaches while avoiding methods that assume a single interpretation, such as the closed-ended questions that are favorites of quantitative survey researchers. Primary methods of collecting data include case study, ethnography, observation, participant observation, and interviewing (both structured and unstructured, group and individual). Primary methods of analyzing data include content analysis, narrative analysis, grounded theory, and phenomenology. The data analysis and results are usually expressed in words rather than other symbols. Most data-gathering and analysis methods can be used regardless of rationalist epistemology; but some are integrated into an epistemological gestalt, for example, Marxist approaches that focus on social structural determinants. If theory-specific methods are identified as different methodologies, the count of available qualitative methods can soar. Yanow and Schwartz-Shea (2006:xx), for example, list 34 interpretive methods.

The oldest approach to data collection and analysis is ethnography, which combines participant observation and interviewing to describe a culture. Most historians suggest ethnography started in the late nineteenth or early twentieth century in anthropology and sociology (for example, Bronislaw Malinowski, Margaret Mead, E. E. Evans-Pritchard, Gregory Bateson, Claude Lévi-Strauss, Franz Boas). Others, however, date the first use of ethnography to the ninth century when a Persian anthropologist (Abū Rayhān Bīrūnī) studied culture in India (Ahmed 1984) or to the sixteenth century when a Franciscan friar (Bernardino de Sahagún) cataloged Aztec culture (León-Portilla 2002).

Padgett's third continuum—mode of presentation of qualitative research (primarily written)—includes many voices or "ethical and emotional modes of expression that writers use to influence how audiences will understand a text" (Lindlof and Taylor 2002:283). Social work authors tend to use a straightforward descriptive approach with the researcher having a neutral voice, called a realist voice by Smith (2006). Reports may also be reflexive, with the focus on the individual writer's standpoint or on the process of making inferences. Sandelowski (1998) suggests that the ideal presentation style reflects the purpose of the research: If the purpose is to describe participants' viewpoints, the description highlights the participants and their multiple voices, with little focus on the researcher; if the purpose is theory development, the description focuses on the process of developing theory, with participants' data as examples rather than the central focus. On the other hand, alternative forms of presentation include confessional tales—the researchers' trials and tribulations, shifting narrative focus from culture to sense-making; impressionistic tales that produce richly developed characters, scenarios, and plots that illustrate themes; and critical tales that depict social structure from the point of view of disadvantaged groups and advocate morally for social, political, and economic justice (Sandelowski 1998; Lindlof and Taylor 2002). Presentation of results also takes nonwritten forms, such as photographs (Molloy 2007; Hergenrather, Rhodes, Cowan, Bardhoshi, and Pula 2009; Munn 2012), rap (William-White 2011), movies (Lindlof and Taylor 2002), and web videos on YouTube (Wesch 2008). (These newer forms of presentation are also often forms of data collection.)

The fourth of Padgett's categories is audience for qualitative research. Pragmatically, the audiences tend to be other qualitative researchers within a particular discipline (e.g., education, psychology, health, political science, organizational management, geography, etc.). However, Alasuutari (2010) argues that, since the fourteenth century, the purpose of research has been governments' need for information so that policy decisions can be depoliticized. He traces shifts in research paradigms to changes in governance and to dissatisfaction with the information provided by the then-dominant approaches. For example, neoliberal government interested in incentivizing individuals to make money needs information that will motivate individuals, not quantitative statistics. Thus, qualitative approaches arose as responses to dissatisfaction with information from quantitative empirical and humanist rational approaches. Later, critical approaches emerged to give voice to marginalized groups and to attempt to change perceptions of dominant groups. Miller, for example, views social work research as advocacy for people who have been marginalized or oppressed (see chapter 3, this volume).

Another audience for qualitative research is the participants themselves. Action research, for example, is explicitly intended to enlighten and empower the participants. At times, it is difficult to find the line between research and community organizing (for examples, see Molloy 2007; Duffy 2011). Other projects rely on participants and their neighbors to validate the research while informing the audience—for example, asking participants to explain their PhotoVoice collages to stakeholders (Ohmer, Warner, and Beck 2010; Freedman, Pitner, White-Johnson, and Hastie 2012).

The notion of qualitative research as continuums in four categories—epistemology, methodology, mode of presentation, and audience (Padgett 2004)—is helpful in sorting out the key elements but does not help much with a definition that can encompass all qualitative research. Consequently, we use dimensions that distinguish qualitative from quantitative research studies (Fraser, Taylor, Jackson, and O'Jack 1991; Fortune and Reid 1999; Padgett 2008). The dimensions include (i) assumptions about truth or shared reality; (ii) the role of objectivity in conducting research; (iii) the researcher's role as an insider (emic) or outsider (etic); (iv) whether data is gathered using predetermined, uniform methods that assume a stimulus has the same meaning to everyone; (v) data analysis using inductive or deductive logic and quantification; (vi) relevance of value-driven research; and (vii) the process of developing knowledge for social work intervention. As outlined in table 2, qualitative research assumes (i) that reality is socially constructed and meaning is subjective, contextual, and relativistic; (ii) the researcher is a human instrument whose self-knowledge and reflexivity are part of the research process; (iii) the researcher as an insider attempts to understand others' social reality; (iv) meaning is constructed

Table 2 Dimensions of Qualitative and Quantitative Research in Social Work

Dimension	Qualitative Research	Quantitative Research
(i) what is reality	Reality is socially constructed and does not have the same meaning to everyone, but meanings can be compared dialectically. Meaning is subjective, contextual, and relativistic. No foundational process by which truth or falsity of constructions can be determined.	There is an objective reality with knowable patterns, yet the world is imperfectly known and imperfectly measurable. There are many ways of inquiring about meaning, including experimentation and observation.
(ii) role of objectivity	Quantification is reductionist and invalid. Researcher is the instrument for understanding, so self-knowledge and reflexivity are important.	Researcher bias is reduced through structured research methods. Knowledge is developed through replication and replacement of old theories, with a community of peers reviewing and criticizing and offering competing theories to explain phenomena.
(iii) role of researcher	Researcher is insider trying to understand construction of meaning (emic). Empathic understanding of social phenomena from individual points of view.	Researcher is outsider (etic) who deduces variables, creates stimuli (e.g., questionnaires) and follows a set of rules for establishing causality.
(iv) how get data	Individual construction of meaning from individual/others (inductive). Use interviewing, observation, records, etc. Methods unstructured, flexible, and may change.	Assumes stimuli have the same meaning to each participant and that it is the meaning researcher intended. Use interviewing, observations, records, and so on. Methods structured, often standardized, are the same for all participants, and do not change during the study.

(v) how analyze and report data	Analysis uses systematic logic, intuition; primarily inductive (data to theory). Data reported primarily in words.	Logic is primarily deductive (theory to data). Quantification: Categorize, count, statistical manipulation ("number crunching"). Rules for causal order. Data reported in statistical tables and words.
(vi) relevance of values	All activity is value-driven so researcher must acknowledge values. Many approaches are explicitly value-driven, for example, Marxist, feminist standpoint. Some use perspective of oppressed to correct oppressors' knowledge.	Attempt neutrality.
(vii) how knowledge is developed	Develop knowledge by constructing individual definitions of social phenomena that are compared dialectically. Good for understanding complex phenomena—depth and contextualized.	Logic-based rules of causal order to draw inferences. Use many methods and designs, replicate results, critique, relate to theory. Knowledge is incremental and requires "critical multiplism" and replication.

Dimensions and descriptions are synthesized from Fraser, Taylor, Jackson, and O'Jack (1991) and Fortune and Reid (1999).

from others using frequently changing methods; (v) logic is primarily inductive, from the data to conclusion, and results are reported in narratives or visual symbols; (vi) research is value-driven and the researcher may use values to understand and change others; and (vii) knowledge is developed by constructing and comparing individual realities.

These dimensions permit an inclusive definition of qualitative research as a range of epistemologies, methods of sampling, data generation, data analysis, and inference. While such a broad multidimensional definition has advantages, it can also lead to poor quality research if researchers do not strive for consistency of research questions, epistemology, and data-gathering/data-analysis methods. Drisko's chapter (chapter 1 in this volume) on standards provides such guidelines for any specific qualitative study.

Qualitative Social Work Research

A second question important to this volume is why *social work* qualitative research? Why not rely on some of the superb and seminal interdisciplinary texts? Social work has been negatively characterized as a discipline that borrows and adapts other fields' knowledge, and it seems to be a source of professional pride to establish its own knowledge-production (see Shaw, chapter 14, this volume). Beyond such reputational concern, there are several reasons for distinguishing social work qualitative research from qualitative research in other fields. One is the oft-cited parallels between qualitative research methods and social work practice. Both qualitative research methods and social work practice assume a goal to understand the other's reality, sensitivity to context, and reflexivity or use of self to gather and process data (Gilgun 1994 and chapter 5, this volume; Postmus, chapter 10). Both require sophisticated interviewing skills, observation skills, and getting perceptions through direct and indirect means (Fortune 1994). Both require similar data-processing methods and logic (Lang 1994; Gilgun chapter 5). The first edition of *Qualitative Research in Social Work* centered on these parallels between practice and qualitative research. Gilgun's (1994:115) famous analogy is that grounded theory research is "natural to social work practitioners, like sliding a hand into a well-made glove."

As compelling as these parallels may be, particularly for qualitative contributions to practice knowledge, the analogy has boundaries. Ultimately, research and practice have different purposes. Research intends to describe so others may understand, while the goal of practice is action and change for a specific individual or group (Fortune 1994). The qualitative researcher suspends the external frame of reference, while the practitioner makes decisions about practice action and in so doing must turn to outside interpretations of normative reality. The purpose of research—even applied research—is to understand the construction of reality, to inform knowledge. That information must be worth studying and communicating whether one calls the meaning for others transferability or generalization. As part of transferability, the researcher's ability to describe results convincingly is paramount; it is extensively discussed as credibility or believability (see, for example, Drisko, chapter 1). In social work practice, the constructed reality is private between the client and practitioner. There is no need or expectation to communicate the reality to others. Indeed, ethics about confidentiality preclude such communication. The data are not given to become public, as they are in research.

A second reason for distinguishing social work qualitative research from qualitative research in general is that it is intended to be applied research; that is, unlike "pure" research intended solely to generate knowledge, we expect topics and results to have some usefulness for social work practice. It is not by accident that the exemplar chapters in this volume deal with child welfare and social service delivery systems with assessment to inform intervention, rather than classroom dynamics (education), cultural groups (anthropology), or civic responsibility (sociology).

Another area where qualitative research in social work research differs from many other disciplines is its wedding with social work values and ethics. Good social work research focuses on topics consistent with these values—vulnerable and oppressed populations, social and economic justice, social problems, health disparities, and so on. Thus topics like family violence, foster care, homelessness, living with a mental illness, and living with HIV/AIDS, while not exclusive to social work, are more likely to be subjects of research in social work. Social work researchers are more likely to evaluate service programs, explore barriers to service, and look at clients' reactions to service. Similarly, social work and qualitative research share emphasis on diversity and culture and on the environmental context that drives individual or group behavior. See, for example, Frame (chapter 18), Rennis et al. (chapter 8), or Riessman (chapter 7), this volume.

One effect of social work's emphasis on vulnerable groups is that some research ethics issues are more salient for social work qualitative research than for other disciplines. How does one's identities as, for example, gay/female/Christian/disabled affect one's understanding of others like or unlike oneself? Can and should one gain access and credibility to both clients and authority-wielding caseworkers? How much do participants have to know about the researcher's intentions? How should the researcher handle conflicts in interpretation among participants? Will a mother lose her children to child protective services if the researcher violates confidentiality? How precise and accurate may thick description be if there is risk of identifying an informant? What are consequences of errors in interpretation by the researcher if the participants are already stigmatized?

These ethical issues highlight the importance of reflexivity in qualitative research. Reflexivity in its extreme form views reality only through the researcher's systematic analysis of his or her reactions or identities (Miller, chapter 3). In its moderate form, reflexivity means being clearly aware of one's viewpoint and monitoring its influence on one's understanding of what is being studied. Many modernist approaches to qualitative research expect the researcher to be reflexive throughout a study, while others question the feasibility of incessant reflexivity throughout the process and limit it to the analysis and writing. In either definition, reflexivity is a tool that enables researchers to interact with the person(s) to be known in challenging situations, to interpret their data, and to address inevitable ethical dilemmas.

Social work values and ethics may also influence selection of epistemology or paradigm. Central social work values are social justice and economic justice. These values lend themselves well to critical and antioppressive approaches such as those Miller describes in chapter 3. Other models do not require such values, but may be open to include them in the purpose and methodology of research. For example, action research has an explicit goal of change that empowers participants, as well as knowledge development (see, for example, Jones, Miller, and Luckey, chapter 9), and some evaluation research has explicit political goals (see Vandenberg and Claiborne, chapter 13). Some qualitative researchers use explicit values to drive their research, for example, Marxist or feminist views of power (Drisko, chapter 4).

In sum, qualitative research in social work may be distinguished from qualitative research in other disciplines by its compatibility to social work practice, its applied nature, and its inclusion of social work values. The latter affects selection of epistemologies and topics and increases ethical risks because of the emphasis on vulnerable and oppressed populations.

Very Brief History of Qualitative Research in Social Work

A final question is: How did qualitative research enter social work? In contemporary accounts of the development of social work research during the last century, qualitative research is not mentioned or mentioned only in passing. Like other social science disciplines in the 1950s and 1960s (Alasuutari 2010), social work researchers concentrated on developing an acceptable and useful scientific approach (Zimbalist 1977; Austin 1999; Graham, Al-Krenawi, and Bradshaw 2000; Zlotnik and Solt 2008). The distinction between qualitative and quantitative research was not as important as the quest for scientific legitimacy. Nevertheless, qualitative research, like quantitative survey research, has been a source of data since social work began. For example, Mary Richman, Sigmund Freud, and Abraham Maslow are viewed as seminal qualitative and case-study researchers (Kirk and Reid 2002; Wertz et al. 2011). Several important studies of the caseworker-client relationship used qualitative and case study methods drawn from sociological methods (Mayer and Timms 1970; Maluccio 1979). Further, Wynne Korr (2011) speculates that social work student internships are called "field work" because the first students at the Chicago School of Civics and Philanthropy completed sociological field studies at places like Hull House.

What changed is that in the 1960s and 1970s disciplines like sociology and anthropology shifted their ethnographic focus from catalogues of physical and social artifacts to less tangible aspects such as worldviews, symbology, and a holistic cultural view of a people (for examples, see Clifford Geertz, Victor Turnbull, or William Foote White). Some began writing bio-confessional ethnographies that included the effects of a culture on the researcher (Claude Lévi-Strauss or Kenneth Read), while others brought new perspectives like post-colonial thought and a focus on the privileged status of the researcher. Some combined ethnography with the political activism of the 1960s (Marshall Sahlins), while others focused on identity politics (Alasuutari 2010). In the late 1970s and 1980s, these new qualitative ideas about the focus and meaning of research were introduced to disciplines like education and psychology and engendered what Yvonne Lincoln calls the "great paradigm wars" (Lincoln 2010:4).

In social work, the paradigm wars began when Martha Heineman[1] published an article entitled "The obsolete scientific imperative in social work research" in 1981. In it, she attacked logical empiricism because it relies on the senses, and human perceptions are innately flawed (Heineman 1981). Her article began a long-running debate between Heineman and prominent social work advocates of logical positivism, as well as among the supporters of logical positivism. Both sides represented the other in its most extreme form and took vituperative umbrage at the "straw men" they had created for the sake of knocking them down. Reamer (1993:128), who details the debates, comments that they were "laced with a form of rancor that has rarely found its way into social work literature." (For more detail, see Reamer, 119–135.) The debates about epistemology raged through the 1980s without generating much actual research, and they have resurfaced occasionally in the twenty-first century (Heineman-Pieper, Tyson, and Pieper 2002). Finally, in 1990, qualitative and quantitative researchers met in Great Barrington, MA, to discuss qualitative methodology and to present completed qualitative studies in social work practice. The resulting text (Sherman and Reid 1994) was the first demonstration of how well qualitative methods can address social work problems.

Organization of This Book

The first section of this volume highlights broad issues pertinent to qualitative research from the unique perspective of social work research. James W. Drisko (chapter 1) offers a road map for understanding qualitative methods and rigor in a social work research paradigm. Because qualitative research does not have standardized protocols like quantitative research, neophytes may be stymied by the freedom and overwhelmed by the data. Standards for quality regardless of the approach or theory are an anchor for the researcher and consumer, and they are particularly useful when one defines qualitative research in the inclusive, multidimensional approach that we have used.

Frederic Reamer's chapter (2) describes the maturation of research ethics in society and among social workers. He demonstrates how core social

[1]Martha Heineman published under different names at various points in her career: Martha Brunswick Heineman; Martha Heineman Field; Martha Heineman; and Martha Heineman Pieper.

work values and mission affect choice of research questions (vulnerable diverse populations and social justice), goals (improve services), sampling (vulnerable populations), data gathering methods that respect clients, and informed consent when participants are vulnerable. He raises issues of special concern for social workers—for example, confidentiality when thick description describes criminal behavior, conflicts of interest when the social worker has an authority relationship to the participants, and social responsibility if participants reveal disturbing data. In the potential morass of ethical dilemmas, Reamer offers several guides for research, including anticipation, understanding of context, awareness of spillover, self-reflection, and guidance from social work values and ethics.

Robert L. Miller, Jr.'s chapter (3) explores epistemology and reflexivity related to researchers' obligations to understand their own multiple identities, the interactions of those identities, and their interrelations with the outside world. Understanding those identities, especially those "less honored," allows the researcher new evaluation points for accessing and considering data. Critical theory provides a framework for examining and criticizing imbalances of power that create oppression. Critical race theory and (feminist) standpoint theory focus this examination of societal power in relation to race and gender, respectively.

The second section of the book deals with epistemologies and approaches to qualitative methods. Padgett (2008) suggests there are primary approaches to qualitative research in social work versus epistemologies (constructivist and critical theory) that were developed recently. This "mixing and matching" makes Drisko's (chapter 1) guidelines for rigor and theoretical consistency even more important. We include in the second section of this volume constructivist epistemology and five primary approaches: mixed inductive-deductive grounded theory, ethnography, narrative analysis, situation analysis, and action research. Briefer descriptions of other methodologies are included in other sections: traditional grounded theory (Abramson and Mizrahi, chapter 21; Ackerson, chapter 16), content analysis (Naccarato and Hernandez, chapter 20), case analysis (Colvin, chapter 19; Shaw, chapter 14), a different form of narrative analysis (Page, chapter 17), and complex mixed methods (Frame, chapter 18). (See table 3.)

To begin the epistemology/approach section, James W. Drisko (chapter 4) describes constructivist research in general as an epistemological stance that social knowledge is a product of knowers—relative, varied, and context-dependent. Groups and individuals "make meaning" through interaction.

Table 3 Location of Content about Qualitative Research Methods

Topic		Chapters
Epistemology or Theoretical Framework	Constructivist	4 Drisko: Constructivist research
	Critical theory	3 Miller: Deconstructing the epistemological question
	Critical race theory	3 Miller: Deconstructing the epistemological question
	Deductive qualitative analysis	5 Gilgun: Grounded theory
	Grounded theory	5 Gilgun: Grounded theory
		16 Ackerson: Coping with dual demands
		21 Abramson and Mizrahi: Collaboration between social workers and physicians
	Systems theory	15 Field: The application of qualitative research
		19 Colvin: Doing the best you can?
	Standpoint theory	3 Miller: Deconstructing the epistemological question
	Situation analysis	8 Rennis et al.: We have a situation here!
	Reformist and radical agendas	14 Shaw: Program evaluation
	Action research	9 Jones et al.: Action research
		13 Vandenburgh and Claiborne: Qualitative program evaluation
	Feminist theory	10 Postmus: Qualitative interviewing
	Use of theory	18 Frame: Parenting and child neglect
Program evaluation		8 Rennis et al.: We have a situation here!
		13 Vandenburgh and Claiborne: Qualitative program evaluation
		14 Shaw: Program evaluation
		15 Field: The application of qualitative research

Methodology: Data gathering and data analysis	Interviews	4 Drisko: Constructivist research
		10 Postmus: Qualitative interviewing
		8 Rennis et al.: We have a situation here!
		16 Ackerson: Coping with dual demands
		19 Colvin: Doing the best you can?
	Participant observation/ ethnography	6 Sands: Ethnography
		14 Shaw: Program evaluation
	Focus groups	11 Wayne: Focus groups
		13 Vandenburgh and Claiborne: Qualitative program evaluation
	Document analysis	6 Sands: Ethnography
		8 Rennis et al.: We have a situation here!
	Visual data	6 Sands: Ethnography
	Direct observation	8 Rennis et al.: We have a situation here!
		18 Frame: Parenting and child neglect
		19 Colvin: Doing the best you can?
	Case study	14 Shaw: Program evaluation
		5 Gilgun: Grounded theory
Methodology: Data analysis	Coding	5 Gilgun: Grounded theory
		7 Riessman: Analysis of personal narratives
		8 Rennis et al.: We have a situation here!
		17 Page: Assessing young children's perceptions of family relationships
		18 Frame: Parenting and child neglect

(continued)

Table 3 Location of Content about Qualitative Research Methods (*continued*)

Topic		Chapters
	Grounded theory/inductive reasoning	20 Naccarato and Hernandez: Scholarships and support
		21 Abramson and Mizrahi: Collaboration between social workers and physicians
		4 Drisko: Constructivist research5 Gilgun: Grounded theory
		6 Sands: Ethnography
		12 Drisko: Qualitative data analysis software
		20 Naccarato and Hernandez: Scholarships and support
		21 Abramson and Mizrahi: Collaboration between social workers and physicians
	Situation analysis	8 Rennis et al.: We have a situation here!
	Narrative analysis	7 Riessman: Analysis of personal narratives
		17 Page: Accessing young children's perceptions
	Software	12 Drisko: Qualitative data analysis software
Other research issues	Ethics	2 Reamer: Ethics
	Sampling	4 Drisko: Constructivist research
		5 Gilgun: Grounded theory
		11 Wayne: Focus groups
		16 Ackerson: Coping with dual demands
	Credibility/validity	1 Drisko: Standards for qualitative studies
		4 Drisko: Constructivist research
		6 Sands: Ethnography
		7 Riessman: Analysis of personal narratives
		16 Ackerson: Coping with dual demands
		21 Abramson and Mizrahi: Collaboration between social workers and physicians

Constructivist research includes more specific approaches (e.g., feminist, narrative, ethnography, and hermeneutics); Drisko outlines their common assumptions and processes for conducting research. He raises key issues for social work researchers: Value premises that challenge the validity of any values while other approaches are grounded in culturally specific values; rigor and quality defined as epistemological internal consistency; credibility of a study conclusion when all voices are equally valid; and clarity of research methods to the participants and readers.

Grounded theory (GT) is a primarily inductive process for organizing data into theory. The researcher analyzes a case to develop patterns and theory, then compares another case to modify the patterns, then compares other cases, and as a final step, compares the newly developed theory to existing research or theory. In pure grounded theory, the researcher immerses him- or herself in the data and works inductively, with no ideas about the outcome. In chapter 5, Jane Gilgun combines grounded theory with deductive conceptualizations or working hypotheses that guide inductive data analysis. She shows how to use deductive qualitative analysis (DQA) when the theory is already well-developed or just a beginning hunch. She also discusses the parallels of GT and DQA to social work practice and suggests applications that bring disenfranchised voices to the public arena.

Roberta Sands's chapter 6 describes ethnography as "qualitative inquiry in which researchers observe the everyday activities of participants in a social setting, group, or community in order to understand . . . them" (p 136). Typically, ethnography includes participant observation, interviewing, note-taking, and systematic data-analysis. Sands describes the nonlinear and recursive ethnographic process, including determining focus, engaging gatekeepers for possible setting, entering the field and explaining one's self to participants, strategies for understanding the culture, different types of documentation, and data analysis, including member checking.

In chapter 7, Catherine Kohler Riessman describes narrative analysis, analyzing the content and structure of individual storytelling. Narrative analysis assumes "that tellers and listeners/questioners interact in particular cultural milieus and historical contexts (p 170)" that may be interpreted. She discusses how to determine segments for analysis and some of the possible points of entry (for example, performative features that indicate how the narrator would like to be seen, social positioning, and salience of events). She illustrates using a woeful tale of divorce that indicates gender roles, marital roles, and social pressures on marriage.

In chapter 8, Lesley Green Rennis, Lourdes Hernández-Cordero, Kjersti Schmitz, and Mindy Thompson Fullilove describe situation analysis as a way of understanding the interior and exterior aspects of a situation, placing high-risk situations within contexts of social, political, and economic forces. Their research involves distinguishing and defining some behaviors (the situation) from the background of actions and events, the embedding context. Their first step is defining the situation—goals of actors, mode of communication, roles, rules of interaction, skills needed in the situation, obstacles, the environmental setting, and defining concepts for participants. The second step is collecting data—learning the history and context; finding obvious and hidden actors; listening to their goals, roles, and so on; studying the physical environment; and observing interactions. The analysis step includes the perspectives of each individual contrasted to the perspectives of others, timelines, links to the embedding context, and overall description. They illustrate with a large-scale evaluation of services for women of color living with HIV/AIDS. Their research in general focuses on urban public health epidemics (AIDS, crack, violence, etc.) and shows how complex qualitative research can link individual, neighborhood, and social problems and suggest large-scale preventive strategies.

In the final chapter (9) in this section, Shirley Jones, Robert L. Miller, Jr., and Irene Luckey describe action research that uses a cyclical process of Look (data gathering), Think (critical reflection), and Act (action). The process includes participation of community members in all aspects of the research, including formulating the goals, making decisions, gathering data, and sharing data. The researchers' roles are facilitating, catalyzing, and teaching community members how to do the action research processes. The chapter includes several case examples from U.S. communities and a wider partnership between people in the United States and South Africa.

The third section includes common methods of data collection and analysis that crosscuts approaches and epistemologies: interviewing, focus groups, and computerized data-analysis software. This section is more practical, pragmatic, how-to-do-it, although it does include some of the epistemological considerations. Judy L. Postmus (10) reflects on the influence of paradigms, sensitivity, and standpoint in conducting qualitative interviews. She discusses the role of power, gender, ethnicity, and class on the interaction between interviewer and interviewee, the skills and preparation needed by interviewers, designing questions, steps of a good interview, pitfalls, and maintaining attention to both content and epistemology-related structure of a qualitative interview.

In chapter 11, Raymie H. Wayne describes focus groups to reveal "what a particular group of people think about complex or sensitive subjects (p 265)." She includes examples of focus group utility, considerations such as composition, topic, recruitment of participants, types and sequencing of questions, stages of group development applied to focus groups, and necessary leader skills.

Finally, James W. Drisko (chapter 12) looks at qualitative software: What it can do and what it cannot do, new possibilities like team analysis and multi-media analysis, and the common steps in using it to organize and analyze data.

The third common qualitative data-gathering technique is participant-observation. It is not dealt with in this section but is discussed in Roberta Sands' chapter on ethnography (6). She describes the nonlinear and recursive ethnographic process, including entering the field, strategies for understanding the culture, documentation, and data analysis.

The fourth section tackles the use of qualitative research methods to evaluate social service programs. Henry Vandenburgh and Nancy Claiborne (chapter 13) give an overview of qualitative program evaluation. Uses include evaluating system-level interventions, stakeholder involvement, community change, and organizational service delivery. Research approaches include grounded theory, action research, and participatory research; typical data-gathering methods include interviews, focus groups, observation, and document review; data analysis can use computer coding to assist. They illustrate with a qualitative evaluation of a public outpatient psychiatric emergency service.

Whereas Vandenberg and Claiborne focus on the how-to of program evaluation, Ian Shaw (chapter 14) focuses on epistemological issues in using qualitative methods for assessing service outcomes. He argues that outcomes evaluation must be purposeful, secure, wide-ranging, and critical; these characteristics are addressed when evaluation is linked to purpose, when there is clear understanding of kinds of knowledge needed, and when evaluation is wide-ranging and resists conventional choices of methodology. Qualitative approaches can provide solutions to design problems—for example, simulations as a substitute for experimental control, can better study microprocesses of change, can identify causal mechanisms and temporal relations, and—through symbolic interaction and interpretivist frameworks—prevent oversimplistic views that ignore context. Shaw also discusses case study methodology and how results can be made relevant to other situations.

In chapter 15, Ralph F. Field focuses on organizational management. In describing participatory strategic management planning and evaluation, he addresses the use of qualitative research skills in complex strategic management and the steps and issues in planning a qualitative evaluation of a community-based preventive health project.

The fifth section includes qualitative studies that contribute to social work knowledge of human behavior, practice, and service delivery. We asked each author to describe his or her methodology and link the methodology to results. Consequently, these chapters demonstrate qualitative methodology in action as well as contribute to knowledge of complex and sensitive issues.

In the first exemplar study, Barry Ackerson (chapter 16) uses traditional grounded theory—theoretical sampling, semistructured interviews, constant comparison, new interviews driven by insight from previous interviews and the data comparison process. The results look at the experiences of mentally ill parents who have successfully raised children, including their fear of seeking help lest the child be removed.

Timothy Page (chapter 17) describes a type of narrative analysis intended to access a child's internal working model of attachment to parental figures (Bowlby 1973). The narrative story-stem technique (NSST) is a standardized story stem that stimulates a child-participant to complete the story using family figurines. The child's narrative responses can be categorized deductively using a priori coding schemas or analyzed inductively to describe the child's individual construction of attachment. The chapter includes a summary of studies that used a priori coding to link attachment to the family caregiving environment and to behavior in other social settings like peer groups. The chapter also includes a narrative from a child with family disruption and how to analyze the attachment themes qualitatively.

In chapter 18, Laura Frame looks at the link between poverty and child neglect among poor urban families. The study includes multilevel approaches to data collection and analysis, approaches that changed as her understanding changed. Ultimately, the study integrated "an inductively-derived description of urban poverty and its effects, a microanalytic study of parent-child interaction, and a process- and content-based analysis of parental narratives related to parenting" (p 446). From the research, Frame developed a model of child protection and neglect in which poverty increases risks, decreases parents' physical and psychological coping, and reduces parents' recognition and response to signals that the child needs care. The chapter is especially strong in showing how theory—especially new interdisciplinary perspectives—can inform and focus qualitative research.

In chapter 19, Julanne Colvin uses intensive case study to investigate not why child neglect occurs but why, once a case is in the child welfare system, the family does not change but stays in the system with the mother "doing the best she can." Colvin interviewed the caseworker and the parent three times, following Seidman's (1998) procedures for making meaning from the context of their lives and the lives of those around them. She also observed parent-child interaction and had the caseworker review the child welfare case records. The study examines the mother-caseworker relationship within the child welfare system and how, over time, it supported lack of change in neglectful behaviors.

Toni Naccarato and Liliana Hernandez look at the other end of the child welfare system: the independent living programs that prepare older foster youth to transition to adulthood and independent living (chapter 20). To assess services needed and outcome, they interviewed key informants who were coordinators of programs that provided support to foster youth in college. They detail the content analysis procedures used to determine key themes inductively. Coordinators' concerns included the students' success in college, youth advocacy, access to resources, and growth and infrastructure of the program.

The final chapter, by Julie Abramson and Terry Mizrahi, describes the development of a typology of collaboration between social workers and physicians (chapter 21). They use grounded theory, with interviews and data analysis intertwined, selecting new participants to provide contrast, developing codes, and eventually dimensions for traditional versus transformational collaborators from each discipline.

Final Comments

This volume is fortunate to have some of the most progressive and expert thinkers applying qualitative methods to social work concerns. Several of the contributors have shaped the qualitative social work research practice canon for over 20 years. Their thinking represents some of the best and most thoughtful work in the field. When we approached them about contributing to this edition, we asked them "to take what they currently know and expand it to create new thoughts and opportunities for idea generation." We hope readers concur that they did so.

We also made concentrated effort to bring in new writers. Several authors recently received their social work doctoral degrees. It is an honor to have some of their first scholarly efforts in this text. The volume is also fortunate to have collaborators from outside the profession to provide multiple frameworks for qualitative methods in the human services: Dr. Ralph F. Field, director of the not-for-profit management department at the University College of the University of Maryland, and Dr. Mindy Fullilove and her team at the Community Research Group from the Mailman School of Public Health at Columbia University. Both provide an additional texture and perspective to social work research and underscore the utility of interdisciplinary thinking.

The hope for this volume was to extend the first edition to generate new ideas, to develop new questions, to demonstrate multiple qualitative approaches to social work questions, and to enhance social workers' research qualitative skills. A goal was to inspire those new to qualitative methodology to consider the many ways of knowing while understanding social work research as a form of practice that is an inherent fulfillment of social work's mission to improve people's level of social functioning.

The second edition was initiated by William J. Reid and Robert L. Miller, Jr., with the support of Jon Michel at Columbia University Press. (Edmund Sherman, the original first editor, had retired.) Shortly after, both Dr. Reid and Mr. Michel died unexpectedly and the book was put on temporary hold. With the support of Mr. Michel's successors at Columbia University Press, Lauren Dockett and then Jennifer Perillo, the project was revived and has now come to fruition. We thank them, the authors who wrote well and then waited patiently and revised as requested, and Katharine Briar-Lawson, the dean at the School of Social Welfare, University at Albany, for their inspiration and support. We hope that, as they would have wished, this volume inspires new and creative qualitative research in social work. We honor their work.

Anne E. Fortune and Robert L. Miller, Jr.
Dedicated to William J. Reid (1928–2003)

References

Ahmed, A. S. 1984. Al-Beruni: The first anthropologist. *RAIN (Royal Anthropological Institute Newsletter)*(60):9–10.

Alasuutari, P. 2010. The rise and relevance of qualitative research. *International Journal of Social Research Methodology*, 13(2):139–155. doi: 10.1080/13645570902966056

Austin, D. M. 1999. A report on progress in the development of research resources in social work. *Research on Social Work Practice*, 9(6):673–707. doi: 10.1177/104973159900900604

Bowlby, J. 1973. *Attachment and loss, Vol. II: Separation: anxiety and anger*. New York: Basic.

Duffy, L. 2011. "Step-by-step we are stronger": Women's empowerment through photovoice. *Journal of Community Health Nursing*, 28(2):105–116.

Fortune, A. E. 1994. Commentary: Ethnography in social work. In *Qualitative research in social work*, E. Sherman and W. J. Reid, eds. 63–67. New York: Columbia UP.

Fortune, A. E. and W. J. Reid. 1999. *Research in social work* (3rd ed.). New York: Columbia UP.

Fraser, M., M. J. Taylor, R. Jackson, and J. O'Jack. 1991. Social work and science: Many ways of knowing? *Social Work Research and Abstracts*, 27(4):5–9.

Freedman, C., R. Pitner, R. L. White-Johnson, and S. Hastie. 2012. "LENS: A strategy for disseminating Photovoice artwork." Paper presented at the Society for Social Work and Research 16th annual conference, Washington, DC.

Gilgun, J. F. 1994. Hand into glove: The grounded theory approach and social work practice research. In *Qualitative research in social work*, E. Sherman and W. J. Reid, eds.115–125). New York: Columbia UP.

Graham, J. R., A. Al-Krenawi, and C. Bradshaw. 2000. The Social Work Research Group/NASW Research Section/Council on Social Work Research, 1949–1965: An emerging research identity in the American profession. *Research on Social Work Practice*, 10(5):622–643.

Grinnell, R. M., Jr. and Y. A. Unrau. 2011. *Social work research and evaluation: Foundations of evidence-based practice*, 9th ed. New York: Oxford UP.

Heineman, M. 1981. The obsolete scientific imperative in social work research. *Social Service Review*, 55(3):371–396.

Heineman-Pieper, J., K. Tyson, and M. H. Pieper. 2002. Doing good science without sacrificing good values: Why the heuristic paradigm in the best choice. *Families in Society*, 83(1):15–28.

Hergenrather, K. C., S. D. Rhodes, C. A. Cowan, G. Bardhoshi, and S. Pula. 2009. Photovoice as community-based participatory research: A qualitative review, *American Journal of Health Behavior*, 33(6):686–698.

Hudson, W. W. 1978. Notes for practice. *Social Work*, 23(1):65.

Kirk, S. A. and W. J. Reid. 2002. *Science and social work: A critical appraisal.* New York: Columbia UP.

Korr, W. (2011). "Hull House research: Narrative and qualitative research for social justice." Paper presented at the 7th International Congress of Qualitative Inquiry: Qualitative Inquiry and the Politics of Advocacy, University of Illinois at Urbana-Champaign, Champaign, IL.

Lai, D. W. L. and C. Thomson. 2011. The impact of perceived adequacy of social support on caregiving burden of family caregivers. *Families in Society, 92*(1):99–106.

Lang, N. C. 1994. Integrating the data processing of qualitative research and social work practice to advance the practitioner as knowledge builder: Tools for knowing and doing. In *Qualitative research in social work,* E. Sherman and W. J. Reid, eds. 251–264. New York: Columbia UP.

LeCompte, M. D. 2002. The transformation of ethnographic practice: Past and current challenges. *Qualitative Research, 2*(3):283–299.

León-Portilla, M. 2002. *Bernardino de Sahagún: First anthropologist* (M. J. Mixco, Trans.). Norman, OK: U of Oklahoma P.

Lincoln, Y. S. 2010. "What a long, strange trip it's been . . .": Twenty-five years of qualitative and new paradigm research. *Qualitative Inquiry, 16*(1):3–9. doi: 10.1177/1077800409349754

Lindlof, T. R. and B. C. Taylor. 2002. *Qualitative communication research methods* (2nd ed.). Thousand Oaks, CA: Sage.

Maluccio, A. N. 1979. *Learning from clients: Interpersonal helping as viewed by clients and social workers.* New York: Free Press.

Mayer, J. E. and N. Timms. 1970. *The client speaks: Working class impressions of casework.* New York: Atherton.

Miller, R. L. 2008. Qualitative and quantitative research methods in social work articles between 1990–92 and 2006–07: A study of *Social Work Abstracts.* Unpublished paper.

Molloy, J. K. 2007. Photovoice as a tool for social justice workers. *Journal of Progressive Human Services, 18*:39–55.

Munn, J. C. 2012. Viewing the world: Visual inquiry in international settings. *Journal of Social Work Education, 48*(1):167–177.

Ohmer, M. L., B. D. Warner, and E. Beck. 2010. Preventing violence in low-income communities: Facilitating residents' ability to intervene in neighborhood problems. *Journal of Sociology and Social Welfare, 37*(2):161–181.

Padgett, D. K. 1998. *Qualitative methods in social work research: Challenges and rewards.* Thousand Oaks, CA: Sage.

——. 2008. *Qualitative methods in social work research: Challenges and rewards,* 2nd ed. Thousand Oaks, CA: Sage.

Padgett, D. K., ed. 2004. *The qualitative research experience.* Belmont, CA: Thomson Brooks/Cole.

Reamer, F. G. 1993. *The philosophical foundations of social work.* New York: Columbia UP.

Rubin, A. and E. Babbie. 2008. *Research methods for social work,* 7th ed. Belmont, CA: Brooks/Cole.

Sandelowski, M. 1998. Writing a good read: Strategies for re-presenting qualitative data. *Research in Nursing and Health,* 21:375–382.

Seidman, I. 1998. *Interviewing as qualitative research: A guide for researchers in education and the social services.* New York: Teachers College.

Shaw, I. and N. Gould. 2001. *Qualitative research in social work: Context and method.* London: Sage.

Sherman, E. and W. J. Reid, eds. 1994. *Qualitative research in social work.* New York: Columbia UP.

Smith, S. 2006. Encouraging the use of reflexivity in the writing up of qualitative research. *International Journal of Therapy & Rehabilitation,* 13(5):209–215.

Thornton, N. and F. P. Hopp. 2011. "So I just took over": African American daughters caregiving for parents with heart failure. *Families in Society,* 92(2):211–217.

Wertz, F. J., K. Charmaz, L. M. McMullen, R. Josselson, R. Anderson, and E. McSpadden. 2011. *Five ways of doing qualitative analysis: Phenomenological psychology, grounded theory, discourse analysis, narrative research, and intuitive inquiry.* New York: Guilford.

Wesch, M. 2008. An anthropological introduction to YouTube by Michael Wescj. Presented at the Library of Congress, June 23, 2008. Retrieved February 21, 2012, from http://www.youtube.com/user/mwesch?feature=watch or http://www.youtube.com/watch?v=TPAO-lZ4_hU.

William-White, L. 2011. Scholarship revolution. *Qualitative Inquiry,* 17(6):534–542. doi: 10.1177/1077800411409886

Yanow, D. and P. Schwartz-Shea, eds. (2006). *Interpretation and method: Empirical research methods and the interpretive turn.* Armonk, NY: M. E. Sharpe.

Zimbalist, S. E. 1977. *Historic themes and landmarks in social welfare research.* New York: Harper & Row.

Zlotnik, J. L. and B. E. Solt. 2008. Developing research infrastructure: The Institute for the Advancement of Social Work Research. *Social Work Research,* 32(4):201–207.

Qualitative Research in Social Work

PART I

THE BIG PICTURE

Standards for Qualitative Studies and Reports

JAMES W. DRISKO

Qualitative research continues to be accepted as a valuable approach in social work and in closely allied disciplines. In 1994, the Council on Social Work Education (CSWE) required that qualitative research methods be taught in all accredited bachelor's and master's level social work programs, a requirement renewed in the Educational Policy and Accreditation Standards in 2002 and again in 2008 (CSWE 2002, 2008). Qualitative interest groups began and rapidly expanded within the Society for Social Work Research, the Council on Social Work Education, and through the interdisciplinary International Congress of Qualitative Inquiry. Juried papers and workshops on qualitative research methods and studies became common at social work conferences, if not more frequent in core professional journals. An international journal, *Qualitative Social Work*, with an emphasis on practice and research started up in 2002, and many new print and electronic journals and resources have been initiated in social work and allied fields.

Despite this growth in interest in qualitative research, there are few U.S. social work texts on the subject and fewer still that cover it in depth. Padgett's (1998, 2008) text offers a sound introduction to several key methods of qualitative research. In contrast, most American social work textbooks offer a very narrow introduction to qualitative research.

The texts fail to portray the range and variety of qualitative research as well as failing to offer much guidance on issues including epistemologies, ethical challenges, sampling, data analysis, and reporting qualitative studies. A few compilations of studies and opinion pieces are also available (Riessman 1994; Sherman and Reid 1994; Shaw and Gould 2002; Padgett 2004), offering a wider portrait of the types of qualitative research social workers undertake. However, little attention is given in these works to establishing standards for qualitative research to guide social work researchers, journal and conference reviewers, and social work educators at all levels. My own standards article (Drisko 1997) set forth a model specific to social work that I have expanded upon in several conference presentations (1999, 2000, 2007). Padgett (1998) identifies several methodological steps that can enhance the rigor of realist qualitative research. Drawing on both our works, Anastas (2004) has addressed standards for qualitative evaluation studies more narrowly. Several conference workshops have been offered on this topic (largely by these three researchers). Nonetheless, no consensus exists on standards for qualitative research in social work.

The lack of standards leads to difficulties at many levels. First, the lack of standards to orient qualitative research makes proposal development more challenging for students and faculty alike. To address this problem, the Group for the Advancement of Doctoral Education has organized discussion of standards for dissertations, many of which included specific expectations for qualitative research. The yield of these discussions has not been widely disseminated, nor widely adopted beyond the doctoral level. The National Institutes of Health, Office of Behavioral and Social Sciences Research (undated), developed a booklet outlining issues in proposal development and review for federally funded qualitative health research. The document, focused largely on ethnographic research, offers an outline of issues to be addressed for federally funded research. These standards, however, are not comprehensive to all the types of qualitative research social workers undertake, nor have they been systematically adopted within social work.

Second, faculty and doctoral students report that their qualitative manuscripts are frequently turned down by social work journals. In many cases, the prospective authors believe their work has not been evaluated using criteria suitable to the content and methods. Instead, they believe qualitative research is often "slammed" by reviewers using inappropriate standards, most often those used for quantitative, statistical research. As Leininger (1994) notes, such reviewers apply no criterion other than a rejection of qualitative research. While rejection of a manuscript often causes authors to doubt the competency of the reviewers, the consistency of the core message—reviews applying inappropriate standards—suggests a lack of clear standards for assessing qualitative research. Such reviews also indicate the lack of a sufficiently expert pool of reviewers for qualitative research. Given that qualitative research is minimally taught at the master's level (Drisko 2008) and is usually taught as a single course at the doctoral level, social work education offers little in the way of preparing future reviewers with deep qualitative expertise. Reviewers with extensive and varied training, research experience, and expertise in qualitative research are few in social work.

Third, the lack of standards combines with the lack of high quality published exemplars to make teaching qualitative research more difficult. Faculty and students are forced to find exemplars of qualitative research in disciplines other than social work. These exemplars may address topics of peripheral interest to the social work profession and they lack a social work perspective. A message is also sent that qualitative research is not highly regarded within the profession, despite the opposite message explicit in the CSWE's accreditations standards.

Finally, all of these challenges jointly act to undermine the development of faculty expertise in qualitative research within social work. Given the lack of support and training for qualitative research, the cadre of knowledgeable and skilled faculty to train future leaders is small. Few opportunities to develop expertise in qualitative research are available, and very few opportunities to teach the content in depth are available at the bachelor's and master's levels. Clear standards, strong materials and exemplars, and a path to develop talent in qualitative research are all needed.

While the focus of this chapter is on standards for qualitative research in social work, it is important to note that interest in standards is conspicuous in many other disciplines as well. Nursing (Burns 1989), education (Guba 1981; Guba and Lincoln 1981), psychology (Chenail 1997) medicine (Berkwits and Aronowitz 1995; Mays and Pope 2000; Barbour 2001), health sciences (Popay 1995; Popay, Rogers, and Williams 1998; Eakin and Mykhalovskiy 2003), linguistics (Lazarton 2003), and governmental social policy development (Spencer et al. 2003) each have recent publications on criteria for evaluating qualitative studies. Several formulations locate qualitative research as a perspective in contrast to "positivism" and/or "science" (Burns 1989; Eakin and Mykhalovskiy 2003). That is, post-positivist and realist qualitative research is ignored or de-emphasized (Smith and Demmes 2000). Since much American qualitative social work research appears realist in epistemology, such standards would not fit well with some of the types of qualitative studies this chapter addresses. In a similar vein, many formulations are criticized as "proceduralist" or "criterionist": emphasizing checklist-style appraisal of particular procedures over broader, synthetic criteria (Barbour 2001; Eakin and Mykhalovskiy 2003). This chapter, in contrast, assumes an initial substantive appraisal of the research question's merits, then identifies a series of choice points—each requiring careful appraisal and judgments about substance, procedure, and internal consistency of the research as a whole. Procedures are relevant as scaffolding, but implementation of them in service of fully meeting the study goals is the focus of evaluation. These criteria are meant to be heuristically useful, not as a checklist or as a straightjacket to creativity and innovation.

The Roles of Data and Interpretation in Qualitative Research

Qualitative research is a diverse terrain, unlike probabilistic quantitative research, which is a single, unified tradition. This diversity makes defining qualitative research challenging. Qualitative research may mean very different things to different people. Tesch (1990) offers a useful map. In describing the types of qualitative data analyses evident in published qualitative research and texts, she proposes a continuum heuristically divided into four sections. First, at the most structured end of the continuum, content analyses apply statistical methods to textual qualitative data. The linkage between the data or evidence to the conclusions is highly structured and mediated by a specified method.[1] Somewhat less structured analyses constitute the middle two sections of Tesch's continuum of qualitative research. The second section centers on the discovery of patterns and regularities. In a similar vein, Crabtree and Miller (1999) call these research types template approaches as they often fit data to *a priori* categories determined before data collection and analysis. Patterns are closely tied to explicit evidence with minimal interpretation. Deductively generated analysis categories are common. Researchers in this section of the continuum apply such formal methods as logical analysis, matrix analysis and narrative analysis (Tesch 1990).

The third section of Tesch's (1990) continuum is yet more interpretive and centers on comprehension of actions and meanings. Crabtree and Miller (1999) label these "editing" approaches and note a priori codes and conceptualization are rarely applied. Here researchers emphasize meaning and intention, which may not include a simple one-to-one correspondence between evidence and interpretation, but a clear chain of inference is provided to justify the interpretation. Inductive analysis is emphasized (though occasionally deductive steps may be included). Data analysis is more interpretive but still follows formally described research methods. Grounded theory, other forms of analytic induction, semiotic analysis, hermeneutic analysis, and phenomenology are all examples of such meaning-focused research method (Tesch 1990). Fourth, at the far end of the continuum, Tesch (1990) locates "reflection": Studies that use data as a springboard for interpretation with little to no explicit analytic structure. Crabtree and Miller (1999) call these immersion approaches. Linkage to empirical evidence may be quite loose or selective as the emphasis is on a personalized, situated analysis. Notably, no formal, named, research methods are necessarily applied. Such studies are often highly self-reflective (Eisner 1997). In social work, Hyde's (1994) reflections on her own organizational qualitative research process are an example of a reflective research report. Similarly, Gilgun (2008) explored her reactions in a reflexive account of working with perpetrators of interpersonal violence. Other examples are found in the journals *Qualitative Social Work, Qualitative Inquiry,* and *Qualitative Research.* Within social work such interpretive work is likely to be directed away from traditional research-oriented journals.

Qualitative Research and Science

That some forms of qualitative research are highly interpretive raises the issue of the role of science in qualitative research. American social work's professional norms have strongly emphasized a scientific approach to knowledge building and testing—as explicitly required by CSWE's curriculum policy statements and accreditation standards. Though definitions of science vary, the core of science is the role of structured observation to test theories. If some forms of qualitative research (though rare in social work) emphasize interpretation with loose linkage to data, they do not seem to be "scientific" as understood within social work. Indeed, some interpretive work is based upon a rejection of a scientific core as the optimal means to develop knowledge about lived, subjective experience. Hermeneutic and interpretive approaches are espoused instead, and vary in structure and formality of methods. This tension between scientific naturalism and hermeneutic approaches is a philosophical issue beyond the scope and purpose of this chapter (Hollis 1994). It does suggest, however, that some excellent qualitative research may purposefully *not* be scientific in order to achieve the goal of incorporating meaning making into the systematic, evidence-based study of people and their activities. On the other hand, other qualitative research may intentionally seek to be part of scientific understanding and evidence based practice (Popay, Rogers, and Williams 1998). Rubin (2008) argues that qualitative research may be a valuable part of evidence-based practice when the practice question centers on understanding the lived experience of persons with a specific difficulty.

While not all qualitative research is necessarily grounded in science, to date the vast majority of American social work qualitative research is so grounded. The problem most apparent in the published qualitative literature in social work is not a rejection of a scientific base, but the failure to produce work of sufficient clarity and rigor to make plain the linkage amongst question, methods, data, and conclusions. My own reviews of the published literature indicate that ethnography and grounded theory are the methods most widely cited by social work qualitative researchers (Drisko 2000a, 2000b, 2003, 2012). Yet Wells (1995) and Oktay (2004) found many deficiencies in the way that grounded theory methods were applied in these studies. Rodwell's (1998) constructivist social work research model also centers on a clear and highly structured testing of conclusions against systematically collected evidence. More common in publications is a minimal description of purposes and methods, frequently including name-dropping of authors or methods—which close inspection may reveal to be inconsistent or incompatible. For example, a grounded theory approach may be claimed, but realized via Miles and Huberman's (1984) quite different, matrix analysis model of data analysis. In American social work publications, problems with conceptual and methodological rigor are currently more apparent in qualitative reports than is a lack of fit with scientific purposes or methods. Rigorous qualitative research may indeed be empirical and scientific.

The hierarchy of research designs promoted by the evidence-based practice (EBP) movement actively devalues qualitative research. While experimental research is certainly a valuable method for testing theory and making cause and effect claims, it is always premised on a complex set of concepts, constructs, and theories that originated in discovery oriented qualitative research. EBP is one valuable form of applied research, but does not displace the need for innovative, basic research to explore and understand new trends and experiences. EBP addresses outcomes and generally promotes methods to enhance internal validity. It does not examine the particular needs of individuals and families that may be portrayed in depth and nuance by qualitative research. Both types of research have merit and worth in orienting professional practice. Neither broad post-modern critiques nor narrow realist claims of effectiveness provides an adequate basis for meeting the information and knowledge needs of a profession (Hammersley 2008). So what standards are appropriate for qualitative studies and reports? The starting point, of course, is the research question.

The Research Question and Its Connection to Epistemology

All research of merit begins with a good question. Criteria for identifying a good question include importance, fruitfulness, timeliness, interest to a specific audience, and utility to problem-solving. Assuming a "good" research question is posed, *how* the question will be examined is the next step. Specific epistemologies are more or less effective at answering specific research questions (Guba and Lincoln 1981; Hartman 1990, 1994; Denzin and Lincoln 1994; Rodwell 1998; Hammersley 2008). Epistemology and related research methods are optimally selected to best address a specific problem for a given purpose and audience.[2] Once an epistemology is selected to address a specific research question, researchers and reviewers should evaluate the merits of the study and report within the epistemology that orients the research. Once a method is selected, researchers and reviewers should evaluate the rigor of the study as it is revealed, missed, or obscured by the chosen methods within the confines of the orienting epistemology. To do so is to appraise and evaluate the research. To do otherwise is to globally critique the research. Critiques do have their place and value, but should not be confused with appraisal of a research report undertaken within its specified parameters and purposes.

Criteria for Planning and Evaluating Qualitative Research

Expanding from my earlier standards article (Drisko 1997), six criteria for evaluating qualitative reports are detailed here (table 1.1). A few of the criteria include several specific elements. Because of the iterative, cyclical nature of most qualitative research, content applicable for one criterion will often be relevant to others as well, or function synergistically with other criteria. The criteria broadly address procedural aspects of research, but always require substantive judgments about (a) the merits of the original research question, (b) key decisions about the research, (c) the internal consistency of the work as a whole, and (d) how well the study answered it.

It is important to note that these criteria simultaneously serve a useful function as guidelines for the development of qualitative research projects. These criteria are intended to guide qualitative researchers in developing and doing studies and to provide a basis for evaluating the resulting reports. While important differences exist among the many qualitative research traditions and the epistemologies applied to the study question, I believe it is possible to identify several concepts and terms that are still generally applicable. This is in large measure because researchers employ the same tools (interviews, observations, analytic strategies) across differences in epistemology, purpose, and audience (Drisko 1999). The criteria are thus intended to be general enough to provide a useful framework across differences of epistemology, purpose, and specific methods when accompanied by overall appraisals of the initial research question.

Criterion One: Specifying the Study's Epistemology

Qualitative research "is not a unified tradition" (Riessman 1994:xii). Indeed, Glaser (1992) notes qualitative research is actually a family of related research approaches. Tesch's (1990) continuum of qualitative data analysis approaches is one effort to help clarify the commonalities and differences in this large family. Given the diversity of qualitative research approaches, clarifying the chosen epistemology is a crucial first step in undertaking internally consistent research. In turn, evaluations of qualitative research must be made within the assumptions, purposes, and goals of the selected epistemological paradigm.

Table 1.1 Orienting and Evaluative Criteria for Qualitative Research and Reports

Beginning with a research question of worth and merit:

(1) Is the epistemology of the study clearly identified?
(2) Are the objectives and the intended audience of the study clearly identified?
(3) Are applicable social work ethics maintained explicitly?
(4) Is the methodology of the study clearly identified and consistent with the stated epistemology and objectives?

    (4a) Is the sampling plan, and rationale for its selection, clearly stated and consistent with the study epistemology and objectives?

    (4b) Does the sampling plan include efforts to include possibly contradictory cases or evidence?

    (4c) Are the means of data collection clearly identified and consistent with the study epistemology and objectives?

    (4d) Are the means of data analysis clearly identified and consistent with the study philosophy, objectives, sample, and collected data set(s)?

    (4e) Is sufficient data made available to make clear how interpretations are linked to the data?

    (4f) Are the data and analysis:

        (1) Credible?
        (2) Confirmable/disconfirmable?
        (3) Meaningful in context?
        (4) Complete? Saturated?

    (4g) How is contradictory evidence included and understood?

    (4h) Are any claims to transferability/generalizability clearly stated and consistent with the study epistemology, objectives, and obtained sample?

(5) Is researcher self-reflection evident? Are biases identified and addressed in a manner consistent with the study epistemology and objectives?
(6) Are the study's analysis, conclusions, and recommendations consistent with, and limited to, the study epistemology, objectives, and presented data?

    (6a) Do the data and analysis support claims of recurrent patterns, meanings, or preliminary theory development?

    (6b) Where development of theory is a goal of the research, is the theory explicit and applicable to orienting practice, policy, or future research?

Identifying the philosophical foundations of a study may be a complex and challenging process. Terminology is variable and often disputed even among philosophers. The intersection of epistemology and ontology may also be complex (House 1991). Denzin and Lincoln (1994) offer four paradigms or philosophical traditions that may serve as the foundation for qualitative research: Positivist/post-positivist approaches, interpretivist/ constructivist approaches, critical approaches, and feminist/post-structural approaches. They exclude ethnic or cultural studies. Greene (1994) identifies four somewhat different paradigms: Post-positivism, pragmatism, interpretivism, and critical or normative approaches. In evaluation studies, Patton's (1986) utilization-focused evaluation is philosophically a pragmatic approach blending quantitative/post-positivist conceptualization and methods with the qualitative data collection and data analysis methods of participant observation and grounded theory. Padgett (2004) applies the pragmatism of Peirce (1986).

The social work literature reveals advocates of many epistemologies and paradigms (Dean 1993; Rodwell 1998; Anastas 1999; Kazi 2002). Heineman Pieper (1989, 1994) and Tyson (1995) identify an overarching heuristic paradigm that appears to frame all research within a realist meta-level construction. Anastas (1999), Floersch (2002), and Kazi (2002) each advance fallibilistic realism as a paradigm that includes the context of the researcher, values theory, and acknowledges multiple internal realities and a "knowable" external world. I have selected realism as the epistemology for a descriptive qualitative study of practice evaluation among clinical social workers (Drisko 2002). Burnette (1994), Drisko (1998), and Padgett (1998) have undertaken pragmatic mixed methods quantitative-qualitative studies. Depoy, Hartman, and Haslett (1999) and Kondrat (2002) apply a critical perspective in social work research. Still other qualitative researchers in social work apply a constructivist epistemology (Healy 1993; Rodwell and Woody 1994; Swigonski 1994; Rodwell 1998). All these models offer valuable and useful frameworks among which social workers may select to orient their qualitative research work. All employ similar research designs and methods, though the nature and meaning of data is understood differently across epistemologies.

Once a philosophical framework is selected, the applied research methods should remain consistent with the identified framework. At this juncture, inconsistencies and/or incompatibilities of epistemology and purpose may arise. For example, Leininger states ". . . one cannot mix research methods across qualitative and quantitative paradigms, but one can mix methods within each paradigm" (1994:101). She notes efforts at triangulation may violate the integrity of the secondary paradigm's epistemological foundations and constitute a misuse of its methods. Thus identification of a study's philosophical foundations is needed to orient researchers and readers alike, as well as to identify and help avoid inappropriate mixing of divergent epistemological premises and methods. Declaring the epistemological foundations of a qualitative study also orients readers and reviewers by clarifying the selected basis for assessing coherence of formulation, method, and analysis in the report. Reviewers and evaluators of qualitative research should consider the internal consistency between philosophical foundation and applied methods as a key test of rigor in qualitative research.

Criterion Two: Identifying the Study Goals and Audience

To guide both researcher and reader, explicit identification of the objectives and audience of the study is the second criterion for orienting and evaluating qualitative research. Greene (1994) advances the view that philosophical paradigms of research differ in the types of questions to which each is optimally applied. She believes each epistemology/philosophy appeals to a somewhat different audience with different interests. That is, large scale, quantitative, confirmatory studies fit well with the interests of macro-level policy planners while qualitative, understanding-oriented studies appeal to meso-level program directors and micro-level practitioners. Yet in social work, Hyde (1994) and Solomon (1994) describe the merits of understanding-oriented qualitative organizational studies. Also in social work, Dean (1993), Gilgun (1994), and Ruckdeshel, Earnshaw, and Ferrik (1994) all point to microscale analysis as particularly useful to practitioners. We should also keep in mind that various journals and funding sources may represent differing audiences with different interests, expectations, and requirements. The objectives and audience of a study should purposefully influence study methods.

For example, qualitative evaluations of cases and particular programs may be very useful and informative to program managers, supervisors, practitioners, and service consumers. The researcher will likely seek a range of divergent viewpoints on program activities and effects. The researcher may study crucial events in depth and detail. Generalization across settings, however, may not be a goal of small scale qualitative studies. Similarly, standpoint research illuminates subjugated or unfamiliar knowledge with great clarity and merit, but may not seek or claim generalizable results beyond identifying sensitizing concepts (Swigonski 1994). Researchers and reviewers best assess the merits of a given qualitative study within its own explicit objectives and purposes, consistent with a specified epistemological framework.

Criterion Three: Explicitly Maintaining Social Work Ethics

Qualitative researchers should work in a manner that conforms fully to social work ethics (National Association of Social Workers 2008) and applicable regulations. Researchers should make explicit in their reports that they sought to do research in an ethical manner. Even brief statements regarding institutional review approval and protections for research participants are still too rare in American social work research reports (qualitative and quantitative alike). Readers and reviewers should be informed of steps taken to protect the interests of research participants.

In this era of lawsuits over informed consent inadequacies and suspensions of university funding over ethical questions, fully applying social work ethical standards and federal regulations might appear an obvious expectation for all researchers. Yet discussion of ethical issues in qualitative research remains little developed within social work and allied fields. Most publications on qualitative research ethics broadly address general concerns with little in-depth, practical discussion of the strengths and limitations of applying traditional ethical standards (i.e., Punch 1994; Christians 2000). In this vein, Lindsley (1997), Christians (2000), and Mauthier et al. (2003) argue for a feminist based "ethic of care" to be applied instead of traditional rule-based ethical standards, consistent with their epistemologies and values. This work is valuable to much qualitative research, yet much more work on the application of ethical principles is needed to guide researchers and those who regulate them.

Larossa, Bennett, and Gelles (1981) argue that most qualitative research would benefit from a thorough risk-benefit analysis and explicitly obtaining informed consent from participants. I would agree fully. At the same time, the ethics literature documents numerous challenges for qualitative researchers involved in formal ethics review processes. Cheek (2000) briefly points out that formal institutional review is required of most funded qualitative research. She also notes that committee members often lack much knowledge of qualitative research methods. Thus extra effort is needed to educate committee members about the iterative nature of much qualitative research, and that samples and data collection methods (even specific questions) may not be fully known prior to undertaking the study. Note that such ethical and methodological "norming" by research ethics boards often parallels the application of inappropriate evaluation standards by editorial reviewers.

Van Den Hoonard (2002) points out that while many qualitative researchers reject the biomedical approach applied by ethics committees, they must nonetheless engage with them. This may pose some difficulties with specific qualitative methods. For example, he notes that research questions may emerge only after engagement with specific populations in some qualitative approaches (i.e., ethnography), or that changes in research methods may follow immersion with participants and setting. He also notes that populations may be far more heterogeneous than initially imaged, requiring changes in research method and adjustments to protections for vulnerable groups. Further, boundary issues are common in qualitative research as researchers seek to give voice to subjugated populations and to engage as equals with participants. These include issues of protecting privacy, entitlement to interpret others' words and actions, and even the power to determine the nature of the final research project. There are many emerging ethical issues in qualitative research warranting further professional discussion and elaboration. Biomedical and even social work research ethics as yet do not provide clear guidance on these issues, nor have guidelines for ethics review committees been developed to address them. This is an area in need of further study and development. Still, despite these challenges, qualitative researchers in social work should follow, apply, and report their efforts to realize ethical standards.

Criterion Four: Specifying the Study Methodology

In all qualitative research and reports, the researcher must clearly identify the methodology employed in the study and demonstrate its consistency with the study's philosophical base. Because of the different epistemologies and philosophical traditions that orient qualitative studies, and their different goals and audiences, somewhat different methods—or interpretations of methods—may be applied. For example, critical studies or feminist studies, based on particular value premises, may employ different methods than do realist studies of the same content area. Pivotal methodological differences center on the nature of the sample, data collection methods, methods of analysis, and methods of data presentation. Different ethical challenges may also be generated by divergent methods.

SAMPLING

Qualitative sampling is an area in need of refinement and elaboration within social work. Samples in many published qualitative studies are minimally described. The adequacy of the sample to meet the researcher's goals is often unclear and unconvincing. Sadly, American social work research textbooks do not describe qualitative sampling well nor detail its iterative nature (Drisko 2003). Detailed descriptions of qualitative sampling methods are also rare in qualitative research texts (Drisko 2003). Specifying a sampling plan and obtaining an adequate sample is vital to rigorous qualitative research.

Researchers should clearly specify the nature of the obtained study sample and the rationale for its selection. In some cases, such as the description of an event or experience, a single-stage sampling plan is adequate. One may illustrate diverse experiences or give testimony meaningfully and effectively without consideration of alternative or contradictory viewpoints. Yet selecting participants who have knowledge of the event or experience requires careful, knowledgeable decision-making. For example, in phenomenology, detailed portrayal of an experience may require only a few key informants. No effort to seek divergent viewpoints or to elaborate theory is inherently needed. In contrast, multiple stage sampling may be required to achieve other research goals. For example, development of a grounded theory about a specific illness will require participants with a range of views and experiences. Glaser and Strauss's concept of theoretical sampling (Strauss and Corbin 1990) is such an iterative approach. In theoretical sampling, changes to the sampling plan are almost always needed to obtain participants with a range of viewpoints on an emergent conceptual dimension. The researcher must actively seek out and include participants who can challenge, test, and elaborate preliminary concepts and theories.

Clearly, differences in study philosophy and objectives will point to different sampling methods. Therefore, researchers must clearly state their sampling methods consistent with the study philosophy.

Sampling is closely linked to the transferability of study findings. The development and testing of general concepts and theories, applicable across persons and settings, requires an analysis of alternative viewpoints, experiences, and circumstances (Drisko 1997). The obligation to seek out, report, and weigh contradictory evidence is an important aspect of establishing the transferability (generalizability) of research. Further, critical case analysis or analysis of extremely deviant cases can be immensely informative in establishing potential transferability of findings (Patton 1987). Such an analysis is only possible if the initial sampling is purposefully done and iteratively elaborated as analysis progresses (Glaser and Strauss 1967; LeCompte and Preissle 1993). Similarly, making a reasonable claim that findings or recommendations are transferable from one setting and context to another requires careful sample selection from divergent contexts. It is worth noting that efforts to seek out and grapple with potentially contradictory evidence will also add to the credibility and verisimilitude of qualitative research. Evaluation of the rigor of qualitative research requires a clear, detailed description of the sampling strategy.

TRANSFERABILITY/GENERALIZATION

Transferability refers to the applicability of findings and conclusions derived from one setting or context to other settings or contexts (Leininger 1994). Social workers and others also use the term generalization in reference to qualitative research (Reid 1994), but some authors believe this term implies a paradigm-specific goal of developing general laws that may not be the chosen goal of any given qualitative study (Lincoln and Guba 1985). The transferability of results beyond the original context, however, is often important to researchers and consumers of qualitative studies. As noted earlier, transferability is premised upon a sampling plan that includes variations in time, setting, and participants. Any claims to transferability must be consistent with the study philosophy, goals, and obtained sample.

A notable limitation of many published qualitative studies is the lack of explicit attention to the transferability of findings. Some qualitative researchers offer vivid, moving, and unique portrayals without comment on the transferability or generalizability of the findings. Quite appropriately,

the yield may be summary "sensitizing concepts" that raise the consciousness and awareness of the reader and are potentially relevant and applicable to other similar settings. However, the consumers of such research are
often left to formulate their own views about the transferability of the findings. As consistent with study goals, qualitative researchers should provide
guidance to the reader on the potential transferability of the findings and
its likely limitations. Such reflection can also increase the credibility of the
research.

DATA COLLECTION METHODS

There are several useful methods for qualitative data collection. Researchers should detail the nature of data collection methods employed to clarify
the nature of evidence used in the study. The transferability, credibility, and
verisimilitude of any qualitative research are shaped by the data under examination. A wide range of named qualitative research approaches draws
on a limited number of data collection methods (interviews, observations,
documents, etc.), but these methods are used with differing emphases. Data
collection methods should be fully consistent with the study philosophy
and goals. Most qualitative approaches employ flexible data collection methods that evolve to meet unexpected data and sources (Anastas 1999). That
is, rather than a single point in time data collection approach, multiple
data collection efforts may be made to gather somewhat different data or to
clarify and elaborate areas left unclear after initial data analysis. These efforts may focus on different data sources and even different data collection
types. Some authors (Denzin 1970; Padgett 2008) suggest triangulation of
data sources. Similarly, observation may be complemented with interviews,
or interviews compared with document and artifacts. However, triangulation usually presupposes a realist epistemology: A constructivist might assume different methods could yield different realities—realities that may
not point to a single understanding. Flexibility of data collection methods
assumes a consistent underlying epistemology for the study.

It is important to bear in mind that sampling, data collection, and data
analysis often form an iterative cycle in qualitative research. Analysis may
identify missing viewpoints and direct changes in sampling. Analysis may
also guide further data collection to elaborate and test preliminary findings and conceptualization. Thus data collection plans and purposes often
change during the course of a qualitative study. As with sampling, a single

fixed plan may not be sufficient to provide adequate evidence for many qualitative research purposes. Coffey and Atkinson (1996) further note that the same data may be analyzed using more than one analytic method (so long as the data are adequate to a thorough analysis).

All data, research notes, memos, and journals should be kept as permanent records that form an audit trail, allowing later examination of the study analysis by others. Though external audit of qualitative research in social work is rare, it may become more frequent as grant-funded projects increase in number. In all cases, detailing—and sharing with the reader—precisely what data has been collected is vital to a study's coherence and completeness.

One reporting challenge is to provide sufficient raw data to allow readers to form their own interpretations. Put another way, readers should have a full and clear map of what evidence leads to the researcher's development of codes, concepts, and theories. Readers and reviewers should be provided enough data to be able to appraise the researcher's conclusions and even to formulate interpretations at odds with those of the researcher. This requires considerable page space and is a challenge to authors and publishers of qualitative reports. Provision of pictures or sound by video or audiotape to reveal actions or nonverbal communications (alternately captured in memos) is both a technical challenge and one of space within a manuscript. Too often, researchers use the sound-bite approach in which a single, brief illustration in a participant's own words is provided. With very limited access to raw data, readers have neither opportunity to ascertain the accuracy and completeness of the researcher's interpretations nor a basis on which to develop their own interpretations. No opportunity to identify unrecognized bias from careful analysis is provided.

A similar challenge emerges around detailing the development of codes and theory. Leininger (1994) notes that claims of recurrent patterns or meanings in qualitative data demand ample documentation. Readers should be provided a grounded map of the researcher's coding efforts, including information on what data was included and excluded from some key codes.

It is worth noting that the requirement to provide ample data and details about the development of codes runs in stark contrast to the quantitative study where researchers typically report data in highly summarized form with interview questions or test items omitted. However, detailing recurrent patterns is crucial to building the credibility of the analysis and conclusions of a qualitative study. Illustrating coding procedures, like providing raw data, requires considerable page space. As such, it may be difficult in a 16- to 20-page manuscript. To provide a model for such a report, I suggest readers look to my study on how clinicians evaluate practice (Drisko 2002). Some reviewers who recommended revision initially felt that the manuscript had "too much raw data" and that I had not done enough "data reduction." Yet one of my research purposes was to illustrate in depth and complexity what participants had actually said. Monograph length reports may provide an alternative and allow greater length for qualitative reports. Solid monograph exemplars in social work include Mallon's (1998) *We Don't Exactly Get the Welcome Wagon* and Floersch's (2002) *Meds, Money and Manners.*

METHODS OF DATA ANALYSIS

Researchers should clearly identify their chosen methods of data analysis and ensure these are consistent with the study philosophy, objectives, and collected data. There are many methods of data analysis available to social work researchers (Tesch 1990; Crabtree and Miller 1999). The most widely cited in American social work publications is Glaser and Strauss's (1967) grounded theory method. However, given present curriculum guidelines, social workers may not know even grounded theory methods in detail. Indeed Wells (1995) and Oktay (2004) suggest published social work research often falls far short of being full grounded theories despite their methodological claims. In response, researchers must offer ample information about coding procedures and other aspects of data analysis within a qualitative report.

The methods of sampling, data collection and data analysis applied in matrix analysis, grounded theory, critical studies, and other qualitative approaches are generally well-developed in the existing literature. They vary in interpretation of qualitative data.

INTERPRETIVE CRITERIA FOR QUALITATIVE DATA ANALYSIS

Broadly applicable interpretive criteria have been offered for assessing data analysis in qualitative studies (Guba and Lincoln 1981; Altheide and Johnson 1994; Leininger 1994; Reid 1994; Rodwell and Woody 1994; Drisko 1998). The applicability of these criteria varies across the philosophical foundations applied in each qualitative research report. Four widely reported criteria are offered here, with variation in salience across different qualitative research approaches and their epistemological premises. These interpretive criteria refer broadly to the methods of capturing and conveying the experiences and meanings of research participants. The four criteria fit well with methods in the middle of Tesch's (1990) continuum (discovering patterns; comprehension of meaning) and with Crabtree and Miller's (1999) template or editing approaches.

The first interpretive criterion is credibility, or believability (Altheide and Johnson 1994; Reid 1994; Drisko 1997; Padgett 1998). Data and analysis must convey fully local participants' knowledge or experience in local context (Leininger 1994). Descriptions of internal knowledge, experiences, and interpretations must be authentic and accurate to the descriptions of the primary participants. The experiences of observers and other forms of data offer external (etic) perspectives that may add to our understandings and interpretations of internal, subjective (emic) knowledge, creating a credible cumulative whole. The whole, as presented to the reader, must be believable and reflect the participants'/informants' world(s), complemented by the researchers' own interpretations and analysis.

Such expectations fit easily within a realist epistemology in which an external reality is supposed and some degree of consistency over time expected. Yet constructivist researchers also apply the criterion to their work and, in some cases, offer technical methods to enhance credibility (Rodwell 1998).

As discussed previously, extensive reporting of raw data in the participant's own words or behavior supports credibility and verisimilitude. Access to raw data allows the reader to decide how credibly the researcher has summarized and interpreted others' experiences and understandings. Given certain epistemological premises, no amount of data ensures credibility, but access to more data certainly enhances it. Additional confirmatory efforts that enhance credibility will be discussed here.

The second interpretative criterion is locating meanings in context (Lincoln and Guba 1985; Leininger 1994; Riessman 1994; Rodwell 1998). Locating meanings within their situational contexts is a strength of rigorous qualitative research. Qualitative data are optimally meaningful within particular contexts or settings. Context may be pivotal to generating meaning and placing participants' understanding. Thus qualitative research and reports convey the local context and perspective. Reports must indicate how meanings or interpretations are consistent with, or conflict with, external interpretations.

Locating meanings in local context enhances the credibility of qualitative research. It is pivotal in standpoint and constructivist research and illuminating in critical theorizing and ethnic studies. The researcher's understanding of evidence should be compared and contrasted with the local meanings established in the participant's own context. In doing so, the researcher also indicates potential limitations to the transferability of data and conclusions.

The third interpretative criterion is confirmability. Confirmability refers to the researcher's efforts to corroborate data as well as to challenge and/or affirm interpretation or theory (Reid 1994; Padgett 1998; Rodwell 1998). Multiple, repeated instances of an event or interpretation, obtained from direct observation or reports from primary sources enhance credibility and confirmability. Note that this criterion assumes some form of consistency of interpretation, an assumption some constructivists would not make. Nonetheless, Rodwell (1998), in describing a constructivist method, suggests that member checks with participants to establish that codes are believable to the primary informants ensures accuracy and enhances credibility. Padgett (1998) suggests triangulation of data sources in Denzin's (1970) sense enhances credibility. The consistency of what is seen and heard with other material sources also establishes confirmability. In addition, triangulation may include multiple methods, data sources, data types, analytic methods, and theoretical perspectives (Denzin 1970).

Reporting confirmation efforts ensures the reader can establish the nature and extent of confirmatory activities. Explicit description of the member checks and other feedback sessions is useful to the reader's ability to evaluate credibility and contexualization. Description of audit trails or similar documenting activities is valuable to peer and external reviewers of the project as whole.

The fourth interpretive criterion is completeness, or saturation. Completeness refers to the comprehensiveness of the data collection and the analysis of the data. Completeness has two important dimensions. First, the researcher must demonstrate thorough, even exhaustive, knowledge of the experiences or events being studied (Patton 1987). The available data should be comprehensive, allowing "thick" and "deep" description and analysis (Glaser and Strauss 1967; Strauss and Corbin 1990; Charmaz 2006). The collected and analyzed data should also reach a point of saturation in which additional data are repetitive and add no more to the study's yield (Leininger 1994). Technically, achieving saturation requires pushing participants to say a little more, observing yet again, and finding no new insight. In data analysis, saturation is achieved when description or conceptual development is credible, located in context, and fully captures variations across settings and conditions. Demonstrating saturation in an article-length manuscript is exceedingly difficult. It is more often asserted than fully established in such short reports.

The second dimension of completeness is that the researcher must provide a comprehensive, saturated report to the reader. The evidence presented to the reader must be credible, located in context, and compelling or useful. The report should also identify and examine variation and contradictions explicitly.

The relative importance of each of these four interpretative criteria may vary with the philosophical frame and objectives of a given study. Nonetheless, qualitative research using template or interpretative analytic procedures will need to address all four interpretive criteria to claim rigor.

Criterion Five: Identifying Potential Biases and Researcher Self-Reflection

Because the researcher is the key tool in qualitative research, explicitly identifying sources of potential researcher bias strengthens the credibility of qualitative reports (Hyde 1994; Reid 1994). Bias in qualitative research refers to influences that impair complete, balanced, or accurate sampling, data collection, data interpretation, and reporting. Qualitative researchers seek to limit bias through recognition and self-awareness. Efforts to identify biases should begin with examination of initial expectations for the study and end with its publication. Therefore, researchers should systematically record or journal and report any biases they recognize. Explicit reporting of potential sources of bias helps alert readers and can enhance the credibility of the report.

A potential source of bias is the initial motivation or funding source for the research. Other sources of potential bias may only become evident during the research process. Notably, problems in sampling and gaps in available data may only become evident late in the research process. For example, in an evaluation of family preservation service outcome from the perspective of clients, I was referred families receiving family preservation services by their social workers (Drisko 1997). In informal discussion, it emerged that staff were concerned that the study was implicitly evaluating their work. I wondered if staff might be referring only families who would likely be affirming of their work, so I sought to counter this possible bias by actively seeking families who were unhappy with services. These families did voice some concerns regarding confidentiality not previously raised. I briefly described this aspect of sampling in the report. A potential source of bias was identified and addressed. At the same time, the reader was alerted to look for examples of criticisms and complaints by the families within the report. Field notes, personal journals, and memos can help document thoughts about biases or limitations in methods. Such steps should be described in the study report.

Qualitative researchers who have personal experience with the content they are studying face a dilemma. One the one hand, personal knowledge helps establish personal bona fides, affords some perspective, enhances awareness of certain details, and raises awareness of certain feelings. On the other hand, one's own experience may differ markedly from the reactions, experiences, contexts, and interpretations of the research participants. Glaser and Strauss (1967) note that personal experience is an important part of theoretical sensitivity but may also lead to bias and misunderstanding without efforts to identify and limit it. Ongoing peer review—by another person who knows the experience and one or more who do not—along with mentoring, member checks, use of negative cases, and self-reflection all support understanding the experiences of others in depth and variety. It provides a mechanism to enhance identification of biases and inform choice regarding the merits and limits of using one's own experiences as a guide to understanding others. For those without personal experience of the research topic, the same techniques may be used to help provide orientation, and to expand openness to feelings and contexts and awareness of missed detail and nuance. Both starting points allow for bias, as well as for failure to understand, but the specific challenges differ. Good research work on bias identification has many parallels to the social work practitioner's reflective use of self: Both practitioner and researcher must continuously reexamine their biases, reactions, and areas of omission with the help of others throughout their work. Innovative approaches to qualitative research, such as autoethnography—though very rare in social work to date, offer additional opportunities for using personal experiences to inform others.

Another area of ambiguity is how much self-reflection and bias identification is enough. Readers and reviewers may always question researcher intentions, methods, and interpretations. Researchers should provide information to make plain potential sources of bias on areas of central importance to the study. However, it is unlikely a simple rule-based formulation will be sufficient to guide such reflection across the variety of qualitative studies. Researcher and reader judgment is always required.

Criterion Six: Maintaining Internal Consistency of Conclusions with Epistemology and Methods

The analysis, conclusions, and recommendations of a qualitative study should be internally consistent with the study's philosophy and objectives, and limited to the presented data. In many ways this final summative criterion defines rigor in qualitative research (Drisko 1999). The goals of qualitative research range from depth exploration of individual viewpoints, to thick description of experiences, to evaluation of cases and programs and the development and testing of theory. Thus qualitative reports will vary widely in the types and extent conclusions and recommendations are offered. Illustrating a subjugated viewpoint may require little discussion by the author. On the other hand, critical analysis of the same viewpoint requires extensive discussion and analysis to yield meaningful and transferable conclusions. Grounded theory or institutional ethnography requires thoughtful and extensive application of many methodological steps to assure the theory is credible, complete, and meaningful in content.

An issue arising in the social work literature is absent or minimal theory development in reports that claim to be based on grounded theory and analytic induction methods (Wells 1995; Oktay 2004). Instead of theory, description is offered without conceptualization. Internal consistency would require reporting of a theoretical perspective to help others understand the events under study and that might frame policy and practice. The yield of such studies must be more than merely descriptive; analysis and conceptual development of a particular type is also required. Indeed, grounded theory requires the active testing of new concepts and theories, not just their production (Glaser and Strauss 1967).

To be rigorous, qualitative researchers must offer conclusions consistent with their chosen philosophical approach, goals, and methods. Such coherence is central to a study's credibility and the utility of conclusions and recommendations it offers. Such coherence is only possible at the end of an ongoing, reflective, critical appraisal of the study throughout the entire course of the project. In some published qualitative research, the discussion and recommendations are overgeneralized or over-transferred beyond the contexts in which they were developed and/or tested. While this may be appropriate when sensitizing concepts or new grounded theories are offered to challenge and extend the thinking of others, it is less appropriate when specific recommendations are made as a basis for practice or policy. Another inconsistency occurs when constructivist researchers reframe co-constructed and potentially mutable meanings into invariant "truths" when implications and recommendations are offered. Here researcher enthusiasm replaces internal consistency of epistemology, data, and interpretation. Such implicit realism (Heron 1996; Coffey and Atkinson 1996 Seale 1999) may come to replace constructed understanding, assuming a single reality over multiple and divergent realities. Researchers may also reify initial value premises, making interesting ideas or interpretations into "facts" over the course of a study or a report (see Seale 1999, chapter 1 for an excellent example). Great care should be taken to maintain consistency of study epistemology, goals, and methods with discussion and implications.

Standards and Qualitative Inquiry: Exceptions

The very idea of standards for qualitative research has recently been hotly contested among qualitative researchers. Some view standards as potential "straitjackets" for an intellectual terrain that should continue to be innovative, challenging, and rapidly evolving. Indeed, one well-known qualitative researcher stated this concern in reaction to a presentation of these standards at a major qualitative research conference (Drisko 2007). Still, others saw them as useful. The core concern is that standards will become, or be used as, a set of conventions that define good work, become reified, and create another power structure that limits variety and innovation. Many qualitative researchers still smart from too few journal outlets for their work and from the many manuscript reviewers that powerfully demonstrate a lack of knowledge and background to do a competent review of the submitted work on its own terms. The current, predominantly quantitative, publication and research funding structure in social work acts as one of these conservative power structures. The ideology and political impact of evidence-based approaches actively devalues qualitative research and often fails to notice or acknowledge how dependent experimental designs are on the innovations, concepts, and theory originally generated by qualitative research. If standards become another route to limit inquiry, innovation, and expression, they may indeed be a bad thing.

After years of my own active reflection and lots of input, pro and con, from colleagues of many disciplines, I still think these standards are a good starting point for teaching and for discussion among active researchers. These standards are intended as broadly applicable guidelines to be used flexibly rather than as a straitjacket. They do have their limitations. They are not a checklist yielding a simple summative assessment; rather they call for internal consistency and transparency in qualitative studies. I am also very committed to improving the quality of social work's qualitative research, which is often intellectually uninformed and methodologically lacking. Two-sentence methodology sections for complex studies are common and inevitably inadequate. Misnamed and incomplete analyses are also common. Themes presented as the only yield of grounded theory methods make a mockery of a valuable research approach. Serious social issues and good ideas deserve better exploration and description. I would like to see more varied and better quality qualitative research in social work.

I think that these standards fit easily with research projects and reports drawing on realist and pragmatic epistemologies. I will also argue that they fit well with many types of constructivist research, especially those that include moderate to large samples and have exploratory or descriptive purposes. Yet given the diversity of qualitative inquiry, there are some studies and reports that these standards do not address well.

Growing interest in critical perspectives, in indigenous methodologies, in participatory action research models, and in performance-based studies and reports make it very difficult to create truly comprehensive standards for qualitative research. Critical analyses seek to clarify and explore topics from new, challenging perspectives. Such efforts at making the invisible visible or at consciousness raising or at perspective changing, may be quite effectively derived from a single case or from thoughtful analysis of theory or through the perspectives of members of oppressed social groups. For example, queer theory, feminist theory, and red pedagogy all offer perspectives social workers need to know and understand to effectively research nondominant groups. Qualitative inquiry can help understand nondominant views, beliefs, and needs. It is also intellectually enlarging to be pushed outside the box. Many valuable critical studies will not fit these standards easily, nor should they. These new frameworks are valuable for developing professional knowledge and for improving practice.

Participatory action research invites a less hierarchical, more democratic, and more inclusive approach to research. Empowering subjects to become true participants in research may lead to new questions and new practical solutions. These methods, and their emphasis on inclusion, fit well with social work's professional values. These standards, however, provide little guidance on appraising or evaluating participation beyond that of the researcher. On the other hand, these standards do not constrain including additional, relevant information about the research process or its results. Detailing how joint participation in designing and completing research projects was undertaken can surely coexist with documenting the internal consistency of research purpose, epistemology, methods, and reporting style.

These standards fit least well with performance or immersive research approaches. Such research or inquiry may not seek to be scientific. Indeed, some scholars promote the use of aesthetic or artistic criteria for their evaluation. While I believe these efforts can be innovative and consciousness-raising, I tend to think of them as inquiry rather than research. The distinction is a subtle one. These standards focus on research efforts within a broad scientific framework. They may not be suitable for the planning and evaluation of other forms of inquiry with different purposes and guiding frameworks. As I stated in 2000, "it's not just anything goes" in qualitative research, but neither is it "one size fits all."

Summary

This chapter details criteria for developing and evaluating qualitative social work studies. The criteria are equally valuable for orienting and guiding qualitative studies through the formulation and implementation phases. These criteria, concepts, and terminology are applicable *across* epistemological approaches and traditions of qualitative research, yet several criteria also emphasize specific issues *within* methods.

The application of evaluative criteria requires multiple judgments about content and quality in addition to addressing each of these criteria. These criteria are intended as a general scaffolding for evaluation, not as a checklist or a straitjacket. Formal evaluation of research projects or research reports will also require additional, content specific judgments.

These criteria for orienting and evaluating qualitative research in social work reports are intended to promote rigor. They may also be useful for teaching qualitative research. Finally, they are intended to serve as standards for editorial reviewers of qualitative studies.

Notes

1. It is important to point out that few true (statistically based) content analyses are labeled as qualitative research in the social work literature. Content analysis is, however, a well-developed research approach for exploring unstructured, qualitative, textual data. Social work students and other authors sometimes use the term content analysis as shorthand for various forms of self-generated derivations of themes from unstructured narrative data. Sadly, the methods by which these themes are generated are rarely specified; they differ markedly from content analysis. Such usage is an indication of a lack of training in qualitative data analysis methods.

2. Note that selecting an epistemology assumes the researcher has been educated sufficiently to be able to view epistemologies as choices with different merits and limitations. It is unclear that social workers generally, even at the doctoral level, are adequately trained to make such choices and to understand their implications in doing qualitative research.

References

Altheide, D. L. and J. M. Johnson. 1994. Criteria for assessing interpretive validity in qualitative research. In *Handbook of qualitative research*. N. K. Denzin and Y. S. Lincoln, eds. 485–499. Newbury Park, CA: Sage.

Anastas, J. 1999. *Research design for social work and the human services* (2nd ed.). New York: Columbia.

——. 2004. Quality in qualitative evaluation: Issues and possible answers. *Research on Social Work Practice*, 15(1):57–65.

Barbour, R. S. 2001. Checklists for improving rigour in qualitative research: A case of the tail wagging the dog? *British Medical Journal*, 332(7294):1115–1117.

Berkwits, M. and R. Aronowitz. 1995. Different questions beg different methods. *Journal of General Internal Medicine* 19:409–410.

Burnette, D. 1994. Managing chronic illness alone in late life: Sisyphus at work. In *Qualitative studies in social work*, C. Riessman, ed. 5–27. Thousand Oaks, CA: Sage.

Burns, N. 1989. Standards for qualitative research. *Nursing Science Quarterly*, 2(4):44–52.

Charmaz, K. 2006. *Constructing grounded theory*. Thousand Oaks, CA: Sage.

Cheek, J. 2000. An untold story? Doing funded qualitative research. In *Handbook of qualitative research* (2nd ed.), N. Denzin and Y. Lincoln, eds. 401–420. Thousand Oaks, CA: Sage.

Chenail, R. 1997. Keeping things plumb in qualitative research. *The Qualitative Report*, 3(3). Online journal article available at http://www.nova.edu/ssss/QR/QR3-3/plumb.html

Christians, C. 2000. Ethics and politics in qualitative research. In *Handbook of qualitative research* (2nd ed.), N. Denzin and Y. Lincoln, eds. 133–155. Thousand Oaks, CA: Sage.

Coffey, A. and P. Atkinson. 1996. *Making sense of qualitative data: Complimentary research strategies*. Thousand Oaks, CA: Sage.

Council on Social Work Education. 2008. *Handbook of accreditation policies and procedures* (6th ed.). Alexandria, VA: Author.

——. 2002. *Handbook of accreditation standards and procedures* (5th ed.). Alexandria, VA: Author.

——. 1994. *Handbook of accreditation standards and procedures* (4th ed.). Alexandria, VA: Author.

Crabtree, B. and W. Miller. 1999. *Doing qualitative research* (2nd ed.). Thousand Oaks, CA: Sage.

Davis, L. 1994. Is feminist research inherently qualitative and is it fundamentally a different approach to research? Yes. In *Controversial issues in social work research*, W. Hudson and P. Nurius, eds. 63–68. Boston: Allyn and Bacon.

Dean, R. 1993. Constructivism: An approach to clinical practice. *Smith College Studies in Social Work*, 63(2):127–146.

Denzin, N. 1970. *The research act: A theoretical introduction to sociological methods*. Chicago: Aldine.

Denzin, N. and Y. Lincoln. 1994. Introduction: Entering the field of qualitative research. In *Handbook of qualitative research*, N. Denzin and Y. Lincoln, eds. 1–17. Thousand Oaks, CA: Sage.

DePoy, E., A. Hartman, and D. Haslett. 1999. Critical action research: A model for social work knowing. *Social Work*. 44(6):560–569.

Drisko, J. 1997. Strengthening qualitative studies and reports: Standards to enhance academic integrity. *Journal of Social Work Education*, 33:187–197.

——. 1998. Utilization-focused evaluation of two intensive family preservation programs. *Families in Society: The Journal of Contemporary Human Services*, 79(1):62–74.

———. (1999). "Rigor in qualitative research." Juried symposium paper (with papers by D. Padgett, J. Anastas, and D. Shelby) presented at the Society for Social Work and Research, Austin, TX.

———. 2000a. Computer-aided data analysis. In *Research Design for Social Work and the Human Services* (2nd ed.) Anastas, J., ed. 503–532. New York: Columbia U P.

———. (2000b). "It's not just anything goes: Qualitative data analysis methods." Juried workshop presented at Social Work and Research Annual Meeting, Charleston, SC.

———. 2001. How do clinical social workers evaluate practice? *Smith College Studies in Social Work, 71*(3):419–439.

———. (2003). "Improving sampling strategies and terminology in qualitative research." Juried paper presented at the Society for Social Work and Research Annual Meeting, Washington, DC.

———. 2004. Qualitative data analysis software: A user's appraisal. In *The Qualitative Research Experience* (revised ed.), D. Padgett, ed. 193–209. Belmont, CA: Wadsworth.

———. (2007). "Standards for qualitative research: A both-and approach." Juried paper presented at the International Congress of Qualitative Inquiry, Champaign-Urbana, IL.

———. 2008. How is qualitative research taught at the master's level? *Journal of Social Work Education, 48*:85–101.

———. (2012). Using ATLAS.ti Software in Qualitative Research. Workshop presented at the Columbia University School of Social Work, New York, NY.

Eakin, J. and E. Mykhalovskiy. 2003. Reframing the evaluation of qualitative health research: Reflections on a review of appraisal guidelines in the health sciences. *Journal of Evaluation in Clinical Practice, 9*(2):187–197.

Eisner, E. 1997. *The enlightened eye: Qualitative inquiry and the enhancement of educational practice.* New York: Prentice Hall.

Floersch, J. 2002. *Meds, money and manners.* New York: Columbia.

Gilgun, J. 2008. Lived experience, reflexivity, and research on perpetrators of interpersonal violence. *Qualitative Social Work, 7*(2):181–197.

———. 1994. A case for case studies in social work research. *Social Work, 39*:371–380.

Glaser, B. 1992. *Basics of grounded theory analysis.* Mill Valley, CA: Sociology.

Glaser, B. and A. Strauss. 1967. *The discovery of grounded theory.* Chicago: Aldine.

Greene, J. 1994. Qualitative program evaluation: Practice and promise. In *Handbook of qualitative research*, N. Denzin and Y. Lincoln, eds. 530–544. Thousand Oaks, CA: Sage.

Guba, E. 1981. Criteria for assessing the trustworthiness of naturalistic inquiries. *Educational Communications and Technology Journal, 29*:75–92.

Guba, E. and Y. Lincoln. 1981. *Effective evaluation*. San Francisco, CA: Jossey Bass.

Hammersley, M. 2008. *Questioning qualitative inquiry: Critical essays*. Thousand Oaks, CA: Sage.

Hartman, A. 1990. Editorial: Many ways of knowing. *Social Work*, 35:3–4.

——. 1994. Setting the theme: Many ways of knowing. In *Qualitative research in social work*, E. Sherman and W. Reid eds. 459–463. New York, NY: Columbia.

Healy, T. 1993. A struggle for language: Patterns of self-disclosure in lesbian couples. *Smith College Studies in Social Work* 63(3):247–263.

Heineman Pieper, M. 1989. The heuristic paradigm: A unifying and comprehensive approach to social work research. *Smith College Studies in Social Work*, 60(1):8–34.

——. 1994. Science, not scientism: The robustness of naturalistic clinical research. In *Qualitative research in social work*, E. Sherman and W. Reid. eds. 71–88. New York: Columbia.

Heron, J. 1996. *Co-operative inquiry: Research into the human condition*. Thousand Oaks, CA: Sage.

Hollis, M. 1994. *The philosophy of social science: An introduction*. New York: Cambridge.

House, E. 1991. Realism in research. *Educational Researcher*, 20(6):2–9, 25.

Huston, P. and M. Rowan. 1997. Qualitative research articles: Information for authors and peer reviewers. *Canadian Medical Association Journal*. 157(10):1442–1446.

Hyde, C. 1994. Reflections on a journey: A research story. In *Qualitative studies in social work*, C. K. Riessman, ed. 169–189. Thousand Oaks, CA: Sage.

Inui, T. and R. Frankel. 1991. Evaluating the quality of qualitative research. *Journal of General Internal Medicine*, 6:485–486.

Kazi, M. (2002). "Realist evaluation for practice." Paper presented at the 6th Annual Conference of the Society for Social Work and Research, San Diego, CA.

Kondrat, M. E. 2002. Actor-centered social work: Re-visioning "person-in-environment" through a critical theory lens. *Social Work*, 47(4):435–448.

Kuhn, T. 1996. The *structure of scientific revolutions* (3rd ed.). Chicago: University of Chicago.

Larossa, R., L. Bennett, and R. Gelles. 1981. Ethical dilemmas in qualitative family research. *Journal of Marriage and the Family*, 43(2):303–313.

Lazarton, A. (2003). Evaluative standards for qualitative research in applied linguistics: Whose criteria and whose research? *The Modern Language Journal*, 87:1–12.

LeCompte, M. and J. Preissle. 1993. *Ethnography and qualitative design in educational research* (2nd ed.). New York: Academic.

Leininger, M. 1994. Evaluation criteria and critique of qualitative studies. In *Critical issues in qualitative research methods*, J. Morse, ed. 95–115. Newbury Park, CA: Sage.

Lincoln, Y. and E. Guba. 1985. *Naturalistic inquiry.* Beverly Hills, CA: Sage.

Lindsley, E. 1997. Feminist issues in qualitative research with formerly homeless mothers. *Affilia, 12*(1):57–75.

Mallon, G. 1998. *We don't exactly get the welcome wagon.* New York: Columbia.

Mauthier, M., M. Birch, J. Jessop, and T. Miller. 2003. *Ethics in qualitative research.* Thousand Oaks, CA: Sage.

Mays, N., and C. Pope. 2000. Assessing quality in qualitative research. *British Medical Journal, 320*:50–52.

Miles, M. and A. Huberman. 1984. *Qualitative data analysis: A sourcebook of new methods.* Beverly Hills, CA: Sage.

National Association of Social Workers. 2008. *Code of ethics.* Washington, DC: Author.

National Institutes of Health, Office of Behavioral and Social Sciences Research. (undated). *Qualitative methods in health research: Opportunities and considerations in application and review.* Retrieved January 4, 2004 from http://obssr.od.nih.gov/publications/qualitative.pdf.

Oktay, J. 2004. Grounded theory. In *The Qualitative Research Experience* (revised ed.), D. Padgett, ed. 23–47. Belmont, CA: Wadsworth.

Padgett, D. 1998. *Qualitative methods in social work research.* Thousand Oaks, CA: Sage.

——. 2008. *Qualitative methods in social work research* (2nd ed). Thousand Oaks, CA: Sage.

Padgett, D. (ed.). 2004. The *qualitative research experience* (revised ed.). Belmont, CA: Wadsworth.

Patton, M. Q. 1986. *Utilization-focused evaluation.* Newbury Park, CA: Sage.

——. 1987. *Using qualitative methods in evaluation.* Newbury Park, CA: Sage.

Peirce, C. S. 1986. *Philosophical writings of Peirce.* New York: Dover.

Popay, J. 1995. Qualitative research and the gingerbread man. *Health Education Journal, 54*:389–392.

Popay, J., A. Rogers, and G. Williams. 1998. Rationale and standards for the systematic review of qualitative literature in health services research. *Qualitative Health Research, 8*(3):341–351.

Punch, M. 1994. Politics and ethics in qualitative research. In *Handbook of qualitative research*, N. Denzin and Y. Lincoln, eds. 83–97. Thousand Oaks, CA: Sage.

Reid, W. 1994. Reframing the epistemological debate. In *Qualitative research in social work*, E. Sherman and W. Reid, eds. 464–481. New York, NY: Columbia.

Riessman, C. K. (ed.). 1994. Preface: Making room for diversity in social work research. In *Qualitative studies in social work*, C. K. Riessman, ed. vii–xx. Thousand Oaks, CA: Sage.

Rodwell, M. and D. Woody. 1994. Constructivist evaluation: The policy/practice context. In *Qualitative research in social work*, E. Sherman and W. Reid, eds. 315–372. New York, NY: Columbia.

Rodwell [O'Connor], M. C. 1998. *Constructivist social work research.* New York: Garland.

Rubin, A. 2008. *Practitioner's guide to using research for evidence-based practice.* New York: John Wiley.

Ruckdeshel, R., P. Earnshaw, and A. Ferrik. 1994. The qualitative case study and evaluation: Issues, methods and examples. In *Qualitative research in social work,* E. Sherman and W. Reid, eds. 251–264. New York, NY: Columbia.

Seale, C. 1999. *The quality of qualitative research.* London: Sage.

Shaw, I., and N. Gould. (eds.) 2002. *Qualitative research in social work.* Thousand Oaks, CA: Sage.

Smith, J. and D. Deemes. 2000. The problem of criteria in the age of relativism. In *Handbook of qualitative research* (2nd ed.),N. Denzin and Y. Lincoln, eds. 877–896. Thousand Oaks, CA: Sage.

Solomon, C. 1994. Welfare workers' responses to homeless welfare applicants. In *Qualitative studies in social work,* C. Riessman, ed.153–168. Thousand Oaks, CA: Sage.

Spencer, L., J. Ritchie, J. Lewis, and L. Dillon. 2003. Quality in qualitative research: A framework for assessing research evidence. London: Cabinet Office, Government Chief Social Researcher's Office. Retrieved May 15, 2004 from http://www.strategy.gov.uk/files/pdf/Quality_framework.pdf.

Strauss, A. and J. Corbin. 1990. *Basics of qualitative research: Grounded theory procedures and techniques.* Newbury Park, CA: Sage.

Swigonski, M. 1994. The logic of feminist standpoint theory for social work research. *Social Work,* 39(4):387–393.

Tesch, R. 1990. *Qualitative research: Analysis types and software tools.* New York: Falmer.

Tyson, L. 1995. *New foundations for social scientific and behavioral research: The heuristic paradigm.* Newbury Park, CA: Sage.

Van Den Hoonard, W. (ed.). 2002. *Walking the tightrope: Ethical issues for qualitative researchers.* Toronto: University of Toronto.

Wells, K. 1995. The strategy of grounded theory: Possibilities and problems. *Social Work Research,* 19(1): 33–37.

[2]

Ethics in Qualitative Research

FREDERIC G. REAMER

Qualitative research in social work has come of age. Especially since the 1980s, social work scholars and practitioners have enhanced their grasp of the rich potential of qualitative research methods and data to further the profession's understanding of human and social problems. Social workers' increased appreciation and use of ethnographic and narrative methods, situational and discourse analysis, participatory action research, and focus groups have done much to advance our understanding of, and ability to address, compelling and daunting challenges related to many areas, such as child welfare, aging, poverty, mental illness, crime and delinquency, health care, domestic violence, and substance abuse (Denzin and Lincoln 2000; Patton 2002; Shaw and Gould 2002; Antle, Regehr, and Mishna 2004; Creswell 2006; Padgett 2008).

Only recently, however, have social workers interested in qualitative research begun to pay explicit and sustained attention to pertinent ethical issues.[1] Limited focus on ethical issues was not unusual for the earliest publications that used or discussed qualitative research methods (Richmond 1917; Hollis 1949; Polsky 1962; Mayer and Timms 1970; Tripodi and Epstein 1980).

This is not to say that social workers have been unaware of ethical issues in research. For decades, social workers have addressed a wide range of ethical issues in research, but they have focused on a variety of protection of human subjects issues that typically arise in conjunction with traditional experimental, quasi-experimental, and quantitative research (Reamer 2006a, 2010). Especially since the 1970s, social workers have wrestled with a range of ethical issues pertaining to the random assignment of research participants to experimental and control groups, the withdrawal of interventions in single system (N = 1) designs, the use of deception, and informed consent. However, literature on unique ethical issues arising out of qualitative research has been notably thin.

Clearly, the tide is changing. For a variety of reasons, social workers are now much more cognizant of, and attentive to, a variety of ethical issues germane to qualitative research. Without question, the widespread codification and formalization of research ethics protocols for more traditional quantitative research are being extended to qualitative research. It has taken some time for this to happen, but it is happening.

The proliferation of ethical standards in research is the result of two major phenomena. The first involves developments in the healthcare field. Perhaps the most significant historical event was the trial of the Nazi doctors at Nuremberg in 1945 following the inhumane experiments they conducted for the benefit of the Third Reich. These proceedings informed the world about the profound harm that can result from unethical research and led to the Nuremberg Code and other international codes of ethics designed to protect research participants (R. Levine 1988; C. Levine 1991).

Two other inglorious episodes in the history of healthcare research also paved the way for major reforms, particularly with respect to the protection of vulnerable populations (Loue 2000; Shamoo and Resnik 2009). The first involved the infamous Tuskegee syphilis study, a 40-year project begun in 1932 by the U.S. Public Health Service to investigate the natural history of untreated syphilis. The project's participants included low-income black men from Alabama who were told that they had "bad blood" and that they would receive free treatments such as spinal taps. These men were not provided with what then was the standard and widely accepted treatment for syphilis, nor were they provided with penicillin when it became available later during the study. The men in the study were not informed about the research design or the various health risks they faced as a result of their participation. Many of the men died. However, the study's unethical design and methods did not come to light until 1972.

The second widely publicized, notorious lapse in research ethics also involved a very vulnerable population: children diagnosed with mental retardation. The children lived at the Willowbrook State Hospital in Staten Island, New York, and were deliberately infected with hepatitis to enable researchers to study the history of the disease when left untreated. The researchers also aimed to evaluate the effects of gamma globulin as a treatment option. Researchers attempted to convince the parents to enroll the children in the study in exchange for admission to the hospital, which had limited space.

Growing awareness of ethical risks in research and occasional ethical misconduct led to a series of influential regulations designed to protect participants from harm. The first prominent guidelines in the United States were introduced in 1966 when Surgeon General William Stewart issued a U.S. Public Health Service directive on human experimentation. This directive announced that the U.S. Public Health Service would not fund research unless the sponsoring institution receiving the federal funds documented the procedures in place to ensure research participants' informed consent, the use of appropriate and ethical research procedures, an adequate review of the risks and medical benefits of the study, and the procedures designed to protect research participants' rights. Also during the 1960s, the World Medical Association issued the Declaration of Helsinki, which elaborated on the informed consent standards contained in the Nuremberg Code in 1946 (Whitebeck 1998).

Other influential documents that have had a profound influence on current ethical standards in research are the *Belmont Report* (National Commission for the Protection of Human Subjects of Biomedical and Behavioral Research 1979) and the *International Guidelines for Biomedical Research Involving Human Subjects* (Council for International Organizations of Medical Sciences 1993). The *Belmont Report* laid out clear guidelines to protect human participants based on three core values: respect for persons, beneficence, and justice (Weijer 1998; Berg 2008). The *International Guidelines for Biomedical Research Involving Human Subjects* promulgated 15 specific standards for researchers, focusing on issues such as informed consent, the extent to which a research project is responsive to community needs, and careful review of a research project's methodology by an ethical review committee.

The second major phenomenon that accounts for the elaboration of ethical standards in research was the emergence of a new field of study in the early 1970s: applied and professional ethics. This unique field, which began primarily with developments related to healthcare ethics (or bioethics) and then spread to other professions, stimulated considerable interest in diverse ethical issues related to, for example, genetic engineering, organ transplantation, end-of-life decisions, involuntary psychiatric treatment, whistle-blowing in government, the limits of clients' right to confidentiality and privacy, informed consent, and deceptive marketing.[2] The burgeoning professional ethics field provided a hospitable environment for practitioners and scholars to explore a variety of complex ethical issues related to research and evaluation.

Social workers' discussions of ethical issues in research have also matured, even though most have not focused explicitly on qualitative methods. Over the years a number of social work research textbooks have acknowledged the importance of research ethics and discuss key ethics concepts (Reid and Smith 1989; Reamer 1998; Grinnell and Unrau 2007; Yegidis and Weinbach 2008; Rubin and Babbie 2010; Thyer 2010), drawing heavily on the evolving ethical standards for experimental, quasi-experimental, and quantitative research projects in the biomedical and social science fields. A critical event for social workers was the ratification of the 1996 *Code of Ethics* of the National Association of Social Workers (NASW 1996). This code, only the third in NASW's history, greatly expanded the number and range of ethical standards pertaining to social work research and evaluation. The 1979 code, which preceded the 1996 code, contained seven ethical guidelines governing research and evaluation; the 1996 code contained sixteen specific ethical standards (Reamer 2006a).

Despite this dramatic growth in social workers' understanding of ethical issues in general and, more specifically, ethical issues in research, practitioners have paid relatively little attention to ethical issues in qualitative research per se (exceptions include Tutty, Rothery and Grinnell 1996; Zeni 2001; Padgett 2008).[3] The purpose of this discussion is to provide a comprehensive, albeit succinct, overview of key ethical issues germane to qualitative inquiry in social work: formulation of research and evaluation questions; sample selection; informed consent; institutional review; research and evaluation design; use of deception and coercion; confidentiality and privacy; preventing distress and harm; conflicts of interest and boundary issues; reporting results; and acknowledging credit. As the discussion will make clear, some aspects of these ethical issues are germane to social work research and evaluation in general and some are unique to qualitative research and evaluation. An overarching theme of this discussion is the key role that values and ethics play in social workers' efforts to use qualitative research as a mechanism to empower informants, strengthen social workers' partnership with informants, and recognize informants' expertise.

Formulation of Research and Evaluation Questions

In order to wrestle with a series of complex ethical issues germane to qualitative research and evaluation, social workers must first settle on the research questions and issues they plan to pursue (Boman and Jevne 2000). On the surface, these choices may not seem to be ethical in nature. However, social workers' very choice of issues to pursue should be guided by the profession's core values, mission, and ethical guidelines. For example, the *Code of Ethics* of the National Association of Social Workers (1999) lists several core values that constitute the profession's moral foundation:

- *Service*: Social workers' primary goal is to help people in need and to address social problems.
- *Social justice*: Social workers challenge social injustice.
- *Dignity and worth of the person*: Social workers respect the inherent dignity and worth of the person.
- *Importance of human relationships*: Social workers recognize the central importance of human relationships.
- *Integrity*: Social workers behave in a trustworthy manner.
- *Competence*: Social workers practice within their areas of competence and develop and enhance their professional expertise.

One can argue that qualitative research and evaluation projects that promote and are consistent with these values (and the code's accompanying ethical standards) are more compelling than projects that are not consistent with these values and do not advance social work's mission. Examples of compelling qualitative research projects consistent with social work values and ethics would include using grounded theory to explore the experiences of vulnerable people who are homeless, living with mental illness, victims of domestic violence, coping with physical disabilities, and parenting foster children; narrative analysis to collect, interpret, and apply information gathered from parents who are grieving the death of a child, and challenges facing social work administrators, supervisors, and community organizers; ethnography to better understand the experiences and needs of clients who live in psychiatric facilities, residential substance abuse treatment programs, and prisons; case studies to better understand how social workers make difficult ethical decisions and explore the experiences of clients, staff, and administrators in family preservation programs or public child welfare agencies; and diverse qualitative methods to conduct evaluations of programs designed to serve elderly clients who have serious mental illness, people living with HIV/AIDS, and children who are deaf. In each of these instances, social workers would have the opportunity to use qualitative research and evaluation tools to enhance the quality and delivery of social services, promote social justice, enhance client dignity and worth, recognize the importance of human relationships, promote social workers' integrity, and improve social workers' competence and expertise. Consistent with these enduring social work values, practitioners' assertive efforts to gather pertinent data from informants provide a rich opportunity to empower informants, recognize their expertise, and involve informants as active partners in the production of knowledge.

Sample Selection

Similarly, social workers should also be mindful of the profession's values and ethical standards when identifying and selecting research and evaluation participants. Social workers have a longstanding commitment to people who are, according to the NASW *Code of Ethics* (1999:1) "vulnerable, oppressed, and living in poverty." Such individuals would include those suffering from mental illness or domestic violence; low-income and homeless people; victims of racial, sexual, and political discrimination; and so on. Thus, qualitative research and evaluation projects that focus on the needs of such individuals, and on the professionals and programs that serve them, are particularly compelling. Including vulnerable people in one's sample provides an opportunity to empower them, recognize their expertise, and engage them in the knowledge-production enterprise.

Social workers conducting qualitative research and evaluation projects should also be guided by the profession's deep-seated commitment to social, cultural, sexual, and ethnic diversity (see sections 1.05 and 6.04 of the

NASW *Code of Ethics* 1999). Whenever feasible and appropriate, samples should include diverse groups and clientele, with adequate representation of the social, cultural, sexual, and ethnic diversity typically encountered by social workers. For example, qualitative case studies or ethnographies involving residents of homeless shelters, soup kitchen patrons, or children in foster care should include a cross-section of clients to ensure adequate representation and diversity. There are ethical reasons for such sample selection that go beyond more technical considerations involving probability sampling techniques and issues of external validity.

Informed Consent

Social workers must be particularly attentive to informed consent issues, particularly because many research and evaluation participants are vulnerable and victims of various forms of oppression, abuse, and neglect. In addition, some potential research and evaluation participants may suffer from mental illness in a way that limits their ability to consent to involvement in a research and evaluation project, may struggle with literacy, or may be immigrants or refugees who have difficulty with verbal and written explanations that rely only on the English language.[4]

The consent of individuals who are invited to participate in case studies, narrative studies, ethnographies, and other forms of qualitative projects must be obtained in a manner consistent with prevailing ethical standards. Formal informed consent guidelines in the human services began with the landmark legal ruling in the 1914 case of *Schloendorff v. Society of New York Hospital,* in which Justice Benjamin Cardozo issued his widely cited opinion that "every human being of adult years and sound mind has a right to determine what shall be done with his own body" (President's Commission for the Study of Ethical Problems in Medicine and Biomedical and Behavioral Research 1982:28–29). A second prominent court ruling, in which the term informed consent was first introduced, was issued in the 1957 case of *Salgo v. Leland Stanford Jr. University Board of Trustees*; this case established doctors' duty to properly disclose ahead of time important information concerning the risks associated with a medical procedure (President's Commission for the Study of Ethical Problems in Medicine and Biomedical and Behavioral Research 1982).

Since these important court decisions, guidelines developed by scholars, government agencies, and private sector organizations have evolved based on a list of core elements that should be included in informed consent procedures in typical research and evaluation projects. These elements are reflected in the NASW *Code of Ethics* (1999:5.02[e,f,h]):

> Social workers engaged in evaluation or research should obtain voluntary and written informed consent from participants, when appropriate, without any implied or actual deprivation or penalty for refusal to participate; without undue inducement to participate; and with due regard for participants' well-being, privacy, and dignity. Informed consent should include information about the nature, extent, and duration of the participation requested and disclosure of the risks and benefits of participation in the research.

> When evaluation or research participants are incapable of giving informed consent, social workers should provide an appropriate explanation to the participants, obtain the participants' assent to the extent they are able, and obtain written consent from an appropriate proxy.

> Social workers should inform participants of their right to withdraw from evaluation and research at any time without penalty.

More specifically, social workers who conduct qualitative research and evaluation must be certain to not use coercion to convince people to participate; ascertain competence of potential participants to consent; obtain participants' consent to specific procedures or actions (as opposed to broadly worded and vague descriptions) using clear and understandable terminology; and respect participants' right to refuse or withdraw consent.

Social workers who conduct qualitative research and evaluation projects face two unique challenges. First, with some qualitative methods, such as naturalistic observation, the data might be compromised if participants are informed of the project before the observations take place. For example, the validity of data gathered by social workers who observe the behaviors of clients in a group home, prison guards, welfare department intake workers, or mental health aides in a psychiatric unit might be severely affected if the clients and staffers are alerted to the purposes and methods of the project before the observations take place. Social workers who face these circumstances should follow the standard in the NASW *Code of Ethics* (1999:5.02[g]):

Social workers should never design or conduct evaluation or research that does not use consent procedures, such as certain forms of naturalistic observation and archival research, unless rigorous and responsible review of the research has found it to be justified because of its prospective scientific, educational, or applied value and unless equally effective alternative procedures that do not involve waiver of consent are not feasible.

Second, the nature of many qualitative research and evaluation projects is such that investigators are not always able to anticipate possible benefits and risks prior to the start of the project. Ordinary informed consent is based on the assumption that researchers are able to disclose potential benefits and risks *before* participants begin their involvement. However, researchers who use qualitative methods often adjust their inquiry, research questions, and data collection procedures at various junctures throughout the project. Behaviors observed, client narratives, and information from ethnographic explorations may lead social work researchers to shift methodological gears in the middle of the project. In these instances, investigators should periodically revisit informed consent throughout a project to ensure that participants are willing to continue their involvement in light of methodological changes (Waldrop 2004; Padgett 2008).

The unique nature of qualitative research has led to refinement of standard informed consent procedures to include what has become known as ongoing consensual decision-making and process consent, which "encourages mutual participation and mutual affirmation between researcher and participant, and offers an opportunity to actualize a negotiated view and make different research arrangements as necessary" (Munhall 1991:52; also see Ramos 1989; Usher and Holmes 1997; Seibold 2000; Smythe and Murray 2000; Ramcharan and Cutcliffe 2001).[5] According to Smythe and Murray (2000:320), process consent "should include the option for participants to withdraw their data following participation. In process consent, explicit procedures are provided for mutually negotiated consent and the process is initiated by the researcher rather than the participant."

Institutional Review

One of the important byproducts of researchers' increased focus on ethical issues was the invention of the concept of institutional review. Institutional review boards (typically known as IRBs, human subjects' protection committees, and research participant protection committees) became popular during the 1970s. Currently, all organizations and sponsors that receive federal research funds are required to have an IRB review the ethical aspects of proposals.[6] An IRB may request additional information and details or may request certain changes in a study's research design before approving a proposal. According to the NASW *Code of Ethics* (1999:5.02[d]), "Social workers engaged in evaluation or research should carefully consider possible consequences and should follow guidelines developed for the protection of evaluation and research participants. Appropriate institutional review boards should be consulted."

Some scholars have argued that traditional IRBs have been much too rigid in their review of proposals for qualitative projects (Stevenson and Beech 1998; Berg 2011). Critics argue that IRBs have been inclined to superimpose review criteria that were first established for traditional quantitative, empirical projects and have not adapted these guidelines to accommodate the unique challenges posed by qualitative projects. As a result, vulnerable people who might be empowered by their participation in qualitative research projects may be excluded from meaningful participation. Ramcharan and Cutcliffe (2001) argue that when review boards consider research proposals they should incorporate a number of "repair procedures" designed to accommodate qualitative methodology:

> *Ethics committee members should not either jointly or severally use methodologies as the only locus for their ethical decision-making.* By implication, they should be open-minded about the potential and prospective gains produced by a number of different research approaches. Second, *to be fair to methodologies with emergent designs, ethics committees should have an organisational form capable of dealing fairly with the ethics of such research* (362; emphasis in the original).

To achieve greater balance and fairness in IRB review, Ramcharan and Cutcliffe (2001) recommend the use of a broader, more diverse range of committee members, some of whom are experienced with and sympathetic to qualitative research; greater selectivity when appointing committee members; and specialized training for board members concerning the methods, strengths, and limitations of qualitative research.

Research and Evaluation Design

In more traditional quantitative research, ethical issues often arise when social workers design projects that explore cause-effect relationships and control for extraneous factors (e.g., demographic attributes, contemporaneous events, measurement effects) by randomly assigning participants to experimental, control, and contrast groups. In single-system or $N = 1$ designs, social workers may attempt to control for extraneous factors by withdrawing and reintroducing an intervention (e.g., A-B-A-B and related designs). Ethically, social workers may be troubled by withholding interventions from a control group or withdrawing potentially meaningful interventions from a single client.

The ethical issues encountered in qualitative research tend to be of a different order. In these projects, the ethical challenges are more likely to concern observing people without fully informing them of one's intentions, developing close relationships with research participants (e.g., when social workers are participant observers), and recruiting vulnerable participants (Smythe and Murray 2000).

Use of Deception and Coercion

It is unusual to find research designs implemented by social workers that incorporate elements of deception and coercion. On the whole, researchers have become much less willing to deceive or coerce research participants in the name of science. One of the legacies of the Tuskegee and Willowbrook experiments, and other infamous inquiries, has been growing awareness of the ethical downside of deception and coercion. Further, some qualitative methods—such as narrative research—are based on a belief that researchers need to develop authentic relationships with participants that are devoid of deception. As Smythe and Murray (2000:323) note,

> Deception normally is not a significant ethical issue for narrative research. Narrative researchers generally have no reason to systematically mislead their research participants at any stage of the research process. They are interested in people's stories, told in their own words, about some aspect of their life experiences, and participants are told this at the outset of a narrative interview. Hence, there is no need for debriefing, in the usual sense of clarifying the "true purposes" of the study, following people's

participation. Narrative researchers typically are forthright and explicit about the purposes of the research from the outset of participation.

Nonetheless, social workers who use qualitative methods should be cognizant of guidelines concerning deception. Because some qualitative methods are much less formal, more creative and innovative, and are more subtle than traditional experimental and quantitative research, qualitative researchers can sometimes be lulled into a false belief that standards concerning the use of deception are looser. Qualitative researchers need to be especially vigilant in their efforts to avoid deceiving and coercing participants. The informal and close relationships that sometimes develop between researchers and participants can lead some researchers to let down their guard and take unwarranted liberties in their methodology, leading them, for example, to withhold important information from research participants that might influence participants' decisions to continue involvement in the research (Ramcharan and Cutcliffe 2001).

Privacy and Confidentiality

Social workers have a longstanding commitment to client confidentiality and privacy. These are among the most venerated values in the profession (Dickson 1998; Reamer 2006b). Over time, the social work profession has developed extensive guidelines concerning the protection of, and limits to, clients' right to confidentiality and privacy. Examples include release of confidential information, if necessary without clients' permission, to comply with state mandatory reporting laws or court orders, protect clients who threaten to harm themselves, and protect third parties who may be harmed by clients.

More recently, social workers have also explored confidentiality issues that arise in the context of research and evaluation. Social work researchers who interview clients and observe clients' behavior may be privy to confidential information that, in a clinical or casework context, might warrant disclosure without clients' consent. Social workers who conduct qualitative research may be especially likely to obtain sensitive confidential information because of their unique relationships with their data sources, for example, when social workers conduct in-depth case studies of clients' emotional and family lives, live as participant observers in clients' neighborhoods and treatment settings, or use narrative analysis in their exploration

Ethics in Qualitative Research

of clients' deeply personal experiences. Qualitative data collected by social workers can include remarkably sensitive details concerning individuals' emotional anguish, vengeful fantasies, criminal conduct, and collegial conflicts. Social workers need to be familiar with prevailing ethics guidelines and vigilant in their efforts to protect client confidentiality, to the extent permitted by ethical standards and the law (Baez 2002).

More specifically, social workers should be cognizant of ethical standards pertaining to the concepts of privacy and confidentiality. Privacy is a broad concept that refers to the right to noninterference in individuals' thoughts, knowledge, acts, associations, and property (Dickson 1998). In a research context, the right to privacy entails participants' right to keep deeply personal information to themselves. According to the NASW *Code of Ethics* (1999:1.07[a]), "Social workers should respect clients' right to privacy. Social workers should not solicit private information from clients unless it is essential to providing services or conducting social work evaluation or research. Once private information is shared, standards of confidentiality apply" (standard 1.07[a]).

Confidentiality rights arise when individuals entrust others with private information. Social work researchers should ensure that research participants understand the nature of their confidentiality rights and any relevant limitations. According to the NASW *Code of Ethics* (1999:5.02[l];1.07[l]):

> Social workers engaged in evaluation or research should ensure the anonymity or confidentiality of participants and of the data obtained from them. Social workers should inform participants of any limits of confidentiality, the measures that will be taken to ensure confidentiality, and when any records containing research data will be destroyed.
>
> Social workers should protect the confidentiality of clients' written and electronic records and other sensitive information. Social workers should take reasonable steps to ensure that clients' records are stored in a secure location and that clients' records are not available to others who are not authorized to have access.

Preventing Distress and Harm

One of the principal consequences of the research-related scandals exposed by the Nuremberg trials and scrutiny of the Tuskegee and Willowbrook experiments has been an earnest commitment among researchers to protect human participants. Guidelines established by the U.S. Public Health Service, the World Medical Association, the National Commission for the Protection of Human Subjects of Biomedical and Behavioral Research, and the Council for International Organizations of Medical Sciences have strengthened researchers' efforts to prevent distress and harm among research participants. The notion of "do no harm" has become an institutionalized, sacred mantra among researchers. The concept is reflected in the NASW *Code of Ethics* (1999:5.02[j]): "Social workers engaged in evaluation or research should protect participants from unwarranted physical or mental distress, harm, danger, or deprivation."

Researchers who use qualitative methods do not need to be concerned about the kind of harm associated with some experimental techniques, such as denying treatment to people randomly assigned to a control group, withdrawing treatment from clients in conjunction with a single-system reversal design (e.g., an ABAB design), or actively deceiving research participants about the actual purpose of the inquiry. The risks in qualitative research are substantially different, and are more likely to be a function of researchers developing very close relationships with the people from whom, and about whom, they are gathering data. Ethnographic research sometimes means spending extensive social time with research participants, where researchers and research participants have opportunities to learn a great deal about one another's personal lives. Narrative inquiry sometimes yields intensely personal details comparable to information that people ordinarily disclose to therapists. Qualitative researchers often have access to the most intimate corners of participants' lives, which could lead some participants to feel overexposed or at risk emotionally. Participants may respond to researchers' queries by revealing details about their lives that they later wish they had not shared.

Participants may also discover that delving into emotionally toxic or painful areas of their lives in response to researchers' questions or prompts is destructive or otherwise counterproductive. For example, narrative research with people who suffer from clinical depression may exacerbate participants' depressive symptoms. Ethnographic research in a community of people who are struggling with substance abuse issues may be very stressful if some participants worry that their illegal drug use may be exposed. Case studies of domestic violence might trigger further conflict and assaults if research interviews lead to intense disagreements and add fuel to simmering family fires. As Usher and Holmes (1997:52) note, "although qualitative research does not generally place the participants at risk from procedures, they may be exposed to data collection that is both intrusive and invasive of sensitive experiences."

Qualitative researchers who have some authority over research participants—for example, social workers who are probation, parole, or welfare office staffers gathering data from individuals on their personal caseloads—need to be careful not to exploit or abuse their power in order to advance their research agendas (Rowan 2000:177). Research participants should never feel coerced to become or remain involved in research projects. One way to minimize this risk, and to enhance the balance of power in participants' relationships with researchers, is to provide as much opportunity as possible for research participants to be involved in the identification and formulation of research questions and design, data gathering, and interpretation of findings. According to Toma (2000), "the research relationship is a partnership. It is not a series of detached observations about subjects by intentionally uninvolved researchers. Instead, subjective qualitative researchers consciously avoid such barriers between themselves and their subjects."

Conflicts of Interest and Boundary Issues

Another compelling risk in qualitative research involves potential and actual conflicts of interest and related boundary issues. Conflicts of interest occur when researchers' determination to gather data clashes with participants' well-being. As in any research project, qualitative researchers must ensure that their research agendas—including any financial, publication, or other incentives—do not take precedence over participants' emotional and physical health, and that the research relationship does not transform itself into a therapeutic relationship (Smythe and Murray 2000). For example, a researcher may use narrative analysis with people who have attempted to commit suicide and discover, during the course of a lengthy research interview, that the respondent is becoming more and more despondent, weepy, and self-critical. A researcher who is using case study techniques to gather data on people living with schizophrenia may find that research interviews with some participants create significant stress and lead to an exacerbation of symptoms. In such instances, social workers are obligated, ethically, to suspend their research agendas (at least temporarily) in order to address participants' needs. When necessary, social workers should refer people in need to appropriate service providers who may be able to provide assistance. The NASW *Code of Ethics* (1999:5.02[i]) stipulates that "Social workers should take appropriate steps to ensure that participants in evaluation and research have access to appropriate supportive services." Seibold (2000:150) shares the ethical challenges she faced when she used qualitative research methods to study the emotional lives of single, midlife women:

> On the two occasions in which the interviews proved cathartic they took on elements of a therapeutic relationship. One woman revealed that she had been a victim of child abuse and another became very distressed when speaking of her relationship with her mother. After the interviews I thought about when and why an interview might or should be terminated. If you terminate an interview are you retreating from a relationship established? What responsibility do you have as a researcher to suggest or facilitate counseling? While in the two cases referred to it did not reach this stage, there was cause to consider the possibility, and whether this would constitute further invasion of privacy.

Social workers also need to be attentive to conflicts of interest and problematic dual relationships that can arise when they recruit their own clients to be research participants. At times, this dual relationship can compromise the quality of social workers' professional service, such as when the social worker's research agenda (for example, to gather data for the social worker's doctoral dissertation) takes precedence over meeting clients' clinical or other needs. According to the NASW *Code of Ethics* (1999:5.02[o]), "Social workers engaged in evaluation or research should be alert to and avoid conflicts of interest and dual relationships with participants, should inform participants when a real or potential conflict of interest arises, and should take steps to resolve the issue in a manner that makes participants' interests primary."

Perhaps the most helpful advice one can offer is for social workers who conduct qualitative research to pay constant attention to their motives, to ensure that their research agenda and methods do not compromise participants' interests or exploit them. In this sense, social work researchers should be what Schon (1983) calls "reflective practitioners"—practitioners who consciously think about, reflect on, and evaluate their actions during their performance.

Reporting Results

In most respects, the ethical issues involved in reporting the results of qualitative inquiry are comparable to those encountered with quantitative research. All social work researchers must be careful to protect the privacy and confidentiality of research participants. Social workers need to ensure that sensitive information—for example, details about criminal activity, drug use, financial difficulties, family conflict, and psychiatric illness—is not available to any unauthorized individuals or organizations. Unless research and evaluation participants have consented to the disclosure of identifying information, social workers should take careful steps to disguise participants' identities and discuss results only with individuals who are permitted to have access to this information. According to the NASW *Code of Ethics* (1999:5.02[k,m]),

> Social workers engaged in the evaluation of services should discuss collected information only for professional purposes and only with people professionally concerned with this information.
>
> Social workers who report evaluation and research results should protect participants' confidentiality by omitting identifying information unless proper consent has been obtained authorizing disclosure.

Social work researchers also have an ethical obligation to report results accurately, avoiding any temptation to modify or alter results for self-interested reasons (for example, to support a personal bias, avoid unflattering publicity or criticism associated with negative program outcomes, or facilitate career advancement). Researchers should not unilaterally modify transcripts of research participants' narrative stories, report ethnographic details that they did not actually observe, or characterize participants in case studies inaccurately. Publication of falsified or altered results damages the profession's integrity, harms participants and other parties whose lives may be affected by misleading publication, and destroys professional careers. As the NASW *Code of Ethics* (1999:5.02[n]) states, "Social workers should report evaluation and research findings accurately. They should not fabricate or falsify results and should take steps to correct any errors later found in published data using standard publication methods."

One of the more challenging ethical dilemmas for qualitative researchers concerns decisions about disclosing results to participants. As a matter of principle, one can argue that research participants have a right to know the results of research and evaluation that involve them. In fact, informing participants of results is yet another way to empower them and engage them as true partners in qualitative research.

In some instances, however, researchers may be tempted to withhold findings that, in their judgment, might be distressing or otherwise harm participants emotionally. For example, a social work researcher who concludes from her ethnographic observations that a resident in a residential program for struggling adolescents is manifesting symptoms of major mental illness may be reluctant to provide the teen with candid feedback. A researcher who conducts a case study of a family in crisis may be reluctant to disclose his suspicions that the father is engaged in an extramarital affair. In these instances, social workers have to carefully and earnestly balance research participants' "right to know" with the professionals' duty to protect participants from harm; social workers should always strive to avoid inappropriate and unjustifiable paternalism. These are exceedingly difficult judgments that require scrupulous, diligent, and good-faith adherence to social work's ethical standards. In these circumstances, social workers may benefit from consultation with thoughtful colleagues.

An additional ethical risk arises out of the fact that research participants may react to seeing their lives described and analyzed in detail in formal and informal publications. Even researchers' best attempts to disguise participants' identities may not be adequate and may not prevent some participants from feeling overexposed (Chase 1996). In addition, participants may feel harmed by what they regard as incomplete or inaccurate portrayals of important aspects of their lives and may want to have some control over the release and publication of results. Smythe and Murray (2000:324) commented on this risk with respect to the use of narrative research:

> Who owns the research participant's narrative? That is, who wields the final control and authority over its presentation and interpretation? The issue of the ownership of data scarcely arises in traditional psychological research, where (as pointed out earlier) one simply gives away one's data to the researcher as part of the standard research participation contract. However, can one give away one's own story in this fashion, especially when it is so heavily invested with one's personal meaning and sense of identity?

Qualitative researchers can follow several steps during the data analysis stage to enhance protection of participants (Smythe and Murray 2000). First, researchers should consult with participants to ensure their transcripts accurately reflect what they said. Second, researchers should monitor, reflect on, and critique the intuitions, analytic methods, and perspectives they used to code the qualitative data. Third, researchers should critically assess the potential impact their interpretations and analyses may have on participants' mental health. Finally, researchers should solicit participants' feedback on the researchers' interpretations of the data before the data are shared with others.

Acknowledging Credit

A final ethical consideration in qualitative research concerns fair and honest acknowledgement of the ways in which others' efforts contributed to the final product. Qualitative research often involves collaboration among agency-based colleagues and between principal investigators and research associates and assistants. In many instances research participants themselves contributed to the research design, data collection, and analysis of results. According to the NASW *Code of Ethics* (1999:4.08[a]), "Social workers should take responsibility and credit, including authorship credit, only for work they have actually performed and to which they have contributed," Further, "Social workers should honestly acknowledge the work of and the contributions made by others (4.08[b]."

Conclusion

The dramatic increase in social workers' use of qualitative research techniques has strengthened and enriched the profession's knowledge base. Ethnographic, narrative, case study, and other qualitative methods have broadened social workers' grasp of a wide range of issues related to direct practice, community organizing, agency administration, social policy, ethnic and cultural diversity, and professional ethics. These developments are part of continuing efforts among social workers to refine and broaden the profession's methods of inquiry. Qualitative research can be used as a powerful intervention tool that promotes respect for informants and empowers them as full participants in the production of knowledge.

Along the way social workers have enhanced their understanding of a wide range of ethical issues germane to qualitative research. Some of these issues are extensions of ethical issues encountered in quantitative research and some are unique to qualitative research. Waldrop (2004:247–248) provides a wise and succinct summary of critical ethics-related lessons she has learned as a result of her extensive qualitative research and her review of colleagues' advice:

1. *Anticipate, anticipate, anticipate.* The importance of thinking through and carefully preparing for qualitative research with at-risk groups cannot be overemphasized. Try to anticipate any ethical dilemmas that could emerge. Plan for dilemmas even if they seem preposterous. Play them out so that you are mentally prepared and ready to handle whatever may occur. Think about the vulnerable population from social, emotional, and moral perspectives prior to entering the field—and your responses should something occur. Consider the standards by which you must act. Your actions are covered by the IRB, professional codes of ethics, and personal morality. They preserve the integrity of your data and analyses, but should be guided by ethical principles of doing no harm. It is ultimately important to go into fieldwork thinking about potential moral and ethical dilemmas before encountering them (Taylor 1987). Prevention is always the best intervention.

2. *Do your homework.* Do not rush into the field. Spend time learning about the experiences, needs, and vulnerabilities of the population that you are studying. Immerse yourself in policy, program, and social issues that affect the population. Get permission to shadow (Ely et al. 1991) key informants (if you can), attend meetings, ask to tour facilities, and interview persons who are knowledgeable about the group. Ask them what you might expect to find (including moral or ethical dilemmas) and what you need to know about the group you are studying.

3. *Be aware of spillover, splatter, and surprises.* Be prepared for something to touch you in an unexpected way. Think of ways to control impulsive responses—some people giggle when faced with extreme distress and others flee the scene. Expect to leave the field or an interview feeling drained and sometimes overwhelmed. Make a commitment before you begin that you will keep your reactions in check until you arrive safely home.

4. *Practice self-discipline.* Write or audiotape notes to yourself about your reactions after every interview, meeting, or day in the field. Watch for themes and patterns over time and be sensitive to changes you observe in yourself—as the research instrument your calibration is critical.

5. *Be a good guest.* "Be alert to proper demands of good citizenship or host-guest relations" (American Anthropological Association *Code of Ethics*, 1998:Standard 3). Honor the home of the person who has invited you to enter—whether it is the plastic tarp of a homeless individual or a room in a nursing home—and thank them for sharing it with you. Resist any urge to comment on odor or filth. Learn to be friendly to animals—pets are important gate-keepers and a source of entrée to the person's life. Be observant, noting photos on the wall and prized possessions. Comment on them—it is considerate and guest-like (while also documenting observations about the person or environment for later recording in your field notes).

6. *Use self-reflections.* Always cross-examine your interviews—what went well and what went poorly—and learn from them (see Tutty, Rothery, and Grinnell 1996:79–82, for helpful suggestions). Use a journal or tape recorder for reflections immediately after you leave an interview or period of observation. Pay particular attention to the parts that made you uneasy.

7. *Practice social responsibility.* If you uncover appalling or dangerous circumstances remember that you have at least four choices: (1) intervene, (2) leave the field, (3) blow the whistle, or (4) continue the study, and use the data to push for macrolevel change when the study is completed (Taylor 1987). These are not mutually exclusive. When in doubt, consider leaving the field temporarily and then deciding on the next best course of action.

8. *Embrace discomfort.* Whenever you feel the telltale butterflies in your stomach, use the ethical uncertainties and ambiguities as signposts along the journey of discovery. Clearly, exploring the needs and complicated life experiences of vulnerable population groups is accompanied by issues that require care and sensitivity. Carefully working with these issues can bring your understanding of the population to an important and desirable new level.

I would add only one key point to this collection of sage counsel: When conducting qualitative research, social workers should be assertive about drawing on the profession's unique set of values, conceptual frameworks, and practice principles. For more than a century, social workers have cultivated an impressive value base and insights that should serve them well when conducting qualitative research. Social work's earnest commitment to matters of social justice, the well-being of oppressed and vulnerable people, social and cultural diversity, human dignity, and self-assessment (use of self) should provide practitioners with invaluable lodestars as they conduct qualitative inquiries.

Notes

1. Indeed, no listing for *ethics* appears in the table of contents, glossary, or index of the first edition of this book (Sherman and Reid 1994).
2. Much has been written about the reasons for the emergence of the applied and professional ethics field in the early 1970s. Most analyses focus on the controversial impact of new technology (e.g., the ethics of genetic engineering, artificial organs, computer privacy); widespread publicity related to prominent scandals (e.g., Watergate); increased awareness of civil and other rights (e.g., welfare, patient, prisoner) as a result of the 1960's activism in these areas; and increased litigation against professionals that alleged ethical misconduct (Callahan and Bok 1980; Sloan 1980).
3. There are other publications rooted in social work and intended for a social work audience that address ethical issues in qualitative research. However, many do not draw directly or explicitly on social work ethics literature or the research ethics guidelines contained in the *Code of Ethics* promulgated by the National Association of Social Workers (see, for example, Waldrop 2004).
4. Social workers should not assume that research and evaluation participants who are not sufficiently competent to provide informed consent at a given point in time will never be competent. For example, psychiatric symptoms often improve as a result of psychotropic medication, and individuals who are not competent because they are under the influence of alcohol or other drugs may be able to provide consent once they become sober. As Usher and Holmes (1997:51) note, "competence to consent, or decision-making capabilities, may vary for one person across time and across tasks; that is to say, a person may be held competent to make one decision but not to make another."

5. According to Josselson (1996:xii–xiii), in many qualitative projects "the concept of *informed consent* is a bit oxymoronic, given that participants can, at the outset, have only the vaguest idea of what they might be consenting to. Doing this work, then, requires that we find a way to encompass contradictions and make our peace with them."

6. There are some exceptions for research that constitutes a routine requirement of an educational or academic program, involves analysis of secondary or existing data in a way that preserves confidentiality, depends on interviews or surveys, or entails observations of public behavior.

References

American Anthropological Association. 1998. *Code of ethics.* Retrieved June 22, 2010 from http://www.aaanet.org/committees/ethics/ethcode.htm

Antle, B. J., C. Regehr, and F. Mishna. 2004. Qualitative research ethics: Thriving within tensions. In *Evidence-based practice manual: Research and outcome measures in health and human services,* A. R. Roberts and K. R. Yeager, eds. 126–136. New York: Oxford UP.

Baez, B. 2002. Confidentiality in qualitative research. *Qualitative Research* 2: 35–38.

Berg, B.L. 2011. *Qualitative research methods for the social sciences* (8th ed.). Upper Saddle River, NJ: Pearson.

Berg, B. L. 2008. *Qualitative research methods* (7th ed.). Boston: Allyn and Bacon.

Boman, J. and R. Jevne. 2000. Pearls, pith, and provocation: Ethical evaluation in qualitative research. *Qualitative Health Research,* 10:547–554.

Callahan, D. and S. Bok, eds. 1980. *Ethics teaching in higher education.* New York: Plenum.

Chase, S. E. 1996. Personal vulnerability and interpretive authority in narrative research. In *The narrative study of lives.* Vol. 4. *Ethics and process in the narrative study of lives,* R. Josselson, ed. 45–59. Thousand Oaks, CA: Sage.

Council for International Organizations of Medical Sciences. 1993. *International guidelines for biomedical research involving human subjects.* Geneva, Switzerland: Council for International Organizations of Medical Sciences with the World Health Organization.

Creswell, J. 2006. *Qualitative inquiry and research design* (2nd ed.). Thousand Oaks, CA: Sage.

Denzin, N. K. and Y. S. Lincoln, eds. 2000. *Handbook of qualitative research* (2nd ed.). Thousand Oaks, CA: Sage.

Dickson, D. T. 1998. *Confidentiality and privacy in social work: A guide to the law for practitioners and students.* New York: Free Press.

Ely, M., M. Anzul, T. Friedman, D. Garner, and A. McCormack-Steinmetz. 1991. *Doing qualitative research: Circles within circles*. London: Falmer.

Grinnell, R. M., Jr. and Y. A. Unrau, eds. 2007. *Social work research and evaluation* (8th ed.). New York: Oxford UP.

Hollis, F. 1949. *Women in marital conflict: A casework study*. New York: Family Service Association of America.

Josselson, R. 1996. *Ethics and process in the narrative study of lives*. Thousand Oaks, CA: Sage.

Levine, C. 1991. AIDS and the ethics of human subjects research. In *AIDS and ethics*, F. G. Reamer, ed. 77–104. New York: Columbia UP.

Levine, R. 1988. *Ethics and regulation of clinical research* (2nd ed.). New Haven, CT: Yale UP.

Loue, S. 2000. *Textbook of research ethics: Theory and practice*. New York: Springer.

Mayer, J. E. and N. Timms. 1970. *The client speaks: Working class impressions of casework*. New York: Atherton.

Munhall, P. L. 1991. Institutional review of qualitative research proposals: A task of no small consequence. In *Qualitative nursing research: A contemporary dialogue*, J.M. Morse, ed. 258–271. Newbury Park, CA: Sage.

National Association of Social Workers. 1996. *Code of ethics*. Washington, DC: Author.

———. 1999. *Code of ethics* (rev.). Washington, DC: Author.

National Commission for the Protection of Human Subjects of Biomedical and Behavioral Research. 1979, *The Belmont report: Ethical principles and guidelines for the protection of human subjects of research*. Washington, DC: U.S. Department of Health, Education, and Welfare.

Padgett, D. 2008. *Qualitative methods in social work research: Challenges and rewards* (2nd ed.). Thousand Oaks, CA: Sage.

Patton, M. Q. 2002. *Qualitative research and evaluation methods* (3rd ed.). Thousand Oaks, CA: Sage.

Polsky, H. 1962. *Cottage six: The social system of delinquent boys in residential treatment*. New York: Wiley.

President's Commission for the Study of Ethical Problems in Medicine and Biomedical and Behavioral Research. 1982. *Making health care decisions: The ethical and legal implications of informed consent in the patient-practitioner relationship* (vol. 3.). Washington, DC: Government Printing Office.

Ramcharan, P. and J. R. Cutcliffe. 2001. Judging the ethics of qualitative research: Considering the "ethics as process" model. *Health and Social Care in the Community*, 9(6):358–366.

Ramos, M. C. 1989. Some ethical implications of qualitative research. *Research in Nursing and Health*, 12:57–63.

Reamer, F. G. 1998. *Social work research and evaluation skills.* New York: Columbia UP.

——. 2006a. *Ethical standards in social work: A review of the NASW Code of Ethics* (2nd ed.). Washington, DC: NASW.

——. 2006b. *Social work values and ethics* (3rd ed.). New York: Columbia UP.

——. 2010. Ethical issues in social work research. In *The handbook of social work research methods* (2nd ed.), B.A. Thyer, ed. 564–578. Thousand Oaks, CA: Sage.

Reid, W. J. and A. Smith. 1989. *Research in social work* (2nd ed.). New York: Columbia UP.

Richmond, M. 1917. *Social diagnosis.* New York: Russell Sage Foundation.

Rowan, J. 2000. Research ethics. *International Journal of Psychotherapy,* 5(2):103–111.

Rubin, A. and E. Babbie. 2010. *Research methods for social work* (7th ed.). Pacific Grove, CA: Brooks/Cole.

Schon, D. 1983. *The reflective practitioner.* New York: Basic.

Seibold, C. 2000. Qualitative research from a feminist perspective in the postmodern era: Methodological, ethical, and reflexive concerns. *Nursing Inquiry,* 7:147–155.

Shamoo, A. and D. Resnik. *Responsible conduct of research* (2nd ed.). New York: Oxford UP.

Shaw, I. and N. Gould. 2002. *Qualitative research in social work.* London: Sage.

Sherman, E. and W. J. Reid, eds. 1994. *Qualitative research in social work.* New York: Columbia UP.

Sloan, D. 1980. The teaching of ethics in the American undergraduate curriculum, 1876–1976. In *Ethics teaching in higher education,* D. Callahan and S. Bok, eds. 1–57. New York: Plenum.

Smythe, W. E. and M. J. Murray. 2000. Owing the story: Ethical considerations in narrative research. *Ethics and Behavior,* 10(4):311–336.

Stevenson, C. and I. Beech. 1998. Playing the power game for qualitative researchers: The possibility of a post-modern approach. *Journal of Advanced Nursing,* 27:790–797.

Taylor, S. J. 1987. Observing abuse: Professional ethics and personal morality in field research. *Qualitative Sociology,* 10:288–302.

Thyer, B., ed. 2010. *The handbook of social work research methods* (2nd ed.). Thousand Oaks, CA: Sage.

Toma, J. D. 2000. How getting close to your subjects makes qualitative data better. *Theory into Practice,* 39(3):177–184.

Tutty, L. M., M. Rothery, and R. M. Grinnell. 1996. *Qualitative research for social workers: Phases, steps, and tasks.* Boston: Allyn & Bacon.

Usher, K. and C. Holmes. 1997. Ethical aspects of phenomenological research with mentally ill people. *Nursing Ethics,* 4(1):49–56.

Waldrop, D. 2004. Ethical issues in qualitative research with high-risk populations. In *The qualitative research experience*, D. Padgett, ed. 236–249. Belmont, CA: Thomson.

Weijer, C. 1998. Research methods and policies. In *Encyclopedia of applied ethics*, R. Chadwick, ed. 853–860. San Diego: Academic.

Whitebeck, C. 1998. Research ethics. In *Encyclopedia of applied ethics*, R. Chadwick, ed. 835–843. San Diego: Academic.

Yegidis, B. and R. Weinbach. 2008. *Research methods for social workers* (6th ed.). Boston: Allyn & Bacon.

Zeni, J., ed. 2001. *Ethical issues in practitioner research*. New York: Teachers College Press.

[3]

Deconstructing the Epistemological Question with a Focus on the Knower

ROBERT L. MILLER, JR.

Locating the Researcher

This chapter emanates from reflections on the evolution from my initial social work research training, my doctoral program. Of the many benefits of my doctoral education, I am most grateful for a statement I heard while developing the dissertation proposal. The statement "If you don't ask the question, the question will not be asked" was the seminal validation to pursue a phenomenon that was virtually nonexistent in the social work, public health, and theological theoretical cannons. My objective was to frame a research question that examined the intersection of spirituality in the lives of African American gay men living with AIDS. The question was shaped by my previous clinical work, doctoral classes (especially the philosophy of science courses), and the support of some wonderful faculty. The research was also motivated by my personal and professional commitments to confront the continued violent and lethal conflation of racism, homophobia, heteronormativity, and aidsphobia that faced African American gay men living with AIDS who possessed a spiritual and religious identity. Those commitments fueled a smoldering determination to pursue the question. There was also a determination to illuminate findings that would acknowledge an extraordinary group of men whose exemplars of courage and faith not only deserved recognition, but would inspire others facing similar challenges. However, it was the philosophy of science courses that gave way to the question of epistemology, which provided the intellectual capacity and increased my emotional courage to pursue the answers of my most central research questions.

It was also during this journey that the social work epistemological debates were becoming less volatile. However, the heat from the debates (fights) had not completely cooled. I was particularly grateful that Ann Hartman's (1990) article, "Many Ways of Knowing" had been published by *Social Work*. Also salient was the arrival of the first edition of the Sage *Handbook of Qualitative Research* (Denzin and Lincoln 1994). What was lacking then and still is not clearly articulated in the social work epistemologic literature is an effort to interrogate or deconstruct the question, "What is the relationship between the knower (the researcher) and the object (or phenomenon) to be known?" Thus the central activity of this chapter is interrogating the role of the knower. Specifically, how might the knower construct and understand a relationship that potentiates a deep understanding of the object to be known? And, in particular, develop an understanding that is consistent with the data provided by the research informant, that is, the one to be known.

By way of disclaimer, this chapter conceptualizes social work research as a form of social work practice. Social work practice continues to be concerned about the location of the social worker in relation to the client. "Starting where the client is" (Jockel 1937) remains a social work practice maxim. In framing a discussion about epistemology in relation to the social work research enterprise, positionality or the location of the researcher in relation to the research question or the one (or the phenomena) being researched is no less relevant. In this instance, the notion of position examines the particular characteristics of the social work researcher. The goal of this chapter is to provide questions for the qualitative researchers to examine as they embark upon the social work research enterprise.

While there are basic questions that epistemology raises, this chapter asserts that the social work mission requires the social work researcher to answer those questions in a social work context. What should researchers know about themselves prior to their engagement in the social work research enterprise? What bearing does the social work researchers' understanding of power, advocacy, and worldviews have on the development and design of their social work qualitative research? How does the social work researcher understand both (1) the motivations for pursuing the research and (2) the potential resulting influences on the research process and outcomes? Ultimately, these and other significant questions like them can direct social work researchers as they initiate the development of research questions that guide their research activities.

To guide these reflections, the chapter first describes a research paradigm. The underlying assumptions of the chapter are provided next. The assumptions are followed by an exploration of the confluence of social work, research, and a coined term "professional epistemology." Professional epistemology includes a focus on the researcher's personal and political identities as well as the resulting identity when the researcher combines those two aspects. These identities and their relationship(s) are conceptualized as resources. Exploration of these resources is framed as an additional goal of the chapter. Because issues of race, class, gender, economic status, sexual orientation, and physical ability as well as other characteristics may potentially influence the researcher's decisions vis-à-vis the research enterprise, critical theory, critical race theory, and standpoint theory are described and explored as factors influencing the researcher. Exemplars utilizing queer theory and spirituality will be used to support the goal of the chapter as well.

The Elements of a Research Paradigm

Ontology explores the question, "What is the nature of the object to be known?" Epistemology examines the question, "What is the relationship between the knower and the object to be known?" Methodology explores the actions involved in answering the question, "How do we learn about the world?" These three ideas or questions are the elements of what is known as a paradigm. Guba (1990:17) defines a paradigm as a basic set of beliefs that guide actions. How one conceptualizes and utilizes their paradigms is an important, though often overlooked, undertaking.

Ignoring the importance of one's epistemological stance in the formation of one's research paradigm is counterintuitive to a quality standard. Developing a conscious understanding of various research paradigms is analogous to understanding what biases are brought to clinical social work practice. Practitioners are always cautioned to examine their judgments related to their clients. While it might be difficult to suspend judgments while practicing social work, it is reasonable to ask practitioners to be conscious of their judgments. It is also reasonable for social workers to examine how their judgments influence how they relate to and treat their clients. Just as understanding how the judgments of social workers influence how they understand clients, researchers' epistemological positions will influence how they formulate their research paradigms and how they conduct their research. The premise of this chapter is that researchers are capable of knowing their epistemologies and are able to articulate those epistemologies prior to conducting research.

Assumptions of the Chapter

This chapter assumes that the reader has some training in and understanding of the epistemological positions of a positivist paradigm, which is most often considered a quantitative research approach. The positivist epistemological perspective experiences a dualist/objective stance. This perspective assumes that research findings are quantifiably and objectively true (Halmi 1996). A positivist epistemology suggests that the researcher can be independent and not influence or be influenced by the one who is being researched. If there is influence in either direction, that influence constitutes a threat to validity of the findings and various strategies are employed to reduce or eliminate those threats (Guba and Lincoln 1994:110).

There is also an assumption that the reader is familiar with the debates in social work research that argue the supremacy of one methodological approach over another. The last assumption is that the reader understands that the decision of a research method is fundamentally dependent upon the research question that is being asked.

Social Work and Research: Professional Epistemology

Social work research is guided by the profession's mission to enhance human well-being and to help meet the basic human needs of all people, with particular attention to the needs and empowerment of people who are oppressed and living in poverty (National Association of Social Workers 1996). People, programs, or policies may be the focus of social work research. Often, the kind of social work research that is conducted by a researcher is as much a statement about their professional worldview as it is about their conceptualization and understanding of the influence they wield. Researchers who have access to power conduct social work research. Moreover, they are able to exercise that power according to their interests, desires, and (often although not always) their funding sources. The research they do is based, in part, on their understanding of a valid research area and the epistemology they employ to address their question.

The Paradigm of Social Work Research as an Advocacy Function

Social work research may be conceptualized as an advocacy function for so-cial work clients. The research activities and the resulting data may provide a context and platform for those who traditionally have been marginalized and oppressed. The researcher may use the qualitative data gathered from these populations to illuminate or reveal conditions or phenomena that have not yet been privileged or previously told. The social work researcher who collects the narratives of disenfranchised clients is positioned to cre-ate opportunities for change. By disseminating the findings, the researcher supports others to create change. Social work researchers who plan and execute research as a way to create change demonstrate a research paradigm that endorses an advocacy function.

The Value of Deconstructing Epistemology

Epistemology is concerned with the relationship between the researcher and the informant. However, the inherent question of epistemology requires a deeper scrutiny, or in fact, deconstruction. This deconstruction invites the researcher to engage in reflexivity as an iterative task prior to entering the re-search enterprise. As social work practitioners are routinely asked to be reflex-ive related to their practice, social work research solicits researchers' reflexivity related to the various personal resources they bring to the research enterprise. Such personal resources may be known by answering the following questions, (1) What are the various identities of the researcher? (2) What are the various relationships created by the researcher among those identities? And (3) how do those identities and their interrelationships have bearing on the research endeavors? Further, this sort of deep reflection is different than the surface thought related to how people might identify themselves. It is an examination of their personal histories to contextualize how they know themselves. In this context, identity is recognized as the result of arousing submerged memories. A confrontation with dangerous (uncomfortable) memory(ies) that change our perceptions of the forces that shape us in turn moves us to redefine our worldviews, our ways of seeing (Kincheloe and Steinberg 2008:146). Framing those individual and collective identities is the first activity set.

The processes of identifying the resources, understanding their meanings individually and in relation to each other, and conceptualizing those meanings in relation to the outside world is a requisite undertaking. While this reflexivity may have been conducted previously, such reflection in light of the research effort may potentiate a different level of understanding in a research context. So in the case of gender identity, the first task for researchers exploring its "first person" meaning is discerning their understanding of gender emotionally and intellectually. This discernment answers the following questions: (1) What does their gender mean to them? (2) How do they experience it for themselves? (3) What is the bodily manifestation of their understanding or how do they live in their bodies in light of how they understand their gender?

After the researchers assess and understand the firsthand experience of their gender, they are then asked to experience their gender in light of some other identity or status. As both of those assessments or analyses are completed, the researchers are encouraged to test those meanings in the context of their environment. They are then charged to ask the questions related to "How do they experience these intermingled identities in the world?" and "How does their understanding of these combined identities influence how they manage in the world?" The experience of meaning making in the context of their race, gender, sexual orientation, physical abilities, economic and class statuses, or other attributes ostensibly increases the researchers' awareness of themselves. This awareness potentially has some bearing on how the researchers frame their preliminary understanding of the informant (object to be known).

This sort of analysis produces a "nested framework" (Tyler 2001:29). He suggests:

> Nested frameworks can refer to the way the overall system or paradigm relates to its broader context, to the paradigm and its embedded components, or to the way the components in the system relate to each other

and to the system itself. These differentiations are arbitrary because a framework and its components are interlinked, but at times it is useful to focus on these aspects in relation to each other.

While Tyler's "nested frameworks" is originally used for consideration on engaged cultural diversity, the action of knowing who you are first—so that you may frame your capacity to know the other and understand their motivations for self-definition—is relevant for this discussion. The term "system" is in fact analogous to the concept of self as well as to those entities for which the self must interact and find in the environment (broader contexts). I am suggesting that the elements of the system or paradigm are the personal identities of the self. Understanding how self system interacts with broader context is in some ways a reframe of the person in environment, specifically for conceptualization in the research endeavor.

A firsthand example of this nest framework concept is the individual entering their social work doctoral program. Most social work researchers have the experience of entering a social work doctoral program that both teaches them how to conduct research and requires that they conduct an independent piece of research prior to earning their doctoral degree. Oftentimes, their research courses are taught with a positivist perspective. The researchers must now examine their core identities in light of their academic training (a new system with which they must interact). This self-reflection may become more challenging because it is a new idea or expectation that was not required in their graduate professional social work training. The complexities may increase if the researchers conceptualize their identities as distinct from the dominant culture in which they live, work, or conduct their research. This may be especially true for researchers of color, sexual minorities, women, or those with disabilities (or other identities, attributes, or statuses that have been marginalized). For some social work researchers who are not part of dominant culture, reflections that inherently portend identification as both researchers/knowers as well as those who are being studied may evoke an unanticipated dichotomy. This may be particularly true for social work researchers who engage in research areas that are typically considered taboo subjects. The irony, of course, is that those taboo subjects are usually found in populations most consistent with the social work mission.

As the social work researchers manage the answers to the various questions related to their identities as knowers, they may or may not be able to reconcile their identities as resources. However, the reconciliation of their various identities potentially results in a highly textured epistemological understanding. Social work researchers whose core identities are not part of the dominant culture but who were trained in academic institutions have developed particular kinds of consciousness and skill sets. The researchers in effect have a confluence of identities and have the capacity to see the world differently, that is, through multiple lenses.

While the confluence of identities is not a new idea, it has received scant attention in the social work qualitative research literature. The fields of education and sociology have explored this idea (Du Bois 1903; Delgado 1995; Dillard 2000). In the early twentieth century, the African American educator, W. E. B. Du Bois described the experience of "ever feeling his two-ness"—two souls, two thoughts, two unreconciled strivings (1903/1953:5) as he sought to understand his surroundings. Although he was educated at Fisk University and earned two degrees from Harvard University, his work chronicles the race discrimination he endured. His experience as a highly trained researcher, combined with his life as an African American man in the first half of the twentieth century, provided Du Bois a unique way to view his circumstances. Delgado (1995:8) suggests this consciousness or epistemology offers a unique positioning. He describes the confluence of various identities as yielding an inherent set of skills, including an ability to speak two languages, learning two cultures, and the ability to think of everything in two or more ways at the same time. He considers such people postmodernists virtually as a condition of their being.

The resulting epistemology that emanates from a multiple consciousness lays the ground for two key ideas. The first is that epistemology is a way of knowing that has both internal logic and external validity (Ladson-Billings 2000). It allows the researcher to examine and test data against multiple evaluation points that may be deeply familiar. The second point is also made by Ladson-Billing (2002) using the work of Shujaa (1997), who suggests that worldviews and systems of knowledge are symbiotic—that how one views the world is influenced by what knowledge one possesses, and what knowledge one is capable of possessing is influenced deeply by one's worldview.

The Utility of Reconsidering Epistemology

As social work researchers develop an epistemological position related to the social work research enterprise, they are encouraged to view the world from multiple vantage points and discern which positions are desirous at any given time. For researchers who find themselves constructed outside of the dominant paradigm, they are positioned to engage in what Wynter (1992) calls an alterity. Alterity refers to the alter ego category of otherness. It allows the researchers to have multiple perspectives without requiring adherence to any perspective. Researchers have the ability to view the world from either a static perspective or from one of the multiple identities (race, class, gender, economic status, etc.) they may choose. Alterity allows for an epistemological stance that is congruent with the confluence of identities.

Alterity also recognizes sources of knowledge based on experience. This epistemology also allows for the recognition of etic and emic knowledge (Pike 1967). Etic knowledge is a knowing on the part of the researcher about a phenomenon from an objective or outsider perspective. Emic knowledge is a knowing on the part of the researcher about a phenomenon from a subjective or insider perspective. While the concepts as ideals are solid, caution is warranted as well. Often when emic knowledge is cited, it is because the researcher may share one or more known identities or characteristics of the informant. However the researcher is always cautioned to take on the position of investigator and to formulate his suspected knowledge of identity or characteristics as a question to be confirmed not assumed.

Because researchers have greater awareness of their identities and subsequent insights into their positionality or location, they are better able to interrogate their preliminary understanding of the phenomena they want to research. From a social work research perspective, conducting research that is consistent with the mission of the profession is an imperative. In an effort to assume an epistemological stance that is reflective of the confluence of researchers' identities, one goal is developing a paradigm that provides humanistic access in studies of sociological microstructures such as local communities, small social groups and individuals (Hamli 1996). To frame these as goals, critical theory, critical race theory, and standpoint theory will be described as epistemologies that help researchers begin to construct their nested frameworks, which may in turn further support their awareness as knowers.

Critical Theory

Critical theory is concerned with power and justice related to the economy. Matters of race, class, gender, ideologies, discourses, education, religion, other social institutions, and cultural dynamics interact to articulate a social problem (Kincheloe and McLaren 2000:281). Further, the ideas that are conceptualized as facts "can never be isolated from the domain of values or removed from some form of ideological inscription" (Kincheloe and McLaren 1994:140). Someone who is guided by critical theory may use his or her research as a way to make commentary or criticism about an imbalance of power. There is an implicit framework of critical theory that suggests that societal structures are predicated on power and that power is rarely evenly distributed. Admittedly, power is an ambiguous topic. However, power is conceptualized as a basic constituent of human existence that works to shape the oppressive forces and productive nature of the human condition.

Kincheloe and McLaren (2000) suggest that Gramsci's term "hegemony" well describes oppressive power and its ability to produce inequalities and human suffering (Lull 1995; Grossberg 1997). They suggest this hegemony recognizes that winning by popular consent is a very complex process and must be researched carefully.

An epistemological view that holds social work research as a practice to create change is consistent with Kincheloe and McLaren's view countering hegemonic practices. Conceptualizing the research effort to combat hegemonic practice may include developing research questions that potentially produce data that expose the misuse of power or highlight the experiences of the marginalized. Another goal is to support the further development of people's self-efficacy as they manage their experiences of race, class, gender, or sexual orientation or other resources that are not routinely honored. The mission of social work provides a foundation for research as practice to promote the increase of people's level of social functioning (Bartlett 1970). Creating a platform for the disempowered to describe their reality and then linking that with action steps to ameliorate the misuse of power is a salient social work goal.

While the work of critical theory concretizes the discussion of power and justice as it relates to the ways of the economy, matters of race, class, gender, social institutions, and cultural dynamics, critical race theory interrogates race specifically in the context of power within the society.

Critical Race Theory

The inclusion of critical race theory in this discussion extends the legal scholarship of researchers concerned with the ways that race and race power are constructed and utilized in the American legal culture specifically, and American society generally (Freeman 1995:xiii). Critical race theory is an outgrowth of critical legal studies that are marked by their utilization of developments in postmodern, poststructural scholarship, especially the focus of liminal or marginalized communities and the use of alternative methodology in the expression of theoretical work. A salient feature of the work is the inclusion of narratives and other literary techniques, while recognizing that the researcher is neither neutral nor objective (Crenshaw, Gotanda, Peller, and Thomas, 1995). Critical race theory is empirically supported and conceptualizes the activities of generating a research question as well as the collection, analyses, and organization of the data as inevitably political[ly] driven (Crenshaw, Gotanda, Peller, and Thomas 1995).

The application of critical race theory in legal research is a rejection of the hegemonic practice of privileging certain voices and experiences. The use of narrative, "challenges the traditional meritocratic paradigm of the academy by attempting to subvert what is viewed as pretenses of 'objectivity,' 'neutrality,' 'meritocracy,' and 'colorblindness'" (Brown 1995:523). It features the narratives of those who are traditionally excluded in legal research. In principle, critical race theory is consistent with both the social work mission as it both endorses the feature of justice, and further, supports the rejection of hegemonic research. And as Laurence Parker (1998) suggests, critical race theory legitimizes and promotes the voices of people of color by using storytelling to integrate the experiential knowledge drawn from history of the "other" into critiques of dominant social order. "The critical centering of race (together with gender, sexual orientation, and other areas of difference) at the location where the research is conducted and discussions are held can serve as a major link between fully understanding the historical vestiges of discrimination and the present day manifestation of that discrimination (Parker 1998:46).

Describing critical theory prior to standpoint theory continues to help researchers reflect on themselves as the knowers. It provides an opportunity to privilege their various identities/assets. It begins to position the researchers to consider the possibility of mutuality. That the researcher is in the position to ask questions about a person or phenomena for which they may share some similarity(ies) is a highly useful opportunity. As the research scans the environment, they may have some additional insight to determine relevant social work research questions. This position further equips the researcher to identify questions that, in the absence of such insight, may result in a missed opportunity (i.e., the researcher may miss important questions that need to be asked).

Standpoint Theory

Standpoint theory highlights (1) the importance of politics of location and position, and (2) how this might intersect with the complexities of more or less conscious social identifications (Fawcett and Hearn 2004). It offers an additional analytic opportunity to examine the relationship between the researcher and the one who is researched. Standpoint theory asks the question "Is it possible to produce accounts of social conditions that are unbiased or less biased?" It recognizes the historic exclusion of women from positivist research. Standpoint theory suggests that experiences produce knowledge and knowledge divorced from experience is colonizing, appropriating, and oppressive (Fawcett and Hearn 2004:203). Knowledge in this framework includes constructing an understanding of others in a society that may happen to be beyond the experience of the researcher conducting the research. It is also concerned with overcoming hegemonic marginalization constructions of others within the research process.

The Knower and the Professional Use of Self

Taken together, critical theory, critical race theory, and standpoint theory provide an intellectual invitation for researchers (including those with identities outside of dominant culture) to further validate a more holistic awareness and utilization of their personal resources/assets in light of their consideration of the phenomenon they want to research. By contextualizing their experiences of oppression and/or marginalization, they are potentially able to frame the phenomenon from a place of empathy, which may inform their intellectual capacity. The theories suggest integrating experiences of marginalization or oppression may increase the capacity of the researchers to see a phenomenon and to react to it both intellectually and affectively. This reaction may yield research questions that penetrate a surface understanding of a phenomenon. This potentially identifies a core problem rather than the symptomatic expressions of the core problem, resulting in more relevant research.

In some ways, allowing our science to be formed by our affective and intellectual cues is parallel to our ability to identify and operationalize a research framework that is analogous to the social work practice expression of professional use of self. As practitioners have empathetically responded to clients who have described difficult circumstances that practitioners may have experienced, such as a difficult divorce, some sort of complicated grief, and so forth, they potentially have a more informed response. While practitioners do not suggest they know what clients are feeling because "they have been through it," they in fact potentially frame their responses to the circumstances from a perspective that is, in part, shaped by their own experiences of similar phenomenon. Practitioners appropriately use their feelings in support of the therapeutic relationship to aid the client. Analogously, many researchers use their understandings of a difficult set of circumstances to inform both the conceptualization of their research agenda/enterprise and their in-depth understanding of the data presented by the research informant. Inherent in this idea are data analytic techniques that help to guard against the researchers' undue bias or overidentification with the data set. The theories suggest that the relationship between the knower and the object or phenomenon to be known may be informed by a disciplined self-understanding. This examination is done from a position of strength and not through a sense of victim status. Standpoint theory is conceptualized by its authors as a social source of knowledge in the context of social power (Collins 1990), which augments critical theory and critical race theory in support of the researchers' understanding of themselves as the knowers.

Exemplars of Integrating These Theories

Bryant Alexander's (2008) work is an exemplar of the integration of these critical theories. His work brings the ideas of various statuses or assets into sharper focus as he examines the issue of holding polar opposites in dynamic tension. He suggests that as a researcher of color who is a black/gay/man/teacher/performer/scholar, his voice embodies his location or positionality as simultaneously experiencing both bondage and freedom.

Held in place by the tensive ties of history's legacy that depicts me as the exotic other, a transplanted aborigine negotiating diaspora in a land that both recognizes and disowns. Not diaspora simply as the disruption of dispersion and longing for an unknown homeland in the bifurcated identity of being an African American, but a queer diaspora that Gayati Gopinath (2005) describes as one that mobilizes questions of the past memory, and nostalgia for radically different purposes . . . Diaspora not as a political or geosocial location, but as a critical lens in which I am always and already looking for the resonant traces of colonial occlusions, those moments when the concerted efforts of exclusion of my racialized and sexualized self are marked as evident and ongoing stratagems of racial domination, serving as an obstacle to my full actualization. I locate myself—within the logics of race and place, time and governance, or situated invasions of geographical and political territories signifying dominance and defeat, deployment and diaspora, captivity and freedom (103).

It is the sort of interrogation of the "past memory and nostalgia" that Kincheloe and Steinberg (2008) suggest comprises the identity to be examined and understood by the knower. It is the knower's efforts in this examination that begin to reveal the understanding of the relationship shared with the one or phenomenon to be known. Bryant's work suggests that recognizing the identities is one part of the process. The subsequent process further reveals an understanding of those assets in the context of the relationship between the researcher and the object of study. The inherent message is that researcher who is both experiencing and managing those polarities cannot be stultified by the oppression. The researcher must use the knowledge to better understand the researcher's reality while attempting to carefully interrogate and understand the experience of the object or the phenomenon to be known, using both the empathy and curiosity to illuminate and privilege the status of the object or phenomenon.

Privileging the status of the object or phenomenon to be known is reflected in the work of Manulani Aluli Meyer (2008). She, along with Dillard (2000), concretizes the relationship between the knower and the one to be known as endorsing features of a spirituality. In fact, Meyer goes so far as to say that "Knowledge that endures is spirit driven. It is a life force connected to all other life forces" (2008:218). Meyer contrasts spirituality with religion.

These are two completely different ideas. What was discovered in the thoughts of others and within my own reflection was the intentionality of process, the value and purpose of meaning, and the practice of mindfulness. These ideas, accessed via deep and enduring respect for our *kupuna*, our lands, our oceans, our language, rituals and families, became the foundation of Hawaiian essence. These are spiritual principles, that if played out as epistemology, help us enter spaces of wonderment, discernment, right viewing, and mature discourse . . . It is a real idea that allows us to ritualize ways to collect medicine, read a text, prepare a meal, or communicate with family. It allows knowing to be an act of consciousness that reaches beyond the mundane into connection and alignment with an essence that finds its renewal throughout the generations. An epistemology of spirit encourages all of us to be of service, to not get drawn into the ego nurtured in academia, and to keep diving into the wellspring of our own awe. In that way, our research is bound in meaning and inspired by the service to others or to our natural environment (2008:219).

Dillard (2000:674–675) frames the discussion in the following manner. She suggests the relationship between the knower and the one to be known is one of

[r]eciprocity and care apparent in the relationships of the research project . . . Such spiritual concerns are articulated epistemologically in that value is placed on individual expressiveness . . . developing the capacity for empathy in research is critical, for attempting to recognize the value of another's perspective, whether or not one agrees with that perspective. Simply put, perspectives have merit and standing simply because they exist, and our role as educational researchers becomes one of recognizing and embracing them as such. In this way, we are encouraged to welcome the conflict inherent in our diversity (of paradigms, methodology, representation), to live within its sometimes seeming ambiguity, and to develop the purpose in research of not just honoring our own version of the practice, praxis and politics of research as truth, but to seek to honor the truth that is created and negotiated in and between ourselves, in relationship with one another as researchers.

Dillard's position echoes the inherent dignity and worth of the individual, which is a cardinal social work value. Ultimately, the text frames the discussion of position to recognize there is greater proximity than distance.

It is in that proximity that the researcher is both encouraged to respectfully acknowledge otherness and implicitly value it as a means of learning more.

The notion of learning from the other implies mutuality. It also has the capacity to evoke an awareness of increased complexity. As Kincheloe and Steinberg (2008:138) suggest, "by understanding the multiple perspectives," we begin "to acknowledge the more we understand about the world (ourselves) the more complex it and we appear to be. We begin to see the multiple causations and the possibility of differing vantage points from which to view a phenomenon." Both Meyer and Dillard agree that the assumptions or the system of meaning-making that the observer consciously or unconsciously employs shapes the observation.

As researchers examine their identities to determine worldviews or various epistemological stances, they might also experience deeper insight into the question, "What is the relationship between the knower and the one to be known?" A more robust understanding of the researchers' power, class, justice, and other social dynamics may surface. Without such an awareness of those forces, research is conducted with the potential for unintended harm in the worst-case scenario or for jeopardizing the acquisition of quality data.

Conclusion

Interrogation of the researcher's position as knower requires both an insight and acknowledgement. The insight includes an understanding of the multiple assets of the knower; chief among them are the power and the privilege to conduct the research. While this might be challenging to embrace, the researcher is encouraged to achieve this critical insight. The acknowledgement includes the responsibility of utilizing his or her power to conduct social work research that fully explores the relationship between the knower and the object or phenomena to be known. This insight and acknowledgement potentially allows the researcher to ask questions that interrogate the core issue(s) that warrants social work research. As the researcher engages in the necessary effort to achieve a relevant sense of themselves as knower, the relationship between the knower and the one or the phenomena to be known becomes more accessible. Ultimately social work research is arguably guided by the mission of social work.

At this point in my research career, that I conduct my research as a social worker explicitly articulates my position in relation to any research question I continue to pursue. Come to think of it, I learned that in my doctoral program too.

References

Alexander, B. K. 2008. Queer(y)ing the postcolonial through the west(ern). In *Handbook of critical and indigenous methodologies*, Norman K. Denzin, Yvonna S. Lincoln, and Linda Tuhiwai Smith, eds. 101–103. Thousand Oaks, CA: Sage.

Bartlett, H. 1970. *The common base of social work practice.* New York: National Association of Social Workers.

Brown, E. M. 1995. The Tower of Babel: Bridging the divide between critical race theory and "mainstream" civil rights scholarship. *Yale Law Journal, 105*:513–547.

Collins, P. H. 1990. *Black feminist thought: Knowledge, consciousness, and the politics of empowerment.* New York: Routledge.

Crenshaw, K., N. Gotanda, G. Peller, and K. Thomas, eds. 1995. *Critical race theory: The key writings that formed the movement.* New York: New Press.

Delgado, R. 1995. Racial realism—after we're gone: Prudent speculations on African in a post-racial epoch. In *Critical race theory: The cutting edge*, R. Delgado, ed. Philadelphia: Temple U P.

Denzin, N. K. and Y. S. Lincoln. 1994. *Handbook of qualitative research.* Thousand Oaks, CA: Sage.

Dillard, C. 2000. The substance of things hoped for, the evidence of things not seen: Examining the endarkened feminist epistemology in educational research and leadership. *Qualitative Studies in Education, 13*(6):661–681.

Du Bois, W.E.B. 1903. The souls of black folk: essays and sketches. Chicago: A.C. McClurg.

Fawcett, B. and J. Hearn. 2004. Researching others: Epistemology, experience standpoints and participation. *International Journal of Social Research Methodology, 7*(3):201–218.

Freeman, A. 1995. Introduction. In K. Crenshaw, N. Gotanda, G. Peller, and K. Thomas, eds. *Critical race theory: The key writings that formed the movement*, New York: New Press.

Gopinath, G. 2005. *Impossible desires: Queer diasporas and South Asian public cultures.* Durham, NC: Duke UP.

Grossberg, L. 1997. Bringing it all back home: Essays on cultural studies. Durham, NC: Duke UP.

Guba, E. G., ed. 1990. *The paradigm dialog.* Newbury Park, CA: Sage.

Guba, E. G. and Y. S. Lincoln. 1994. Competing paradigms in qualitative research. In *Handbook of qualitative research*, N. K. Denzin and Y. S. Lincoln, eds. 105–117. Thousand Oaks, CA: Sage.

Halmi, A. 1996. The qualitative approach to social work: An epistemological basis. *International Social Work, 39*:363–375.

Hartman, A. 1990. Many ways of knowing. *Social Work* 35:3–4.

Jockel. E. 1937. Movement toward treatment in the application interview in a family agency." *Journal of Social Work Process* 1(1): 32–40

Kincheloe, J. L. and P. McLaren. 1994. Rethinking critical theory and qualitative research . In *Handbook of qualitative research*, N. K. Denzin and Y. S. Lincoln, eds. 138–157. Thousand Oaks, CA: Sage.

——. 2000. Rethinking critical theory and qualitative research. In *Handbook of qualitative research*, (2nd ed), N. K. Denzin and Y. S. Lincoln, eds. 279–313. Thousand Oaks, CA: Sage.

Kincheloe, J. L. and Steinberg, S. 2008. Indigenous knowledges in education: Complexities, dangers, and profound benefits. In *Handbook of critical and indigenous methodologies*, N. K. Denzin, Y. S. Lincoln, and L. T. Smith, eds. 134–156. Thousand Oaks, CA: Sage.

Ladson-Billings. G. 2000. Racialized discourses and ethnic epistemologies. In *Handbook of qualitative research*, (2nd ed), N.K. Denzin & Y.S. Lincoln, eds. 257–277. Thousand Oaks, CA: Sage.

Lull, J. 1995. *Media, communication, culture: A global approach.* New York: Columbia UP.

Meyer, M. A. 2008. Indigenous and authentic: Hawaiian epistemology and the triangulation meaning. In *Handbook of critical and indigenous methodologies*, N. K. Denzin, Y. S. Lincoln, and L. T. Smith, eds. 217–232. Thousand Oaks, CA: Sage.

National Association of Social Workers. 1996. Code of Ethics. Accessed March 4, 2010 http://www.socialworkers.org/pubs/code/default.asp.

Parker, L. 1998. Race is . . . race ain't: An exploration of the utility of critical race theory in qualitative research in education. *International Journal of Qualitative Studies in Education*, 11:45–55.

Pike, K. 1967. *Language in relation to a unified theory of the structure of human behavior.* The Hague: Mouton.

Shujaa, M. (1997). "Transformation of the researcher working toward liberation." Paper presented at the Annual Meeting of the American Educational Research Association, San Diego, CA.

Tyler, F. 2001. *Cultures, communities, competence and change.* New York: Kluwer Academic/Plenum.

Wynter, S. 1992. *Do not call us "Negroes": How "multicultural" textbooks perpetuate racism.* San Francisco: Aspire.

PART II

APPROACHES TO QUALITATIVE RESEARCH

[4]

Constructivist Research in Social Work

JAMES W. DRISKO

Strictly speaking there are no such things as facts pure and simple.

—*Alfred Schütz, Collected Papers, Volume 1*

Some authors now argue that all qualitative research must be constructivist research (Denzin and Lincoln 2005). Yet in social work, very little constructivist research is evident. A search of *Social Work Abstracts* in June 2012 yielded almost 22,350 hits for the term "research" but only 117 for "constructivist." "Constructivist social work research" yields 21 hits, including dissertations, reflections on research methods, and case-based practice analyses. Most constructivist research comes in under the radar, labeled instead as postmodern, critical, narrative, and poststructural research or inquiry. Rodwell's [O'Connor's] (1998) excellent, but hard to find, textbook *Social Work Constructivist Research* is the sole American social work text on this topic. Morris's (2006) research methods text includes constructivist research as one of four focal paradigms. The limited presence of constructivist social work research likely reflects the recent intensive emphasis on large-scale, grant-funded research notable in American academic social work. At the same time, considerable work in allied disciplines and by some European, Canadian, Israeli, and Australian social workers shows growing interest in this area.

There is no single, standard type of constructivist research. There are instead many different and very divergent voices, applying both old and new methods and creating widely varied research reports. This variety is a strength of constructivist research, but poses a challenge for the student and those unfamiliar with constructivism and its connections to research methods.

Defining Constructivist Research

Constructivist research is defined by an epistemological stance that social knowledge is the active product of human "knowers," that knowledge is relative, varies across people and their social groups, and is context dependent (Berger and Luckman 1966). Experiences in the natural and the social world are idiosyncratically constructed using the interpretive categories of one's reference group. There are multiple realities, multiple worlds, based on peoples' varied interpretative constructs and categories. The reality of the external world is not denied by constructivists; rather knowledge of the world is understood as related to the ways in which we actively organize our experiences of it (Glaserfeld 1984). Constructivists view any social circumstance as open to multiple ways of knowing and evaluation: Any given person's frame of reference and purposes will define what constitutes a "better" interpretation of the event or experience. Still, in application within social work, the worth of constructivist research knowledge is most often defined pragmatically by its usefulness (Rodwell 1998).

Constructivist research generally explores meaning making: how people understand and define both social situations (Schwandt 1994) and each other (Gergen 1994). Knowledge and meaning are understood as dependent on the active construction and interpretation of knowers situated in social groups. Thus social truth and knowledge are always linked to perspective and context (Schwandt 1994). People are understood as active learners who apply socially constructed meanings to make sense of situations and experiences (Hiller and DiLuzio, 2004).

Constructivists point out that much socially shared understanding and contextualization is evident even in the objective physical sciences. Scientists, for example, are groups of experts who bring a shared way of making meaning to the interpretation of events that may be mysterious to most laypeople. Latour and Woolgar (1986) studied medical researchers at the Salk Institute and found their interpretations of "wiggly lines" generated by machines to be unpersuasive evidence to their untrained (uninitiated?) observations. No direct sensory observation of the events these lines represent is possible, and an extended chain of constructs, logic, technology, and interpretation is applied by the scientists to make sense of their technology's yield. Latour and Woolgar argue that the "reality is formed as a consequence of stabilization [of differences]" (1986:180). That is, within this skilled social group of medical researchers, members share ideas about what constitutes meaningful research methods and factual results, all based on social constructions. Similarly, Best (2003:47) examined the social construction of statistics, arguing that "statistics—even official statistics . . . are products of social activity . . . not facts that simply exist." In the everyday social world, constructivists assume differences in meaning making across social groups and across individuals, though commonalities may exist. Gergen (1994) states that the constructs people use to understand the world are social artifacts, created by groups in specific cultural, political, and historical contexts. Many diverse reference groups exist, each with different ways of assigning value and meaning. Exploring the constructs used by people to make meaning of experience is a key focus of constructivist qualitative research.

A defining tension in constructivism centers on multiple perspectives on knowledge and the nature of reality. If there are multiple realities, how do we justify a claim to social knowledge? In large measure, the authenticity, viability, and utility of the realities voiced by research participants serve as the basis for knowledge claims in constructivist research (Manning 1997). This has led to the development of new ways of thinking about validity and the quality of constructivist research (Lincoln and Guba 1986; Lather 1993; Kvale 1995).

While the emphasis in most constructivist research is on the construction of knowledge (Ruckdeschel 1985), some approaches (i.e., Rodwell 1998) put more emphasis on methods of data verification while others (i.e., Lather 1995; Guba and Lincoln 2005) view any collected data as "text" to be processed and used to create additional texts that are presented to readers—as yet additional texts (Ricoeur 1979). To such strong constructivists, text is a construct: There is no difference in mode of experience between persons, texts, and artifacts (Dennett 1991). To strong constructivists, social constructions are entities with status equal to people and their actions.

Communities of Knowers

Constructivists view social groups as active influences in the development and socialization of the individual knower. Reference groups actively shape the core interpretative categories that are broadly shared among group members. By providing order, reference groups make social interaction possible. In turn, the group shapes each individual self. The nature of child rearing, the nature of family and extra-family social interactions, language, economics, politics, religion, art, music, and texts all shape interpretation within a community of knowers. The self is not an island unto itself, but constantly embedded in a complex web of relationships with others and ideas.

This web of relationships is dynamic and evolves with changes in physical and social context and in interaction with one's reference group and other, different, social groups. For example, in contemporary American culture, people are frequently members of many social reference groups. The groups interact in a dialectical fashion, with tensions between them posing both challenges and opportunities. Individuals who are members of multiple references groups must make sense of the different meanings and interpretations they confront. These opportunities and challenges cause tensions and, at best, promote creative change.

Not only the social group, but each individual, is an active maker of meaning. Individuals may diverge somewhat from the meanings and understandings shared by their reference groups. Such variation is based on unique individual experiences. Experiences that highlight differences between the constructs of a valued reference group and one's individual identity are often challenging for the individual, causing cognitive and social dissonance. For example, being lesbian or gay, or having a history of childhood sexual abuse—experiences often not sanctioned by, or often visible to, the larger reference group—may lead the individual to use constructs that are not widely familiar or shared among the reference group. Individuals are unique, active interpreters of the social and physical environment and of each other. If (and if, how well) we can come to know other knowers is a central question in philosophy and an area of theorizing and research for constructivists.

The nature and format of constructivist qualitative research also varies widely. While most reports in social work and other allied professions are extended text narratives, novel methods of reporting are increasingly common in nonapplied disciplines. Multimedia reports and performance narratives are increasingly evident, along with explicit linkages to jazz, theatrical performances, woven rugs, pictures, and other artifacts. The journal *Qualitative Inquiry* is a key vehicle for such works of qualitative performance.

Values and Constructivist Research

An interpretivist epistemology and a relativist ontology inherently offer little guidance on values and ethics. Indeed, the core premise of constructivist research is antifoundationalist—questioning any fixed claim of authority as located within particular cultural values and power relations. However, many constructivist researchers and theorists place emphasis on particular values, norms, and purposes. Their chosen values are not inherent to constructivism but rather are combined with it. Such critical or normative perspectives emphasize a focal issue or population selected a priori, based on the researcher's own standpoint and interests. For example, Marxist research explores ownership and power relationships while feminist research examines the situation of women. Guba and Lincoln (2005) distinguish constructivist, critical, and collaborative paradigms though in practice many researchers link a constructivist epistemology with specific value positions of their own choosing. For instance, Denzin and Lincoln (2005) state that all research is an inherently political act; Smith (1999) views research as among the worst aspects of Western colonization of indigenous peoples. Such value positions, however, are combined with constructivism rather than a central part of constructivism, in which multiple views and voices can always challenge any claim to a fixed core value or foundational premise.

At the same time, some characteristics of the research process have led constructivists to emphasize certain values within the research act. Emphasis on equality, collaboration, and the possibility of free choice are widely (though not inherently) linked to constructivist social work endeavors (Fisher 1991). Viewed from this perspective, the construction of a research report can be seen as a shared, collaborative enterprise between researcher and participants. Constructivist researchers who adopt these value positions emphasize equality between researcher and participants and an interactive, participatory, vision of the construction of the research endeavor. Research questions, data, findings, and report/re-presentation can all be understood as co-constructed in collaborative endeavors between researcher and participants (Guba and Lincoln 2005). Since the participants live and know the "emic" experience, they are given equal value to the researcher's skill as "etic" witness/translator/giver of testimony to others embedded in another context. Since there is no subject-object dichotomy, joint participation is often emphasized (Guba and Lincoln 2005). Joining these value positions with constructivism has important consequences for research methods.

Further, because people may come to adopt different perspectives on any event, there is always the possibility of free—and potentially unexpected—choice in human action (Fisher 1991). Openness to the views of others and reflexivity regarding one's own values create the opportunity for creativity and change. Social relations are not viewed as simple, linear, and deterministic, but rather as complex, situated webs of interaction with potential for free choice and liberation.

A different view is voiced by Brinkmann and Kvale (2005) who point to ethicism in qualitative research. They find problematic the claims that qualitative research is ethically good in itself, or at least ethically superior to "uncaring" quantitative approaches. They also challenge the idea that empathic interviews are ethically optimal and even argue for the use of "actively confronting" interviews. They view ethical issues as inescapable in research. Instead, they argue, the focus of attention should be broadened from the ethics of the researcher to the ethics of the report and its developed knowledge.

Specific to social work, Gilgun and Abrams (2002) advance the view that qualitative research in social work has applied feminist and emancipatory values consistent with the profession's core values. They also note that qualitative research can apply culturally specific values and illuminate diverse frames of reference. Research applied to these ends is consistent with social work's core purposes. Dean and Fenby (1989) also argue that constructivist epistemology fits well with social work's values and action focus. Thus constructivist research can be joined with social work's professional values and purposes.

Indeed, Mertens and Ginsburg (2008), studying a marginalized group, found constructivist research a valuable fit with their emancipatory purposes. They also note that such work may be enhanced when members of the research team take on somewhat differentiated roles in interaction with participants to ensure that varied data is collected and that transformative processes are successfully emphasized.

Institutional review boards may not understand, and may actively restrict, researchers planning constructivist research. For example, while planning constructivist research and incorporating democratic, participatory values, Leisey (2008) was disallowed by an institutional review board (IRB) from using simple snowball sampling to sample for domestic violence victims. This was despite her stated goal of seeking to give voice to members of this group. She also notes that in her view, constructivist research requires a new informed consent process at every contact with a participant because of the educational and catalytic dimension of being part of the research. That is, participants' self and views may have changed or elaborated after each contact. Therefore, a new consent is undertaken to acknowledge that a somewhat different, more informed, person may be making the decision to participate at a later point. Institutional review, and ongoing consent processes, may require expansion and adaptation when used in constructivist research.

Who Defines the Research Question?

A key power dynamic in research resides in the definition of the research question. In the traditional model, the researcher generates the research question. The authority of the researcher to frame the question is unexamined and etic constructs may be (mis)applied to groups in which they have little relevance, or in which they may be understood as degrading or harmful (Smith 1999; Schlutsmeyer and Pike 2002).

In relational constructivist research, questions are generated interactively between researcher and participants. That is, the participants are empowered to frame, or to help frame, the research question (Freeman 2001). Such co-construction levels the playing field, making researcher and participants co-creators and joint learners. The equality in power is further understood as helpful in gaining the authentic participation of others and as ethically necessary (Schlutsmeyer and Pike 2002). Yet Guba and Lincoln (2005) locate such interactive generation of research questions as part of a collaborative paradigm that they distinguish from their view of the constructivist paradigm.

Reference group differences and power differences between the researcher and the participants, however, ultimately leave the researcher with responsibility for the research report. The researcher represents others in the researcher's own terms. The researcher serves as a witness and also as a translator of experiences and understandings across different social groups. Yet, not infrequently, the researcher's interpretations and reports can run the risk of creating and portraying a group that does not exist (Said 1978), reflecting one's own culture and times more than the other.

The researcher's etic report of the emic views and experiences of others can never be an objective or complete view of another reality. Given the assumption of multiple realities and dynamic meanings, the researcher may be said to assume authority, even to act with hubris, to portray the experiences of others. Thus the joint framing of research questions, and interactive efforts to maximize verbatim reporting of participants' voices, may aid in the creation of a more worthy and more useful research report. Simple correspondence validity as portrayed in the traditional textbook manner is neither sought nor expected.

Problematizing Research Methods

In the textbook image, research methods are presented as a straightforward set of tools from which the researcher makes selections for specific uses. Stated this way, the toolbox metaphor fails to convey the contexts and power relationships in which the creation of these methods was originally located. The researcher's own methodological choices may also be masked or unnoticed. Further, the complexity of the actual applications and interpretations of research methods is often minimally described in research reports. Embedded in this vision is a dichotomy between subject and object, and tools and their yield. Until the past two decades, this vision served to shield research methods from critical reflection and deep analysis (Atkinson, Coffey, and Delamont 2003). A constructivist view would suggest that research methods are social constructions developed in interaction and dialogue within specific communities of knowers that are open to multiple, divergent uses and interpretations. Therefore, research methods, like any aspect of research, reflect meaning making; their use enacts the power relations between researcher and participants. Optimal use of all research methods requires reflexive review by the researcher and, perhaps, by research participants, too.

Atkinson, Coffey, and Delamont (2003) point out that constructivists may interpret the results of interviews as creating a different type of knowledge than from observations. Therefore, rather than expecting that the results of interviews and observations may be simply triangulated with each other to produce a convergent result, they may instead create distinct views of the social world. The relationship between the data collected with the two different tools is not simple. Indeed, to constructivists the data may be understood as incommensurable in Kuhn's (1962/1996) sense— created by different methods with different premises and constituting different and incompatible realities. In turn, claiming that triangulation is a technique to enhance the validity of results requires extensive explication; it is not a simple claim based on the yield of unproblematic research tools.

Constructivist Research Methods and Research Approaches

An odd dichotomy is evident in the portrayal of constructivist research methods. Some authors point to a lack of guidance for researchers, while others label a wide and varied set of named research approaches as constructivist. For example, from one perspective Hoskins (2002:238) states: "Perhaps most challenging for those unfamiliar with this kind of interpretive, relational research is that . . . there are no concrete 'how tos' for proceeding." Yet from the other perspective, authors view ethnography (Van Manen 1988), hermeneutics (Rodwell 1998; Hoskins 2002), case studies (Rodwell 1998), narrative analysis (Mishler 1986; Riessman 1993), grounded theory (Rodwell 1998; Charmaz 2000), biography, autoethnography (White 2001), emancipatory evaluation (Whitmore 2001), feminist research (Sprague 2005), queer theory and studies (Gamson 2000), connoisseurship (Eisner 1998), certain fictional narratives (Gilgun 2004), and performances (Denzin 2003) *all* as potential constructivist research methods. Thus there are multiple "how to" guides—although not necessarily ones that consistently are joined with an explicitly claimed constructivist epistemology. To further complicate matters, various authors may combine constructivist epistemology and methods with value positions of their own selection, making for a critical-constructivist hybrid position.

It is probably safe to say that many research methods (separately or in combination) may be used in constructivist research, depending on the researcher's perspective and purposes (Morris 1994). To aid readers, a rationale for the use of specific methods, strong internal consistency, or congruence among question, methods, and report, and provision of a transparent road map to clarify connections between evidence and conclusions should be provided (Drisko 1997; this volume).

How Is Data Collection Done?

As noted here, data collection in constructivist research has been tied to a wide range of research methods. Interviews, focus groups, participant observation, and artifacts are widely used. Reflections on one's own experience and participation are also recorded extensively. Arvay (2002) points to co-construction of the initial data collection performance by researcher and participants, followed by an interactive cycle of researcher and participant reflection and analysis of the initial data. The products of this cycle, too, are treated as data, and used by the researcher in writing one story as the final, "blended text" (Arvay 2002:218).

Rodwell (1998) details a similar data collection approach using a wide range of structured and unstructured methods, even standardized instruments, tied to hermeneutically informed grounded theory generation. Interviews, focus groups, observations, and nonhuman data sources may all be employed. Self-reflection and planned use of peer reviews and member checks (review of the data and preliminary analysis by colleagues and the original participants) is emphasized as well. The goal is for the researcher and participants to learn from each other during a hermeneutic cycle of data collection and systematic reviews. Similarly, data analysis involves both interrogating the data and negotiating with participants to bridge differences in meaning and understanding. Preliminary data analysis may identify needs for iterative changes in sampling and data collections methods. The final yield is a better understanding of the participants' views and constructs by the researcher and, in turn, a more useful and revealing report to future readers.

Sampling

Very little attention has been paid to sampling in constructivist research. Such sampling is purposive in nature and may be theoretically informed at the outset (Rodwell 1998). Constructivist researchers seek complexity and expect multiple voices and views (called polyvocality or multivocality). Frequently, preliminary data analysis points to the need to alter the initial sampling plan, to expand the number and perspectives of participants, and/ or to alter times and locations of data collection (Drisko 2003). Beyond participants, locations and times, one can also imagine the utility of sampling different theories, values, or cultural standpoints in some constructivist research (Drisko 2003). Ongoing reflection and reflexivity can be joined with member checks and peer review to propel reformulation of the sampling plan as well as guiding data analysis.

Defining approaches to sampling, and their related rationales, is an area in need of further development in constructivist research. For transparency, authors should provide a rationale for why the chosen sample was selected and how reflection led to its alteration (if any). While a single case, or small group of participants, may offer evocative and revealing perspectives on the views of people unknown or unfamiliar to the reader, a rationale for the selection of the particular sample should be offered by the researcher. That is, researchers using single cases might make clear how they find multiple realities and polyvocality in the single case (see, for example, Riessman 1989). Learning from the interactive dialogue may help the researcher guide others in understanding how context, culture, and individual development may shape the views offered in a given research report.

Data Analysis

Given the increasingly wide range of constructivist research reports, it should not be surprising that a wide range of data analysis methods is used by their creators. All these methods seek complexity rather than simplicity and multiple views or polyvocality rather than single answers. Self-reflection or reflexivity is a common aspect of the researcher's data analysis process, though reports vary widely in how much of the researcher's identity and process is reported to the reader. Documentation of reflexivity in published constructivist reports ranges from a brief orientation to the researcher's background to a developing genre of autoethnography in which the researcher writes solely of their own socially situated experience from their own frame of reference (White 2001).

Riessman (1993) makes use of narrative analysis to analyze data in her work. Riessman (1989) also offers systematic analysis of individual cases of domestic violence, reporting key stories told in full by women. Using Mischler's narrative methods, she identifies the structure of the telling of the story, noting conventions employed by the teller and examining the unfolding line of narrative. She adds to this systemic analysis many connections to prior theories of domestic violence and offers her personal reactions, both to the tale and its telling. Riessman has also drawn on large numbers of narratives of divorce (1990) and infertility (2000) to simultaneously offer both unique portraits of individual lives and more generalized, aggregate insights into practical and policy issues in these areas. These reports, however, run to book length.

Rodwell [O'Connor] (1998) has used grounded theory methods in constructivist evaluation. In her work, collected data is systematically peer-reviewed and member-checked to ascertain that it does convey the meanings intended by participants and to ensure the views of the researcher do not unduly shape the research report in a manner that undermines the purposes and views of the participants.

Several authors offer self-reflective constructivist chapters that center on the researcher's learning during the research process. Hyde (1994) reports heavily on how her experience offered further insight on organizational development in a woman's organization. Ruckdeschel, Earnshaw, and Firrek (1994) provide immersive thick descriptions of social work in renal dialysis settings with strong self-reflection by the authors. White (2001) offers an autoethnography reflecting on her emerging understanding of the impact of attachment theory and agency process in teamwork in child welfare services. These reports immerse the reader in the author's experiences, illustrated with accounts of pivotal events and theoretical reflection. The constructs employed by the author are examined in detail, but the constructs and views of others may be much less systematically developed.

New approaches to immersing readers in the experiences of others (of "strangers") are developing within disciplines close to social work, but are less evident within mainstream American social work journals. Gilgun (2004) offers a story of how a child molester understands and approaches his victim in a fictionalized version of a story told to her by an incarcerated child molester. No formal research method is stated, no constructs are identified, and the boundaries between her fictionalized account and the molester's told story are left unclear (in part to assure his confidentiality). Yet the reader is offered a rare insight into the dynamics of child molestation, how rape is rationalized as care, and how parents are led to understand events in a manner that covers for the perpetrator. Such reports may be understood as immersion research in the terminology of Crabtree and Miller (1999), or as Eisner's (1998) "connoisseurship." Abma (2002) points out that newly emerging narrative forms of representation are often misunderstood in the health sciences. One can easily imagine that such pieces may be inappropriately reviewed (slammed?) by academic peer reviewers who fail to understand or appreciate their specific research purposes and innovative reporting conventions.

The most frequent form of constructivist research report in American social work takes a fairly traditional form but is understood from a constructivist perspective. Data analysis is minimally described, more implicit than explicit, leading to the reporting of several themes. Raw data is too often presented via brief sound bites of a sentence or less. It is not always clear how multiple perspectives and realities are evident in the summarized data, raising issues of internal consistency and credibility. Indeed, such reports could be read as creating/reporting a single reality, which is inconsistent with a constructivist epistemology. The state of the art in American social work is not yet strong, but is developing. As noted in the chapter introduction, citations of constructivist social work research are very few in number to date.

Also frequent in the American social work literature is what might be called constructivist inquiry or scholarship—explorations of a topic or method from several perspectives, often from a particular critical value viewpoint, with varying degrees of linkage to newly collected data. Such reports offer perspective and insight, and generate new ways of looking at an idea, an event, or a value position. Such reports often explore the role of the investigator's personal perspective as a shaping influence on the event and the report. They offer engaging and fruitful immersion into the multiple perspectives of constructivist academic work and demonstrate applications of constructivist thinking. What is less clear is that such reports constitute empirical research in the sense of a systematic examination of newly generated data. They can, however, be understood as hermeneutic interpretations of prior work and perspectives, though such an orienting analytic framework may be, or may not be, explicitly stated. Hermeneutics offer a rich approach to constructivist research, one that could be better exploited within academic social work.

To some readers and reviewers, evocative or immersive research reports—those closest to the thick description of phenomenology in their format—may not appear to be research. Such reactions are more likely to reports that are solely descriptive and include no explicit method or analysis to frame or locate the descriptive content. Authors must take care to ensure their purposes and choices are clear to editors, peer reviewers, and readers.

Quality and Rigor in Constructivist Research

If constructivist research reports seek to convey the perspectives and understanding of others and themselves in formats appropriate to the content, how do we determine the quality of the work? In constructivist research, great variation is expected in report format, content, identification of—and explicit reflection on—methods, and extent of data about participants and even the researcher. The very diversity of constructivist research poses a challenge for the development of standards or expectations for reports.

Rigor in qualitative research may be broadly understood as the internal consistency of question, epistemology, research purposes, intended audience, ethics, methods, and report (Drisko 1997; 1999; this volume). In addition, projects and reports will vary in the thoroughness with which each area is addressed. That is, a report may claim a constructivist epistemology but fail to identify the constructs used by the participants or fail to articulate multiple perspectives and voices. Alternately, a report may give voice to multiple perspectives on a social issue but fall into making "one size fits all" policy recommendations that do not seem to honor the variety of voices and meanings reported. In such cases, the constructivist research report falls into implicit realism and lacks internal epistemological consistency.

Seeking epistemological internal consistency in a project should guide both the researcher doing the project and the reader of the report. Bearing in mind that constructivists view the reader as an active interpreter of the material presented, the researcher still should help orient the reader with a road map of what the researcher sought to do. Providing such a road map also helps the reader judge if the researcher was successful in achieving the intended research purposes. It offers readers and editorial reviewers guidance in assessing the report on its own terms. Of course, the active readers are the final creators (Eco 1979), who may choose not to adopt the researcher's stated purposes and instead interpret based on their own premises and interests.

Credibility and Validity in Constructivist Qualitative Research

Not surprisingly, there are varied ideas about the credibility or validity of constructivist research. While some authors (i.e., Guba and Lincoln 1989, 2005) choose to use different terminology for qualitative research, many others continue to use the term validity while expanding the boundaries of the term. Some authors apply a skeptical postmodernist approach to validity, doubting both universal and localized "truths" and viewing any legitimizing meta-narratives as naive (Lyotard 1984). Others take a more affirmative position, doubting universal truths but accepting "the possibility of specific, local, personal and community forms of truth with a focus on daily life and local narrative" (Kvale 1995:21). Still others take a transgressive position, arguing that validity in constructivist research should actively seek to stretch our ideas about validity (Lather 1993).

Taking an affirmative position, Kvale (1995) identifies three different views of validity in qualitative research. The first approach is related to the craftsmanship and procedural integrity of a study, established by careful checking, questioning, and theorizing on the phenomena of interest. This position is evident in the work of Glaser and Strauss (1967), as well as the work of Rodwell (1995) in social work. Extensive interactive efforts are employed to ensure credibility/validity, including member checks, use of multiple data types, and researcher self-reflection and peer review. Triangulation across data types and data collection methods (i.e., interviews, observations, artifacts, documents) is commonly employed. Kvale's second approach goes beyond such correspondence criteria of validity to emphasize meta-level interaction and communication about the phenomena under study. Such communicative validity is not simple persuasion but is actively established in challenging interaction, even argument, among "competent others" (Eisner 1991). Eisner (1998, 2001) argues for the use of criteria from the visual and literary arts in appraising qualitative research via processes of connoisseurship and expert criticism. Yet Kvale (1995) notes that some qualitative research approaches include research participants and the general public in the pool of competent others who serve as the interpretative community. This creates a counterpoint between socially sanctioned experts and the expertise of common people's lived experience. Who is authorized to engage in the determination of communicative validity, how the communication takes place, and the purposes of the interaction can vary widely.

Kvale's (1995) third view of validity is a pragmatic one, emphasizing the utility of knowledge. This view fits well with the knowledge needs and challenges facing applied professions such as social work. Drawing on sources ranging from Marx and Freud to contemporary qualitative researchers Patton (1980) and Wahl (1982), Kvale argues that more than communicative validation is required for professional knowledge. The justification of professional knowledge rests on its usefulness in application to specific target populations: It must generate useful results. Pragmatic validation also requires that knowledge is accompanied by action (Kvale 1995). Even more compelling is that interventions based on the researcher's interpretations lead to changes in client's behavior. Kvale notes that the application of professional knowledge in the social world has tacit, relational, and intersubjective aspects that are difficult to frame as formal rules. Thus who determines what constitutes knowledge and practice, as well as the nature of the changes to be achieved, are important power issues in appraising the pragmatic validity of qualitative research.

Pointing to the limitations of traditional approaches to validity, Lather's (1993) transgressive forms of validity seek to alter the nature of validity in keeping with several ideas in constructivism and critical theory. Drawing on Deleuze, she identifies four new forms of validity; all are very different from traditional correspondence validity. The first is ironic validity which "foregrounds the insufficiencies of language . . . produces truth as a problem . . . and resists the hold of the real" (Lather 1995:54). The second form is paralogical validity which "fosters difference and heterogeneity . . . [is] concerned with undecidables, limits, paradoxes . . . [and] searches for the oppositionality in our daily practice (55) . . ." The third form is rhizomatic validity, which "unsettles from within, taps underground . . . puts conventional discursive procedures under erasure, breaches congealed discourses (55) . . ." Lather's (1995:55) fourth form is voluptuous validity which "goes too far toward disruptive excess . . . creates a questioning text that is bounded and unbounded, closed and opened . . ." These new validity metaphors seek to help researchers go beyond easily available discourses, to help researchers examine the "various effects of opening up and closing down" in research practice (Lather 1995:56). Note that Lather's typology is playful and creative: It forces the reader to rethink the purposes of research, its methods, and the format of research reports. All are intended as stimuli, as heuristic devices, to gain multiple perspectives on research, and to help frame research reports in a multivocal constructivist fashion. Indeed, Lather (1995) applies all four types to a piece of her own work, finding richness in both the intellectual ancestry and the complex stories of women with HIV/AIDS. The results join empirical findings of depth and heart with a revealing metaphor—solid academic roots presented in a format meant to make the reader work and think.

Lincoln and Guba (1986) identify fairness and several forms of authenticity as appropriate standards for appraising the validity of constructivist research. Fairness addresses the requirement for evenhanded portrayal of multiple perspectives on the focal research issue. While a reasonable expectation, it is unclear how such fairness fits with immersive reports taking only a single perspective. Such reports could inherently appear to lack fairness. Similarly, fairness raises the issue of how many different views need to be represented to meet the standard. Who would judge the adequacy of a fair portrayal, and by what standards, is left unresolved by Lincoln and Guba. Fairness is a provocative concept, but raises questions that do not easily fit with a multivocal, relativist position in application.

Authenticity takes several forms: ontological, educative, catalytic, and tactical (Guba and Lincoln 2005). Ontological and educational authenticities refer to raising consciousness and understanding in the research participants and in the researcher, respectively. Catalytic authenticity refers to the expectation that the research led to action by participants toward greater social justice. Tactical authenticity refers to the expectation that the researcher helps participants learn to work the political system in which they reside. All these forms of authenticity validity fit well with an action research perspective. However, these authenticity standards apply particular, external value premises to constructivist research. They bring in values most social workers would support, since they are generally consistent with social work's core values. Yet they serve, in effect, as imported foundational values. Such foundational values, of course, are always open to challenge in a constructivist epistemology. Applying these standards would also require authors to include specific information in constructivist research reports.

Clearly the concept of validity in constructivist research is being actively examined from multiple perspectives. The fruitfulness of research in generating new and useful ideas, in vividly conveying the unfamiliar, in offering new perspectives is heavily emphasized in constructivist research. At the same time, a tension may be emerging between the needs and purposes of academic disciplines and the needs and purposes of applied professions such as social work. Kvale (1995) points out that the social sanction for professions requires that social workers keep in mind the pragmatic expectations for results. Similarly, House (1980:255) states that the validity of evaluation rests, in part, on its being "normatively correct" or producing desired results, which could conflict with the authenticity standards. Social workers doing constructivist research must engage with the tension among transgressive, correspondence, communicative, and pragmatic forms of validity as well as the demands of funders and the public who seek practical results. Within these arcs of tension, there is exceptional opportunity for social workers to elaborate, extend, and remake the person-in-environment perspective from widely varied perspectives to the benefit of the profession and the public alike.

Writing Up Constructivist Research

There is no single valid form for all constructivist research purposes and audiences. Multiple texts—and multiple types of texts—are to be expected in constructivist research. Multiple voices may be represented via polyvocal texts weaving varied perspectives and viewpoints (i.e., Riessman 1993; Lather 1995). Indeed, dissatisfaction with the traditional research report format and organization has led to innovative formats for constructivist research reports. Experimentation with varied report formats in turn allows reflection on the traditional format.

Using Van Maanen's (1988) typology, realist tales are the least likely form for constructivist research. Nonetheless, they are frequently found in social work publications and can be valuable in guiding practice and raising consciousness. For example, Tijerina (2009) offers a constructivist report of issues related to Mexican-American women's adherence to hemodialysis. Lacking, however, is a polyvocal perspective. Dettlaff and Rycraft (2008) offer the views of multiple stakeholders on health care disproportionality within a realist tale framework. Beyond social work journal outlets, two more widely used constructivist report formats are impressionistic description and confessional tales. Impressionistic tales seek to help the reader enter the world under study, to tell a compelling tale that highlights what the author found important. Reporting of research methods tends to be given secondary importance to the story. Phenomenological thick description, life stories, and narrative analyses are often impressionistic descriptions. Gilgun's (1999) "Fingernails Painted Red" combines the told story of a murderer with the reflections and actions of the researcher as well as commentary on methods for sitting with horrific content in research. Confessional tales focus on the experiences of the author. They are usually written in the first person and seek to highlight the views and processes of the researcher. Self-reflection and reflexivity are heavily emphasized. Research processes and methods are often one of several foci within the report. Researchers report the challenges they confronted, the strategies used to address these challenges, and appraise the strengths and limitations of the new strategies. Terrell and Staller's (2003) "Buckshot's Case" tells the co-constructed story of a social worker working with a poor defendant whose life was on the line in Alabama.

Van Maanen's typology addresses reports employing fairly traditional formats. Additional innovations include the use of diaries, novels, or fictional stories, poems, or combinations of these forms. Note that the use of fictional approaches and poetry will likely be combined with little to no content on research methods per se. Reports may also include images, audio, film, or video. Such media may be very useful where oral traditions or performance are more common than are written texts.

Portraying multiple voices or perspectives simultaneously requires the generation of new reporting formats for constructivist research. Some authors use computer-based hypertext presentations to overcome the linear, sequential nature of the written text. Hypertext links allow readers to make choices regarding how to move around the text and other materials, allowing creation of diverse stories that are neither simple nor predictable. Offering multiple perspectives within a written text has been done using multiple, nonsequential narratives interspersed one upon the other; through the use of extensive footnotes to give ample voice to the author's reactions and perspectives; and through multi part narratives that weave back and forth from the voices of participants, to multiple theoretical and methodological perspectives, to the views and reactions of the author. Such innovative "messy texts" seek to challenge the boundaries between science and literature and to portray human experiences in their complexity (Marcus and Fischer 1986). Such constructivist reports seek to shake up the reader's ways of understanding, to deconstruct, and to point out dialectics. A few strive for "getting us all lost" (Lather 2001:485) by using density and even opacity of language, as well as the structure of the report, to push readers to take different perspectives.

The relative success of such innovative report forms and formats is difficult to assess at this early point in the development of the new genres. While arguing for experimentation, Tierney (1995) notes that even experimental writing should be done well; that experimentation is not an excuse for lack of clarity, obfuscation, or a boring report. Tierney also points out that if authors are to have impact they must be read and valued by an audience. Very few experimental texts are evident in American social work journals and only some as chapters in books. Some appear in the international journal *Qualitative Social Work* (authored both by social workers and scholars from allied disciplines). There appears to be no opportunity to present hypertexts, or to include images, audio or video as electronic files in social work's professional journals. Even current electronic journals overwhelmingly emphasize text-based reports. However, the inclusion of interactive CDs or DVDs in textbooks and the development of electronic versions of journals suggest that channels for the dissemination of nontextual materials may be emerging.

Photovoice is a participatory research method in which participants are asked to represent their community or point of view by taking photographs, and creating short explanatory narratives to go along with their photographs (Molloy 2007). Exhibits of photographs and narratives are displayed for the general public, often with opening celebrations. Photovoice seeks to allow marginalized people to share their images and views, as well as empowering them through the research and reporting process. A related alternative form of reporting research is evident in the 2004 movie *Born into Brothels: Calcutta's Red Light Kids*. Children of sex workers were given video cameras to document their daily lives. Their chosen videotaped experiences form the core of this Academy Award winning film. Other alternative forms of multimedia research reports may now be videos found on YouTube. New avenues for the reporting of nontextual research need to be developed to keep pace with innovations in research and in social inquiry.

Issues for Constructivist Research in Social Work

"Of course the performance turn in Anglo-American theory has not been embraced everywhere, nor is there a massive rush to take up post-interpretive, post-foundational evaluative paradigms" (Denzin 2003:245). As noted in the opening of this chapter, constructivist social work research is minimally evident in American literature. In this current era, funding for the applied professions is closely tied to practical results and pragmatic applications. Strong academic and economic forces are hypervaluing experimental research and actively devaluing the all other forms of research (Tanenbaum 2003; Reed and Eisman 2006). Yet social work interventions must optimally draw on complex and sophisticated understandings of the people we serve and their increasingly varied social and cultural contexts. Rubin (2008:39ff) argues that a valid focus of evidence-based practice (EBP) may be to use research to understand the experiences of clients. This use of "evidence" is in addition to seeking more traditional EBP information about the effectiveness of diagnostic tests and treatments. In this territory of understanding lived experience lies the strength of constructivist research. It can help us be more open in our ways of thinking, more attentive to context, increasingly aware of subtlety in communication, and more creative in our methods. It can help professionals understand the processes and contexts in which improvement occurs, or fails to occur. As such, it can help us improve conceptualization, policy, and services.

While there may be a growing infrastructure of social work educators and practitioners who apply constructivist epistemology to practice, there appears to be much less support for doing constructivist research and for training future constructivist researchers. Interest appears strong, but training opportunities are few. Social work researchers need to be inventive to find funding for innovative approaches. Social work's professional organizations need to become more supportive of varied forms of social work scholarship. The arrival of *Qualitative Social Work* suggests that a growing marketplace for innovative scholarship exists. More sources for support, affirmation, and positive examples are needed for constructivist research in social work.

Constructivist research can bear witness, offer testimony, provide perspective, raise consciousness, spur creativity, promote conceptualization, and motivate action. All these are consistent with the values, aims, and purposes of professional social work. Constructivist research can develop and explore subjective, subjugated and intersubjective knowledge that can both guide micro-level practice and shape macro-level policy perspective.

References

Abma, T. 2002. Emerging narrative forms of knowledge representation in the health sciences: Two texts in a postmodern context. *Qualitative Health Research*, 12(I):5–27.

Arvay, M. 2002. Putting the heart back into human science research. In *Studies in meaning: Exploring constructivist psychology*, J. Raskin and S. Bridges, eds. 210–223. New York: Pace UP.

Atkinson, P., A. Coffey, and S. Delamont. 2003. *Key themes in qualitative research: Continuities and changes.* Lanham, MD: AltaMira.

Berger, P. and T. Luckmann. 1966. *The social construction of reality.* Garden City, NY: Doubleday.

Best, J. 2003. Audiences evaluate statistics. In *Social problems: Constructivist readings*, D. Loseke and J. Best, eds. 43–50. New York: Aldine de Grutyer.

Briski, Z. and Kauffman, R. 2004. (Producers and directors). Born into Brothels: Calcutta's Red Light Kids. [Motion picture]. Calcutta, West Bengal, India: Redlight Films and HBO/Cinemax Documentary.

Brinkmann, S. and S. Kvale. 2005. Confronting the ethics of qualitative research. *Journal of Constructivist Psychology, 18*(2):157–181.

Charmaz, K. 2000. Constructivist and objectivist grounded theory. In *Handbook of qualitative research* (2nd ed.), N. Denzin and Y. Lincoln, eds. 509–535. Thousand Oaks, CA: Sage.

Crabtree, B. and W. Miller, eds. 1999. *Doing qualitative research.* Thousand Oaks, CA: Sage.

Dean, R. and B. Fenby. 1989. Exploring epistemologies: Social work action as a reflection of philosophical assumptions. *Journal of Social Work Education, 25*(1):46–54.

Dennett, D. 1991. *Consciousness explained.* Harmondsworth, UK: Penguin.

Denzin, N.K. 2003. *Performance ethnography: Critical pedagogy and the politics of culture.* Thousand Oaks, CA: Sage.

Denzin, N. and Y. Lincoln. 2005. Introduction: The discipline and practice of qualitative research. In *Handbook of qualitative research* (3rd ed.), N. Denzin and Y. Lincoln, eds. 1–32. Thousand Oaks, CA: Sage.

Dettlaff, A. and J. Rycraft. 2008. Deconstructing disproportionality: Views from multiple stakeholders. *Child Welfare, 87*(2):37–58.

Drisko, J. 1997. Strengthening qualitative studies and reports: Standards to enhance academic integrity. *Journal of Social Work Education, 33*:187–197.

——. (1999). "Rigor in qualitative research." Paper presented at the Society for Social Work and Research Annual Meeting, Austin, TX.

——. (2003). "Improving sampling strategies and terminology in qualitative research." Paper presented at the Society for Social Work and Research Annual Meeting, Washington, DC.

Eco, U. 1979. *The role of the reader.* Bloomington: IN: University of Indiana.

Eisner, E. 1991. *The enlightened eye: Qualitative inquiry and the enhancement of educational practice.* New York: Macmillan.

——. 1998. *The enlightened eye: Qualitative inquiry and the enhancement of educational practice* (2nd ed.). Upper Saddle River, NJ: Merrill.

——. 2001. Concerns and aspirations for qualitative research in the new millennium. *Qualitative Research 1*(2):135–145.

Fisher, D. 1991. *An introduction to constructivism for social workers.* New York: Praeger.

Freeman, E. 2001. *Substance abuse intervention, prevention, rehabilitation, and systems change strategies: Helping individuals, families and groups to empower.* New York: Columbia UP.

Gamson, J. 2000. Sexualities, queer theory and qualitative research. In *Handbook of qualitative research* (2nd ed.), N. Denzin and Y. Lincoln, eds. 347–365. Thousand Oaks, CA: Sage.

Gergen, K. 1994. *Realities and relationships: Soundings in social construction.* Cambridge, MA: Harvard UP.

Gilgun, J. 1999. Fingernails painted red: A feminist, semiotic analysis of "hot" text. *Qualitative Inquiry,* 5:181–207.

——. 2004. Fictionalizing life stories: Yukee the wine thief. *Qualitative Inquiry,* 10:691–705.

Gilgun, J. and L. Abrams. 2002. The nature and usefulness of qualitative social work research: Some thoughts and an invitation to dialogue. *Qualitative Social Work,* 1(1):39–55.

Glaser, B. and A. Strauss. 1967. *The discovery of grounded theory.* Chicago: Aldine.

Glaserfeld, E. von. 1984. An introduction to radical constructivism. In *The invented reality: How do we know what we believe we know?* P. Watzlawick, ed. 17–40. New York: Norton.

——. 1996. Introduction: Aspects of constructivism. In *Constructivism: Theory, perspectives, and practice,* C.T. Fosnot, ed. 3–7. New York: Teachers College.

Guba, E. and Y. Lincoln. 1989. *Fourth generation evaluation.* Newbury Park, CA: Sage.

——. 2005. Paradigmatic controversies, contradictions, and emerging confluences. In *Handbook of qualitative research* (3rd ed.), N. Denzin and Y. Lincoln, eds. 191–216. Thousand Oaks, CA: Sage.

Hiller, H. and L. DiLuzio. 2004. The interviewee and the research interview: Analysing a neglected dimension in research. *Canadian Review of Sociology and Anthropology,* 41(1):1–26.

Hoskins, M. 2002. Towards new methodologies for constructivist research: Synthesizing knowledges for relational inquiries. In *Studies in meaning: Exploring constructivist psychology,* J. Raskin and S. Bridges, eds. 225–244. New York: Pace UP.

House, E. R. 1980. *Evaluating with validity.* Beverly Hills, CA: Sage.

Hyde, C. 1994. Reflections on a journey: A research story. In *Qualitative studies in social work,* C. Riessman, ed. 169–189. Thousand Oaks, CA: Sage.

Kuhn, T. 1962/1996. *The structure of scientific revolutions* (3rd ed.). Chicago, IL: University of Chicago.

Kvale, S. 1995. The social construction of validity. *Qualitative Inquiry,* 1(1):19–40.

Lather, P. 1993. Fertile obsession: Validity after poststructuralism. *Sociological Quarterly, 34*: 673–693.

——. 1995. The validity of angels: Interpretive and textual strategies in researching the lives of women with HIV/AIDS. *Qualitative Inquiry,* 1:41–68.

——. 2001. Postmodernism: Post-structuralism and post(critical) ethnography: Of ruins, aporias and angels. In *Handbook of ethnography,* P. Atkinson, A. Coffey, S. Delamont, J. Lofland and L. Lofland, eds. 477–492. Thousand Oaks, CA: Sage.

Latour, B. and S. Woolgar. 1986. *Laboratory life: The construction of scientific facts.* Princeton, NJ: Princeton UP.

Leisey, M. 2008. Qualitative inquiry and the IRB: Protection at all costs? *Qualitative Social Work,* 7:415–427.

Lincoln, Y. and E. Guba. 1986. But is it rigorous? Trustworthiness and authenticity in naturalistic evaluation. In *Naturalistic evaluation,* D. Williams, ed. 73–84. San Francisco, CA: Jossey Bass.

Lyotard, J. 1984. *The postmodern condition: A report on knowledge.* Manchester, UK: U of Manchester.

Manning, K. 1997. Authenticity in constructivist inquiry: Methodological consideration without prescription. *Qualitative Inquiry, 3*(1):93–115.

Marcus, G. and M. Fischer. 1986. *Anthropology as cultural critique: An experimental moment in the human sciences.* Chicago, IL: University of Chicago.

Mertens, D. and P. Ginsburg. 2008. Deep in ethical waters: Transformative perspectives in qualitative social work research. *Qualitative Social Work,* 7:404–503.

Mishler, E. 1986. *Research interviewing: Context and narrative.* Cambridge, MA: Harvard UP.

Molloy, J. 2007. Photovoice as a tool for social justice workers. *Journal of Progressive Human Services, 18*(2):39–55.

Morris, T. 1994. Alternative paradigms: A source for social work practice research. *Arete. 18*(2):31–44.

——. 2006. *Social work research methods: Four alternative paradigms.* Thousand Oaks, CA: Sage.

Patton, M. Q. 1980. *Qualitative evaluation methods.* Beverly Hills, CA: Sage.

Peled, E. and R. Leichtentritt. 2002. The ethics of qualitative social work research. *Qualitative Social Work, 1*(2):145–169.

Raskin, J. and S. Bridges. 2002. *Studies in meaning: Exploring constructivist psychology.* New York: Pace UP.

Reed, G. and E. Eisman. 2006. Uses and misused of evidence: Managed care, treatment guidelines, and outcomes measurement in professional practice. In *Evidence-based psychotherapy: Where practice and research meet,* C. Goodheart, A. Kazdin and R. Sternberg, eds. 1303. Washington, DC: American Psychological Association.

Ricoeur, P. 1979. The model of the text: Meaningful action considered as a text. In *Interpretive social science: A reader*, P. Rabinow and W. Sullivan, eds. 73–101. Berkeley: U of California P.

Riessman, C. 1989. From victim to survivor: A woman's narrative reconstruction of marital sexual abuse. *Smith College Studies in Social Work*, 59(3):232–251.

——. 1990. *Divorce talk: Women and men make sense of personal relationships.* New Brunswick, NJ: Rutgers UP.

——. 1993. *Narrative analysis.* Newbury Park, CA: Sage.

——. 2000. "Even if we don't have children [we] can live": Stigma and infertility in South India." In *Narratives and the cultural construction of illness and healing*, C. Mattingly and L. Garro, eds. 128–152. Berkeley, CA: U of California P.

Rodwell [O'Connor], M.K. 1998. *Social work constructivist research.* New York: Garland.

Rubin, A. 2008. Practitioner's guide to using research for evidence-based practice. Hoboken, NJ: Wiley.

Ruckdeschel, R. 1985. Qualitative research as a perspective. *Social Work Research and Abstracts*, 21(2):17–21.

Ruckdeschel, R., P. Earnshaw, and A. Firrek. 1994. The qualitative case study and evaluation: Issues, methods and examples. In *Qualitative research in social work*, E. Sherman and W. Reid, eds. 251–264. New York: Columbia UP.

Said, E. 1978. *Orientalism.* New York: Bantam.

Schlutsmeyer, M. and N. Pike. 2002. Ownership and research: The appropriation of psychological data. In *Studies in meaning: Exploring constructivist psychology*, J. Raskin and S. Bridges, eds. 181–200. New York: Pace UP.

Schütz, A. 1962. *Collected papers. Volume I: Studies in social theory.* The Hague, Netherlands: Nijhoff.

Schwandt, T. 1994. Constructivist, interpretivist approaches to human inquiry. In *Handbook of qualitative research*, N. Denzin and Y. Lincoln, eds. 118–137. Thousand Oaks, CA: Sage.

Smith, L. 1999. *Decolonizing methodologies: Research and indigenous peoples.* Dunedin, NZ: U of Otago P.

Sprague, J. 2005. *Feminist methodologies for critical researchers: Bridging differences.* Lanham, MD: AltaMira.

Tanenbaum, S. 2003. Evidence-based practice in mental health: Practical weakness meets political strengths. *Journal of Evidence in Clinical Practice*, 9:287–301.

Terrell, J. and K. Staller. 2003. Buckshot's case: Social work and death penalty mitigation in Alabama. *Qualitative Social Work*, 2(1):7–23.

Tierney, W. 1995. (Re)presentation and voice. *Qualitative Inquiry*, 1(4):379–390.

Tijerina, M. 2009. Mexican-American women's adherence to hemodialysis treatment: A social constructivist perspective. *Social Work*, 54(3):232–242.

Van Manen, J. 1988. *Tales of the field: On writing ethnography.* Chicago: U of Chicago P.

Wahl, D. 1982. Handlungsvalidierung [Validation through action]. In *Verbale Daten* [Verbal Data], G. Huber and H. Mandl, eds. 259–274. Weinheim, Germany: Beltz.

White, S. 2001. Auto-ethnography as reflexive inquiry. In *Qualitative research in social work*, I. Shaw and N. Gould, eds. 100–155. Thousand Oaks, CA: Sage.

Whitmore, E. 2001. "People listened to what we had to say": Reflections on an emancipatory qualitative evaluation. In *Qualitative research in social work*, I. Shaw and N. Gould, eds. 83–99. Thousand Oaks, CA: Sage.

Grounded Theory, Deductive Qualitative Analysis, and Social Work Research and Practice

JANE F. GILGUN

This chapter updates an earlier version published more than 16 years ago (Gilgun 1994c). I kept an emphasis on grounded theory research, and I added information on deductive qualitative analysis, which involves hypothesis-testing and theory-guided research in the conduct of qualitative research. These additions are responsive to funders and dissertation committees who are more likely to support research that begins with conceptual models and testable hypotheses. Grounded theory and deductive qualitative analysis have common roots within the Chicago School of Sociology and work well for knowledge-building in social work. Social work academics and activists made contributions to the Chicago School and thus can claim to be part of the original formulations of analytic induction, on which grounded theory is based. Deductive qualitative analysis is an updated version of analytic induction.

Grounded theory and deductive qualitative analysis are important ways to do social work research. They can contribute to knowledge-building not only in the three main areas of social work direct practice—assessment, intervention, and evaluation—but also in other domains where social workers practice, such as policy research, program development and evaluation, community organizing, social development, advocacy, and studies of program implementation. The findings of grounded theory (GT) and deductive qualitative analysis (DQA) are a good fit with the research agenda of social work because they arise out of the interaction of researchers with research participants, show multiple meanings and multiple dimensions of human phenomena, and, at their best, show connections between concepts and theories and their concrete indicators in the natural world. Social work's emphasis on social justice comes to life when researchers seek the meanings that research participants attribute to social issues that are part of their lived experience. The emphasis of GT and DQA on multiple meanings and perspectives sensitizes researchers to the worlds of direct practitioners, which typically are complicated, untidy, sometimes confusing, often intrusive, and sometimes traumatizing (Gilgun 2008, 2010b, 2012, in press).

In addition, the procedures of GT and DQA are similar to many of the procedures of direct practice and practice in other domains as well, including processes of interviewing and observing; developing and testing hypotheses in response to complex, situated phenomena; skills in organizing massive amount of data; and emphasis on values such self-determination and doing no harm. Learning how to do these types of research and using the findings may feel natural to social work practitioners who seek research training in graduate programs, like sliding a hand into a well-made glove. In fact, some claim that the procedures of this style of research are similar to excellent everyday thinking (Corbin and Strauss 2008).

The purpose of this chapter is to demonstrate the importance of GT and DQA to the development of knowledge relevant to social work direct practice. Although the focus is limited to direct practice, the ideas may be tested for fit with other domains of practice. The chapter begins with a discussion of the procedures for doing these two forms of qualitative analysis, moves on to a demonstration of parallels between these procedures and the assumptions of direct practice, and then provides an overview of the kinds of products that researchers can develop from these two approaches. While there are many ways to do qualitative research, I chose to focus on two approaches, both of which have roots in the Chicago School of Sociology, that, in turn, has connections to social work research in the first part of the twentieth century (Bulmer 1984; Deegan 1990; Gilgun 1999b, 2012).

Definitions

For the purposes of this discussion, hypotheses are statements of relationships between concepts or variables. Concepts are the components of hypotheses and are abstractions from concrete descriptions of processes and other phenomena. Theories are composed of interrelated hypotheses. They are provisional and subject to further testing and modification. A set of related theories become models when they are thought to account for how something works. Models may be theoretical; that is, researchers have not tested them. They typically are based on multiple sources of information, such as research, theory, practitioner expertise, personal experience, and personal and professional values.

Direct practice is any form of social work that involves face-to-face contact and interaction with service users. This includes child welfare; children's mental health; work in shelters, group homes, and residential treatment programs; therapy with families, couples, and individuals; group work; and community organizing in the many other domains in which social workers do their practice.

Deductive Qualitative Analysis

Many researchers assume that to do qualitative studies, they have to begin their research with no hypotheses to test and, in so doing, bypass hypothesis testing and theory-guided research (Gilgun 2005b, 2010a). This widespread impression stems at least in part from the idea of emergence, linked to procedures of GT (Glaser and Strauss 1967; Glaser 2010; Corbin and Strauss 2008) where researchers assume that researchable questions and valuable findings will arise through immersion in the worlds of informants (e.g., research participants). Yet, researchers interested in particular bodies of research and theoretical models cannot nor should they be expected to start anew, or act as if they don't already know something about their areas of interest. There is no reason why they cannot test their theories and models qualitatively or do theory-guided research. Furthermore, dissertation committees are unlikely to approve studies that do not build on what is already known, nor are funders inclined to commit money to such studies (Gilgun 2005b, 2010a).

Deductive qualitative analysis recognizes these issues and provides guidelines for doing research that begins with an initial conceptualization that can range from a parsimonious model or theory to a rather loose set of ideas. I use the term *deductive qualitative analysis*, after trying out many others, because my experience had led me to conclude that having a prior conceptual framework is an important way to do qualitative research. I pieced together the procedures of DQA from earlier work on analytic induction (Znaniecki 1934; Lindesmith 1947; Cressey 1953) and the thinking of philosophers John Dewey (1910) and Karl Popper (1969).

The unit of analysis of DQA is the case. Cases are individual units. The cases themselves can be simple or complex. Simple cases are composed of a single person or other individual phenomenon of interest. Complex cases are composed of two or more entities of interest, such as case studies of couples, families, agencies, counties, provinces, countries, and regions of the world.

In DQA, coding, analysis, and interpretation can be done any number of ways, such as the generic three-level codes described in works on GT (Strauss 1987; Strauss and Corbin 1998; Corbin and Strauss, 2008) or the kinds of analysis associated with interpretive phenomenology (Benner 1994; Crist and Tanner, 2003) that include several levels of analysis such as the identification of themes and the construction of exemplars and paradigm cases. Group analysis of data is effective because researchers can discuss emerging understandings with other people who have different life experiences, training, knowledge, and perspectives. In this way, it is more likely that the findings will account for the complexity and variations of social phenomena. Group analysis of data originates at least with Charles Booth's studies of the London poor in the latter part of the nineteenth century (Webb and Webb 1932).

Typically, analysis includes three levels of writing. The first level is writing up individual cases in their complexities. The second level is making comparisons between and across cases. The third level is comparing the conclusions of the first two levels of analysis with existing research and theory and any personal and professional experiences that might be relevant. Researchers then change their hypotheses to fit these findings and ground these revisions in data. The procedures are similar for each successive case. The final product is a hypothesis or a set of hypotheses that fit the cases on which researchers developed them.

Induction and Deduction

My use of the term deduction in this paper is modeled after Dewey (1910), who provided a discussion of what he calls "complete thinking," which involves both deduction and induction. Deduction is a process of testing working hypotheses, for the purposes of "confirming, refuting, and modifying" them (82). Hypotheses are working hypotheses when researchers do not think of them as final conclusions, but as emerging understandings that are open to further testing and change. Induction is the processes of creating abstractions from concrete data, which is probably impossible to do independently of deductive thinking because we notice and overlook phenomena depending upon the prior ideas we carry with us (Blumer 1969; Gilgun 1999b, 2010a). Nonetheless, inductive thinking represents an attempt to put aside researchers' own views and promote active listening and open-minded consideration in research interviewing, observations, and document analysis. Glaser (1978) has offered the concept of theoretical sensitivity and Blumer (1986) the idea of sensitizing concepts to help us understand how prior ideas are part of processes that some consider to be inductive.

Dewey's pragmatist philosophy influenced the Chicago School of Sociology (Bulmer 1984; Deegan 1990) whose faculty and students developed the procedures of analytic induction (AI). It is important to note that some Chicago School faculty members were social workers, such as Hull House residents Sophonisba Breckinridge and Edith Abbott (Abbott 1910; Abbott and Breckinridge 1916; Deegan 1990). In addition, the Chicago School faculty—including Dewey—was in ongoing dialogue for years with Jane Addams and other residents of Hull House about the conduct of urban research and on the pragmatist philosophy of experience and action (Bulmer 1984; Deegan 1990, 2006; Gilgun 1999b, 2012).

Analytic induction recognizes the movement between induction and deduction and the importance of modifying theory to fit available evidence. To ensure that theories are adequately tested, transformed, refined, and even refuted, researchers who do analytic induction engage in negative case analysis (Cressey 1953), a sampling method that involves the selection of cases that have promise of undermining the emerging understandings that researchers construct over the course of data collection and analysis. When researchers see that some findings contradict their hypotheses, they change their hypotheses to fit these new findings. Thus hypotheses may show patterns and variations within the phenomena of interest. This method fits with Popper's (1969) idea of conjectures, refutations, and reformulations that Popper believes is the fundamental process of science. The method also has the potential to account for multiple possible variations in human phenomena, such as how persons cope with adversities or how people from non-Western cultures respond to Western medical procedures. One size, one pattern does not fit all.

In earlier writings, I used the term analytic induction to describe what I am now calling DQA (e.g., Gilgun 1995, 2001a, 2001b). Analytic induction is the procedure that researchers used on now classic studies, such as the work of Becker, Geer, Hughes, and Strauss (1961), Cressey (1953), and Lindesmith (1947). The primary reason I prefer the term *deduction* is my belief that induction is not possible as an initial step in the doing of research. In order to sort particular observations from innumerable possible observations, researchers do not begin as blank slates, as noted earlier. Something helps them notice particular phenomena and not others. I view this something as prior knowledge, sensitizing concepts, conceptual frameworks, or cognitive schemas; call them what you will, they orient researchers as to what to notice and what to overlook. Even Glaser and Strauss (1967), widely considered premier and pioneering inductive qualitative researchers, acknowledge the impossibility of researchers being blank slates in a footnote in their well-known text. Induction, then, is a misnomer in this type of research.

A second reason I decided to put together procedures that I call deductive qualitative analysis was to invite researchers trained in logico-deductive methods to do qualitative research. For too long, the idea that qualitative research does not begin with a conceptual model has been dominant. Social work researchers have a wealth of theory-, research-, and practice-based knowledge that can be put to use in qualitative studies the purpose of which are to document and understand the complexities of person-environment interactions. Even personal experience and values have their places in knowledge building. None of these models, no matter how constructed, can be taken for granted. They must be tested not only for fit but for lack of fit with particular persons in particular places, at particular times. In this way, results that researchers develop will be closely linked to experiences of service users and thus will be useful to policy, programs, prevention, and intervention.

A third reason I encourage DQA in my teaching and writing is the widespread perception that AI is based on obsolete philosophies of science that promote the idea that researchers should seek causal and universal hypotheses that are invariant and that researchers can construct such hypotheses on as few as one or two cases (Gilgun 2001a, 2010a). Because of these claims, the term has a "spoiled identity." Some commentators (Robinson 1951; Manning 1982; Goldenberg 1993; Vidich and Lyman 2000) dismissed AI because of the claims of universality and invariance. As a result, the term analytic induction has rarely been used for about 50 years. Glaser and Strauss (1967) mention the procedure but dismiss it with little commentary.

Types of Initial Conceptual Models

In DQA, the initial conceptual model with which researchers begin their studies may range from tightly defined to rough and unfocused, as mentioned earlier. One possible type of initial conceptual model is highly abstract and parsimonious, based on previous research and theory and from which researchers construct hypotheses to be tested qualitatively. This type of hypothesis testing appears not to have been done in social work as of yet, but it is a viable approach.

A second type of conceptual model is composed of a loose set of ideas and concepts derived from one or more sources such as previous research and theory, professional experience, and personal experience. Researchers can put this model to many different uses, such as to develop open-ended hypotheses that bring some focus to the study, use the model to do pattern matching, or use the theory as a guide in exploring new areas of understanding. In pattern matching, researchers use the conceptual model as a screen that they place over their findings (Campbell 1979). They then compare the patterns of the conceptual model with the patterns of the findings they construct from data.

An example of hypothesis-testing based on a loose framework is my analysis of the moral discourse of incest perpetrators, where I began with hypotheses I developed from theories of feminist moral development and ended with revised hypotheses that I constructed from my analysis (Gilgun 1995). An example of pattern matching is my work with Brommel on emotion display rules and the accounts prison inmates gave of their violent behaviors in families and communities (Gilgun and Brommel, 2004). We first developed a framework that delineated possible ways that men display their emotions, and then we compared this framework to how the men actually expressed their emotions. An example of theory-guided research is the analysis of Abrams (2003) on young women's gender identity negotiations. Abrams used a loose conceptual framework to illuminate and interpret her analysis.

A third type of DQA begins with roughly formulated ideas and hunches, sometimes based on professional and/or personal experience. The guidance that this type of DQA provides is that of a general orientation or framework. Elizabeth Bott's (1957) work on family social networks is a classic example; she used Lewin's ecology theory as her initial general framework, had no hypotheses to test, and ended with a richly described social network theory, where she shared her processes of theorizing in some detail. Undoubtedly, there are many other ways to use conceptual models at the onset of qualitative research, and there are probably more to be developed.

Researchers have to be on the alert to ensure they are not fitting their findings into pre-established categories, or imposing theory onto findings (Glaser and Strauss 1967). Negative case analysis and group analysis of data, discussed earlier, guards against this. The final product of theory-testing efforts in qualitative research is a set of concepts and interrelated hypotheses that have been subjected to rigorous analysis. During the course of testing and analysis, researchers typically fold into the model additional related research and theory that enhance and clarify the meanings and significance of the components of the model that are under development, which is the third level of analysis mentioned earlier. Such a well-documented and well-tested model can be developed for assessments, interventions, policy and programs. They can also be subjected to statistical analysis. As Lenzenweger (2004) stated in his discussion of taxometric analysis, a salient issue in statistical analysis is the adequacy of the underlying model. Deductive qualitative analysis is a significant way to construct conceptual models. As researchers explore the potential of this approach, relevant, generative theories about phenomena relating to social work will continue to grow.

Grounded Theory Approaches

The purposes of GT, according to Strauss and Corbin (1998:13), are to "Build rather than test theory" and to "identify, develop and relate the concepts that are the building blocks of theory." A key idea is the emergence of the research problem as a result of immersion in the field. Strauss, who earned a PhD in sociology from the University of Chicago in the mid-1950s, carried on many of the traditions of the Chicago School of Sociology. Thus DQA and GT have some research traditions in common (Gilgun 2001b, 2005b).

To generate grounded theory, researchers enter the field, according to Glaser (1992), with "an open mind to the emergence of the subjects' problem" (23), with a trust that the central problem will emerge, and with a commitment "not to know" until it does (24). Many influences "core out" the central problem, such as the researchers' training, the location of the study, the nature of the research subjects, funding, among others. Both Strauss and Glaser maintained a career-long interest in basic social processes, derived from Lazarfeld's elaboration analysis and symbolic interaction theory (Glaser and Strauss 1967; Glaser 1978, 1992; Strauss 1987; Strauss and Corbin 1998). Thus emergence might not be an accurate term because we see in texts what we have already been sensitized to see; our own favored theories and other coring out influences shape our interpretations of texts. Nonetheless, the point here is to make every effort to understand and theorize informants' (research participants') points of view and attempt to refute and reformulate them.

The Original Formulation

In its original formulation, an initial conceptual model was not part of GT. The originators considered such models preconceptions and a way of attaining "a grounded modifying of theory" (Glaser and Strauss 1967:2). In their first book-length publications, Glaser and Straus (1967) and Glaser (1978) expressed concern that when researchers start with a preconception, they will force data into the model rather than to construct concepts and hypotheses based on their observations or what research respondents tell them. My experience as a researcher has shown that negative case analysis, discussed earlier and based on the ideas of conjectures, refutations, and reformulations, and group analysis of data help researchers to avoid such forcing.

Glaser and Strauss (1967) proposed GT in response to the kinds of theory that they said were prevalent at the time: highly abstract, disconnected from relevant social problems, non-modifiable, and whose sources were not always clear. They also had concerns about the imposition of theory onto observations and the tacking on of theory at the end of a report based on atheoretical research.

Later Formulations

Over time, Strauss softened his stance on the place of prior research and theory in the conduct of GT (cf. Strauss and Corbin 1998; Corbin and Strauss, 2008), while Glaser (1992) remained committed to the earlier idea. In his last formulation, published after his death in 1995, Strauss and his co-author Juliet Corbin (Strauss and Corbin 1998), offered several different uses of research and theory before entering the field and while engaged in analysis and interpretation. I will highlight some of them.

One use of research and theory is as sources of research questions and problems to be studied, although the focus of the study should eventually be on the concerns of respondents as identified through fieldwork. They also acknowledged that prior knowledge may sensitize researchers to particular questions and concerns, which is akin to Blumer's (1986) idea of sensitizing concepts that help researchers to identify patterns and meanings in data.

Another use of preconceived theory is what I have called deductive qualitative analysis (DQA). For Strauss and Corbin (1998:12), researchers use preconceptions when they want to "elaborate and extend an existing theory." In the later edition of their coauthored book, Corbin and Strauss (2008) wrote with approval about the work of a researcher who used a prior framework, namely one of Strauss's grounded theories, to structure her own research. She used Strauss's grounded theory throughout her research, from the initial conceptualization to the choice of measurement instruments. Citing discussions with me about the use of prior frameworks, Corbin in Corbin and Strauss (2008:39) said that "Though it is these authors' preference not to begin our research with a predefined theoretical framework or set of concepts, we acknowledge in some instances theoretical frameworks can be useful."

My preferences depend upon my research issue. In my long-term research on the development of violent behaviors and the meanings of violence to perpetrators, I immersed myself in the field with no "predefined theoretical frameworks or sets of concepts." I did have a strong value-based framework based on social justice and care and a conviction that violence is wrong. The purpose of my research is primary prevention, which is an emancipatory, social justice and care stance (Gilgun 2010a). Over the course of many years, I have developed what appears to be a complex theory that involves the procedures that Corbin and Strauss (2008) prefer.

The full scope of the theory is yet unpublished, although I have published many pieces over the years. I developed DQA because of its efficiency and its common sense for researchers who want to do and sometimes must do focused qualitative research, "must do" because of external constraints (Gilgun 2004a).

Another use of related research and theory that Strauss and Corbin endorse is its use in data analysis and interpretation. They said that a commitment to a particular theoretical model can blind researchers to other possible interpretations of their data. They gave as an example the experience of a student researcher "who had difficulty *not* seeing exchange theory" (Strauss and Corbin 1998:69) in his interviews with African American adolescent boys about their negotiations for sex with their female peers. In class discussions, other students shared their interpretations, including ideas of negotiation and manipulation, gender role expectations, and consumerism. The student left the class with new ideas about how to interpret his interview material. This analysis shows the commitment of grounded theorists to group analysis of data so as to broaden and sharpen their interpretations.

Data Collection

Methods of data collection typical in GT and in other forms of qualitative research as well, including DQA, are interviews, observations, and document analysis. Videotapes and audiotapes can also be analyzed, as well as archived narrative material such as oral histories, photographs and other graphic materials, and case records.

Many researchers use a combination of methods. Open-ended interviewing is particularly amenable to soliciting the points of view of informants (subjects). Observation and interviewing often brings researchers into the social world of informants. For this reason, GT and DQA research commonly are naturalistic, that is, taking place in everyday settings where people live their lives. Note taking, either during or immediately after interviewing or observing, and mechanical recording through audio or video are typical methods of capturing data. Note taking is called field notes. Researchers often embed observer comments and memos within field notes. Observer comments are spontaneous reactions in the forms of thoughts, emotions, or insights that come to them as they write their field notes or that they recall they had in the process of data collection. Memos usually come at the end of field notes and are analytic attempts at inter- pretation, including making connections between the emerging findings and related research and theory. Bogdan and Biklen (2007) have an excel- lent discussion of field notes, observer comments, and memos. In some instances, informants themselves provide written data, such as when they write out their own life histories (Bulmer 1984; Taylor and Bogdan 1998).

Theoretical Sampling

Sampling in GT is theoretical, which means that sampling depends on what researchers want to know next, and they guide their choice of next case by what they find in their comparisons within and across cases (Glaser and Strauss 1967; Strauss and Corbin 1998). Rarely is there reason to do random or convenience sampling in GT, although descriptive qualitative researchers may make use of these methods. In doing theoretical sampling, researchers select a homogeneous sample on which to focus. They continue interviewing and/or observing and/or analyze textual and graphic records until they find that they are learning little or nothing that adds to their emerging understandings. They are at the point of theoretical saturation. Researchers then reflect on what comparisons they need to make next to deepen their understanding. These reflections lead to a decision of which kind of sample to recruit next. An example is in a study I did on incest perpetrators and the women who were married to them (Gilgun 1992), where I wanted to isolate qualities that differentiated incest perpetrators from persons with similar social histories.

Coding

Strauss and colleagues' coding scheme is a set of generic procedures that can be used in research other than GT, such as oral histories and other nar- rative approaches. For example, they originated a coding scheme that at first accounted for two levels of analysis (Glaser and Strauss 1967; Glaser 1978) and then added selective coding as the third (Strauss and Corbin 1998). The first level is open coding, where researchers search transcripts, field notes, and other texts for meaning units, which they label. These labels are the codes. The second level consists of axial coding, where researchers decide whether a concept is substantial enough to become a core concept, where a core concept is code around which researchers can develop an analysis (Strauss 1987; Strauss and Corbin 1998). An example of a core concept is emotion regulation, where it is likely that in any given text that focuses on emotion, emotion regulation will tie together many aspects of emotion and its expression. The third level of coding is selective, which researchers do after they have chosen the core concepts and want to dimensionalize them. Selective coding involves fleshing out of the core concepts by finding in the texts as many relevant instances of the phenomena that the concepts represent.

Research Questions and Hypotheses

Another point that the originators of GT made is their understanding of qualitative research questions and hypotheses. From their point of view, the purpose of research questions is to provide a general focus to the research, a focus that will sharpen as researchers engage with respondents, listen to their stories, and observe them in interaction with others. The idea of independent and dependent variables is rare in qualitative research. Instead, researchers want to know how respondents experience something, think about something, or respond to something, and researchers look for the processes involved. Hypotheses can be written in any number of ways. The hypotheses that Strauss and Corbin and other qualitative researchers use are statements of relationships that link two or more concepts, as stated earlier. For example, a hypothesis I tested in my research on the moral discourse of incest perpetrators (Gilgun 1995:268) was "Incest perpetrators have special regard for themselves and do not have regard for the impact of incest on their victims." Persons unfamiliar with qualitative methods might not recognize this as a hypothesis at all.

Summary

Although widely thought of as an approach that eschews the formulation of conceptual frameworks prior to entering the field, contemporary grounded theorists at least entertain this as a possibility. Deductive qualitative analysis is my attempt to encourage researchers to test, refine, reformulate, refute, and replace theoretical models qualitatively. This approach acknowledges the importance of logico-deductive methods, although I depart in many ways from traditional ways of doing this kind of research. Qualitative thinking underlies all science. Qualitative analysis is a way of thinking, whether or not the research begins with a conceptual model or develops what appears to be a new one in the process of doing the research.

Finally, GT is a far more detailed set of procedures for doing qualitative research than is DQA. What DQA adds is an invitation to do deductive research, suggestions for several different types of deductive qualitative research, guidelines for ensuring that researchers do not impose preconceptions onto their findings (search for negative evidence/conjectures and refutations), and guidelines for ensuring that findings account for diversities (negative case analysis). Many of the notions and procedures of GT fit well with DQA, including the coding scheme that GT encourages, the notions of core concepts and their dimensions, definitions of hypotheses, commitment to identifying and representing the points of view of informants, and open-mindedness as to how researchers present their findings, among many others. The notions of processes, contexts, and consequences are embedded within GT, and although researchers may not use these terms, much of qualitative research involves these ideas.

Links to Direct Practice

The following characteristics are typical within GT and DQA. Other forms of qualitative research, such as narrative analysis (Riessman 1993, 2008) and oral histories (Martin 1995), frequently have some of these qualities as well. Many of these characteristics are also procedures that are present within direct practice.

Connections with Others

Qualitative approaches allow researchers to connect with other people in deeply personal ways. The two main types of qualitative methods, in-depth interviewing and observation, bring researchers into close contact with lived experiences of the persons with whom we do research. These interactions often involve personal and sometimes painful topics that can evoke powerful emotions in researchers and informants. In such evocative situations, researchers have opportunities to explore deep meanings of the phenomena of interest and thus develop new theories and understandings that have rich and nuanced dimensions (Gilgun 2008, in press).

The knowledge we gain, therefore, is not information that simply passes through the central processors of our brains. It also arises from our hearts and often our deeply held emotions. Understandings gained through an engagement of heart and mind have an immediacy that potentially connects to the hearts and minds of audiences. Giesela Konopka (1958 1963, 1966, 1988), who died in December 2003 at the age of 93, practiced this kind of social work research. She said, "Get to know people. Live there with them. Let them talk" (Konopka, personal communication, September 2001).

The persons who are social work's constituencies—children who have been maltreated, poor minorities of color, homeless families, persons with mental illness, and frail elderly, among many others—are typically disenfranchised and excluded from the political system. Their voices are routinely suppressed within the many arenas in which their fates are debated and shaped--public opinion, the mass media, legislatures, and sometimes even social service agencies.

Researchers, like other social workers, share a professional and cultural authority that permits us, if we so choose, to bring these voices to the forefront of public decisions and debates (Weick 2000). This power to speak for others is by nature a problematic and unequal power arrangement and a subject of discussion by many within and outside the discipline of social worker (cf. hooks 1990). Witkin (1999), editor of *Social Work* during the end of the twentieth century and the beginning of the twenty-first, recognized the urgency of including the voices of clients within the arenas in which their interests are at stake.

There are at least three potential pitfalls to the closeness of contact, however, with safeguards for both. One pitfall is the risk of a loss of an analytic stance. Researchers need to stay in tune with informants while at the same time maintaining a focus on concepts and hypotheses that are to be explored and tested. Sometimes the material informants provide is compelling to the point where researchers are drawn so far into the worlds of informants that researchers do not explore other aspects of informants' experience. The result is a limited description of phenomena. Researchers can lose the balance between being in tune and being overwhelmed.

Informants in subsequent cases, however, usually do not focus on precisely what informants from previous cases have focused on. Therefore, over the course of conducting several case studies, researchers can identify multiple aspects of phenomena, and the possible narrowness of findings in one case is corrected by findings in subsequent cases. Most grounded theorists—and qualitative researchers in general—interview informants more than once. This has many advantages, including clarifying and extending discussions from previous interviews and comparing what other informants have said, and refining and amplifying emerging understandings.

A second possible pitfall related to closeness to data in GT and DQA approaches is emotional reactions to research findings. Many researchers investigate sensitive issues, such as treatment of persons in institutions, wife battering, rape, and child abuse. Researchers often have strong personal reactions to such content. This, too, can lead to a loss of analytic stance. Grounded theorists, therefore, in order to maintain an analytic stance, can benefit from working in teams. Discussion with other team members not only can help researchers deal with personal reactions, but it also can help researchers process their findings, leading to further insight into the world of informants, as discussed earlier.

A third pitfall is the possibility of ethical lapses in the conduct of research. Social work researchers are bound to the National Association of Social Workers (NASW) *Code of Ethics* (Gilgun and Abrams 2002). Researchers have full responsibility for the ethical conduct of their research, no matter what informants might do or appear to do. There are many possible ethical breaches, including boundary violations that researchers commit and boundary violations that researchers permit and even encourage. The first principles of ethical conduct are to do no harm and to protect the well-being of others. The task of human subjects committees is the protection of human subjects, and, of course, every university-based qualitative study must have their approval and oversight. Beyond this, however, social work researchers must understand the power differential between themselves and their informants. They must also understand that their status may result in informants complying rather than giving full informed consent. Thus I recommend that researchers encourage informants not to answer any question they do not want to answer and to stop talking about an issue if they start feeling uncomfortable. I routinely tell informants this and ask them if they would like to stop if I think they are going outside of their zone of safety.

Researcher self-disclosure, if well-timed, may contribute to the quality of the research. Yet, with the emotion-laden nature of qualitative research, it is important for researchers to make sure that they maintain their analytic stance and not let themselves slide into self-disclosure that is self-indulgent and shuts out informants. Also important ethically is not to develop friendships with informants. In addition, sexual relationships are a serious ethical breach and are grounds for the loss of licenses to practice social work.

Contextualized Findings

The grounded nature of qualitative research extends in several directions. Sampling strategies and comparisons within and across cases lead to findings that encompass multiple aspects of phenomena. Rarely are concepts defined unidimensionally. The goal of describing multiple aspects of phenomena almost automatically leads to embedding those described phenomena in their contexts. Findings become inextricably linked to context. The "thick description" (Geertz 1973) characteristic of GT and DQA means that findings are presented multidimensionally and in ways that show the phenomena as part of a context (Gilgun 1992; Gilgun and Abrams 2002).

Patterns and Theories

Pattern theory is produced by GT and DQA, which Kaplan (1964) describes as hypotheses arranged in horizontal relationships to each other (not arranged hierarchically with the most abstract first); the later-stated hypotheses are deductions. Pattern theory often is context-specific, and therefore can be at a fairly low level of abstraction. Yet, pattern theory attempts to account for dominant and not so prevalent patterns.

The rich, descriptive data that qualitative methods yield also lends themselves to the development of typologies, a strategy for organizing findings that show similarities, differences, and overlaps between and within classes of phenomena. Typologies are particularly helpful in educational and clinical settings, where practitioners are confronted with complex human behaviors. Often interventions, such as medication, educational strategies, and forms of therapy, are linked to classifications that typologies can provide. Robinson et al. (2001) used observations of family physicians' responses to patients' emotional distress and developed a four-quadrant typology: the Technician, the Friend, the Detective, and the Healer. They noted that this typology can contribute to physician training, and it can also provide direction to future research that asks such questions as whether physician style is linked to outcome and whether patients select physicians who suit their personal preferences. A classic example of the use of typologies is E. F. Frazier's *The Negro Family in Chicago* (1932) where he classified American "Negroes" as migrants, old settlers, and nouveaux riches.

Pattern theory is quite different from hierarchical theory, which is characteristic of much logico-deductive research. Hierarchical theory is composed of a relatively small number of highly abstract principles from which hypotheses are deduced. These hypotheses then are tested, usually using highly complex mathematical formulas on a relatively small number of variables, which are abstracted from context. Hierarchical theory, especially when combined with probability theory, seeks to account only for findings thought to be dominant, and relegates less dominant patterns to the status of error term or outlier. An example of hierarchical theory is the following:

> The most consistent findings from studies of family structure and socialization are that single parents exert weaker controls and make fewer demands on children than married parents, while stepparents provide less warmth than do original parents (Thomson, McLanahan, and Curtin 1992:368).

These general statements are important because they provide an overview of social phenomena, but they are difficult to apply to individual cases unless practitioners are aware of the importance of looking for exceptions to these normative statements. Findings stated like this do not account for parents who are exceptions to these patterns, and they invite thinking that one pattern fits all cases. Therefore, they invite stereotyping. Contextual variables and individual experiences and perceptions also are not taken into account. Evidence for such statements is not based on in-depth studies of parents' experience, but usually on one-time telephone or in-person structured interviews, which, of course, do provide valuable information, but are not rich or in-depth, a fact that practitioners must keep in mind as they use such findings. Without thinking of exceptions and testing for fit, such statements—when practitioners apply them to practice—risk ignoring individualization and discounting information that is important to specific contexts.

In many senses, therefore, the findings of GT and DQA are more idiographic than nomothetic. They are focused on understanding individual situations and testing to see if findings can illuminate other situations. The process of testing to see if previous findings are relevant to a new situation is called pattern-matching, where the findings of one case are tested for their fit on succeeding cases (Campbell 1979). The findings make no claim to be generalizable to all members of a class. Even the findings of nomothetic research cannot claim that their findings will fit a particular situation. This is the ecological fallacy (Rubin and Babbie 2010). What might be true in general of a group may not be true of individual members of that group (Runyan 1982). Cronbach (1975) pointed out that findings in any type of research situation must be treated as working hypotheses when applied to local settings. The process of pattern-matching results in a type of generalizability called *analytic,* which is much different from probabilistic generalizations—most commonly taught in research and statistics courses (Gilgun 1994a; 2005b).

Logico-deductive research, associated with hierarchical theory, is more nomothetic, meaning the search is for general laws, abstracted from time, place, and specific persons. Social work practice benefits from both types of research findings—idiographic and nomothetic. Pattern theory, however, may be more useful to social work practice for three reasons: one, it matches the specificity of the contexts in which social workers practice; two, it encourages pattern-matching rather than generalizing to situations that have not yet been investigated; and, three, it accounts for as many patterns as can be discovered, encouraging the individualization of specific cases.

Even if findings were based on every known type of instance of a phenomenon, however, qualitative theory development is premised on the idea that researchers test each finding for its fit in new situations. The new situation could differ significantly from all other instances on which the findings are based. Because findings of qualitative research are open ended, they are continually subject to modification.

Parallels to Direct Practice

There are many parallels between direct practice and the procedures of GT and DQA. These parallels are important for at least two reasons. The first is related to research utilization. Practitioner use of research findings may be enhanced when research methods match practice contexts. A second reason for the importance of these parallels is the possibility that, with appropriate training in the use of qualitative methods, social work practitioners can become qualitative researchers. The following are some of the parallels between GT, DQA, and direct practice.

- The focus on the perspectives of informants is congruent with the social work principle of starting where clients are and paying attention to client perspectives throughout the course of practice, with research a form of practice.
- By definition, social work direct practice involves direct engagement with clients. Social workers, like qualitative researchers, strive for empathy, characterized by a balance between being in tune with clients and maintaining an analytic stance. Both the practice of social work and the practice of GT and DQA require this as well.
- GT research and DQA, like social work, often take place in natural settings—for social workers, this would be in the homes and communities of clients.
- The emphasis on viewing informants as inextricably part of a wider context fits with the social work perspective of focus on the client-environment interface.
- Detailed descriptions of individual cases fit with the social work injunction to individualize assessment, treatment, and evaluation to fit specific client situations.
- The combination of induction and deduction approaches parallels how social workers think about cases. Practitioners use previous research and theory as well as practice wisdom while attempting to avoid forming preconceptions about clients. Practitioners want to understand clients in their particularities—using the notion of individualization—as do practitioners of DQA and GT.
- Social workers come to conclusions about clients through direct contact and after gathering data from many different sources. The

conclusions are tentative, and open to modification as new information becomes available.

- Direct practitioners routinely consult with other practitioners to ensure that they have a balanced and comprehensive picture of clients and their situations; this parallels group analysis of data.
- Social workers bring hypotheses with them into new situations, but for the purposes of seeing whether they are helpful in the conduct of practice. They are fully ready to modify these hypotheses to fit the situation. This parallels pattern-matching in GT and DQA.
- The data collection methods of interviewing, observation, and document analysis are used by social workers as well as qualitative researchers.
- The use of field notes, observer comments, and memos are similar to process recording and problem-oriented case record keeping.

Some of the procedures of social work, DQA, and GT, therefore, are complementary. This complementarity bodes well for the future of GT and deductive qualitative approaches in social work research.

Padgett (1998:374) noted several ways in which "social work practice differs from qualitative research." She makes some good points, such as differences in goals between research and practice, differences between clients and participants in research, training issues, and the multiplicity of underlying assumptions in practice and research. She was concerned that some social work researchers appeared to draw potentially problematic parallels between qualitative research and practice. She wanted to provide some balance to an overemphasis on parallels.

Padgett's (1998, 1999) perspectives complement mine. In the earlier version of this chapter, I focused only on parallels and not on differences. As Padgett said, "the parallels are undeniable" (1998:380), but a balanced view is important. I will comment, however, on some of her ideas, those on which I have other perspectives on the fit of DQA and GT with direct social work practice.

Padgett (1998) stated that qualitative approaches do not use preexisting conceptual frameworks. As I have shown, DQA is designed to do just that. She stated that the ethical responsibilities of researchers and practitioners differ in regard to confidentiality. As I stated earlier, social work researchers must abide by all the mandates of the NASW *Code of Ethics*, including reporting laws and duty to warn. Government regulations permit some exemptions from this, but I believe for social work researchers that the *Code of Ethics* prevails in all research situations.

Although Padgett (1998) makes a good point that social work qualitative researchers learn from clients, I believe that effective social work practitioners also learn from clients (Gilgun 2005b; 2010b). Beyond this, however, researchers do not have responsibilities for attempting to influence client behaviors. In addition, we do not have legal mandates to enforce laws, as child protection social workers do, for example, although researchers are obligated to report to law enforcement actual or threatened harm to informants that we learn about through our research. This actually has been a relief to me. One of the hardest parts of practice for me had been the sense of failure I felt when I seemed unable to be of help to clients. When research informants appear to gain from participating in research, I am glad for them, but informant change is not the goal of research. Gathering information is. Clients are not research informants, and research informants are not clients.

I have also shown in the earlier discussion that researchers have a great deal of authority and power in relationship to informants, and that the similar ethical breaches are possible in qualitative research and in direct practice. Padgett (1998), I believe, underemphasizes this power. Writing about our own clients poses serious ethical issues, as Padgett noted. However, where would Freud have been if he had not done so, and where, in fact, would clinical practice in general be? With this said, if social work practitioners want to write about clients, they must study and follow the NASW *Code of Ethics*, go through an ethical review within their own agencies, and also review other codes of ethics, such as the code of the American Psychological Association. While there are differences between qualitative research and practice, the parallels are clear.

Applications to Practice Research

GT and DQA can facilitate the development of knowledge useful in many types of social work practice settings. My own research, that now spans more than 25 years, has resulted in several types of products that are useful for practice, such as theoretical models. These models include one that integrates research on resilience, schema theory, gender studies, and brain research and is meant to guide assessment of families and children where the children have a range of adjustment issues (Gilgun 2005a); a second that guides practitioners to assess for issues related to neurobiology, executive function, attachment, trauma, and self-regulation (NEATS) in ecological and development perspectives (Gilgun 2010b), and a third that shows the significance of resources in models of risk that I tested statistically (Gilgun, Klein, and Pranis 2000).

My qualitative research has resulted in typologies related to perpetrators of child sexual abuse (Gilgun 1994b), effects on adversities on human development (Gilgun 1996a, 1996b), and effects of sexual abuse on the sexual identity development of men who experienced such abuse in childhood (Gilgun and Reiser 1990).

Another product is descriptive research relevant to assessment such as how perpetrators of child sexual abuse view their victims (Gilgun and Connor 1989), on resilience as process (Gilgun 1999a), and the multiple effects on me and my thinking that resulted from doing qualitative research on violence (Gilgun 2008; 2010c). I have developed and tested several clinical assessment tools that are also useful for practice evaluation (Gilgun 1999a; Gilgun et al. 1999; Gilgun 2004a) and, with many collaborators, a self-assessment called the Readiness to Adopt Self-Survey (RASS), for parents considering adopting children with special needs (Gilgun and Keskinen 2005). Finally, my research using both GT and DQA has resulted in some practice guidelines for work with children and their families when the children have problematic sexual behaviors (Gilgun, Jones and Rice 2005; Gilgun 2006).

Discussion

Grounded theory and DQA can provide important information that is useful to direct practitioners. Both the procedures and products of these two approaches have parallels to practitioners' experience of their work with clients, although—as Padgett (1998) pointed out—they are differences as well. Thus these procedures and products are familiar to practitioners, and there is every reason to hope that practitioners will find the products of qualitative research useful to them in their practice. Grounded theory is useful when researchers want to identify lines of research that are significant to informants. To do so, they do what can be considered preliminary studies.

Deductive qualitative analysis is the approach of choice when researchers start their research with a conceptual framework, typically composed of a literature review, a précis of the guiding ideas of the research, and research questions to answer and/or hypotheses to test.

My career as a qualitative researcher spans more than 25 years. During this time, I used the procedures of both GT and DQA and focused primarily on the development of violent behaviors, the meanings of violence to perpetrators, and how persons overcome adversities. Although doing qualitative research involved enormous challenges and a great deal of ongoing learning that continues to this day, its procedures seemed to have come naturally to me. I do not know if my training and experience in direct practice was a factor in my easy transition from practitioner to researcher, but after all these years I continue to see parallels between how I did my practice and how I do qualitative research using procedures of GT and DQA.

My research was guided by theory, but routinely, as best I could, I made attempts to set aside my own assumptions and theoretical orientations and attempted to listen with an open mind to what informants were saying. I purposely sought cases that I hoped would provide evidence that would lead me to modify my findings and even refute them. I sought out co-researchers whose perspectives were different from mine and who therefore could challenge my assumptions and add new ideas to my interpretations. I found that beginning with a conceptual framework was helpful at times; otherwise, I may have been unable to identify concrete instances of the phenomena in which I was interested. At other times, my theoretical frameworks were not useful. I was left with a lot of information that was interesting and important in and of itself but I had little idea how to organize it or how to use it. I found at those points that exploring research and theory that might be relevant was helpful.

Thus over the years, I have read many bodies of research to help me understand the significance of what informants told me. This research includes theories and research on risk and resilience, emotional development, sexual development, social information processing theory, cognitive science, gender theory, theories of human agency, and brain research, to name just some.

In summary, GT and DQA have much to offer social work research. There appears to be more interest than ever in qualitative approaches, and it is clear to me that social work can never have too much practice-relevant research. Social work direct practitioners already have many of the skills required to do qualitative research. We can never have too many well-trained social work researchers.

References

Abbott, E. 1910. *Women in industry.* New York: Appleton.

Abbott, E. and S. P. Breckinridge. 1916. *The tenements of Chicago, 1908–1935.* Chicago: U of Chicago P.

Abrams, L. S. 2003. Contextual variations in young women's gender identity negotiations. *Psychology of Women Quarterly,* 27(1):64–74.

Becker, H. S., B. Geer, E. C. Hughes, and A. L. Strauss. 1961. *Boys in white: Student culture in medical school.* Chicago: U of Chicago P.

Benner, P., ed. 1994. *Interpretive phenomenology.* Thousand Oaks, CA: Sage.

Blumer, H. 1969/1986. *Symbolic interactionism: Perspective and method.* Englewood Cliffs, NJ: Prentice-Hall. Reprinted in paperback, 1986. Berkeley, CA: U of California P.

Bogdan, R. and S. K. Biklen. 2007. *Introduction to qualitative research for education* (3rd ed.). Boston: Allyn and Bacon.

Bott, E. 1957. *Family and social network.* New York: Free Press.

Bulmer, M. 1984. *The Chicago School of Sociology.* Chicago: U of Chicago P.

Campbell, D. T. 1979. "Degrees of freedom" and the case study. In *Qualitative and quantitative methods in evaluation research,* T. D. Cook and C. S. Reichardt, eds. 49–67. Beverly Hills, CA: Sage.

Corbin, J. and A. Straus. 2008. *Basics of qualitative research* (3rd ed.). Thousand Oaks, CA: Sage.

Cressey, D. 1953. *Other people's money.* Belmont, CA: Wadsworth.

Crist, J. D. and C. A. Tanner. 2003. Interpretation/analysis methods in hermeneutic interpretive phenomenology. *Nursing Research,* 52(3):202–205.

Cronbach, L. 1975. Beyond the two disciplines of scientific psychology. *American Psychologist,* 30:116–127.

Deegan, M. J. 1990. *Jane Addams and the men of the Chicago School of Sociology, 1892–1918.* New Brunswick: Transaction.

Deegan, M. J. 2006. The human drama behind the study of people as potato bugs: The curious marriage of Robert E. Park and Clara Cahill Park. *Journal of Classical Sociology* 6:101–122.

Dewey, J. 1910. *How we think.* Amherst, NY: Prometheus.

Frazier, E. F. 1932. *The Negro family in Chicago.* Chicago: U of Chicago P.

Geertz, C. 1973. *The interpretation of culture*. New York: Basic.

Gilgun, J. F. 1992. Hypothesis-generation in social work research. *Journal of Social Service Research*, 15:113–135.

——. 1994a. A case for case studies in social work research. *Social Work*, 39:371–380.

——. 1994b. Avengers, conquerors, playmates, and lovers: A continuum of roles played by perpetrators of child sexual abuse. *Families in Society*, 75:467–480.

——. 1994c. Hand into glove: Grounded theory and social work practice research. In *Qualitative research in social work*, E. Sherman and W. J. Reid, eds. 115–125. New York: Columbia UP.

——. 1995. We shared something special: The moral discourse of incest perpetrators. *Journal of Marriage and the Family*, 57:265–281.

——. 1996a. Human development and adversity in ecological perspective: Part 2: Three patterns. *Families in Society*, 77:459–576.

——. 1996b. Human development and adversity in ecological perspective: Part 1: A conceptual framework. *Families in Society*, 77:395–402.

——. 1999a. Mapping resilience as process among adults maltreated in childhood. In *The dynamics of resilient families*, H. I. McCubbin, E. A. Thompson, A. I. Thompson, and J. A. Futrell, eds. 41–70. Thousand Oaks, CA: Sage.

——. 1999b. Methodological pluralism and qualitative family research. In *Handbook of marriage and the family* (2nd ed.), S. K. Steinmetz, M. B. Sussman, and G. W. Peterson, eds. 219–261. New York: Plenum.

——. (2001a). "Case study research, analytic induction, and theory development: The future and the past," Paper presented at the Preconference Workshop on Theory Construction and Research Methodology, National Conference on Family Relations, Rochester, NY.

——. 2001b. Grounded theory, other inductive methods, and social work methods. In *Handbook of social work research*, B. Thyer, ed. 345–364. Thousand Oaks, CA: Sage.

——. 2004a. Qualitative methods and the development of clinical assessment tools. *Qualitative Health Research*, 14(7):1008–1019.

——. 2004b. The 4-D: Strengths-based assessments for youth who've experienced adversities. *Journal of Human Behavior in the Social Environment*, 10(4):51–73.

——. 2005a. Evidence-based practice, descriptive research, and the resilience-schema-gender-brain (RSGB) assessment. *British Journal of Social Work*, 35(6): 843–862.

——. 2005b. Qualitative research and family psychology. *Journal of Family Psychology*, 19(1):40–50.

——. 2006. Children and adolescents with problematic sexual behaviors: Lessons from research on resilience. In *Current perspectives on working with sexually aggressive youth and youth with sexual behavior problems*, R. Longo and D. Prescott, eds. 383–394. Holyoke, MA: Neari.

——. (2008). Lived experience, reflexivity, and research on perpetrators of interpersonal violence. *Qualitative Social Work*, 7(2):181–197.

——. 2010a. Methods for enhancing theory and knowledge about problems, policies, and practice. In *The Sage handbook of social work research*, K. Briar, J. Orme, R. Ruckdeschel, and I. Shaw, eds. 281–297. Thousand Oaks, CA: Sage.

——. (2010b). "The nature of practice in evidence-based practice." Paper presented at the Pre-Conference Workshop on Theory Construction and Research Methodology, Annual Conference, National Council on Family Relations, Minneapolis, MN.

——. 2010c. Reflections on 25 years of research on violence. *Reflections: Narratives of professional helping*, 16(4), 50–59.

——. 2012. Qualitative family research: Enduring themes and contemporary variations. In *Handbook of marriage and the family* (3rd ed.), G. F. Peterson and K. Bush, eds. New York: Plenum.

Gilgun, J. F., S. Keskinen, D. J. Marti, and K. Rice. 1999. Clinical applications of the CASPARS instruments: Boys who act out sexually. *Families in Society* 80(6): 629–641.

Gilgun, J. F. and L. Abrams. 2002. Commentary on Denzin: The nature and usefulness of qualitative social work research. *Qualitative Social Work*, 1(1):39–55.

Gilgun, J. F. and S. Brommel. 2004. "Emotion display rules in the accounts of violent men." St. Paul, MN: University of Minnesota, School of Social Work. Unpublished manuscript.

Gilgun, J. F. and T. M. Connor. 1989. How perpetrators view child sexual abuse. *Social Work*. 34:249–251.

Gilgun, J. F., D. Jones, and K. Rice. 2005. Emotional expressiveness as an indicator of progress in treatment. In *Emerging approaches to work with children and young people who sexually abuse*, M. C. Calder, ed. 231–244. Dorset, UK: Russell House.

Gilgun, J. F. and S. Keskinen. 2005. "Readiness to Adopt Children with Special Needs." Accessed December 5, 2007. Scribd.com. *http://www.scribd.com/doc/22159852/Readiness-to-Adopt-Children-with-Special-Needs-User-Manual*.

Gilgun, J. F., C. Klein, and K. Pranis. (2000). The significance of resources in models of risk, *Journal of Interpersonal Violence*, 14:627–646.

Gilgun, J. F. and E. Reiser. 1990. The development of sexual identity among men sexually abused as children. *Families in Society*. 71, 515–523.

Glaser, B. 1978. *Theoretical sensitivity*. Mill Valley, CA: Sociology.

——. 1992. *Basics of grounded theory analysis: Emergence vs. forcing*. Mill Valley, CA: Sociology.

——. 2010. Doing formal theory. In *SAGE handbook of grounded theory*. A. Bryant and K. Charmaz, eds. 97–118. Thousand Oaks, CA: Sage.

Glaser, B. and A. L. Strauss. 1967. *The discovery of grounded theory*. New York: Aldine.

Goldenberg, S. 1993. Analytic induction revisited. *Canadian Journal of Sociology*, 18(2):161–176.

hooks, b. 1999. *Yearning: Race, gender, and cultural politics*. Cambridge, MA: South End Press.

Kaplan, A. 1964. *The conduct of inquiry*. San Francisco: Chandler.

Konopka, G. 1958. *Eduard C. Lindeman and social work philosophy*. Minneapolis, MN: University of Minnesota.

——. 1963. *Social group work: A helping process*. Englewood Cliffs, NJ: Prentice Hall.

——. 1966. *The adolescent girl in conflict*. Englewood Cliffs, NJ: Prentice-Hall.

——. 1988. *Courage and love*. Edina, MN: Burgess.

Lenzenweger, M. F. 2004. Consideration of the challenges, complications, and pitfalls of taxometric analysis. *Journal of Abnormal Psychology*, 113(1):10–23.

Lindesmith, A. R. 1947. *Opiate addiction*. Bloomington, IN: Principia.

Manning, P. K. 1982. Analytic induction. In *Qualitative methods*, volume II of *Handbook of social sciences*, R. B. Smith and P. K. Manning, eds. 273–302. Cambridge, MA: Ballinger.

Martin, R. R. 1995. *Oral history in social work: Research, assessment, and intervention*. Thousand Oaks, CA: Sage.

Padgett, D. K. 1998. Does the glove really fit? Qualitative research and clinical social work practice. *Social Work*, 43(4):373–381.

——. 1999. The research-practice debate in a qualitative research context. *Social work*, 44(3):280–283.

Popper, K. R. 1969. *Conjectures and refutations: The growth of scientific knowledge*. London: Routledge and Kegan Paul.

Riessman, C. K. 1993. *Narrative analysis*. Thousand Oaks, CA: Sage.

——. 2008. *Narrative analysis for the human sciences*. Los Angeles: Sage.

Robinson, W. D., L. A. Prest, J. L. Susman, J. Rouse, and B. F. Crabtree. 2001. Technician, friend, detective, and healer: Family physicians' responses to emotional distress. *Journal of Family Practice*, 50(10):864–870.

Robinson, W. S. 1951. The logical structure of analytic induction. *American Sociological Review*, 16:812–818.

Rubin, A. and E. Babbie. 2010. *Research methods for social workers* (7th ed.). Belmont, CA: Brooks/Cole.

Runyan, W. M. 1982. *Life histories and psychobiography. Explorations in theory and method*. New York: Oxford UP.

Strauss, A. and J. Corbin. 1998. *Basics of qualitative research: Techniques and procedures for developing grounded theory* (2nd ed.). Thousand Oaks, CA: Sage.

Strauss, A. L. 1987. *Qualitative analysis for social scientists*. New York: Cambridge UP.

Taylor, S. J. and R. Bogdan. 1998. Introduction to qualitative research methods. (3rd ed.). New York: Wiley.

Thomson, E., S. S. McLanahan, and R. B. Curtin. 1992. Family structure, gender, and parental socialization. *Journal of Marriage and the Family,* 54:368–378.

Vidich, A. J. and Lyman, S. M. 2000. Qualitative methods: Their history in sociology and anthropology. In *Handbook of qualitative research* (2nd ed.), N. K. Denzin and Y. S. Lincoln, eds. 37–84. Thousand Oaks, CA: Sage.

Webb, S. and B. Webb. 1932. Gender and age in fieldwork and fieldwork education. *Social Problems* 26:509–522.

Weick, A. 2000. Hidden voices. *Social Work,* 5(5):395–402.

Witkin, S. L. 1999. Editorial: Constructing our future. *Social Work,* 44(1):5–8.

Znaniecki, F. l934. *The method of sociology.* New York: Farrar and Rinehart.

[6]

Ethnography

ROBERTA G. SANDS

Nothing is stranger than this business of humans observing other humans in order to write about them.

Ruth Behar, *The Vulnerable Observer*

Ethnography is a tradition of qualitative inquiry in which researchers observe the everyday activities of participants in a social setting, group, or community in order to understand and write about them. Derived from the work of anthropologists who left their home societies to study far-off cultures, today ethnography is undertaken by researchers from a variety of disciplines—many of whom study sectors of their own societies. Social work has benefited from ethnographic research of scholars from its own (e.g., Pithouse 1987; Riemer 1999; Floersch 2002; Hall 2003) and other disciplines (e.g., Estroff 1981; Anderson 1990; Liebow 1993).

This chapter describes ethnography and how it can be accomplished by social work researchers in settings relevant to the profession. The chapter is organized around the following topics: (1) brief historical background; (2) definitional issues; (3) characteristics of ethnographic research; (4) research methods; (5) the research process; (6) data analysis and presentation; and (7) strengths, limitations, and opportunities for social work research. The chapter concludes with a summary.

Brief Historical Background

Ethnography grew out of the discovery of exotic human settlements outside Western society. As Vidich and Lyman (2000) explain, early ethnographic accounts were written by missionaries, colonial governors, and explorers, who viewed the people of other races and cultures they had encountered from a Eurocentric perspective. During the early 1920s, the Polish-born, British anthropologist Bronislaw Malinowski (1884–1942) developed and described an intensive, participatory, scientific approach to ethnographic fieldwork, insisting that social practices be understood in terms of their larger social context ("holism"), and asserting that the aim of ethnography is to come to know "the native's point of view" (Malinowski 1922:25; Macdonald 2001). Since Malinowski, British ethnography has gone through periods of consolidation, consensus, incorporation of new approaches, and self-criticism, the latter consisting of discussions about anthropologists' apparent complicity with colonialism, the exclusion of women's voices, the relative importance of ethnographic practice over written texts (Macdonald 2001), and a critique of methodological trends within ethnography that threatens to diminish its character as a social science (Hammersley 1992).

Franz Boas (1858–1942), an immigrant from Germany, advanced anthropology in the United States. He laid out the parameters of the discipline and, like Malinowski, developed scientific field methods that could be used to learn about nonliterate cultures (Lesser 1968). A subgroup of American sociologists from the Chicago School of Sociology (Deegan 2001) fostered the development of urban ethnography in the United States. Two University of Chicago faculty members, Robert E. Park (1864–1944) and Ernest W. Burgess (1886–1966), promoted the study of everyday social interactions in particular sectors of urban communities through dissertations conducted by their students from 1917 to 1942 (Vidich and Lyman 2000; Deegan 2001). The intellectual underpinnings of these studies came from Park and Burgess's ideas about natural areas of the city (now called social ecology) and the Chicago School's symbolic interactionism, based on the ideas of George Herbert Mead, W. I. Thomas, and others (Deegan 2001). Later exemplars of the Chicago School include Erving Goffman, Anselm Strauss, and Howard Becker. (For a more complex rendering of the history of the Chicago School, see Howard Becker's "The Chicago School, So-called" [1999].) Notably, the work of the Chicago School of ethnographers was supported by social workers at the university and in the community, particularly Edith Abbott, Sophonisba Breckinridge, and Jane Addams (Deegan 2001). Outside of Chicago, W. E. B. Du Bois (1899/1996) described an African American community in Philadelphia; Robert and Helen Lynd (1929, 1937) produced two studies of a community they called Middletown; and

William Foote Whyte (1943) portrayed residents of an Italian neighborhood in Boston (Vidich and Lyman 2000).

These ethnographic studies were written at a time when sociologists expected ethnic and racial minorities to assimilate into American society (Vidich and Lyman 2000). When it became evident that assimilation had failed, particularly for African Americans, the paradigm changed for a while to one of pluralism. With the increased influence of postmodern thinking on qualitative research in recent years, further change is taking place. Articles in Clifford and Marcus's (1986) edited volume, *Writing Culture*, raise questions about the partiality of the ethnographic truths, the tendency of ethnographers to present their interpretations as "the" interpretation, and the ways in which ethnographers transform their own visions into text (see especially Clifford 1986). This discussion, supported by other works (e.g., Marcus and Fischer 1986; Clifford 1988; Geertz 1988) ushered in a crisis in representation that challenged ethnographers to be more aware of the impact of race, gender, and class on their writing and to acknowledge their own role in the production of the text (Denzin and Lincoln 2005). This chapter will identify some of these problematic issues in ethnography and provide references for readers who wish to explore debates within the field further.

Definitional Issues

Ethnography is a process and a product (Tedlock 2000). The process entails fieldwork—the intensive study of the everyday life of a group, community, or organization in their natural contexts where the researcher comes to know and understand the experiences of participants and the norms of the group being studied. Assuming the stance of a professional stranger (Agar 1980), the researcher becomes immersed in a culture and learns what it is like to experience life the way participants do. In order to achieve an ethnographic understanding, the researcher uses a variety of methods and, ideally, spends a relatively extensive period of time in the field. The research product, an ethnography or ethnographic report, describes and interprets the group, community, or organization, including its patterns of relationships and the ways in which the parts are related to each other and the whole.

Central to the ethnographic project is an understanding of the culture of the entity that is being studied (Geertz 1973; Van Maanen 1988). Culture may be viewed as a dynamic system (Wax 1971) characterized by shared knowledge, beliefs, behaviors, and ways of life (Fetterman 1989). A given culture has its own patterned ways of perceiving, believing, acting, communicating, and evaluating phenomena (Goodenough 1970). Likewise, subcultures that exist within a larger, dominant culture have their own cultural ways. Because cultural patterns are beneath the surface, taken for granted, or tacitly known, they are not immediately discernible. Researchers attempt to perceive cultural patterns by observing actions and listening to talk (Van Manaan 1988). Language is integral to understanding culture. Specific settings and subgroups have specialized vocabularies that are known and understood by members. In order to make sense of a culture or subcultural group, ethnographers attempt to learn its language and what special terms mean to those who use it.

The primary goal of the ethnographer is to create a descriptive account of the culture and to interpret it to an audience. The researcher seeks multiple iterations of similar sequences of actions and a variety of data sources to identify cultural categories and patterns and understand their significance to those who are insiders to the culture. A challenging undertaking in itself, the process is problematic. Because "what we call our data are really our own constructions of other people's constructions of what they and their compatriots are up to" (Geertz 1973:9), researchers are implicated in the process of recording and interpreting data. Their constructions are influenced by their own positionality (socio-economic status, race, gender, and age) in relation to the social locations of the researched. Social work researchers are also influenced by their professional values and knowledge; and as social scientists, they draw from research paradigms, concepts, and theories with which they are familiar.

Like other qualitative researchers, ethnographers identify with particular research paradigms, perspectives, or political orientations (cf. Guba and Lincoln 2005) that, in turn, have a bearing on what they see and record as data, how they interpret findings, and decisions they make about taking political action in relation to the researched group. Ethnographers identifying with constructivism, for example, might consider the ways in which the group he or she is examining constructs meaning from their experience, knowledge, and social interactions. Postmodern ethnographers might think deeply about diverse contextualized, localized "truths" within cultures and attend to inconsistencies and contradictions (cf. Power 2004:858). Critical ethnographers look at power relations and patterns of domination and subjugation as they are expressed in social structure and in some cases will become directly involved in political struggles (Foley and Valenzuela 2005). Feminist researchers, too, are concerned with power relations, but they also focus on voice, the participant's agency, and ethical issues related to their work (Skeggs 2001). At the same time feminist ethnographers cultivate empathetic, egalitarian relationships in the field, they acknowledge that they put research participants at risk of exploitation (Stacey 1988) or being spoken for in the authoritative voice of the ethnographer (cf. Clifford and Marcus 1986; Lather 2001).

In general, ethnographers begin their studies with an inductive approach, allowing patterns, themes, and cultural processes to become evident in the course of the study (LeCompte 2002). The role of theory in ethnographic research has been deliberated about in the literature. Hammersley (1992:13) states that "all descriptions are theoretical in the sense that they rely on concepts and theories," and finds "theoretical descriptions" useful in the "application" of theories. In such cases, the ethnographer would be tying known concepts and theories to the data. On the other hand, Marcus (1998) is concerned that theory can unduly influence the shape of a study, interfering with the process of discovery. LeCompte asserts that ethnographers do not enter the field "empty-headed" (2002:266) and may have a tacit or implicit theory or will use theory at the inception of the study. Zaharlick and Green (1991) advise those who begin a study with one or more theories to use them provisionally—putting them on hold so they do not control or limit data that are collected. While collecting and analyzing data, these theories may turn out to be irrelevant, and other theories or concepts may better explain the data.

Ethnography is sometimes confused with other terms or is used imprecisely. *Ethnology* is an anthropological approach related to ethnography that compares aspects of one culture with those of another, past or present, leading to hypotheses about elements of culture that are generic and those that are specific to a given culture (Zaharlick and Green 1991). *Ethnomethodology* is the study of ways in which people make sense of everyday experience (Garfinkel 1967). Researchers using this approach today tend to focus on the underlying structure of meaning making in "naturally occurring talk and social interaction" (Holstein and Gubrium 2005:487) and use methods drawn from conversation analysis and discourse analysis. Rather than trying to get inside a social world, which is the ethnographer's aim, ethnomethodologists seek to illuminate how people accomplish talk (Gubrium and Holstein 1997).

At times the term "ethnography" is used "in a general sense that is broadly equivalent to 'qualitative method'" (Hammersley 1992:8). The term is also used loosely to describe folk art or artifacts or to describe case histories that encompass a cultural perspective. Here the term is used to refer to a study involving a relatively long-term, intensive engagement in a physical field site or sites where the researcher engages in participant observation, along with other methods, in order to learn about the culture. Such an approach is time intensive and emotionally demanding. Other researchers, however, interpret the words field and culture more broadly than I do. LeCompte (2002), for example, argues that in the context of today's complex, fluid, multiethnic, Internet-connected world, the field is not restricted to a particular geographic location. Accordingly, the ethnographer can study communities that share ethnicity or a particular social problem but do not necessarily interact face-to-face with each other in a setting. LeCompte adds that in view of emigration, environmental changes, and the expansion of technology, the concept of culture needs to be revised to account for the intermingling of peoples, ideas, and culture. Accordingly, she states, ethnographers of the twenty-first century should focus on the production of identities and personal agency.

Some clinical reports and qualitative studies incorporate ethnographic methods, such as time-limited participant observation or ethnographic interviewing, but are not as intensive as the approach I am describing in this chapter. For example, Seeley (2004) described the use of an ethnographically adapted approach to short-term, intercultural clinical practice that explores the cultural meanings of "categories and conceptions of mind, self, relationship, and disorder" (142). Another example comes from my study of women with severe mental illness who were mothers (Sands 1995). During the first few months of this research, I engaged in participant observation at a child care center that was associated with the supported housing in which the mothers lived. This preliminary period provided me with an opportunity to see how the mothers interacted with their children and the staff when the mothers dropped off and picked up their children, and to learn how the staff perceived both. By being present at the center and assisting with the care of the children, I was able to develop friendly relationships with the mothers and children, creating comfort and trust when I invited the women to be interviewed.

Within ethnography, there are related genres that are applications, blends, and extensions of ethnography and other fields. These include institutional ethnography, ethnography of communication, ethnographic microanalysis, autoethnography, performance ethnography, and narrative ethnography. With *institutional ethnography*, ethnographic data are used to investigate the linkages among local practices, organizations, and overriding forms of coordination or rules (Smith 1987; DeVault and McCoy 2001). The *ethnography of communication*, developed by linguistic anthropologists, entails the examination of variation in communication style among speech communities (Gumperz and Hymes 1964; Hymes 1974; Saville-Troike 1989), whereas *ethnographic microanalysis* is the contextualized study of social interaction, using audiovisual recordings (Erickson 1992, 2006). *Autoethnography* is a personal narrative that displays how the writer's personal experiences, along with those of others, are connected to culture (Ellis and Bochner 2000). With *performance ethnography*, a blending of performance studies and ethnography, one studies a culture or cultural activity, takes notes on observations, and enacts interpretations to an audience (Alexander 2005). The enactments draw attention to cultural practices that are oppressive and can become a means to stimulate awareness of social injustices and a need for social change (Denzin 2003; Alexander 2005). A recent addition, *narrative ethnography*, has to do with the situated nature of stories, and thus is concerned with the story, the storytelling process, and the narrative environment (Gubrium and Holstein 2008, 2009). More information about these fields can be found in the references cited.

Characteristics of Ethnographic Research

The emergence of autoethnography, performance ethnography, and narrative ethnography raises questions about the boundaries between ethnography and other fields of endeavor, such as autobiography, drama, and politics. Here I am characterizing ethnographic research as naturalistic, reflexive, inclusive of emic and etic perspectives, holistic, and incorporating a special stance of the researcher (see, e.g., Fetterman 1989; Hammersley and Atkinson 2007). This section will discuss each of these topics.

Ethnographic research is naturalistic in that, to the extent possible, it entails the observation of individuals as they pursue their everyday activities and the following of sequences of action in the contexts in which they ordinarily occur. Rather than manipulating conditions by setting up artificial laboratory experiments, the ethnographer focuses on events as they unfold. The ethnographer may, however, study natural experiments such as an organization instituting a change (Hammersley and Atkinson 2007).

The presence of researchers in naturalistic settings can affect the events and interactions that follow, especially in the beginning of a study. Moreover, the researcher's own assumptions, biases, and values may influence their processes of data gathering and analysis. In order to account for and manage these challenges, ethnographers attempt to be reflexive, that is, they acknowledge and describe their own role and others' reactions to their presence in reflexive journals and their research reports. For example, Marleen McClelland and I devoted a chapter of our ethnographic study of interprofessional team communication to the "Voices of Researchers" (McClelland and Sands 2002). We documented and discussed the impact of our respective theoretical interests and professional orientations, the behavior around our use of the camcorder, and our interactions with team members of our respective professions (physical therapy and social work) on the research.

Another characteristic of ethnographic research is its attention to emic and etic perspectives. Derived from the linguistic terms phonemic and phonetic (Pike 1954), *emic* and *etic* refer respectively to insider and outsider perspectives. Ethnographers give primacy to understanding the perceptions of insiders, the participants in a study. This is because insider knowledge makes it possible for one to gain access to the language, normative practices, and meaning system of a group. Nevertheless, outsider perspectives, which are external to the participants, events, settings, or situations under study, are relevant and can enrich the study. Individuals who are outsiders to the norms of the group or event may raise questions about tacit assumptions that are taken for granted by insiders. In our study of interprofessional teams, we found that in the field neither emic nor etic perspective was fixed (Sands and McClelland 1994; McClelland and Sands 2002). Participants and each of us moved in and out of insider and outsider positions depending on our prior knowledge, professional identification, and length of time with the team or study.

Ethnographic research is also holistic. Accordingly, the investigator attempts to obtain a comprehensive understanding of the social, political, economic, and historical contexts of participants or events. The researcher must "see beyond an immediate cultural scene or event in a classroom, hospital room, city street," or other site (Fetterman 1989:29) to a larger whole (Green, Dixon, and Zaharlick 2003). This necessitates asking questions, consulting documents, and exploring cultural dimensions and systems that are connected with the one under study. When writing the ethnographic report, the research demonstrates how the parts and whole cohere (or contradict each other, if that is the case).

The stance of researchers engaged in ethnographic research is unique. "Professional strangers," they treat the field setting as if it were strange, even if it is familiar (Agar 1980). When they enter research sites, ethnographers act like outsiders who do not know what is expected of whom, under what circumstances, and how. Rather than assuming that this culture is like their own, researchers allow the particular beliefs, values, and practices of the culture to surface (Hammersley and Atkinson 2007). In addition, researchers present themselves as learners or novices, open to being taught by participants, who are experts in their own culture. A further aspect of the researcher's role is that it demands both engagement and disengagement. When engaged in participant observation, one becomes part of the setting under study. Data analysis, however, requires distance. Managing these two activities requires the capacity to move back and forth between these two processes. The next section will explain the research methods that can help ethnographers navigate engagement.

Research Methods

As with other traditions of qualitative research, ethnography uses multiple research methods of data collection and a variety of data sources. This section begins with a discussion of the interviewer as human instrument. Then it proceeds to discuss participant observation, the principal data collection method used in ethnography, and field notes. Next interviewing is taken up. This section also describes documents and visual data.

Human Instrument

With ethnography, researchers use themselves to study others. The research engages the senses, thoughts, and emotions. Ethnographers use their interpersonal skills when they interact with participants and draw from their values and judgment when they select from a wide range of stimuli those aspects of a situation that they consider data. Data analysis, too, engages the person of the researcher—or researchers, when there is a research team.

To traditional social science researchers, personal involvement on the part of the investigator in the research is problematic. They worry about the data becoming contaminated and perceive a risk that the ethnography will turn out to be autobiography. In recent years, ethnographers have turned this critique on its head. For one thing, it has become common for members of a culture to study their own group. These ethnographers tend to position themselves within a standpoint epistemology and use their own reactions as a resource (Denzin 1997, Chapter 3). Autoethnography, mentioned earlier, takes advantage of the insider's perspective and uses it to enhance understanding of the culture (Ellis and Bochner 2000). Furthermore, ethnographers are beginning to share their emotional reactions with readers, making themselves vulnerable (Behar 1996).

Participant Observation

Participant observation refers to a researcher's being present and part of the setting she or he is studying. The ethnographer examines the scene and its surroundings and tries to understand what is going on. This method is particularly effective "for studying processes, relationships among people and events, the organization of people and events, continuities over time, and patterns, as well as the immediate sociocultural contexts in which human existence unfolds" (Jorgensen 1989:12). Observation allows one to see processes that participants ordinarily do not describe in interviews because they are taken for granted; this facilitates understanding of the culture by enabling one to perceive interactions in context. Participant observation over an extended period of time allows one to see, hear, and get a feel for the full range of diversity among people, events, and activities, so that one can determine what is typical and what is atypical (Erickson 1992). Further, sustained observation facilitates the development of field relationships and promotes access to an emic perspective.

Researchers describe a continuum of participant observer roles that range from complete participant, participant as observer, observer as participant, and complete observer (Gold 1958; Junker 1960; Hammersley and Atkinson 2007). A *complete participant* conceals his or her identity as a researcher and joins the group. One might, for example, become a member of a cult or political organization. This approach provides the most access to insider information, but it poses serious ethical problems and risks. If the researcher is not honest with the host group about his or her research role, she or he puts comembers or the group itself at risk of having their trust violated or secrets betrayed. In addition, the complete insider is susceptible to overidentifying with the group and losing his or her outsider perspective. A *participant as observer* is open about his or her researcher role and may also carve out a role within the setting (e.g., assistant teacher). The *observer as participant* is primarily an observer who has brief encounters with participants, whereas the *complete observer* observes from a distance without interacting with participants. In her classic study of women on welfare, Stack (1974) came close to the complete participant position when she joined the women on welfare she was studying in their practice of child sharing. Stack, however, was open about her researcher role. In our study of interprofessional teams, Marleen McClelland and I found ourselves shifting among various roles during the course of our research (McClelland and Sands 2002). For example, while following evaluations of children who were being assessed consecutively by different professionals, I provided staff with general information on what transpired in a previous examination when I was asked. At times, however, I was a complete observer, viewing children being evaluated through one-way mirrors in isolated viewing rooms. On some of these occasions, I was able to observe other observers—parents and professionals—who made comments about the child's responses while sitting in the viewing room.

Field Notes

Ordinarily, ethnographers record their observations in the form of field notes, which are taken during or after days in the field. Researchers vary in what they consider field notes, how they write them, and how they feel about what they write (Jackson 1990). Furthermore, field notes are contested because they are the writer's constructions, often worked over and transformed, not raw data (see Clifford and Marcus 1986; Sanjek 1990). Still, the notes do offer the researcher and, after they are transformed into ethnographic reports, his/her readers, partial truths (Clifford 1986).

Like other authors (Emerson, Fretz and Shaw 1995; Hammersley and Atkinson 2007), I recommend that one take down brief jottings while in the field and expand upon them in narrative form in a word processing file as soon as possible afterwards. I have recorded my handwritten jottings in small, unobtrusive spiral notebooks. I keep a running record of what I see and hear, including the time frame, on the pages to the right of the spiral and use the left side for comments. My comments are about my research methods, theory, personal feelings, and the language of the culture. For example, I have commented on what I can and cannot see from where I was sitting; and I have recorded my discomfort over being asked about my findings before I had completed my study. Later, I write narrative summaries of my observations (based on notes on the right side of the page), adding context to my brief jottings. I have used comments on the left side of the page as a basis for writing a journal. My journal is the place in which I record my evolving interpretations, examine my methods and how they may have affected what I saw, and reflect on my feelings, biases, and positionality.

Computers help in the process of creating field notes that are legible and can be coded. Although many ethnographers continue to take handwritten field notes that they record in field notebooks and write narrative descriptions later, some are taking laptop computers or smaller electronic devices with them in the field. Researchers should consider whether the presence of a laptop computer (or field notebook) is too intrusive to the setting. Alternatively, one might consider taking one of these to the field but using it only when one has a private moment or space.

Beginning participant observers often wonder what they should observe and record in field notes. Spradley (1980) identified three features common to all social situations that are a good starting point—place, actor, and activities. Accordingly, one might begin by describing the physical surroundings that one sees. (What is within eyesight? What is in the foreground? What is in the background?) One way to capture this in field notes is to construct drawings, maps, or diagrams. For example, I drew seating charts when I was observing interprofessional team meetings. One can also describe the actors or participants. (What are their roles or jobs? What do they look like? How are they dressed? What are their approximate ages, their genders, and other salient characteristics?) If one is observing an activity, one might record the sequence of events, who is involved, interactions and actions that occur, and the consequences.

Geertz (1973:9–10) describes the acquisition of deep cultural knowledge and its inscription into ethnographic text as "thick description." The ethnographer seeks a complex, nuanced understanding of the underlying meaning of a situation that is observed. Here I am using the term to convey that field notes (i.e., jottings), the source of thick descriptions that are incorporated into narratives and written ethnographic reports, should be detailed, textured, and close to what one observes and the context of the event, so that the researcher has a basis for interpreting it. Thus one would include sequences of action, dialogue, nonverbal gestures between people, sounds, sights, odors, and whatever other contextual data seem relevant. As Laird (1994:186) points out, the context takes in "the nests of context and power relations, the familial and social worlds in which meaning is generated. . . . We cannot understand the said and the unsaid . . . without understanding the surrounding forces that make possible the said and mandate the unsaid." Sometimes insights into these forces can be obtained from interviews.

Interviewing

Interviewing is integral to participant observation and a separate activity. Ethnographers conduct informal interviews during or after observing and make specific arrangements to conduct formal interviews. Informal interviews with individuals who are insiders to the culture take place in natural contexts (e.g., after a team meeting, on the way to a doctor's appointment, in the cafeteria, etc.), when spontaneous talk is appropriate to the circumstance. The researcher is friendly and listens to what the participant says and responds with interest, curiosity, and follow-up questions. The interviewer might use these opportunities to inquire about the meaning of a linguistic expression, group interaction, procedure, or event that was observed. Informal interviewing is not only a means to obtain information; it also provides an opportunity for the researcher to enact the role of learner and demonstrate interest in the participants and their setting. The interviewee may find informal interviews comfortable times in which to share their knowledge. Because of the informality of these occasions and their spontaneity, it is awkward to take field notes while they are occurring. One needs to train oneself to remember the details and record them as field notes later.

Informal interviewing can be built into a study by *shadowing* or accompanying selected participants while they pursue the ordinary events of their daily lives. One might meet a participant early in the morning while the family is having breakfast or is sending children off to school, observe children at school or a parent at work, and/or join the family in a celebration. For example, Iversen and Armstrong (2006) and her team "hung out" with families and shadowed parents at their workplaces and children at school in their study of the experiences of participants in manpower training programs who were moving from welfare to work. Social work researchers might spend time with clients, accompanying them to social agencies where they can observe the settings and clients' interactions with service providers. Observation over extended periods of time allows for a greater range of experience, more in-depth examination, and the opportunity to observe outcomes.

Ethnographers also conduct *formal interviews*, which have a more specific focus. Participants may be asked to describe their experience at the setting or personal experiences with the problem that is under study, or they may be asked about their life histories. The selection of interviewees and the questions that are asked should be consistent with the purpose of the project. Liebow (1993) took life histories of 20 long-term homeless women he observed in shelters. Patton (2002) provides guidance on sampling of interviewees, whether the study is ethnographic or otherwise. Formal interviews may be audiorecorded and transcribed.

Ideally, formal interviews are conducted privately. Attention should be paid to establishing rapport, explaining the purpose of the interview, and obtaining informed consent. Written consent forms should explain how confidentiality will be ensured and, if the interview is recorded, how tapes or digital information will be protected and how long they will be held. The interview itself may be structured around a set of prepared questions or topics or may revolve around questions that have been evolving in the course of the study. (University internal review boards usually require researchers to submit specific questions or at least a list of topics they plan to ask.) Open-ended questions provide structure at the same time they offer participants control over what they choose to share (Kadushin and Kadushin 1997). Such questions also promote free association, which stimulates story-telling and open up areas of inquiry that are new to the project. Closed-ended questions can get at specific issues and provide structure to reticent interviewees.

Ethnographic interviewing is the type of interviewing that has been associated with ethnography. In his classic book on the subject, Spradley (1979) explains how ethnographic interviews can be used to elicit categories or folk terms, which provide a window into the culture. Spradley discusses three kinds of questions—descriptive, structural, and contrast questions. Descriptive "grand tour" questions, which help the conversation get started and orient the researcher to the culture, encourage participants to speak broadly about a place, time period, or sequence of events (e.g., "Would you explain a typical day to me?"). "Mini tour" questions are similar but more focused (e.g., "Would you describe what your mornings are like?"). Structural questions are used to elicit information about the categories that are meaningful to a cultural group (e.g., "I've heard psychologists talk about a 'battery of tests' that they use to test children. What kinds of tests do psychologists in this clinic use in their battery of tests?"). Contrast questions seek to determine how cultural categories that are similar in some ways differ in other ways (e.g., "How are the ABS and WISC-III different?"). The three types of questions can be commingled and asked in a friendly, conversational way.

Some ethnographers conduct interviews with *key informants*—individuals who have specialized knowledge, are in a position of authority, or have a great deal of work experience with the population or problem under study. For example, as part of an ethnographic study of people who abuse prescription drugs, one might interview physicians and pharmacists who have knowledge about medication and experience with this population. Key informants can help researchers understand a problem more fully and recommend relevant sites and interviewees. Bernard (1994:168) suggests choosing "trustworthy informants who are observant, reflective, and articulate." Interviews with key informants may be summarized or audiorecorded and transcribed.

Documents

Considering that ethnographic research today occurs largely in literate societies, written documents produced by the cultures studied are important data sources (Atkinson and Coffey 2004). Social work agencies in particular generate annual reports, memoranda, financial reports, organizational charts, case records, personnel policies, minutes of staff meetings, and, in some cases, their own newsletters. Ethnographic research can be further enriched with documents such as public policies, newspaper articles, conferences related to the research topic, and websites. Further, one may come upon other sorts of documentary data accidentally, for example, when a parent hands the researcher a story a child wrote for school, or one notices an interesting item posted on a neighborhood bulletin board. Written autobiographical accounts, letters, and diaries, newspapers, and archival data can provide depth and context to an ethnographic study.

As Atkinson and Coffey (2004) state, documents are cultural products that need to be considered social constructions. Nonetheless, they provide useful information to the ethnographer. "We should examine their place in organizational settings, the cultural values attached to them, their distinctive types and forms" (58). Like verbal interactions, written documents use the culture's specialized language and make reference to other texts (documents, organizations, laws, etc.) that are related to the culture (intertextuality). Thus a review of documents can open up additional areas of inquiry and facilitate holism.

Visual Data

As suggested in the earlier discussions about participant observation and field notes, the visual field is integral to ethnographic research. Emmison (2004) asserts that visual signs (e.g., traffic lights) inform people how they are to accomplish their daily activities, and thus are relevant to research aimed at understanding a culture. He points to a wide range of visual data that can be made use of in research, including photographs, clothing, body language, eye contact, maps, directional signs, billboards, cartoons, advertisements, the design of hospitals, and the arrangement of public spaces. To that list, I add drawings created by members of a cultural setting. These data sources are ordinarily present in field sites or in documents. Additionally, the ethnographer can create visual data by taking photographs (with informed consent, of course). Photographs provide a visual record of people, places, artifacts, and activities at a moment of time.

Like photographs, videorecordings portray and freeze a scene, providing contextual data that can be reviewed after leaving the field. Video recordings have the added advantage of capturing sound, particularly talk, as well as nonverbal behaviors and movement. Camcorders and audiorecorders can be used, with the participants' consent, in interviews and group meetings. Used in tandem with field notes, they can be revisited to hone in on potentially relevant findings. Obviously, camcorders are obtrusive, but they have the advantage of capturing a great deal of interactional data. We used camcorders to record team meetings and evaluations related to case studies of particular children in our ethnographic research on interprofessional team communication (McClelland and Sands 2002). Initially, the professional staff was uncomfortable with our recording team meetings, but after a while, they seemed to forget that they were being recorded. For large meetings, we used two camcorders—each positioned at a different location, and employed an audiotape recorder for back up. (This proved to be a good strategy. Mechanic failure does occur in field work.) Having video and audio recordings had the further advantage of helping us document our research process.

The Research Process

The research process is nonlinear and recursive. Nevertheless, there is a definable beginning and an endpoint and activities in between. This section describes the various components of the process, including data analysis.

As with other genres of research, one begins with curiosity about a problem, population, process, situation, or issue. For example, one may wonder how mothers with severe mental illness care for themselves and their children, how immigrants manage their dual identities, or how child welfare workers manage heavy caseloads. In order to transform curiosity about a problem into research questions, exploration is needed.

One way to explore a problem is to consult the literature. This can help the researcher understand the problem more deeply and determine whether others have investigated this problem and, if so, what aspects they examined and what they disregarded. If there is a paucity of professional literature on a topic, one might read about related problems or populations. There may not be much written about how immigrants from Chad manage their dual identities, but literature on other African immigrant groups may be helpful. Look especially for prior ethnographic studies. In order to become sensitized to the problem, one may also read accounts directed at popular audiences—such as articles in the popular press or magazines and works of fiction (Hammersley and Atkinson 2007), or view relevant videotapes, television programs, or websites. Emerging social problems often appear in the popular media before they are studied by social scientists.

There is a difference of opinion among qualitative researchers about the extent to which one should review literature prior to conducting a study. Strauss and Corbin (1990; Corbin and Strauss 2008) recommend reading some but not all the technical literature in the beginning, and then throughout the project, particularly after categories relevant to an emerging theory have been identified. Speaking from the perspective of classical grounded theory, Glaser (1992) warns researchers that reading in advance of conducting a study promotes the development of preconceived ideas, which can bias a project. He does recommend reading after the theory has emerged. In my opinion, it is impossible to enter the field without preconceived ideas. It is the researcher's responsibility to become aware of and acknowledge his or her prior theories, assumptions, and biases and to avoid imposing these on the data where they do not fit and to be open to alternative perspectives.

Another way to explore a problem is to conduct informational interviews with individuals who are familiar with the population or issue. Depending on one's topic, these may be social workers, administrators, or members of a disenfranchised group. These individuals might be asked about what they have observed and provide the names of other individuals who may be helpful. Volunteering at a site that is relevant to one's research topic is an excellent way to gain insight into a problem and to narrow one's focus. If one builds positive relationships at this site, one may be able to conduct a pilot study on some aspect of this program or setting. Although pilot research may differ from one's final project, prior research does help one determine whether one's ideas are feasible and can help one to settle on the focus of one's study.

Once researchers narrow down their focus, they can begin to develop a provisional set of research questions that outline what they want to learn and understand through a study (Maxwell 1996). Generally these are process-oriented, open-ended questions that ask who, what, how, when, and where certain phenomena occurs. The questions are worded in such a way that different outcomes are possible. For example, our study of interprofessional teams was guided by these questions:

- What is the nature of participation in interprofessional teams? How do professionals on these teams interact with and make sense of their interactions with each other?

- How do families interact with and make sense of their interactions with professionals on teams?
- What knowledge do participants bring to bear in interactions within interprofessional teams and between teams and clients?
- When interprofessional teams interact with each other and clients, whose voice counts? (McClelland and Sands 2002:3)

Research questions may be refined or reworked during a pilot research study and, where warranted, modified during the course of implementing a study.

Once one has some direction, one looks into settings that are conducive to answering the research questions. One should consider what is stable about the setting and what is subject to change. Enclosed environments such as emergency services, domestic violence shelters, and hospitals offer environments in which to observe patterned interactions among staff and between staff and clients, but there is instability in the client population. If one wants to focus on the client's perspective, one may want a setting in which clients have the opportunity for long-term stays, such as residential treatment centers and schools for children with severe emotional disabilities. Carros (1997) conducted a study of a neonatal hospital team in which team membership was relatively steady. Its stability made visible the impact of the neonatal unit's move from one part of the hospital to another, as well as changes in Medicare reimbursement, on team interactions.

Exploration of a research setting involves interacting with gatekeepers, individuals who control access to an organization or group. When meeting with such individuals, researchers should present a clear picture of the kind of study that they envision and, in particular, the demands this may make on the setting and the potential benefits. In the course of the conversation, researchers might also inquire whether there are issues that the organization is interested in exploring. This opens the door for a convergence of goals and acceptability, at least by the gatekeeper. Hammersley and Atkinson (2007), however, warn investigators that the people who grant access, such as administrators, may be protective of their organizations and thus may deliberately point researchers in some directions and block access to others.

Entering the field should be given some prior thought. One should consider how one is going to describe oneself, what kind of role one is going to assume, and how one is going to proceed. One might also consider how one will dress. The student role is compatible with that of the learner stance of the ethnographer (Hammersley and Atkinson 2007). Alternatively, one may describe oneself as a researcher. Before starting her dissertation research, Koppelman (2004) worked as a volunteer tutor at a residential treatment program for substance abusing women and their children. Participants also were told that she was a graduate student. By the time she began to interview mothers and staff, they knew her as someone who was friendly, helpful, honest, and trustworthy. If the setting is an agency or organization, one should also give thought to how staff will regard one's presence. Despite efforts to assure them otherwise, staff at the site of the interprofessional team study voiced concern that they were being evaluated (McClelland and Sands 2002). A further point to keep in mind is that everyone is positioned somewhere (Hammersley and Atkinson 2007) and is viewed in terms of an ascribed status; thus participants are likely to react to one's race, gender, age, and physical appearance.

Once one has decided on a problem, setting, and/or group, one should develop a strategy in which to make systematic observations. Lincoln and Guba (1985) outline three phases of naturalistic research—(1) orientation and overview, (2) focused exploration, and (3) member checking. During the first phase, one learns one's way around the setting without committing oneself to a particular direction. One explores the terrain, does some observing and interviewing, and begins to develop relations with participants. Evaluation of data collected during this period should suggest areas for more focused study in the second phase. The second phase is a prolonged period of concurrent data collection and analysis. Then comes member checking, determining where the participants concur with the findings and where there are commonalities and differences in the meaning of the findings. In ethnographic research, these phases are not discrete. Even though orientation occurs at the beginning, new data gathered in the course of the study can result in changes within the second phase. Member checking can be accomplished throughout the study.

After one is sufficiently oriented, one decides on a course of observation. During the first phase of my research on interprofessional teams, following approval by the university's institutional review board (IRB), I obtained informed consent and began to observe, take field notes, and audiotape two biweekly intake assessment teams (Sands 1990). After observing some discipline-specific evaluations of children and reporting sessions to parents, I identified criteria for the case evaluations I would observe during the second phase and worked out a mechanism with staff to obtain the parents' consent in advance. After identifying children for my case studies, I worked out the logistics for shadowing parents and children on days when the children came to the center for discipline-specific assessments. At the end of the study, I conducted member-checking interviews with a representative sample of professionals and students who had been observed during the preceding academic year. Member checking led to a refinement of hypotheses that had emerged in the course of fieldwork and an understanding of the diverse disciplinary perspectives and how they coalesced and varied.

Regardless of what one is studying, participant observation should be purposeful and systematic. One should think through how frequently one is going to observe, the time of day, and the activities. Consider observing when programs or personnel are new or where there is a transition from one condition to the others. I found that focusing on new team members, a social worker and a pediatrician, who were trying to decipher the norms of the culture, gave me access to these norms (Sands 1989; McClelland and Sands 2002). If one's research site is a hospital, shelter, or treatment program, one should consider sampling times of the day and week. At night and on weekends one sees a different side of a program.

If one is planning to conduct formal interviews as part of the ethnography, one should think about how, when, and where these will take place and with whom. If there are sensitive issues involved in the study, such as abuse, mental illness, or HIV, strenuous efforts at building trust should take place prior to suggesting an interview. In all cases, procedures to protect confidentiality should be explained and informed consent should be obtained. Even with such efforts, some individuals may change their minds about participating and others may refuse to be audiorecorded. Researchers should think through whether they are willing to take notes rather than record an interview.

Researchers generally design their studies, including their research questions, topics to be explored in interviews, and methods, in advance of implementing the study. It is likely, however, that some aspects of the study will change in the course of implementation. Ethnography is a "dynamic, interactive-reactive" evolving process in which decisions are made in the process of data collection (Zaharlick and Green 1991; Green, Dixon, and Zaharlick 2003). The field presents demands and opportunities that one cannot predict or spell out specifically in advance.

Data Analysis and Presentation

With ethnography, data analysis is concurrent with data collection and continues afterward. The researcher regularly examines and reflects upon the data that have been collected and records emerging ideas about regularities in the data (themes or patterns) and potential hypotheses in field notes, journal entries, or memos. At the end of data collection, all the data are reviewed (including documents, field notes, and visual data) in relation to original research questions and the themes, patterns, and hypotheses that have been identified. This examination includes a comprehensive examination of convergent and divergent data. Where research teams are used, the team engages in a dialogical process in which convergent and divergent perceptions of the data are identified and thoroughly discussed.

The process of reading and rereading field notes and other data cannot be overemphasized. Consider reading in different ways. For example, one might read all data chronologically regardless of the type of data. Another approach is to examine all data that are about a particular individual, group, or theme, or review all key informant interviews. One might also read one's entire journal or memos. This process, especially when it occurs after one has some distance from the field, can increase familiarity with the data and stimulate new ideas about the meaning of the data. This process also yields a list of codes, their definitions, and parameters for assigning them.

Considering that ethnographers generally collect a great deal of data, a system of organizing and coding data is needed. Notes should be dated and classified as field notes, journal entries, memos, interviews, and so on. Loose-leaf notebooks, files, file cabinets, and boxes can be used to store and organize notebooks, tapes, and documents. Computers lend themselves to the efficient management and coding of data. There are a number of computer programs that are currently available that facilitate coding written files, linking themes, and the development of theory (see chapter 12 in this volume).

Throughout the study and following data collection, one reads or rereads theoretical writings that address some of the patterns one has identified in the data. The researcher (or team) then considers how an array of theories explains the data and ways in which they fit and do not fit. The use of multiple theories to explain the same data, theoretical triangulation (Denzin 1989), is not aimed at establishing validity; rather, it is a means to expand the perspectives from which the data can be understood. Likewise, other types of triangulation—methodological, data, investigator, and interdisciplinary triangulation (Denzin 1989; Janesick 1994)—do not need to be used for purposes of corroboration. As Bloor (1997) argues about methodological triangulation, triangulation is problematic as a technique of validation. Because the same social circumstances cannot be replicated in everyday life, it is unreasonable to expect two methods to be of the same order and yield the same quality of results. On the other hand, triangulation can help elucidate the complexity of a social setting and thus enrich understanding. Awareness of where the triangulation is convergent, divergent, or complementary (Erzberger and Prein 1997; Perlesz and Lindsay 2003) and where each perspective contributes unique or illuminating information (Sands and Roer-Strier 2006) stimulates additional questions that one may ask of the data.

The process of reading, comparing, coding, and triangulating data usually yields findings. Like other qualitative researchers, the ethnographer looks for a narrative or storyline (Strauss and Corbin 1990; Corbin and Strauss 2008) that provides an overarching organizing frame for the study. The storyline should be conceptual and take into account the part-whole relationship. In addition, the ethnography includes themes that stress different facets of the story. In a written ethnography, the themes may be the subjects of different chapters or sections.

Once findings are theoretically and thematically understood, one should consider presenting preliminary findings to individuals or groups that were part of the study—as a courtesy and as a means of member checking. If the research was conducted at an agency or group of agencies, such a presentation serves as a means of giving something back to people who have offered assistance to the study and of expressing gratitude. It also provides participants with an opportunity to respond to the findings. Through questions and interaction about the presentation, the researcher can assess where the findings resonate with the participants and where there is a difference of opinion. Differences of opinion can be explored with the group or individuals and by revisiting the data. Member checking may also be accomplished by showing participants drafts of chapters and asking them to comment. Like triangulation, member checking is controversial as a means of corroboration. Bloor (1997) found a number of problems associated with "member validation." For one, the methods used and the occasions in which member responses are elicited are different from those in which the data were gathered. Secondly, the perspectives of researchers and members of what is salient may be different. Third, participants' perceptions may change over time. On the other hand, member checking can yield new data. Thus rather than a means of verification or validation, it "can be viewed instead as further important data, an occasion for extending and elaborating the researcher's analysis" (Bloor 1997:48).

Debates about the truth value of data and the authority of the ethnographer (Lincoln and Denzin 2000) have opened up a variety of ways of communicating the ethnographic findings. Traditional ethnographies are descriptive and may also include photographs, contain excerpts from field notes, and use quotations from transcriptions. Tables and diagrams that depict the theoretical perspectives and findings are also incorporated into ethnographic reports (cf. McClelland and Sands 2002). Van Maanen (1988) reported three ways in which ethnographers can describe their study—realist, confessional, and impressionist tales. The realist tale, narrated in the third person, suppresses the "I" and tries to be true to the subject matter. It portrays the culture in an objective way, maintaining authorial authority. The confessional tale, written in the first person, highlights the experiences of the field worker. Here the author discloses stories about the fieldwork and reveals his or her own humanness. The impressionist tale, which has elements of the other two, is a personal account of moments in the field. It uses literary standards to create characters, feeling, and atmosphere, while departing from the literal. In addition to these approaches, ethnographers have been using innovative methods such as dramatic performance, poetry, and multivoiced methods of presentation (see Lincoln and Denzin 2000; Richardson 2000). These alternative means offer new avenues for creativity.

The choice of method of presentation is related to the audience or context of presentation (Zaharlick and Green 1991). Audiences differ in their knowledge of the subject matter, assumptions, and values, all of which can influence their receptivity to the research. For many academic audiences, including dissertation committees, a realist tale, strong in theory would be appropriate. An audience of other qualitative researchers may be open to a confessional tale or some of the performance methods delineated earlier. Clinical practitioners are likely to be responsive to case descriptions. Administrators may be interested in the programmatic and policy implications of the research. Consider, too, the advantages of visual and audiovisual aids in relation to each audience.

Strengths, Limitations, and Opportunities

Ethnographic research offers an in-depth look at a group, community, or organization in action. In contrast with qualitative studies that are based primarily on one-time interviews, ethnography provides a contextualized perspective over the extended time period in which it is conducted. The single interview, like a snapshot, captures an occasion, but this moment may be uncharacteristic and may not account for the varying contexts of social life and changes that develop over time. Ethnography makes it possible for one to have numerous occasions to view the same individuals, places, and entities in various combinations. Persistent observation over time, in tandem with other methods, elicits potentially rich sources of data out of which to support complex, nuanced findings.

Ethnographic research can be exciting and exhilarating. Every day provides new opportunities to learn about other cultural settings whether these are organizations, communities, or groups. The process of disentangling the meaning system of another culture and generating hypotheses is intellectually challenging. In learning about others, one learns about oneself. On the other hand, this research genre makes huge demands on one's time and emotions. It requires the engagement of all of one's cognitive, emotional, and sensory faculties, which can be exhausting. If one is working alone, it can be lonely. Investigating some areas of inquiry can threaten one's safety. One may also find oneself in ethical dilemmas if one observes events or behaviors that are illegal or immoral. When it comes to writing the ethnography, one can become overwhelmed with the amount of data one has collected.

Critics of ethnography point to its subjectivity. They believe that, because the ethnographer becomes part of the world he or she is researching, the research findings are likely to be infused with personal preconceptions, political goals, reactions, and values. Some ethnographers respond to this argument by asserting that all research is affected by values and has political consequences; others assert that reflexivity allows one to monitor one's own subjectivity (Patton 2002; Padgett 2008). I have found that immersion in the field, openness to understanding the perspectives of others, having at least one other co-investigator, together with a willingness to be reflexive, thwart the persistence of my own preconceptions and the imposition of my values on the data.

Social workers considering or engaged in ethnographic research are likely to find a goodness of fit between their professional training and the "doing" of this form of research. Educated to observe, listen, and interview, social workers have know-how that is transferable to ethnographic field-work. Social work practitioners' ability to examine and make effective use of their own selves can serve them well. Their experience collecting and analyzing data from multiple sources equips them to pursue this research approach. Their nonjudgmental attitude and appreciation of diversity are conducive to building field relationships. Moreover, social work's person-in-environment perspective is compatible with the holism that is integral to ethnography (Fetterman 1989). Other scholars have debated the affinity between ethnography and social work practice (see e.g., Fortune 1994; Goldstein 1994).

There are abundant opportunities for social workers to conduct ethnographic research in social work settings and amidst those with whom they work. Whether one is interested in health, mental health, aging, developmental disability, families and children, poverty, or a social problem like HIV or homelessness, there are agencies, advocacy organizations, and meeting places that are suitable for an ethnographic study. Curiosity, perseverance, and the excitement of the field draw interested scholars to a fascinating genre of qualitative research.

Summary

Ethnography is the intensive study of a setting, community, or group. Both a process and a product, the process involves participant observation over time and the infusion of other methods; and the product is the ethnography or ethnographic report. Like other qualitative researchers, ethnographers situate themselves and their studies in particular paradigms, typically constructivist, postmodern, feminist, or critical theory. A variety of other theoretical perspectives and concepts may be brought into play in data analysis.

This chapter described salient characteristics of ethnographic research—naturalism, emic and etic perspectives, reflexivity, holism, and the special stance of the researcher. It also described research methods. Ethnographers use themselves as research instruments as they engage in participant observation, writing field notes, interviewing, reviewing documents, and examining visual data.

The research process is nonlinear and recursive. One begins with curiosity and explores a problem or population through literature and meeting with knowledgeable people in the community. Volunteer work and pilot studies in relevant community settings can help one get started. Ethnographic research is guided by research questions that may be refined as the study proceeds. Researchers need to negotiate access to potential settings and populations and determine the kind of role they will assume as ethnographers. Participant observation should be purposeful and thought should be given about sampling time as well as events. Formal and informal interviews should also be purposeful.

Data analysis is ongoing and concurrent with data collection, facilitating the emergence of themes and hypotheses. Numerous readings of the data in various ways can enhance understanding and stimulate the development or refinement of hypotheses. Triangulation of methods, data, investigators, and theories can enhance understanding of the complexity of the research setting or group and open up new areas of inquiry. Data analysis, like data collection, can be an exhilarating experience. There is an intellectual excitement in putting the pieces together in ways that one had not anticipated early in the study. The researcher as well as the research is enriched by the ethnographer's discoveries.

References

Agar, M. 1980. *The professional stranger: An informal introduction to ethnography.* Orlando, FL: Academic.

Alexander, K. B. 2005. Performance ethnography: The reenacting and inciting of culture. In *The Sage handbook of qualitative research* (3rd ed.), N. K. Denzin and Y. S. Lincoln, eds. 411–441. Thousand Oaks, CA: Sage.

Anderson, E. 1990. *Streetwise: Race, class, and change in an urban community.* Chicago: U of Chicago P.

Atkinson, P. and A. Coffey. 2004. Analysing documentary realities. In *Qualitative research: theory, method and practice,* D. Silverman, ed. 56–75. Thousand Oaks, CA: Sage.

Becker, H. S. (1999) The Chicago School, so-called. *Qualitative Sociology,* 22:3–12.

Behar, R. 1996. *The vulnerable observer: Anthropology that breaks your heart.* Boston: Beacon.

Bernard, H. R. 1994. *Research methods in anthropology: Qualitative and quantitative approaches* (2nd ed.). Thousand Oaks, CA: Sage.

Bloor, M. 1997. Techniques of validation. In *Context and method in qualitative research,* G. Miller and R. Dingwall, eds. 37–50. Thousand Oaks: Sage.

Carros, N. 1997. "Multidisciplinary team interaction: An ethnographic study of a neonatal intensive care multidisciplinary team." Doctoral dissertation, University of Pennsylvania School of Social Work.

Clifford, J. 1986. Introduction: Partial truths. In *Writing culture: The poetics and politics of ethnography*, J. Clifford and G. E. Marcus, eds. 1–26. Berkeley, CA: U of California P.

——. 1988. *The predicament of culture: Twentieth-century ethnography, literature, and art*. Cambridge, MA: Harvard UP.

Clifford, J. and G. E. Marcus, eds. 1986. *Writing culture: The poetics and politics of ethnography*. Berkeley, CA: U of California P.

Corbin, J. and A. Strauss. 2008. *Basics of qualitative research* (3rd ed.). Los Angeles: Sage.

Cresswell, J. W. 1998. *Qualitative inquiry and research design: Choosing among five traditions*. Thousand Oaks, CA: Sage.

Deegan, M. J. 2001. The Chicago School of ethnography. In *Handbook of ethnography*, P. Atkinson, A. Coffey, S. Delamont, J. Lofland, and L. Lofland, eds. 11–25. London and Thousand Oaks: Sage.

Denzin, N. K. 1989. *The research act* (3rd ed.). Englewood Cliffs, NJ: Prentice Hall.

——. 1997. *Interpretive ethnography: Ethnographic practices for the 21st century*. Thousand Oaks, CA: Sage.

——. 2003. *Performance ethnography: Critical pedagogy and the politics of culture*. Thousand Oaks, CA: Sage.

Denzin, N. K. and Y. S. Lincoln. 2005. Introduction. In *The Sage handbook of qualitative research* (3rd ed.), N. K. Denzin and Y. S. Lincoln, eds. 1–32. Thousand Oaks, CA: Sage.

DeVault, M. L. and L. McCoy. 2001. Institutional ethnography: Using interviews to investigate ruling relations. In *Handbook of interview research: Context and method*, J. F. Gubrium and J. A. Holstein, eds. 751–776. Thousand Oaks, CA: Sage.

Du Bois, W. E. B. 1899/1996. *The Philadelphia Negro: A social study*. Philadelphia, PA: U of Pennsylvania P.

Ellis, C. and A. P. Bochner. 2000. Autoethnography, personal narrative, reflexivity: Researcher as subject. In *Handbook of qualitative research* (2nd ed.), N. K. Denzin and Y. S. Lincoln, eds. 733–768. Thousand Oaks, CA: Sage.

Emerson, R. M., R. I. Fretz, and L. L. Shaw. 1995. *Writing ethnographic fieldnotes*. Chicago: U of Chicago P.

Emmison, M. 2004. Visual data. In *Qualitative research: Theory, method and practice* (2nd ed.), D. Silverman, ed. 246–265. Thousand Oaks: Sage.

Erickson, F. 1992. Ethnographic microanalysis of interaction. In *The handbook of qualitative research in education*, M. D. LeComte, W. L. Millroy, and J. Preissle, eds., 201–225. San Diego, CA: Academic.

——. 2006. Definition and analysis of data from videotape: Some research procedures and their rationales. In *Handbook of complementary methods in education
research*, J. L. Green, G. Camilli, and P. B. Elmore, eds. 177–191. Washington,
DC: American Educational Research Association.

Erzberger, C. and G. Prein. 1997. Triangulation: Validity and empirically-based hypothesis construction. *Quality and Quantity*, 31:141–154.

Estroff, S. 1981. *Making it crazy*. Berkeley, CA: U of California P.

Fetterman, D. M. 1989. *Ethnography step by step*. Newbury Park, CA: Sage.

Floersch, J. 2002. *Meds, money, and manners: The case management of severe mental
illness*. New York: Columbia UP.

Foley, D. and A. Valenzuela. 2005. Critical ethnography: The politics of collaboration. In *Handbook of qualitative research* (3rd ed.), N. K. Denzin and Y. S. Lincoln,
eds. 217–234. Thousand Oaks, CA: Sage.

Fortune, A. 1994. Commentary: Ethnography in social work. In *Qualitative research
in social work*, E. Sherman and W. J. Reid, eds. 63–67. New York: Columbia UP.

Garfinkel, H. 1967. *Studies in ethnomethodology*. Englewood Cliffs, NJ: Prentice Hall.

Geertz, C. 1973. *The interpretation of culture*. New York: Basic.

——. 1988. *Works and lives: The anthropologist as author*. Stanford, CA: Stanford UP.

Glaser, B. G. 1992. *Basics of grounded theory analysis: Emergence vs. forcing*. Mill Valley, CA: Sociology.

Gold, R. 1958. Roles in sociological field observations. *Social Forces, 36*:217–223.

Goldstein, H. 1994. Ethnography, critical inquiry, and social work practice. In *Qualitative research in social work*, E. Sherman and W. J. Reid, eds. 42–51. New York:
Columbia UP.

Goodenough, W. H. 1970. *Description and comparison in cultural anthropology*. Chicago: Aldine.

Green, J. L., C. N. Dixon, and A. Zaharlick. 2003. Ethnography as a logic of in-
quiry. In *Handbook of research on teaching the English language* (2nd ed.), J. Flood,
D. Lapp, J. R. Squire, and J. M. Jensen, eds. 201–224. Mahwah, NJ: Lawrence
Erlbaum.

Guba, E. G. and Y. S. Lincoln. 2005. Paradigmatic controversies, contradictions,
and emerging confluences. In *The Sage handbook of qualitative research* (3rd ed.),
N. K. Denzin and Y. S. Lincoln, eds. 191–215. Thousand Oaks, CA: Sage.

Gubrium, J. F. and J. A. Holstein. 1997. *The new language of qualitative method*. New
York: Oxford UP.

——. 2008. Narrative ethnography. In *Handbook of emergent methods*, S. Nagy
Hesse-Biber and P. Leavy, eds. New York: Guilford.

——. 2009. *Analyzing narrative reality*. Los Angeles: Sage.

Gumperz, J. and D. Hymes. 1964. The ethnography of communication. *American
Anthropologist, 66*(6):Pt. II.

Hall, T. 2003. *Better times than this: Youth homelessness in Britain*. London: Pluto.

Hammersley, M. 1992. *What's wrong with ethnography? Methodological explorations*. New York: Routledge.

Hammersley, M. and P. Atkinson. 2007. *Ethnography: Principles in practice* (3rd ed.). New York: Routledge.

Holstein, J. A. and J. F. Gubrium. 2005. Interpretive practice and social action. In *Handbook of qualitative research* (3rd ed.), N. K. Denzin and Y. S. Lincoln, eds. 483–505. Thousand Oaks, CA: Sage.

Hymes, D. 1974. *Foundations of sociolinguistics: An ethnographic approach*. Philadelphia, PA: University of Pennsylvania.

Iversen, R. R. and A. L. Armstrong. 2006. Jobs aren't enough: Toward a new economic mobility for low-income families. Philadelphia, PA: Temple University.

Jackson, J. E. 1990. "I am a fieldnote": Fieldnotes as a symbol of professional identity. In *Fieldnotes: The making of anthropology*, R. Sanjek, ed. 3–33. Ithaca, NY: Cornell UP.

Janesick, V. 1994. The choreography of qualitative research design. In *Handbook of qualitative research*, N. K. Denzin and Y. S. Lincoln, eds. 209–219. Thousand Oaks, CA: Sage.

Jorgensen, D. L. 1989. *Participant observation: A methodology for human studies*. Newbury Park: Sage.

Junker, B. 1960. *Field work*. Chicago: U of Chicago P.

Kadushin, A. and G. Kadushin. 1997. *The social work interview: A guide for human service professionals* (4th ed.). New York: Columbia UP.

Koppelman, N. 2004. *Defying dependence: Women with addictions facing welfare, child welfare, and substance abuse treatment systems*. Ph.D. dissertation, University of Pennsylvania.

Laird, J. 1994. "Thick description" revisited. In *Qualitative research in social work*, E. Sherman and W. J. Reid, eds. 175–189. New York: Columbia UP.

Lather, P. 2001. Postbook: Working the ruins of feminist ethnography. *Signs: Journal of Women in Culture and Society*, 27(1):199–227.

LeCompte, M. 2002. The transformation of ethnographic practice: Past and current challenges. *Qualitative Research*, 2(3):283–299.

Lesser, A. 1968. Boas, Franz. In *International encyclopedia of the social sciences*, vol. 2, D. L. Sills, ed. 99–110. New York: Macmillan.

Liebow, E. 1993. *Tell them who I am: The lives of homeless women*. New York: Free Press.

Lincoln, Y. S. and N. K. Denzin. 2000. The seventh moment: Out of the past. In *Handbook of qualitative research* (2nd ed.), N. K. Denzin and Y. S. Lincoln, eds. 1047–1065. Thousand Oaks, CA: Sage.

Lincoln, Y. S. and E. G. Guba. 1985. *Naturalistic inquiry*. Beverly Hills, CA: Sage.

Lynd, R. S. and H. M. Lynd. 1929. *Middletown: A study in contemporary American culture*. New York: Harcourt, Brace.

———. 1937. *Middletown in transition: A study in cultural conflicts*. New York: Harcourt, Brace.

Macdonald, S. 2001. British social anthropology. In *Handbook of ethnography*, P. Atkinson, A. Coffey, S. Delamont, J. Lofland, and L. Lofland, eds. 60–79. Thousand Oaks: Sage.

Malinowski, B. 1922. *Argonauts of the Western Pacific: An account of native enterprise and adventure in the archipelagoes of Melanesian New Guinea*. New York: Routledge.

Marcus, G. E. 1998. *Ethnography through thick and thin*. Princeton, NJ: Princeton UP.

Marcus, G. E. and Fischer, M. M. J. 1986. *Anthropology as cultural critique: An experimental moment in the human sciences*. Chicago: U of Chicago P.

Maxwell, J. A. 1996. *Qualitative research design: An interactive approach*. Thousand Oaks, CA: Sage.

McClelland, M. and R. G. Sands. 2002. *Interprofessional and family discourses: Voices, knowledge, and practice*. Cresskill, NJ: Hampton.

Padgett, D. K. 2008. *Qualitative methods in social work research* (2nd ed.). Los Angeles, CA: Sage.

Patton, M. Q. 2002. *Qualitative evaluation and research methods* (3rd ed.). Thousand Oaks, CA: Sage.

Perlesz, A. and J. Lindsay. 2003. Methodological triangulation in researching families: making sense of dissonant data. *International Journal of Social Research Methodology*, 6(1):25–40.

Pike, K. L. 1954. *Language in relation to a unified theory of structure of human behavior*. Part I: Preliminary edition. Santa Ana, CA: Summer Institute of Linguistics.

Pithouse, A. 1987. *Social work: The organisation of an invisible trade*. Avebury: Gower.

Power, E. M. 2004. Toward understanding in postmodern interview analysis: Interpreting the contradictory remarks of a research participant. *Qualitative Health Research*, 14(6):858–865.

Richardson, L. 2000. Writing: A method of inquiry. In *Handbook of qualitative research* (2nd ed.), N. K. Denzin and Y. S. Lincoln, eds. 923–948. Thousand Oaks, CA: Sage.

Riemer, F. J. 1999. Quick attachments to the workforce: An ethnographic analysis of a transition from welfare to low-wage jobs. In *Social work research methods: Building knowledge for practice*, S. A. Kirk, ed. 305–315. Washington, DC: NASW.

Sands, R. G. 1989. The social worker joins the team: A look at the socialization process. *Social Work in Health Care*, 14(2):1–15.

———. 1990. Ethnographic research: A qualitative research approach to study of the interdisciplinary team. *Social Work in Health Care*, 15(1):115–129.

——. 1995. The parenting experience of low-income single women with chronic mental disorders. *Families in Society*, 76(2):86–96.

Sands, R. G. and M. McClelland. 1994. Emic and etic perspectives in ethnographic research on the interdisciplinary team. In *Qualitative research in social work*, E. Sherman and Reid, W. J., eds. 32–51. New York: Columbia UP.

Sands, R. G. and D. Roer-Strier. 2006. Using data triangulation of mother and daughter interviews to enhance research about families. *Qualitative Social Work: Research and Practice*, 5(2):237–260.

Sanjek, R., ed. 1990. *Fieldnotes: The makings of anthropology*. Ithaca, NY: Cornell UP.

Saville-Troike, M. 1989. *The ethnography of communication: An introduction* (2nd ed.). New York: Basil Blackwell.

Seeley, K. M. 2004. Short-term intercultural psychotherapy: Ethnographic inquiry. *Social Work*, 49(1):121–130.

Skeggs, B. 2001. Feminist ethnography. In *Handbook of ethnography*, P. Atkinson, A. Coffey, S. Delamont, J. Lofland, and L. Lofland, eds. 426–441. Thousand Oaks: Sage.

Smith, D. E. 1987. *The everyday world as problematic: A feminist sociology*. Boston: Northeastern UP.

Spradley, J. P. 1979. *The ethnographic interview*. New York: Holt, Rinehart and Winston.

——. 1980. *Participant observation*. New York: Holt, Rinehart and Winston.

Stacey, J. 1988. Can there be a feminist ethnography? *Women's Studies International Forum*, 11(1):21–27.

Stack, C. 1974. *All our kin: Strategies for survival in a black community*. New York: Harper and Row.

Strauss, A. and J. Corbin. 1990. *Basics of qualitative research: Grounded theory procedures and techniques*. Newbury Park, CA: Sage.

Tedlock B. 2000. Ethnography and ethnographic representation. In *Handbook of qualitative research* (2nd ed.), N. K. Denzin and Y. S. Lincoln, eds. 455–486. Thousand Oaks, CA: Sage.

Van Maanen, J. 1988. *Tales of the field: On writing ethnography*. Chicago: U of Chicago P.

Vidich, A. J. and S. M. Lyman. 2000. Qualitative methods: Their history in sociology and anthropology. In *Handbook of qualitative research* (2nd ed.), N. K. Denzin and Y. S. Lincoln, eds. 37–84. Thousand Oaks, CA: Sage.

Wax, R. 1971. *Doing fieldwork: Warnings and advice*. Chicago: U of Chicago P.

Whyte, W. F. 1943. *Street corner society: The social structure of an Italian slum*. Chicago: U of Chicago P.

Zaharlick, A. and J. L. Green. 1991. Ethnographic research. In *Handbook of research on teaching the English language arts*, J. Flood, J. M. Jensen, D. Lapp and J. R. Squire, eds. 205–225. New York: Macmillan.

[7]

Analysis of Personal Narratives

CATHERINE KOHLER RIESSMAN

It is a common experience for investigators to craft interview questions carefully only to have participants respond with lengthy accounts, long stories that appear on the surface to have little to do with the questions. I became aware of this in the early 1980s while researching the topic of divorce. After completing a household interview with a divorcing spouse, I would note upon listening to the tape that a respondent had gone "on and on." Asking a seemingly straightforward question (e.g., "What were the main causes of your separation?"), I expected a list in response but instead got a "long story." Those of us on the research team interpreted these stories as digressions.

Subsequently, I realized that participants were resisting our efforts to fragment their experiences into thematic (codable) categories—our attempts, in effect, to control meaning. There was a typical sequence to the moments of resistance: The long story began with the decision to marry, moved through the years of the marriage, paused to reenact especially troubling incidents and ended often with the moment of separation (Riessman 1990a). If participants resisted our efforts to contain their lengthy narratives, they were nonetheless quite aware of the rules of conversational storytelling. After coming to the end of the long and complex story of a

Reprinted from *Handbook of interview research: Context and method*, 2002, Jaber F. Gubium and James A. Holstein, eds. 695–710. Thousand Oaks, CA: Sage.

marriage, a participant would sometimes say, "Uh, I'm afraid I got a little lost. What was the question you asked?" With such "exit talk," the interviewer could move on to the next question.

Looking back, I am both embarrassed and instructed. These incidents underscore the gap between the standard practice of research interviewing on the one side and the life world of naturally occurring conversation and social interaction on the other (Mishler 1986). Although dehumanizing research practices persist, feminists and others in the social sciences have cleared a space for less dominating and more relational modes of interviewing that reflect and respect participants' ways of organizing meaning in their lives (DeVault 1999; see also Reinharz and Chase 2002). We have made efforts to give up communicative power and follow participants down their diverse trails. The current wellspring of interest in personal narrative reflects these trends.

The Narrative Turn

The burgeoning literature on narrative has touched almost every discipline and profession. No longer the province of literary study alone, the "narrative turn" has entered history (Carr 1986; Cronon 1992; White 1987), anthropology and folklore (Behar 1993; Mattingly and Garro 2000; Rosaldo 1989; Young 1987), psychology (Bruner 1986, 1990; Mishler 1986, 2000b; Polkinghorne 1988; Rosenwald and Ochberg 1992; Sarbin 1986), sociolinguistics (Capps and Ochs 1995; Gee 1986, 1991; Labov 1982; Linde 1993), and sociology (Bell 1988, 1999, 2000; Chase 1995; Boje 1991; DeVault 1991; Frank, 1995; Holstein and Gubrium 2000; Williams 1984). The professions, too, have embraced the narrative metaphor, along with investigators who study particular professions. These include law ("Legal Storytelling" 1989), medicine (Charon 1986; Greenhalgh and Hurwitz 1998; Hunter 1991; Hyden 1997; Kleinman 1988), nursing (Sandelowski 1991), occupational therapy (Mattingly 1998), and social work (Dean 1995; Laird 1988). Storytelling, to put the argument simply, is what we do when we describe research and clinical materials, and what informants do with us when they convey the details and courses of their experiences. The approach does not assume objectivity; rather, it privileges positionality and subjectivity.

Narrative analysis takes as its object of investigation the story itself. I limit discussion here to first-person accounts in interviews of informants' own experience, putting aside other kinds of narratives (e.g., about the self of the investigator, what happened in the field, media descriptions of events or the "master narratives" of theory).[1] My research has focused on disruptive life events, accounts of experiences that fundamentally alter expected biographies. I have studied divorce, chronic illness, and infertility, and I draw on examples from my work throughout the chapter.

Narrative analysis, however, is not only relevant for the study of life disruptions; the methods are equally appropriate for research concerning social movements, political change, and macro-level phenomena (see Cándida Smith 2002; Czarniawska 2002). Because storytelling "promotes empathy across different social locations," regarding the U.S. abortion debate William Gamson (1999:5) argues, for example, that storytelling has counteracted excessive abstraction, bridging policy discourse and the language of women's life worlds; storytelling has fostered the development of constituencies—communities of action. Ken Plummer (1995:174) puts it vividly: "Stories gather people around them," dialectically connecting the people and social movements. The identity stories of members of historically "defiled" groups, such as rape victims, gays, and lesbians, reveal shifts in language over time that shape, and were shaped by, the mobilization of these actors in collective movements. Examples here are "Take Back the Night" and gay rights groups (see Kong, Mahoney and Plummer, 2002). "For narratives to flourish, there must be a community to hear . . . for communities to hear, there must be stories which weave together their history, their identity, their politics" (Plummer 1995:87).

Storytelling is a relational activity that encourages others to listen, to share, and to empathize. It is a collaborative practice and assumes that tellers and listeners/questioners interact in particular cultural milieus and historical contexts, which are essential to interpretation. Analysis in narrative studies opens up forms of telling about experience, not simply the content to which language refers. We ask, "Why was the story told that way?" (Riessman 1993).

The study of personal narrative is a type of case-centered research (Mishler 2000b). Building on the kind of analysis articulated most vividly by C. Wright Mills (1959), the approach illuminates the intersection of biography, history, and society. The "personal troubles" that participants represent in their narratives of divorce, for example, tell us a great deal about social and historical processes—contemporary beliefs about gender relations and pressures on marriage at a junction of American history (Riessman 1990a). Similarly, coming out stories, in which narrators proclaim their gayness to themselves and to others, reveal a shift in genre over time; the linear, "causal" modernist tales of the 1960s and 1970s have given way in contemporary stories to identities that blur and change (Plummer 1995). Historical shifts in understanding and growing politicization occur in the stories of women with cancer whose mothers were exposed to diethylstilbestrol (DES) during their pregnancies (Bell 1999). Illness narratives reveal "deeply historicized and social view[s] of health and illness," as Vieda Skultans (1999:322) shows with post-Soviet women patients' accounts of hardship, whose explanations are erased in their physicians' biomedical definitions of problems. As Mills said long ago, what we call "personal troubles" are located in particular times and places, and individuals' narratives about their troubles are works of history as much as they are about individuals, the social spaces they inhabit, and the societies they live in. The analysis of personal narratives can illuminate "individual and collective action and meanings, as well as the processes by which social life and human relationships are made and changed" (Laslett 1999:392).

Defining Narratives for Analysis

There is considerable variation in how investigators employ the concept of personal narrative and, relatedly, in the methodological assumptions investigators make and the strategies they choose for analysis. These are often tied to disciplinary background. In one tradition of work, typical of social history and anthropology, the narrative is considered to be the entire life story, an amalgam of autobiographical materials. Barbara Myerhoff's (1978) work offers an early example of the life story approach and illustrates its potentials and problems. Myerhoff constructs compelling portraits of elderly Eastern European Jews who are living out the remainder of their lives in Venice, California. She builds these portraits from the many incidents informants shared with her during extended fieldwork. She artfully "infiltrates" her informants, "depositing her authorial word inside others' speech" to speak her truth without "erasing the others' viewpoint and social language (Kaminsky 1992:17–18). In this genre, the stories that informants recount merge with the analyst's interpretation of them, sometimes to the point that stories and interpretation are indistinguishable.

In a very different tradition of work, the concept of personal narrative is quite restrictive, used to refer to brief, topically specific stories organized around characters, setting, and plot. These are discrete stories told in response to single questions; they recapitulate specific events the narrator witnessed or experienced. William Labov's (1982) work illustrates this approach. For example, Labov analyzes the common structures underlying a series of bounded (transcribed) stories of inner-city violence told in response to a specific question. Narrators recapitulate sequences of actions that erupt and bring the danger of death. The approach has been extended by others who include more than brief episodes to analyze a variety of experiences (Attanucci 1991; Bamberg 1997a; Bell 1988; Riessman 1990b).

In a third approach, personal narrative is considered to encompass large sections of talk and interview exchanges—extended accounts of lives that develop over the course of interviews. The discrete story as the unit of analysis of Labov's and others' approach gives way to an evolving series of stories that are framed in and through interaction. Elliot Mishler (2000b), for example, studied the trajectories of identity development among a group of artists/craftspersons that emerged from his extended interviews with them. The approach is distinguished by the following features: presentation of and reliance on detailed transcripts of interview excerpts, attention to the structural features of discourse, analysis of the coproduction of narratives through the dialogic exchange between interviewer and participant, and a comparative orientation to interpreting similarities and contrasts among participants' life stories (see also Bell 1999).

Despite differences in these approaches, most investigators share certain basic understandings. Narration is distinguished by ordering and sequence; one action is viewed as consequential for the next. Narrators create plots from disordered experience, giving reality "a unity that neither nature nor the past possesses so clearly" (Cronon 1992:1349).[2] Relatedly, narrators structure their tales temporally and spatially; "they look back on and recount lives that are located in particular times and places" (Laslett 1999:392). The temporal ordering of a plot is most familiar and responds to the characteristic Western listener's preoccupation with time marching forward, as in the question, "And then what happened?" But narratives can also be organized thematically and episodically (Gee 1991; Michaels 1981; Riessman 1987). Narrators use particular linguistic devices to hold their accounts together and communicate meaning to listeners (for a review see Riessman1993:18–19). Human agency and imagination are vividly expressed:

With narrative, people strive to configure space and time, deploy cohesive devices, reveal identity of actors and relatedness of actions across scenes. They create themes, plots, and drama. In so doing, narrators make sense of themselves, social situations, and history (Bamberg and McCabe 1998:iii).

If all talk in interviews is not narrative (there are questions and answers about demographic facts, listings, chronicles, and other nonnarrative forms of discourse), how does an investigator discern narrative segments for analysis? Sometimes the decision is clear: An informant signals that a story is coming and indicates when it is over with entrance and exit talk (Jefferson 1979). In my divorce interviews, for example, responding to a question about the "main causes" of separation, one man provided a listing and then said, "I'll clarify this with an example," an utterance that introduced a lengthy story about his judging a dog show, an avocation his wife did not share. He exited from the story many minutes later by saying, "That is a classic example of the whole relationship . . . she chose *not* to be with *me*." As the story was especially vivid, I used it along with others to theorize about gender differences in expectations of companionate marriage in the contemporary United States (Riessman1990a:102–108).

Stories in research interviews are rarely so clearly bounded, however, and often there is negotiation between teller and listener about placement and relevance, a process that can be analyzed with transcriptions that include paralinguistic utterances ("uhms") false starts, interruptions, and other subtle features of interaction. Deciding which segments to analyze and putting boundaries around them are interpretive acts that are shaped in major ways by the investigator's theoretical interests.

Deciding where the beginnings and endings of narratives fall is often a complex interpretive task. I confronted the problem in a study of stigma and infertility as I began to analyze a woman's narrative account of her multiple miscarriages. The research was conducted in Kerala, South India, and elsewhere I describe the fieldwork (Riessman 2000a, 2000b). At a certain point in the project, I began to focus on identity development for women beyond childbearing age, how older women construct identities that defy stigma and the master narrative of motherhood.

Below, I present a portion of an interview with a woman I call "Gita," who is 55 years old, married, childless, Hindu, and from a lower caste. Because of progressive social policies and related opportunities in Kerala, Gita is educated, has risen in status, and works as a lawyer in a small

Table 7.1

| Cathy: | Now I am going to go back and ask some specific questions. Were you ever pregnant? | Scene 1 |

Gita: Pregnant means—You see it was three years [after the marriage]
then I approached [name of doctor]
then she said it is not a viable—[pregnancy].

==

So she asked me to undergo this operation, this D&C
and she wanted to examine him [husband] also.

Then the second time in 1974—in '75,   Scene 2
next time—four months.
Then she wanted [me] to take bed rest
advised me to take bed rest.

Because I already told you   Scene 3
it was during that period that [name] the socialist leader
led the gigantic procession against Mrs. Indira Gandhi,
the Prime Minister of India, in Delhi.

And I was a political leader [names place and party]
I had to participate in that.

So I went by train to Delhi
but returned by plane.
After the return I was in [name] Nursing Home
for 16 days bleeding.

And so he [husband] was very angry   Scene 4
he said "do not go for any social work
do not be active" this and that.
But afterwards I never became—[pregnant]

==

Then my in-laws, they are in [city]   Scene 5
they thought I had some defect, really speaking.
So they brought me to a gynecologist,
one [name], one specialist.

She took three hours to examine me
and she said "you are perfectly—[normal], no defect at all"
even though I was 40 or 41 then.
"So I have to examine your husband."

Then I told her [doctor] "You just ask his sister."
She was—his sister was with me in [city],
So I asked her to ask her to bring him in.
He will not come.
Then we went to the house
so then I said "Dr. [name] wants to see you."
Then he [husband] said "No, no, I will not go to a lady doctor."
Then she [sister-in-law] said she would not examine him
they had to examine the—what is it?—the sperm in the
laboratory. But he did not allow that.

municipality. The interaction represented in this extract took place after she and I had talked (in English) for nearly an hour in her home about a variety of topics, most of which she introduced. These included her schooling, how her marriage was arranged, and her political work in the "liberation struggle of Kerala." We enter the interview as I reintroduce the topic of infertility. My transcription conventions are adapted from those recommended by James Gee (1986).[3]

Although Gita could answer my question "Were you ever pregnant?" directly with a yes, she chooses instead to negotiate a space in the interview to develop a complex narrative. She describes terminated pregnancies, going to a political demonstration, and coming home to her husband's anger, whereupon the scene shifts to the actions of her in-laws and her husband's refusal to be examined for infertility. This was unlike other women's accounts about failed pregnancies in my interviews. Although temporally organized, Gita's plot spans many years and social settings, and emotions related to the events are absent. She makes no reference to sadness, disappointment, or other feelings common to narratives of miscarriage and infertility.

In an effort to interpret this segment of the interview, I struggled to define its boundaries. Initially, I decided to conclude my representation of the narrative with what seems like a coda at the end of Scene 4: "But afterwards I never became—[pregnant]." The utterance concludes the sequence about pregnancies—the topic of my initial question. Ultimately, however, I decided to include the next scene, which communicates various family members' responses and the reported speech of Gita's husband ("No, no, I will not go to a lady doctor"). The change in decision coincided with a theoretical shift in my thinking about identity construction. I became interested in how women in South India resist stigma when infertility occurs (Riessman 2000b). It was crucial, then, to include the episode about the in-laws, the interaction with the gynecologist, and the husband's response to the request that he be tested.

Although not my focus here, the narrative excerpt could have been analyzed as an interactional accomplishment, that is, as a joint production of the interviewer and the respondent. Such a focus would require retranscription so as to include all of my utterances (deleted and marked with = = in the interview excerpt), the ways I elicited and shaped the narrative (for examples of this approach, see Bell 1999; Capps and Ochs 1995; Mishler 1997; Riessman 1987; Poland 2002). The narrative also could have been analyzed with a primary focus on cultural context, centering on the prominent role of the wife's in-laws, for example, in defining and managing infertility in India (for an example, see Riessman 2000a). And the narrative could have been analyzed in terms of problems it solves for the narrator—an angle into the text I will develop shortly—and other problems that narrative creates. Investigators interested in psychological processes, narrative therapy, and change (White and Epston 1990; Josselson and Lieblich 1993; McLeod 1997) might explore Gita's account of infertility for its closed, sealed off features; Gita displays a set of understandings that seem to defy redefinition and change. Or silence about emotions might be a focus. These are just a few of the analytic strategies available.

Across the board, the discernment of a narrative segment for analysis— the representations and boundaries chosen—is strongly influenced by the investigator's evolving understandings, disciplinary preferences, and research questions. In all of these ways, the investigator variously "infiltrates" the text. Unlike some of the life story approaches mentioned earlier, especially Myerhoff's, my approach here includes detailed transcripts of speech so that readers can, to a much greater degree, see the stories apart from their analysis.[4] The selves of storyteller and analyst then remain separate (Laslett 1999).

Analyzing Narrative as Performance

Personal narratives serve many purposes—to remember, argue, convince, engage, or entertain their audiences (Bamberg and McCabe 1998). Consequently, investigators have many points of entry. Personal narratives can be analyzed textually (Gee 1986; Labov 1982), conversationally (Polanyi 1985), culturally (Rosaldo 1989; Mattingly and Garro 2000), politically/historically (Mumby 1993; White 1987), and performatively (Langellier 1989).[5] It is the last of these analytic positions that I emphasize primarily here. A story involves storytelling, which is a reciprocal event between a teller and an audience. When we tell stories about our lives, we perform our (preferred) identities (Langellier 2001).

As Erving Goffman (1959, 1981) suggests with his repeated use of the dramaturgical metaphor, social actors stage performances of desirable selves to preserve "face" in situations of difficulty, thus managing potentially "spoiled" identities. Relatedly, gender identity is performed, produced for and by audiences in social situations. To emphasize the performative element is not to suggest that identities are inauthentic, but only that they are situated and accomplished in social interaction.

Applying these insights to interviews, informants negotiate how they want to be known by the stories they develop collaboratively with their audiences. Informants do not reveal an essential self as much as they perform a preferred one, selected from the multiplicity of selves or personas that individuals switch among as they go about their lives. Approaching identity as a "performative struggle over the meanings of experience" (Langellier 2001:3) opens up analytic possibilities that are missed with static conceptions of identity and by essentializing theories that assume the unity of an inner self.

Personal narratives contain many performative features that enable the "local achievement of identity" (Cussins 1998). Tellers intensify words and phrases; they enhance segments with narrative detail, reported speech, appeals to the audience, paralinguistic features and gestures, and body movement (Bauman 1986). Analysts can ask many questions of a narrative segment in terms of performance. In what kind of a story does a narrator place herself? How does she locate herself in relation to the audience, and vice versa? How does she locate characters in relation to one another and in relation to herself? How does she relate to herself, that is, make identity claims about who or what she is (Bamberg 1997b)?

Social positioning in stories—how narrators choose to position audiences, characters, and themselves—is a useful point of entry because "fluid positionings, not fixed roles, are used by people to cope with the situations they find themselves in" (Harré and van Langenhove 1999:17). Narrators can position themselves, for example, as victims of one circumstance or another in their stories, giving over to other characters rather than themselves the power to initiate action. Alternatively, narrators can position themselves as agentic beings who assume control over events and actions, individuals who purposefully initiate and cause action. They can shift among positions, giving themselves active roles in certain scenes and passive roles in others. To create these fluid semantic spaces for themselves, narrators use particular grammatical resources to construct who they are. Verbs, for example, can frame actions as voluntary rather than compulsory. Other grammatical forms intensify vulnerability (Capps and Ochs 1995). These positionings of the self in personal narratives signify the performance of identity. They are enacted in an immediate discursive context, the evolving interview with a listener/questioner, and can be analyzed from detailed transcriptions.

I illustrate this approach by returning to Gita's narrative account in the transcript excerpt above. In the larger research project from which the transcript is taken, I show how the cultural discourse of gender defines women by their marital and child bearing status. In South India, married women face severe stigma when they can not, or choose not to, reproduce (Riessman 2000b). Self-stigma was a recurring theme in my interviews, even as historical developments in contemporary India are enabling some women to resist the "master narrative" of motherhood. Gita deviated from the general pattern. She was beyond childbearing age, and the absence of motherhood did not seem to be a particularly salient topic for her (I was always the one to introduce it); she did not express sadness or negative self-evaluation about not having had children, as younger women did. It turned out that Gita had built a life around principles other than motherhood; she is a lawyer and political activist. Close examination of the narrative reveals precisely how she constructs this preferred, positive identity, solving the problem of stigma and subordination as a childless woman in South India. She resists the dominant cultural narrative about gender identity with an autobiographical account that transforms a personal issue into a public one (Richardson 1990).

Gita carefully positions the audience (me) and various characters in constructing her story, which is, as I noted earlier, a complex performance that I have represented in five scenes. Each scene offers a snapshot of action located in a particular time and setting. Unlike narratives in the discrete story approach (Labov 1982), Gita's narrative is complex in its organization. Attention to how scenes are organized within the performance is my analytic point of entry.

The first two scenes are prompted by an audience request ("Were you ever pregnant?"), my attempt to position Gita in a world of fertility. She reluctantly moves into the role of pregnant woman in these brief scenes, quickly chronicling two pregnancies several years apart (the outcomes of which I attempt to clarify, in lines deleted from the transcript). She does not provide narrative detail, elaborate meanings, or describe emotions associated with the miscarriages; the audience must infer a great deal. Gita constructs the first two scenes with only one character aside from herself, her doctor. She "approached" the doctor, who "asked" her to have a D&C. In a quick aside, she states that the doctor wanted to examine the husband, but we infer that this did not happen. With this utterance, Gita prefigures her husband's responsibility, anticipating the final scene and the moral of the narrative. Gita again casts the doctor as the active agent in Scene 2; she "wanted" and "advised" Gita to take bed rest. Through her choices of verbs and the positioning of characters, Gita constructs scenes in which she has a relatively minor role. From the lack of narrative detail, the audience assumes that the events in the plot up to this point are not particularly salient for Gita.

The narrator's position and the salience of the events change dramatically in the third scene. Gita shifts topics, from pregnancy "to what I already told you," which is the primacy of her political world. She now constructs a scene in which *she* is the central character, the agent of action, a "political leader" in her Kerala community who "had to" participate in a demonstration in Delhi against Mrs. Indira Gandhi, who was seeking reelection. Verbs frame the narrator's intentional actions, situated as political exigencies, and there is considerable narrative elaboration, which is a sharp contrast to the spare, "passive" grammar of the previous scenes, in which Gita was the object of the doctor's actions.[6] As Gita locates her private fertility story in the larger public story of India's socialist movement, the audience is not left wondering which is more important. Ignoring her doctor's advice "to take bed rest" during her second pregnancy, she traveled to Delhi to participate in a mass demonstration, which probably involved a three-day train trip in 1975. Despite her return by plane and a 16-day nursing home stay for "bleeding," the audience infers that Gita lost the pregnancy (a fact I confirm a few moments later in lines not included here). She constructs a narrative around oppositional worlds—family life on one side and the socialist movement of India on the other. The personal and the political occupy separate spheres of action and, as such, do not morally infringe upon each other.

Moving along, in the next two scenes Gita shifts the plot to the family world. In Scene 4, she again introduces her husband as a character and reports that he was "very angry" at her "social work," meaning her political activism. She communicates a one-way conversation; Gita does not give herself a speaking role. She positions herself only as the object of her husband's angry speech. We do not know what she said to him, if anything. Her passive positioning in this scene contrasts with her activity in the previous one. Is she displaying here the typical practice in South Indian families, which is that wives are expected to defer to their husbands' authority (Riessman 2000b)? If so, her choice of language is instructive; he said "this and that." Could she be belittling her husband's anger and directives? She concludes Scene 4 with a factual utterance: "But afterwards I never became—[pregnant]."

In the fifth and final lengthy scene, Gita introduces new characters—her parents-in-law, an infertility specialist, a sister-in-law—and an intricate plot before the narrative moves toward its moral point, which is that Gita's infertility is not her responsibility. The final scene is most elaborate, suggesting importance. Gita's performance of identity is quite vivid here. She begins by constructing a passive, stigmatized position for herself: Her in-laws "brought" her for treatment to a gynecologist in the major South Indian city where the parents live because "they thought I had some defect." As in earlier scenes involving pregnancy, others suggest or initiate action.[7] She intensifies meaning and thematic importance with repetition ("defect") in the next stanza; the gynecologist determined after a lengthy examination that Gita has "no defect at all." She is "perfectly" normal. Blame for her infertility, Gita intimates, resides elsewhere. Using the linguistic device of reported speech, she performs several conversations on the topic of getting her husband tested. Everyone is enlisted in the effort—gynecologist, sister-in-law—but he refuses: "No, no, I will not go to a lady doctor." Nor is he willing to have his sperm tested in a laboratory. (Gita returned several other times in our interview to his refusal to be tested.) The narrator has crafted a narrative performance in which she has no responsibility whatsoever.[8] Readers might question Gita's attributions. She ignored her physician's advice to "take bed rest" during her second pregnancy, choosing to travel instead to Delhi. She gave primacy to political commitments, valuing work in the socialist movement over her gendered position in the home. She was also "40 or 41" years old when she was finally examined by a specialist. Age may have been a factor. Gita had conceived twice, but could not sustain pregnancies, implying a possible "defect." Gita's performance, however, suggests how she wants to be known as a "perfectly" normal woman "with no defect at all." The way she organizes scenes within the narrative performance, the choices she makes about positioning, and the grammatical resources she employs put forth the preferred identity of committed political activist, not disappointed would-be mother.

Later in the interview (in a portion not extracted here), she supported this interpretation. Resisting once again my positioning of her in the world of biological fertility, she said explicitly, "Because I do not have [children],

I have no disappointments, because mine is a big family." She continued with a listing of many brothers, their children, and particular nieces who "come here every evening . . . to take their meals." With these words, she challenged my bipolar notions of parenthood—either you have children or you don't. Gita performs a gender identity that resists the master cultural narrative in place in her world: that biological motherhood is the central axis of identity for women. Elsewhere, I historicize Gita's life chances and locate her in an evolving cultural discourse about women's "proper" place in modern India, a "developing" nation that is formulating new spaces other than home and field in which women may labor (Riessman 2000b).

The analytic strategy I have illustrated is generalizable. Narrators can emplot events in their lives in a variety of ways. They "select and assemble experiences and events so they contribute collectively to the intended point of the story . . . why it is being told, in just this way, in just this setting" (Mishler 2000a:8). How narrators accomplish their situated stories conveys a great deal about the presentation of self (Goffman 1959). To make the process visible, we can analyze scenes in relation to one another, how narrators position characters and themselves, and we can "unpack" the grammatical resources they select to make their moral points clear to the listener. Interpretation requires close analysis of how narrators position audiences, too, and, reciprocally, how the audience positions the narrator. Identities are constituted through such performative actions, within the context of the interview itself as a performance. Audiences, of course, may "read" events differently than narrators do, resulting in contested meanings.

The "Truths" of Personal Narrative

I stated at the outset that my approach to narrative analysis assumes not objectivity but, instead, positionality and subjectivity. The perspectives of both narrator and analyst can come into view. As the Personal Narratives Group (1989) articulates, "truths" rather than "the" truth of personal narrative is the watchword.

Not all scholars who work with personal narratives would agree (see Atkinson 2002; Fontana 2002; Cándida Smith 2002). Daniel Bertaux (1995:2) believes that "every life story contains a large proportion of factual data which can be verified," for example, with respect to the dates and places of biographical events. Locating himself in the "realist" research tradition, Bertaux argues that informants' stories collected from the same milieu can serve as documentary sources for investigating the world "out there." Although acknowledging that informants do not "tell us the whole truth and nothing but the truth," Bertaux (1995:2) claims that by collecting many stories from the same milieu, a researcher can uncover "recurrent patterns concerning collective phenomena or share collective experience in a particular milieu."

Those working from social constructionist or performative perspectives approach the issue of truth differently. Verification of the "facts" of lives is less salient than understanding the changing meanings of events for the individuals involved, and how these, in turn, are located in history and culture. Personal narratives are, at core, meaning-making units of discourse. They are of interest precisely because narrators interpret the past in stories rather than reproduce the past as it was.

Returning to Gita's narrative account of infertility, it is irrelevant whether the events "really" occurred just as she reports them. Gita was one informant in a larger project about identity for childless women, and she clearly performs one strategic solution to the problem infertility poses for her; she is "perfectly" normal, with "no defect at all."

As noted earlier, it is possible to question her causal attributions. It also goes without saying that the passage of time since the miscarriages has softened their emotional impact, and consequently she can be silent about her feelings. As all narrators do, Gita presents past events from the vantage point of present realities and values. Not unlike other women I interviewed who were beyond childbearing age, she minimizes the significance of biological motherhood and emphasizes, instead, occupational and political identities. The truths of narrative accounts lie not in their faithful representation of a past world, but in the shifting connections they forge among past, present, and future.

The complex relationships among narrative, time, and memory are currently a vital topic of research and theorizing (Freeman 1998, 2002; for a review, see Hinchman and Hinchman 1997). Storytelling among those with chronic illnesses offers a case in point (Morse 2002). Serious illness interrupts lives (Charmaz 1991) and occasions the "call for stories" (Frank 1995:53). Friends want to know "what happened," and stories provide maps for the ill themselves "to repair the damage that illness has done to the ill person's sense of where she is in life, and where she may be going" (Frank

1995:53). Yet the storylines or plots into which the seriously ill pour their experience may be at variance with biomedical plots. Patients with incurable cancers, for example, construct "restitution" narratives that suggest positive end points, whereas others represent themselves in "chaos" narratives where continuity between past and future is unclear (Frank 1995). Oncologists are often asked about time, and they construct narratives of hope for families that blur endings and leave the future ambiguous (Good et al. 1994). For both practitioner and patient, a storyline locates the threatening illness in an imagined life trajectory (Mattingly 1994; Riessman 1990b).

The meanings of life events are not fixed or constant; rather, they evolve, influenced by subsequent life events. According to Mishler (1999:5), "As we access and make sense of events and experiences in our pasts and how they are related to our current selves, we change their meanings." Ends beget beginnings, in other words (Mishler 2000a). Personal narratives—the stories we tell to ourselves, to each other, and to researchers—offer a unique window into these formations and reformations: "We continually restory our pasts, shifting the relative significance of different events for whom we have become, discovering connections we had previously been unaware of, repositioning ourselves and others in our networks of relationships" (Mishler 1999:5).

A useful way to see how identities can shift over time is to look at "turning points" in stories—moments when the narrator signifies a radical shift in the expected course of a life. For example, in my research on divorce, it was common for informants to report moments when they realized retrospectively, "This is it"—the marital relationship had crossed a line beyond repair. Such turning points often coincided with incidents of physical violence, directed toward either the spouse or a child. One woman said: "That was the last straw. You just don't hit me . . . I wasn't going to stay around to be hit again." Another woman, who had been physically abused for years, spoke of "the final blow": Her husband "punched our oldest daughter across the living room . . . if he was going to start doing that to the kids, that was it." A divorcing man told a long narrative about his wife's open infidelity, culminating in a moment when he hit her. He said to himself "This is it . . . there wasn't any reason to be there other than to hurt" (Riessman 1990a). Such turning points fundamentally change the meaning of past experiences and consequently individuals' identities. "They open up directions of movement that were not anticipated by and could not be predicted by their pasts"—an insight Mishler (1999:7–8) applies to the narratives of sexual abuse survivors. Past abuse is given new significance as women move out of destructive relationships and construct new identities.

The "trustworthiness" of narrative accounts cannot be evaluated using traditional correspondence criteria. There is no canonical approach to validation in interpretive work, no recipes or formulas. (For a review of several approaches that may be useful in certain instances, see Riessman 1993:64–69.)

Conclusion

I began this chapter with an account of my difficulty in doing research interviews with individuals whose lives had been disrupted and being initially annoyed at interviewees' lengthy and convoluted responses. Since then, many investigators have given a name to my problem—these were "narratives"—and offered analytic solutions for working with interview responses that do not require fragmenting them. The field now named *narrative analysis* has grown rapidly, and no review can be complete and summarize the many types of work that are evident today. I have purposively bounded the field, focusing on the personal narrative and emphasizing the performative dimension, but I have also pointed the reader toward other perspectives. (For reviews and typologies of research strategies, see Cortazzi 1993; Langellier 1989; Mishler 1995; Riessman 1993.)

Narrative analysis has its critics, of course (Atkinson 1997; Atkinson and Silverman 1997). Its methods are not appropriate for studies of large numbers of nameless, faceless subjects. The approach is slow and painstaking, requiring attention to subtlety: nuances of speech, the organization of a response, relations between researcher and subject, social and historical contexts. It is not suitable for investigators who seek a clear and unobstructed view of subjects' lives, and the analytic detail required may seem excessive to those who orient to language as a transparent medium.

Narrative methods can be combined with other forms of qualitative analysis (for an example, see Riessman 1990a), even with quantitative analysis.[9] Some fancy epistemological footwork is required, because the interpretive perspective that typically underlies narrative work is very different from the realist assumptions of some forms of qualitative analysis and certainly of quantification. Combining methods forces investigators to confront troublesome philosophical issues and to educate readers about them. Science cannot be spoken in a singular, universal voice. Any

methodological standpoint is, by definition, partial, incomplete, and historically contingent. Diversity of representations is needed. Narrative analysis
is one approach, not a panacea; it is suitable for some situations and not
others. It is a useful addition to the stockpot of social research methods,
bringing critical flavors to the surface that otherwise get lost in the brew.
Narrative analysis allows for the systematic study of personal experience
and meaning. The approach enables investigators to study the "active, self-
shaping quality of human thought, the power of stories to create and re-
fashion personal identity (Hinchman and Hinchman 1997:xiv).

Narratives are a particularly significant genre for representing and analyzing identity in its multiple guises in different contexts. The methods
allow for the systematic study of experience and, for feminist researchers
such as myself, the changing meanings of conditions that affect women
disproportionately, including domestic violence, reproductive illness, and
poverty. Personal narratives provide windows into lives that confront the
constraints of circumstances. Attention to personal narratives in interviews
opens discursive spaces for research subjects, representing them as agents
acting in life worlds of moral complexity.

Author's Note: I thank Elliot Mishler, Paul Rosenblatt, Jay Gubrium, and Jim
Holstein for comments on earlier versions of this chapter. The Narrative
Study Group provided valuable input for my analysis of Gita's narrative.

Notes

1. There are, of course, narrative sites other than interviews (see Ochs, Smith,
   and Taylor 1989; Polanyi 1985; Gubrium and Holstein 2000).
2. There is lively philosophical debate in this area about whether primary experience is "disordered"—that is, whether narrators create order out of chaos
   (see Hinchman and Hinchman 1997:xix–xx).
3. I have grouped lines about a single topic into stanzas, which I have then
   grouped into scenes. Because of the narrative's direct performative reference, I have organized it into "scenes" rather than "strophes," as Gee (1986)
   does. I have deleted brief exchanges between Gita and me, questions I ask to
   clarify what she has said, which are marked ==.
4. Transcriptions, of course, are themselves theory-laden; how we choose to represent spoken dialogue is not independent of theoretical goals (see Ochs
   1979; Mishler 1991; Kvale 1996:chap. 9; Poland 1995).

5. Lisa Capps and Elinor Ochs (1995) provide a compelling analysis of conversations with a single narrator over several years. They combine textual and conversational approaches in their study of the discourse of a woman suffering from agoraphobia (severe panic attacks).

6. The verb construction *had to* is, in fact, ambiguous. It might refer to others' expectations that Gita participate in the political demonstration, a consequence of her leadership role in the community, or it might refer to an "inner" compulsion to participate, arising out of her own political conviction and priorities. The narrative context supports the latter interpretation.

7. Infertility is a family event in the Indian context, and husbands' relatives often suggest and initiate treatment for daughters-in-law, including medical and religious cures (Riessman 2000a, 2000b).

8. The physiological responsibility for infertility in this and the other cases is unclear. India's infertility clinics require both spouses to be tested, and about a third of the time the problem lies in the sperm. Elsewhere, I have described Indian women's management of male responsibility; they do not disclose it to deflect stigma but, in an effort to keep families together, absorb the "fault" themselves (Riessman 2000b).

9. The material in this paragraph is adapted from Riessman (1993:70).

References

Atkinson, P. 1997. Narrative turn or blind alley? *Qualitative Health Research* 7:325–344.

Atkinson, P. and D. Silverman. 1997. Kundera's *Immortality:* The interview society and the invention of self. *Qualitative Inquiry* 3:304–325.

Atkinson, R. 2002. The life story interview. In *Handbook of interview research: Context and method,* J. F. Gubium and J. A. Holstein, (Eds.). 121–140. Thousand Oaks, CA: Sage.

Attanucci, J. 1991. Changing subjects: Growing up and growing older. *Journal of Moral Education* 20:317–328.

Bamberg, M. G. W, ed. 1997a. Oral versions of personal experience: Three decades of narrative analysis (special issue). *Journal of Narrative and Life History* 7(1–4).

——. 1997b. Positioning between structure and performance. In Oral versions of personal experience: Three decades of narrative analysis (special issue), edited by M. G. W. Bamberg. *Journal of Narrative and Life History* 7:335–342.

Bamberg, M. G. W. and A. McCabe. 1998. Editorial. *Narrative Inquiry* 8(1):iii–v.

Bauman, R. 1986. *Story, performance, and event: Contextual studies of oral narrative.* Cambridge: Cambridge UP.

Behar, R. 1993. *Translated woman: Crossing the border with Esperanza's story.* Boston: Beacon.

Bell, S. E. 1988. Becoming a political woman: The reconstruction and interpretation of experience through stories. In *Gender and discourse: The power of talk.* A. D. Todd and S. Fisher, (Eds.). Norwood, NJ: Ablex.

——. 1999. Narratives and lives: Women's health politics and the diagnosis of cancer for DES daughters. *Narrative Inquiry* 9(2):1–43.

——. 2000. Experiencing illness in/and narrative. In *Handbook of medical sociology,* 5th ed. C. E. Bird, P. Conrad, and A. M. Fremont (Eds.). Upper Saddle River, NJ: Prentice Hall.

Bertaux, D. 1995. A response to Thierry Kochuyt's "Biographic and empiricist Illusions: A reply to recent criticism." *Biography and Society* (annual newsletter of Research Committee 38, International Sociological Association), 2–6.

Boje, D. M. 1991. The storytelling organization: A study of story performance in an office-supply firm. *Administrative Science Quarterly* 36:106–26.

Bruner, J. 1986. *Actual minds, possible worlds.* Cambridge, MA: Harvard UP.

——. 1990. *Acts of meaning.* Cambridge, MA: Harvard UP.

Cándida Smith, R. 2002. Analytic strategies for oral history interviews. In *Handbook of interview research: Context and method.* J. F. Gubium and J. A. Holstein (Eds.). 711–732. Thousand Oaks, CA: Sage.

Capps, L. and E. Ochs. 1995. *Constructing panic: The discourse of agoraphobia.* Cambridge, MA: Harvard UP.

Carr, D. 1986. *Time, narrative, and history.* Bloomington: Indiana UP.

Charmaz, K. 1991. *Good days, bad days: The self in chronic illness and time.* New Brunswick, NJ: Rutgers UP.

Charon, R. 1986. To render the lives of patients. *Literature and Medicine* 5:58–74.

Chase, S. E. 1995. *Ambiguous empowerment: The work narratives of women school superintendents.* Amherst: University of Massachusetts.

Cortazzi, M. 1993. *Narrative analysis.* London: Falmer.

Cronon, W. 1992. A place for stories: Nature, history, and narrative. *Journal of American History* 78:1347–1376.

Cussins, C. M. 1998. Ontological choreography: Agency for women patients in an infertility clinic. In *Differences in medicine: Unraveling practices, techniques, and bodies.* M. Berg and S. Mol. Durham (Eds.). NC: Duke UP.

Czarniawska, B. 2002. Narrative, interviews, and organizations. In *Handbook of interview research: Context and method.* J. F. Gubium and J. A. Holstein (Eds.). 733–750. Thousand Oaks, CA: Sage.

Dean, R. G. 1995. Stories of AIDS: The use of narrative as an approach to understanding in an AIDS support group. *Clinical Social Work Journal* 23:287–304.

DeVault, M. L. 1991. Talking and listening from women's standpoint: Feminist strategies for interviewing and analysis. *Social Problems* 37:96–116.

———. 1999. *Liberating method: Feminism and social research*. Philadelphia: Temple UP.

Fontana, A. 2002. Postmodern trends in interviewing. In *Handbook of interview research: Context and method*. J. F. Gubium and J. A. Holstein (Eds.). 161–176. Thousand Oaks, CA: Sage.

Frank, A. W. 1995. *The wounded storyteller: Body, illness, and ethics*. Chicago: U of Chicago P.

Freeman, M. 1998. Mythical time, historical time, and the narrative fabric of the self. *Narrative Inquiry* 8(1):1–24.

———. 2002. The presence of what is missing: Memory, poetry, and the ride home. In *Between fathers and sons: Critical incident narratives on the development of men's lives*. R. J. Pellegrini and T. R. Sarbin (Eds.). 165–176. New York: Haworth.

Gamson, W. A. (1999.) "How story telling can be empowering." Presented at the Conference Toward a Sociology of Culture and Cognition, Rutgers University, New Brunswick, NJ.

Gee, J. P. 1986. Units in the production of narrative discourse. *Discourse Processes* 9:391–422.

———. 1991. A linguistic approach to narrative. *Journal of Narrative and Life History* 1:15–39.

Goffman, E. 1959. *The presentation of self in everyday life*. Garden City, NY: Doubleday.

———. 1981. *Forms of talk*. Philadelphia: U of Pennsylvania P.

Good, M.-J. D., T. Munakata, Y. Kobayashi, C. Mattingly, and B. J. Good. 1994. Oncology and narrative time. *Social Science and Medicine* 38:855–862.

Greenhalgh, T. and B. Hurwitz (Eds.). 1998. *Narrative based medicine: Dialogue and discourse in clinical practice*. London: BMJ.

Gubrium, J. F. and J. A. Holstein (Eds.). 2000. *Institutional selves: Troubled identities in a postmodern world*. New York: Oxford UP.

Harré, R. and L. van Langenhove. 1999. Introducing positioning theory. In *Positioning theory*. R. Harré and L. van Langenhove (Eds.). 14–31. Malden, MA: Blackwell.

Hinchman, L. P. and S. K. Hinchman. 1997. Introduction. In *memory, identity, community: The idea of narrative in the human sciences*. L.P. Hinchman and S. K. Hinchman (Eds.). Albany: State U of New York P.

Holstein, J. A. and J. F. Gubrium. 2000. *The self we live by: Narrative identity in a postmodern world*. New York: Oxford UP.

Hunter, K. M. 1991. *Doctors' stories: The narrative structure of medical knowledge*. Princeton, NJ: Princeton UP.

Hydén, L. C. 1997. Illness and narrative. *Sociology of Health and Illness* 19:48–69.

Jefferson, G. 1979. Sequential aspects of storytelling in conversation. In *Studies in the organization of conversational interaction*. J. Schenkein (Ed.). New York: Academic.

Josselson, R. and A. Lieblich (Eds.). 1993. *The narrative study of lives*, Vol. 1, *The narrative study of lives*. Newbury Park, CA: Sage.

Kaminsky, M. 1992. Introduction. In *Remembered lives: The work of ritual, storytelling, and growing older*. B. Myerhoff (Ed.). Ann Arbor: University of Michigan.

Kleinman, A. 1.988. *The illness narratives: Suffering, healing, and the human condition*. New York: Basic.

Kong, T. S. K., D. Mahoney, and K. Plummer. 2002. Queering the interview. In *Handbook of interview research: Context and method*. J. F. Gubium and J. A. Holstein (Eds.). 239–258. Thousand Oaks, CA: Sage.

Kvale, S. 1996. *InterViews: An introduction to qualitative research interviewing*. Thousand Oaks, CA: Sage.

Labov, W. 1982. Speech actions and reactions in personal narrative. In *Analyzing discourse: Text and talk*. D. Tannen (Ed.). Washington, DC: Georgetown UP.

Laird, J. 1988. Women and stories: Restorying women's self-constructions. In *Women in families: A framework for family therapy*. M. McGoldrick, C. Anderson, and F. Walsh (Eds.). New York: Norton.

Langellier, K. 1989. Personal narratives: Perspectives on theory and research, *Text and Performance Quarterly* 9:243–276.

——. 2001. "You're marked": Breast cancer, tattoo, and the narrative performance of identity. In *Narrative and identity: Studies in autobiography, self and culture*. J. Brockmeier and D. Carbaugh (Eds.). Amsterdam: John Benjamins.

Laslett, B. 1999. Personal narratives as sociology. *Contemporary Sociology* 28:391–401.

Legal storytelling (special issue). 1989. *Michigan Law Review* 87(8).

Linde, C. 1993. *Life stories: The creation of coherence*. New York: Oxford UP.

Mattingly, C. 1994. The concept of therapeutic "emplotment." *Social Science and Medicine* 38:811–822.

——. 1998. *Healing dramas and clinical plots: The narrative structure of experience*. New York: Cambridge UP.

Mattingly, C. and L. C. Garro. (Eds.). 2000. *Narrative and cultural construction of illness and healing*. Berkeley: U of California P.

McLeod, J. 1997. *Narrative and Psychotherapy*. Thousand Oaks, CA: Sage.

Michaels, S. 1981. "Sharing time": Children's narrative styles and differential access to literacy. *Language and Society* 10:423–442.

Mills, C.W. 1959. *The sociological imagination*. New York: Oxford UP.

Mishler, E. G. 1986. *Research interviewing: Context and narrative*. Cambridge, MA: Harvard UP.

——. 1991. Representing discourse: The rhetoric of transcription, *Journal of Narrative and Life History* 1:225–280.

——. 1995. Models of narrative analysis: A typology. *Journal of Narrative and Life History* 5:87–123.

——. 1997. Narrative accounts in clinical and research interviews. In *The construction of professional discourse*. B. L. Gunnarsson, P. Linell, and B. Norberg (Eds.). London: Longman.

——. (1999). "Time's double arrow: Re-presenting the past in life history studies." Presented at Radcliffe Murray Center conference, Lives in Context: The Study of Human Development, Cambridge, MA.

——. (2000a). "Narrative and the paradox of temporal ordering: How ends beget beginnings." Presented at the Conference on Discourse and Identity, Clark University.

——. 2000b. *Storylines: Craftartists' narratives of identity.* Cambridge, MA: Harvard UP.

Morse, J. M. 2002. Interviewing the ill. In *Handbook of interview research: Context and method.* J. F. Gubium and J. A. Holstein (Eds.). 317–330. Thousand Oaks, CA: Sage.

Mumby, D. K. 1993. *Narrative and social control: Critical perspectives.* Newbury Park, CA: Sage.

Myerhoff, B. 1978. *Number our days.* New York: Simon and Schuster.

Ochs, E. 1979. Transcription as theory. In *Developmental pragmatics.* E. Ochs and B.B. Schieffelin (Eds.). New York: Academic.

Ochs, E., R. Smith, and C. Taylor. 1989. Dinner narratives as detective stories. *Cultural Dynamics* 2:238–257.

Personal Narratives Group, eds. 1989. Truths. In *Interpreting women's lives: Feminist theory and personal narratives.* Bloomington: Indiana UP.

Plummer, K. 1995. *Telling sexual stories: Power, change and social worlds.* New York: Routledge.

Poland, D. B. 1995. Transcription quality as an aspect of rigor in qualitative research. *Qualitative Inquiry* 1:290–310.

——. 2002. Transcription quality. In *Handbook of interview research: Context and method,* J. F. Gubium and J. A. Holstein (Eds.). 629–650. Thousand Oaks, CA: Sage.

Polanyi, L. 1985. Conversational storytelling. In *Handbook of discourse analysis,* Vol. 3. T. A. van Dijk Ed. 183–201. London: Academic.

Polkinghorne, D. E. 1988. *Narrative knowing and the human sciences.* Albany: State University of New York.

Reinharz, S. and S. E. Chase. 2002. Interviewing women. In *Handbook of interview research: Context and method,* J. F. Gubium and J. A. Holstein (Eds.). 221–239. Thousand Oaks, CA: Sage.

Richardson, L. 1990. *Writing strategies: Reaching diverse audiences.* Newbury Park, CA: Sage.

——. 1990a. *Divorce talk: Women and men make sense of personal relationships*. New Brunswick, NJ: Rutgers UP.

——. 1990b. Strategic uses of narrative in the presentation of self and illness. *Social Science and Medicine* 30:1195–1200.

——. 1993. *Narrative analysis*. Newbury Park, CA: Sage.

——. 2000a. "Even if we don't have children [we] can live": Stigma and infertility in South India. In *Narrative and cultural construction of illness and healing*, C. Mattingly and L. C. Garro. (Eds.). Berkeley: U of California P.

——. 2000b. Stigma and everyday resistance practices: Childless women in South India. *Gender and Society* 14:111–135.

Riessman, C. K. 1987. When gender is not enough: Women interviewing women. *Gender and Society* 1:172–207.

Rosaldo, R. 1989. *Culture and truth: The remaking of social analysis*. Boston: Beacon.

Rosenwald, G. C. and R. L. Ochberg, eds. 1992. *Storied lives: The cultural politics of self-understanding*. New Haven, CT: Yale UP.

Sandelowski, M. 1991. Telling stories: Narrative approaches in qualitative research. *Image: Journal of Nursing Scholarship* 23(3):161–166.

Sarbin, T.R., ed. 1986. *Narrative psychology: The storied nature of human conduct*. New York: Praeger.

Skultans, V. 1999. Narratives of the body and history: Illness in judgement on the Soviet past. *Sociology of Health and Illness* 21:310–128.

White, H. 1987. *The content of the form: Narrative discourse and historical representation*. Baltimore: Johns Hopkins UP.

White, M. and D. Epston. 1990. *Narrative means to therapeutic ends*. New York: Norton.

Williams, G. 1984. The genesis of chronic illness: Narrative reconstruction. *Sociology of Health and Illness* 6:175–200.

Young, K. G. 1987. *Taleworlds and storyrealms: The phenomenology of narrative*. Boston: Martinus Nijhoff.

[8]

"We Have a Situation Here!"

Using Situation Analysis for Health and Social Research

LESLEY GREEN RENNIS, LOURDES HERNÁNDEZ-CORDERO,
KJERSTI SCHMITZ, AND MINDY THOMPSON FULLILOVE

This chapter describes situation analysis, a method that allows researchers to gain a deeper understanding of an issue with the end goal of recommending targeted intervention strategies. Situation analysis examines a selected interpersonal episode or complex state of affairs (the situation) in the context of the larger narrative of which it is a part (the embedding drama). Using situation analysis, we can understand how larger social systems influence and constrain smaller ones, how epidemics impact individuals and families, and how seemingly isolated incidents are connected to one another. In short, situation analysis creates a detailed description of the situation and links that particular situation to the larger drama of which it is a part in order to identify the factors driving the situation and highlight the most useful points for intervention. Situation analysis is ideal for social work because of its emphasis on vulnerable populations, on the person-in-situation, on interactions between individuals and the physical and service environments, and on targeting interventions.

Our team, the Community Research Group (CRG) of Columbia University and New York State Psychiatric Institute, has used situation analysis to study care for women with AIDS (CRG 1999); neighborhood violence (M. T. Fullilove et al. 1998); neighborhood renovation (Fullilove, Green, and Fullilove 1999); fatal school shootings (Fullilove, Arias, and Nuñez

2003); and urban renewal (M. T. Fullilove 2001).[1] This chapter is based on the methods we learned to use while conducting those studies.

We first became interested in the concept of situations based on the work of Zwi and Cabral (1991). They recommended that the identification of high-risk situations would be an aid in the prevention of AIDS. They proposed that high-risk situations were, ". . . the range of social, economic and political forces affecting groups, placing them at particularly high risk of HIV infection" (1527). Much of social science and nearly all of biomedical research has ignored the larger context. Yet this advice made sense to us. We had been studying emerging health problems in poor communities since 1986 and had already seen how changing contexts shifted patterns of disease.

In the period between 1986 and 2000, we studied epidemics that arrived one after the other: AIDS, crack cocaine, violence, trauma-related mental illness caused by violence, multi-drug resistant tuberculosis, asthma, and obesity and lack of exercise (Fullilove, Fullilove, Bowser, et al. 1990; Fullilove, Wiley, Fullilove, et al. 1992; Fullilove, Lown, and Fullilove 1992; Fullilove, Fullilove, Smith, et al. 1993; Wallace, Wallace, Andrews, et al. 1995; Fullilove, Fullilove, Northridge, et al. 1999). At the same time, our research revealed that, in poor neighborhoods, social and physical conditions were in rapid decline: Dilapidated housing was being lost to fire, creating a severe housing famine; families were becoming smaller and smaller, as two-parent families became the minority and one-parent families the majority of all families; and, with the progression of deindustrialization without a concomitant enhancement in educational opportunity, legitimate employment declined and work in the underground economy escalated; as drugs became a common feature of everyday life, the police presence increased, and more and more people were sent to prison (M. T. Fullilove 2000).

Serial epidemics, massive outbreaks of violence, collapse of families and neighborhoods: How were we to understand these events and their impact? At first, we were interested in understanding each process on its own terms. But as the epidemics piled up in the poor neighborhoods we were studying, we realized that this one-at-a-time approach was misleading. We needed to put the AIDS epidemic in the context of the crack epidemic, just as we needed to put the epidemic of violence-related mental illness in the context of crack and AIDS. Zwi and Cabral's (1991) recommendation to understand these high-risk situations in context helped us situate each epidemic within a much larger context of multiple social, political, and economic forces.

Subsequently, as we examined each epidemic in context, we realized situations are events of great interest in and of themselves. It was the line of sociological research conducted under the rubric of defining the situation that gave us tools to understand the situation (Stebbins 1986). In effect, the definition of the situation takes the researcher into the interior of an interpersonal episode so that the interactions may be named and interpreted. This illustrious body of work has delineated the factors that compose a situation, providing a strong foundation for fieldwork. Thus while Zwi and Cabral (1991) were urging scientists to look at the larger context—what we might call the exterior of the situation—the definition of the situation takes us to the heart of the interaction, a versatile and useful scientific tool. The method of situation analysis has been developed by the contributions of many scholars, highlighted by a classic paper by J. Clyde Mitchell (1983), and developed in the studies conducted by such scholars as Fagan and Wilkinson (1998), Meyrowitz (1968), and Triandis, Chen, and Chan (1998).

To understand both the interior and exterior of the situation, we adopted situation analysis. Using this method, we can understand the ways in which spatial change influences city life (Héon-Klin et al. 2000). We can detail the ways in which an outbreak of illness is affecting neighborhood life (Watkins and Fullilove 1999). We have the ability to grasp the complex intercultural strains that follow a terrorist act in a large city (Fullilove, Hernández-Cordero, Madoff, and Fullilove 2004).

This chapter will present situation analysis in three parts: In the first section, we will review the basic concepts of the situation and its definition; then we will describe how a situation analysis is conducted; and finally, we will illustrate these ideas with an example from our own work.

Situations: Definitions and Contexts

"We Have a Situation Here!"

Imagine the scene in the movie, *Saving Private Ryan*, in which American soldiers are threatening to kill a German prisoner. One of the Americans, trying to stop the murder, shouts, "Sergeant! We have a situation here!" The sergeant, who was attending to other matters, immediately takes charge and diffuses the tension.

By saying, "We have a situation here!" one person signals to another that something is happening that demands attention and management.

"We have a situation here!" is a command statement, and people respond by acting: They run to see an accident; they pick up a telephone to get more information; they shout commands to others who need to act; or they begin to ask questions of those around them.

Thought Experiment #1

Imagine what you would like to know after reading these headlines that appeared in newspapers and magazines in 1998–99:

- Kosovo situation worsens as Serbs press offensive, *New York Times*, March 21, 1999
- One family's situation, *New York Times*, February 28, 1999
- Situation normal, *New York Times*, October 24, 1998
- Definition of soldiers' situation could determine their treatment, *USA Today*, April 2, 1999
- "We know the situation," *Wall Street Journal*, October 30 1998
- Talking through difficult situations, *USA Today*, August 4, 1998
- Commodities corner: Tense situation, *Barron's*, July 22, 1998
- FAA on top of the situation, *USA Today*, May 14, 1998

We have established two facts: (1) that the sentence "We have a situation here!" incites action and (2) the action may be to act or to learn more about the situation. That is because situation is an indefinite noun. A situation is, as noted by Webster's, an unusual state of affairs, a particular or striking complex of affairs.

Webster's Dictionary offers the following definitions for the word *situation*.

- 1a: the way in which something is placed in relation to its surroundings; b: site (archaic: locality)
- 2: (archaic: state of health)
- 3a: position or place of employment: post, job; b: position in life: status
- 4: position with respect to conditions and circumstances (the military ~ remains obscure)
- 5a: relative position or combination of circumstances at a certain moment; b: a critical, trying, or unusual state of affairs: problem; c: a particular or striking complex of affairs at a stage in the action of a narrative or drama.

Defining the Situation

If a situation is an affair, we might well ask, "But what is the affair?" In do-ing so, we are engaging in an important, indeed universal, human act by which we go from the general sense that something is up to a precise ac-count of what is taking place. Social scientists call this process defining the situation. We may say that this is the process by which an individual comes to understand the structure of events going on around him. As a cognitive exercise, it is an effort to separate the signal from the noise, to differenti-ate figure from ground, to link the dots that reveal a given shape. People are always defining situations. It is such an important act that English and other languages contain hundreds, if not thousands, of words and phrases that name situations. Some common examples are: ambushed, marooned, invaded, deprived, bedazzled, and displaced. These important words are shorthand for complex affairs: People can both name the situation from the constellation of events and list the events from the situation name.

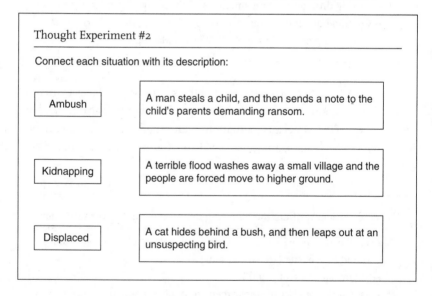

Thought Experiment #2

Connect each situation with its description:

| Ambush | A man steals a child, and then sends a note to the child's parents demanding ransom. |

| Kidnapping | A terrible flood washes away a small village and the people are forced move to higher ground. |

| Displaced | A cat hides behind a bush, and then leaps out at an unsuspecting bird. |

The great advantage of defining a situation is that it delineates from the universe of all possible next steps a relatively small number of highly relevant actions. At this point, people can act in a much more focused way pointed at achieving a resolution of the crisis. Once all the actors have en-gaged with the problem, the situation will play out according to the actors' skills, resources, setting, and culture.

> Thought Experiment #3
>
> Define what might happen next in each of the situations in Thought Experiment #2.
>
> Are the actions the same?
>
> If different, why are they different?

Sociologist Michael Argyle proposed a functional theory of situations, built on a synthesis of various schools in situation research. He proposed that situations can be studied by understanding the following features:

> ... the goals (there may be more than one), the elements of the repertoire in terms of their modality (verbal and nonverbal actions and sequences of behavior), the roles (players and positions, leadership, division of labor), the rules governing the interaction (including any sanctions and norms operating), the skills and difficulties needed, the environmental setting (including social proximity, crowding, orientation, color, furniture, decoration, and equipment), and the concepts used, which he refers to as salience dimensions (Ross and Ferreira-Pinto 2000:63–64).

> When you are investigating a situation:
>
> - Learn the goals of each of the different characters;
> - Identify the set of steps that people followed;
> - Learn more about the roles people played;
> - Get people to explain the rules that governed their actions;
> - Try to figure out what skills people brought to the situation;
> - Investigate the obstacles they faced;
> - List the physical and social characteristics of the setting; and
> - Learn about people's values, ideas, and concepts.

Because people have imperfect methods for gathering data and decoding its meaning, the actual definition of a situation may be wrong. This does not stop people from acting. In fact, one of the earliest and most intriguing observations about situations —and one that has informed 80 years of subsequent work in this area (Argyle 1981; Stebbins 1986)—is the Thomas theorem, which posits, "If men define situations as real, they are real in their consequences" (1928:571–572). The Thomases pointed out that people acting on a misperception can make a mistaken idea come true. For example, unfounded rumors can precipitate a run on a bank and cause it to fail. At the heart of the study of situations is an appreciation for the ways in which "what I thought I saw" is not only an essential guide to group and individual action but also helps us understand how the unreal can suddenly become real.

The Embedding Context

In the preceding paragraphs, we have suggested that we define situations by distinguishing some behaviors from a background of actions and events. This background activity is the embedding context for the situation under study, but it must be studied in its own right. The embedding context has many dimensions, such as politics, culture, history, social and physical structures, and social constructs of race, class, and gender. It refers to the macro forces influencing the micro interactions we study in a given situation. For example, politics and power relationships define who has access to and control of resources. The history of a neighborhood, a city, a region, and a country (and increasingly global history as well) has created local realities that frame the current encounter. Social structures such as family, church, government, and their permutations and ever-changing rules of conduct influence players' loyalties, rights, and responsibilities. Physical structures shape the relationships between the physical space within which the drama takes place and its surroundings. Social constructs of race, class and gender guide interactions as well. Each and every one of these dimensions—and the tensions and conflicts among them—create the embedding context.

Many of these factors have objective aspects, but perceptions and perspectives operate at group, as well as individual, levels of scale. Specifically, groups develop cultural interpretations of situations that govern their recognition and management of group life. One part of the group's logic has to do with naming segments of activity that organize behavior, what environmental psychologist Roger Barker calls "behavioral settings." Barker (1968) postulates that any group of people, living together in a given place over a period of time, will develop an array of behavioral settings, each with its own roles and rules. These behavioral settings govern the actions of people who enter the setting. The organization of a baseball game offers one simple example of this principle—a player who is engaged in the behavioral setting of a baseball game will not attempt to kick the ball while he is at bat.

This system of cuing facilitates the vast majority of human interactions, but depends for its success on intersubjective agreement about the workings of the world. Such concordance increases the likelihood that people, sharing the same information about a situation, will reach similar conclusions about what is going on. People holding differing assumptions about meaning are much more likely to differ in their conclusions, leading to what Goffman (1974) has called frame disputes. Frame disputes become increasingly more likely—and more difficult to resolve—as the level of scale shifts from two or three people to episodes involving different countries or groups of countries. When subjectivities come into conflict, chaos can result.

Thought Experiment #4

Imagine a man who is sitting in the shade of a bush near a stream. Suddenly, he sees a child running by and realizes the child is in danger of falling into the stream. The man leaps out from behind the bush and grabs the child. The child says, "Hey, you ambushed me!" but the man replies, "No, I saved you."

Who is right?

What happens next?

Is there any way in which such perceptual disagreements can be avoided?

Thus the embedding context of a situation is composed by people's collective ideas and objective realities, as well as their historical experience and current environment. In order to understand the embedding context, it is essential to develop a thorough understanding of these factors.

How to Do Situation Analysis

In order to carry out situation analysis, we must be able to answer the questions: What is the definition of the situation? What is the context within which it is located? And how are the situation and the context informing one another? In figure 8.1, we illustrate the relationship between the specific situation with its many component parts, and the context within which it is embedded.

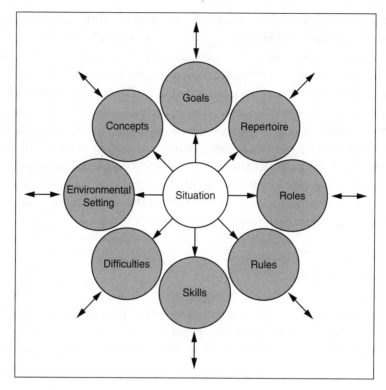

Figure 8.1

Collect Data

We propose the metaphor of a play as a way to explain what information to collect. First, imagine that the situation is one act within a larger play. Your goal is to understand both the single act and the entire play. To do this, you must accomplish four tasks: (1) master the story of the play, (2) listen to what the characters have to say, (3) study the stage set, and (4) watch the action.

MASTER THE STORY OF THE PLAY

The study of the situation should extend backwards in time, to include a historical perspective on the place. In mastering the story of the play, we provide the analysis with historical and social context. In fact, because situations are not only embedded in the immediate physical environment in which they occur but are also globally positioned, defining the situation should attempt to understand the ways in which the local is part of the global.

Archival research methods are useful in understanding the play. To complete this part of the research, you should:

1. Collect ephemera—newspaper stories, leaflets, Post-it notes, and other artifacts. These should be meticulously collected, and considered as part of the investigation of the problem.

2. Gather quantitative data—demographic and economic statistics should be obtained from a variety of sources such as health and planning departments, economic development offices, and libraries.

3. Collect maps and photos—physical descriptors of the area as it changes through time enrich our data.

4. Learn about the cultures of the people who are engaged in the situation. What languages do they speak? How long have they lived in the area? These provide critical kinds of information about larger social, economic, and geographic forces producing change and conflict.

LISTEN TO WHAT THE CHARACTERS HAVE TO SAY

Any given problem involves groups of obvious and hidden actors. The design of a situation study would certainly include conversations with people who have articulated interest or have been identified by third parties as players in the situation. A situation may also have hidden actors, and one of the roles of the researcher is to find those hidden actors. These may be individuals acting separately from other players, but who indirectly affect the situation. They may not have been identified at the beginning of the study, but they, or a subset of them, can be included in the study as they are identified.

Talking with the cast of characters provides you with the players' perspective on the situation—their definition, interpretation, and perceived role. In order to get the story from the point of view of the player, a researcher should:

1. Identify stakeholders—start by creating a list of types of players based on their role in the situation (i.e., policymakers).

Try these action verbs for learning objectives:

- Define
- Identify
- Relate
- Apply
- Compare
- Contrast

2. Outline a series of learning objectives—based on your knowledge of the embedding context and the way the situation has been defined, create a list of learning objectives. Recruit players: Use snowball sampling techniques to identify one or more individuals in each category. Remember that the interviews are useful for filling in information about all of the items on Argyle's list:

- Learn the goals of each of the different characters
- Identify the set of steps that people followed
- Learn more about the roles people played
- Get people to explain the rules that governed their actions
- Try to figure out what skills people brought to the situation
- Investigate the obstacles they faced
- List the physical and social characteristics of the setting
- Learn about people's values, ideas, and concepts

3. Conduct semistructured interviews—use the learning objectives to guide the conversation. Revisit your interview guide as data collection continues. For a more specialized form of interviewing, focus groups can be carried out.

STUDY THE STAGE SET

Getting to know the location of the situation presents the physical possibilities that the situation may follow. This refers to public spaces in which social interaction occurs—buildings or other structures that may serve as places to meet or barriers to interaction. Thus a key part of a situation analysis is the definition and description of the location of the events.

Visits to the location are essential, and the exploration of the terrain should be documented with maps, photographs, and diagrams. When visiting the scene, a researcher should:

1. Take a walk—visit the place where the situation takes place and make notations in a journal. On your first visit, be sure to make a list of 15 sentences of aspects of the location that caught your attention.
2. Create materials—obtain a map (i.e., from the city planning office) and divide the area of study in quadrants.
3. Invite stakeholders to participate in visiting the area—identify a group of stakeholders willing to guide you through the neighborhood and/or participate in a mapping exercise.
4. Conduct a mapping exercise—invite stakeholders to participate in a walk-through of the area. Assign a quadrant of the area under study to groups of three to five participants.
5. Debrief—hold a debriefing discussion after the mapping exercise. Record their comments about the area.

WATCH THE ACTION

As we triangulate the data gathered through the other three tasks, observing group interaction helps validate our budding interpretation of the situation. Comparing and contrasting the ways in which individuals react to each other can help problematize overly simplistic assumptions and guide the iterative process of data collection.

The Analysis

In qualitative research studies, analysis is directed at coding themes and organizing those themes into a logical pattern. In the analysis of a situation, the following tasks are added to that list:

1. *Ascertain the story and the perspective of each individual participant.* Each person has a working definition of the situation that we must be able to describe and integrate into the larger study. Acknowledge that there will be at least as many takes on the situation as there are players and researchers.

2. *Compare and contrast the perspectives of the individuals.* Each player will have the "truth" as seen from his/her vantage point within the situation. Look at the ways in which the stories are the same or different, intersect or diverge, corroborate or negate one another. Remember that the story of how the situation unfolds is not simply the narration of events. Assess the ways of seeing the world that each player has and how they lead to tension and conflict.

3. *Create a timeline of events.* Identify the sequence in which the events of the story unfold.

4. *Find links to the larger, embedding context.* Pay attention to ways in which people describe the world around them. Follow the trail indicated by these comments. Document the links between the particular episode and the general processes.

5. *Prepare a nuanced description of the situation and its embedding context.* Weaving together objective and subjective, narrative and symbol, person and place creates a whole that is greater than the sum of its parts. Rich description leads to a more complete understanding of the situation. We often tell our students that the answer is not in the data. By that we mean that the answer is found as a result of the synthesis of the data, but it cannot be derived in a deductive manner from the comments of interviewees or the observations of the researcher. The answer, which is meta to the data, will be reached by an inductive process that rests on—but is not identical to—the creation of thick description of who, what, when, where, why, and how.

The Vicious Circle: Using Situation Analysis to Understand Women's Access to HIV/AIDS Services

Identifying the Situation

In 2000, the Health Resources and Services Administration (HRSA) wanted to evaluate the effectiveness of its Ryan White Comprehensive AIDS Resources Emergency (CARE) Act service delivery systems for women of color living with HIV/AIDS. HRSA started with the question, "How well is the Ryan White CARE Act serving the needs of minority women?" It was well known that women of color were relatively disadvantaged both in

U.S. society and among those seeking care for HIV/AIDS. Between 1985 and 1994, the number of AIDS cases among women tripled. Overwhelmingly, this increase occurred among women of color: 77% of women living with AIDS were African American or Latina. In 1999, this upward trend in reported HIV/AIDS cases among women of color showed no signs of abating. For the first time, more females than males were diagnosed with HIV among 13- to 19-year-olds—six out of 10 new HIV infections occurred in this age group. Among 20- to 24-year-olds, young women accounted for 44% of new infections reported that year. It was clear that these women were also likely to be poor, politically disempowered, and lacking adequate food, housing, and child care. We labeled this problem a "situation."

The Situation

Women of color are disproportionately infected with HIV and lack adequate care.

Collecting Data

In response to HRSA's question, our group embarked on a two-month intensive study of programs, neighborhoods, and services for women of color living with HIV/AIDS. We undertook a situation analysis in five urban areas: Los Angeles, Miami, St. Louis, San Antonio, and New York (Meyrowitz 1968). The first step of the analysis was to visit these five areas and familiarize ourselves with HIV/AIDS services in each setting. Seeing the places of care, as well as getting from one place to another, oriented us to the environmental setting. In addition to visiting the places of care, we learned about the neighborhoods that were home to the women who were receiving care. Transportation systems, the location of other services, and the well-being of neighborhoods were some of the features of the local environment that were of interest to us. These visits supplied a good deal of objective information but also stirred the researchers' feelings, particularly about social inequities.

The Setting

Five metropolitan areas: Los Angeles, Miami, New York, St. Louis, and San Antonio.

In the second step of the research process, we were concerned with the identification of people with different roles in the situation (i.e., decision-makers, service providers, advocates, and consumers). We used HRSA grant applications to identify those in the first three categories, and they, in turn, referred us to those in the last category. In interviews with each of these actors, we were able to collect information about rules, skills, orientation, and concepts.

The Roles
_____

- Decision-makers
- Service providers
- Advocates
- Consumers

We asked questions about the day-to-day needs of women of color living with HIV/AIDS, about how the current system was falling short of meeting these needs, and about the women's lives outside of HIV/AIDS. This supplied us with a great deal of information about the subjective and intersubjective aspects of the study.

The Questions
_____

What is the system of care in this city?

How do women get connected to the services they need?

Third, we were interested in observing the interactions of actors with different roles. We observed interactions among service providers and consumers, sat in on staff meetings, and noted how consumers interacted with staff as they utilized services. Direct observation offers a different kind of information about rules and roles from that available through individual report. Specifically, it allows the observer to get a clearer sense of the concordance between the individual's stated goals and real interpersonal performance. These observations provided subjective (observer), intersubjective (symbols used in conversation), and objective (details of the process) information for our analysis.

The Observations

Staff meetings

Provider/consumer contact

Consumers interacting with each other

Consumers obtaining care

Finally, we were interested in reviewing documents, such as grant proposals, brochures created by local organizations; and ephemera collected during our visits, all of which provided additional information on the ways in which people presented themselves and their ideas to others. Documents are objective, in the sense that they exist and what is written on them can be corroborated by others, but they help with decoding subjective and intersubjective aspects of the situation because of the symbolic nature of all communication.

The Archival Data

Proposals

Newspapers

Brochures

Pamphlets

Newsletters

What Did We Learn?

On the basis of this information, we were able to conduct our situation analysis. We learned that women with HIV/AIDS had to manage a difficult illness while also managing the larger problems caused by racism and poverty. One woman captured the hardships of her life in the following words:

> As a black woman with children, I am trying to do the best I can, but I have three children who are not in day care. And if I am trying to keep the appointment for one of the children or for myself, I have to

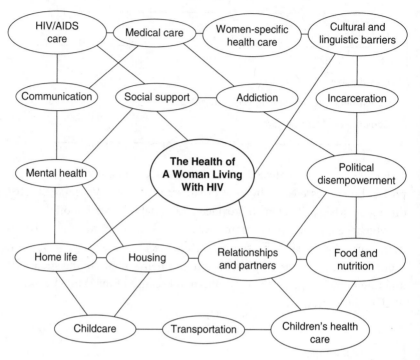

Figure 8.2

take everybody. And I can't take the two because they are affected, not infected, so I am not going to go. This is difficult, and these are the issues that need to be addressed.

The people we interviewed agreed that women faced a complex set of problems. These problems—which have been identified many times in the literature on AIDS and related illnesses—create a web of needs, which we illustrate in figure 8.2. The web of needs, in the words of one provider, was structured at multiple levels of scale:

Most women are the primary caretakers of their families and the primary income earners. They are undereducated and underemployed. They not only have to face disclosure issues, but also issues related to race and poverty. Daily, they have to stack all these issues on top of one another and sort out what they will address.

We observed some care settings that had done a remarkable job of organizing an array of services that helped women manage the complex problems they faced, including their own medical care. But we also found that these settings were the exception, rather than the rule.

We asked what it would take to replicate the model care programs. We were informed about a list of problems. Many services, particularly substance abuse treatment and mental health services, were inadequately funded. Essential elements of healthy living, like child care, affordable housing, healthy food, and safe streets, were also in short supply, and out of the price range of most women living with HIV/AIDS. Finally, AIDS spending decisions were made as a result of a political process that was largely inaccessible to women. One woman living with HIV told us:

> We need more representation of women on committees when different things are coming up and decisions are being made. Our health care is being based on how men have been taken care of in the past, and we are quite a bit different. We need to have a larger say-so on what is being decided.

Indeed, we were convinced that increased political engagement was essential, but difficult to achieve, given the larger circumstances of women's lives: the enormous burdens they had to manage and their lack of political skills. One might say that a vicious circle had been created, in which women's political disadvantage placed them at high risk for infection. Once infected, their political disadvantage placed them at high risk for inadequate care, which, in turn, placed them at high risk for other infections and diseases that follow in the path of collapse of the immune system. There was, to our eyes, a profound parallel between political engagement as immunity and T-cell function as immunity. Breaking out of social marginalization was the key to better health, but the burdens of marginalization made such political engagement quite challenging.

Impact of the Study

Through our analysis, we were able to identify and examine many issues that often fail to surface on the radar screen of typical AIDS service, yet undermine the health and well-being of women living with the virus. We reported this analysis to HRSA, which distributed the findings to many HIV/AIDS providers and activists across the country. One important outcome was an increase in the number of efforts to support women's political engagement by providing women with training, babysitting, transportation, and other necessary resources. Another useful outcome was a series of publications that described the kinds of programs that seemed most able to meet the web of needs of women with HIV/AIDS. Thus the analysis of the situation revealed important targets for intervention that had the potential to create a new process for interaction.

Conclusion

Recognition and analysis of situations is a useful tool for understanding complex social problems. Situation analysis brings together many of the tools of qualitative research: interviewing, analyzing documents, visiting locations, and observing groups in action. The use of multiple methods helps to ensure that the results are sound. The close examination of links between the particular situation and its larger embedding context allows us to understand the ways in which social structures cause and/or shape interpersonal conflict. It is only by understanding the contribution of structure that we can begin to predict what will happen next and how that possible future might be averted. Thus situation analysis is a useful tool for social scientists who hope to apply their findings in order to alleviate human inequality and unnecessary suffering.

Acknowledgments

We are grateful to those Columbia University Mailman School of Public Health students who, by their hard work in Qualitative Research Methods I, Fall 1999, and/or Qualitative Research Methods II, Spring 2000, helped us decipher the meaning and utility of situations.

Note

1. For examples from other groups, we recommend Fernández-Kelly (1994), Behar (1993), Sclar (1990), and Stam and Ross (1989).

References

Argyle, M. 1981. The experimental study of the basic features of situations. In *Toward a psychology of situations: an interactive perspective*, D. Magnusson, ed. Hillsdale, NJ: Lawrence Erlbaum, pp. 63–83.

Barker, R. 1968. *Ecological psychology*. Palo Alto: Stanford UP.

Community Research Group. 1999. Women's Equity in AIDS Resources (WEAR) study: A report to the Health Resources and Services Administration HIV/AIDS Bureau. New York: New York State Psychiatric Institute and Columbia University.

Behar, R. 1993. My Mexican friend Marta, who lost her womb on this side of the border. *Journal of Women's Health*, 2(1), 85–89.

Fagan, J. and D. L.Wilkinson. 1998. Guns, youth violence, and social identity in inner cities. *Youth Violence*, 24:373–456.

Fernández-Kelly, P. 1994. Towanda's triumph: Social and cultural capital in the transition to adulthood in the urban ghetto. *International Journal of Urban and Regional Research*, 18:88–111.

Fullilove, M. T. 2000. Death and life of a great American city. *International Journal of Mental Health*. 28(4): 20–29.

——. 2001. Root shock: The consequences of African American dispossession. *Journal of Urban Health*, 78:72–80.

Fullilove, M. T., G. Arias, M. Nuñez, et al. 2003. What did Ian tell God? School violence in East New York. In *Deadly lessons: Understanding lethal school violence*, M. H. Moore, C. Petrie, A. A. Braga, and B. L. McLaughlin, eds. Washington, DC: National Academies.

Fullilove, M. T., R. E. Fullilove, M. Smith, K. Winkler, C. Michael, P. Panzer, and R. Wallace. 1993. Violence, trauma and post-traumatic stress disorder among women drug users. *Journal of Traumatic Stress*, 6:105–115.

Fullilove, M. T., L. L. Green, and R. E. Fullilove. 1999. Building momentum: An ethnographic study of inner-city redevelopment. *American Journal of Public Health*, 89:840–844.

Fullilove, M. T., V. Héon, W. Jimenez, C. Parsons, L. L. Green, and R. E. Fullilove. 1998. Injury and anomie: The effects of violence on an inner-city community. *American Journal of Public Health*, 88:924–927.

Fullilove, M. T., L. Hernandez-Cordero, J. S. Madoff, and R. E. Fullilove. 2004. Promoting collective recovery through organizational mobilization: The post-9/11 disaster relief work of NYC RECOVERS. *Journal of Biosocial Science*, 36:479–489.

Fullilove, M. T., A. Lown, and R. E. Fullilove. 1992. Crack 'hos and skeezers: Traumatic experiences of women crack users. *Journal of Sex Research*, 29:275–287.

Fullilove, M. T., J. Wiley, R. E. Fullilove, E. Golden, J. Catania, J. Peterson, K. Garrett, D. Siegel, B. Marin, S. Kegeles, T. Coates, and S. Hulley. 1992. Risk for AIDS in multi-ethnic neighborhoods of San Francisco: The population-based AMEN Study. *Western Journal of Medicine, 157*(1):32–40.

Fullilove, R. E., M. T. Fullilove, B. Bowser, and S. Gross. 1990. Risk of sexually transmitted disease among black adolescent crack users in Oakland and San Francisco, CA. *JAMA 263*:851–855.

Fullilove, R. E., M. T. Fullilove, M. E. Northridge, M. L. Ganz, M. T. Bassett, D. E. McLean, A. A. Aidala, D. H. Gemson, and C. McCord. 1999. Risk factors for excess mortality in Harlem: findings from the Harlem Household Survey. *American Journal of Preventive Medicine, 16*(3S):22–28.

Goffman, E. 1974. *Frame analysis.* Cambridge, MA: Harvard UP.

Heon-Klin, V., E. Sieber, J. Huebner, and M. T. Fullilove. 2000. The influence of geopolitical change on the well-being of a population: The Berlin Wall. *American Journal of Public Health, 91*:369–374.

Meyrowitz, J. 1968. *No sense of place.* Cambridge, MA: Oxford UP.

Mitchell, J. C. 1983. Case and situation analysis. *Sociological Review, 31*:187–211.

Ross, M. W. and J. Ferreira-Pinto. 2000. Toward a public health of situations: The re-contextualization of risk. *Cadernos Saúde Pública, 16*:59–71.

Sclar, E. D. 1990. Homelessness and housing policy: A game of musical chairs. *American Journal of Public Health, 80*:1039–1040.

Stam, B. and J. Ross. 1989. Understanding behavior in escalation situations. *Science 246*:216–220.

Stebbins, R. 1968. The definition of the situation: A review. In *Social behavior in context*, A. Furnham, ed. Boston: Allyn & Bacon.

Thomas, W. and D. Thomas. 1928. *The child in America.* New York: Alfred A. Knopf.

Triandis, H., X. Chen, and D. Chan. 1998. Scenarios for the measurement of collectivism and individualism. *Journal of Cross-Cultural Psychology, 29*:275–289.

UNICEF DPRK. October 2003. Analysis of the situation of the children and women in the Democratic People's Republic of Korea. Pyongyang, North Korea: UNICEF DPRK.

Wallace, R., D. Wallace, H. Andrews, R. Fullilove, and M. T. Fullilove. 1995. The spaciotemporal dynamics of AIDS and TB in the New York metropolitan region from a sociogeographic perspective: Understanding the linkages of central city and suburbs. *Environment and Planning A 27*:1085–1108.

Watkins, B.X. and Fullilove M.T. 1999. Crack cocaine and Harlem's health. *Souls: A Critical Journal of Black Politics, Culture, and Society, 1*(1):36–48.

Zwi, A. and A. Cabral. 1991. Identifying "high risk situations" for preventing AIDS. *British Journal of Medicine 303*:1527–1529.

[9]

Action Research

An Intervention for Change, Development, and Advocacy in a Global Society

SHIRLEY J. JONES, ROBERT L. MILLER, JR., AND IRENE LUCKEY

Globalization[1] and its impact on the social and economic conditions of the world, the need for better sensitivity to cultural and religious differences, and a general sense of powerlessness related to community building and bringing about change (Netting, Kettner, and McMurtry 1998; Worthington 2000; Jones and Austin 2010) are just a few issues and concerns that need to be addressed in the twenty-first century. Action researchers and helping professionals, such as social workers, can help motivate individuals, groups, communities, and organizations to become more proactive regarding their lives and encourage them to better address the social and economic concerns that impede them and their community's growth and development (Jones and Zlotnik 1998).

This chapter highlights action research and how it is utilized as an intervention for change and development. Action research is a fluid term that involves interacting with and involving participants in the research process. This article focuses on action learning as an important component of action research and as a means to ensure effective participant[2] education and empowerment. Case studies are presented to point out elements and components of action research and the role of the researcher as a facilitator/catalyst and educator in the process. Limitations in funding and recognition for action research are discussed, specifically noting how such limitations affect the advancement of action research as a valued, viable research method. The need for inclusion of action research in research courses and the use of action research to bring about effective change and development in the twenty-first century are emphasized.

Background and Definition

Kurt Lewin, a German-born social and experimental psychologist, is widely regarded as a founder of action research as presently used in the fields of education, business, and most recently, health, social work, and law. Action research method gained popularity in the United States in industrial settings, community development, and education (Murphy, Scammell, and Sclove 1997; O'Brien 2003). During the 1960s, action research suffered a decline in interest due to its association with radical political activism. But it has since gained popularity in the realms of community-based and participatory action research (Park 2006). In 1976, the International Participatory Research Network was started. The Network, in association with the International Council for Adult Education, helped to give visibility to a set of concepts and practices, which have continued to impact social movements and social policy scholars to the present time (Hall 1997).

There is no standard definition for action research. Wagner (1993) describes it as the systematic gathering of information by concerned professionals and consumers of services who seek to document problems or effect change; Green et al. (1997) view action research as both a method and a process. Several researchers (Schenck 1996; Israel, Schulz, Parker and Becker 1998; Netting and McMurtry 1998; Kettner, Moroney, and Martin 1999; Israel et al. 2005) point out that action research enables individuals and communities to work in concert with others to develop plans to ensure the implementation of effective variations or alterations. O'Brien (2003) emphasizes that action research is learning by doing. This research method aims at contributing to the concerns of people in an immediate problematic situation. Similarly, Stringer (1999) and Inglis (1994) point out that action research is a collaborative approach to inquiry or investigation that is a "hands and hands-on" versus a "hands-at-length" technique. Action research, in this article, refers to a cluster of applied research methods and processes (i.e., participatory research, collaborative inquiry, emancipatory research, and action learning).

Criteria for action research includes pursuing action and research while engaging in a cyclic process that alternates action with critical reflection. Stringer (1999), Dick (2002), O'Brien (2003), and Israel et al. (2005) provide principles related to action research. They include the following:

- building on participants' strengths and resources;
- collective decision-making about the direction of the research;
- awareness of the nature of the process from the beginning, including all personal biases and interest;
- equal access to information generated by the process for all participants; and
- creation of a process that maximizes opportunities for involving all participants.

For this article, the participatory nature of action research broadens the identification of stakeholders including participants, coplanner, cosponsors, and fund-raisers.

Action research generates identifiable outcomes. Some outcomes of action research identified by Green et al. (1997), Dick (2002), and Israel et al. (2005) include the following:

- education and skill building,
- participation in decision-making,
- developing knowledge from experiential learning and research,
- having a clearer sense of the issues from those most affected, and
- empowering participants so that they are able to take action for change and development.

Critics of participatory research have existed through the years. Some critics' questions relate to the political nature of action research while some concerns relate to what has been called "the lack of rigor and scientific application" of this research method. Furthermore, it has been argued that action research "is not a 'method' or a procedure for research but a series of commitments to observe and problematize through practice a series of principles for conducting social inquiry" (Smith 2001:9).

Park (2006:84) argues that the action research method is "not just a convenient instrument for solving problems through technically efficacious means. But is also a social practice that helps marginalized people attain a degree of emancipation as autonomous and responsible members of society." Action research methods include a variety of data collection methods generally common to the qualitative research paradigm that include: keeping a research journal, document collection and analysis, participant observation recordings, questionnaire surveys, structured and unstructured interviews, and case studies (O'Brien 2001). The overarching feature of the method is the commitment of researchers to developing close and trusting relationships with community partners, their shared dedication to working for positive social change, and their willingness to reflect upon the challenges and contradictions of participatory action research (Brydon-Miller, Kral, Maguire, Noffke, and Sabhlok 2011). While this position differs dramatically from a positivist perspective, the method enjoys a recognized tradition and custom.

The authors of this article have adopted a participatory perspective from research that entails action-oriented activity. Specifically, the authors have observed action research being used successfully in African countries such as South Africa and Tanzania. In these countries, this research method has aided in the facilitation of community processes, inter- and intra-community familiarity, collective understanding of community issues, identification of community strengths, decisions on necessary changes, implementation of certain changes, and monitoring them based upon the community's own frame of reference (Collins 1999). This research has served to promote mutual collaborative relationships for effective policies, programs, change, and development; notably action research has helped to empower disenfranchised, oppressed, and poor individuals, groups, communities, and organizations both nationally and internationally. This article uses van Dyk's (2000:50) description of empower, ". . . the feelings of being able to do things that were not previously possible . . . the ability to do things not previously within one's competence and the opening up of opportunities that were previously denied."

Action Research as an Intervention Aimed at Change and Development

An overarching principle of action research is the worth and development of all people, which serves as the underpinning for change and development. It recognizes the inequitable relationship between those who create and dominate knowledge and those being researched. It incorporates the exchange and collaboration between researchers and the researched. It is viewed not only as a process of creating knowledge, but simultaneously developing consciousness and mobilizing for action all who participate (Murphy, Scammell, and Sclove 1997). It focuses on shared power and decision-making rather than the domination of the process by researchers (Murphy, Scammell, and Sclove 1997; Collins 1999; Tomson et al. 2005).

Colin van Rooyen (2000) of South Africa in writing about research for social change cautioned that action research is not a recipe for social change. He points out that that this research method is a democratic approach to investigation and learning. It is a tool (to be taken up by individuals, groups, and movements) that is aimed at social change. Van Rooyen used this method of research to develop a project that intertwined research and intervention in a poor, crime-ridden area in the province of KwaZulu-Natal, South Africa. The Crime Reduction in Schools Project's (CRISP) goal is to develop strategies that make a positive contribution toward reducing crime among young people and the development of reciprocal partnerships between schools, universities, and community organizations. Participants address the nature and outcome of crime; share personal crime experiences; facilitate partnerships with the police, school officials, and the general community; and design and develop research strategies and tools to help develop policies and programs for change and development. The project's outcomes includes the right of participation of all interested in the problem or concern, appreciation of the strengths and expertise of the youth in addressing crime, and the empowerment of all participants.

Education as a Primary Stage of Action Research

Action research, a facilitator for change and development, incorporates a spiral versus a linear process that Stringer (1999) describes as Look (gathering relevant information, building a picture, describing the situation), Think (exploring and analyzing, interpreting and explaining), and Act (planning, implementing, and evaluating). This process can be viewed as a map that relates to the traditional research practices of data gathering, analyzing, theorizing, reporting, and evaluating (Stringer 1999).

Stringer (1999) and van Rooyen (2000) note that there is no step-by-step design or routine for action research that exists to the extent that it can be applied universally. Both authors describe action research method as being nonlinear in nature; and, therefore, it may not always permit a neat, orderly activity that allows participants to proceed step-by-step to the end of the process. For example, people involved in action research may find themselves working backward through routines and stages, repeating processes, revising procedures, rethinking interpretations, moving from stages or steps, and making innovative changes in direction (Stringer 1999). However, with this information as background, the authors' experiences with action research suggest that a primary step or stage of action research (as applied to change) is the education of people affected by the proposed change. Knowledge as education is power (Park 2006), and people should know collectively what their concerns are regarding the situation/problem and what direction they want to change. They should be encouraged to provide input based on their own perspectives (Murphy et al. 1997; Collins 1999; Park 2006; and Dick 2002).

Case Studies

Three case studies illustrate the spiral process Springer (1999) identified as Look (how people and organizations can be provided with information to observe), Think (how people and organizations may be given opportunities to explore and analyze), and Act (how people and organizations may be encouraged to plan, implement, and make suggestions about their problems/concerns). This process helps to better educate participants about issues affecting their lives and introduces them to new ideas and research methods such as action research.

Case #1. Project South, based in Atlanta, Georgia, is an example of a community-based organization helping to prepare local people to be informed participants. The project uses popular education that focuses on life experiences and addresses issues people face every day. Workshops are held to provide information on issues and concerns such as poverty, globalization, and community economic development (Look). Community people are introduced to logic, observation, and theory through a tool called "Timeframe" that views the problem or concern in the context of economic history, policy history, and popular movement history (Think). Timeframe was developed through the collaborative efforts of the Columbia Heights Action Research Project, Project South, the Institute for the

Elimination of Poverty and Genocide, and Howard University Graduate Sociology Department. The purpose of this tool is to educate grassroots participants about issues affecting their lives (Look) by helping them to ask critical questions, process new ideas, theories, and information (Think) and make responsible decisions regarding their lives in a global society (Act). Project South is also planning to reclaim the purpose and function of debate to further engage their membership in analysis and thinking and to enrich the popular education program (Project South Periodical Spring 2010).

Case #2. Loka Institute in Washington, DC, provides another example of a community-based organization that helps educate individuals and communities for decision-making and advocacy. A community workshop was held by Loka Institute (September 10–11, 2004) to focus on the public participation provision of the 21st Century Nanotechnology Research and Development Act passed by Congress in 2003. The act authorized up to $3.7 billion for federal research and development. The participants in the workshop were helped to understand nanotechnology as ". . . a set of techniques used to manipulate matter at the scale of atoms and molecules" (Look). The workshop participants were given opportunities to reflect on their concerns about this new technology. Some participants' concerns included the scientific uncertainty surrounding nanoparticle toxicity, the lack of regulations, whether the environmental and social costs of nanotechnology outweigh its many benefits (ETC Group 2004b), and the overall implications for poor and marginalized communities. Community participants who attended the workshop asked critical questions of the experts, identified community interests and concerns (Think), and made recommendations that could enable the federal government to effectively promote and sustain public participation in the evolution of nanotechnology policy (Act) (ETC 2004b; Weiss 2004). The department of nanotechnology at the University at Albany is reaching out to grassroots teenagers to take part in planned programs to provide education regarding the technology and prepare students for employment opportunities in the field.

Case #3. A teleconference entitled "Research for Action: University and Community Partnerships" was arranged to help organizations such as institutions of higher education become better informed about the role of informed inquiry and information particularly as it relates to educating their constituents (i.e., students and faculty) so that they are freer to use different research methods to promote development and change in their local communities. Collaboratively sponsored by the School of Social Welfare, University at Albany, the Participatory Action Research Center at Cornell University, and the University of Missouri-Columbia, the teleconference was planned and conducted by both students and faculty. The major purpose of this teleconference was to educate administrators, faculty, and students about using action research as a means to encourage better collaborative partnerships between the university and the community (Look). Experts on action research were invited to be guest speakers. Workshop participants were asked questions and reflected on the information provided (Think). Interestingly, given the economic downturn, the university administrators were motivated to attend this workshop because they viewed the teleconferencing technology as a cost savings to their university. Direct and indirect outcomes from the planning and implementation (Act) of this teleconference included an increased appreciation on the part of the teleconference participants regarding action research; collaborative student-faculty partnerships for research and publication (Bashant 1998); development of a consortium of students and faculty; increased interest of faculty and community-based agencies in action research; more university involvement in community outreach; increased university recognition of faculty and students engaged in action research; the addition of action research to the curriculum offerings in the schools of social welfare and public health at the University of Albany, and information regarding the technology and economics necessary to conduct teleconferences.

The three case studies presented illustrate the role of informed inquiry and information as an important means for educating participants to learn more about problems and/or situations through the use of the action research process. This knowledge helped participants to better reflect on possible solutions to the problems and/or situations and to identify ways to take action for change and development. The use of tools such as Timeframe, workshops, focus groups, and teleconferences can help assist the researcher (as facilitator/catalyst) to educate and train participants in a comfortable and effective manner. These tools can assist all involved to gather information (Look), define, describe, and analyze the situation (Think), and plan and implement action (Act).

Action Learning as a Bridge to Education: Procedures and Stages of Action Research

It has been argued that "correct" knowledge in and of itself does not lead to change. Other forces, such as culture, societal conditions, social perception, and mental attitudes, also play important roles in change and development (Smith 2001). Action learning provides hands-on opportunities that offer another tool to ensure effective education and increase sensitivity to culture, societal conditions, and mental health. It can promote the creative integration of learning, thinking, and doing and it helps to integrate theory and practice (Taylor and Francis Group 1999). This learning process is both a means and an end because it can assist in gathering relevant information for all stakeholders. Professor Reginald Revans, one of the originators of action learning, used it as a tool to work with managers and organizations in order to assist them in understanding their own behavior and to be aware of their lack of relevant knowledge (Revans 2011). Action learning enables the researcher to carry out basic procedures and stages of action research, and facilitate empowerment of all participants.

Action learning is a part of the cyclic nature of action research. It permits action to alternate with reflection and therefore allows for experiential learning, empowerment, change, and development. O'Brien (2001:9) refers to action learning as "contextual action research . . . insofar as [action learning] entails the structural relations among actors in a social environment . . . and it tries to involve all affected parties and stakeholders." For example, action learning has the ability to help each participant to understand the working of the whole and to act as mutual decision-makers, project designers, and coresearchers (Stringer 1999). In this regard, action learning can serve as a bridge to other steps and stages involved in action research.

The interrelationship between action and reflection as well as the contextual aspect of action is illustrated through a project sponsored by the School of Social Welfare at the University at Albany entitled the U.S.–Africa Partnership for Building Stronger Communities. The project illustrates how action learning underpins and helps to correlate activities that assist participants to gather information (Look), to explore and analyze (Think), and to accomplish their task (Act). The project shows how action learning can be supportive to the researcher in the role of facilitator/catalyst in that it ensures a participatory process and therefore can be empowering to all stakeholders.

The U.S.–Africa Partnership for Building Stronger Communities Project

An illustration of the interrelationship between action and reflection, as well as contextual aspects of action research, is seen through the U.S.–Africa Partnership for Building Stronger Communities Project. The project began in 2000 and continues today, with an aim to promoting stronger U.S.–African relationships by engaging, educating, empowering and preparing leaders (e.g., students, faculty, and community-based practitioners) to function in a global society. The mission and key goals of the project include promoting stronger international relationships; introducing the participants to culture, diversity, differences, and leadership; and educating participants about national and international policies and programs to facilitate change and development. Underpinnings of the project include action learning and research, participation and empowerment theories, and strength perspectives. Basic principles of participation, empowerment, access to information, and action are embedded in the philosophy of the entire project. Three major activities were designed to interrelate with one another in order to achieve the mission and goals of the project. Each activity is designed to incorporate theories and perspectives, support learning of the participants, and provide them with opportunities for informed inquiry, reflection, and action for change and development.

The structure of the U.S.–Africa Partnership for Building Stronger Communities Project requires the interrelationship of the three major activities of the program, that is, the Summer Study Tour to Africa[3] (which is incorporated in an advanced social policy course), the virtual and actual focus group meetings, and the collaborative partnerships for research, publication, and advocacy.

Project Interrelationship Model

Figure 9.1 shows the inter- and intra-relationship of the U.S.–Africa Partnership for Building Stronger Communities Project's three activities: (1) Summer Study Tour to Africa (SSTA), which is incorporated in an advanced social policy course, (2) actual and virtual focus group meetings, and (3) collaborative partnerships for research, publication, and advocacy. The process of Look, Think, and Act surrounds all three of these activities, in order to

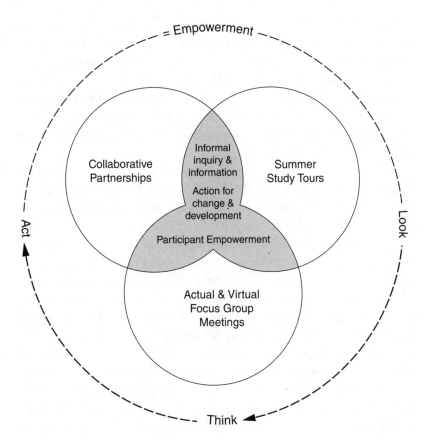

Figure 9.1 Relationship of the U.S.–Africa Partnership for Building Stronger Communities Project's main components: Study tours, focus group meetings, and collaborative partnerships.

provide informed inquiry and information, action for change and development, and participant empowerment.

THE SUMMER STUDY TOUR TO AFRICA

The Summer Study Tour to Africa (SSTA) is structured to provide opportunities for learning and working together for a diverse group of people, (i.e., age, class, race, culture, educational background and experience). It has become part of a for-credit elective course offered by the Office of International Education and the School of Social Welfare at the University at Albany. The study tour provides opportunities for participants to visit hospitals, schools, orphanages, government and nongovernment agencies, and deprived communities. SSTA participants are able to apply their interest in, and knowledge and skills of, social policy formulation, implementation, and evaluation. The hands-on experiences related to the SSTA and the union and collaboration of participants and instructor encourage informed discussions, formal and informal reflection, and direct and indirect action (Dick 2002; O'Brien 2003).

SSTA participants are prepared for the study tours through formal readings, lecturers, and videotapes that describe the culture, policies, programs, and specific issues related to the African countries they visit. During the SSTA, they are asked to keep a personal journal and are involved in daily group sessions so that they can reflect on their learning experiences in Africa. In special cases, some students enrolled in the course are unable to go on the SSTA. They receive the same preparation and are required to further their learning through extensive library research. Course participants help plan and facilitate teleconferences from Africa to the United States. This activity helps to unite all participants enrolled in the course around planning and international issues such as HIV/AIDS, education, poverty, and economic development. All course participants unite at the final course session, where they all share their learning experiences and present their research papers on international social policies. The course participants reflect on their presentations, their learning, the skills developed, and possible action to be taken (Look, Think, Act). All stakeholders involved in this activity are encouraged to share their learning experiences with others (Act). One planned activity used to facilitate shared learning is a brown bag luncheon where students and others exchange information about issues related to Africa and other developing countries and show their photos of the SSTA. Some major outcomes of the SSTA activity include the participants' increased sensitivity to values, perspectives and theories, such as the worth and dignity of all people; conscious use of self; diversity including difference, culture, religion, class, and gender; poverty; conflict; a strengths perspective; and chaos theory. Excursions to African townships, meetings with grassroots and rural people, visits to social and governmental agencies, the group dynamics and behaviors encountered during the SSTA, reflection and formal discussions, and workshops enable the participants to develop a greater consciousness of themselves in relation to their usefulness in identifying problems and effecting change. Their hands-on learning experience helps to shape their ideas regarding social and economic problems, application of culture and human needs, and their ability to impact policy formulation and implementation. Reflection regarding hands-on learning helps to stimulate learning and provides a mechanism for exchange of information and establishment of collaborative partnerships with grassroots people, government, social agencies, and institutions of higher education. The SSTA activity incorporates the Look, Think, and Act elements of action learning and research.

FOCUS GROUP MEETINGS

Virtual and actual focus group meetings facilitate the sharing and gathering of information on a variety of issues. African and American scholars are guest speakers in virtual (teleconferenced) and actual (in country) focus group meetings and conferences aimed at sharing and exchanging information and advocating for better international/interdisciplinary policies and programs. The international scholars exchange and share information about global issues, such as women's roles in economic development, HIV/AIDS, international education, and the World Bank's documented and undocumented policies (i.e., privatization of Ghana's water[4]). Such efforts require collaborative work, cosponsored planning, and implementation between institutions in the United States and Africa.

From 2001 to 2008, the Information and Technology Department (ITD) at Peninsula Technikon in Bellsville, South Africa (now known as Cape Peninsula University of Technology), and the School of Social Welfare and the School of Public Health at the University at Albany pooled their expertise and financial resources to use teleconferencing as a method of holding international focus groups meetings. Virtual and actual focus group meetings were incorporated into the SSTA activity (2001–2008), offering students and others not able to take part in the study tours a means to unite with their colleagues and an opportunity to meet their African counterparts. The televised discussions enabled them to assess what they learned during their library research or through nonprint media. In addition, the teleconferences served to connect faculty, students, and university administrators with grassroots people.

A case in point is the teleconference workshop conducted by Information and Technology Department (ITD) at the Cape Peninsula University of Technology, the School of Social Welfare at the University at Albany, and the Women on Farms Project in South Africa. The workshop was held in Bellsville, South Africa, on July 10, 2004, for a group of teenage girls (members of the Women on Farms Project) and was entitled "Use of Technology as a Means of Empowerment." The teleconference workshop introduced the girls to technology and further empowered them through education and skills development (Look). The teleconference was one of ITD's many efforts to reach out to the community. It also served to bridge two countries—South Africa and the United States—and provided a forum to unite urban-based students and faculty with rural-based residents (Act). All involved in the teleconference were able to reflect on and discuss how to sustain the lessons learned at the workshop (Think), suggest how to support the girls in advancing their knowledge and skills of computers and other technologies, and encourage the girls to share their new knowledge and skills with their peers and adults working on farms. Students and faculty from the United States promised to keep in contact with the girls via e-mail, fax, and mail. In order to broaden and sustain this outreach project, as well as the overall virtual focus group meetings, grant funding is needed. As demonstrated here, the components of Look, Think, and Act were woven into the fabric of the virtual and actual focus group meetings.

COLLABORATIVE PARTNERSHIPS FOR RESEARCH AND ADVOCACY

Collaborative partnerships for research and advocacy are both an activity and a goal of the U.S.–Africa Partnership for Building Stronger Communities Project. For example, an actual focus group meeting held in Ghana (2002) brought together African and U.S. students to discuss the issue of privatization of water in Ghana (Look). The workshop discussed the pros and cons of privatization of water in Ghana and analyzed the role of the World Bank and other Western donors (see note 4) and their impact on policies and programs in Ghana and other developing countries (Think). The U.S. students were assigned to write their research papers on the World Bank's policies related to privatization of water in Ghana. The papers were shared with students at the School of Social Work in Ghana and with the Ghana Association of Social Workers (GAOSW). This collaboration informed the social workers in Ghana about the need to develop an informed civil society that includes students and community-based practitioners (Act).

Collaborative partnerships[5] with community-based agencies and institutions of higher education in Nigeria led to collaborative research efforts regarding the development of civil societies and training on conflict resolution. Partnerships with Nigerian nongovernmental organizations (NGOs) have enabled collaborative grant writing to sponsor the education and training of grassroots people so that they will be better prepared to help formulate and evaluate government policies and programs and to advocate for effective change and development. Grassroots people were included in the development of the proposed grants and sensitivity was given to their participation in all activities of the U.S–Africa Partnership for Building Stronger Communities Project.

Action research encourages exchange and sharing of information with the general public and with others who need to be informed. To that end, two televised premieres of the *Presidential Tours of Africa Series* (sponsored by The Africa Society of the National Summit on Africa and the Discovery Channel) were held in 2002 and 2003 by the U.S.–Africa Partnership for Building Stronger Communities Project. Dissemination of both televised premieres sparked additional interest in Africa. Additionally, all those involved with the project were asked to share their experiences and knowledge with others, such as church, school, civic, and professional organizations. This request resulted in project participants showing videos of their SSTA at community and other events, and students also presented their research papers on African policies and programs to their peers in other classes. One of the project's participants implemented a forum on the African Growth Opportunity Act (AGOA) with the New York State Bar Association. Other participants in the project have collaborated on research projects and have made presentations at national and international conferences.

In March 2010, the Collaborative Partnership for Research and Advocacy activity served as a model for a conference entitled "Public Health and Child Welfare: Implications for a Society's Security." The conference was designed to use collaboration and constructive dialogue to help develop common wisdom about public health and child welfare and its implications for peace and security of countries such as the United States and South Africa. The collaborative partnerships included the New York National Guard, the University at Albany, the State University of New York at Cobleskill, the University of South Africa, and the Cape Peninsula University of Technology. Teleconferencing was aided by webcasting and web streaming. This collaborative partnership activity embraced the Look, Think, and Act components of action learning and research by sharing information about HIV/AIDS, reporting on the number of children, families, communities, and countries impacted by this illness, identifying national and international agencies addressing HIV/AIDS, and advocating for government and grass roots community partnerships for preventive research and adequate public health and child welfare services (both on a national and international level).

Action Learning Process Incorporated Within the U.S.–Africa Partnership for Building Stronger Communities

Figure 9.2 illustrates the spiral nature of action learning, which is a key underpinning of the U.S.–Africa Partnership for Building Stronger Communities Project.

Action learning (experiential, hands-on learning) offers the participants of the Summer Study Tour to Africa (as well as participants of the virtual and actual focus group meetings and the collaborative partnerships for research, publication, and advocacy) rich experiences for learning (Look) and for reflection. Planned and unplanned reflection (Think) helps the project participants develop ideas for change (Act). This action includes teleconferences and forums to discuss such issues as women engaged in development and the African Growth and Opportunity Act (AGOA) as well as ideas for research and publication.

Further opportunities for reflection help the participants to plan, analyze behavior/problems, collaborate, and advocate for change and development (Act). Evaluation is an ongoing process that leads to further experiences (including hands-on) and refinement of the overall project.

Roles of Project Director: Facilitator/Catalyst, Educator

The project director of the U.S.–Africa Partnership for Building Stronger Communities Project has served as a facilitator and a catalyst to ensure that the theoretical underpinnings are incorporated into the overall project and that all involved stakeholders are cognizant of the project's mission and goals. The project directory utilizes action learning to integrate didactic and hands-on principles and learning, structures and fosters individual and group participation and reflection, and encourages participant involvement

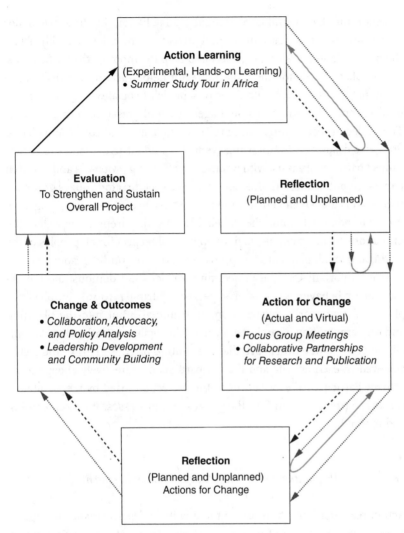

Figure 9.2 Action learning processes in the U.S.–Africa Partnership for Building Stronger Communities.

In the diagram, heavy dashed lines represent moving smoothly from one portion of the process to the next. The light dotted lines followed by a solid gray line indicate a second scenario where portions of the process may have to be repeated in order to address difficulties and conflicts encountered. The solid black line represents the culminating participant empowerment.

in action for change and development. As facilitator, the director's major responsibility is to oversee the overall project in a manner that will sustain the mission and goals of the project and help to empower the participants. In the role of facilitator, the project director helps sustain the collaborative relationships developed with African schools of social work, universities, government and non-government agencies, and grassroots organizations. The project director works with project participants and community-based groups to cosponsor fund-raising events for student scholarships to Africa. Project participants assist with writing joint funding proposals and research papers for publication. In this regard, the project director utilizes group dynamic skills to foster an environment for people to effectively work together. A case in point is helping the stakeholders see the strengths as well as the limitations in all situations, to develop mutual respect for all peoples of the world, and to adopt a win-win approach in areas of conflict resolution.

It is important that the project director does not demonstrate the demeanor or behavior of boss or supervisor (Stringer 1999). Emphasis is placed on teamwork, collaboration, and mutual input into the planning and implementation of project activities. The facilitator/catalyst works with all the stakeholders to ensure that the routine of Look, Think, and Act is achieved in each activity and that all participants effectively engage in an activity. Participants' experiences in the project are used by the facilitator/catalyst to prepare them for other stages and processes of action learning and research.

The Project's Preparation for the Next Stage of Action Research

Action research looks to improve the quality and performance of organizations and projects (O'Brien 2003). Using this statement as a guiding principle, the project director of the U.S.–Africa Partnership for Building Stronger Communities Project used action research to evaluate and update the overall project. Several cycles of activities have provided the project participants with experiences in the action learning process. In the participants' efforts to learn, explore, reflect, and take action, they have been introduced to the elements of evaluation.

The evaluation of the project (2007–2008) was conducted in concert with the consultation of expert action researchers, a planning committee, a doctoral student, and a master level student as well as project stakeholders.

The key goals of the evaluation were obtaining information to improve and sustain the project, distributing information about the project to a variety of stakeholders, and educating the project stakeholders so that they can serve as change agents. Data was collected via evaluation questionnaires, focus group meetings, and co-planner/collaborative partnership surveys. The participatory nature of the research and evaluation process allowed for continued learning and implementation of the Look, Think, and Act methodology to occur. An important outcome of the evaluation report was to provide the project director with relevant data necessary to assess the strengths and weaknesses of the project and to make recommendations for adjustments that should be incorporated to ensure the project's continuation. As an agent of change, the founding director (who developed and sustained the project for 10 years), elected to select a new project director (2009) to continue the progress that had been achieved. The founding director now serves on the fund-raising committee of the U.S.–Africa Partnership for Building Stronger Communities Project; its goal is to help maintain the project by providing scholarships for students who need financial assistance in order to participate in the SSTA.

The current director is developing relationships with additional countries. Action research, including Look, Think and Act, is used in the context of both understanding issues concerning the provision of social work services in Africa, as well as building new relationships in the East African region. Going forward, the project will continue employing the methodology of Look, Think, and Act to conceptualize and address issues such as HIV/AIDS prevention in a context that honors Africa's history and cultures. Action research will continue to be a salient teaching tool along with sustaining collaborative partnerships.

Limited Government and University Recognition of Action Research

Presently, university and government recognition of action research is limited. Action researchers face barriers that researchers using traditional methods of research do not. For example, action researchers and other change agents are often faced with the limitation of university and government recognition and funding when using action research methods. This is especially true if the focus of the research is directed toward change and development. In addition, many universities and government organizations more readily recognize and fund research that they view as rigorous or scholarly. Luckey (1998) points out that quantitative research, a positivistic approach of seeking facts through a collection of objective quantifiable data under experimentally controlled conditions, is usually accepted more than qualitative research. Action research as a method of qualitative research is still largely not considered as rigorous or reliable as classic research methods. Luckey (1999) goes on to say that this point of view often leaves action researchers without the necessary funds to carry out their research activities.

A major concern of university professors interested in action research is the difficulty in securing promotion and tenure. Also, masters and doctoral students interested in action research often find it difficult to find faculty members who are knowledgeable about action research methods. Jones (1998) notes that, unfortunately, universities recognize traditional research methods as the most valued means worthy to meet the criteria for students' learning.

Many community-based organizations have expressed concerns regarding the lack of recognition and funding they receive from governmental agencies and universities for their use of action research (Loka Institute 2004). This lack of funding has implications for local, national, and international community building and development, and it can serve to prevent change agents from using action learning and research for promoting individual, group, and community change and development.

The U.S.–Africa Partnership for Building Stronger Communities Project has had to rely on creative funding, which includes private fund-raising and in-kind contributions (i.e., volunteering of time and services and the use of community facilities, equipment, and vehicles). However, even with the limitation of university and government funding and recognition, this article advocates for recognition of action research because it serves communities and benefits universities by providing learning experiences and opportunities as well as offering community service opportunities to students and faculty (Schenck 1996; Jones 1998). Armstrong (1998) is positive about her advocacy for action research. She notes that the conceptual model represented by participatory (action) research rarely informs the design or conduct of public health research. She goes on to point out that participatory processes are receiving more attention by some funding agencies and that there is evidence of the participatory processes in public health's involvement of community advisory boards and attention to community capacity building.

Limitations of university and government recognition and funding of action research suggest that action researchers must view themselves as change agents. In this role, they need to be the voices of change through publications and conference presentations and documenting outcomes of their research. They should advocate for action research to be included as a valued research method and seek to promote action research as a means for change and development in this era of social, cultural, technical, and economic globalization.

Implications of Action Research for Change Agents in a Global Society

Now, more than ever, opportunities are needed to sensitize individuals, groups, and communities to a more mosaic world, which has resulted from the breaking down of borders due to globalization. Action learning and research focuses on the worth and dignity of all people and the principle of participation. These concepts translated into action can help bring people of different cultural backgrounds and ages together. Additionally, action learning and research can assist in developing strong civil societies. Components of action learning and research that emphasize informed inquiry, reflection, and empowerment can be used to encourage people and communities to take part in decision-making with regard to issues and concerns that impact their lives and that of their families and communities. Efforts to encourage people and communities to collaboratively address peace and security can be facilitated through the process of collective decision-making and the maximizing of opportunities to involve all participants. Furthermore, action learning and research can assist in education and training related to mediation and reconciliation, which are important components in achieving peace and security. Thus action learning and research have implications for change agents (i.e., action researchers, social workers and other helping professionals, and policymakers) and for the promotion of change and development. It is timely to use action learning and action research as a means to help communities and their residents become empowered so that they will be able to be more self-sufficient and able to effectively address issues and problems that affect their lives. Action researchers recognize the strengths, worth, and dignity of all people and understand the power of information and mutual participation (Brueggemann 1996). In this era of globalization, they can help to create opportunities for change and development using their knowledge and skills in action learning and research (Netting et al. 1998).

Notes

1. The phenomenon of globalization entered our lexicon in the 1980s as a new form of worldwide interconnectedness, especially in the organization of production. This phenomenon is complex and has many definitions. It can be viewed from a social, cultural, technological, economic, and political perspective. For example, social globalization has been referred to as a means of global integration in which diverse peoples, economics, cultures, and political processes are subjected to international influences. Economic globalization is related to the expanding international trade in goods and services that has accelerated over the past quarter century with the booming of computer technology, the reduction of trade barriers, and the growing political and economic power of multinational corporations (Jones and Austin 2010).

2. It should be noted that in this article, the term participant refers to students, community-based practitioners, grass roots communities, stakeholders, and those engaged in or subject to the U.S.–Africa Partnership for Building Stronger Communities Project's evaluation.

3. On each Summer Study Tour to Africa (SSTA), participants do not arrive in countries empty-handed. They provide schools, hospitals, and orphanages with school supplies (purchased by the SSTA participants) and hand-quilted blankets and toys (made by quilting guilds located throughout the United States).

4. Ghana (as well as other African nations) have polluted and limited streams of water. Lack of individual and community funds makes it difficult to provide sources of clean drinking water. The World Bank (2000) recommended that Ghana (in order to reduce its huge debts from loans secured through the World Bank and others) privatize its water. However, due to the poverty of majority of Ghana's residents, this recommendation generated national and international protest (Jones and Austin 2010).

5. Collaborative partnership for this paper refers to a mutual and respectful form of partnership and teamwork that aims for collective wisdom. The authors' perspective for this type of partnership comes from the principles of action learning and research and from the ancient South African philosophy of *ubuntu* that draws on the fact that we are one human family in need of one another (Lundin and Nelson 2010).

References

Armstrong, J. (1998). "Identifying barriers to participatory research: Funding for public health research." Paper presented at focus group meeting on *Action Research as a Means to Support University and Community Partnerships*. Sponsored by the State University of New York at Albany, Cornell University, and the University of Missouri at Columbia.

Bashant, J. (1998). "Action learning: Faculty-student partnership." Paper presented at focus group meeting on *Action Research as a Means to Support University and Community Partnerships*. Sponsored by the State University of New York at Albany, Cornell University, and the University of Missouri at Columbia.

Brueggemann, W. G. 1996. *The practice of macro social work*. Chicago: Nelson-Hall.

Brydon-Miller, M., M. Kral, P. Maguire, S. Noffke, and A. Sabhlok. 2011. Jazz and the banyan tree: Roots and riffs on participatory action research. In *The Sage handbook of qualitative research* (4th ed.), N. K. Denzin and Y. S. Lincoln, eds. 387–400. Thousand Oaks, CA: Sage.

Collins, K. 1999. *Participatory research: A primer*. South Africa: Prentice Hall South Africa.

——. 2004. *Powerful collaborations: Building a movement for social change*. Washington, DC: Loka Institute.

——. 2002. Action research international. *Journal of Action Research* [on-line journal]. Retrieved September 22, 2004 at http://www.scu.edu.au/schools/gcm/ar/ari/ari-hist.html.

ETC Group. 2004b, June. *The little big down: A small introduction to nano-scale technologies*. Canada: Action Group on Erosion, Technology and Concentration. Retrieved September 20, 2004 at http://www.etcgroup.org.

——. 2004a, April. *Nano's troubled waters*. Canada: Action Group on Erosion, Technology, and Concentration. Retrieved September 20, 2004 at http://www.etcgroup.org.

Green, L. W., M. A. George, M. Daniel, C. J. Frankish, C. P. Herbert, W. R. Bowie and M. O'Neil. 1997. Background on participatory research. In *Doing community-based research: A reader*, D. Murphy, M. Scammell, and R. Sclove, eds. 53–66. Amherst, MA: The Loka Institute.

Hall, B. (1997). "Reflection on the origins of the International Participatory Research Network and the Participatory Research Group in Toronto, Canada". Paper presented at the Midwest Research-To-Practice Conference in Adult, Continuing and Community Education, Michigan State University, Lansing, MI.

Inglis, S. 1994. *Making the most out of action learning*. Brookfield, VT: Gower.

Israel, B. A., A. J. Schulz, E. A. Parker, and A. B. Becker. 1998. Review of community-based research: Assessing partnership approaches to improve public health. *Annual Review of Public Health*, 19:173–202.

Israel, B., E. Eng, A. Schulz, and E. Parker. 2005. *Methods in community-based participatory research for health*. San Francisco, CA: Jossey-Bass.

Jones, S. J. (1998). "Research for action: University and community partnership." Unpublished paper used to plan and design a focus group meeting on *Action Research as a Means to Support University and Community Partnerships* held on October 22, 1998, at the State University at Albany and a teleconference on *Research as a Means to Engage, Enrich and Sustain Communities* held on July 5, 2000, at the University of Pretoria, South Africa.

Jones, S. J. and S. A. Austin. 2010. Globalization and Africa: Development challenges and implications for helping professionals in *Globalization, Social justice, and the helping profession*, W. Roth and Katharine Briar-Lawson, eds. Albany: State University of New York. 119–134.

Jones, S. J. and J. L. Zlotnik, eds. 1998. *Preparing helping professionals to meet community needs*. Alexandria, VA: Council on Social Work Education.

Kettner, P., R. Moroney, and L. Martin. 1999. *Designing and managing programs: An effectiveness-based approach* (2nd ed.). Thousand Oaks, CA: Sage.

Loka Institute. 2004. About us. Retrieved August 11, 2005 at http://www.loka.org.

Luckey, I. (1998). "Empowerment research with community groups." Paper presented at focus group meeting on *Action Research as a Means to Support University and Community Partnerships*. Sponsored by the State University of New York at Albany, Cornell University, and the University of Missouri at Columbia.

Lundin, S. and B. Nelson. 2010. *Ubuntu*. New York: Broadway Book Publishers.

Murphy, D., M. Scammell, and R. Sclove. 1997. *Doing community-based research: A reader*. Amherst, MA: Loka Institute.

Netting, E.F., P. M. Kettner, and S. L. McMurtry. 1998. Social work macro practice. New York: Longman.

O'Brien, R. 2001. Um exame da abordagem metodologica da pesquisa acao [An overview of the methodological approach of action research]. In *Teoria e pratica da pesquisa acao* [Theory and practice of action research], Roberto Richardson, ed. Joao Pessoa, Brazil: Universidade Federal da Paraiba. (English version) Available: http://www.web.ca/robrien/papers/arfinal.html. (Accessed August 17, 2010.)

———. 2003. *An overview of the methodological approach to action research*. Retrieved September 22, 2004 at www.web.net~robrien/papers/arfinal.html.

Park, P. 2006. Knowledge and participatory research. In *Handbook of action research: concise paperback edition*, P. Reason and H. Bradbury, eds. 83–93. Thousand Oaks, CA: Sage.

Project South. 2002. Movement building timeline. Retrieved September 22, 2004, at projectsouthdc@earthlink.net or http://www.projectsouth.org.

Project South Periodical Spring 2010 http://www.projectsouth.org/movement-building-projects/download March 14, 2010.

Revans, R. 2011. *ABC of action learning*. England: Gower.

Ryder, M. 2003. Action research. Retrieved September 22, 2004 at http://www.carbon.cudenver.edu/~mryder/itc/act_res.html.

Schenck C. J. 1996. *Community development*. Pretoria: U of South Africa P.

Smith, M. K. 2001. Kurt Lewin, groups, experiential learning and action research, in *The encyclopedia of informal education*, online at http://www.infed.org/thinkers/et-lewin.htm. August 2010

Stringer, E. T. 1999. *Action research*. Thousand Oaks, CA: Sage.

Taylor & Francis Group. 1999. *Action research living*. New York: Taylor & Francis.

Tomson, G., C. Paphassarang, K. Jönsson, K. Houamboun, K. Akkhavong, R. Wahlström. (2005). Decision-makers and the usefulness of research evidence in policy implementation a case study from Lao PDR. *Social Science & Medicine* 61(6):1291–1299.

van Dyk, A. C. 2000. *Welfare science and social welfare policy*. Pretoria: U of South Africa P.

van Rooyen, C. (2002). "Research for change partnerships and strengths as foundations for change in the crime reduction in schools project. Paper presented at focus group meeting on *Action Research as a Means to Support University and Community Partnerships*. Sponsored at the University of South Africa, Pretoria, South Africa.

Wagner, J. 1993. Educational research as a full participant: Challenges and opportunities for generating new knowledge. *Qualitative Studies in Education, 6*(1):3–18.

Weiss, R. "For science, nanotech poses big unknowns." *Washington Post*, February 1, 2004.

Worthington, R. 2000. *Rethinking globalization: Production, politics, action*. New York: Peter Lang.

PART III

METHODS OF DATA COLLECTION AND ANALYSIS

Qualitative Interviewing

JUDY L. POSTMUS

. . . a crown princess, like a queen, can succeed only by staying apart. Separation, elevation, delegation.

—Anidori-Kiladra Talianna Isilee, Crown Princess of Kildenree,
The Goose Girl

Similar to the crown princess in this fairy tale, researchers sometimes think that to be successful and objective interviewers, they must remain apart from respondents by elevating their "expert" status above those interviewed. However, when thinking about interviewing subjects in a qualitative study, researchers are permitted to participate in a truly remarkable enterprise—one that puts the researcher into the learner position and the subject into the expert position. As the princess learned in *The Goose Girl*, by subjugating herself and shedding her crown and power, she was able to finally understand, appreciate, and advocate for others based on their own experiences as working-class folks (Hale 2003).

For researchers, one purpose of interviewing others is to understand someone else's life experiences from his/her point of view. Interviewing draws social workers to qualitative research because they have many of the skills necessary to conduct such interviews. Social workers interview clients, consumers, or patients to collect much information about them and to assess the challenges in their lives.

Should a skilled social worker read more about interviewing? This chapter provides a practical guide to qualitative research interviewing through the perspective of a social worker with experience interviewing others as a practitioner and as a researcher, and it is written for social workers who desire to learn from others and to satisfy that innate curiosity to understand someone else's perspective on life. Additionally, because our professional commitment is to work with and improve the lives of oppressed populations, this chapter focuses on interviewing individuals whose voices usually are overlooked or discounted so that we may give voice to those individuals. In sum, this chapter will afford social workers the opportunity to learn the essence of qualitative research using interviewing that helps others' voices be heard and to realize they have many of the skills necessary to conduct interviews as researchers.

This chapter starts with a brief discussion on the debates among qualitative researchers regarding the paradigmatic issues with a focus on the pragmatic approach adopted by this author. The chapter then reviews the challenges faced by the qualitative interviewer, identifies the training and skills needed to conduct qualitative interviews, reviews the decisions the interviewer must make prior to interviewing, and concludes with a brief description of the steps involved in the actual interview process.

While this chapter focuses on qualitative interviewing, the decisions to make, the skills needed, and the challenges faced are similar to quantitative interviewing. The biggest difference lies in the type of questions; quantitative methods require that questions are asked in a consistent and accurate manner with quantifiable responses offered by the participant whereas qualitative interviewing does not restrict the type or format of questions. Throughout this chapter, the person responding to the interview, namely the interviewee, the respondent, or the research subject, will be referred to as the participant.

Finally, this chapter focuses on interviewing individuals. Other forms of interviewing exist including focus groups and group interviewing. Focus group interviewing consists of gathering a small group of individuals to answer questions on a specific topic. The most salient feature of this method is the presence of group interaction among participants in response to researchers' questions, wherein participants can add to or revise their responses based on learning from other group members (Morgan and Krueger 1993). The goal of the focus group interview is to collect data on the questions posed and not to reach a consensus or to solve a problem. "The object is to get high-quality data in a social context where people can consider their own views in the context of the views of others" (Patton 2002:386). Different from focus groups, group interviewing consists of unstructured, conversational interviews without particular questions that need to be answered. For further information on conducting focus groups, see the next chapter in this volume, chapter 11, by Raymie H. Wayne.

The Paradigm Debate

The debate over which paradigm should be used to inform research and ways of knowing has raged for years among academics throughout the world. From positivist and empiricist, to constructivist and postmodern, to post positivist, interpretivist, and critical, the debate continues as to which one qualitative researchers should ascribe (Padgett 2008). Rather than choosing one paradigm, this chapter takes a pragmatic approach to qualitative interviewing—an approach discussed by Padgett (2008), Patton (2002), and Teddlie and Tashakkori (2009).

What exactly is a pragmatic approach to qualitative research? Tashakkori and Teddlie (2009) and Padgett (2008) list a few basic tenets including:

- There is no absolute truth since personal (and sometimes political) values drive research methods; facts are truly theories.
- Any set of data can have a wide range of interpretation.
- The difference between quantitative and qualitative methodologies lies with how data are collected, analyzed, and interpreted. The choice between methods should be driven by the research question and not by a particular paradigm (Padgett 2008).

The pragmatic approach allows researchers to move within and between researchers ascribing to different paradigms—a lifesaving tactic for doctoral students navigating dissertation committees with members ascribing to and religiously supporting various paradigms. This approach also allows the reader to learn and apply the information contained in this chapter about qualitative interviewing while personally ascribing to his or her own paradigm. For those interested in further discussions about the different paradigms and the long-standing and interesting debate among qualitative researchers, please see Denzin and Lincoln (2005) as a starting point.

Challenges to Address

Regardless of the chosen paradigm, the qualitative interviewer will be faced with challenges about the methods prior to the commencement of interviewing individuals. These challenges, described more fully here, include choosing flexibility versus consistency, managing complex and sensitive topics, and remembering the role of power, gender, ethnicity, and class.

Flexibility Versus Consistency

The challenge of flexibility versus consistency is usually addressed when determining the structure or type of questions to ask. If the choice is to conduct a standardized interview with structured research questions, then flexibility in pursuing new topics is lost; however, the results from the interview include consistent answers that can then be compared. Probes and the possibility of bias are limited when the same questions are asked of every participant. However, this limits the flexibility and spontaneity of the researcher who wants to explore uncharted territory by limiting the pursuit of other topics not anticipated but discovered during the interview (Patton 2002).

Why, then, conduct structured interviews? The answer to this question lies in what researchers view as reliable and valid research. By having structured interview questions, the instrument can be inspected and validated by others such as a dissertation committee, human subjects committee, or a journal review panel. Additionally, if more than one interviewer is involved, the use of structured questions will minimize the variation between interviewers, again reducing bias. Finally, with structured questions, the participants answer the same questions allowing for complete answers to the questions and for comparability between participants (Patton 2002).

Then why would one sacrifice reliability, validity, and consistency for the sake of flexibility? The answer lies with the original research question and the intent of the researcher. If the researcher has concrete questions based on previous research literature or theory and wants more information from others about these specific questions, then using structured interview questions makes sense. However, if the researcher truly wants to learn from participants' perspectives, thoughts, and emotions, then the researcher leaves those participants in charge of the interview process and encourages the discussion of new and uncharted territory. Unfortunately, this unstructured method often leaves the researcher open to criticism from colleagues, dissertation committees, and institutional review boards who usually want to know what questions will be asked in advance prior to granting approval to the study. The challenge, then, is for the researcher to reflect on what is more important to answer the original research question—flexibility or consistency.

Managing Complex and Sensitive Topics

In social work research, the topics explored are often complex and sensitive such as domestic violence, HIV/AIDS, sexual abuse, or family relationships. During interviews, participants may experience strong emotions while they relive their experiences and feelings about these painful events. Face-to-face interviews offer researchers the opportunity to monitor the reactions of participants and to adjust the questions and timing of the interview. Nonverbal cues such as crying, fidgeting in a chair, or a change in tone of voice can signal the researcher that the participant is possibly uncomfortable with the subject matter. Social workers are trained to recognize these nonverbal cues and to ask questions about the messages given.

The challenge, then, for the social work researcher is to know when to continue asking questions, when to adjust the interview, or when to stop the interview. Often, practitioners know these nonverbal cues and use them to challenge clients to work through tough issues or retreat if the discussion is too much for the client. Yet as a researcher, it is important to avoid the practitioner role in which the client's emotional pain is alleviated or self-awareness becomes enhanced (Tutty, Rothery, and Grinnell 1996). Instead, the cues dictate if the participant can finish the interview or not; the focus is still on collecting information from the participant for the purposes of the study. That is not to say that interviewers should be calloused and insensitive; rather, they can adjust the timing of the interview to be sensitive to the feelings of the participant and offer referrals and information about services available in the community to help participants deal with these issues more effectively.

As an example, I interviewed incarcerated women to learn about their adult and childhood victimization experiences as part of a National Institute of Justice (NIJ) grant (Postmus 2002; Postmus and Severson 2006). While the interview questions were standardized questions as part of this mixed methods study, the questions dredged up feelings for one of the participants who started crying about her victimization experiences. I stopped the interview and offered her tissues. The practitioner in me wanted to explore and alleviate her emotional pain. What was she remembering or thinking about that brought tears to her eyes? However, the researcher in me focused on the purpose of the study—namely to collect data on her experiences. So I asked if she needed a break or wanted to stop the interview. Through tears, she stated she wanted to continue. After the hour-long interview, I reminded her that there was a support group available for her and other women incarcerated at the prison for her to further talk about her experiences and address some of the emotional pain she displayed through her tears. This woman may have had some insight from the interaction with me; however, my role was not to help her gain insight into her pain. Instead, my role was to collect information about her experiences and allow her voice to contribute to the knowledge about victimization experiences of incarcerated women.

If this had been a qualitative interview with an unstructured question format, my approach may have been different. I may have stopped to ask what she was thinking that led her to tears. Her responses could have led the discussion to another level of inquiry—or not. Regardless, the goal for the researcher is to learn as much as possible from the participant about a particular level of inquiry. While seemingly callous, the struggle for social work researchers is to not engage in social work practice with participants but rather to team with other resources to provide that service.

The Role of Power, Gender, Ethnicity, and Class

Whatever the training, skills, and background of the interviewer, the interaction between the researcher and the participant may unfold in different ways depending on the gender, ethnicity, and class of all those involved in the interview (Warren 2002). Qualitative interviewers must consider the role power will play in the interviews and who will maintain the power. Quantitative interviewers often determine the questions, the pace, and the context of the interview, viewing the participants as "passive vessels of answers" (Holstein and Gubrium 1995:7). In contrast, qualitative methods offer the researcher the opportunity to distribute all or a portion of the power and decisions behind the interview. The challenge for researchers is to determine how comfortable they are with not keeping power or control over the interview. Most often, researchers think they are sharing power when in fact, because of their gender, race, education, or social class, they may not realize their own inherent power and how that power impacts the interaction and information collected. Participants' lack of power may influence their answers in which they provide imperfect, ambiguous, or incomplete information (Shuy 2002).

Indeed, Briggs (2002) takes the power dynamics in interviews one step further by criticizing how researchers and those that interview others hold power over what is collected, how it is analyzed, and how it is presented, all the while disguising themselves as objective and rational. "Interviews are structured by power asymmetries and by conventions that produce discursively complex material that is geared toward the institutional ends for which it was created. . . . construing the interview itself as the locus of knowledge production places audiences and analysts alike in the grip of a powerful illusion" (Briggs 2002:919).

Thus interviewers must be aware of the power they hold based on their position, class, gender, or ethnicity. Social workers are taught to pay attention to power dynamics or at least to the differences between the practitioner and the client. The same social work awareness of differences and the impact on our practice is needed in qualitative interviewing. The following sections review some of the challenges to consider when conducting interviews across cultural and gender boundaries.

CROSS-CULTURAL INTERVIEWING

Cross-cultural interviewing "refers to the collection of interview data across cultural and national borders" (Ryen 2002:336). Cultural borders include differences in class, ethnicity, and religious status. The challenge researchers face is to encourage participants from different classes or ethnic or religious groups to join with the researcher and describe their experiences, knowledge, and feelings. Establishing and maintaining rapport—crucial to get an accurate portrayal of the participant's experiences—becomes more challenging when there is a history of hierarchy, exploitation, racism, or sexism (Ryen 2002). The researcher must be diligent to avoid becoming the expert and taking or remaining in the power position if the goal is to encourage accurate information from the participant.

In addition to being aware of the position of power held, the researcher must also focus on the verbal and nonverbal communication challenges that emerge when conducting cross-cultural interviews. Speaking another language requires more than vocabulary and grammar since linguistic styles are different in different contexts. "The problem may not necessarily be a matter of posing the right questions, but one of the researcher's communicating questions to the interpreter in culturally appropriate ways that invite further communication" (Ryen 2002:344).

Nonverbal communication skills are crucial for anyone conducting interviews but may pose additional challenges for researchers conducting cross-cultural interviews. Breaks and silences may be misinterpreted as cues to prompt more discussion or that the participant is confused when in reality, long pauses may be part of everyday conversations. "Language—spoken and unspoken words, sounds, utterances, gestures, signs, and other forms of speech and action used to communicate—is the primary vehicle through which, in which, we construct our worlds, give order and meaning to our lives, and relate to each other" (H. Anderson 1997:201). Thus understanding the power dynamics based on class, ethnicity, or gender will enhance the interaction between the interviewer and the participants.

Again, social workers learn how to establish rapport with clients early on including clients who are different from them. Indeed, social work training and education prepare us to think about cultural diversity. The challenge for social workers is to remember these skills when interviewing participants for research.

FEMINIST INTERVIEWING

When interviewing women, regardless of the gender of the interviewer, the researcher must be aware of the challenges that may hinder the interview process. Much has been written about doing feminist research including strategies for interviewing and analyzing data (Devault and Gross 2007). The first challenge is to be aware of the assumptions inherent in feminist interviewing including the assumption that, while all women's experiences are gendered, no two women's experiences are identical (Reinharz and Chase 2002). Women's perspectives are often conflicted—with one view framed in values and concepts that reflect men's dominant position in the culture and the other framed from their personal experiences (Anderson and Jack 1991). Thus researchers need to learn to listen to both what is said and what is left unsaid instead of focusing on the next question or structuring questions in such a way that minimizes responses of women participants.

Listening to women requires skills that focus on the unique experiences and perspectives women bring (Anderson and Jack 1991). Anderson and

Jack (1991) list three ways to help researchers listen to women's point of view. First, listen to the woman's moral language by examining the relationship between her self-concept and cultural norms. Next, attend to what she leaves unsaid; that is, be alert to spontaneous pauses or stops, or any recounting or reframing of what was just said. This alerts the interviewer that the individual is struggling with what she thinks versus what she is supposed to say. One such example includes the use of the phrase "you know." Sometimes this phrase indicates that the person is fumbling for words; however, it may signal a request for understanding and a desire to join with the interviewer (Devault and Gross 2007). Finally, listen to the logic of the narrative by noticing any consistencies, contradictions, or recurring themes and how they all relate to each other (Anderson and Jack 1991).

Traditionally, social science research has focused on men; researchers should be aware that women, who may have never had the opportunity to express themselves or to be heard, may not know what to do when given that opportunity (Reinharz and Chase 2002). Women and men learn to communicate by imitating others and passing on the lessons learned to next generations. Minister (1991) describes this tradition of learning communication skills as a frame that allows the individual to label and define experiences. Girls, who are more closely supervised by adults, learn to create and maintain relationships of closeness and equality, criticize others in acceptable ways, and interpret the speech of other girls in an accurate fashion (Minister 1991). Boys, on the other hand, learn to use communication as a way to assert a position of dominance, attract and maintain an audience, and assert oneself when other speakers have the floor (Minister 1991). Thus researchers must learn to not only encourage women to talk about their experiences but also be aware of the impact the telling of these experiences may have on the participants and be prepared to offer referrals to resources when the impact is overwhelming (Reinharz and Chase 2002).

Training and Skills

What are the training and skills needed to be a good interviewer? Gilgun (1994) has suggested that qualitative interviewing fits social workers "hand in glove." She notes that, like social workers, researchers must start where the client is, focus on the individual and maximize the details, use both deductive and inductive thinking before drawing conclusions, be aware of the verbal and nonverbal cues, and explore thoughts, memories, feelings, and opinions in a safe environment (Gilgun 1994).

However, Padgett (1998) has challenged the notion that social workers can easily transfer their clinical skills to research skills for interviewing participants. While she acknowledges some duplication in skills, she also identifies a paradigm shift in which assumptions and goals are different for the clinician compared to the researcher. The goal for practitioners includes providing quality services to the client with attention paid to the functions and requirements of the agency or setting (Padgett 1998). For instance, when conducting a client intake, the practitioner focuses on the client's strengths, challenges, and limitations in light of the services the agency can offer. Thus for a client entering a domestic violence shelter, the worker focuses on her domestic violence experiences and, because of time and form constraint, may not delve into other topics suggested by the client.

Another difference lies in the power dynamics between the participant/ client and researcher/practitioner. The researcher encourages the participant to take on the teacher and informer role while the researcher becomes the learner. The participant knows that the only agenda the researcher has is to learn about their experiences—not to determine if they are appropriate for services, to solve their problems, nor to establish a working relationship beyond one or possibly two interviews. The researcher's ultimate goal is to learn from the participant and to contribute knowledge and understanding based on what the participant and other participants describe from their experiences (Tutty, Rothery, and Grinnell 1996; Padgett 1998).

As an example, I experienced this shift in paradigm during the qualitative interviews I conducted for my dissertation. After working in the field for more than 15 years, I was nervous as I prepared for interviews with battered women on welfare. Exploring victimization experiences was not daunting to me, a skilled and seasoned practitioner. The nervousness stemmed from my concern that I would end up acting as a practitioner instead of a researcher. After interviewing 29 women and learning much from their experiences with victimization and welfare, I also saw this paradigm shift in my own skills. I learned that since my role with these incredible women was just to learn from them and offer them $20 for their time, I was able to encourage women to tell me more about their experiences than they have ever told any practitioner. Having the freedom from filling out an intake form or having any confines from agency function allowed me to learn as much as the women wanted to discuss. Plus, the women could be comfortable knowing that I did not want anything more from them besides their stories; they did not have to say the right thing to get the needed services (e.g., shelter, food, counseling, day care). Since that first study, I continue to find that women are more than willing to tell of their abuse if given the opportunity, the freedom, and the safety needed to divulge horrible experiences at the hand of an intimate partner.

Thus the skills needed to conduct qualitative interviews include more than just the skills needed to be a good practitioner. Researchers must also be aware of the influence of their own language on the interview process (May 1991). Questions may begin with nonspecific language until terms and meanings are identified, taking into account "the subtle sociocultural differences in verbal and nonverbal styles when planning and executing interviews" (May 1991:197). For example, how is coping defined? Participants may answer that question by providing varying definitions and meanings based on their own experiences and knowledge, which, in turn, will contribute to how coping is defined. Thus the interview may not start with the description of coping skills but rather a description of how the participant views and defines coping (May 1991).

Another skill needed is to be able to establish rapport quickly to encourage participants to talk. Practitioners often have more than one time to discuss concerns of clients. Indeed, at times, social workers postpone asking the hard questions until they have established rapport, often waiting for two to three sessions to pass. Researchers, on the other hand, have to develop rapport, demonstrate empathy, and ask very personal or tough questions all within the span of one to two hours. Thus, for social work researchers, their skill of establishing rapport must be evident quickly so that research participants feel comfortable describing their personal experiences.

How does one learn this skill of quickly establishing rapport? From personal experiences, I have learned that if I am genuine about my intent, truly care about the person in front of me, and demonstrate quickly that I am the learner in the relationship with no motive other than to learn from the participant, then I am able to create a safe and comfortable environment in even the most public venues. Often, I rely on not only my verbal communication skills but also my nonverbal cues that indicate my openness to learn from the participant. For example, in my interviews with battered women on welfare (Postmus 2002), I distinctly remember one woman who talked about her abuse experiences and what she told the worker from the welfare system. Interestingly, she stated that she did not tell them about her sexual abuse experiences but felt comfortable telling me. Her reason? She relied on nonverbal cues from the welfare worker who indicated that she was already appalled by the abuse experiences. The woman concluded that the worker would not be able to handle any more information. However, she felt safe enough to talk about her sexual abuse experiences with me while she wore a lapel microphone to record every word and while sitting in a crowded restaurant. So my nonverbal communication, telling her that I was safe and strong enough to hear her deepest secrets, encouraged her to talk freely. Social workers are trained to get others to talk. The key is to enhance that training to encourage others to talk in a short amount of time.

Finally, other training and skills needed for interviewers may depend on the type of questions asked. Both practitioners and researchers need knowledge about the interview topics and self-awareness to monitor one's biases and reactions to participants. However, for researchers, the knowledge and self-awareness needed are different because of the nature of research interviewing. For example, if the research study is on victimization experiences, interviewers must be trained to minimize and manage any emotional distress for the safety and emotional health of both the participant and the interviewer (Sullivan 2004). Intensive and continual exposure to other people's victimization experiences may affect the interviewer—especially if there is no time to process the information in between interviews (Sullivan 2004). While a practitioner may also experience similar reactions to a client's victimization experiences, usually there is time to process the experiences with the client over a period of time. Additionally, there may be more supports in place, such as other colleagues, that may mitigate the impact. Researchers, on the other hand, may interview multiple participants in a short period of time, collecting intimate and grizzly details of horrific abuse or trauma experiences. It is important for interviewers and those supervising the research to watch for signs of interviewer distress, including distancing themselves and limiting the engagement with participants, presenting common emotional and physical symptoms of stress, or expressing problems in relationships with family and friends (Slattery and Goodman 2009). Ongoing support and training will alleviate some of the distress.

Decisions to Make

Prior to actually interviewing participants for a research study, several decisions must be made including the overall purpose of the study, the structure of the interview, how to conduct the interview, and the specific questions to ask. The final decisions made depend on the research questions and whether or not the use of interviewing is even warranted. Each of these decisions is discussed in the following sections.

Purpose

From a pragmatic approach, determining whether to use quantitative or qualitative interviewing often depends on what the researcher hopes to uncover from the interview. If the purpose of the study is to uncover facts and concrete experiences in a numeric fashion that enhances already obtained knowledge, then the use of specific questions with limited answers as part of quantitative methods is warranted. However, if deep information and new understanding are desired, then qualitative interviewing would be best. In other words, to gain different perspectives, to learn new information that goes beyond commonsense explanations, to be a student interested in gaining knowledge from a veteran informant, or to grasp different meanings of some activity, event, place, or cultural experience, in-depth interviewing is warranted (J. M. Johnson 2002).

For example, when designing a study to explore the experiences of battered women on welfare with the Family Violence Option (FVO), the better method to gather this information was qualitative interviewing (Postmus 2004). Lawmakers passed the FVO, an amendment to the Personal Responsibility and Work Opportunity Reconciliation Act, in response to the prevalence of battered women on welfare and the concerns about the ability of battered women to meet welfare requirements. The FVO allows states the flexibility to respond to battered women on welfare and provide waivers from Temporary Assistance to Needy Family (TANF) program requirements. When developing this study in 2001, there was little known about the FVO, the effectiveness of the implementation, or the experiences of battered women with the FVO and the welfare system. Gilgun (1994) suggests that qualitative methodologies are useful when studying policy formulation and implementation—especially a new policy such as the FVO.

Additionally, qualitative methodologies are useful when working with an at-risk population—one that is difficult to access in large numbers, such as battered women on welfare. The information collected from battered women's experiences on welfare and with the FVO provided a beginning knowledge of battered women's perspectives on the FVO.

Types of Interviews

Once the decision to uncover in-depth information is made, then the next decision is to determine the type of interview method to use. Standardized, structured, or conventional interviews require the development of specific questions that are asked of everyone participating in the research study. The assumptions are that the questions asked are sufficiently comprehensive to get all the information desired and worded well enough for all to understand, and that the meaning of each question is identical for each person (Tutty, Rothery, and Grinnell 1996). The trick is to use questions that create an atmosphere that encourages participants to talk about their experiences while at the same time controlling for bias to validate the results (Holstein and Gubrium 1995). Bias emerges from interviewers who are not capable of suppressing personal opinions or avoiding stereotyping participants, or from the interview setting and the interaction between participant and researcher—not from the respondent "who, under ideal conditions, serves up authentic reports when beckoned to do so" (Holstein and Gubrium 1995:8). By minimizing variation among researchers or among answers, the conventional approach to interviewing decreases biases by reducing flexibility and spontaneity while maximizing efficiency (Patton 2002). Participants are not intricately involved in the interaction; instead, they are "passive vessels of answers" that provide facts and details of their experiences (Holstein and Gubrium 1995:7).

Another type of interview method is the unstructured, informal conversation in which spontaneous questions and follow-up probes are useful to gain a thorough understanding of the perceptions and experiences of participants. Using this method allows researchers to develop, adapt, and generate questions appropriate to a given situation, in accordance with the research questions that guide the study (Tutty, Rothery, and Grinnell 1996). Often considered to be an open-ended interview, the questions are not predetermined since not all participants find equal meaning in them.

The goal is to encourage the participants to disclose feelings, thoughts, and experiences as well as opinions; the interview itself produces meaning while the interactions between the participants and the researcher are constantly developing (Holstein and Gubrium 1995).

Finally, researchers can combine methods by developing semistructured or guided interviews in which there are some predetermined questions that function as reminders of topics to explore with participants. This combination has the advantages of both the structured and unstructured interview; it addresses the bias that may be created by having predetermined topics asked of everyone, yet is not so structured that participants cannot provide their own meaning for the question that drives their answers. The decision on which method to choose depends on the research questions and the type of information sought from participants.

For example, in the interviews with battered women on welfare, I used a combination of questions, including standardized closed and open-ended questions along with probes, that allowed the battered women to expand on their answers to provide a fuller picture. The standardized questions allowed me to ask participants about their experiences with the welfare system and specific parts of the FVO yet the probes provided flexibility to pursue other topics not thought of when creating the interview questions.

How to Conduct the Interview

Another decision to make includes how to conduct the interview—namely, whether to conduct face-to-face interviews or telephone interviews. There are strengths and limitations to each of these methods—these rely heavily on the type of information desired, whether there is a need for consistency, the complexity of the topics, and any financial, time, and location constraints (Shuy 2002). Shuy (2002) reviewed the research literature that examined which works better—in-person or telephone interviewing. The results indicate that in-person interviews generate more accurate responses, primarily owing to the comfort of talking face-to-face with the interviewer. Other benefits of in-person interviewing include the increased likelihood of self-generated answers, better response rates, and more thoughtful responses especially when dealing with complex or sensitive topics. On the other hand, the advantages of telephone interviewing include the reduction of interviewer effects, better interviewer uniformity, greater standardization of questions, improved cost efficiency, and better researcher safety. Thus the decision regarding whether to conduct the interviews using a telephone or face-to-face method largely depends on what the researcher hopes to accomplish or collect from the interview.

This decision on whether to conduct the interview over-the-phone or in person can be exemplified by the research done on domestic violence. Researchers have used different methods to interview battered women with special attention given to their safety needs and their comfort in answering different questions about personal experiences. For their study, McNutt and her colleagues (McNutt, Carlson, Persaud, and Postmus 2002) chose to interview women over the phone. These women came from a primary health clinic and were asked about their abuse experiences, if they had experienced abuse. The rationale for conducting telephone interviews was to make the interview experience as nonthreatening as possible and to encourage women to be candid in their responses. Telephoning more than 500 women also saved tremendous time and costs associated with meeting face-to-face (McNutt et al. 2002).

On the other hand, for our NIJ study (Postmus and Severson 2006), we chose to conduct face-to-face interviews with 423 women. While we were aware of the extra time and money needed, our rationale included our desire for the women to feel a connection—albeit a short one—to the interviewer when discussing personal matters. We wanted to make the interview more meaningful for the women and help them believe that as the expert of their own experiences, we as interviewers can learn a great deal from them. How does a one-hour interview with a stranger create a meaningful experience? By being genuine about our reasons for the study, demonstrating our desire to learn from women through our opening statements on the purpose, benefits, and risks involved, we were able to create a safe, confidential, and anonymous environment that encouraged women to describe intimate details of their victimization histories. In fact, a few of the women interviewed divulged that this was the first time they told anyone about their abuse.

In a final example, I also combined telephone and face-to-face interviews in a longitudinal study with survivors of abuse (Postmus and Plummer 2010). We conducted three interviews over a period of 11 months with women recruited from 10 different states and 14 domestic violence service providers in those states. For the first interview, we decided to conduct face-to-face interviews with the intent of establishing rapport and a relationship with these participants. For the second interview, we conducted telephone interviews as a way to save time and money from traveling to different locations. For the final interview, we again used face-to-face interviews as a way to close the relationship with the participants. In between interviews, we also had monthly contact with participants, calling or e-mailing them. After 11 months, we were able to maintain a 77 percent retention rate—a significant feat considering the population (survivors of abuse) and their location (10 states). Thus, when deciding how to conduct the interviews, it is important to understand the rationale behind choosing between face-to-face or telephone interviewing.

Designing the Questions

The type, sequencing, and wording of questions will also influence the success of the interview; in other words, good questions will get good answers (Corbin and Strauss 2008). Patton (2002) describes different types of questions to ask including those about experiences and behaviors as well as about opinions—the intent being to understand the experiential, cognitive, and interpretive processes of participants. Other questions can focus on feelings, knowledge or factual information, or the individual's senses including what is seen, heard, touched, tasted, and smelled (Tutty, Rothery, and Grinnell 1996; Patton 2002). Sensitizing questions are useful to establish rapport with participants and to develop an environment that encourages their full disclosure. Examples of sensitizing questions include role-playing or simulation questions in which one asks the participant to respond to the interviewer as if he or she were someone else (Patton 2002). For example, in my interviews with battered women, one of the questions used was "Imagine your best friend, who is also a domestic violence victim, is applying for welfare for the first time. What would you tell her that would best prepare her for the process?" This question gave the women an opportunity to simulate helping someone else experience the process of applying for welfare by giving advice based on their own experiences. Grand tour questions or describing a typical day can help the participant walk the interviewer through a particular day. Finally, free recall listing requires participants to list all of the things they can think of regarding a given topic; this elicitation technique allows the researcher to determine if everything on a particular topic is covered (Johnson and Weller 2002).

Probes and follow-up questions often deepen the responses and inform the participant about the level of information wanted. Probes include detail-oriented questions, cues to keep the participant talking—such as the nodding of the head, clarification of statements, or compare and contrast statements—are all used with the intent of gathering more information from interview participants. "Probing is a skill that comes from knowing what to look for in the interview, listening carefully to what is said and what is not said, and being sensitive to the feedback needs of the person being interviewed" (Patton 2002:374).

The order or sequencing of questions is also important to consider. Starting with noncontroversial or present experiences, behaviors, or activities allows the participant time to adjust to the interview and divulge personal information. Next, the researcher should follow up with questions that focus on interpretations, opinions, feelings, and knowledge. Questions can be framed in the present, past, or future; however, questions about the present are easier to respond to than the past, and future questions are less reliable, calling for speculation (Patton 2002). Limit background and demographic questions by including them at the end of the interview.

The wording of questions is also important to consider. If wanting to ask open-ended questions, ensure that they truly are open and allow the participant to determine how he or she wants to respond. Closed-ended questions are also common on qualitative interviewing; ensure the timing and spacing of these questions to prevent the interview from turning into an interrogation. Questions should also be singular in nature; only one idea per question. Ask clear questions using terms and language with which the participant is most familiar. Finally, watch the use of "why" questions; these questions "presume cause-effect relationships, ordered world, perfect knowledge, and rationality" (Patton 2002:363).

Finally, when creating questions, one must also keep in mind the status of the participants. For example, when interviewing children, their age and cognitive abilities must be taken into consideration when creating questions. When interviewing "elites" or those who have authority or power (e.g., agency directors, policymakers), questions and the interview process may need to be adapted because the participant may want to control the questions asked—similar to how they grant interviews to the press (Marshall and Rossman 2006).

Steps of an Interview

There are multiple steps involved in interviewing, including steps prior to, during, and after the interview. First, prepare for the interview by recruiting participants through the use of screening criteria and informing them of the purpose of the interview, any risks and benefits to participation, and the role of confidentiality. Ensure that all the logistical questions are answered including the time, place, length, use of tape recorders, incentives, and identifying information. Be prepared with all the necessary paperwork such as consent forms and interview questions, including extra copies for participants. Finally, be prepared for logistical problems that may occur such as batteries wearing down, ink running out, or too much noise that drowns out the participant's voice. In my interviews with battered women on welfare, the best investment I made was to purchase a lapel microphone that captured everything the women said regardless of whether the interview setting was quiet or noisy.

Once prepared, the first few minutes of the interview are crucial for engaging the participant and establishing rapport. The process may start with small talk in an effort to put the participant (and the researcher) at ease with each other. The interview then starts with introductions and the interviewer describing the purpose of the interview. Review the human subjects consent form with special attention given to the purpose of the study, the benefits and risks of participation, and the measures taken to ensure confidentiality. Reiterate that the information he or she gives is important and discuss how the information will be used. Talk about the participant's role in the study—that they are a partner in collecting the information and telling others. For example, when I interviewed battered women on welfare, I told them that their experiences and stories would help other battered women on welfare and improve the implementation of the FVO. Their partnering with me gave voice to the women—voices that are often overlooked in research and policy development (Hagen and Davis 1994; Nichols-Casebolt and Spakes 1995).

Once the interview begins, one must be aware of the spoken and unspoken cues given by the interviewer and the participant, the surroundings, and the interviewer's thoughts and feelings about the participant and the answers. Provide reinforcement and feedback with words of thanks, nodding of the head, and reassuring the importance of the information given. Learn to be comfortable with silence and not be satisfied with monosyllabic answers. Throughout the interview, be cordial, respectful, and appreciative of the time given for the interview.

Upon conclusion of the interview, bring closure to the interaction by summing up the purpose and ask if the participant left anything unsaid. Give referrals or other sources of information for the participant to turn to for additional emotional, physical, or spiritual support. Once the participant leaves, one should reflect about the interview—thinking of things learned about the participant, the interaction, and oneself. Some researchers encourage the use of journaling thoughts and ideas that emerge immediately after the interview (Tutty, Rothery, and Grinnell 1996).

Conclusion

While interviewing someone seems simple for most, for the social work researcher doing qualitative interviewing, the art of interviewing is not as simple as it seems. Decisions must be made—such as whether to use structured or unstructured interviews, how to conduct the interviews, and the questions to ask—all influenced by the overall purpose of the study, the amount of flexibility or consistency desired, the sensitivity of the topics, and the power dynamics between the participants and the researcher. Some of the skills needed to be a successful research interviewer are the same as those of the social work practitioner, including strong communication skills (both verbal and nonverbal) and the ability to establish rapport. Yet a researcher also needs different training and skills that focus not only on the goals and objectives of the study, but also on the power dynamics of the interview so that the researcher is put in the learner position. Learning from others and telling their stories benefits those who tell their stories and those who report them to a wider audience. Good qualitative interviewing skills are crucial for ensuring that accurate stories are portrayed.

Social workers are trained to work with people—especially oppressed populations whose voices are rarely heard. Social workers have learned about establishing rapport and engaging others to talk about personal issues. They have learned how to be aware of their own biases and positions of power when working with others who are different from them. This knowledge affords social workers the beginning skills needed for qualitative interviewing. But one must not stop with these skills and think that these skills will automatically lead to being a good researcher interviewer.

One must be aware of the paradigm or approach taken for the research, as well as the potential challenges and the decisions to be made before beginning research. In essence, good interviewers must tap into their innate curiosity about the lives of others and bring forth participants' voices to inform policy, practice, and research.

References

Anderson, H. 1997. *Conversation, language, and possibilities: A postmodern approach to therapy*. New York: Basic.

Anderson, K. and D. C. Jack. 1991. Learning to listen: Interview techniques and analyses. In *Women's words: The feminist practice of oral history*, S. B. Gluck and D. Patai, eds. 11–26. New York: Routledge.

Briggs, C. L. 2002. Interviewing, power/knowledge, and social inequality. In *Handbook of interview research: Context and method*, J. F. Gubrium and J. A. Holstein, eds. 911–922. Thousand Oaks, CA: Sage.

Corbin, J. and A. Strauss. 2008. *Basics of qualitative research: Techniques and procedures for developing grounded theory* (3rd ed.). Thousand Oaks, CA: Sage.

Denzin, N. K. and Y. S. Lincoln, eds. 2005. *The Sage handbook of qualitative research* (3rd ed.). Thousand Oaks, CA: Sage.

Devault, M. L. and G. Gross. 2007. Feminist interviewing: Experience, talk, and knowledge. In *Handbook of feminist research: Theory and praxis*, S. N. Hesse-Biber, ed. 143–154. Thousand Oaks, CA: Sage.

Gilgun, J. F. 1994. Hand into glove: The grounded theory approach and social work practice research. In *Qualitative research in social work practice*, E. Sherman and W. J. Reid, eds. 115–125. New York: Columbia UP.

Hagen, J. L. and L. V. Davis. 1994. Women on welfare talk about reform. *Public Welfare*, 52:30–43.

Hale, S. 2003. *The goose girl*. New York: Bloomsbury.

Holstein, J. A. and J. F. Gubrium. 1995. *The active interview* (Vol. 37). Thousand Oaks, CA: Sage.

Johnson, J. C. and S. C. Weller. 2002. Elicitation techniques for interviewing. In *Handbook of interview research: Context and method*, J. F. Gubrium and J. A. Holstein, eds. 491–514. Thousand Oaks, CA: Sage.

Johnson, J. M. 2002. In-depth interviewing. In *Handbook of interview research: Context and method*, J. F. Gubrium and J. A. Holstein, eds. 103–119. Thousand Oaks, CA: Sage.

Marshall, C. and G. B. Rossman. 2006. *Designing qualitative research* (4th ed.). Thousand Oaks, CA: Sage.

May, K. A. 1991. Interview techniques in qualitative research: Concerns and challenges. In *Qualitative nursing research*, J. M. Morse, ed. 188–201. Newbury Park, CA: Sage.

McNutt, L. A., B. E. Carlson, M. Persaud, and J. L. Postmus. 2002. Cumulative abuse experiences, physical health and health practices. *Annals of Epidemiology*, 12(2):123–130.

Minister, K. 1991. A feminist frame for the oral history interview. In *Women's words: The feminist practice of oral history*, S. B. Gluck and D. Patai, eds. 27–41. New York: Routledge.

Morgan, D. L. and R. A. Krueger. 1993. When to use focus groups and why. In *Successful focus groups: Advancing the state of the art*, D. L. Morgan, ed. 3–19. Newbury Park, CA: Sage.

Nichols-Casebolt, A. and P. Spakes. 1995. Policy research and the voices of women. *Social Work Research, 19*(1):49–55.

Padgett, D. K. 1998. Does the glove really fit? Qualitative research and clinical social work practice. *Social Work, 43*(4):373–381.

——. 2008. *Qualitative methods in social work* (2nd ed.). Los Angeles, CA: Sage.

Patton, M. Q. 2002. *Qualitative research and evaluation methods* (3rd ed.). Thousand Oaks, CA: Sage.

Postmus, J. L. 2002. *In their own words: Battered women, welfare, and the Family Violence Option.* (Doctoral dissertation). Albany: State University of New York.

——. 2004. Battered and on welfare: The experiences of women with the Family Violence Option. *Journal of Sociology and Social Welfare, 31*(2):113–124.

Postmus, J. L. and S. B. Plummer. 2010. *Validating the Allstate Foundation's national model on helping survivors of violence achieve economic self-sufficiency: Final report.* New Brunswick, NJ: Rutgers University, School of Social Work, Center on Violence Against Women and Children.

Postmus, J. L. and M. E. Severson. 2006. *Violence and victimization: Exploring women's histories of survival.* Washington, DC: Dept. of Justice, Office of Justice Programs, National Crime Justice Reference Service.

Reinharz, S. and S. E. Chase. 2002. Interviewing women. In *Handbook of interview research: Context and method*, J. F. Gubrium and J. A. Holstein, eds. 221–238. Thousand Oaks, CA: Sage.

Ryen, A. 2002. Cross-cultural interviewing. In *Handbook of interview research: Context and method*, J. F. Gubrium and J. A. Holstein, eds. 335–354. Thousand Oaks, CA: Sage.

Shuy, R. W. 2002. In-person versus telephone interviewing. In *Handbook of interview research: Context and method*, J. F. Gubrium and J. A. Holstein, eds. 537–555. Thousand Oaks, CA: Sage.

Slattery, S. M. and L. A. Goodman. 2009. Secondary traumatic stress among domestic violence advocates: Workplace risk and protective factors. *Violence Against Women,* 15(11):1358–1379.

Sullivan, C. M. 2004. Ethical and safety considerations when obtaining information from or about battered women for research purposes. *Journal of Interpersonal Violence,* 19(5):603–618.

Teddlie, C. and A. Tashakkori. 2009. *Foundations of mixed methods research: Integrating quantitative and qualitative approaches in the social and behavioral sciences.* Thousand Oaks, CA: Sage.

Tutty, L. M., M. A. Rothery, and R. M. Grinnell, Jr. 1996. *Qualitative research for social workers.* Boston: Allyn & Bacon.

Warren, C. A. B. 2002. Qualitative interviewing. In *Handbook of interview research: Context and method,* J. F. Gubrium and J. A. Holstein, eds. 83–101. Thousand Oaks, CA: Sage.

[11]

Focus Groups

RAYMIE H. WAYNE

Focus groups are a data collection method used to reveal people's thoughts, perceptions, and experiences related to topics of interest to the researcher. Focus group methods grew out of the work of Paul Lazarsfeld, Robert Merton, and colleagues at the Bureau of Applied Social Research at Columbia University. The methodology was developed to study listeners' reactions to propaganda and radio news programs during World War II (Kidd and Parshall 2000). Although first adopted by the marketing field, focus groups have become a useful data collection tool in the social sciences (Maynard-Tucker 2000). A recent content analysis of social work abstracts from 1988–2002 shows a steady increase in the number of references to focus groups (Cohen 2003). In fact, 38 percent of the focus group references were from the final three-year period of the study (2000–2002). As the popularity of focus groups increases, it will become more important that social workers be able to conduct and critique focus group research. By explaining the nuts and bolts of focus group design, this chapter will help social work students, practitioners, and researchers engage in and critique focus group research.

Characteristics of Focus Groups

Focus groups can be used to reveal what a particular group of people think about complex or sensitive subjects. For example, Drake used focus groups to "obtain worker and client views of key competencies in child welfare services" (1994:595). Likewise, Stock and Morse (1997) conducted focus groups to learn about community members' opposition to school-based health care programs (SBHCPs). Focus groups can be particularly useful in situations such as these, where participants may not have previously tried to articulate their views on the subject at hand and can thus benefit from a group dialogue as they find their own words. In fact, a characteristic of focus group research is that the data are generated through group discussion and interaction. Focus group research is unique in that participants "have the opportunity to stimulate, support, and build on each other's ideas on the topic" (Balch and Mertens 1999:267). Other important characteristics of the focus group designs cited here are that the researchers began their projects with articulated research questions, held multiple groups, and limited the number of participants present at each session. Additional characteristics are commonly a part of focus group research.

The following are primary characteristics of most focus group research:

- Purpose of group meetings is to get information about how the participants think or feel about a specific item of interest (i.e., a program or common experience). In short, there is a research question.
- Multiple groups, each with different participants, are held to ensure reliability.
- Each group meets one time for a limited time, usually 90 to 120 minutes.
- Each group consists of a limited number of participants selected based on criteria that relate to the research question. Six to 12 participants is usually recommended.
- Each group meeting follows the same structured agenda.
- Agendas consist of questions that, if answered by the participants, will yield data that answers the research question.
- Trained and neutral moderators actively keep the group on task.
- Participant interaction is used to generate data, including verbal interaction and group dynamics.
- Group discussions are recorded and the dialogue is coded and used for a purpose relating to the research project.

An ideal focus group plan would incorporate all of the aforementioned characteristics. However, qualitative research (or any research on human subjects, for that matter) is rarely that perfect and some variation occurs. For example, Lonek and Way used repeated focus groups with clinicians to get their "impressions of what leads to successful referral of clients with dual diagnoses to services in the community" (1997:108). The first session was used to explore the therapeutic process that underlies client referrals while in the second session the researchers "reviewed and validated clinicians' initial responses and probed for additional details" (108). Whereas focus groups typically only meet once, the researchers in this case used a second meeting to increase the validity of the data.

In another study, Hagen and Owens-Manley (2002) used focus groups to gain an understanding of frontline welfare workers' perspectives on issues that impact how Temporary Assistance to Needy Families (TANF) is implemented. Instead of using a structured agenda, the researchers created seven case studies that were ranked by the focus group participants and served to launch the discussion. The researchers organized the discussion around four major topic areas. In this study, the structured agenda was replaced with a topic guide. Krueger (1998) identified the topic guide as an acceptable alternative to the structured agenda if the focus group moderators are experienced facilitators. The use of the case studies and the topic guide allowed the researchers to follow the lead of the focus group participants. This variation from the focus group methodology outlined earlier is appropriate when the participants know each other well and/or the researcher is concerned that a predetermined agenda might close off important (but not thought of) areas of investigation.

The possibility of adjusting focus group methodology to meet the demands of a particular project is one of the method's greatest strengths. However, the confusion created by the aforementioned flexibility causes people to use the term to describe any group of people gathered together to discuss a single issue, for example, team brainstorming or large open political forums (Straw and Smith 1995). These are not focus groups because they are not guided by a research question and do not meet most of the criteria for focus groups. In conducting focus groups for research purposes, a key is to use the criteria flexibly to improve the research or to make a project doable without sacrificing the fundamental attributes of focus groups. If enough of the focus group criteria become morphed (or ignored), at some point the group is no longer a focus group. For example, when participant interaction is inhibited, focus groups can instead become individual interviews in a group setting (Wilson 1997). Similarly, if the number of attendees is not limited, the intended focus group could become some type of open forum.

When to Use a Focus Group

Focus groups have many uses. Focus groups can be used as a part of an engagement/assessment process, an evaluation process, or as a part of an exploratory research design. Practitioners can use focus groups to assess the need for certain programs, or the goodness of fit of proposed solutions to specific community problems (Griggs and Stewart 1995; Brueggemann 2002). Straw and Smith (1995) recommend that focus groups be used during the beginning phases of program implementation as an engagement technique and to obtain information about the goodness of fit between the new program and the community. Similarly, Williams, Bonnell, and Stoffel (2009), used focus groups to understand the needs of university library patrons and to gain information about how to develop a user-friendly web page. Kidd and Parshall (2000) note that focus group methodology may be particularly useful for studying issues that impact vulnerable populations. Their goodness of fit with the previously mentioned phases of social work practice make focus groups a good match with participatory research strategies. Gong, Baron, Ayala, Stock, McDevitt, and Heaney (2009) described a participatory process for formulating health and safety policy initiatives that included the use of focus groups. For researchers, focus groups are especially useful when little is known about a topic and one wishes to generate hypotheses for further testing. As will be discussed under the sampling strategies heading, focus group data is only generalizable under limited circumstances, usually only to a small group of people.

The Lonek and Way (1997) study previously cited is a good example of using focus groups to generate testable hypotheses. The researchers were interested in learning how clinicians balance supportive and confrontive statements with patients that are dually diagnosed. To ensure that their research would be relevant for clinicians in the field, Lonek and Way conducted focus groups with the practitioners. Lonek and Way (1997:108) reported that "in essence [the practitioners] became coinvestigators by generating a series of clinical hypotheses that we could test in data derived from their sessions." Furthermore, the focus groups helped the researchers to refine their research questions and to choose suitable research methods.

In summary, focus groups fit well with many aspects of social work practice and research. They are appropriately used if the research question pertains to people's perceptions and experiences. Focus groups provide depth of data rather than breadth, and the results often have limited generalizability. Focus groups are an excellent tool for generating hypotheses for further testing.

Once it is decided that focus groups are the best data collection method to answer the research questions, it is time to decide who should participate in the groups, how many groups to have, what the agenda will consist of, and more. The remainder of this chapter focuses on the "how to" of focus groups. The rationale that supports each of the techniques is also presented. By learning the "why" behind the "what," the reader will be able to make better judgments when real world obstacles require straying from the ideal practices (Cohen, Garrett, Meier, Phillips, and Wayne 2003).

Multiple Groups

Multiple groups must be held for two reasons. First—as discussed in more detail to follow—within each group, participants should be as homogeneous as possible. Most often the research question will require the discovery of several unique perspectives (i.e., men and women, children of different ages). Because homogeneity is important in relation to the focus group topic, it is likely that separate groups will need to be held for laypeople and professionals, caregivers and spouses, and so on, depending on the topic. The rationale for creating homogeneous groups is explained in the next section. Secondly, holding more than one focus group for each population segment ensures greater reliability. Just as a survey researcher would not generalize the results from a single survey response, a focus group researcher cannot draw conclusions about a larger population from a single focus group meeting. Any single group may have contained a particularly persuasive group member that influenced the thoughts (or words) of everyone present. Holding more than one focus group for each population segment allows the researcher to see if the same themes emerge again and again or if a group was influenced by a strong (and atypical) group member or other dynamic.

Whom to Invite to Focus Groups

Group Composition

Focus group composition should be based upon the knowledge of group dynamics that promote participant interaction and disclosure of information. There is a popular belief that focus group participants should represent diverse populations in order to produce more generalizable information. In fact, each focus group should be as homogeneous as possible, to encourage participants to feel comfortable quickly. The more comfortable participants are, the more likely they will be to share personal information. There are two aspects to consider when creating homogeneous groups. The first relates to the participants' worldview regarding the topic of the group. The second pertains to members' status in and outside of the group. Each aspect is examined in more detail in the following discussion.

TOPIC

Here the goal is to create groups where participants are likely to have similar perspectives on the topic at hand. For example, in the Stock and Morse study about barriers to SBHCPs (referred to earlier) the researchers conducted separate focus groups with students, parents, faculty and administration, community leaders, and SBHCP clinic staff. Each population was likely to have a different worldview and language when it came to discussing a school-based program. By creating homogeneous groups, it was likely that the participants felt comfortable more quickly and were more inclined to speak openly and honestly. Additionally, the homogeneity and common worldview probably led to some basic understandings that left more time for exploring the research issue in depth.

STATUS

Focus groups do not occur in a social vacuum. Participants all have outside roles and statuses that can make them either respected or discounted in group settings. A member whose status is perceived as high might (unintentionally) impact other members' statements or thoughts, thereby distorting the data. For example, a stay-at-home mom may refrain from discussing how she handles her children's colds if a physician is in the group and gives an answer first. One way to avoid this is by sorting the sample by known status indicators and creating the groups accordingly. An example follows. Wanting to learn more about the HIV/AIDS case management process in a particular region, Chernesky and Grube (2000) conducted focus groups with case managers and their supervisors. To increase the validity of the responses, the researchers ran separate groups for the case managers and for the supervisors. If they had mixed the groups, a case manager might have felt inhibited about disagreeing with a supervisor about the nature of the work, or a supervisor might have deferred to a case manager on certain details instead of expressing her own view.

Sampling Strategies

There are several sampling strategies that are commonly used to recruit focus group participants. Two of the most common sampling strategies are purposive and snowball sampling. Purposive sampling consists of handpicking key members based on specific characteristics that relate to the study's purpose (Fortune and Reid 1999). Snowball sampling involves starting "with a few individuals who meet the study criteria and [asking] them to suggest the names of additional individuals who meet the criteria" (Fortune and Reid 1999:212). Each person who is accepted into the study is invited to recommend more people until the sample is large enough. Snowball sampling is an especially good fit if the focus groups are part of a participatory research strategy (see the section, "Participatory Research" in chapter 13, this volume). Most focus group sampling procedures place greater emphasis on recruiting people with the correct characteristics than on random sampling. For that reason, one should be very cautious when trying to generalize from focus group findings. As previously stated, focus groups are well suited for generating hypotheses that can later be tested using quantitative methods.

In his child welfare study, Drake (1994) used purposive sampling for his pilot groups and then random sampling for the remaining groups. Similarly, Stock and Morse (1997), in their study about opposition to SBHCPs, used a key informant to create lists of appropriate people (the sampling frame). The researchers randomly selected the focus group participants from the list. Other variations, however, are also possible. Hagen and Owens-Manley (2002) allowed frontline welfare workers to self-select by distributing an invitation to all workers and requesting that interested parties sign up to participate. Chernesky and Grube (2000) also allowed participants to self-select. They invited all HIV case management programs in their target area to send program staff to the focus groups. By way of example, it has been demonstrated that there are many ways to recruit focus group participants. The important point is to weigh the pros and cons of all possible methods and to make an intelligent judgment as to how to proceed.

Both purposive and snowball sampling are likely to yield focus group participants who know each other. This has benefits and drawbacks that vary greatly depending on the sensitivity level of the topic. Kitzinger (1995) suggests that group members who have a prior relationship are able to engage in collective remembering, (i.e., prompt each other's memories, or challenge selective or filtered memories, thereby improving the validity of the research). However, if the topic is of a personal and potentially embarrassing nature, participants may be reluctant to be truthful in the presence of acquaintances and colleagues.

In summary, focus group participants should be homogeneous in relation to the group's purpose and members' statuses. It is important that participants feel that they each have a unique contribution to make and do not defer to an "expert" in the group. Purposive and snowball sampling strategies are commonly employed in focus group research and can lead to groups of people who have relationships outside of the group. Having focus group participants who know each other can impact the validity of the data both positively and negatively. On the one hand, participants can correct each other and improve the accuracy of the statements that are made from memory. On the other hand, participants may be less inclined to share embarrassing information.

The Focus Group Agenda

The focus group should begin with a brief statement of the purpose of the group, what the data will be used for, and with whom it will be shared. Informed consent, especially if the group is being recorded, should be obtained orally and in writing at the start of the group. While it is important not to skip any of these tasks, it is equally important to get them out of the way as quickly as possible so that focus group participants can begin speaking. If the facilitator speaks for too long at the start of the meeting, the participants can assume a passive noncommunicative role. It is therefore important to get to the interactive portion of the meeting as quickly as possible.

Question Sequencing

The focus group questions and their sequencing create the structure and environment that facilitates and enhances participants' creative thinking (Krueger 1998). Krueger (1998) identified five types of questions that are designed to elicit the maximum amount of information in a short time period. The five question categories, in order of their appearance are: opening, introductory, transition, key, and ending. Used in this order, the questions move from the broad association level to personal insights. Each of Krueger's question types is defined in detail here. A sample agenda with each question type follows the explanations.

OPENING QUESTION

The opening question is a simple fact-based question that participants can answer easily and is likely to draw on commonalities among the participants. This question is usually answered in a round-robin format. The purpose of the question is to get all participants to speak early in the group. Be careful to avoid questions that denote a status such as job title, number of years employed as a nurse, and so on. A general tip is to stay away from questions that require numerical answers. Although seemingly benign, these latter questions could establish someone as an "expert" early in the group. Very little time is spent on this question, usually less than five minutes.

INTRODUCTORY QUESTIONS

An introductory question is used to introduce the participant to the topic. The question should be general and asked to the group as a whole (no more round-robin). The purpose of this question is less about generating data and more about getting the group comfortable and oriented. A focus group agenda may contain one or two introductory questions. Once again, not a lot of time is spent on introductory questions; usually about five minutes is sufficient.

TRANSITION QUESTIONS

The transition questions serve, as the name suggests, as a link from the previous question to the main questions that the researcher is interested in having answered. These questions create a flow that enables participants to continue thinking about the focus group topic in more depth. One or two transition questions are usually sufficient. Five to ten minutes, depending on the total amount of time allotted for each focus group meeting, is adequate for transition questions.

KEY QUESTIONS

Most focus groups will have three to five key questions. These questions get to the heart of the research question. At least 50 percent of the time allotted for the focus group should be reserved for the key questions.

ENDING QUESTIONS

Ending questions serve two important but closely related functions. They give the participants a sense of closure and a chance to correct any misconceptions. Typical ending questions involve a summary of what was said and then ask about the accuracy of the summary. Another important ending question is to ask if there was something that should have been asked but was not. It is difficult, but important, to save enough time for the ending questions. Nothing is less genuine than to ask for feedback and then announce that the group is out of time. A minimum of ten minutes should be reserved for ending questions.

Table 11.1 provides examples of focus group questions created by Harrity and Wayne (1999). The goal of the focus groups was to identify community projects that would improve mental health care in the region. The researchers were interested in learning what activities took the mental health workers away from providing services, what activities could be added to improve services, and what types of projects would garner the support of the professional community. Notice that the agenda included a detailed time schedule that enabled the facilitator to save enough time for the key

Table 11.1 Sample Focus Group Agenda

Mental Health Workers

9:30–9:40	**Cushion Time**
9:40–9:45	Introductory remarks (purpose)
9:45–9:50	**Opening Question (round-robin)**

"Tell us who you are, what agency you represent, and the newest service your agency is offering."

| 9:50–9:55 | **Introductory Question (open to the group)** |

"What was your first impression of mental health services in northwestern Connecticut?"

| 9:55–10:05 | **Transition Question** |

"What is your favorite job responsibility in your current position?"

| 10:05–10:45 | **Key Question(s)** |

"In the next two weeks, what are you or your staff going to spend time doing that you wish you did not have to do?"

"In the next two weeks, what activities do you wish you had more time to focus on?"

"Picture in your mind an action-oriented committee that gets things done. You are an integral member of this committee. What is the committee working on?"

| 10:45–11:00 | **Ending Question** |

"How well does ___ [brief summary] ___ capture what was said here?"

"Is there anything that we should have talked about but did not?"

questions and the ending question. To ensure that the focus groups did not begin behind schedule the researchers reserved ten minutes at the start of the group for latecomers to arrive and get settled.

Stages of Group Development

Understanding the stages of group development enables focus group researchers to skillfully create and implement a focus group agenda. Furthermore, understanding the theory that supports the questioning sequencing permits the facilitator to make on the spot judgments about the best use of the agenda in order to further the information getting goals.

Stage theories of group development assert that all groups cycle through phases, each with its own distinct theme and tasks (Tuckman 1965; Garland, Jones, and Kolodny 1976). Many social scientists have written about the stages of group development, each assigning different names to describe the same phenomena (Ephross and Vassil 2005). Perhaps because they rhyme, Tuckman's stages are among the most popular and are used here to show how the stages of group development support the question sequencing protocol on the previous pages. Concepts and descriptive language borrowed from Garland, Jones, and Kolodny (1976) are used in the definitions of the stages. Tuckman's five stages are forming, storming, norming, performing, and adjourning. Each stage and its significance in relation to the facilitator's tasks, is described in more detail here.

FORMING

During the first stage of group development, members initially approach groups with a high level of self-consciousness. This initial stage is characterized by member ambivalence about being a part of the group. One does not yet know what the rules of the group will be and how to behave in a way that meets the social expectations of the others in the room. These feelings are present as soon as one enters the room, even before the meeting has officially begun.

Facilitator Tasks. The focus group facilitator has several tasks during this phase, all of which revolve around helping people to feel comfortable. The facilitator should engage all participants as they enter the room and help people to feel comfortable. Simple questions that get participants to chat will help warm the participants for the work that follows. Once the focus group has officially begun, the brief introductory statements about the group's purpose should be geared toward making people feel comfortable. Additionally, it is important to convey the expectation that group members will speak frankly about the topic, even if it means disagreeing with other group members. Hopefully, by establishing the rules quickly and by beginning with an opening question that gets everyone to talk, participants will feel comfortable early in the life of the focus group.

STORMING

Following the period of self-consciousness, members typically tune into and test the developing norms and culture and assess which behaviors will be rewarded or shunned. Also during this stage, members may try to establish themselves as experts on the topic and take extreme views on issues. Power struggles are common during this stage.

Facilitator Tasks. The role of the facilitator during this stage is to create an environment where people can disagree openly. The facilitator also wants to establish that everyone's opinion counts equally and wants to make sure that power is shared among group members. One way to encourage honest and open disagreement is to ask for different perspectives on an issue that was just explored from a single viewpoint. This is especially important to do if someone with a high status offered the initial opinion. The facilitator should also try to help group members not get locked into a single and extreme stance on a topic this early in the life of the group.

NORMING

This stage is characterized by feelings of closeness. Members understand the rules of the group and know or sense the roles that different individuals will play. Members adapt their behaviors and statements to comply with the group norms. This is also a time when people begin to reveal personal information.

Facilitator Tasks. It is essential throughout the norming process that members be helped to maintain their individuality and resist the temptation to morph their opinions to comply with group norms. At this point the facilitator is moving into the key questions to capitalize on the tendency of group members to reveal information during this stage of group development.

PERFORMING

This stage, as it name suggests, is a highly productive stage. It is characterized by more rational thought than its somewhat emotional predecessor. This is a good phase for problem-solving activities.

Facilitator Tasks. The main work for the facilitator here is to keep the group on schedule and on task. If everything has gone smoothly up until now, the group should be functioning well and working on answering the questions as asked by the facilitator.

ADJOURNING

Much like the first stage, forming, the adjourning stage is characterized by ambivalence. If it was a good group experience, members may not want the session to end. They may feel a rush to complete the task, in this case wishing to make sure that their take on the issue is understood.

Facilitator Tasks. The facilitator's primary task at this stage is to provide a sense of closure. This can be done by providing an accurate summary of what was said during the focus group and by asking for additional comments. Throughout the focus group the facilitator should have kept a close eye on the time, so that this last piece is not rushed. Finally, the facilitator should conclude the group by thanking participants and reminding them how the information will be used. Table 11.2 details the stages of development of a typical focus group.

In summary, focus groups follow a structured agenda that begins with the participants' broad association and ends with their personal experiences and reflections about the topic. The rationale for question sequencing is consistent with the stages of group development. Understanding the stages of group development will enable the focus group facilitator to concentrate on key tasks at key times and to increase the likelihood of generating valid data during the course of the focus group.

Skills of a Focus Group Facilitator

Although all aspects of focus group design and implementation are important, the skill level of the facilitator is frequently cited as the most important component (Maynard-Tucker 2000). As with many types of groups, the focus group facilitator should be lively, likable, interested, engaged, flexible, perceptive, and analytical. These personality traits will keep a high energy level in the room and will help to keep the participants engaged. Natural curiosity will help the facilitator to probe unclear or unfinished remarks. The attentive facilitator will be able to tune into and act on subtle messages that are sometimes conveyed through body language, tone of voice, or quietness. The flexible facilitator will be able to take full advantage of the focus group context by allowing participants more or less time than planned to explore specific topics, thereby increasing the amount of data that is generated.

Table 11.2 Stages of Focus Group Development

Stage of Group Development	Member Task (Theme)	Question Type	Connection
Forming	Self-consciousness. Ambivalence	Opening (round-robin)	People are feeling self-conscious and need to know the rules. Round-robin establishes a norm that everyone in this group speaks.
Storming	Testing. Role development	Introductory and transition (open to group)	Facilitator establishes that everyone's perspective matters. Limits the creation of an "expert." Facilitator responds to participant testing by welcoming all perspectives on an issue.
Norming	Coalescing	Transition and key	Participants reveal information. Facilitator gets to important data collection questions.
Performing	Problem solving	Key	Participants move into problem-solving mode. Facilitator asks the hardest questions, requiring the energy and expertise of the participants.
Adjourning	Rushing to complete. Ambivalence	Ending	Participants look for closure and a feeling of accomplishment, which is provided through the ending questions.

Note: Labels are from Tuckman, B. W. 1965. Developmental sequences in small groups. *Psychological Bulletin*, 63:384–399. Member tasks from Tuckman (1965) and Garland, J. H. Jones, and R. Kolodny. 1976. A model for stages of development in social work groups. In S. Bernstein (ed.), *Explorations in group work: Essays in theory and practice.* Boston: Charles River Books.

There are several key tasks of the focus group facilitator that apply throughout the life of the group and not just during specific phases as previously discussed. It is obvious that the facilitator must create a safe environment where participants feel comfortable providing honest responses to the questions asked. The facilitator is more likely to succeed in creating a safe environment if she is able to tune into group dynamics. A good facilitator will be skilled in paraphrasing and clarifying participant responses as well as articulating commonalities and distinctions among participant statements. Focus group facilitators should be comfortable with silence. This means being able to wait for participants to gather their thoughts and the energy to speak without rushing in to fill the silence. A facilitator who fills in the silence risks setting a norm where she answers her own questions. Clearly, the facilitator must have good oral and written communication skills. Finally, the focus group facilitator must have a good sense of time. As previously mentioned, the focus group agenda is carefully planned to maximize the value of the participants' time and to move people through a thought process in quick fashion. A facilitator who loses track of time will need to rush through the most important part of the agenda (the key questions) and will not leave enough time for the ending question(s).

Another aspect that relates to facilitation is note taking. Some facilitators find that using a flip chart is helpful. As a focal point, the flip chart can help the facilitator retain the leadership function throughout the session. The flip chart can also demonstrate the facilitator's ability to paraphrase and listen. A drawback of the flip chart is that, by becoming the focal point, it has the potential to limit participant interaction. Additionally, it requires that the facilitator be able to analyze statements on the spot. Regardless of what notes are taken during the session, the facilitator should write a set of notes immediately after each group to attempt to capture as much of her thinking during the session as possible. Memories fade quickly, especially the visual cues that can be helpful when interpreting remarks.

Logistics

There are several logistical items that, although simple, can greatly improve the quality of focus groups. The importance of location, room setup, name tags, and refreshments are discussed in more detail as follows.

Location

It is important to find a neutral setting for hosting the focus groups. While it may be convenient to use a meeting room at the agency where participants work or receive services, participants may limit their comments based on the behavioral cues that are present in that setting. Additionally, being in a new place can stimulate creative, out-of-the-box thinking. In addition to being neutral, the location should be easy to find, have plenty of easy parking, and be quiet and welcoming. Libraries, town halls, and local chambers of commerce are often good places to consider.

Room Setup

It is ideal to have a large round table that comfortably seats the number of participants and the facilitator. If a round table is not possible, any table is better than no table. The table helps people to feel comfortable (physically and psychologically) and provides a space for the facilitator's notes, the recorder, and for the participant's refreshments. If possible, the registration table should be outside the focus group room so that any latecomers can be taken care of without disruption to the whole group.

Name Tags/Table Tents

Participants can be given name tags or table tents. In general, table tents (8-½-by-11-inch pieces of card stock folded lengthwise) are preferred, as the type can be bigger and the facilitator will be more likely to be able to refer to people by name without squinting! A useful tip is to prepare the table tents ahead of time and to type each person's name on both sides of their tent. Often people will set the tent so that they can see their own name. By having the name on both sides, one can avoid having to correct someone at the start of the group.

Refreshments

Food and beverages should always be offered. Food and beverages can help with icebreaking and help people to feel cared for. In general, eating is a social activity and can encourage chattiness before the group begins.

Report Production

The written analysis or report should be created as soon as possible after the focus groups have concluded, and it should be written by the person or people who facilitated the groups (Rothwell 2010). Creating the report promptly reduces the risk that important nuances will be forgotten. Similarly, if written by the facilitators, the report is more likely to properly contextualize statements.

Focus group reports should include a methodology section that contains the overall research design, including the sampling strategies that were utilized. The remainder of the report might include a summary of findings, analysis, implications, and/or recommendations, depending on the purpose of the groups and the intended uses of the reports (Henderson 1995). The summary of findings should include the themes that were discovered during the groups followed by quotes from participants that support the researcher's interpretation. Carey and Smith (1994) recommend including conversations among members in the final report to demonstrate the context in which the interesting comments occurred. As with all social work assessments, descriptors of how the data was presented (i.e., body language, tone, expressions of conflict and emotion) are an important part of the content and should be included in the narrative (Henderson 1995). Additionally, any obviously omitted information should also be acknowledged; for example, no one mentioned that the largest mental health agency in the region just laid off 15 social workers.

Conclusion

Focus groups are a data collection method used in qualitative research. They are best used to understand people's perceptions and experiences of specific phenomena and to generate hypotheses for further testing. The methodology can be adjusted to be useful in many contexts. All adjustments, however, should be made with the knowledge of the theory behind the rule, so that the data gathering purpose is not compromised.

A focus group research design must include a research question, multiple groups, a limited number of participants in each group, and the use of verbal interaction as the data source. Often focus group participants will be recruited through purposive and snowball sampling techniques. Most focus groups follow a strict agenda comprised of questions that lead the participants from broad associations to personal insights about the topic.

Successful focus groups require a skilled facilitator and attention to logistical details. If done properly, focus groups can be an excellent data collection tool in qualitative research.

References

Balch, G. I. and D. M. Mertens. 1999. Focus group design and group dynamics: Lessons from deaf and hard of hearing participants. *American Journal of Evaluation* 20(2):265–277.

Brueggemann, W. G. 2002. *The practice of macro social work* (2nd ed.). Belmont, CA: Wadsworth.

Carey, M. A. and M. W. Smith. 1994. Capturing the group effect in focus groups: A special concern in analysis. *Qualitative Health Research*, 4(1):123–127.

Chernesky, R. H. and B. Grube. 2000. Examining the HIV/AIDS case management process. *Health and Social Work* 25(4):243–253.

Cohen, C. 2003. [Focus group usage in social work publications]. Unpublished raw data.

Cohen, C., K. Garrett, A. Meier, M. Phillips, and R. H. Wayne. (2003). "Focus group research and social work: Challenges, commonalities and opportunities." Invitational Presentation at the 25th Annual International Symposium on Social Work with Groups, Boston, MA.

Drake, B. 1994. Relationship competencies in child welfare services. *Social Work,* 39(5):595–602.

Ephross, P. H. and T. V. Vassil. 2005. *Groups that work: Structure and process* (2nd ed.). New York: Columbia UP.

Fortune, A. E. and W. J. Reid. 1999. *Research in social work* (3rd ed.). New York: Columbia UP.

Garland, J., H. Jones, and R. Kolodny. 1976. A model for stages of development in social work groups. In *Explorations in group work: Essays in theory and practice,* S. Bernstein (ed.). Boston: Charles River.

Gong, F., S. Baron, L. Ayala, L. Stock, S. McDevitt, and C. Heaney. 2009. The role for community-based participatory research in formulating policy initiatives: Promoting safety and health for in-home care workers and their consumers. *American Journal of Public Health,* 99(S3), S531. Retrieved from MasterFILE Premier database.

Griggs, H. and B. Stewart. 1995. An innovative method for improving program planning. *Education,* 116(2):189–193.

Hagen, J. and J. Owens-Manley. 2002. Issues in implementing TANF in New York: The perspective of frontline workers. *Social Work, 47*(2):171–182.

Harrity, P. and R. H. Wayne. (1999). "Utilizing focus groups to identify collaborative opportunities for AHECs." Paper presented at the National AHEC Workshop, Louisville, KY.

Henderson, N. R. 1995. A practical approach to analyzing and reporting focus groups studies: Lessons from qualitative market research. *Qualitative Health Research 5*(4):463–578.

Kidd, P. S. and M. B. Parshall. 2000. Getting the focus and the group: Enhancing analytical rigor in focus group research. *Qualitative Health Research 10*(3):293–309.

Kitzinger, J. 1995. Introducing focus groups. *British Medical Journal 311*(7000): 299–303.

Krueger, R. A. 1998. Developing questions for focus groups. In *The Focus Group Kit*, vol 3 D. L. Morgan and R. A. Krueger, eds. Thousand Oaks, CA: Sage.

Loneck, B. and B. Way. 1997. Using focus groups of clinicians to develop a research project on therapeutic process for clients with dual diagnoses. *Social Work, 42*(1):107–111.

Maynard-Tucker, G. 2000. Conducting focus groups in developing countries: Skill training for local bilingual facilitators. *Qualitative Health Research, 10*(3):396–411.

Rothwell, E. 2010. Analyzing focus group data: Content and interaction. *Journal for Specialists in Pediatric Nursing, 15*(2):176–180. doi:10.1111/j.1744-6155.2010.00237.x.

Straw, R. B. and M. W. Smith. 1995. Potential uses of focus groups in federal policy and program evaluation studies. *Qualitative Health Research, 5*(4):421–428.

Stock, M. R. and E. V. Morse. 1997. Barriers to school-based health care programs. *Health and Social Work 22*(4):274–282.

Tuckman, B. W. 1965. Developmental sequences in small groups. In *Psychological Bulletin, 63*:384–399.

Williams, S., A. Bonnell, and B. Stoffel. 2009. Student feedback on federated search use, satisfaction, and web presence: Qualitative findings of focus groups. *Reference and User Services Quarterly, 49*(2):131139. Retrieved August 13, 2010 from Academic Search Premier database.

Wilson, V. 1997. Focus groups: A useful qualitative method for educational research? *British Educational Research 23*(2):209–225.

[12]

Qualitative Data Analysis Software

An Overview and New Possibilities

JAMES W. DRISKO

Computer-aided qualitative data analysis has increasingly become part of research projects in social work and in allied fields (Lewins and Silver 2007; Hwang 2008; Sin 2008). At its core, computer software helps researchers organize, manage, and analyze the large volume of data common to qualitative projects. It can be used with a wide range of analytic methods and techniques (Weitzman and Miles 1995; Drisko 2004; King 2010). It makes no analytic decisions; these remain fully the manual responsibility of the researcher. Computer software is used optimally by researchers who possess a sound knowledge of qualitative research methods (Dey 1993; Kelle 1995; Drisko 1998; di Gregorio and Davidson 2008). It will be no asset to researchers who lack knowledge of qualitative research methods (Konopasek 2007). Yet at the cutting edge, computer software offers whole new vistas for qualitative research, expanding the types of data it addresses and the forms through which knowledge is developed and communicated.

This chapter will provide an overview of qualitative data analysis software, its purposes, its merits, and its limitations. The chapter has three main sections. It will open with a conceptual overview of what qualitative data analysis software does. A brief summary of the process of using the software will follow. The chapter will close with a guide to locating, choosing, and learning about qualitative data analysis software packages.

It is worth noting that the core features of contemporary software packages have evolved and converged to a point where the basic tools are well developed in all of the most common products (Lewins and Silver 2007, 2009; Peters and Wester 2007). That is, any of the widely used software packages will help knowledgeable qualitative researchers organize, manage, code, and retrieve their data efficiently. The differences among the software packages have to do more with ease of use and additional features than with major differences in their core feature sets. Current advertisements emphasize colorful displays of coded options and other features that may be of interest to a few researchers but are certainly not vital to most forms of basic qualitative data analysis. What most distinguishes contemporary software packages from each other are features to open and analyze specific types of multimedia and nontext files and to manage group research projects. In this area, important differences exist and may serve as compelling reasons to choose one package over another. These choices will be specific to one's research interests, data types, and publication plans.

What Does Qualitative Data Analysis Software Do?

This question has a two-part answer. On one hand, computer software can be a valuable aid to organizing and analyzing qualitative data sets (Weitzman and Miles 1995; Kelle 1995; Drisko 1998; Lewins and Silver 2007). In this role, it speeds and aids the traditional work of pencil-and-paper qualitative analysis. It is efficient and very useful but not really ground-breaking. These features of software are most commonly noted and explored in commercial advertisements and in academic summaries.

On the other hand, computer software makes possible a whole new world of multimedia qualitative research endeavors (Drisko 2005; Lewins and Silver 2009). In this second role, it is truly ground-breaking and points to much greater scope and depth than is possible with pencil-and-paper projects. Computer software can organize, analyze, and display images, and audio and video files directly, without transcription to text. This allows for the use of much richer and varied data sets than does traditional flat text. Posture, gesture, intonation, and expression can all be directly and richly conveyed rather than sketched in the words of the researcher. A linkage to geographic mapping software allows researchers to locate and contextualize their work anywhere on the planet. Analysis of Internet sites and documents directly as html and pdf data files allows researchers to draw on contemporary modes of communication without having to alter raw data into simplified texts. Many new types of research become possible.

Yet the options made possible by qualitative software have actually outpaced the ability of ordinary academic outlets to publish these new forms of work. Research models and publication media and formats will have to expand and change to keep pace with these new tools. I will examine the two distinctive roles for qualitative data analysis software in order.

Organizing and Analyzing Text-Based Qualitative Research Efficiently

The most widely used software packages first help researchers manage their research projects (Dey 1993; Weitzman and Miles 1995; Wickham and Woods 2005; Lewins and Silver 2007). Computer software helps to electronically organize large amounts of data and allows for easy backups of both data and associated analytic work. These features help make qualitative research more systematic and efficient (Kelle 1995). Next, computer software helps researchers explore and code data (Weitzman and Miles 1995). This speeds the marking and retrieval of meaningful passages or segments of data. It also provides a flexible method for making connections among meaningful data, revising codes and connections as needed, and for easily saving iterations of analytic work. These features can help make qualitative studies both more systematic and more transparent (Dey 1993; Kelle 1995; Lewins and Silver 2007).

Because computer software creates hyperlinks between the raw data and user-defined codes, it allows virtually instant retrieval of researcher-identified text passages or segments of electronic files. Such features speed recall, which in turn can help maintain connections to the larger, shaping context. They can also help with the identification of patterns within the data set. The process of moving from concrete, grounded evidence to more abstract concepts is enhanced. The shift from analysis of individual cases to aggregated analysis is also facilitated and documented (Weitzman and Miles 1995).

Further, most contemporary qualitative data analysis software allows for creation of memos or annotations to most elements of the data set (Kelle 1995; Lewins and Silver 2007). This aids transparency by clarifying and documenting analytic decisions and links researcher reflexivity to specific elements of the data set. Simple and complex searches of the data set as a whole, and querying within coded materials, is made quick and thorough. Finally, most software packages include network development or mapping features that allows users to create and revise descriptive and conceptual displays of the connections within the data set. These features allow researchers to organize the more abstract, conceptual yield of coding schemes and to make them more accessible to others (Weitzman and Miles 1995; Lewins and Silver 2007). At the same time, links to the original data are always maintained and are easily available via hyperlink, grounding conceptual development in raw data. Organization and data management is enhanced, as is the completeness of searches and queries. Efficiency is improved.

What Computer Software Does Not Do

These core features mimic and enhance the traditional paper-and-pencil approaches to qualitative data analysis. What they add is instant ability to explore, search, and efficiently back up the entire project as it evolves. However, the software makes no analytic decisions for the researcher: Identification of meaningful passages and development of codes is entirely done manually by the researcher (Dey 1993; Drisko 1998; Lewins and Silver 2009). This time-consuming and intellectually demanding work is organized, but not completed, by the software. Unlike statistical software, qualitative data analysis software does not do the analysis; it merely facilitates it.

Computer software does not teach researchers the methods of qualitative research, nor enforce any particular method of analysis (Lewins and Silver 2009). It is increasingly generic in function rather than tied to a specific research approach such as grounded theory or ethnography. Computer software requires that the researcher be very knowledgeable about the analytic methods and procedures they use. Further, it does not automatically reduce researcher bias, nor improve the reliability or credibility of the analysis. Computer software is often cited in the methods sections of qualitative reports, but the use of software in no way guarantees a meaningful or rigorous analysis. It may offer some modest overtones of thoroughness but these can be appearances only if the software is not used thoughtfully. The optimal use of computer software draws upon a solid foundation in qualitative research methods and the ongoing support of peer reviewers who appraise, interrogate, and challenge the researcher's analytic decisions.

Computer software is not always necessary for doing qualitative research. It does, however, offer two important new research options that are as yet both poorly understood and underutilized. First, computer software makes team-based qualitative research much more practical and, sometimes, makes it possible. Second, it opens up many new opportunities for multimedia data analysis and display. These features of qualitative data analysis software are not frequently taught nor effectively promoted. Indeed, they are often omitted in descriptions of software features, and—at this time—may be ahead of the curve with regard to how academic and publishers think. But they offer wonderful possibilities for the very near future.

Making Multisite Team Qualitative Research Feasible

An often overlooked innovation made possible by computer software is geographically dispersed, multisite, group qualitative research. Before software, research teams would need to box and mail coded paper copies of their work to share changes with colleagues. Since a 90-minute interview can run to a 60-page typed transcript, a relatively small study might generate 600 pages of data and many more pages of memos and journal notes. The receiving researcher would have to integrate their colleagues' new work with their own paper copies or start a whole new merged version from original documents. The process was possible, but surely not easy. It also might have to be completed several times as the project progressed. My own experience and comments from colleagues indicate that the practical challenges to sharing large volumes of paper data were many: Pets could undo days worth of work in moments, one slip with a box of data could cause hours of frustrating collating, and loss or damage to paper data in transit was common. Such daunting tasks made team-based qualitative research difficult and, in turn, very infrequent. With computer software, both the data set and the saved coding work can be compressed and sent by e-mail to research colleagues. Using the same software, team members can open and view the work of other team members almost instantly.

Select software packages further allow the merging of analytic work among team members as well. That is, work done by one researcher in

New York may be electronically merged with work done by another researcher in Cairo and a third in Sydney. Researchers can select which features of a project to merge or to leave as is. For example, they may select to add only new data documents, or combine coding work for all team members along with new documents, or merge annotations all at once or selectively. Researchers can also track the names of the researcher team member who made each analytic decision both in individual work and in the new merged data set.

Since making copies of both the work of each individual and of the merged team effort is simple, and generates only a small electronic file, backups of all work are made easy by computer software. This allows large-scale revisions to the team project as necessary with minimal time investment. With computer software, the work of the entire team can be shared easily with virtually no limitations due to distance. The combining of team work can be almost instantaneous, reducing a major paper undertaking to an easy electronic one. Yet this valuable contribution of qualitative data analysis software has not been widely noticed, or much capitalized on, by researchers. It is nonetheless a major and valuable contribution of computer software to qualitative research possibilities.

Research Beyond Text: The Multimedia Future Is Here, Now

Where qualitative data analysis software really opens new possibilities is in research with nontext, or multimedia, data sets. Some contemporary software packages allow researchers to use electronic images, audio files, and video files directly as data. Also easily managed are electronic copies of mixed-media Internet documents, spreadsheets, databases, and geographic location images. There is no paper-and-pencil method for displaying, let alone analyzing, much of this data. Computer software literally makes possible the use of many important contemporary data types in qualitative research. Greater scope of information can be included in qualitative research, making for richer and more nuanced data from which to learn about the social world. Reduction of complex data to flat text is not required, helping to realize the research goals of credibility, richness, and verisimilitude in qualitative research.

Qualitative data analysis software allows the segmenting and coding of images by marking specific two-dimensional sections of images. Portions of an image are defined within a square frame and coded, using a process much like cropping an image. In this way, a specific focus is identified within the entire image. Multiple and overlapping portions can be marked on a single image. Audio and video files are segmented into time spans starting at a particular moment in time and ending after a specific time elapses. Passages of a user-defined duration are coded in a manner similar to those used to edit videos for home use. The process requires some experience to master, but is not difficult. Computer software tracks and links segments of images or passages of video in exactly the same manner as it tracks and links segments of written text. Code names may be applied; annotations may be attached; the segment itself may be revised later; the code name may also be changed later.

One key difference centers on how the data is displayed. Text, of course, can be printed out from electronic file to paper hard copy. Images, audio, and video often require means of electronic display. Paper media cannot match the information density and richness of audio, pictorial, and video data. Still, the quality of available data, its conceptual foundations, and how effectively vital information is conveyed will distinguish research with merit from rambling slide shows. One picture or video may be worth a thousand words, but only if what it conveys is important and useful to realizing the researcher's purposes.

The Challenges of Publishing Multimedia Qualitative Research

While computer software can help organize the analysis of multimedia data sets, the media in use for academic publication do not yet allow for the publication and display of multimedia qualitative research. The modes and media of academic publication have not kept pace with recent changes in technology, severely limiting the use of richer data types in qualitative research. Academics are very sensitive to the means of publication for their work. "Publish or perish" may be understood as a quite literal process. If avenues for the efficient display and publication of one's work are limited, they may be passed over even if such new technologies and media have strengths and possibilities not provided by existing outlets.

Some qualitative data analysis software makes available an efficient technology for the analysis of more diverse and more information-rich data than is available via flat text. But if the obsolete data projectors available at conferences cannot display coded video successfully, and print-only journals offer no means for publishing audio data sets, a wonderful tool may be undermined and ignored. I presented a multimedia "paper" at the Society for Social Work and Research conference in 2005. The presentation opened with photographic images, as one aspect of an exploration of ethical and "taste" issues in coverage of the Indian Ocean tsunami and its devastation. Using PowerPoint software, I simply displayed selected images, along with newspaper statements from reporters and letters from readers to let them speak for themselves, requiring no spoken narration. The pictures literally told the story (though I carefully chose what was conveyed for a very specific purpose). Using a now obsolete version of ATLAS. ti qualitative data analysis software, I then explored the information limits of written text by contrasting transcripts with the richer spoken oration and video it summarized. (Again, I carefully and purposefully selected materials that capitalized on the differences in information richness between the audio, video, and written data.) Computer software has for several years offered analytic and information display opportunities that have neither been well understood nor widely utilized by academic researchers. Ironically, even the electronic versions of academic journals in social work center on the marketing of written text documents rather than on making full use of the possibilities of other electronic media.

Recent devices such as the Kindle and the Nook e-book readers aim solely to display print text. Their purpose is to replace books but not to enhance and expand them. (Of course, laptop and netbook computers have been intended for years as both readers and multimedia display devices!) Small, multipurpose tablet computers may point to a truly multimedia future that could draw along academic publishers over time (Enderle 2010). Qualitative data analysis software is already up to the task. Researchers need to find its optimal uses, and publishers need to create appropriate media outlets for new forms of research reports.

Using Qualitative Data Analysis Software

Qualitative data analysis software is increasingly easy to use (Lewins and Silver 2007; La Rocca 2009). Yet it is also true that it has a considerable learning curve and requires that the user has a solid background in qualitative research methods. Optimal use of advanced features requires considerable expertise in qualitative research methods, detailed knowledge of one's data, and skill in using computer software (Johnston 2006). The first four software packages I explored in 1995 came on one or two floppy disks. Some seemed to require expertise in DOS and immense patience. Others, even then, used icons and drop-down menus to make many features readily available. Today all qualitative data analysis software employs highly visual interfaces to guide the user in locating and using basic research functions. Convenience has increased, but not all users find the software intuitive. To provide a look into using the software, a brief walk-through of the steps of creating and working with a project may be helpful. I will focus on ATLAS. ti as my personal favorite, but remind readers that for most basic uses, the steps are generic across programs.

A Tour of a Software-Based Qualitative Analysis Project

An important preparatory step is to collect the electronic data files and make sure they have been proofed and are in final form. It is possible to edit text documents within most qualitative data analysis software, but it is wise to preen them first. Images, audio, video, pdf documents, and spreadsheets cannot (yet) be edited once imported into qualitative data analysis software. The task of preparing documents is different enough from coding and other analysis that it seems to be preferable to do it as a separate preparatory step, all at once, before copying any electronic files into the computer software.

Getting Started

After installing the qualitative software, one opens the software and starts a new project. The software tracks and stores all analytic decisions in a single computer file. This file is created and named as the container for each project. Bear in mind that computer software can manage several different projects at once, so naming each project with an intuitive label is important. However, this project file does not include the raw data files. Therefore, the next step is to assign the raw data files into the analysis software. The raw data files are copied into a specific folder location. The data files are not altered during analysis; only the project file evolves as analysis progresses. Still, it is wise to keep backup copies of the data files in another location for safekeeping (optimally in a different building). Once the data is copied into the data folder, a few clicks assign or link these files with the named project. They are then available in the qualitative data analysis software.

Making Memos and Annotations

Memos or a journal are used to document one's ideas, reflections, and questions about the research project from start to finish. Computer software allows the easy creation of memo files that document initial ideas, musings, concerns, and possible biases. A few clicks open text windows that can address the project as a whole or can be linked to specific elements of the project (such as documents or codes). It is good practice to start each new project with a memo that documents the researcher's overall expectations, hopes, and/or hypotheses to begin and document the reflexive process. Such entries strengthen qualitative research by helping researchers identify their potential biases and create ways to explore and offset them. Researchers can add later entries or memos related to the project as a whole or to specific elements of the project. Linking such memos to specific aspects for the analysis also helps to document analytic decisions. Dating each entry adds precision and documents the project's chronology. All such memos become part of the project file, allowing easy access and quick backup.

The Coding Process

With the project populated with data files and a beginning project memo saved, the researcher opens a data file and begins the analysis. This usually centers at first on identifying meaningful passages of text or sections of multimedia data. The researcher highlights a section of text or other media, usually through an easy "click and drag" process. The identified (usually highlighted) passage is next labeled with a code name for later retrieval. If it fits one's chosen research approach, coding also starts the process of categorization or conceptual development. Tools to create codes are available via icons or small floating windows.

Marking meaningful passages and coding them is the single most time consuming part of qualitative data analysis. As a result, computer software offers several different methods for coding. One great feature of ATLAS. ti is "drag and drop" coding that lets researchers code a passage simply by dragging the code name onto a highlighted passage. This technique is fast and easy, and very efficient once a number of codes have been created. Multiple coding options allow researchers to find approaches that best fit their analytic needs and personal styles. They also save time.

Search Functions

To search for all instances of a word or concept, computer software offers a range of search functions. The simple search functions allow searching for specific words or sets of related terms all at once. One might search for the word "why" to find explanations, or combine "why" and "since" and "because" into a single search process. Computer searching aids thoroughness of examination, but researchers must make sure the resulting hit is meaningful in context. For example, some searches may find words used in an unusual and irrelevant context or used by the interviewer, which may not be considered data.

Output Options and Backing Up Your Work

Computer software can save and output coded materials in many formats. Lists of codes, word frequencies, codes along with all the passages they summarize, or texts with coding attached may all be printed to paper, to computer screen, or saved as electronic files for later review and use. In this way, output from computer software can mimic paper and pencil methods as well as offering many additional output options.

Software can also save and back up the research project on a regular basis. This can build peace of mind as well as creating an iterative audit trail documenting analytic decisions over the course of the project. ATLAS. ti has a wonderful "pack and go" feature called the copy bundle that creates compressed versions of both analytic project files and data files for saving or sharing with colleagues. Copied bundles can later be opened on one, or several, different computers on which ATLAS.ti is installed, recreating the entire project quickly and efficiently.

Queries Within Coded Materials

More advanced search functions, known as queries, allow for exploration within already coded materials. Boolean queries allow location of passages of text or multimedia files coded with user-defined combinations of code names. Such Boolean queries allow for location of all passages with *both* one code *and* another, one code *or* another, or one code *but not* another. In this manner, researchers may examine if relationships within coded materials fit certain existing or developing concepts and theories. Another form of query examines materials coded as superordinate and subordinate to each other, helping to explore and clarify hierarchical relationships among content and concepts. Still another form of query allows for the exploration of the proximity among content in coded passages. For example, a researcher may query to see if passages coded as "trauma" follow passages codes as "the traumatic event" or "the perpetrator" within a range of five lines or within a single paragraph. All queries are best used when theory suggests certain patterns within coded data. They require strong content knowledge on the part of the research for optimal use.

Creating Subsets of Materials to Focus Analysis

Qualitative data analysis software can also filter documents, meaningful passages, and codes into subsets for analysis. For example, a subset of documents representing only the female participants may be created and analyzed or reviewed separately from that of the data on male participants. This increases focus on the selected issue and reduces the volumes of data to be examined. Subsets of codes can be created to help review the consistency or reliability and completeness of coding on a specific topic. This is both efficient and effective.

Identifying and Visually Portraying Relationships Within the Data

Once meaningful passages of data have been coded, researchers may wish to identify and display the relationships among these passages. Computer software offers tools to create links between and among coded elements of the data, as well as with other parts of the project such as memos or even entire data files. At the simplest level, a researcher might wish to link several codes that are component elements of a superordinate concept. For example, various types of trauma, coded separately, might be linked to the overarching general concept of trauma. Alternatively, the many sources of resiliency used to cope with and overcome the effects of trauma might be broken out as distinct influences. These sources of resiliency might be understood not as components of an overarching category but as separate influences that each shape coping and recovery. In ATLAS.ti, a researcher can establish links among codes, segments of data, documents, and memos. By default, Glaser and Strauss's (1967) set of basic relationships are available as labels to identify the type of relationship identified. These include "is a part of," "is a cause of," "contradicts," and "cycles." One can also select "no name" or create user-defined relationship labels for specific research purposes.

Once relationships are created, they can be displayed as network maps portraying the content and relationships visually. Network maps move analysis from establishing grounded linkages between codes and raw data to a more abstract level of conceptualization. They can also convey complex relationships among large amounts of information effectively. La Rocca (2009) argues that network maps can also be used to effectively convey the analytic decisions involved in large-scale ethnographic studies. At the same time, a mouse click can shift the focus back to the original data in which the analysis is grounded. Network maps can be exported as graphic images files for presentation and additional analysis.

Word Counts and Statistical Functions

One further function of qualitative data analysis software is the ability to perform some basic statistical functions. One such function is the ability to create lists of word frequencies within the data set or a specific document. Such features are useful for rudimentary content analysis. On the other hand, software specifically designed for content analysis is more fully featured and includes tools to create concordances and indices that general purpose software does not.

ATLAS.ti can generate output to SPSS or Excel for statistical analysis. The limitation of such tools is that the coding of the data is much more time consuming in the qualitative software that it would be using SPSS. It is a feature of limited utility.

Multimedia Analytic Tools

ATLAS.ti allows the direct analysis of images, audio, and video. As previously noted, these features are available in only a few other qualitative data analysis packages. Segmenting such files is fairly straightforward but lacks great precision. That is, marking video segments at a very precise time may take several attempts to do so successfully. With experience, one gains skill quickly. The reward is the ability to use information rich data files without transcription. The downside is the limited availability of publication options. Further, there is the simple fact that watching video occurs in real time: Five minutes of video will always take five minutes to watch. Reading text transcripts is often much faster. Still, the information captured by audio and video may allow additional secondary analyses, making collected data both more revealing and efficient.

Only a few software packages allow direct analysis of Adobe Acrobat pdf files. These files often combine images and text in complex formats. One may wish to analyze not only the content but the organization and layout of the combined multimedia images. To do so requires software to display the files accurately, coupled with tools for their segmentation and coding. ATLAS.ti and NVivo provide such tools. Since pdf files are a common format for government documents and service manuals, this tool is very helpful for research involving the comparison of enacted programs with their published claims and procedures. It is a real help for many forms of evaluation research.

ATLAS.ti also allows for the association of Google Earth geographic information files with other forms of qualitative data. That is, Google Earth images and maps may be linked to descriptions of neighborhoods or specific resources such as bus routes and locations of supermarkets. Here computer software allows very detailed location information using GPS coordinates as well as photographic images of specific locations (Fielding and Cisneros-Puebla 2009). For ethnographic studies, a new dimension of information is made available.

Learning to Use Qualitative Data Analysis Software

Computer software offers a wealth of tools for the qualitative researcher. Some parallel pencil-and-paper procedures, others are newly available due to the additional capacities of electronic files and computer equipment. Using such software has a learning curve and takes some concentrated effort (Drisko 2004). While one can learn it on one's own, taking a workshop is often a useful way to break the ice and learn by doing with feedback. Both commercial and academic options are available. In addition, there are many helpful print and multimedia tutorials for the major software packages. These tutorials can help users learn the software and explore its unfamiliar features as needed.

While comfort with technology is increasing with time, users may find lack of knowledge of qualitative research methods to be another major limitation to using computer software. Since the software only organizes and manages a research project, the researchers must make many independent decisions as the project is implemented. It is my sense that users sometimes leave computer software behind because they lack sufficient education in qualitative research methods and data analysis procedures. Many novices appear to hope that software will help structure their research work. Sadly, it does not. Having a wide range of analytic tools available will be of little help if one's data is thin, or one's knowledge of how to design and implement a qualitative study is limited. Training and mentoring in qualitative methods coupled with using software is an ideal combination. Understanding and using the computer technology may pose challenges for some older students, but has become an almost "taken for granted" set of everyday tools for many younger, technology-savvy students.

Several studies show that users either come to master and use this software or set it aside and return to traditional approaches (Agar 1991; Lee and Fielding 1995). The only limitation to the choice not to use qualitative data analysis software is that one is limited in the data types and sources one may use in research. In the very near future, not using software may be a choice that severely limits the qualitative researcher. Given the rise in popularity and volume of mailing list, Facebook, and YouTube in contemporary culture, information rich sources of data may become unavailable to researchers who do not utilize multimedia data analysis tools.

Choosing among Software Packages

The best software package is the one that will do the tasks you want done easily and in a manner that fits your style. Just as some users prefer

WordPerfect over Word and others choose Word 2003 over Word 2007 or Word 2010, the best qualitative data analysis software should fit your needs and style optimally. Unfortunately, it takes some time to use and get to know several packages in order to make a personalized decision. This may not be a realistic endeavor for many researchers. Instead, researchers draw on the views of colleagues or publications that are surely valuable but that may not adequately address personal preferences and needs. The good news is that most of the widely used computer software packages are increasingly easy to use and are remarkably flexible. The bad news is that personal preferences may make a competent software product unappealing for some users.

There are some excellent guides for appraising qualitative data analysis software. The best overview of all the options is still the Weitzman and Miles (1995) sourcebook. While the details about product features are dated, the book provides an excellent and comprehensive overview of the different kinds of software that can be used in qualitative data analysis. Meyer and Avery (2009) note that even Excel can be a tool for organizing field work materials—an option Weitzman and Miles described and compared to other products many year earlier. Their sourcebook is demanding but comprehensive. It can help researchers find and make use of existing and familiar tools in many ways. The book's major limitation is that it does not address analysis of multimedia files.

Lewins and Silver (2009) offer irregularly updated comparisons and reviews of qualitative data analysis software. Their product comparison is a great starting point for newcomers looking to choose among widely used software products. (Be sure you have the latest version as older ones remain available online.) Both authors are part of the Computer Assisted Qualitative Data Analysis (CAQDAS) project at the University of Surry in the United Kingdom. Their summaries and reviews are available at the CADQAS project website or via an Internet search.

Lewins and Silver (2007) also offer a helpful introductory text that compares and contrasts several widely used computer software packages. The book is very clear and well illustrated with software screenshots. The authors are experienced software users with strong qualitative research knowledge who point out many practical, user-focused, differences among the most widely used software packages. Once again, those with greater knowledge of qualitative methods will be better able to understand the relevance of features to their specific research needs.

There are also many online software comparisons. My view of these documents is that the researcher's own preferences seem to have an exaggerated influence on the features they find most useful or efficient and also those that are found wanting. In turn, these online documents can be informative but should be viewed critically for limitations and biases. I have used ATLAS.ti for many years and find it keeps data prominent on screen, has many icons to allow quick access to features, and it handles many kinds of multimedia files fully and successfully. But others prefer the more project focused "metaphor" of NVivo and argue it handles large text files better than does ATLAS.ti. HyperRESEARCH runs natively on Apple OS. ATLAS.ti, NVivo, and MAXQDA are Windows products (but ATLAS.ti and NVivo can run on Apple OS with Windows emulator software; MAXQDA makes no such claim). Users do need to try out any software product before purchase to see how it works on your equipment and how it feels for your style and needs. All major products offer free downloads of trial or demo versions that allow users to install the product and try it out. I encourage such trials for anyone considering the use of the products. If possible, it is still better is to see a hands-on demonstration of how skillful researchers have used the software in their own research.

The manuals for some software products are available for free download from the product's website. These manuals are long, detailed, and often appear very technical. They do, however, provide extensive listings of product features that allow potential users to examine how they work and to see if they will meet specific research needs. Always be sure that the manual is current. It is quite common that new features are explained in separate files instead of an entire manual update. Be sure to look for the manual and also for any additional updates on specific features.

A listing of online resources is provided at the end of this chapter. These include the major software packages and one that is useful for specific multimedia applications (creating transcriptions on a computer and analysis of video files.) As software products evolve rapidly, and new options emerge frequently, an online search should be undertaken to ensure any print description of software is accurate and up to date.

Qualitative data analysis software can make research more efficient and more thorough. It also makes possible a wide range of new multimedia and group research opportunities. Still, qualitative data analysis software may not be necessary for some research projects. Optimal software use requires solid knowledge of qualitative research methods and some dedication to learn the software. In turn, it points to new and exciting possibilities for the next generation of qualitative research.

Online Resources

The University of Surrey's Computer-Aided Qualitative Data AnalysiS (**CAQDAS**) site provides helpful software comparisons and information about the use of many software products. http://caqdas.soc.surrey.ac.uk/

ATLAS.ti This site provides the latest information about ATLAS.ti along with tutorials, newsletters, and a free, downloadable trial version. Designed for Windows operating systems, but can be run on Apple OS with emulation software. http://www.atlasti.com

NVivo This site provides the latest information about NVivo along with tutorials and a free, downloadable trial version. Designed for Windows operating systems, but can be run on Apple OS with emulation software. http://www.qsrinternational.com/products_nvivo.aspx

HyperRESEARCH This site provides the latest information about HyperRESEARCH along with tutorials and a free, downloadable trial version. HyperRESEARCH was designed as a cross-platform program and runs on both Apple OS and Windows operating systems (without any extra software). A Linux version may be forthcoming. http://www.researchware.com/

MAXQDA This site provides the latest information about MAXQDA along with tutorials, and a free, downloadable trial version. MAXQDA was designed for the Windows operating system. http://www.maxqda.com/

Transana This site provides the latest information about Transana, a software product designed to transcribe and analyze audio and video files (not mainly text). Transana is an open source product, designed as a cross-platform program and runs on both Apple OS and Windows operating systems. http://www.transana.org/

References

Agar, M. 1991. The right brain strikes back. In *Using computers in qualitative research*, N. Fielding and R. Lee, eds. 181–194. Newbury Park, CA: Sage.

Dey, I. 1993. *Qualitative data analysis: A user-friendly guide for social scientists*. New York: Routledge.

di Gregorio, S. and J. Davidson. 2008. *Qualitative research design for software users*. New York: Open University.

Drisko, J. 1998. Using qualitative data analysis software. *Computers in Human Services*, 15(1):1–19.

——. 2004. Qualitative data analysis software: A user's appraisal. In *The qualitative research experience* (revised ed.), D. Padgett, ed. 193–209. Belmont, CA: Wadsworth.

——. (2005). "Using images, sound and video in research: The tools are available now!" Juried workshop presented at the Society for Social Work and Research Annual Meeting, Miami, FL.

Enderle, R. Amazon's new Kindle is worth the upgrade. Retrieved July 29, 2010, from www.digitaltrends.com/gadgets/amazons-new-kindle-is-worth-the-upgrade.

Fielding, N. and C. Cisneros-Puebla. 2009. CAQDAS-GIS convergence: Toward a new integrated mixed method research practice? *Journal of Mixed Methods Research*, 3(4):349–370.

Glaser, B. and A. Strauss. 1967. *The discovery of grounded theory.* Chicago: Aldine.

Hwang, S. 2008. Utilizing qualitative data analysis software: A review of Atlas.ti. *Social Science Computer Review*, 26(4):519–527.

Johnston, L. 2006. Software and method: Reflections on teaching and using QSR NVivo in doctoral research. *International Journal of Social Research Methodology*, 9(5):379–391.

Kelle, U. 1995. An overview of computer-aided methods in qualitative research. In *Computer-aided qualitative data analysis: Theory, methods and practice*, U. Kelle, ed. 1–17. Thousand Oaks, CA: Sage.

King, A. 2010. Membership matters: Applying membership categorisation analysis (MCA) to qualitative data using computer-assisted qualitative data analysis software. *International Journal of Social Research Methodology*, 13(1):1–16.

Konopasek, Z. 2007. Making thinking visible with Atlas.ti: Computer assisted qualitative analysis as textual practice. *Historical Social Research/Historische Sozialforschung*, 19:276–298.

La Rocca, G. 2009. Organizing ethnographic information: The Role of CAQDAS. (Organizzare l'informazione etnografica. Il ruolo dei CAQDAS.) *Rassegna Italiana di Sociologia*, 50(1):133–160.

Lee, R. and N. Fielding. 1995. User's experiences of qualitative data analysis software. In *Computer-aided qualitative data analysis: Theory, methods and practice*, U. Kelle, ed. 29–40. Thousand Oaks, CA: Sage.

Lewins, A. and C. Silver. 2007. *Using software in qualitative research.* Thousand Oaks, CA: Sage.

——. 2009. Choosing a CAQDAS Package (6th ed.). CAQDAS Networking Project and Qualitative Innovations in CAQDAS project. Retrieved May 2, 2011 from http://eprints.ncrm.ac.uk/791/1/2009ChoosingaCAQDASPackage.pdf.

Meyer, D. and L. Avery. 2009. Excel as a qualitative data analysis tool. *Field Methods,* 21(1):91–112.

Peters, V. and F. Wester. 2007. How qualitative data analysis software may support the qualitative analysis process. *Quality and Quantity,* 41(5):635–659.

Sin, C. 2008. Teamwork involving qualitative data analysis software: Striking a balance between research ideals and pragmatics. *Social Science Computer Review,* 26(3):350–358.

Weitzman, E. and M. Miles. 1995. *Computer programs for qualitative data analysis: A software sourcebook.* Thousand Oaks, CA: Sage.

Wickham, M. and M. Woods. 2005. Reflecting on the strategic use of CAQDAS to manage and report on the qualitative research process. *Qualitative Report,* 10(4):687–702.

PART IV

QUALITATIVE PROGRAM EVALUATION

Qualitative Program Evaluation

Overview

HENRY VANDENBURGH AND NANCY CLAIBORNE

Organizational evaluation provides information for stakeholders about the details of a program, aiding them in decision-making that enhances quality of life in affected organizations and communities (Julian 2005). Systemic evaluation is a structured series of steps that can target the local, community, or policy levels. Given such a wide scope, methodological approaches for evaluation vary considerably. This chapter gives a brief overview of types and methodological approaches to evaluation and offers a case example from a county psychiatric emergency service.

Evaluation methodology includes conceptualization, research design, measurement, data collection, and data analysis. The foremost reason for selecting a method is the purpose of the evaluation. The purpose directs the questions asked and the research design, which requires understanding the initiative's goals and objectives, its structure, the expected impact on the target group(s), and the performance criteria designated by stakeholders. The scope of the evaluation is shaped by the number of partners, the resources available, and the time frame. The design ultimately establishes when and from whom measurements will be gathered (data collection) and how the data will be analyzed.

Purposes of Evaluation Studies in Social Work

Social welfare evaluations have been applied to a wide range of activities. These include (1) policy-to-practice initiatives sponsored by government entities, (2) system-level involvement and interventions, (3) involvement of consumers and stakeholder groups in ground-level planning and implementation, (4) community planning and infrastructure development to support new programs, (5) community programs, and (6) provider needs assessment and program evaluation (McDonel Herr, English, and Brown 2003).

The first purpose, evaluation of policy-to-practice initiatives, usually involves efficacy research (rigorous randomized studies) in applied settings. Evaluating policy-to-practice initiatives focuses on the successful transfer of evidenced-based practices to specified populations, geographic regions, and institutions. It also includes knowledge synthesis, which makes information available rapidly, both so that providers can adopt effective practices and policymakers can implement system-level changes. For example, in 2004, the Massachusetts Department of Social Services (DSS) launched a policy initiative using a team-based structure to deliver services to children and families. The teaming initiative intended to decrease isolation and stress among front-line child welfare workers. Did the policy-to-practice initiative yield better outcomes for children and families? Foldy, Ung, Wernick, and Gregorio (2005) evaluated the new service delivery structure using a mix of surveys, group team interviews, individual interviews, and observation of the team meetings to identify how team members viewed the change as well as factors that enabled or inhibited team effectiveness.

Second, evaluating system-level interventions is used to recognize and reduce barriers that negatively impact service users' outcomes. Such a system-level approach requires evaluating the relevant entities within a community and their subsequent collaborations. An example of such a community collaboration effort is Lawson et al.'s (2007) case study evaluation of five youth development partnerships. Each partnership had five core outcomes: (1) Enhance and maintain the community development partnership; (2) increase opportunities, services, and supports for young people; (3) increase youth engagement; (4) facilitate organizational change; and (5) facilitate community policy change. These outcomes indicate community change because if they are achieved, it means, for example, that holistic programs and services are developed and appropriate knowledge of youth development and best practices are threaded into existing youth-serving organizations. Such systems-level capacity-building requires leadership programs, responsive training, consultation, and technical assistance to help individuals and groups acquire new knowledge and competencies, while "unlearning" less appropriate competencies. In this study, one systems-level barrier to collaboration resided in the characteristics of the partnership. The partnership required a shift from a process orientation to a results orientation (partnerships are a means to specific outcomes). Prior to this shift, partners expected short-term results, which did not advance opportunities for youths. A results-oriented, developmental strategy allowed greater emphasis on organizational collaboration over long periods of time, thus facilitating community policy changes.

The third purpose of evaluation methods is to involve consumer and stakeholder groups in making choices, planning, and constructing new services. A common expectation is that the new services will be less restrictive, more flexible, and more creative. This ground-level planning approach is embedded in a participatory philosophy promoting the involvement of consumers and stakeholders in service delivery decisions. For example, Werrbach, Withers, and Neptune's (2009) evaluation describes the creation of a children's mental health system of care by the Passmaquoddy tribe. The tribe coordinated agencies and formal and informal community resources. Tribe members were engaged to create a culturally competent system and overcame historical and contemporary issues that were barriers to its creation.

A fourth purpose, initiatives that support community change, focuses on community planning, problem-solving, and infrastructure development. Evaluations measure the level of community policymakers' and influential stakeholders' engagement, as well as community-wide involvement. For example, Behar and Hydaker (2009) assessed 25 federally funded sites for their readiness to develop and deliver a system-of-care model for children with emotional disorders. They identified organizational and community factors that required changes for successful implementation, including leadership, local partners' network, shared goals, collaboration, families and youth partnerships, accountability, evaluation, and planning for expanded services.

A fifth purpose is assessing a community program through its governance structure. The focal point is the ability of the governance structure to coordinate implementation across constituents by collaborating with diverse organizations within the community (Mesaros 2005). Typical measures include implementation activities, organizational linkages, and impact on target populations. To learn how one state coordinated implementation of Temporary Assistance to Needy Families (TANF) for HIV-positive women, Keigher and Stevens (2011) conducted repeated in-depth interviews that explored the women's efforts to secure health care, income and social services. The women were below the poverty level and experienced the double stigma of having HIV and receiving welfare. Other entitlement programs providing income and related services were intermittent. The program was unable to coordinate the services needed, which, when combined with the illness, resulted in exhaustion, anger, and demoralization.

The sixth purpose of social welfare evaluations is needs assessment and program evaluation for a provider to obtain information for decision-making and stakeholder approval. Needs assessment gathers information about consumer and community unmet needs, usually for strategic planning purposes and for a single program. Because of its ability to consider a rich array of data, qualitative program evaluation has become a key tool for needs assessment.

For example, a health consortium and university collaborated on an assessment of needs for mental health services among Latino and immigrant populations in Montgomery County, Maryland (Primary Care Coalition 2011). They conducted focus groups with participants from the consortium agencies, starting with the tricky issue of defining mental health in various Spanish-speaking cultures. They also completed structured interviews with key informants from grassroots organizations and stakeholders. The data were analyzed and presented for commentary in several forums: university-based researchers, community-based topical specialists, and community consortium members, who had an additional task of recommending service changes. The rich results suggested culturally attuned projects to (1) combat mental health stigma, (2) increase resiliency among community members, (3) reduce violence, alcoholism, and increase treatment adherence, and (4) work within cultural beliefs to increase understanding of psychotropic medications and engagement in mental health treatment.

Qualitative Program Evaluation

The types of evaluation described earlier can be done with qualitative, quantitative, or mixed methods. When is it most appropriate to use qualitative methods? Qualitative techniques such as observations or open-ended interviews can generate a rich picture of how the program or project being studied operates. If done well, the resulting evaluation is as valid and potentially reliable as using any other method. Although typically more time-consuming and costly than other approaches, qualitative methods have the advantage of presenting a very complete view of their objects of study. They can capture the idiosyncratic reasons for a program functioning well or poorly, thus helping avoid premature conclusions about what works and what does not. Because qualitative evaluation is particularly good at capturing the rich details and unique features of programs, it is particularly suited to formative evaluations (evaluations that occur during the operation of a program) and process evaluations (evaluations that observe the workings of the program underway).

Qualitative evaluation is less well suited to monitoring the quantitative outputs of a program such as indicators of financial solvency, consumers served, and so on. Summative evaluations (typically evaluations that measure outcomes) should also use quantitative approaches unless outcomes are directly palpable. Still, mixed methods can supplement quantitative approaches in important ways. For example, if cost and time savings are the primary consideration, quantitative methods are appropriate. Nevertheless, qualitative methods can enrich understanding of the meaning of cost and time to the providers and recipients.

Approaches to Qualitative Program Evaluation

At its most basic, qualitative analysis of programs could be accomplished crudely by an evaluator "hanging out" in the setting where the program operates, observing what goes on, and writing up his or her impressions. This laid-back approach is likely to miss much, however. It might overlook the answers to key questions about how the program operates; many central features of the program may be hidden or inaccessible; the program's problems may be concealed from casual observation. Nothing would make it certain that the evaluator would identify key program features, processes, and issues. A structured method of qualitative program evaluation can help overcome these issues. We will examine three structured approaches frequently used (among many available): grounded theory, action research, and participatory research.

Grounded Theory

Grounded theory uses large amounts of qualitative data to build up an empirical theory of how an organization functions. It typically uses a series of steps to develop a picture of the situation and its features. Following Strauss and Corbin (1990), the first step is to examine the data carefully for patterns that suggested common themes (open coding). The second step is to examine it in more detail to delineate relationships, and third, linkage categories (axial coding). Fourth, the evaluator attempts to establish actual causal connections among phenomena, as well as the contexts for the phenomena and their relationships. This process of "formulating a paradigm" (Strauss and Corbin 1990) requires considering the following issues (in order):

1. Causal conditions: The events or incidents leading to the observations.
2. Context: The specific set of properties pertaining to a phenomenon.
3. Intervening conditions: The broader structural context in which the phenomenon is inserted.
4. Action/interactional strategies: Purposeful, goal oriented, procedural behavior designed to affect events pertaining to the phenomenon.
5. Consequences: The resultant set of phenomena, once action/interaction has taken place.

Turner (1981), in interpreting Glaser and Strauss (1967), suggests the following stages: (1) The evaluator uses available data to develop categories (nominal classifications) that fit the data closely. (2) The evaluator fills (saturates) these categories by accumulating all of the examples from interviews and observational data that fit each category. (3) The evaluator abstracts a definition for each category by stating the criteria for putting further instances of this specific type of phenomena into the category. (4) The categories frame follow up observations based upon questions raised when the evaluator sees the data in the light of the categories. (5) The evaluator further exploits the categories by inspecting them to see if they suggest additional categories, suggest more general or specific instances, or suggest their opposites. One notes and develops links between categories by becoming aware of the patterned relationships between them, and by developing hypothesis about these links. (6) The evaluator considers when the links hold by theorizing about these relationships and the contexts that condition them. (7) The evaluator connects the categories and their interconnections to existing theory. An additional step recommended by Glaser and Strauss (1990) is to look for extreme conditions to test whether new instances fit the emerging relationships.

In a grounded theory approach, the evaluator typically waits to define the research questions after the theory has been formulated. Thus grounded theory offers an extremely rich picture of an organization, but one that is likely to be expensive and time-consuming to obtain. (For more about uses of grounded theory, see chapter 5, by Gilgun, in this volume.)

Action Research

Action research is a process where an intervention and research take place simultaneously (Alvares and Gutierrez 2001; Israel et al. 2003). The evaluator can emphasize either the action portion of the activity or the research portion of the activity. Because it is often rooted in the perceptions of consumers, community groups, or employee groups, action research tends to be bottom-up, rather than top-down. The stakeholders who like this type of evaluation are thus likely to be clients of organizations or "lower participants" in them. The research tends to be qualitative and to have a rolling or processual nature. Typically, action research is used to adjust the activities of organizations as they seek to accomplish goals, not all of which may have been goals at the beginning of the research. Unlike grounded theory, which has scientific aspirations because of its close relationship to the facts of the empirical observations and its willingness to generate theory from these facts, action research emphasizes praxis, the idea that a group's ongoing activities need study to monitor their efficacy, but not from the point of view of abstract empiricism (Mills 1959/2000) or standing outside of events and metering them.

One action research design, the Snyder Evaluation Model (Snyder 2005), suggests that action research has three components:

1. A process evaluation that assesses how the organization functions.
2. An outcome evaluation that assesses how effective a program is.
3. A short cycle evaluation that sets up feedback loops for self-improvement as an intermediate step.

Snyder believes that quantitative as well as qualitative measures should be used in action research, and that evaluation should begin with the process evaluation. The short cycle stage allows for ongoing correction as time progresses, and outcome evaluation can be used as the program matures. It is clear that action research is practical and pragmatic, even if it does not always offer the most objective point of view possible. (An example of action research on the international level is in chapter 9 of this volume, by Jones, Miller, and Luckey.)

Participatory Research

Participatory research extends the idea of action research. Here, the researchers are typically part of the organization, community, or collaboration carrying out the project. They are thus full partners with the actors. Often such projects attempt to transform the community as well as its context through processes of education about collective action. Because of the "embeddedness" of the researcher(s) in community activities, collaboration and mutual trust hopefully overcome cross-cultural or organizational setting resistance to the researcher(s) (Baum, MacDougall, and Smith 2006). Ideally, participants forget that the researcher is in an evaluative role, and begin to consider him/her part of the usual setting.

Participatory research incorporates the participants' perspectives in order to produce insights about the ways in which participants' needs can be met. It is highly value-oriented, as opposed to merely pragmatic. Therefore, interventions devised must be compatible with the participants' values.

Most participatory evaluations include the following characteristics:

1. Priority is given to conditions identified by the community or collaboration members.
2. Empowerment and critical awareness are used to urge members to obtain resources and to change the contexts in which they find themselves.
3. Because the research is embedded, members use their experience to validate whether or not change has occurred.

As the evaluation proceeds, the researcher and members "co-learn," that is, they jointly develop knowledge of the situation and an explanation for it. In collaboration, both researchers and members contribute experience, knowledge, and the ability to identify needs, as well as possible planning, implementation, and evaluation solutions.

Participatory research can also embrace political activism and thus may resist objectivity (Reason and Bradbury 2006). Such participatory research seeks to reverse existing power relations, and rejects the idea that researchers can monopolize certain skills. Typically, it incorporates four stages: (1) assess community needs and resources; (2) action plan; (3) action taking; (4) project outcomes.

Clearly, politically active participatory research is likely to lead to interesting and dynamic results. However, its partisan nature could open it up to charges that it is not very objective, let alone scientific. It is possible, also, that the results could be more or less true for participants but not for other stakeholders. As an example of bottom-up research, it is thus likely to privilege consumers of social programs. But it is also possible that the perspectives of other social groups not present need to be assessed as well. For example, a mental patient consumer group might advocate for a policy of completely voluntary medication in community programs, but other community members might desire that medication be given involuntarily under some circumstances, because some unmedicated patients may pose a danger to themselves or others.

An example of a community-based participatory research study was conducted by Austin and Claiborne (2011). The researchers were participants in a community effort to develop a health ministry program in four northeastern urban black churches. Participant observations, meeting notes, and a focus group were used to develop awareness of needs, create the health ministry, and then design and implement a culturally competent health promotion program for management of type 2 diabetes. Because the researchers were part of the collaboration, overt participant observation was used to understand the contextual meanings occurring in the planning meetings. As part of co-learning, notes of each planning meeting were analyzed with the health ministry coordinators. An unconventionally large focus group (23 participants) was conducted. The group was large because the collaboration members reasoned that a larger group would afford active cross-discussion and greater information. In keeping with participatory principles, the researchers agreed to this format. The focus group included church ministers, the health ministry chairpersons, the program coordinator, and 16 participants representing the four churches. The participants were asked about program goals, what they learned, what they liked about the program, what aspects of the program worked well, and recommendations for improving the program. Such participatory methodology made available a quality and depth of information regarding the creation of a health collaboration and educational program, diabetes management, as well as the pressures, influences, and group norms motivating coping behaviors.

Data-Gathering in Qualitative Program Evaluation

Qualitative program evaluation uses a wide range of techniques for gathering data, as does quantitative evaluation. However, the most common are structured or semistructured individual interviews, group interviews and focus groups, observation, and review of existing documents.

Structured Individual Interviews

Some form of structured or semistructured individual interviews is utilized in most evaluations to yield either qualitative and/or quantitative data. The measurement tool, characteristically a questionnaire, requires that the evaluator ask each individual participant similar questions in a similar manner. The questionnaire may be given face to face, on the telephone, through mailings, or with the aid of the Internet. The questions themselves may be yes/no, scaled response, fill-in-the-blank, or open ended. Highly structured interviews will have more questions with pregenerated answers. Qualitative evaluations typically use more open-ended questions because they provide no structure for the answer and do not generate data for statistical analysis. However, the questions should be focused enough to elicit the kind of information the evaluator needs. Such open-ended questions usually require transcription and subsequent coding by themes, making them more appropriate for small numbers of participants. For example, Claiborne et al. (2009) used open-ended questions to understand relationship patterns among selected northern Peruvian non-governmental organizations (NGOs). Questions to executive directors were organized to elicit information regarding the linkages and relationship patterns among NGOs in the same local geographic region, the national region, with their international stakeholders, and with local and national government agencies. Box 13.1 includes an example of the questions about relationship with other NGOs in the same local region.

Box 13.1 Questions for a Structured Interview with NGO Executives:
Relationship among Local NGOs in Peru

1. What is the NGO's relationship with other local NGOs? How many
    other local NGOs do you have contact with? Do formal communi-
    cations mechanisms exist? If yes, what are they and how often do
    they occur?

2. What type of cooperating activities does the NGO have with other
    local NGOs? Does the NGO: Share information with other local
    NGOs? Refer clients across NGOs? Coordinate across NGOs or
    programs, such as synchronizing efforts, sharing common ter-
    minology, or standardizing forms? Are programs co-located? Are
    there collective community building activities? Are there legal con-
    tracts with other NGOs?

3. What resource relationship does the NGO has with other local
    NGOs? (Resource relationship includes nonmonetary and mon-
    etary categories.)

    3.1. Does the NGO have nonmonetary resources relationships
          with other local NGOs? What kinds? For how long? How
          much have these relationships increased or decreased in the
          last five years? Have they been helpful? Do they impose any
          restrictions or accountability expectations?

    3.2. Does the NGO have monetary resource relationships with
          other local NGOs? How long has the NGO had these relation-
          ships? What are the mechanisms for obtaining grants or con-
          tracts? How much money is involved?

4. How do the NGO's administrators and line staff perceive col-
    laborating with other local NGOs? Is the collaboration important?
    Why? What are the advantages and disadvantages of collaboration?
    What are the barriers? Was the collaboration successful or satisfy-
    ing? What factors are critical? What factors help managing power
    negotiations? What factors help overcome barriers? What are fac-
    tors help obtain nonmonetary or monetary resources?

5. What impact does the collaboration with other local NGOs have
    on this NGO? How does it influence this NGO's mission? What
    changes does it cause in management or organizational structure?
    Does the collaboration bring greater or less efficiency? Does the
    collaboration improve or diminish programs quality, service deliv-
    ery, or management capability?

Source: Claiborne et al. 2009

Group Interviews and Focus Groups

Group interviews and focus groups are similar to each other in that both interview a number of people at the same time. An important difference is that in the group interview, the emphasis is on the questions asked and the individuals' responses. However, in focus groups, the evaluator relies on the interaction of the group participants based on selected topics presented to them (Krueger and Casey 2009). In both, an interview guide is used to elicit group and individual responses to questions. The guide is predetermined by the evaluation goals, and the subjective experiences and opinions elicited from the participants yield the data. In chapter 11 in this volume, Raymie H. Wayne gives more detail about conducting focus groups—for example, sequence of topics, number of participants, and length and number of meetings.

Perhaps the biggest challenge for evaluators using group interviews or focus groups is selecting appropriate participants. Especially for focus groups, because the emphasis is on the group interaction, individuals selected must share experiences about the topic being evaluated. Consideration needs to be given to the diversity of participants (gender, age, status, ethnicity, etc.). A more diverse group may stimulate interaction among participants and generate multiple perspectives for the evaluator. However, homogenous groups may feel more comfortable with each other, thus providing more information. Sometimes, the participants are preselected due to their roles and their involvement with the project. Ultimately, however, the evaluator must find a balance between participants who feel comfortable with each other but who are diverse enough to encourage interaction. The Claiborne et al. (2009) study of Peruvian NGOs included focus groups as well as individual interviews. Focus groups were conducted to understand collaboration efforts from the perspective of the line staff. Box 13.2 includes examples of the focus group guide and questions.

Observations

Observations offer an evaluator the opportunity to see what actually occurs in a setting, versus what others report. The evaluator often makes field notes using "thick description," that is, immediately writing down or dictating as much as the researcher can immediately remember of what is

Box 13.2 Guide for a Focus Group with Line Staff of NGOs: Relationship among Local NGOs in Peru

Narrative/Introduction

Good morning. My name is _____ . I am conducting a study with Peruvian and U.S. researchers of relationship patterns among northern Peruvian NGOs. We are interested in understanding how your NGO functions and your relationship with other local, regional, and international NGOs—as well as with government agencies. We hope that findings from this study will support and enhance your agency.

As part of our study, we are asking you to provide us information about your collaboration experiences and your opinion about how your services impact consumers.

Our discussion should last about one hour. I will guide the discussion and make sure everyone has a chance to speak. This is _____, one of the researchers on the project, who will take notes during the discussion and operate the tape recorder.

Before we begin, we should all introduce ourselves. Please tell us your name.

Now that we have introduced ourselves, let me explain the ground rules. They are very simple:

- Please try to give everyone a chance to speak.
- Be open and honest.
- Be specific and talk about your own experiences.
- There are no right or wrong answers; all responses are valued.
- Once we begin, please do not mention any names. This is to ensure confidentiality. _____ will *not* write down any names and we will erase from the tape recording the names of anyone you might mention.
- While your responses are confidentially held by the researchers, you should realize that there will be other focus group participants present who may or may not share information outside of the focus group, including information that you may feel is sensitive or private.

Are there any ground rules you would like to add?

Please remember that you are the experts, and we are here to learn from you. So, please feel free to tell us your opinions and experiences.

Focus Group Guide

I. Successful experiences related to collaboration

  1. What successes have you experienced related to collaboration relationships?

      a. Assume that you are the evaluator. What specific indicators of successful collaboration would you identify?

      b. Please describe, in detail, your success stories. In other words, detail your accomplishments.

      c. What were the key ingredients in your success stories?

      d. In retrospect, how did you blend these key ingredients to produce these successes?

II. Strategies for overcoming barriers in collaboration

  2. What barriers have you experienced within your agency regarding collaboration efforts? What strategies did you use to overcome them? Did these strategies work? Why, or why not?

  3. What barriers have you experienced with your collaboration partners? What strategies did you use to overcome them? Did they work? Why, or why not?

  4. Think back to the very beginning of your work. If you knew then what you know now, is there anything you would do differently?

III. Collaboration impacts on agency operations

  5. How has collaboration impacted your agency operations? (For example, financial, mission, organizational structure (authority/reporting lines), management, delivering services, etc.)

  6. What are the positive effects of collaboration on the agency? Please describe these in detail. What made these positive effects possible?

  7. What are the negative effects of collaboration on the agency? Please describe these in detail. What strategies did you use to overcome them? Did they work? Why, or why not?

IV. Improvements to services and outcomes for consumers due to collaboration

  8. When you think about the services you provide to consumers, tell us about your success stories. How do you know if you are successful or not (your criteria)? How does your supervisor know if you are successful with consumers?

  9. Have collaborations with other agencies have improved services to consumers? What are these improvements? What made these improvements possible?

10. What problems did collaborations cause regarding services to consumers? How did you address them? Did these strategies work? Why, or why not?

11. Does your agency have a formal evaluation for consumer outcomes? How is the evaluation conducted across your program or the agency? Who performs this evaluation? How is the information used? Do you find it useful?

Source: Claiborne 2009

observed plus any conversation that occurs. Writing notes away from the site makes the evaluator's presence as a researcher less obtrusive. Observations combined with various types of interviews allow the researcher to triangulate the setting, in other words, to obtain a more complete picture by using more than one method. Observations typically involve how staff interact with each other, such as in team meetings, or how they interact with clients or important stakeholders. Observations can also occur during operational meetings such as board meetings, management meetings, meetings among multiple agency collaborators, or community meetings. In Luske's (1990:15–16) research of an inpatient psychiatric setting, he described his one-and-a-half-year observation as:

> . . . I was a participant observer in all aspects of the setting for a few days a week and also worked part-time on the night shift.
>
> Maintaining access to a setting is an ongoing process of eliciting staff and resident's trust and cooperation. My basic approach in the field was to sit around the facility and casually talk with residents and staff as they went about their activities. These talks ranged from passing comments to bull sessions lasting over an hour, and often involved two or more people.

Document Review

Document review involves surveying a program's work plans and technical reports to extract qualitative data from them in the same manner as extracting data from observations or interviews. Typical documents include mission statements, strategic plans, budgets, work records, and even past evaluation documents. Minutes of meetings and e-mail documents often provide decision-making processes that furnish a contextual background to the evaluation. Portions of these documents can be transcribed and processed just as though they were the text of interviews or materials obtained through observation.

Processing the Data Obtained

Processing data in qualitative evaluation usually means putting data into categories called codes. These codes provide the basis for formulating features pertaining to the program and can be linked to other codes by causal inference. Analytic memos should be generated as well to capture the relationships observed or hypothesized. The procedures for coding using a grounded theory approach were described earlier in this chapter. If data from interviews, observations, or documents are in the form of transcribed text materials, a qualitative software program such as ATLAS.ti or NVivo-9 (formerly NUD*IST) may be used to analyze the data. (Chapter 12, by Drisko, includes further discussion of qualitative data analysis software.)

Coding

Coding is assigning portions of text (or even whole documents) to categories. Codes may be simply denotative or they may be more interpretative. For example, NVivo allows one to code by highlighting a word or phrase that then becomes the code, by assigning a previously constructed code, or allowing the software to search and code automatically, as used to be done with word processors. Automatic coding is the least useful, usually, because the researcher is not able to use his or her judgment about which codes to assign.

Codes and the next level of categorizing—called nodes in NVivo—may also be coded, hyperlinked, searched, and so on. Accessing a node gives one a basic sense of how qualitative research is turned into a finished product. All of the highlighted text that was coded under that node is displayed sequentially. To write about the theme indicated by the node, one can select the text in that node, paste it into a word processing document, and inter-connect the text quotes with analytic statements. Of course, the quality of coding and ultimately the study conclusions are heavily dependent on the researcher's ability to code consistently, understand latent content, and make valid linkages among the codes, as well as the theoretical approach that guides the coding. Several chapters in this volume include examples of coding: Gilgun's chapter 5, Reissman's chapter 7, Naccarato and Hernan-dez's chapter 20, and Abramson and Mizrahi's chapter 21.

In program evaluation, the stakeholders and researchers often have specific questions in mind, so the time-consuming coding and qualitative analysis may be foreshortened in comparison to a full-blown ethnogra-phy or theory-building effort. The evaluation questions guide the coding process and to some extent influence the categories, whereas a full-blown study would use any and all information about the setting.

The following case illustrates an evaluation using mixed quantitative-qualitative analysis within an action research framework. It demonstrates the utility of different data-gathering approaches and issues in the relation-ship of the evaluator to participants and stakeholders who have different views of the organization.

Case: Program Evaluation of a County Psychiatric Emergency Service

One author was asked to do an organizational program evaluation of the general processes of a county psychiatric emergency service (PES). The program evaluation utilized a mixed method (quantitative and qualita-tive) based on the action research approach. Management also desired to know the answer to a specific question about days of inpatient residence at the local state hospital occasioned by patients passing through the PES. This was the only outcome (quantitative) measure. The process and short-cycle outcome evaluations from the Snyder Model (Snyder 2010) were combined because of the short time frame involved (about a month.) The researcher initially observed counselors meeting with clients and the op-eration of a ten-bed crisis stabilization unit. The operation seemed very smooth-running, except for the fact that counselors were obliged to answer crisis telephone calls at the same time as counseling walk-in patients. But when the researcher interviewed each of the workers and the administra-tor, utilizing an open-ended in-depth format, a different picture emerged.

The administrator made all of the clinical decisions for the PES's two units, allowing her little time to attend to organizational or management issues in spite of the fact that several other workers had licenses as therapists and could have made these decisions. This would have freed the administrator to manage the unit more generally. The difference between the data from the observation and from in-depth interviews illustrates the importance of triangulation, or using mixed methods of data collection to verify results.

In addition, in the individual interviews, many workers were dissatisfied that they could not obtain clinical supervision for clinical licensure. Another issue was the fact that the computer program in use to identify patients and record information about them was very slow—so slow, in fact, that counselors found it of little use when trying to access a returning patient's relevant history. At the same time, the program had many screens to fill out with information as well as redundant paper forms, which took time away from clients.

The range and depth of the issues revealed to the researcher were productive because of using the individual structured interview with open-ended questions. In this case, a focus group would not have attained pertinent information regarding the operations of the organization. The researcher, hired by management, would have been identified as a conduit to the administrator. Therefore, expressing negative feeling could be perceived as "unsafe" by some participants. Safety concerns here included loss of job, loss of status, and loss of influence, or being labeled as "a troublemaker or negative worker." These might also have impaired salary increases. In a focus group, some participants may identify those expressing negative feelings and repeat what is discussed to the administrator. This is especially a concern when there is conflict between management and workers, between individual units within the organization, or among workers. In an individual interview, the researcher can more easily reassure participants that information given will be confidential and that they will not be identifiable to others. It is also easier to establish a rapport and trust with participants in such individual interviews. The participant usually becomes more relaxed, and thus forthcoming with information on his/her perspectives and opinions.

An additional data-gathering method was review of key documents pertinent to the operations of the PES. Intake forms, telephone logs, admission forms, and policy and procedure documents were reviewed for content, replication, and task purposes. The computer system was assessed in the same manner. The documents and assessment of the computer system provided important information regarding the expected function of workers and administration, time elements regarding interface with callers and clients, and a holistic picture of the PES's operations. These documents also served to validate information from the individual interviews.

The program evaluation included a recommendation section, as is common for operationally-oriented program evaluations, especially those using an action research approach. Recommendations included (1) that a clinical supervisor be designated for each of the two clinical units and that the use of forms and the intake computer program be reexamined; (2) that separate counselors undertake phone and face-to-face intake tasks; and (3) that clinical supervision hours be provided for workers seeking licensure. The evaluation's key findings shaped the recommendations to make changes feasible within the existing organizational structure, yet offer capacity building suggestions, which was one of the motivations for conducting the evaluation.

Conclusion

Qualitative program evaluation provides a rich, full analysis of a program's workings. It is particularly useful for process evaluation, where a program is being evaluated while underway or situations where programs desire to self-correct while in process. It is generally less useful for evaluating outcomes unless they are very clear. Qualitative program evaluation promotes the interests of consumers and the public as well as management—although, unlike other qualitative research, it is often directed by stakeholder questions. Qualitative program evaluation is flexible enough to be conducted with multiple theoretical frameworks, including explicitly value-driven action research, and at the same time it can use varied data sources and data-gathering methods to validate participants' perspectives. Thus qualitative program evaluation can be an effective method of assessing programs and projects.

References

Alvares, A. R., and L. M. Gutierrez. 2001. Choosing to do participatory research: An example and issue of fit to consider. *Journal of Community Practice.* 9(1):1–19.

Austin, S. and N. Claiborne. 2011. Faith Wellness Collaborative: A community-based approach to address type II diabetes disparities in an African American community. *Social Work in Healthcare*, 50(5):360–375.

Baum, F., C. MacDougall, and D. Smith. 2006. Participatory action research. *Journal of Epidemiological Community Health*, 60(10):854–857.

Behar, L. B. and W. M. Hydaker. 2009. Defining community readiness for the implementation of system of care. *Administration and Policy in Mental Health*, 36(6):381–392.

Claiborne, N., J. Liu, H. Vandenburgh, J. Hagen, A. Mera Rodas, J. M. Raunelli Sander, J. G. Adanaque Zapata, and M. J. Zurita Paucar. 2009. Northern Peruvian NGOs: Patterns of interorganizational relationships. *International Social Work*, 52(3):327–342.

Foldy, E. G., T. Ung, L. Wernick, and D. B. Gregorio. (2005). "Team learning and effectiveness in child welfare practice, preliminary report #1." Unpublished report, Wagner Graduate School of Public Service, New York University.

Glaser, B. G. and A. L. Strauss. 1967. *Discovery of grounded theory: Strategies for qualitative research*. Hawthorne, NY: Aldine de Gruyter.

Israel, B. A., A. J. Schulz, E. A. Parker, A. B. Becker, A. Allen, and J. R. Guzman. 2003. Critical issues in developing and following community-based participatory research principles. In: *Community-based participatory research for health*. M. Minkler and N. Wallerstein, eds. 56–73. San Francisco, CA: Jossey-Bass.

Julian, D. A. 2005. Enhancing quality of practice through theory of change-based evaluation: Science or practice? *American Journal of Community Psychology*, 35(3–4):159–169.

Keigher, S. M. and P. E. Stevens. 2011. Catch 22: Women with HIV on Wisconsin's Temporary Assistance to Needy Families (TANF) program: A qualitative narrative analysis. *Journal of HIV/AIDS & Social Service*, 10(1):68–86.

Krueger, R. A. and M. A. Casey. 2009. *Focus groups: A practical guide for applied research*. Thousand Oaks, CA: Sage.

Lawson, H. A., N. Claiborne, E. Hardiman, M. Surko, and S. Austin. 2007. Deriving theories of change from successful community development partnerships for youth. *American Journal of Education*, 114(1):1–40.

Luske, B. 1990. *Mirrors of madness: Patrolling the psychic border*. New York: Aldine De Gruyter.

McDonel Herr, E. C., M. J. English, and N. B. Brown. 2003. Translating mental health services research into practice: A perspective from staff at the US Substance Abuse and Mental Health Services Administration. *Alzheimer's Care Quarterly*, 4(3):241–254.

Mesaros, W. 2005. Making evaluation integral to your asset-building initiative: Employing a theory of action and change. [Online] Available from: http://www.

search-institute.org/research/knowledge/MakingEvaluationIntegral.html. Accessed July 13, 2010.

Mills, C. Wright. 1959/2000. *The sociological imagination.* New York: Oxford UP.

Primary Care Coalition of Montgomery County and the Georgetown University Center for Trauma and the Community. 2011. *Reflective engagement in the public interest: A collaborative mental health research agenda in the community, final report.* http://www.primarycarecoalition.org/?q=system/files/Collaborative+Research+Agenda.pdf . Accessed February 6, 2012.

Reason, P. and H. Bradbury. 2006. *Handbook of action research: The concise paperback edition.* Thousand Oaks, CA: Sage.

Snyder, P. 2005. Snyder evaluation model. [Online] Available from: www.scu.edu.au/schools/gcm/ar/arp/snyder-b.html. Accessed July 13, 2010.

Strauss, A. L. and J. Corbin. 1990. *Basics of qualitative research.* Newbury Park: Sage.

Turner, B. A. 1981. Some practical aspects of qualitative data analysis: One way of organizing the cognitive processes associated with the generation of grounded theory. *Quantity and Quality,* 15:225–247.

Werrbach, G., M. Withers, and E. Neptune. 2009. Creating a system of care for children's mental health in a Native American community. *Families in Society: The Journal of Contemporary Social Services,* 90(1):87–95.

[14]

Qualitative Program Evaluation

Departures, Designs, and Futures

IAN SHAW

Not being good at statistics; a choice constrained by preference, obligation, or feasibility for small-scale or local research ventures; an assumption that having been trained as a social worker one is thereby equipped with good qualitative research skills; and a commitment to undertaking participatory or justice-based evaluation—these are all arguments I have heard over the years given by beginning and, on occasion, established evaluators for electing to adopt qualitative methodology. On the other hand, one does not have to search far to find reasoning that proceeds along the lines that evaluation is primarily about accountability. Accountability requires measures of effectiveness; and in order to assess program effectiveness, the gold standard is the randomized control trial. These are all misplaced, even damaging, reasons for choosing one methodology over another.

In this chapter, my aim is to marshal the best persuasive case I can muster for purposeful, wide-ranging, critical, and secure qualitative program evaluation. There is, I sense, a subtle wind of change that may prove hostile to this position. The weariness—or possibly simply mental sleepiness—that most mentions of the word *paradigm* evoke, the distaste for a strong methods agenda that marks some critical approaches to evaluation, and a mis/ reading of some powerful critiques of ethnography within social science (e.g., Hammersley 1992) are but some of the reasons for the unfriendly reception sometimes afforded to strong qualitative commitments. Indeed, if this volume proves agenda-setting in the same way achieved by its predecessor, it will have achieved much in the current climate.

It is this reading of social work and the social sciences that prompts me to fashion this chapter more broadly than a good-practice guide to choosing methods of program evaluation. Qualitative program evaluation will be purposeful and secure when it is based on an alert sense of the kinds of knowledge within social work, and an informed judgment regarding the knowledge claims that stem from research and evaluation.[1] It will be wide ranging and critical when it resists conventional or taken for granted choices of method in any given circumstances. I develop and illustrate these lines of thinking during this chapter.

Points of Departure and Arrival for Qualitative Program Evaluation

Insofar as our interest lies in evaluation for social work, it will demand an articulation with the purposes of social work rather than, for example, resting in justifications that lie within the research act itself. The ramifications of this apparently common-sense claim are considerable. For example, social work will no longer be seen as a client state of social science research, but as engaged in a reciprocal shaping and re-shaping relationship with all forms of disciplined inquiry (cf. Shaw 2005, 2007). To pick but two connected central strands of this, what are the types of knowledge in social work and the human services? How might we make judgments regarding the quality of particular knowledge claims? There is no firm agreement on either of these questions. Pawson and colleagues, in a recent contribution to a multi-stranded UK knowledge review, suggest a classification (Table 14.1) based on the purposes of social work and social care[2] knowledge (Pawson, Boaz, Grayson, Long, and Barnes 2003).

This approach is primarily useful as a way of thinking about social work knowledge. It is probably less useful as a device for assessing published evaluative research. This is partly because of practical considerations, such as lack of detail in research abstracts, and partly because much evaluation is often marked by complex, multi-purpose intentions.

Efforts to classify social work knowledge have been thin on the ground so far. There has been more work on applying ideas of purpose to the wider field of evaluation of policies, programs, and projects. A current handbook

Table 14.1 The Purposes of Knowledge in Social Work and Social Care

Knowledge Purpose	Knowledge Content
Proactive assessment and trouble-shooting	Measures to assess client needs, problem sources, and existing best practice
Program and organizational improvement	Action approaches to clarify, improve, and develop ongoing practice
Emancipatory aims and promoting user control	Emancipatory research; empowerment of service users by adopting their values and challenging oppressive structures
Oversight, monitoring, and compliance	Information management for benchmarking, auditing, and regulating provision
Program effectiveness	Formal research to discover what works—why, when, and wherefore
Circulating tacit wisdom for practice decisions	Promoting skills, reflexive judgment, and active decision-making through experience and training
Social science theory and knowledge development	Generating concepts and general propositions to enlighten the policy community

Source: Adapted from Pawson et al. 2003:22.

of social work research organizes the role and purpose of evaluation and research around distinctive intellectual traditions and ways of thinking and knowing within evaluation (Shaw, Briar-Miller, Orme, and Ruckdeschel 2010). Each tradition represents a particular role or purpose for evaluation in society. The five broad purposes are as follows:

1. Providing objective, impartial evidence for decision-making, and providing public accountability.
2. Generating or enhancing theory and knowledge about social policy, social problems, and how best to solve them.
3. Instrumentally improving practice and organizational learning.
4. Highlighting the quality of lived experience and advancing practical wisdom and good practice.
5. Promoting justice/social change.

Such statements will necessarily be pluralistic, as evaluation and research have many countenances, multiple vested audiences, and diverse ideologies. They will also necessarily be dynamic because evaluation is intrinsically linked to changing societal and scientific ideas and ideals. Starting from the purpose of knowledge does not, needless to say, tell us what choice to make regarding methodology. This point cuts both ways. An accountability purpose, for instance, does not inherently entail a quantitative evaluation design, any more than promoting justice or social change necessarily requires a qualitative strategy. But it does have substantial methodological implications, by cautioning us against treating choice of method as directed just by commonsense practice, or restricting the range of methodology for any given purpose within an unduly narrow range of choices.

Ideas about evaluation purpose should also be premised on judgments about the nature of evaluation and research and the kind of knowledge claims that follow most naturally from any method choice. To come to the point, when will we wish to choose a qualitative methodology as all or part of our evaluation work? This question is too often treated in a dreadfully simplistic manner, to suggest that if we are interested in outcomes we will choose a quantitative design, with an element of control in the design, whereas if we are interested in understanding processes we will go for qualitative strategies. You may sense from the previous paragraph that I find it difficult to find much that is positive to say about this position. A somewhat more developed position is given in a standard book on program evaluation (Shadish, Cook, and Leviton 1990). Qualitative designs will make sense, suggest the authors, when:

- The evaluator wants breadth.
- Few questions are known ahead of the evaluation.
- The evaluation will be used by readers who cannot experience the program themselves.
- Evaluators can forgo higher quality answers to more specific questions.
- A succinct summary of results will not be a priority.
- Generalizations across sites are not a priority.
- Discovery is a higher priority than confirmation.
- The evaluation client will regard qualitative evaluation as credible.

While this is an improvement on the either/or simplicity dismissed a moment ago, there seems to be an underlying "second class" dimension to most of these criteria. Most of the points are stated negatively. We are left with an impression of qualitative evaluation as an imprecise, ill-focused, descriptive, inductive exercise, strong on vicarious experience, but chronically at risk of failed credibility in the eyes of the people who count—the clients. A much better approach is to recognize the diversity of knowledge claims that may stem from different methods. Williams (1986) collated the criteria by which we may decide if a qualitative or naturalistic evaluation is appropriate. In so doing, he provided an extensive and powerful battery of reasons for electing to adopt qualitative evaluation designs that has not been bettered in subsequent writing. It will be appropriate, he suggests, in circumstances when:

- Evaluation issues are not clear in advance.
- Official definitions of the evaluand are not sufficient, and insider (emic) perspectives are needed.
- Thick description is required.
- It is desirable to convey the potential for vicarious experience of the evaluand on the part of the reader.
- Formative evaluation aimed at improving the program, policy, or practice is appropriate.
- The outcome includes complex actions in natural settings.
- Evaluation recipients want to know how the evaluand is operating in its natural state.
- There is time to study the evaluand through its natural cycle. The true power of naturalistic evaluation is dissipated if there is not time to observe the natural functions of the evaluand in their various forms.
- The situation permits intensive inquiry, without posing serious ethical obstacles.
- The evaluand can be studied unobtrusively, as it operates, and in an ethical way.
- Diverse data sources are available.
- There are resources and consent to search for negative instances and counter evidence.
- There is sufficient customer and end user agreement on methodological strategy.

I would take this approach one step further. A risk in Williams's otherwise excellent list of criteria is that we will take different qualitative methods to bring shared, homogenous qualities to the evaluation task. There is, of course, an important sense in which qualitative research has a coherence that is well worth arguing for. While the case for the strengths that qualitative inquiry brings to evaluation has to be exemplified rather than asserted, it generally entails a unifying focus on naturally occurring events, the local groundedness and contextualization of evaluation, the flexibility and responsiveness of study design, and the potential for disclosing complexity through holistic approaches. Yet the knowledge claims from each qualitative method are not equivalent and there is a need to develop the case for a dialectical mix of methods *within* qualitative research. This will need to proceed through the development of a set of critical features of knowledge for different qualitative methodologies. A helpful starting point for this is a paper of some years ago by McKeganey and colleagues, in which they discuss the benefits and limitations of interviewing and observation methods as part of a study of professional decision-making when people may be offered a place in a home for the elderly (McKeganey, MacPherson, and Hunter 1988). There is much work to be done in this area; initial analyses needs to be extended to the full range of qualitative strategies and tied to the critical features of their associated knowledge claims (cf. Greene and Caracelli 1997:12–13).

Qualitative Evaluation Designs and Social Work Outcomes

My second point in the chapter introduction rested on a claim that qualitative evaluation will be wide-ranging and critical when it resists conventional or taken-for-granted choices of method in any given circumstances. In the following section, I want to make this point initially through developing what may seem the most demanding test case—that qualitative evaluation will sometimes be the methodology of choice when the focus of the evaluation is on social work outcomes. I illustrate how qualitative methods can contribute indispensably to outcomes research in four ways:[3]

- Design solutions.
- Sensitivity to the microprocesses of practice and programs.
- Applications of symbolic interactionism and ethnomethodology.
- Qualitative data analysis.

We should not conclude, however, that qualitative research is better equipped than more traditional approaches to generate foundationalist knowledge of policy and practice outcomes. This would be crass. "*Nothing* can guarantee that we have recalled the truth" (Phillips 1990:43). Nor is this a plea to replace one uniformitarian orthodoxy with another. On the one hand, a notion that only qualitative methods can examine unique, complex cases is clearly not accurate because there is an interesting history of idiographic and ipsative quantitative methods for individual case analysis in psychology in the work of people such as Rogers, Allport, Cattell, and Kelly. Likewise, I am not convinced that all forms and traditions of qualitative methodology lend themselves equally or even directly to evaluative purposes. Stake no doubt had this in mind when he remarked with characteristic elegance that "to the qualitative scholar, the understanding of human experience is a matter of chronologies more than of cause and effect," and that "the function of research is not . . . to map and conquer the world but to sophisticate the beholding of it" (Stake 1995:39, 43).

Evaluability Assessment

Before sketching out these four stances toward qualitative evaluation on outcomes, a preliminary question occurs. Are there any steps we can or should take to resolve whether an evaluation is feasible? Wholey (1994:16) identifies several problems that, if not resolved, will render any evaluation nugatory. He suggests that

- Lack of agreement on goals, objectives, side effects, and performance criteria will lead to an evaluation that focuses on nonrepresentative or nonrelevant questions.
- Unrealistic goals and objectives, given the level of program resources and activities will lead to a program that inevitably fails.
- When relevant information regarding the program cannot be made available, the evaluation will be inconclusive.
- If policymakers or managers are unwilling or unable to act on the basis of evaluation in order to change the program, then the result will be "information in search of a user."

Assessment of evaluability shows whether a program can be meaningfully evaluated and also if such evaluation is likely to lead to action to maintain or change the policy, program, or practice evaluated, or some future evaluand. Wholey's analysis of the problems and their consequences is generally helpful, although it tends to be based in a managerial and customer-led framework that carries with it several associated problems.[4] He underscores the factors that prevent an unproblematic application of a goals and outcomes model of evaluation, and makes clear that there are some evaluation-related activities that will enable a better understanding and improvement of the evaluation process. Evaluability assessment will not always be appropriate. It presupposes the possibility of a consensual strategy for evaluation, and as such perhaps best fits a model of qualitative evaluation that is based on a responsive stance toward key stakeholders and interest constituencies.

Pulice (1994) illustrated a stakeholder-focused evaluability assessment in his discussion of qualitative evaluation methods in the public sector with seriously mentally ill adults in the first edition of this book. He recommended identifying relevant constituency groups at all levels and completing preliminary interviews with key informants on the reason for the evaluation request, the likely time frames, and their views regarding intended uses of the evaluation. He also advised a literature search of legislation, agency documents, and committee reports "to determine the nature and content of documentation relative to the evaluation question" (Pulice 1994:307). He suggested that the evaluator/s develop a preliminary taxonomy of the identified constituency groups in terms of their likely role as advocates, planners, facilitators, monitors, or managers. Finally, he recommended conducting semistructured interviews that focus on the broad evaluation questions, which could include the use focus groups.

Evaluability assessments will reflect the underlying perspectives of the evaluators. For example, critical evaluators may wish to explore—with a view to mitigating—the potential for imposing their own worldviews on those participating in the evaluation. Where such imposition seems unavoidable, it may be decided that evaluation is not feasible. Evaluators who commence from a constructivist and relativist standpoint will wish to explore the feasibility of an authentic evaluation that takes local context into account, and empowers stakeholders. Rodwell and Woody (1994:319) believe that

Constructivist methods to determine evaluability are very appropriate when the goal is to have all possible stakeholding groups involved in the process, while having problems emerge from observation, from experiences, and from the data.

They describe a proposal for an evaluation of a clinic setting that went astray. "We ignored the context of our deeds" (Rodwell and Woody 1994:324). When the proposal was made, following the evaluability assessment, it was turned down on the grounds that it did not follow the research policy of the agency; that it threatened the homeostasis of the organization through having too broad a focus, and too short a time frame to accomplish it; and that such detailed study was not needed but that the agency wanted comparison studies with similar services and using quantitative methods. The authors believe their failure stemmed in part from not taking criteria of authenticity into account. Such assessments can "create a referent in a not so rational program evaluation environment" (Rodwell and Woody 1994:326).

Design Solutions

By way of illustration of how qualitative evaluation designs have a pay-off for outcomes studies, it is important to reflect on the use of simulations. Simulations offer a rather different design solution for qualitative evaluation, and have the potential to provide "a unique and innovative tool that has not yet been widely applied" (Turner and Zimmerman 2004:335). They have two main applications—first, as an evaluative test for service discrimination, and second, as a qualitative proxy for control within a natural setting. It is the second application that is more relevant for present purposes. One particular example of simulation—the simulated client—represents an advance on the use of vignettes in policy research. Those who evaluate the process of professional practice come face to face with the invisibility of practice. How may we learn the ways in which social workers—or for that matter lawyers, teachers, and general medical practitioners—practice? How would different professionals deal with the same case? Wasoff and Dobash (1992, 1996) used a promising innovatory method, which has been too little noticed, in their study of how a specific piece of law reform was incorporated into the practice of solicitors. The use of simulated clients in "natural" settings allowed them to identify practice variations that could be ascribed with some confidence to differences between lawyers rather than the artifacts of differences between cases.

Suppose, for example, that one wishes to carry out a qualitative evaluation of decisions made by housing managers, medical staff, and social workers regarding the allocation of care management packages. Evaluators using simulated clients would prepare a small number of detailed case histories designed to test the practice decisions under consideration. Without any covert elements, a researcher or evaluator takes on the role of the client in the case history. The housing manager, relevant medical staff, and social workers each interview the "client" within the natural setting of their work.

Microprocesses

The late Bill Reid had some helpful things to say on how the close inspection of microprocesses sheds light on outcomes. He was attracted by the potential of change-process research. He did not reject the role of controlled experiments but concluded that "practical and ethical constraints on experiments necessitate a reliance on the naturalistic study of these relations" (Reid 1990:130). This entails a focus on the processes of change during the period of contact between the professional helper and the client system. Rather than relying on aggregated, averaged summary measures of outcomes, this approach returns to the content-analysis tradition in social research, through a greater focus on micro-outcomes.

A systemic view of intervention is at its root, in which professionals and service users are viewed in a circular, mutually influencing interaction. In this model "conventional distinctions between intervention and outcome lose their simplicity" (Reid 1990:135). "It then becomes possible to depict change-process research as a study of strings of intermixed . . . interventions and outcomes" (136). While Reid defended experiments, he suggested a more naturalistic stance when he said that "averages of process variables that are devoid of their contexts at best provide weak measures" (137).

A different and interesting argument for using qualitative methods as a means of understanding microprocesses has been suggested by McLeod in a thoughtful assessment of the potential of qualitative methods for understanding outcomes of counseling. He suggests that qualitative interviews are more likely to elicit critical perspectives than questionnaires, arising from the "demand characteristics" of extended interviews. "In terms of producing new knowledge that contributes to debates over evidence-based therapy, it would appear that qualitative evaluation is better able to explore the limits of therapeutic *ineffectiveness*" (McLeod 2001:178). Combined with their potential for eliciting positive relations between intervention and outcome, he concludes that "Qualitative interviews appear to be, at present, the most sensitive method for evaluating the harmful effects of therapy and also for recording its greatest individual successes" (179).

Ethnography and Interactionism

A menu of interactionist and broadly interpretivist approaches to evaluation helpfully discourages oversimplifications in the choice of methods to assess service outcomes. They do so in large part by prioritizing the importance of understanding local context. Gale Miller's work yields an example that enriches our understanding of the importance of context in qualitative outcomes evaluation. He discusses ways in which institutional texts constructed to explain past decisions inevitably gloss over the openness and complexity of the decision-making process (Miller 1997). He gives the mundane example of evaluation research on a bowel-training program in a nursing home. The evaluation consisted of counting when and how patients had bowel movements. The program was judged to have a successful outcome if patients used a toilet or bedpan and ineffective for those who continued soiling beds. One patient had soiled her bed. However, ethnographic methods enabled the researcher to observe a nursing aide contesting the definition of this incident as "failure," on the grounds that the patient knew what she was doing and had soiled her bed as a protest act against staff favoring another patient. This illustrates how mundane, everyday life is illuminated by observing the context of text construction. This would not have found a way into the formal outcome record. Text production in institutions is "micropolitically organized," and this includes textual outcome records.

Social work evaluation takes place within temporal, social, relational, cultural, faith, governmental, political, institutional, ethical, intellectual, spatial, and practice contexts. Evaluation occurs in place and time. It inhabits these contexts in ways that are, by and large, parallel to and reciprocal with evaluation in other professions, disciplines, and fields of study that share to a significant degree a commitment to comparable purposes of research. Time and place are not only the contexts within which social work evaluation happens but also the character-formers of evaluation and the (unduly neglected) focus and concern of the act of inquiry (Shaw 2010).

Analyzing Outcomes

Qualitative social work journal articles have tended to overclaim—and badly oversimplify—the influence of grounded theory on the practice of research. Yet a serious engagement with grounded theory and the logic of comparison opens up one of the few dedicated efforts by qualitative methodologists to understand and respond to the standard logics of causality in John Stuart Mill and others (cf. Dey 2004). Fresh energy has been devoted, especially in the United States, to qualitative strategies for analyzing outcomes and reaching cautious inferences about cause and effect. John and Lyn Lofland (1995:136, 138) express the view that

> Qualitative studies are not designed to provide definitive answers to causal questions . . . (but) it can still be an appropriately qualified pursuit.

Miles and Huberman (1994:147) are even less reserved. "The conventional view is that qualitative studies are only good for exploratory forays, for developing hypotheses—and that strong explanations, including causal attributions, can be derived only through quantitative studies." They described this view as "mistaken," and insist that qualitative evaluation research can

1. Identify causal mechanisms.
2. Deal with complex local networks.
3. Sort out the temporal dimension of events.
4. Cycle back and forth between different levels of variables and processes, and is well equipped to do so.
5. Provide a way through analytic induction of testing and deepening single case explanations.

Causal accounts will be local and "now-oriented" (Lofland and Lofland 1995:141). Miles and Huberman (1994) develop analytic methods that address causal attribution in both single and multiple case explanations. For example, they advocate the use of field research to map the local causal networks that informants carry in their heads, and to make connections with the evaluator's own emerging causal map of the setting. Such maps start from causal fragments that lead to linked building of logical chains of evidence. Such causal networks

> Are not probabilistic, but specific and determinate, grounded in under-standing of events over time in the concrete local context—*and* tied to a good conceptualization of each variable (Miles and Huberman 1994:159).

Patton gives an example of how we can explore linkages between process and outcome. This is done by developing categories of types and levels of outcomes and of program processes. The categories are developed through orthodox thematic qualitative analysis. The relationships between processes and outcomes may come either from participants or through subsequent analysis. The following extract gives an illustration of how this approach can operate.

> Suppose we have been evaluating a juvenile justice program that places delinquent youth in foster homes. . . . A *regularly recurring process theme* concerns the importance of "letting kids learn to make their own decisions." A *regularly recurring outcome theme* involves "keeping the kids straight . . ." By crossing the program process ("kids making their own decisions") with the program outcome ("keeping the kids straight"), we create a data analysis question: What actual decisions do juveniles make that are supposed to lead to reduced recidivism? We then carefully review our field notes and interview quotations looking for data that help us understand how people in the program have answered this question based on their actual behaviors and practices. By describing what decisions juveniles actually make in the program, the decision makers to whom our findings are reported can make their own judgments about the strength or weakness of the linkage . . . (Patton 2002:472–473)

Patton (2002:152) also emphasizes the potential of narrative analysis to illuminate outcomes. Even taking for granted an accountability purpose, stories provide the critical context for interpreting.

> Well-crafted case studies can tell the stories behind the numbers, capture unintended impacts and ripple effects, and illuminate dimensions of desired outcomes that are difficult to quantify.

Insofar as identifying individualized outcomes is apposite—and it often is—then quantitative, standardized measures may be inappropriate.[5] For example, programs are often aimed in some form at improving individual autonomy and independence. But "independence has different meanings for different people under different life conditions . . . What program staff want to document under such conditions is the unique meaning of the outcomes for each client" (Patton 2002:158). Hence, while qualitative evaluation cannot resolve the problems of causal conclusions any more than quantitative evaluation, it can assess causality "as it actually plays out in a particular setting" (Miles and Huberman 1994:10).

Case Studies

The review of qualitative evaluation for outcomes has led us into a diversity of methodological approaches. A counterbalance to this approach is provided in the following paragraphs through a consideration of the logic of case study evaluation in social work, and the specific issues that this design solution poses.

> The case for case studies in qualitative evaluations rests on a confluence of their responsive political-value stance and their underlying interpretivist assumptions (Greene 1994:538).

Case studies in evaluation emerged in the 1970s in the education field. "Case study was a metaphor that appealed to those who were looking for a way of integrating the comprehensive data requirements that emerged from the various critical reviews of the evaluation tradition" (Simon 1987:61–62). In the evaluation context, case study was not simply a loan from existing social science traditions dating back to the Chicago School. For better or worse, evaluators were preoccupied with issues of audiences, time limits, and power relationships, which encouraged a collaborative model of research.

Hakim (1988:61) remarks that, "The case study is the social research equivalent of the spotlight or the microscope; its value depends crucially on how well the study is focused." Case studies are flexible and multipurpose. They may be descriptive, exploring and providing portraits of little known entities. They may also be selective, pursuing more richly detailed accounts of processes at work. They may also be designed to achieve a form of experimental isolation of selected social factors within a real life context. But whichever general purpose guides the adoption of case study evaluation, decisions about case study designs must address five issues. First, what will count as a case? Second, will evaluation address a single case or multiple cases? Third, what will be the units of analysis? Fourth, what logic of generalization will be adopted? Finally, what is the intended relationship between practitioner values and evaluator values? We will briefly consider each of these.

First, what counts as a case? Stake (1995:133) says

> The case is a special something to be studied, a student, a classroom, a committee, a program, perhaps, but not a problem, a relationship, or a theme. The case to be studied probably has problems and relationships, and the report of the case is likely to have a theme, but the case is an entity. The case, in some ways, has a unique life.

Unfortunately, case study evaluation sometimes has suffered at the hands of its qualitative advocates. Atkinson and Delamont (1993:207) complain appositely of a tendency to looseness in talk of cases.

> What counts as a "case" is . . . much more problematic than "case-study" researchers seem to allow for . . . It is . . . quite meaningless for authors of the case-study persuasion to write as if the world were populated by "cases" whose status and existence were independent of methodological and theoretical concerns.

Stake's bet-hedging definition exhibits some of this vagueness. Yet precedent suggests that case studies may be carried out with individuals, communities, social groups, organizations, and institutions, and certain events, roles, relationships, or interactions (Hakim 1988).

Second, case studies may address either single or multiple cases. There are various rationales for focusing on a single case. Yin (2009) distinguishes critical cases (which allow the testing of a well-formulated theory), extreme or rare cases, and revelatory cases (a phenomenon hitherto inaccessible to scientific investigation). For example, voluntary welfare agencies may set up projects that reflect a novel model of intervention that they wish to develop; local educational authorities may set up small numbers of innovative but relatively costly curriculum innovations; and government departments routinely introduce innovative or imported forms of dealing with offenders. Studies of critical or rare cases are possible in these instances. Changing public attitudes to the benefits or risks of a hitherto unimpeachable project may open up the possibility of revelatory case study evaluations in a previously no-go area of practice.

Innovations are more frequently relatively widespread and therefore allow the possibility of multiple rather than single case studies. Human services innovations often fall into this category. By definition, these are unlikely to be critical, rare, or revelatory cases.

Multiple case studies can be achieved by setting up "projects which are specifically designed as a series of ethnographic studies in different settings, selected on criteria developed from existing theory to provide the most significant dimensions for comparison" (Finch 1986:185). Finch suggests the advantage of a central team that provides a steer to the analytic themes and categories at the design stage, but does not dictate the research methods. Alternatively, multiple case studies could be done sequentially by planning cumulative comparative studies. While we should not expect this to yield an easy linear development of knowledge, it does provide opportunity for interdisciplinary evaluation and would be a significant advance on most current case study evaluation.[6]

Multisite case studies may well be interested in cases at more than one level. Yin uses the term *embedded* to describe case studies where there is more than one unit of analysis, and this is the third aspect of design decision that evaluators need to resolve.

The fourth case study design issue is the logic of generalization from case studies.[7] Qualitative researchers have emphasized the importance of the locally relevant story, and the applicability of the story to other contexts has tended to be a judgment left to others. Miller and Crabtree (1994:348) put is as follows: "Local context and the human story . . . are the primary goals of qualitative research and not 'generalisability.'" The focus of the generalization problem will be different according to whether case studies have a primarily descriptive or explanatory purpose. Either way, Yin (2009) rightly warns against inappropriate borrowing of survey logic when planning case studies. He regards conceptions of statistical generalization as the method of generalizing the results of the case as a fatal flaw. When selecting multiple cases, the logic is not that of sampling but of replication. In this strategy, each case must be selected so that it either (a) predicts similar results (a literal replication) or (b) produces contrasting results but for predictable reasons (a theoretical replication).

A different but common theoretically guided approach to generalization is analytic induction. The method proceeds by employing the notion of a generic problem, which is applied through explicit and implicit comparisons of instances (Atkinson and Delamont 1993). The use of this constant comparative method, including the identification of critical and deviant cases, enables the identification of common features between cases. This brief description of analytic approaches illustrates that inferences about generalization are logical ones rather than statistical. Qualitative methods lend themselves more readily to logic of this kind, because "the place of generalization in social work is closer to the constructivist, naturalistic orientation . . . than to the position of logical positivists" (Reid 1994:470).

An approach to generalization quite unlike the aforementioned is associated with logic that seeks to bridge the experience yielded by the research and the experience of the research participants and audience. Stake and Trumbull (1982:2) have evaluative research in mind when they say:

> We believe that program evaluation studies should be planned and carried out in such a way as to provide a maximum of vicarious experience to the readers who may then intuitively combine this with their previous experience.

These are "self-generated knowings, naturalistic generalisations, that come when, individually, for each reader, each practitioner, new experience is added to old" (5). It is the evocation of personal experience that leads, in their view, to the improvement of practice.

Approaches based on personal experience are difficult to assess, and are open to the criticism that they diminish the possibility of generalizing inferences that challenge the wider, structural status quo. These approaches tend to assume a consensual moral framework, and fit well with Stake's emphasis on stakeholder case studies. The basic ideas are challenging, but they need development.

Finally, we should note that models of statistical generalization have occasionally been used effectively with multiple case studies. Sinclair reported a large-scale study of hostels for young male offenders, which utilized an impressive range of mainly qualitative data sources to draw conclusions regarding the effect of hostel environments on offenders (Sinclair 1970). He and colleagues went on to argue that

> The comparison of a large number of institutions within a single study enables a serious weakness of descriptive case studies to be overcome. This is the difficulty of linking the precise features of the care provided with its immediate and long term effects (Tizard, Sinclair, and Clarke 1975:3).

Tizard and colleagues reported a series of studies of residential establishments which showed variations of ideology, organization, staffing and resident response. Provided resources are adequate, multisite case studies provide rich opportunities for theoretically informed qualitative evaluation. Yet we must remain cautious. Geertz's conclusion (1973:25) about anthropology will often stand for social work. "What generality it contrives to achieve grows out of the delicacy of its distinctions, not the sweep of its abstractions."

Finally, we noted Simon's observation that the emergence of case studies in educational evaluation included a preoccupation with power relationships, and encouraged the emergence of collaborative models of case studies. Democratic evaluation models in Britain and the United States developed in a political context that supported discovery approaches in education. This fostered the early recognition that case studies may have an emancipatory potential "based on respect for the autonomy of the individual and a rationale of stimulated self-improvement" (Simon 1987:83). In other words, the case study was seen as having educational potential in itself.

Case studies that are broadly emancipatory have also been developed in social work. Bogdan and Taylor (1994) reported a multisite case study evaluation of forty programs that aimed to promote the integration into the community of people with learning disabilities and multiple disabilities. They aimed to develop a model of evaluation that partially resolves the conflicting orientations of practitioners and researchers, by combining appropriately skeptical rigor with research that will "help conscientious practitioners—people who are leading the reforms in the direction of integration" (Bogdan and Taylor 1994:295).

They studied each of the forty projects through a rolling program of eight brief case studies a year over five years. The sites were selected through purposive sampling methods that combined asking key informants to nominate good programs, and then undertaking telephone interviews. They wished to identify innovative and exemplary programs rather than build a probability sample. "We consciously tried to find places that can teach us about how people with severe disabilities can be integrated into the community" (298). Consistent with their theoretical orientation, they started with a deliberately vague definition of integration.

> We treat the concept of integration as problematic, something to be investigated rather than assumed. We want to learn about how agencies . . . define and accomplish integration (Bogdan and Taylor 1994:297).

Their approach resulted in much easier access; and, ironically, people were more candid about dilemmas of practice than they may otherwise have been. Short reports were produced in the professional press on each project, and when the reports focused on negative aspects of less than exemplary agencies, agencies were allowed the choice of whether or not their names were mentioned. They were interested in generalizing—"patterns that transcend individual cases" (Bogdan and Taylor 1994:300). They were also interested in theorizing, and "developing sensitizing concepts and grounded theory that transcend the commonsense ideas of the people we study," although they do not discuss how they think generalizing works or offer any reflection of the relationship between lay and scientific concepts.

The Futures Market in Qualitative Program Evaluation

I have aimed to provide an illustrative rather than comprehensive demonstration of the case for purposeful, wide-ranging, critical, and secure qualitative program evaluation. Qualitative program evaluation, I have suggested, will be purposeful and secure when it is based on an alert sense of the kinds of knowledge within social work, and an informed judgment regarding the knowledge claims that stem from research and evaluation. It will be wide ranging and critical when it resists conventional or taken-for-granted choices of method in any given circumstances. I have suggested how we might develop a big picture view of the kinds of knowledge that both social work and evaluation seek to claim. I have illustrated in moderate detail how this may shape and enrich decisions regarding the feasibility of evaluation, the evaluation of social work outcomes, and the development of case study evaluation.

I have also suggested that ways of doing qualitative evaluation will be pluralistic and dynamic. If so, where might—and should—qualitative program evaluation be heading? Insofar as we have any control over such directions, we should

1. Continue to engage the development of theoretically and philosophically informed mixed methods.
2. Be methodologically innovative and continue to elaborate the knowledge claims that we can make from different qualitative methods.
3. Give much greater attention to the relations of methods and culture.
4. Maintain, extend, and deepen a reformist and radical agenda for the process of qualitative evaluation.
5. Develop an empirical agenda for understanding how qualitative evaluation works.

Mixed Methods

There have been constructive, if cautious, dialogues regarding the relative merits and characteristics of quantitative and qualitative methodologies in social work. For example, Bill Reid in the United States and Ian Sinclair in the UK have developed mediating positions. Reid (1994:477) sought to "redefine the nature of the mainstream so that qualitative methodology is a part of it not apart from it." He regarded quantitative research as strong when dealing with linkages, control, precision, and larger data sets, while qualitative research is able to depict system workings, contextual factors, and elusive phenomena, and provide thorough description. "Neither method is superior to the other, but each provides the researcher with different tools of inquiry" that can be set against a single set of standards (Reid 1994:477; cf. Shaw 2004).

It would be highly premature, however, to conclude that the debates should now be closed, and we should simply get on with evaluation research without wasting time on the profession of "philosophical and methodological worry" (Becker 1993:226). For example, it is sometimes wrongly assumed that using multiple methods will lead to sounder consensual conclusions in an additive fashion. Naïve versions of triangulation arguments are sometimes resorted to in support of this argument (cf. Bloor 1997 for a helpful discussion of triangulation as a means of judging validity). One of the most insightful discussions of the problems raised by this assumption is Trend's early classic account of a program evaluation designed to test the effectiveness of direct payment of housing allowances to low income families (Trend 1979). In one case study, the quantitative data suggested that the program was producing major improvements in housing quality. Yet all the qualitative data indicated the program would fail. The major part of Trend's paper records his assiduous sifting of the data in an attempt to discover a plausible explanation that did not simplistically cut the Gordian knot, either by prioritizing one kind of data above the other through paradigm arguments, or by premature syntheses. His conclusion still stands as a warning against such easy solutions.

> The complementarity is not always apparent. Simply using different perspectives, with the expectation that they will validate each other, does not tell us what to do if the pieces do not fit (1979:83).

His advice was

> That we give the different viewpoints the chance to arise, and postpone the immediate rejection of information or hypotheses that seem out of joint with the majority viewpoint (84).

The interrelationship of qualitative and quantitative methods is not only, nor even primarily, about choice of methods. It is about single cases or comparison, cause and meaning, context against distance, homogeneity and heterogeneity. It entails judgments about validity and the criteria of quality in social work research, the relationship of researcher and researched, and measurement. Methodological choice is also inextricably relevant to issues of the politics and purposes of social research, values, participatory forms of research, interdisciplinary inquiry, and the uses of research.

The position that is likely to prove most creative for qualitative evaluation is that described by Greene and Caracelli (1997) as dialectical. This position accepts that philosophical differences are real and cannot be ignored or easily reconciled. We should work for a principled synthesis where feasible, but should not assume that a synthesis will be possible in any given instance. This represents

> A balanced, reciprocal relationship between the philosophy and methodology, between paradigms and practice. This . . . honors both the integrity of the paradigm construct and the legitimacy of contextual demands, and seeks a respectful, dialogical interaction between the two in guiding and shaping evaluation decisions in the field (Greene and Caracelli 1997:12).

One possible undesirable consequence is that an emphasis on the value of multiple, integrated methods may lead to a dilution of one or the other—a lowest common denominator position. It may also lead to a tendency that I have warned against already—to treat qualitative methodology (or quantitative) in an unduly homogenous way. Stake's confession should not be ignored. "I have not had much luck in using qualitative and quantitative studies to confirm each other. The criteria of the one get lost in the events of the other. Consistencies, enrichments in meaning, can be found but, I think, seldom confirmations."[8]

Methodological Depth and Innovation

A second necessary focus of attention follows from the realization that qualitative methodology may not be as soundly based as first impressions suggest. There are twin risks of routinization and dilution. There is a "follow-my-leader" tendency whereby fruitful approaches such as focus groups or narrative analysis become the uncritical routine method of choice. Qualitative social work research is also at risk of dilution. In the countries with which I am most familiar, a high proportion of master's dissertations[9] draw on qualitative methods, but few such dissertations include anything other than semistructured interviews and focus groups. There may also be cause for misgivings about the gradual proliferation of research and evaluation consultancy firms, with the associated risk of routine implementation of off-the-shelf designs. There are, however, positive developments. The gradual growth of social work membership in networks such as the American Evaluation Association, the crystallizing of qualitative interest groups in membership organizations such as the Society for Social Work and Research, and the establishment of qualitatively oriented journals such as *Qualitative Social Work* all presage a closer attention to consolidating and developing good qualitative research and evaluation practice. Earlier in this chapter, I emphasized the need for careful work on the knowledge claims that may plausibly be associated with different qualitative methods.

Culture and Methods

There has been a certain amount of concern with what is described as cultural competence in evaluation (e.g., Thompson-Robinson, Hopson, and SenGupta 2004). However, this is mainly focused on cultural diversity within the United States. One problem for me, in the late 1980s, was the realization that much of the Arab world's evaluative research by doctoral students tended to be heavily reliant on quantitative methods, especially survey designs. I would now include with this the presence of a strongly realist model of research, and what is usually referred to as a correspondence theory of the relationship between inquiry and truth. That seemed to be to me both paradoxical and unsettling.

Paradoxical, for example, because survey research demands capacity relating to population information, language, and data analysis that sometimes is in short supply. With its stress on external validity, survey research requires adequate sampling frames and working populations that are often not available in the Arab world, even in urban areas. I heard interesting anecdotes about how access to samples was informally negotiated—not that perfect sampling frames are just lying around in Western countries, waiting for the researcher to pick them up. Indeed, an ironic consequence of the high status of the Western export model of social research is that importers may be tempted into an overly sanguine belief about the ease and quality of survey research in the West. Challenges facing research in Arab cultures may be simply the challenges facing Western research writ large.

But also unsettling is that a plausible case may be made for saying that survey methodology reflects in a quite subtle manner a paradigm of Western pluralism that sits uncomfortably with societies whose members hold distinctive values regarding social solidarity and homogeneity, authority, and the appropriate form of knowledge transmission. To Western eyes, conventional and technical, relatively value-free methods of analysis will almost routinely uncover evidence of variance and will enable the production of tables that will differentiate people according to this or that category.

Yet far from being neutral, such methods of analysis probably assume a pluralist model of society where, within certain boundaries, expressions of differences of opinion and behavior are acceptable and a reflection of "normal" society.

Culture and methods include issues of gender (Al-Makhamreh and Lewando-Hundt 2008). Most doctoral social work research in the Arab world (I do not know about social research in general) tends to be conducted by men. This illustrates the particular challenge faced in hearing the voices of women as family members and users of services. But the problem is not easily resolved, particularly if you favor the merits of qualitative inquiry as a means of researching such questions. Take, for example, focus groups—in almost all cases these would be single-sex groups. Or take semi- or unstructured interviews for a subtler problem. Even if interviews are conducted and taped by women, the possibility that men may listen to and analyze the voice deposit of the women poses serious difficulties. Once again we discover that what are largely technical questions to Western social science researchers are much more than this for many people. Developing culturally indigenous qualitative research and evaluation methods that retain and enhance a critical edge is a long-term challenge for social work colleagues in the southern as well as the northern world (Mafile'o 2004).

Reformist and Radical Agenda

I described at this chapter's start a commitment to undertaking participatory or justice-based evaluation as a probably misplaced, even damaging, reason for choosing qualitative evaluation methods. Having said this, I would still wish to defend the view that qualitative methodology enriches the political, moral, and value dimensions of social work evaluation. I am not discussing the case for emancipatory or reformist evaluation, but rather addressing the specific question of whether such a commitment entails an associated commitment to qualitative methods. Several considerations are relevant to this question (cf. chapter 10 of Shaw and Gould 2001 for a full discussion); but most important for our present purposes, a diminished concern with methodological cogency has often been associated with an advocacy position on research, where instrumental procedures take second place to wider political issues. Lorenz (2000:8) summarizes this position as follows.

It is not the choice of a particular research method that determines social work's position socially and politically. Rather it is the ability to engage critically in the political agenda of defining the terms on which knowledge and truth can be established which should form the basis for the search of appropriate research approaches in social work.

In a thoughtful analysis of research in relation to race and cultural diversity, Stanfield (1994:168) concludes that "even in the most critical qualitative research methods literature there is a tendency to treat 'human subjects' as the passive prisoners of the research process."

Others have taken a less distrustful position, and have argued that qualitative methodology is usually the most congenial strategy for advocacy-oriented research, although methodology by itself is never sufficient. Lather (1986a) takes this position. She refuses to demonize holders of different paradigm positions, and complains about the fuzziness of emancipatory researchers on the need for data credibility checks. She also argues for an empirical stance that is "open-ended, dialogically reciprocal, grounded in respect for human capacity, and yet profoundly skeptical of appearances and 'common sense'" (Lather 1986b:269).

Others have been still more optimistic regarding the affinity of qualitative methodology with moral or political agenda. Riessman (1994:114), for example, has written about narrative methods through which "an individual links disruptive events in a biography to heal discontinuities—what should have been and what was." She makes a more general link between qualitative methodology and liberatory positions. "Because qualitative approaches offer the potential for representing human agency—initiative, language, emotion—they provide support for the liberatory project of social work (Riessman 1994:xv). My own position is that qualitative research informed by critical concerns "must neither ignore instrumental issues nor privilege them" (Vanderplaat 1995:94).

What Is Happening Out There?

Finally, we should develop and pursue an empirical agenda for understanding how qualitative evaluation actually plays out in the real world. This is in part a straightforward remedying of a deficiency in our information knowledge, but, more significantly, it is likely to shape our understanding. It is possible, even likely, for example, that evaluation practice diverges from best practice as found in social work programs, journals, and textbooks. Peled and Leichtentritt (2002), for instance, found that qualitative social work studies rarely utilized widely accepted qualitative research validity criteria. Kirk and Reid (2002:17) lamented that we know little about social workers' actual epistemologies in practice. A focus of this kind would yield a number of gains. First, it would shed light on the kinds of knowledge actually deployed in social work. Second, it would bring together program evaluation and different forms of direct practitioner evaluation. Evaluation theory, in the United States at least, has tended to subordinate practitioner evaluation to program evaluation. Finally, it would feed in to the practice-theory relationship in evaluation (e.g., Christie 2003).

Niels Bohr, the Danish physicist, was among those who remarked to the effect that "Prediction is very difficult, especially about the future (Bohr n.d.)." Bearing in mind that caution, newer issues, and the differentiation and expansion of existing ones can be provisionally identified. The challenge of faith issues may prove a major trial for social work evaluation. The significance of developments in Information Communications Technology (ICT) and the Internet will figure extensively. The relationship of the state and social work evaluation is not easy to anticipate. The present predominance of social work research and evaluation as a Western phenomenon may alter as one consequence of the world recession in the latter years of the first decade of this century. Countries such as China, Brazil, and India may well emerge as leading economic powers that hence become significant in how the state/citizen relationship plays out in social work evaluation.

Notes

1. I may betray my Britishness in my studied avoidance of a strong distinction between *research* methods and *evaluation* methods, though I do not think the point is material for this chapter.
2. The expression "social care" is widely used in the UK when the expression "human services" would be used in the United States. The scope of each is not the same, but they share an intention to express the location of social work within a (much) wider field of personal service interventions.
3. I have made this case at greater length in Shaw 2003.

4. I have developed a critique of Wholey's position in Shaw 1999:82–83; 124–126.

5. I acknowledge that advocates of single system designs have often made a corresponding argument.

6. The study of multisite evaluation in UK schools reported some years ago by Burgess and colleagues can be extrapolated to corresponding circumstances in social work (Burgess et al. 1994). Sinclair (1970) can also be read as a multisite case study.

7. For a review of how issues of generalization may be thought through in qualitative inquiry, see Payne and Williams (2005).

8. Quoted from a posting on EVALTALK—the discussion list of the American Evaluation Association—June 26, 2001.

9. A 15,000- to 20,000-word research requirement for completion of a master's degree in the UK and elsewhere.

References

Al-Makhamreh, S. S. and G. Lewando-Hundt. 2008. Researching "at home" as an insider/outsider: Gender and culture in an ethnographic study of social work practice in an Arab society. *Qualitative Social Work*, 7:9–23.

Atkinson, P. and S. Delamont. 1993. Bread and dreams or bread and circuses? A critique of case study research in evaluation. In *Controversies in the classroom*, M. Hammersley, ed. 204–221. Buckingham, UK: Open University.

Becker, H. 1993. Theory: The necessary evil. In *Theory and concepts in qualitative research: Perspectives from the field*, D. Flinders and G. Mills, eds. 218–229. New York: Teachers College.

Bloor, M. 1997. Techniques of validation in qualitative research. In *Context and method in qualitative research*, G. Miller and R. Dingwall, eds.37–50. London: Sage.

Bogdan, R. and S. Taylor. 1994. A positive approach to qualitative evaluation and policy research in social work. In *Qualitative research in social work*, E. Sherman and W. J. Reid, eds. 293–302, New York: Columbia UP.

Bohr, N. n.d. Prediction is very difficult . . . Quotation commonly attributed to Neils Bohr but also attributed to others. Retrieved September 30, 2012, from http://en.wikiquote.org/wiki/Niels_Bohr. For other attributed authors, see: http://www.larry.denenberg.com/predictions.html and http://en.wikiquote.org/wiki/Niels_Bohr (retrieved September 30, 2012).

Burgess, R., C. Pole, K. Evans, and C. Priestley. 1994. Four studies from one or one study from four? Multisite case study research. In *Analysing qualitative data*, A. Bryman and R. Burgess, eds. 129–145. London: Routledge.

Christie, C. A. 2003. *The practice-theory relationship in evaluation*. San Francisco: Jossey-Bass.

Dey, I. 2004. Grounded theory. In *Qualitative research practice*, C. Seale, G. Gobo, J. F. Gubrium and D. Silverman, eds. 80–93. London: Sage.

Finch, J. 1986. *Research and policy: The uses of qualitative methods in social and educational research*. London: Falmer.

Geertz, C. 1973. *The interpretation of cultures*. New York: Basic.

Greene, J. 1994. Qualitative program evaluation: Practice and promise. In *Handbook of qualitative research*, N. Denzin and Y. Lincoln, eds. 530–544. Thousand Oaks, CA: Sage.

Greene, J. and V. Caracelli. 1997. *Advances in mixed method evaluation: The challenge and benefits of integrating diverse paradigms*. San Francisco: Jossey-Bass.

Hakim, C. 1988. *Research design*. London: Allen and Unwin.

Hammersley, M. 1992. On feminist methodology. *Sociology*, 26(2):187–206.

Kirk, S. A. and W. J. Reid. 2002. *Social science and social work*. New York: Columbia UP.

Lather, P. 1986a. Issues of validity in openly ideological research. *Interchange*, 17(4):63–84.

———. 1986b. Research as praxis. *Harvard Educational Review*, 56(3):257–277.

Lofland, J. and L. Lofland. 1995. *Analyzing social settings*. Belmont, UK: Wadsworth.

Lorenz, W. (2000). "Contentious identities—social work research and the search for professional and personal identities." Paper from ESRC seminar series, *Theorizing social work research*. http://www.nisw.org.uk/tswr/lorenz.html.

Mafile'o, T. 2004. Exploring Tongan social work: *Fakafekau'aki* (connecting) and *Fakatokilalo* (humility). *Qualitative Social Work*, 3(3):239–257.

McKeganey, N., I. MacPherson, and D. Hunter. 1988. How "they" decide: Exploring professional decision making. *Research, Policy and Planning*, 6(1):15–19.

McLeod, J. 2001. *Qualitative research in counseling and psychotherapy*. London: Sage.

Miles, M. and A. Huberman. 1994. *Qualitative data analysis: An expanded sourcebook*. Thousand Oaks, CA: Sage.

Miller, G. 1997. Contextualizing texts: Studying organizational texts. In *Context and method in qualitative research*, G. Miller and R. Dingwall, eds. 77–91. London: Sage.

Miller, W. and B. Crabtree. 1994. Clinical research. In *Handbook of qualitative methods*, N. Denzin and Y. Lincoln, eds. 331–376. Thousand Oaks, CA: Sage.

Patton, M. Q. 2002. *Qualitative research and evaluation methods*. Thousand Oaks, CA: Sage.

Pawson, R., A. Boaz, L. Grayson, A. Long, and C. Barnes. 2003. *Types and quality of knowledge in social care*. London: Social Care Institute for Excellence.

Peled, E. and R. Leichtentritt. 2002. The ethics of qualitative social work research. *Qualitative Social Work*, 1(2):145–169.

Phillips, D. 1990. Postpositivistic science: Myths and realities. In *The paradigm dialog*, E. Guba, ed. 31–45. Newbury Park: Sage.

Pulice, R. 1994. Qualitative evaluation methods in the public sector: Understanding and working with constituency groups in the evaluation process. In *Qualitative research in social work*, E. Sherman and W. J. Reid, eds. 303–313. New York: Columbia UP.

Reid, W. 1994. Reframing the epistemological debate. In *Qualitative research in social work*, E. Sherman and W. J. Reid, eds. 464–481. New York: Columbia UP.

———. 1990. Change-process research: A new paradigm. In *Advances in clinical social work research*, L. Videka-Sherman and W. J. Reid, eds. 130–148. Silver Spring, MD: NASW.

Riessman, C. K., ed. 1994. *Qualitative studies in social work research*. Thousand Oaks, CA: Sage.

Rodwell, M. and D. Woody. 1994. Constructivist evaluation: The policy/practice context. In *Qualitative research in social work*, E. Sherman and W. J. Reid, eds. 315–327. New York: Columbia UP.

Shadish, W., T. Cook, and L. Leviton. 1990. *Foundations of program evaluation: Theories of practice*. Newbury Park: Sage.

Shaw, I. 1999. *Qualitative evaluation*. London: Sage.

Shaw, I. 2003. Qualitative research and outcomes in health, social work and education. *Qualitative Research*, 3(1):57–77.

———. 2004. William J. Reid: An appreciation. *Qualitative Social Work*, 3(2):109–115.

———. 2005. Practitioner research: Evidence or critique? *British Journal of Social Work*, 35(8):1231–1248.

———. 2007. Is social work research distinctive? *Social Work Education*, 26(7): 659–669.

———. 2010. Places in time: Contextualizing social work research. In *Sage handbook of social work research*, I. Shaw, K. Briar-Lawson, J. Orme, and R. Ruckdeschel, eds. 210–228. London: Sage.

Shaw I. and N. Gould. 2001. *Qualitative social work research*. London: Sage.

Shaw, I., K. Briar-Lawson, J. Orme, and R. Ruckdeschel, eds. 2010. *Sage handbook of social work research*. London: Sage.

Simon, H. 1987. *Getting to know schools in a democracy*. London: Falmer.

Sinclair, I. 1970. *Hostels for probationers*. London: HMSO.

Stake, R. 1995. *The art of case study research*. Thousand Oaks, CA: Sage.

Stake, R. and D. Trumbull. 1982. Naturalistic generalizations. *Review Journal of Philosophy and Social Science*, 7:1–12.

Stanfield, J. 1994. Empowering the culturally diversified sociological voice. In *Power and method: Political activism and educational research*, A. Gitlin, ed. 166–180. New York: Routledge.

Thompson-Robinson, M., R. Hopson, and S. SenGupta. 2004. *In search of cultural competence in evaluation.* San Francisco: Jossey-Bass.

Tizard, J., I. Sinclair, and R. Clarke, eds. 1975. *Varieties of residential experience.* London: Routledge.

Trend, M. G. 1979. On the reconciliation of qualitative and quantitative analyses. In *Qualitative and quantitative methods in evaluation research,* T. Cook and C. Reichardt, eds. 66–86. Beverly Hills: Sage.

Turner, M. and W. Zimmerman. 2004. Roleplaying. In *Handbook of practical program evaluation,* J. Wholey, H. Hatry, and K. Newcomer, eds. 310–339. San Francisco: Jossey-Bass.

Vanderplaat, M. 1995. Beyond technique: Issues in evaluating for empowerment. *Evaluation,* 1(1):81–96.

Wasoff, F. and R. Dobash. 1992. Simulated clients in "natural" settings: Constructing a client to study professional practice. *Sociology,* 26(2):333–349.

———. 1996. *The simulated client: A method for studying professionals working with clients.* Aldershot, UK: Avebury.

Williams, D. D. 1986. When is naturalistic evaluation appropriate? In *Naturalistic evaluation,* D. D. Williams, ed. 85–92. San Francisco: Jossey-Bass.

Yin, R. K. 2009. *Case study research: Design and methods.* Thousand Oaks, CA: Sage.

15

The Application of Qualitative Research to Organizational Decision Making

RALPH F. FIELD

Management is as much an exercise in qualitative methods as it is a process of commanding and controlling organizations. Although not formally trained in qualitative research methods and subject to the pitfalls of poor or nonexistent training, many managers apply techniques derived from qualitative methods to create and manage work teams, formulate strategic plans, and troubleshoot every day problem-solving (Skinner, Tagg, and Holloway 2000; Perry 2004; Gummesson 2007). What then do those who are trained in qualitative methods do when they find themselves in managerial roles? How can social workers trained in qualitative research use their skills to manage programs and organizations? Illustrating the application of qualitative methods to strategic management within the context of a specific case, a disability prevention program, helps to answer this question.

What follows is based on the author's experience of 18 months as an evaluation consultant engaged by a public health program to develop an evaluation strategy for community-based preventative health projects. The description of that experience illuminates the details of a participatory, strategic management process based on qualitative methods for use in decision making—also known as action research (for additional discussion of action research, see chapter 13 by Vandenburgh and Claiborne and chapter 9 by Jones, Miller, and Luckey in this volume). Different qualitative and small group development techniques were used to propel office leadership toward crafting and articulating an evaluation strategy consistent with a state Office of Disability Prevention's operating capacity, culture, and mission, and its position in its environment.

In the mid-1990s, a state-level public health department's Office of Disability Prevention began a program of creating a set of model demonstration projects that decentralized disability prevention to the community level. The program was funded by the state along with substantial grants from the U.S. Department of Health and Human Services and the Centers for Disease Control. The program was designed to yield replicable model projects representing part of a decentralization movement to bring human services into communities and neighborhoods. Bryant, Frothofer, Brown, Landis, and McDermott (2000) have discussed these activities in social marketing terms, while Fielding, Luck, and Tye (2003) detailed this process for reorganizing public health in Los Angeles County, California. However, unlike other model projects, those that the Office produced were more often public relations events designed to garner local political support. After twelve months of funding, the Office and program management were urged by their funders to graft an evaluation component onto the ongoing program that was not producing the originally intended projects.

It is important to note that the following narrative traces a sequence of events up to the point of designing a program evaluation. The case study does not extend through the design and implementation of the evaluation itself. The case study also is bounded by specific interventions and a theory of organization and decision making rooted in systems theory; the specific evaluation representing an organization's adaptation to change.

This chapter is sectioned into seven main parts. The following section is a discussion of systems theory of organizations, which precedes sections on decision making and strategic management. The fifth section is a discussion of the application of qualitative research methods and strategic management. The remainder of the chapter is a discussion of strategic management and qualitative research methods in the context of the very specific case of the department of public health's Office of Disability Prevention's response to its funders' recommendation that the Office evaluate its disability prevention program.

Organizations Are Systems

The classic definition of organizations holds that they are identifiable social entities existing for distinct and explicit purposes (Scott 2004). Organizations work to achieve specific objectives that logically follow from their purpose. Ideally, all interactions within an organization are patterned on the structure of work and activities having the greatest probability of goal attainment. More recent conceptualizations of organizations recognize that they are dynamic groupings of people interacting with one another to achieve stated and unstated objectives (McAdam and Leonard 1999; Daniel and Brown 2000).

The Office of Disability Prevention was such a dynamic group of people who worked to implement several different sets of activities or programs. What characterized and gave personality to the Office was the existence of personal networks evident in office-based birthday parties, socializing away from the office, and even matchmaking on the part of the director and professional staff. These relationships among individuals created a cohesive organization that was oriented to achieving both the official mission of preventing disabilities and a day-to-day mission of creating public relations events to garner more funds.

In contemporary management studies, interactions within and between organizations are frequently understood to be open systems with respect to a dynamic environment (Harrison 1994; Scott 2004). Organizational actions either enhance or detract from the ability to adapt to change. Two key concepts of a theory of open systems are interdependency and holism. An organization is studied in terms of all of its elements and the interdependency of its elements, as well as its interdependency with other systems (Delen, Dalal, and Benjamin 2005). The environment is the physical, economic, social, political, cultural, and technological context within which systems interact.

Features of open systems also include inputs (resources such as the raw material, information people, and knowledge that an organization needs to survive and thrive); outputs (products, services, and programs); and throughputs (processes, technology, tools, knowledge, and skills) that transform inputs into outputs (Gharajedaghi 1999). The Office's program inputs were grant funds, expertise, leadership, and advice from a variety of communities throughout the state. Inputs passed through the organization and were transformed into demonstration projects that were public relations events and led to more grant applications. The environment consisted of laws, economy, other health department program offices, communities, political constituencies, funding sources, and local, state, and national economies. Any change within the Office or within its environment would necessitate change in the Office and its programs. Thinking in terms of systems enabled mangers to decide how best to adapt operations and programs to changes in their organization's capacity and environment. Office management quickly grasped this idea when their actions and concerns were explained as a process of adapting to their funder's request for an evaluation strategy.

Decision Making

Decision making lies at the heart of the managerial task and defines in large part the nature of leadership. Leadership is, in part, the ability to articulate and make choices (Northouse 2007). How decisions are made reflects the way an organization is structured to fulfill its purpose. Furthermore, making decisions is an exercise of judgment (Bazerman and Moore 2009). In turn, judgment is about assigning variable worth to different actions, people, and things with reference to a set of standards. Leadership collects information, weighs it against standards, and chooses a course of action, thereby making judgments as to the best use of resources and the direction the organization takes.

Decision making is not purely rational. It is bounded by the realities of the moment, knowledge, skills, emotions, and desires of the decision maker (Simon 1957). It follows that decision making is quasi-rational: self-interest, reason, and will power set the boundaries within which decisions are made (Thaler 2000). Furthermore, self-interest is tempered by altruism; reason is bounded by imperfect knowledge; and willpower is influenced by immediate concerns more so than future issues. The end result is that purely rational decisions give way to decisions that seem reasonable. That is, decision-makers *satisfice*: They do not examine all possibilities, just those that "meet an acceptable level of performance" (Bazerman and Moore 2000:5). The Office's decision to produce public relations events was a result of immediate concerns and a way to balance self-interest and altruism.

Strategic Management

The decision to pursue public relations-style events was one of expediency. It unfortunately had the unintended consequence of prompting key funders to request an evaluation of the disability prevention program. This precipitated a crisis that required a strategic response. The issue was less that of which type of evaluation to implement and more of a strategic issue of how to integrate an approach to evaluations within the fabric of the Office. This strategic issue concerned how the Office could best deal with the external intrusion of funders. Systems theory provided a systematic approach to identifying an appropriate organizational response to the request for an evaluation by instituting a systems thinking approach to strategic management as an adaptive response to change (Haines 2000; Roney and Lehman 2008).

Strategic decision-making is an adaptive response of an organization to changes in its environment. It proceeds from individual to group to organization and external relations within the environment. It is bonded to organizational leadership and requires a system of management through which leadership directs staff, secures external income, responds to external forces, and adjusts to changes in organizational capacity (Waldman, Ramirez, Hovse, and Puraman 2001). Strategic management is a disciplined and occasionally inspired improvisation of organizational practices to attain objectives within vibrant and occasionally unfriendly environments. A strategy is an explicit plan of action ingrained in all of the daily actions, values, and perceptions of an organization's members (Swindler 1986). Strategy increases the probability that what is done today will result in a desirable outcome tomorrow. Strategies and strategic plans are adaptive mechanisms. "A well-formulated strategy helps to marshal and allocate an organization's resources into a unique and viable posture based on its relative internal competencies and shortcomings, anticipated changes in the environment, and contingent moves by intelligent opponents" (Mintzberg 1994:23)." In this context, strategic management is a process of engaging an organization's (company's or agency's) people to care and belong to something bigger than themselves (Mintzberg 2009).

The best possible strategic fit ensures that all organizational actions conspire to achieve the agency's mission. For nonprofit organizations and public agencies, fulfilling missions and mandates is paramount to achieving success (Bryce 2000). Brinckerhoff (1994), writing about mission-based management, lays out the elements of nonprofit management from board governance, budgeting, human resource use, and income generation to ensure that each element lends itself to mission. A strategy matches an agency's strengths and weaknesses to the threats and opportunities presented by the environment to achieve mission (Koteen 1997). Strategic planning is a systematic process for setting priorities and creating commitment for choosing the best response to the circumstances of a dynamic and occasionally hostile environment.

Qualitative Methods and Strategic Management

Strategic management uses both quantitative and qualitative methodologies (Hoskisson, Hitt, Wan, and Yiu 1999). A key element in this approach is active listening in which the observer listens to those around him/her to identify what the speaker identifies as the truth (Brady 2003). Active listening is used in a variety of fields, notably health cases, to ascertain the reality of a patient's world (Davidhizar 2004; Robertson 2005). However, in working to develop an evaluation strategy *in situ*, with active participation of the Office staff, using qualitative methods called for Office management and staff to play to their strengths. They understood qualitative methods. Strategic management was presented to them as a context within which to apply their knowledge. Rather than using their skills for research, they were guided through this process to ensure the Office fulfilled its mission by identifying an appropriate evaluation strategy. This approach allowed participants to combine operations, leadership and research roles, and knowledge of qualitative methods and clinical fieldwork approaches with their management positions (McNiff and Whitehead 2002). In action research, the researcher as manager is a change agent in a process of participatory research in which all become active subjects in, not objects of, research. It has been used in the assessment of social service outcomes (McIntyre- Mills 2010). Action research has provided a framework within which educators embrace research and educational reform (Smith and Clark 2010). It also has been used, for example, to address social welfare issues such as homelessness (Mulroy and Lauber 2004). Interpretations of organization and group behavior were fixed within systems theory. Strategy was defined as an adaptive response to change; the process of creating strategy was determined to be a dynamic learning process (McGarth 2001).

Practitioner/Observer

The practitioner-observer within the framework of strategic management allows for disciplined and focused application of qualitative research methods to strategic decision-making. The importance of qualitative methods in management is related to the necessity of making meaningful and effective decisions to ensure that the purpose of the organization is fulfilled. Creswell (2008) notes several features of research design such as the identification of potential audiences (i.e., organizational or program stakeholders) can be applied to management decision-making. Other features include: Acknowledgment that data is being collected in a natural setting in which the manager is a key player; the use of multiple and humanistic methods of data collection; the recognition that the search for relevant data is emergent rather than prefigured (i.e., avoiding reliance on specific and highly prescriptive program or business models); analysis is interpretive; the issue or pending decision is viewed holistically (systems perspective); and data is collected and analyzed in a reflective manner (the manager knows that s/he is not separate from the data gathering).

Strategic Planning Protocol

Once an organization is conceived as a system, it is possible to apply a systems-based strategic management and strategy development protocol that results in decisions that satisfice. While the decisions may not be purely rational, the process, undertaken in good faith, ensures a level of transparency in the strategic decision-making process. Transparency and participation in decision-making tend to lead to acceptance of a decision as legitimate.

The protocol was outlined as follows:

1. Begin by determining whether the issue or event, about which decisions will be made, is strategic;
2. If leadership determines it to be a strategic issue, then a data collection and assessment process begins with an analysis of the organization's environment;
3. This is followed by an assessment of the organization's capacity, competences, and processes;

4. Next, the specific interaction of the organization with its environment is assessed to identify a set of alternative actions that might achieve the best strategic fit;
5. Once a slate of alternatives is proposed, each is assessed in terms of the organization's mission, the feasibility for undertaking the action, and the desirability of the action; and,
6. The selected alternative is then implemented and assessed in terms of its impact and outcomes.

While this sequence represented a logical progression from ideas to action, in truth, leadership's initial intervention in organizational operations could have begun at any point in the process that provides an opportunity for strategic management. In the case of the disabilities program, the initial intervention began toward the end of the sequence with a request to the consultant to recommend an evaluation methodology after the program has been initiated. From that point on, the protocol was employed to align the disability program with original grant expectations and the mission of the Office of Disabilities Prevention.

The Case: The Office of Disability Prevention

The state department of public health, the Office of Disability Prevention, and the program were managed by public health and social work professionals familiar with qualitative methods as a result of clinical training and epidemiologists more accustomed to statistical analysis. In all, there was one Office director who relied on a consultant to help her exercise her leadership role, seven professionals, an office management staff of four, and 12 junior level social workers who divided their time between the office and field services. All had learned management on the job. Consequently, they had difficulty applying management concepts as well as making the connection between their formal, professional schooling and training.

Background

The disability prevention office and the demonstration program had a well-defined leadership that exercised control within the program office. This centered on the person of the Office director who, as a public health professional trained in sociology, was able to command respect for her technical skills. She exercised her power through several different sets of personal relationships that partially coincided with the formal office structure. A part of her technique was to conduct impromptu meetings for the entire Office and occasional meetings with senior professional staff. The formal structure provided a rationale for her leadership, while the use of rewards and ridicule as well as anger in personal relationships ensured that her decisions and the decisions of key allies were carried out. The existence of this dual command structure showed that the Office director had the ability to make choices with regard to interpreting the department's mission and program resource allocation. In spite of her ability, decision-making was inherently political, isolated from most senior and junior staff, and had little regard for tangible community-based results. Everyone was satisfied with the demonstration program if it seemed as if there was progress (with progress defined as successful grant writing and good public relations).

The department of public health as a public agency had a mandate to promote and protect the health and safety of the state's residents through risk identification, public education, preventing and controlling diseases and injuries, and protecting residents from exposure to environmental hazards. The mandate permeated all official work and relationships, including the community demonstration program of the Office of Disability Prevention. In practice, Office leadership pursued a strategy to secure public grants to create projects that served as public relations vehicles in order to present the program in the best possible light to state legislators, community activities, and the press. The "strategy-in-practice" assumed that favorable public perceptions of the program would result in increased grant funding. As a result, attention to the details of grant implementation was limited. This was most evident in the public awards events staged by the Office. Each event showcased a community leader, project, or public official and was heavily covered by local press. These ego-stroking events flattered those who had the potential to derail the programs and the Office's fund-raising. It was partly in reaction to these events that the Office was requested by its principal donor to develop a program evaluation.

Scope of Work

The author began the consultancy with a scope of work created by himself jointly with the Office in which Office leadership and staff committed to a specific process of work, taking responsibility for different portions of the work. The intent of the scope of work was for the Office to become a full partner in the identification of an evaluation strategy rather than a passive observer who either accepts or rejects a final product. The Office had to take ownership of both the process and the product from the very beginning. As a research-practitioner with managerial expertise, the author's task was to shift the focus of the work from himself to the program. The scope of work accomplished this by taking on the qualities of a contract in which program management obligated itself to create and implement an evaluation methodology through a strategic management exercise. This marked a subtle shift away from thinking that the consultant and his activities were external to recognition that the entire process was internal within the Office. This shift in perception was indicated by the use of possessives (such as "our" scope of work, "our" evaluation, and "our" progress) when program managers talked about the evaluation. Similarly, when colleagues from the department of public health assessed the program, program management exhibited ownership over the process with such phrases as "see what we have done" or "you cannot just tell us what to do." Just as telling as the language was the proprietary nature of the relationship that program management exhibited over the consultant. The consultant was expected to participate in program and office activities that went beyond the boundaries of a consultancy such as being expected to comment on different aspects of management, attending meetings that had no bearing on the evaluation methodology, and being present at social gatherings such as office-based birthday parties.

The Management Problem

The Office of Disability Prevention raised an interesting research problem: How would managers without professional management training, but responsible for an organization, adapt to organizational change? Given the nature of the work setting and the consultant's assignment, the research problem needed to be reframed as a management issue. What was most intriguing about the management problem was the nature of the work of disability prevention. The demonstration program, in addition to marshalling community resources, involved the application of intellectual capital. That is: The combined knowledge of public health and social work professionals had to be brought to bear on the task of preventing disabilities through particular organizational and managerial interventions. The specific management issue facing the Office of Disability Prevention was to identify the best possible evaluation strategy that could be applied to the program of demonstration projects. The problem would be resolved after teasing out the explicit and implicit aspects of managerial decision-making in the Office of Disability Prevention to identify those moments when qualitative methods could be best adopted as an integral part of management. To do this, the Office was redefined as a learning organization in which culture and structure are geared to support learning and initiative to advance the organization (Walczak 2005). This meant identifying those sequences of office and program life into which an analytically based, strategy development process could be spliced. Once a way to engage management in the development of an evaluation strategy had been identified, two interlinked management issues surfaced. These were how best to identify an appropriate approach to program evaluation methodology and how to ensure that the decision to use that methodology would be considered legitimate by professionals within the Office.

Framing the Management Problem

The answer to how best to proceed with the work readily presented itself in the Office's mode of work and within the knowledge base of Office management. While the Office director managed through personal networks, she would bring her networks together in large Office-wide meetings to discuss work. These meetings were supplemented from time to time with smaller meetings with other managers and professional staff. Most everyone in the Office treated decisions that arose from discussion in these settings, no matter how autocratic in the making, as legitimate decisions. Already a part of the tempo of daily and weekly life in the Office, group settings presented ample opportunity to engage Office management and professional and junior staff in a process of identifying an evaluation strategy. This was further reinforced by the fact that the management and professional staff's training in qualitative social science and clinical techniques included experience in small group development and team-based work. The consultancy would be carried out in settings that mimicked the meetings. This helped institutionalize a strategy development process within the Office culture and legitimize the resulting strategy.

Determining Strategic Importance

After the introduction of basic concepts and outlining the approach to strategy development, the first task was to determine whether or not designing an evaluation was a strategic or an operational issue. This was achieved by asking questions about a specific set of criteria that required unequivocal "yes" or "no" responses. While there was discussion around each of the criteria, each question generated an unambiguous negative or positive assessment of specific factors related to strategic management. The criteria were encapsulated in the following questions put to Office leadership:

1. Would a program evaluation methodology issue have implications for organizational policy? No. Decisions made about program evaluations were not policy decisions;

2. Would a program evaluation methodology influence the Office's overall position in its environment? Yes. A well thought out program evaluation methodology might increase the Office's competitiveness vis-à-vis other agencies and organizations vying for grant and contract money;

3. Would a program evaluation methodology substantially influence long-term implementation of projects and programs? Yes. Information and data concerning program efficiency and effectiveness would influence long-term implementation by offering opportunities for mid- and endpoint corrections.

4. Would a program evaluation methodology influence the position of Office and program leadership and the definition of duties? No. The leadership of the Office of Disabilities Prevention and program managers' positions were secure within the state budgeting system. Several of the key players within the Office also had secure political backing that guaranteed security of tenure.

5. Would a program evaluation influence the Office's ability to fulfill its mission and goals? Yes. The formal mission and goals to reduce disabilities were dependent upon a successful program.

6. Would an evaluation methodology represent nonroutine behavior as opposed to routine behavior? Yes.

7. Would a program evaluation methodology imply the possibility of the Office's death? No.

On balance, retrofitting an evaluation methodology to an existing program by the disabilities program was clearly a strategic issue. It had implications for the success of the program as well as the reputation and competitiveness of the Office. As a tangible expression of the Office's— and by extension the Department of Health's—stated purpose, success or failure of the program would determine how well the mission was realized.

Confirming the Mission

Once Office and program management realized that creating an evaluation methodology was a strategic issue, the Office began a process of authoring an evaluation. The first task in this process was to articulate their mission. A useful mission would provide a rationale for an organization, define its work, and establish its core values and desires for the future (Kearns 2000). Therefore, the mission needed to reflect the essence of an organization at its most mundane. While the Office and the public health department had a stated mission mandated by public authority, they did not have a working mission to guide management and staff in the day-to-day activities to achieve stated program objectives. The stated mission seemed remote from how work was actually carried out. Many on the staff did not know the mandated mission. To rectify this, management and staff agreed to participate in several exercises to identify their daily mission and to ensure it reflected their public mandate. In essence, these exercises were designed to answer the question: "What business are we in?" The exercises also were designed to demonstrate that everyone in the Office contributed to the mission or the business of disability prevention.

Discussion about the mission was important for the Office of Disabilities Prevention for two reasons. First, a discussion about the mission might uncover disagreements indicating problems for any future course of action. Second, and most importantly, a well-articulated mission that expressed the consensus of Office leadership and staff would serve as the ultimate standard, against which programs and projects could be judged.

Two qualitative techniques were used to explore the Office's management and staff understanding of their mission. Both techniques relied on small group research methods. The use of two techniques was necessary to establish the validity of the results. The first technique was based on cognitive mapping (Ackermann, Cropper, Cook, and Eden 1990; Eden 1990), which

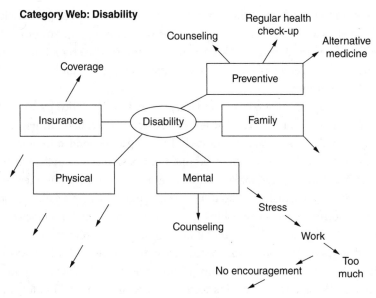

Figure 15.1

has been used in management research (Eden and Huxham 1988) and in information systems research (Siau and Tan 2006); the second was based on nominal group techniques formulated for use in organizational development (Delbecq, Van de Ven, and Gustafson 1995; Eisele 2007). The techniques were employed in this work to produce mutually agreed-upon data from which a working mission that reflected the Office as a whole could be created.

To create a cognitive map of the Office's mission, participants first were asked individually to list a series of words triggered by the phrase "disabilities prevention." Next, each person rank ordered their list from most to least important. They then centered their most important word on a piece of paper and mapped the relationships of their ideas to one another. This created a created an image of their thoughts in the form of a category web with different ideas placed in relationship to one another. What follows is a category web centered on the idea of health (see Figure 15.1).

Each person created his or her own individual map and then shared them with one another in an open setting to create a group map. This activity was designed to create a consensus image of the Office's workaday image. However, in the process of creating a group map, two distinct maps emerged indicating two different groups within the Office, each with a different interpretation of the mission. One group considered the mission to be tied to creating events to curry favor with key department of public health officials and state and local opinion leaders. The second group interpreted the mission as a social service mission to field resources to target population groups.

The appearance of a conceptual fault line within the Office provided an opportunity for a discussion that led to a search for a coherent image. Although the discussion was not heated, the two groups tended to view one another as having little credibility beyond their positions within the Office's hierarchy. However, the application of group cognitive mapping created a means to sustain a dialogue about the mission that took participants outside of their normal work relationships. This formed the basis for a discussion about the dimensions of the Office's work on disability prevention.

A discussion to bind relationships across the conceptual divide was facilitated by the application of a nominal group technique. As with cognitive mapping, the application of this technique brought participants together for a structured group discussion. The first part of the discussion was the presentation of the session topic. Disability Office leadership and staff were asked once again to define their mission based on what they had accomplished in the cognitive mapping exercise. This time the discussion was restricted to specific questions: Who are we? What do we do? Who do we do it for (or to)? After each question had been asked in a general meeting, staff who did not share the same conceptual map of a mission were paired off to discuss the questions. Given the constraints of Office-wide participation, much of the discussion was one-sided. Those in command positions tended to dominate the conversation, while those in subordinate positions tended acquiesce to their superiors' interpretations.

All responses to the three questions were recorded and displayed. Once all the responses had been recorded, all duplicates were eliminated. Then each unique response was assigned a number by each participant ranging from one (representing most important) to five (for least important.) Numbers were tallied for the entire group. Responses for the three questions represented a rough consensus that drew in elements from the two competing interpretations of the Office's mission:

1. Who are we? "We are public service and social welfare workers."
2. What do we do? "We show the community how to organize to live better, safer, and healthier lives."
3. Who do we do it for? "We work for the community."

The third response was sufficiently vague to require further discussion to define "community." The definition of community that seemed to reflect the office as a whole was that community was the networks of people with disabilities, unmarried mothers, and front-line social workers.

After working through the various statements and data from the group session, a working mission was crafted and presented to the Office as a whole as their creation. It was accepted as such. The mission provided a standard against which prospective evaluation strategies could be assessed and not simply be a reaction to the funder's request. The Office and program had created a conceptual platform from which to survey and assess their circumstances in anticipation of decisions about the form and substance of a program evaluation methodology. The working mission was: The Office of Disability Prevention applies the knowledge and techniques of social workers, scientists, and public health professionals to assist people with disabilities, poor communities, and community health workers to better to teach people about disability prevention.

The resulting mission was not the product of unanimous agreement. However, this process did serve the purpose of creating explicit agreement about the elements of a mission in a semi-public setting. This has had two effects. The first was to extend the commitment of the leadership as expressed in the scope of work into the wider work setting and of garnering some buy-in from subordinate staff into leadership's decisions. The second was to expose management to the positions and thoughts of junior and field staff, forcing management to take into consideration how any particular evaluation strategy might actually be implemented.

Shaping the Strategy

The evaluation strategy began to take shape in this next phase of the process. Leadership and staff were guided through a process of data gathering for use in identifying several different alternative evaluation strategies. They began by assessing their environment and then their own organizational capacity with the objective of creating strategic fit.

ENVIRONMENT

In order to identify a suitable evaluation strategy and methodology, it was necessary for Office leadership and management to understand the context within which the Office of Disability Prevention carried out its programs. This was done through environmental scans. Typically, environmental scans focus managers' attention on external factors that currently influence and may influence their organization in the future. This is well illustrated in management texts such as Thompson and Strickland (2003). First, leadership and staff were facilitated in a process of treating one another as key informants about the environment (Patton 2002). In effect, they taught one another what they knew of environmental aspects that influenced their work (Gilchrist and Williams 1999.

The environmental scan was conducted in two phases. In the first phase, Office staff and leadership scanned their environment to identify political pressures from within the state, community expectations, the general public, funding agencies such as the Centers for Disease Control (CDC), economic trends, medical trends, as well as demographic trends such as birth and death rates that might influence the Office's ability to fulfill their mission. Data were categorized as key success factors (KSFs). A KSF is something that all other entities in the environment must do, and do well, in order to survive. Not surprisingly, Office leadership noted that all the successful public and private agencies engaged in public health and disability prevention had to raise money through grants and contracts. Grantsmanship was a very important KSF for the Office. Other key success factors included a public health knowledge base and skill set; the ability to establish useful community relations; competence in intra-departmental relations; and utilization of consultants and content experts such as social workers.

In the second phase, the environment was scanned with reference to three categories of information (Bryson 1995). They were: forces and trends that influenced the environment and all entities within that environment; key resource controllers; and actual or potential collaborators and competitors. Forces and trends were further classified as political, economic, social, and technological factors that influenced the behavior of the Office of Disability Prevention. Leadership and staff also identified changes in factors such as public policy, funding patterns, and rates of inflation, and the rise of expectations for diversity, and digital work environments.

Leadership was particularly interested in key resource controllers outside of the department of public health. These were, for example, funders who controlled access to program funds and set standards for program outcomes. This also included competitors and collaborators. At this point, the interest in competitors and collaborators foreshadowed the type of evaluation strategy

the office would consider, creating a temptation to truncate the strategic planning process and proceed directly to the identification and implementation
of the evaluation. It was then necessary to point out that the Office would be
committing itself to a strategy without understanding whether or not it had
the resources and skills to implement such a strategy or whether or not the
evaluation strategy fit with the mission of the Office and its programs.

Throughout the strategic planning exercise, Office leadership and staff
treated the environmental assessment as an iterative process, while other
elements of strategy development were being carried out. As data were
being continuously refined, two environmental factors stood out has having the greatest influences on the program. First, there was little concern
about disability prevention among those who were disabled or were at
risk of disability. Instead, they were more concerned about services and
responses to disabilities after they occurred. Second, the pool of community groups and channels for information dissemination were exceedingly
limited. The same groups of people were called on to assist in all of the department of public health's community-based work. In conducting a series
of environmental scans, the Office reconceptualized what it already knew
about its community environment as a "cottage industry of community
representatives" that was sustained by small grant programs from the Office and the public recognitions events.

At the end of each environmental assessment, the staff and leadership
were requested, as a group, to categorize external influences as either opportunities or threats. In truth, this process did not expose any surprises. Leadership and staff had a very good understanding of the environment. What
it did though was to make their collective knowledge explicit and accessible
to others in the organization, and place it within a theoretical framework
that allowed them to exploit that knowledge. Prior to this process, leadership and staff thought of their office as a unique stand-alone group to which
things happened. Funding was something that happened to the Office, Just
as policy was something that happened. Understanding the dynamic nature
of their environment and the porous nature of organizational boundaries
allowed staff and leadership to think more systematically and proactively.

ORGANIZATIONAL CAPACITY

Knowledge of the environment, while necessary, was not sufficient for crafting strategy. A workable evaluation strategy also required an understanding

of the Office's capacity to adapt to change: How effectively was it managed (Allision and Kaye 1997). A workable strategy would represent the best fit for the Office with its environment. Therefore, the next step was to understand the Office's capacity to manage programs and change within its environment. This process was distilled into two questions that Office staff and leadership were requested to ask of themselves: (1) What is it that we do? (2) How do we do it? These questions were asked about the tangible and intangible assets and behaviors that characterized the Office of Disability Prevention. This included an assessment of the quantitative elements of the organization such as the number of personnel, salaries, reserves, technology, and so forth.

Most organizations have a fairly good grasp of their tangible capacity (annual budgeting and auditing activities provide a ready impetus to maintain counts of people and things). The intangible elements such as organizational culture, social networks, and work processes are much more difficult to illuminate because they were implied within the relationships that sustained the workplace.

Given that the assessment of Office capacity and assets took place in the course of daily operations, leadership and staff were positioned to be key informants to one another just as they had in the environmental assessment. At this time in the consultancy, the facilitation of self-study groups in the guise of Office meetings was well established. As with the environmental analysis, Office staff, along with their leadership, were to asked to list, then rank order what they perceived to be the Office's strengths and weakness, providing examples. The results were assessed in a series of round-robin discussions. Based on their self-assessment, staff created a fairly comprehensive sense of their collective capacity. They recognized their ability to garner information on disability prevention, create public awareness materials, and raise funds for projects. What was most heartening was that they had reached a point in the process where they could reflect on their activities. As a result of their discussions, they not only recognized what were some of their strengths but also what hindered them in achieving their objectives, chief among which was poor program management. Prior to this process, they had not considered program management as a key determinant of success.

Their self-assessment generated data that also was conceptualized in terms of core competencies. A core competency is something that an organization does better than any other organization. Core competencies are the basis of competitive edge. In working with Office staff to assess their core competencies, it was necessary to recognize that knowledge about social services, public health, and public Information campaigns lay at the heart of their operations. There was, however, no straight line between competency and competitive edge. Instead their knowledge represented sets of relationships that management could not control at all times. For example, their knowledge about small independent groups who advocated for the rights of the disabled did not automatically translate into programs because the local groups decided within themselves whether or not they wished to cooperate with public agencies.

In addition to knowledge, other core competencies included the Office's ability to raise funds (through expertly written and researched proposals) and their knowledge of disability prevention. As in the environmental analysis, Office management and staff engaged in several iterations of self-assessment, including focus groups. In addition to fundraising and their knowledge base, they recognized their superior ability to create networks (although limited) of community leaders, disability advocacy groups, and public sector service professionals. The Office realized that they very effectively acted as an interface between public, private, and nonprofit groups grappling with disability and disability prevention issues.

The sets of relationships resources and knowledge organized by the Office captured the work dynamic. It was presented to the Office by the consultant as a value chain. The concept of the value chain was derived directly from systems theory. A value chain is the sequence of tasks through which inputs become outputs. The Office's value chain began with inputs of knowledge, resources, and contacts with other organizations. Outputs represented value added benefits the Office was placing into the environment in the form of public information and programs, such as public relations events. Outputs also included proposals for programs that retuned inputs for the Office in the form of grant money.

STRENGTHS, WEAKNESSES, OPPORTUNITIES, AND THREATS: THE INTERSECTION OF THE ENVIRONMENT AND CAPACITY

The strengths, weaknesses, opportunities, and threats (SWOT) analysis began by organizing the data in terms of highs and lows (Bryson 1995). This is an analysis of internal and external factors that provided information for a simple, but powerful, assessment. It established a database that leadership used to decide upon a specific and appropriate set of strategic options (Thompson and Strickland 2003. In conducting a SWOT, all the data from environmental and organizational assessments were organized in the four categories of strengths, weakness, opportunities, and threats. The SWOT required further reflection and discussion about the Office of Disability Prevention and the demonstration program. For example, the "highs" relating to the Office's own capabilities were classified as strengths. "Lows" relating to the environment were classified as threats. Given that systems theory explains organizational adaptation (or maladaptation) in terms of interdependencies with organizations and between organizations within an observable environment, the Office stood poised to decide the best way to identify how to utilize its strengths (and deflect attention from its weaknesses) in such a way to best interact with external resources and other systems to decide on an evaluation strategy.

Although past experience is not always a good predictor of future experiences, categorizing the highs and lows is an analytical process that highlights some of the precedents the Office had established that could be expected to influence future action. Participants were asked to recall the highs and lows experienced by the Office within a three-year period. Their recollections were written on index cards. The cards were then affixed above or below a line taped on a wall. The distance from the line indicated each card's perceived degree of highness or lowness. Recollections of highs and lows such as winning a competitive grant or the collapse of a community recognition event because an official had not been invited were representative of results of the analysis.

As a group, the participants analyzed the results of the highs and lows by asking the following set of questions:

1. What opportunities have we had? Which have we taken advantage of and which have we neglected? What were the results of taken and missed opportunities?
2. What threats have we had to counter? Which have we handled well and which have we not handled well? What were the results?
3. What strengths have used to counter threats and take advantage of opportunities? What has been the result?
4. What weakness became apparent when we faced threats and opportunities? What was the result?

Asking participants in a group setting these questions enabled participants to catalogue key organizational attributes and environmental impacts and engage in scenario development. By moving the timeline forward into the future, the participants engaged in a simple forecasting exercise to create a basis for the Office to envision how the contexts might be implemented within evaluation methodologies. Strictly speaking, this was not a predictive exercise, but it did provide a disciplined framework for assessing possible future situations and outcomes. As a result of this activity, everyone concluded that, while funding would continue to be uncertain, they would have the capacity to write solid proposals, disability prevention programs would still be needed, the political context would remain stable, and the network of concerned parties would grow.

The beauty of thinking in terms of SWOT is its methodological flexibility. It can be created with quantifiable data and or qualitative data, as long as the basic rules of research are applied: Clear definition of purpose and a researchable question, transparent and consistent methods, and a way to validate findings. To validate the results of the "high–low" exercise and begin the creation of a SWOT matrix, a snow card exercise was conducted (Greenblat and Duke 1981). This technique engaged the group in the coding and analysis of data uncovered through earlier analytical techniques.

The snow card exercise began with a series of questions to establish the organization's actions within its environment. Participants reflected on the findings of their high–low analysis by again asking what they determined to be the major external or future opportunities; what were the major external or future threats; what were the major internal or present strengths; and what were the major internal or future weaknesses. For each question, participants were asked to silently brainstorm their responses then choose their best responses (any number from three to ten) and write each response onto an index card (the snow card.) The cards were attached to the wall and clustered by SWOT theme. Once all the clusters were created, they were rearranged until the participants agreed that the arrangement reflected their understanding of the organization's unique strengths, weaknesses, and opportunities.

Table 15.1 summarizes the SWOT analysis.

THREATS, OPPORTUNITIES, WEAKNESSES, AND STRENGTHS:
DETERMINING STRATEGIC OPTIONS

At this point, Office leadership and managers were ready to identify a set of alternative evaluation strategies. They began with only two options. They

Table 15.1 Strengths, Weaknesses, Opportunities, and Threats (SWOT) Analysis Summary

STRENGTHS	• Knowledge about disability prevention
	• Local community access
	• Open to new ideas (willingness to undertake a strategy process)
	• Access to funding sources
	• Ability to secure grants and contracts
WEAKNESSES	• Lack of evaluation strategy
	• High staff turnover
	• Limited intraoffice communication
	• Command and control structure
OPPORTUNITIES	• Need for disability prevention knowledge in communities
	• Local resource groups
	• No local public sector competitor
	• Requests for assistance from disability groups
THREATS	• Narrow base of local groups associated with the Office
	• Potential changes in public policy
	• Demands from funders for more control over programs
	• Nonprofit competitors

could undertake an unspecified evaluation strategy or forgo an evaluation and deal with the consequences. Given that the former option was not a viable alternative because of external pressures, the Office took the next step by creating create a matrix of options. The threats, opportunities, weaknesses, and strengths (TOWS) matrix paired the Office's strengths and weaknesses with the threats and opportunities (Weihrich 1992). For each pairing, participants asked a set of questions of the data. Answers suggested a particular strategy. For example, when strengths were paired with opportunities, the participants asked: "What activity (strategy, program, or project) results from a specific strength taking advantage of a specific opportunity?" Similarly, they were asked how they might leverage opportunities to compensate for organizational weaknesses.

The TOWS matrix created by key decision-makers in the Office appears here. Cells labeled strengths, weaknesses, opportunities, and threats are

Table 15.2 Matrix of Strategic Options

	Strengths	Weaknesses
	• Knowledge about disability prevention • Local community access • Open to new ideas (willingness to undertake a strategy process) • Access to funding sources • Ability to secure grants and contracts • Access to public officials	• Lack of evaluation strategy and knowledge • High junior staff turnover • Limited intraoffice communication • Command and control structure
Opportunities • Need for disability prevention knowledge in communities • Local resource groups • No local public sector competitor • Requests for assistance from disability groups • Interested grantors • Potential collaborators	**SO** • Submit a grant application to create an evaluation that would be administered through local disability networks • Submit a proposal that would fund the training and data collection of a cadre of locally based evaluators.	**WO** • Create partnership with nonprofit with strong evaluation skills to spearhead statewide evaluation
Threats • Narrow base of local groups associated with the Office • Potential changes in public policy • Demands from prime funder for more control over programs • Nonprofit competitors	**ST** • Request state officials to intervene with funder to modify evaluation requirement • Secure funding to transform Office into a resource for others to use for evaluation	**WT** • Request guidance from funders on range, scope, design, and implementation of an evaluation

self-explanatory. Cells labeled SO, WO, ST, and WT represent strategic options: Strengths used to leverage opportunities; opportunities used to compensate for weaknesses; strengths used to protect against threats; and rectifying weaknesses to counter threats.

The advantage of identifying a set of alternative actions using the TOWS matrix was that each of the alternatives was grounded in the realities of the Office of Disability Prevention as perceived and validated by the Office leadership and staff. None of the alternatives were alien to the Office. Moreover, the use of qualitative methods to create a set of possible approaches to creating and implementing an evaluation strategy, while time consuming, allowed Office leadership and staff to generate the data for themselves in such a way that they learned a process through which major programs could be designed and explored.

THE OPTIMUM STRATEGY

With a range of realistic alternative strategies, Office leadership could make a decision on which evaluation strategy to choose. That is, the Office could determine the best strategic fit in which its capabilities could interface with its environment with optimal efficiency and effectiveness. Each potential evaluation strategy was considered in terms of several criteria. These were the degrees of risk that the Office was willing to accept; how well each option would lend itself to the fulfillment of the mission; and the degree of fit each represented. In addition to the degree of acceptable risk, judgment was passed on the desirability and feasibility of each of the options. Whether or not a particular option was desirable was determined by what the Office leadership valued. Feasibility involved questions of capacity, political realities, available funding, and the willingness of potential partners to participate in an evaluation.

The ultimate criterion in selecting a strategy was the mission. Leadership had to be very clear about which of the strategic alternatives would be most effective in fulfilling their mission. At the same time, the most appropriate evaluation strategy had to be consistent with the Office's public mandate. Leadership very clearly understood that their work-a-day mission was of paramount importance: It represented what they actually did. Office leadership, in consultation with their overseers in the department of public health agreed that a strategy that utilized strengths to maximize opportunities represented the best course of action. They decided to solicit external funding to support the design of an evaluation to be implemented through affiliated community groups. The proposed evaluation was a summative, participatory evaluation that strengthened local groups and provided ample examples for successful public relations. The details of the evaluation and its implementation were carried at a later date and were beyond the scope of this particular consultancy.

Summary

Funds for the evaluation were solicited from a community foundation interested in the local development aspects of the disability prevention demonstration projects. The grant monies were allocated to assist the Office and allied community groups in the design and implementation of a very simple impact evaluation. The Office with its access to statewide data and the research capabilities of national groups supplemented findings with statistical data. The locally administered assessments were in essence "one-shot" investigations of work completed to date. Each assessment was a measure of local awareness, attitudes, and behaviors related to disability prevention. While sophisticated in design, the assessments enabled the Office to extend its newfound skills in strategic management to its local constituents. The end result was a strengthening of community leadership in assessing needs and progress. This was accomplished by providing a theoretical and social context for the application of qualitative research skills.

Although this entire process extended over 18 months, it did not represent 18 months of continuous work. Strategy meetings were called on a regular schedule. However, in light of the need for the process to adapt itself to the requirements and rhythms of the Office, schedules were written with enough flexibility to take into account the demands of report and grant writing as well as community events. The entire process infused concepts of strategic management throughout a public sector agency in which leadership and staff were, first and foremost, public health and social workers. While most were familiar with qualitative and group-based research methods, they did not know how to apply their skills to the operations and responsibilities of their office. The strategy development process as part of a management exercise wedded leadership and the staff's skills to a framework for strategically managing their activities.

References

Ackermann, F., S. Cropper, J. Cook, and C. Eden. 1990. Policy development in the public sector: An experiment. *Working Paper No. 89/2*, Strathclyde, UK: University of Strathclyde.

Bazerman, M. H. and Moore, D. 2009. *Judgment in managerial decision making*. 7th ed. New York: Wiley.

Brady, M. 2003. *The wisdom of listening*. Boston, MA: Wisdom.

Brinckerhoff, P.C. 1994. *Mission-based management: Leading your not-for-profit into the 21st century*. Oak Park, IL: Alpine Guild, Bryant, C. A., M. S. Frothofer, K. R. Brown, D. Landis, and R. J. McDermott. 2000. Community-based prevention marketing: The next steps in disseminating behavior change. *American Journal of Health Behavior, 24*:61–68.

Bryce, H. J. 2000. *Financial and strategic management for nonprofit organizations: A comprehensive reference to legal, financial, management and operations rules for nonprofits*, 3rd ed, San Diego, CA: Jossey Bass.

Bryson, J. M. 1995. *Strategic planning for public and nonprofit organizations: A guide to strengthening and sustaining organizational achievement*, San Francisco CA: Jossey-Bass.

Bryson, J. M. and B. C. Crosby. 1992. *Leadership for the common good: Tackling public problems in a shared power world*. San Francisco: Jossey-Bass

Creswell, J. W. 2008. *Research design: Qualitative, quantitative, and mixed methods approaches*. Thousand Oaks, CA: Sage.

Daniel, J. S. and L. L. Brown. 2000. A complex systems approach to organization. *Current Directions in Psychological Science, 9*:69–74.

Davidhizar, R. 2004. Listening—a nursing strategy to transcend culture. *Journal of Practical Nursing 54*:22–34.

Delbecq, A. L., A. H. Van de Ven, and D. Gustafson. 1975. *Group techniques program planning*. Glenview, IL: Scott-Foresman.

Delen, D., N. Dalal, and P. Benjamin. 2005. Integrated modeling: The key to holistic understanding of the enterprise. *Communications of the ACM, 48*:107–113.

Eden, C. 1990. Using cognitive mapping for strategic options development and analysis (SODA). In *Rational Analysis for a Problematic World*, J. Rosendhead, ed. Chichester, UK: Wiley.

Eden, C. and C. Huxham 1988. Action-oriented management research. *The Journal of the Operational Research Society, 39*:889–1003.

Eisele, P. 2007. A field experiment comparing different workgroup techniques. *Perceptual and Motor Skills 104*:171–183.

Fielding, J. E., J. Luck, and G. Tye. 2003. Reinvigorating public health core functions: Reconstructing Los Angeles County's public health system. *Journal of Public Health Management and Practice*, 9:7–15.

Flood, D. 2010. The relationship of "systems thinking" to action research. *Systematic Practice and Action Research* 23:269–290.

Gharajedaghi, J. 1999. *Systems thinking: Managing chaos and complexity: A platform for designing business architecture*. Boston, MA: Butterworth Heinemann.

Gilchrist, V. L. and Williams, R.L. 1999. Key informant interviews. In *Doing qualitative research*, 2nd ed. B. F. Crabtree and W. L Miller, eds. 71–88. Thousand Oaks, CA: Sage.

Goto, G., H. Pelto, D. Pelletier, D., and J. Tiffany 2010. "It really opened my eyes." The effects on youth peer educators of participating in an action research project. *Human Organization* 69:192–213.

Greenblat, C. and R. Duke. 1981 *Principles and practices of gaming simulation*. Newbury Park, CA: Sage.

Gummesson, E. 2007 Qualitative research in management. *Management Decisions*, 44:167–180.

Haines, S. 2000. *The systems thinking approach to strategic planning and management*. Boca Raton, FL: CRC.

Harrison, M. I. 1994. *Diagnosing organizations: Methods, models, and processes*. Thousand Oaks, CA: Sage.

Higginbotham, J. B. and K. K. Cox. 1979. *Focus group interviews*. Chicago: Marketing Associations.

Hoskisson, R. E., M. A. Hitt, W. P. Wan, and D. Yiu. 1999. Theory and research in strategic management: Swings of a pendulum. *Journal of Management*, 25:417–456.

Kearns, K. P. 2000. *Private sector strategies for social sector success: The guide to strategy and planning for public and nonprofit organizations*. San Francisco, CA: Jossey-Bass.

Koteen, J. 1997. *Strategic management in public and nonprofit organizations: Managing public concerns in an era of limits*. Westport, CT: Praeger.

Ladkin, D. 2004. Action research. In *Action research in qualitative research practice*, C. Seale, G. Goto and J. Gubrium, eds. Thousand Oaks, CA: Sage.

McAdam, R. and D. Leonard. 1999. The contribution of learning organization principles to business process re-engineering. *Knowledge and Process Management*, 6:176–183.

McGarth, R. G. 2001. Exploratory learning, innovative capacity, and managerial oversight. *Academy of Management Journal*, 44:118–130.

McIntyre-Mills, J. 2010. Participatory democracy and well-being: Narrowing the gap between service outcomes and perceived needs. *Systematic Research Practice and Action Research* 23:21–35.

McNiff, J. and J. Whitehead. 2002. Action research in organizations. *Management Learning*. Thousand Oaks, CA: Sage.

Mintzberg, H. 1994. *The rise and fall of strategic planning*. New York: Free Press.

———. 2009. Rebuilding companies as communities. *Harvard Business Review*, 87:140–157.

Northcutt, N. and D. McCoy. 2004. *Interactive qualitative analysis: A systems method for qualitative research*. Thousand Oaks, CA: Sage.

Northouse, G. 2007. *Leadership theory and practice*, 3rd ed. Thousand Oaks CA: Sage.

Oster, S. 1995. *Strategic management of nonprofit organizations*. New York: Oxford UP.

Patton, M. Q. 2002. *Qualitative research & evaluation methods*. Thousand Oaks, CA: Sage.

Perry, C. 2004. Action research in marketing. *European Journal of Management*, 138:310–326.

Pijl, K. and H. Sminia. 2004. Strategic management of public interest organizations. *Voluntas*, 15:137–157.

Robertson, K. 2005. Active listening: More than just paying attention. *Australian Family Physician* 34:1053–1081.

Roney, C. W. 2004. *Strategic management methodology: Generally accepted principles*. New York: Praeger.

Roney, C. W. and D. Lehman. 2008. Self-regulation in goal striving: Individual and situational moderators of the goal-framing of performance tasks. *Social Psychology*, 38:2691–2703.

Schmid, H. 2004. Theory for management practice in human service organizations. *Administration in Social Work, 28*:97–115.

Scott, R. W. 2004. Reflections on a half century of organizational sociology. *Annual Review of Sociology, 30*:1–22.

Siau, K. and X. Tan. 2006. Use of cognitive mapping techniques in information systems. *Information Technology Newsletter, 17*: 26–34.

Simon 1957.. *Models of Man: Social and Rational*. New York: Wiley.

Skinner, D., C. Tagg, and J. Holloway 2000. The pros and cons of qualitative approaches. *Management Learning, 31*:145–161.

Smith, J. and G. Clark. 2010. Action research in business classrooms; another lens to examine learning. *American Journal of Business Education, 13*:347–360.

Swindler, A. 1986. Culture in action. *American Sociological Review, 51*:273–286.

Thaler, R. H. 2000. From homo economicus to homo sapiens. *Journal of Economics Perspectives* 14:133–141.

Thompson, A. A. and Strickland, A.J. 2003 Strategic management: Concepts and cases, 12th ed). New York: McGraw-Hill College.

Walczak, S. 2005. Organizational knowledge management structure. *The Learning Organization*, 12:330–339.

Waldman, D. A., G. G. Ramirez, R. J. Hovse, and P. Puraman. 2001. Does leadership matter? CEO leadership attributes and profitability under conditions of perceived environmental uncertainty. *Academy of Management Journal*, 44:128–141.

Weihrich, H. 1982. The TOWS matrix: A tool for situational analysis. *Long Range Planning*, 15:52–64.

PART V

GENERATING NEW KNOWLEDGE
FOR SOCIAL WORK

16

Coping with the Dual Demands of Psychiatric Disability and Parenting

The Parents' Perspective

BARRY J. ACKERSON

The experience of parenting by individuals who have severe mental disorders (e.g., schizophrenia, major depression, and bipolar disorder) has rarely been addressed from the viewpoint of these parents. While there is extensive literature on parenting and the development of parenting skills, most of the research on parents with psychiatric disabilities focuses on their pathology and the potential for harm to their children (Gopfert, Webster, and Seeman 1996; Jacobsen and Miller 1999; Mowbray, Bybee, Oyserman, MacFarlane, and Bowersox 2006). Although some parents with severe mental disorders may present a potential risk to children in their care, often it is only those families that experience a serious crisis who receive attention because of their involvement with the child welfare system (Blanch, Nicholson, and Purcell 1994). The experiences of parents who manage to cope with their mental disorder and successfully raise their children have not been a focus of research. Although community mental health services have enabled many individuals with psychiatric disabilities to live productive lives in their communities, the parenting role of many of these clients has typically been overlooked by the mental health system (Nicholson and Blanch 1994; Oyserman, Mowbray, and Zemencuk 1994; Zeman and Buila 2006). We are just beginning to appreciate the importance of parenthood for these individuals, along with the challenges they face in confronting the complex demands of parenting and their psychiatric disability (Mowbray, Oyserman, and Ross 1995; Sands 1995; Fox 1999; Venkataraman and Ackerson 2008).

This chapter describes a qualitative study on mental illness in parents that has been previously published in the literature (Ackerson 2003a). A qualitative, exploratory design was appropriate for this study because it investigated a phenomenon that is not well understood from the parents' perspective, and built upon prior qualitative research on this topic. For example, Sands (1995) interviewed mothers with chronic mental illness living in an urban area in the eastern United States. Most of the participants in her study were African Americans with low incomes. In contrast, participants in this study lived in small cities and rural communities in a midwestern state, all were European American, and while some have low incomes, others hold blue-collar or white-collar jobs. Despite these differences in the two samples, the two studies are similar in that participants were interviewed about their experiences as parents with a psychiatric disability and how their mental disorder and parenting affect each other.

Other qualitative studies used focus groups with mothers diagnosed with a severe mental disorder who have young children. A study in the northeastern United States (Nicholson, Sweeney, and Geller 1998) examined these mothers' experiences with their families, exploring the quality of social support they received from family members. The researchers found that family members did often provide important social support to these women, but that these relationships were complex and not entirely positive. Another study in Australia (Bassett, Lampe, and Lloyd 1999) also used focus groups to explore the parenting experiences of mothers with severe mental disorders who had children under age five. Major themes that emerged were loss of custody, trauma of hospitalization, social isolation, stigma, care of the child if the mother becomes ill, access to community services, need for consistent staff, and each mother's relationship with their children. Many of the themes found in these previous studies also emerged during the interviews in the 2003 study.

Although results of qualitative inquiry do not generalize to a larger group, they are inherently valid representations of individuals' views of their experiences (Rapp, Kisthardt, Gowdy, and Hanson 1994). Use of qualitative methods also provides a better understanding of how these parents socially construct their experiences by allowing them to discuss these experiences in an open-ended, narrative fashion. This study augmented previous qualitative studies by exploring similar questions but with a different demographic group and in a different geographic and cultural setting. One key difference is that the sample was not limited to parents of young children. By including parents whose children are now adolescents or young adults, the interviews were able to incorporate a broader historical perspective of these parents' experiences that had not been explored in previous studies. This is an example of the theoretical sampling technique used in this study and is discussed in greater detail in the methodology section.

Qualitative Methods

Grounded Theory Methods

A qualitative research design was used in this study in order to obtain a deeper understanding of the topic from the participants' point of view. The goal is to identify recurring themes and concerns as a particular group (e.g., parents with psychiatric disabilities) experiences them. The purpose in using this research method is to understand, rather than predict (Royse 2008). A qualitative design is relevant in areas where there are gaps in understanding a social phenomenon and is particularly useful for understanding the phenomenon from mental health consumers' perspective (Rapp, Kisthardt, Gowdy, and Hanson 1994).

This study used grounded theory techniques for data gathering and analysis. Because the goal was to describe and develop a richer understanding of a phenomenon rather than to develop an underlying theory, it is best described as using grounded theory methods than being a pure grounded theory design. The grounded theory techniques of theoretical sampling and constant comparison were used in conjunction with the use of semi-structured interviews that elicited a narrative history from the participants.

Sampling Methods

Theoretical sampling refers to a sampling strategy that is based upon theoretical or conceptual themes rather than sampling that is based upon general characteristics in order to generalize to a broader population.

Theoretical sampling provided the basis for sampling decisions for the initial round of interviews and the follow-up interviews. Because we were focusing on issues pertaining to parents with mental illness, it was necessary to establish some diagnostic criteria for sampling. Theoretical literature on the nature and causes of mental illness is very broad. For this study, we were interested in understanding the parenting experiences of those individuals described in the mental health literature as having a serious and persistent mental illness (SPMI). Therefore, criteria for inclusion in the sample required a history of treatment and at least one hospitalization for a severe mental disorder, which was defined as either a psychotic disorder (e.g., schizophrenia) or a severe mood disorder (e.g., major depression or bipolar disorder). Persons with other psychiatric disabilities, such as alcohol or substance abuse and personality disorders, were included only if they had a primary diagnosis that fit this criteria. The participants were recruited from community mental health centers throughout central Illinois and from several mental health consumer and family support groups.

Because other studies have focused on parents of preschool or school-age children, the decision was made to use a broader sampling criterion that included parents of children who are now adolescents or young adults. The rationale for this decision was that we wanted to obtain a longer historical perspective of the parents' experiences and to better understand how these issues played out over a greater period of time in their children's development. A decision was also made to include parents who had lost custody of their children, as well as those who currently had custody of at least one child. The decision to include parents whose children are now older allowed for the inclusion of parents who had either temporarily lost or voluntarily relinquished custody of one or more children for a period of time, but who later regained custody of at least one child. This also gave us an opportunity to explore this issue in greater depth than a narrower time frame would have allowed. We also included parents who had permanently lost custody due to their mental illness.

The theoretical rationale for these sampling decisions was to expand upon the perspectives reported in other recent qualitative studies on this topic. For example, several previous studies where custody concerns have been mentioned focused on parents living in poverty and those who were involved with the child welfare system. We wanted to explore whether other parents with psychiatric disabilities also share these concerns and to identify factors that these parents believed enabled them to either maintain or regain custody of their children. In addition, the greater age range of the children in these families allowed us to develop a historical and developmental perspective that has not been reported in other studies.

Participants

Thirteen parents who have a psychiatric disability agreed to participate in the study. Nine of the participants were active clients of community mental health centers across central Illinois, so we were able to confirm their diagnosis and treatment history with their treatment provider. The other four participants were recruited through mental health consumer support groups in the area. These individuals provided detailed information regarding their diagnosis and treatment. This information was discussed in-depth during the recruitment and interview process. Three of these four participants had a confirmed diagnosis that met the research criteria for a severe mental disorder, while one participant's diagnostic information was unclear. She no longer has active psychiatric symptoms nor receives active mental health treatment, but she did have a documented hospital stay and several years of treatment for psychotic symptoms in the past. This mother is an active member of mental health consumer groups and represents a population that is often overlooked in research—individuals who achieve a high degree of recovery following treatment for a psychotic disorder. Despite the fact that her clinical history and life experiences were different from the other participants in the study, the decision was made to include her insights and experiences in order to compare and contrast them with those of the other participants.

Our sample of thirteen parents consisted of twelve women and one man. Three are currently married while the remaining ten are separated, widowed, or divorced. Ten of the participants have at least a high school education, with four reporting anywhere from one year of college to graduate studies. Seven of the parents reported losing custody of their children at some point and another one reported having joint custody, but that her children's primary residence was with their father following her divorce. Four of those who lost custody later regained custody of at least one child, two permanently lost custody as a result of divorce (one of these was the only father in our sample), and one gave up her children for adoption. Five parents reported at least one child who has a psychiatric or behavioral disorder of some type.

Interviews

During the first round of interviews, participants were asked to provide background information and to briefly discuss their treatment history. The interviewer then used a semistructured interview schedule that posed a series of questions and follow-up probes asking participants to discuss how their psychiatric disability had affected them as parents. These queries were followed by questions about how their experiences as parents, in turn, influenced their mental disorder. Otherwise, these interviews were relatively open-ended and allowed the parents to formulate their ideas and responses as part of an interactive interview process. During these initial interviews, it became apparent that the participants viewed their experiences with their disorder, their personal relationships, and their experiences as parents as inextricably interwoven. As a result, the structure of the interviews evolved into a narrative history form, with probes and follow-up questions serving to guide the discussion. The interviewer continued to use the interview schedule as a guide, but allowed the discussion to flow more naturally as the parent told their story in a narrative form. Follow-up questions and probes were used to fill in any questions on the schedule that may not have been directly addressed in the narrative history.

Data Collection and Analysis

Data gathering and analysis used the constant comparative method and theoretical sampling techniques developed by Glaser and Strauss (1967). Constant comparison is a systematic method for gathering, recording, and analyzing qualitative data in which narrative data are analyzed and coded concurrently with the gathering of additional data (Strauss and Corbin 1990). In adopting the constant comparative method, the research team went through several stages of coding to analyze the narrative data. The first stage, open coding, involved carefully reading transcripts of the recorded data, line by line, with open assignment of categories ascribed to the data. During this stage, the researcher and the research assistant coded the interviews individually. A process of evolving and negotiating categories and themes occurred during this stage. These discussions led to the next stage of axial coding. In this stage, data were reorganized in new ways by making connections between the categories and by constructing broader themes. Concurrent with the coding of the initial interviews, themes that emerged guided sampling decisions and the development of questions for follow-up interviews.

In order to further explore the themes that were identified during coding, a second round of interviews was conducted. Data collection decisions for the follow-up interviews were guided by the theoretical sampling concepts discussed earlier in this section (Strauss and Corbin, 1990). The goal of theoretical sampling is to sample concepts, incidents, or behaviors that are significant in light of the developing ideas and themes that can sharpen the researchers' conceptualization. With this in mind, five parents were selected whose initial interviews suggested greater exploration of the developing themes that had been identified during open and axial coding and who represented a cross-section of the initial sample. Four of these five participants agreed to participate in the follow-up interviews.

Second round interview questions were more structured and focused on theoretical topics, but continued to be open ended and again engaged the participants in a narrative discussion of their experiences. First, parents were asked to confirm background information and to elaborate on any diagnostic or treatment information that may have been unclear in the initial interview. They were then presented with a synthesis of the initial interview and asked to verify or comment on the categories and themes that had been identified. Themes that were explored fell into three categories: relationship with children, sources of support, and the strain of single parenthood. The category of relationship with children contained three specific themes: discipline, boundary issues, and role reversal. Sources of support included informal supports, such as family or friends, and formal supports, such as social service agencies. The strain of single parenthood included economic and emotional difficulties that resulted from divorce, as well as ongoing concerns and struggles regarding custody.

While the follow-up interviews were being conducted, axial coding continued to be done with the original interviews. Following the second round of interviews and the ongoing data analysis, saturation of categories occurred. The final stage of selective coding was performed with connections made between the various themes and categories.

Findings

Problems with Diagnosis and Treatment

Because the interviews began with an exploration of each individual's experiences with her or his psychiatric disability, it was not unexpected that over half of them (eight) described difficulties related to their treatment. What was notable is that many of them struggled for years with either an uncertain diagnosis or a misdiagnosis that further complicated their attempts to manage their disorder. As a result, their ability to fulfill their role as a mother or father was jeopardized. The theme of unrecognized or inadequately treated mental illness resounded through many of the interviews. One participant stated

> It was never recognized that I had a mental illness. Everybody felt like this was a behavior. . . . Snap out of it. . . . You should be over it by now. I didn't really get the right diagnosis until after my kids were practically raised.

This particular mother went through a series of therapists and counselors and was diagnosed with a personality disorder before finally receiving a correct diagnosis of bipolar disorder. Unfortunately for this parent, her children were in late adolescence before the correct diagnosis was made. Similarly, many of the parents interviewed reported suffering for years with an incorrect diagnosis or experienced inadequate treatment, which impaired their ability to be an effective parent during acute episodes of their illness. Another parent reported

> I've been diagnosed [with] everything. . . . One said I was a paranoid schizophrenic and the other one said no I wasn't. . . . You know, when you get a different doctor, they see what they think they see, and do the best they can, you know . . . and some of them want to medicate you to death, and, you know, not deal with your problems and not talk to you. I had one doctor . . . he gave me too much shock and I was in a coma for three weeks.

Many participants recognized that their symptoms during acute episodes compromised their parenting skills. One parent reported, "Before

I started medicine . . . I was on the couch for many months . . . barely taking care of them." For many parents, this created a crisis situation for their families when their condition became severe enough to require hospitalization. The manner in which these parents coped with these crises is discussed further in the sections on social support and custody issues. It was also clear that for the majority of these parents their acute symptoms abated with proper diagnosis and treatment. However, they continued to struggle with the handicap of being labeled with a mental disorder.

Effects of Stigma

The harmful effects of stigma for individuals with psychiatric disability have been well documented in the literature (Corrigan 2004) as well as by advocacy groups such as the National Alliance for the Mentally Ill (NAMI). For this reason, it is not surprising that stigma and discrimination emerged as recurrent themes in the interviews. However, it is noteworthy that stigma was also described as a significant issue by the one parent who has achieved a high level of recovery, indicating that this was a common experience for all of our participants regardless of the severity of their symptoms. Stigma impacts parents with mental disorders in several ways. First, it has a chilling effect on their willingness to seek help and engage in treatment. This aspect of stigma is directly related to the earlier theme of problems with misdiagnosis and treatment. As one parent put it

> I had problems, but my husband wouldn't listen to me. I self-diagnosed myself as schizophrenic. . . . Yeah, I just diagnosed myself . . . and I didn't want to go to a psychiatrist because I thought he would lock me up and I wanted to raise my kids.

Stigma was also discussed within the context of the parents' concerns about losing custody of their children. They expressed reluctance to seek treatment due to fear of losing custody if diagnosed with a psychiatric disorder. In fact, those parents who went through a divorce reported having their diagnosis used against them. This was sometimes done through formal court custody decisions, but was just as likely to involve acquiescence on the part of the parent when faced with a threat by their former spouse. For those parents who experienced either a temporary or permanent loss of custody via the child welfare system, most felt that their diagnosis was also used against them by child welfare workers. Thus their adverse experiences associated with custody concerns and fear of losing their children reinforced their perceptions of discrimination due to the stigma of their mental illness.

The theme of stigma was also expressed through the parents' concerns for their children. One parent described the harassment and verbal abuse that her adolescent daughter, who has also been diagnosed with depression, experienced at school and in her neighborhood. As a result of this harassment, the mother and her daughter became reclusive, further compounding the social withdrawal that accompanies their disorder. Other parents discussed general concerns about the subtle types of discrimination their children might (and sometimes did) experience at school or in their neighborhoods as a result of their parent's illness. One mother expressed concerns about her children, despite the fact that she is an outspoken mental health consumer advocate and has been free of symptoms for many years. Although she was not ashamed to speak about her own experiences, she was concerned about the impact her advocacy might have on her children's relationships with peers.

Chaotic Interpersonal Relationships

All the study participants had been married at some point, and all but two subsequently went through a divorce. One exception is the parent who experienced a psychotic episode at an early age and did not marry or have children until several years later when she had already achieved a high level of recovery. In contrast to the other parents, whose divorces exacerbated their illness, she discussed the relationship with her husband as a protective factor in helping to cope with her disorder and to prevent relapse. The other exception was a woman whose husband had died just a few years ago. She viewed his death and her subsequent grief as being the stressors that triggered her mood disorder. All the other participants saw their psychiatric disability affecting their relationships in one of two ways. They either viewed their disorder as contributing to the difficulties they were experiencing in their relationships, or they believed their symptoms were exacerbated by these relationship problems. One mother described this interaction between her disorder and the problems in her relationship in the following manner.

I got the medicine, but I only took it for a short while because that's when the divorce hit. . . . He thought I was crazy. . . . When your mind is sick, it is like you are under water just waiting for it to pass and finally you come up for air, you are waiting for it to pass, how long am I going to be under this time? That's what it's like. . . . He couldn't understand or anything. He was tired of it, he said, "I can't take you mentally anymore." . . . I was just crushed. . . . Eventually I couldn't decipher reality from non-reality and I finally put myself in the hospital.

In addition to difficulties maintaining a relationship with their significant other, many of the parents also reported strained relationships with their parents or siblings. On the one hand, these family members were a key source of support during times of crisis, especially in regard to child care. However, their relationship to the participant was at times strained due to these demands, and these family members were often described as being very critical and emotionally unsupportive. This theme is explored further under the heading of social support.

Strain of Single Parenthood

A few other qualitative studies of parents with psychiatric disabilities have identified single parenthood as a significant theme (Sands 1995; Bassett, Lampe, and Lloyd 1999). This was also a recurrent theme throughout the interviews in this study. Whether participants viewed their symptoms as being exacerbated by the break up of their marriages or whether they also saw their disorder as contributing to their failed relationships, the end result was the same. At a time when they found themselves most emotionally vulnerable and under stress due to their loss of a significant other, they typically experienced a major emotional or psychiatric crisis. The one exception was the participant whose acute phase of her illness preceded her marriage and children by several years and who did not divorce. She believed that the success of her marriage enhanced her recovery and that her husband acted as a protective factor during times of stress, reporting

So, part of it is I feel that I am more aware of how stressors affect people's lives . . . having children and parenting has not been a particular stressor. . . . I have a wonderful support network, my husband is fabulous in being

a support. . . . I would say that far and away is the most important thing.
I couldn't imagine doing it without that openness and support.

In addition to the support of her spouse, which was missing in all the other
interviews, she cited other forms of social support as key factors, "I have a
great friendship network. . . . Having a work setting that accommodates day
care, parental concerns, makes a big difference."

During times of crises, these parents often found themselves caring
for one or more children while dealing with the financial and emotional
problems that accompany single parenthood. One mother expressed the
financial hardship by saying, "I know one thing that is very hard on a
single parent. When he left, the money left. My security went and their
security went." Another parent described her struggle with these dual
demands during an acute episode of her mood disorder following her
divorce.

I tried to get work and the kids were giving me problems because they
were demanding more attention now that they knew I was in trouble. I
didn't know what to do. . . . I was starving but it didn't matter to him, he
just wanted me to take care of them like I always had.

Custody Issues

Eleven of the thirteen participants expressed concerns about losing their
children through either divorce or child welfare. The two exceptions were
(a) the atypical case whose marriage and childrearing came several years
after she recovered from the acute phase of her illness, and (b) another
parent whose symptoms became acute following the death of her husband
four years prior to the interview. Seven of these 11 parents had actually lost
custody on at least a temporary basis, but only three had lost custody on a
permanent basis. Although custody concerns were an ongoing stressor for
most of the participants in the study, they were particularly acute during
times of a psychiatric crisis. It was during times of crisis that these parents
needed support from family or friends for the care of their children. Because
of their temporary inability to adequately care for their children, they were
vulnerable to losing their children. A theme that echoed throughout the
interviews was that parents with a psychiatric disability appreciate having

someone take care of their children during times of crisis or hospitalization. However, they are very concerned that these incidents may be used against them in custody decisions as a result of either divorce or involvement with the child welfare system.

Relationships with Children

Three themes emerged under this category: discipline, boundary issues, and role reversal. These three themes were interwoven throughout the various narratives. These specific themes were grouped within a more general category because of the manner in which the various narratives described the interactive nature of these three factors. Discipline is a key parental responsibility that requires judgment and restraint that may be compromised by psychiatric disabilities. Many of the parents interviewed admitted to having some problems in this area and were more likely to see themselves as too lax or permissive than too harsh. This was expressed by several parents with statements such as, "I look back and see that I maybe should have set a few more rules," or "I was never good about rules . . . my biggest problem was consistency and discipline." Some of them viewed this as a consequence of their own perceptions of inadequacy and the guilt they felt about being a parent with a mental disorder. One mother expressed a sense of guilt due to the impact her psychiatric disability and chaotic relationships had on her children, "I was not good at saying no, because I felt sorry for them . . . [because they had been through so much] I tried to make their life easier."

A common experience the interviewed father had with many of the mothers was loss of custody. He expressed his lax approach to discipline by saying, "I would let them do things that she wouldn't let them do. . . . I was able to be more lenient with them. I didn't have to discipline them or anything." Many of the parents described a tendency to be more lenient as a result of only seeing the children during visitations and wanting to enjoy the brief periods of time they spent with their children. One mother who lost custody as a result of her divorce said

> Because our time initially was so little together, why spend it yelling and screaming and making them do chores when they're gone in two days. . . . When they came to my house we were going to have fun.

A few parents reported problems with excessive discipline that occurred during an acute episode of their illness. One parent reported

> I only spanked them when they got into something that could hurt them. . . . Sometimes when I was sick I would go overboard with the spankings. . . . So as far as discipline goes, I used to discipline them when I was sick, and it was wrong. So now I don't punish when I'm sick. . . . I shy away because I've done it in the wrong way before.

A few other parents also recalled instances when their psychotic or manic symptoms made them dangerous to their children. In these instances, professional intervention and support from a family member or friend who could temporarily take care of the children were needed. However, the more frequent theme found in the interviews was a lax or permissive approach to discipline that was accompanied by a special sense of closeness between the parent and their children.

Many parents characterized their relationships with their children as a special bond that helped them get through tough times. They typically described this bond as something that developed over time as a result of going through the hardships the family faced. One mother characterized her relationship with her daughter following the death of her husband in the following manner.

> Well, it's made us closer. She used to be a daddy's girl. She wouldn't have anything to do with me . . . and since he died we have become closer. I support her in every which way there is that I can possibly think of, and she supports me.

Although they acknowledged that their children often had more expectations placed on them and faced special burdens due to the participant's psychiatric disability, these parents believed the hardships eventually led to a closer, mutually interdependent relationship with their children. However, during the data coding process, the parents' descriptions of close bonds with their children also suggested themes of role reversal and boundary issues.

Role reversal was apparent in two respects. First, during times when the parent was experiencing an exacerbation of their symptoms, older children often had to act as a parent in assuming responsibility for taking care of younger children or helping with household chores. One mother described her relationship with her daughter during an acute phase of the mother's illness by saying

> You know, she was doing the parenting! And she took care of [her brother], in terms of taking him around in the wagon. . . . She became the little parent sometimes, and because she had that little bit of responsibility or something, it made it even worse for me to parent her!

In another example of this, one mother described the following scenario that occurred during her major depressive episodes.

> My kids have had to come home and, you know, had to help with the housework and "well mom's not well so we have to fix supper tonight," or you know, things around the house . . . and it was tough on me, having to ask my kids. . . . I mean, all of them helped a great deal.

Role reversal was evident when the child and parent would switch caregiver roles during times when the parent was incapacitated. This ranged from doing household chores such as cooking for the parent, to cueing the parent to take their medicine or alerting the parent or other adults that the parent's symptoms were becoming worse. One mother described her dependence on her daughter in the following way.

> That was difficult for my daughter. . . . During the week I would sit [my son] beside me and I would watch cartoons or whatever, a lot times my head was really out of it. . . . My daughter had to help, she still thinks that was the pits. [At other times when her symptoms became worse] they would tell me. I would tell them to tell me; I would say, "Tell me if I am not making sense, because I need to know, it is important."

All of the participants reported a sense of a special closeness with their children even though their relationships with their children were strained at times due to these extra demands. In some respects, these parents' narratives reflect a healthy and mutually beneficial relationship. However, it also appeared that some of the discussions of these relationships were excessively idyllic and suggested problems with establishing appropriate boundaries between parent and child. As shown in some of the earlier

quotes, several parents reported difficulties in exerting parental authority due to the role reversal that occurred during acute episodes of their
disorder.

Boundary issues also emerged when some parents described relationships
with their children as filling the void created by divorce or chaotic relationships. One mother referred to her sons by saying, "Who needs a husband!
My kids did it." A clearer example of problems in establishing clear boundaries due to psychiatric symptoms is exemplified in the following comments
by one mother, "But me and [one of her sons] were like soul mates. Anything
that happened to him, I could feel it. . . . He is like an angel."

Therefore, it was difficult to discern in a few interviews whether the
special bond that many of the parents described was a sign of healthy affection and mutual support, or whether it was an indication of impaired
cognition and perceptions due to the parent's mental disorder. It is possible that many of these parents do have a healthy and reciprocal relationship with their children. However, social workers should be aware of this
issue and should include an assessment of clearly established boundaries
between parents and their children when working with persons who have
psychiatric disabilities.

Social Support

Parents who had a strong social support network—whether it was family,
friends, or church—were able to cope with crises better than those who
were more socially isolated. The most important issue they identified is having someone who can step in and help with the children during times of a
psychiatric crisis or hospitalization. Parents who did not have this support,
either because they did not seek it out or because it was not readily available,
were more likely to have lost custody of their children at least temporarily. In
addition, neighbors and friends were also mentioned as people who would
step in and supervise the children or assist with household chores that the
parent viewed as being essential to the children's well-being. Other types
of support identified as important were emotional support from friends or
family and financial support from an ex-spouse or their relatives. Finally,
the few individuals who are currently in a stable relationship reported that
the emotional support they receive from their spouse plays a significant
role in their ability to cope with their illness and their responsibilities as

a parent. This protective, buffering effect existed even for parents whose past histories included chaotic relationships, divorces, and acute episodes of their disorder.

Female family members, usually mothers or sisters, were most frequently mentioned as the individuals who provided support in times of crisis. However, several participants also mentioned their ex-spouse or the ex-spouse's relatives, such as their mother-in-law, as providing support in times of crisis. Informal support, such as from family and friends, was mentioned much more frequently than formal, professional sources of support (such as case managers, social workers, or social service agencies). However, clients actively involved with psychosocial rehabilitation services through their community mental health center were more likely to mention professional forms of support.

Although most of our participants readily acknowledged their sources of support, they also described their relationships with those in their support network in complex terms. This was particularly true when their primary source of support was family or an ex-spouse. Similar to the findings by Nicholson, Sweeney, and Geller (1998), most participants described mixed relationships with relatives. On the one hand, parents or siblings provided a good deal of financial and child-rearing support for the children, but they were not often described as a good source of emotional support for the mentally ill parent. Several participants characterized their relationships with their family in the following manner.

> They did step in and help me out, but sometimes their good intentions were the worse thing for me. Sometimes they tended to take over and they had the children a lot . . . also they got on me a lot . . . [and told me to] snap out of it.

> My sister, I got support from her, and she took care of the kids when I stayed in the hospital for three months. . . . My sister, my families are mixed about me being sick.

> I believe it takes a village to raise a child. Even though I didn't appreciate my family at times, and my ex-husband, I felt that everybody was important for my kids. . . . Even though I knew what they were saying, I didn't counteract it with "No your mom isn't crazy." . . . I didn't need that bickering. . . . They weren't supportive of me.

Pride in Being a Parent

All the parents who spent any period of time raising their children described the self-esteem they derived from the parent role. They expressed this through such statements as

> I think the joy of being a parent, for me, adds to mental health.

> I think I am more complete because I am a parent.

> It has helped me. I am proud to be a mother; I am happy to be a mother; I love being a mother.

> I enjoy working, but when it comes right down to it, it's my kids that are most important.

Every participant in the study, including the parent who voluntarily gave up her child for adoption, expressed genuine concern for her or his children. This was evident in a number of ways. Most of the parents who lost custody described some effort to maintain contact despite separation. Those who permanently lost custody or gave up their children for adoption reported reconnecting after the children became adults. Typically, the children initiated these contacts, indicating the importance of these relationships to them as well. Many of these parents are now providing some type of support for their adult children. Typically, this support has come in the form of serving in the grandparent role or by providing emotional support and was reported by parents who had lost custody as well as those who had maintained custody.

Methodological Implications

Because this study focused on the parents' perspectives, further research involving the children, spouses, or ex-spouses, and other members of the parents' social support network is needed. The themes of role reversal and social support that were discussed by the parents in this study involve complex social interactions that place demands on other members of the family. Previous research examined caregiver burden experienced by family members of persons with severe mental disorders (Veltro, Magliano, Lobrace, and Maj 1994; Mueser, Webb, Pfeiffer, Gladis, and Levinson 1996). However, none of these older studies focused on families where the mentally ill individual is also a parent.

Future interviews that explore the experiences of other family members who are impacted by the parents' illness would help to provide a more complete understanding of how parents who have a severe mental disorder cope with their illness and the demands of parenting. For example, studies that include the spouse or partner, as well as other members of the extended family, may provide a broader understanding of the complexities of these parents' social support networks. Because individual narratives are inherently biased from the point of view of the person being interviewed, interviewing other members of the parent's social support network provides a means for triangulation of the data through multiple perspectives of the same phenomenon.

Interviews with children of these parents could provide a mirroring perspective that complements the parents' perspective. Boundary issues, discipline, and role reversal emerged as important issues in these parents' relationships with their children. Role reversal may be a concern if too many demands are being placed on a child at too early an age, but it may also be a source of considerable support for both the parent and child. The stories of mutual reliance described in many of the narratives in the current study (Ackerson 2003a) implied a beneficial impact on the children by fostering their sense of responsibility and maturity as well as creating a stronger parent–child bond. From the parents' perspective, the ability of an older child to help with household chores or to supervise younger children provided a safe home environment during times when the parent experienced greater impairment due to their illness. However, this issue needs to be studied further from the child's perspective in order to understand the potential burden they experience as a result of boundary issues and role reversal. For example, does the child also view their relationship with the parent as special and mutually reliant? How do they view the burden of responsibility placed on them when role reversal occurs? Do other members of the family's support system help mediate the child's caregiver burden? A good example of a qualitative study that incorporates the child's perspective along with the parent's is a more recent study by Venkataraman and Ackerson (2008) that focused on mothers with bipolar disorder.

Any study that relies on client memories and recall of past events is subject to some bias and distortion. Nonetheless, use of narrative history offers an opportunity to develop a richer understanding of a phenomenon over time that is difficult to capture with quantitative methods.

One example of this can be seen in the narratives of several of the participants in this study who experienced incorrect diagnoses and ineffective treatment for their bipolar disorder. Bipolar disorders are often misdiagnosed initially because the more severe symptoms are often mistaken for psychosis, while the less severe symptoms are either overlooked or seen as a personality disorder or substance abuse. A recent survey of individuals with bipolar disorder (Mondimore 1999) found that 73 percent of them reported at least one incorrect diagnosis prior to being correctly diagnosed. In a quantitative design, a researcher may try to control for problems in diagnosis through the use of clinical screening instruments. In contrast, narrative history in this study was a useful data gathering tool that allowed the participants to describe their experiences over time. Although some of the specific facts may have been distorted or overemphasized by the person being interviewed, the impact of this issue on the parent's ability to cope with the demands of parenting was clearly evident in a way that would be difficult to capture with a survey or other quantitative method. Because we were more interested in the lived experience of these parents, we were able to capture the problem of misdiagnosis more thoroughly than if we has just focused on correctly assigning an individual to a specific diagnostic category.

Use of qualitative interviewing methods was very helpful in capturing the longitudinal perspective of our participant's stories. We also included a wide age range for the parents' children in our sampling criteria in order to capture this longitudinal perspective. Through use of open-ended interviews and constant comparison coding of the narratives, we were able to get a deeper understanding of the interactive relationship between each parent's psychiatric symptoms and their relationship with their children. The cyclical nature of these disorders and their impact on the individual's ability to function adequately in the parenting role was made clearer as they became engaged with the researcher during the course of the interview. As themes began to emerge, probes during the interviews became more focused and elaborative but continued to elicit narratives from the parents that provided insight into their personal experiences and concerns. Furthermore, the process of asking these parents to tell their stories to an interested stranger was described by several participants as very empowering.

References

Ackerson, B. J. 2003. Coping with the dual demands of severe mental illness and parenting: The parents' perspective. *Families in Society*, 84:109–118.

Bassett, H., J. Lampe, and C. Lloyd. 1999. Parenting: Experiences and feelings of parents with a mental illness. *Journal of Mental Health*, 8(6):597–604.

Blanch, A., J. Nicholson, and J. Purcell. 1994. Parents with severe mental illness and their children: The need for human services integration. *Journal of Mental Health Administration*, 21:388–396.

Corrigan, P. 2004. How stigma interferes with mental health care. *American Psychologist*, 59:614–625.

Fox, L. 1999. Missing out on motherhood. *Psychiatric Services*, 50:193–194.

Glaser, B. and A. Strauss. 1967. *The discovery of grounded theory*. Chicago: Aldine.

Gopfert, M., J. Webster, and M. V. Seeman (Eds). 1996. *Parental psychiatric disorder: Distressed parents and their families*. Cambridge: Cambridge UP.

Jacobsen, T. and L. J. Miller. 1999. Attachment quality in young children of mentally ill mothers: Contribution of maternal caregiving abilities and foster care context. In *Attachment disorganization*, J. Solomon and C. George, eds. 347–378. New York: Guilford.

Mondimore, F. 1999. *Bipolar disorder: A guide for patients and families*. Baltimore, MD: Johns Hopkins UP.

Mowbray, C., D. Bybee, D. Oyserman, P. MacFarlane, and N. Bowersox. 2006. Psychosocial outcomes for adult children of parents with severe mental illness: Demographic and clinical history predictors. *Health and Social Work*, 31:99–108.

Mowbray, C. T., D. Oyserman, and S. Ross. 1995. Parenting and the significance of children for women with a serious mental illness. *Journal of Mental Health Administration*, 22:189–200.

Mueser, K. T., C. Webb, M. Pfeiffer, M. Gladis, and D. F. Levinson. 1996. Family burden of schizophrenia and bipolar disorder: Perceptions of relatives and professionals. *Psychiatric Services*, 47:507–511.

Nicholson, J. and A. Blanch. 1994. Rehabilitation for parenting roles for people with serious mental illness. *Psychosocial Rehabilitation Journal*, 18:109–119.

Nicholson, J., E. M. Sweeney, and J. L. Geller. 1998. Mothers with mental illness: I. The competing demands of parenting and living with mental illness. *Psychiatric Services*, 49:635–642.

——. 1998. Mothers with mental illness: II. Family relationships and the context of parenting. *Psychiatric Services*, 49:643–649.

Oyserman, D., C. T. Mowbray, and J.A. Zemencuk. 1994. Resources and supports for mothers with severe mental illness. *Health and Social Work*, 19:132–142.

Rapp, C. A., W. Kisthardt, E. Gowdy, and J. Hanson. 1994. Amplifying the consumer voice: Qualitative methods, empowerment, and mental health research. In *Qualitative research in social work*, E. Sherman and W. J. Reid, eds. 381–395. New York: Columbia UP.

Royse, D. 2008. *Research methods in social work*, 5th ed. Chicago: Nelson-Hall.

Sands, R. 1995. The parenting experience of low-income single women with serious mental disorders. *Families in Society*, 76(2):86–96.

Strauss, A. and J. Corbin. 1990. *Basics of qualitative research*. Newbury Park: Sage.

Veltro, F., L. Magliano, S. Lobrace, and M. Maj. 1994. Burden on key relatives of patients with schizophrenia vs. neurotic disorders: A pilot study. *Social Psychiatry and Psychiatric Epidemiology*, 29:66–70.

Venkataraman, M. and B. J. Ackerson, 2008. Parenting among mothers with bipolar disorders: Strengths, challenges, and service needs. *Journal of Family Social Work*, 11:389–408.

Zeman, L. D. and S Buila. 2006. Practice wisdom on custodial parenting with mental illness: A strengths view. *Journal of Family Social Work*, 10:51–65.

17

Assessing Young Children's Perceptions of Family Relationships

Theory and Applications of the Narrative Story-Stem Technique

TIMOTHY PAGE

The narrative story-stem technique (NSST) (Buchsbaum et al. 1992) is the generic term for a semiprojective method of assessing young children's perceptions of family relationships using open-ended story stems. The NSST was developed by attachment researchers in the field of developmental psychology to specifically study children's perceptions of their attachment relationships (Bretherton, Ridgeway, and Cassidy 1990; Bretherton and Oppenheim 2003). Applications of attachment theory to social work practice have generated vibrant interest in recent years because of the critical importance of attachment in the lives and social problems of our client populations. Yet social work is only beginning to absorb either the evidence base for attachment theory or assessment tools that can pinpoint potential interventions. In addition, there are few approaches to understanding the young child's perspective. This chapter contributes to these gaps by focusing on recent advancements in an attachment-based assessment of young children.

The NSST operates very much like an interview in that it poses a set of standardized problems and questions to child respondents. In this case, however, the interview format consists of story stems depicting familiar family scenarios, which are enacted with toy figures. Children create responses to these questions in the form of spontaneous narratives, which are coded according to the researchers' questions of interest. To distinguish the NSST from more traditional quantitative measures, children's narrative responses to the story stems are not necessarily coded in an a priori, fixed format of mutually exclusive response sets (although they may be). They are instead often coded to capture the very personal and creative desires of the child subject. This is, therefore, an example of flexible research methodology (Anastas 1999), where the nature of responses provided by participants may, as in a feedback loop, influence the examiner to revisit and refine a priori assumptions about how to organize, synthesize, and present the data. In this chapter, the conceptual and theoretical foundation, empirical support for, and applications of the NSST will be presented, along with recommendations regarding its use in social work practice and research.

Conceptual Framework

Clinicians working with young children have long recognized that play materials and activities must be an essential part of their interventions. In the early twentieth century, psychoanalytic psychotherapists theorized that children's play is projective of their intrapsychic conflicts, and ultimately actual life experiences (Schaefer and O'Connor 1983). More contemporary cognitive-behavioral approaches to clinical practice with children also recognize the utility of incorporating children's capacities for play into interventions, such as in providing a method of systematic desensitization in a controlled setting (Morris and Kratochwill 1998). Developmentalists regard play as the primary medium through which children learn to explore their world, investigate new roles and behavior, and learn to communicate experience with others (Ashford, LeCroy, and Lortie 2001). Despite a broad clinical acceptance of the need and the utility of incorporating play activities in assessment and intervention, there has been relatively little empirical study of the ways in which children actually create meaning in their play that reflects their life experiences. This gap is an important issue that the NSST was designed to address, and will be discussed in more detail in this chapter.

Play and Cognitive Development

Children's capacities to engage in play activities mature as their cognitive and social capacities mature (see Farmer-Dougan and Kaszuba 1999).

Children's maturing capacities for symbolic representation, in particular, reflect an important developmental advance in understanding that one thing can be imagined to represent some other thing. By approximately the age of three, children acquire the ability to mentally represent their worlds in sequential event schemas—basic memory structures that identify actors and action, circumstances and motives (see Bretherton and Munholland 2008). These capacities gradually become organized into narrative forms of character and plot involving setting, and problem and story resolution. Indeed, it appears that the capacity to think and perceive in narrative form is essential for learning and interpreting daily experience (Fivush 1993) because it provides a necessary structure for the organization and application of information stored in memory. In developing the NSST, attachment researchers incorporated the understanding of these achievements into Bowlby's conceptualization of internalized representations of attachment figures, the central theoretical construct upon which the NSST is based. A brief explanation of the importance of this construct to this method follows.

ATTACHMENT THEORY AND INTERNAL WORKING MODELS

By approximately the end of the first year of life, a normally developing child has acquired a specific type of attachment to the caregiver(s) with whom the child is familiar (for a review of this literature, see Cassidy 2008). This achievement emerges from the child's innate predisposition to seek proximity to familiar caregivers when distressed, and the nature of the relationship history. Children whose caregivers consistently respond with appropriate and sensitive care tend to develop secure attachments to them. Children tend to develop insecure attachments when their caregivers inconsistently perceive and respond to their needs, especially in maltreating circumstances.

Later, in toddlerhood, in a normally developing child's life, the organized memories of experiences with attachment figures increasingly function—in optimal circumstances—to provide the child with a sense of emotional security in times of distress. Among other things, this allows the child to explore his world at greater distances and enter into new social spheres, independent of the attachment figure's presence. Bowlby (1973) referred to the cognitive capacity for this achievement as the child's "internal working model" of the attachment relationship. He used this term to reflect the relative enduring nature of the synthesized memories of relationship experiences with the attachment figure, while at the same time communicating that these memories are always available for new input and updating when significant new experiences in close relationships are encountered.

Internal working models are conceptualized as organized cognitive representations of relationship qualities, more than representations of individual attributes (Sroufe and Fleeson 1986; Bretherton and Munholland 2008). Internal working models of specific attachment relationships become generalized models of the child's behavioral repertoire in the expression of attachment needs, and of his/her expectations of others in responding to those needs. As such, internal working models serve a vital predictive function for the child for the likely response of significant others to the child's needs, and, in reciprocal fashion, of the child's own sense of worthiness in being responded to when distressed (Bowlby 1973).

The theoretical significance of internal working models of attachment relationships to life span development is therefore considerable. Attachment research at the level of representation (Main, Kaplan, and Cassidy 1985), thus became an important focus in recent decades in order to better understand these processes. Several semiprojective measures have been developed in response to this interest that assess significant aspects of young children's internal working models of attachment relationships, including the use of ambiguous thematic apperception test (TAT)-like drawings in the Separation Anxiety Test (Main, Kaplan, and Cassidy 1985); projective, unstructured doll play (Murray, Woolgar, Briers, and Hipwell 1999); and an interview format involving puppets (Cassidy 1988).

The NSST is among the methods explicitly designed to gain access to children's internal working models of their attachment relationships and other relational representations. Such a method of assessment is vitally important, given that young children are typically unable to verbally express such perceptions. The NSST has become the most widely used of these methods, with a steadily growing empirical literature that has revealed much about the nature and significance of this developmental achievement. In the following sections, highlights of this literature will be discussed, after first describing the procedural applications of the NSST.

General Procedures for the Administration of the Narrative Story-Stem Technique

Age of Subjects

As noted earlier, the NSST was originally designed as a measure of preschool children's perceptions of attachment relationships, for children as young as 36 months. Since its inception, however, it has been used in published reports, with minor modifications, with children as old as 11.5 years (Granot and Mayseless 2001). At the extremes of this age range, developmental capabilities may be an important consideration in the use of the NSST. The youngest children must be capable of understanding and expressing themselves through the basic structure of narratives. Some children at the upper age limit may view the procedure as too childish. Others, even up to age 12, however, very willingly accept and respond well to the measure, especially those with developmental or social delays, as the majority of social work clientele often tends to be (Steve Farnfield, 2002, personal communication).

Basic Characteristics of the Story-Stem Protocol

While most children as young as three years old are capable of understanding and responding to simple narrative structures, they typically find this difficult to do purely on a verbal level (Mize and Ladd 1988). The NSST therefore presents its story stems with the aid of family figures and props to enable children to visualize the stories and manipulate the figures as they are enacted. There is some variation in the choice of props used by researchers, depending on the requirements of the individual stories used, but they generally consist of father and mother figures, a grandmother, two siblings the same gender as the study child, a friend of the child, and the family dog. Other props (e.g., car, furniture, etc.) are included as needed. It is important, however, that the props be very simply made. Elaborate or commercially recognizable props tend to distract the child away from the narrative and cause them to focus too much on the toy itself (Bretherton and Oppenheim 2003). Human-like figures are commonly used, as are animal figures such as bears (Page and Bretherton 2001) or pigs (Hodges et al. 2003). When human-like figures are used, many believe it is important that the race represented by the figures match the child participant's race. The story protocol is administered on a child-sized table big enough for the enactment of distance and vigorous activities, yet small enough for the child to sit comfortably and reach across when desired.

At the conclusion of the presentation of each story stem, the examiner asks the child to "Show me and tell me what happens now," encouraging the child to create a spontaneous narrative in reply. Each story stem contains an identified central problem or conflict, and standardized prompts are used to encourage the child to attend to this. In a story about the parents leaving for an overnight trip, for example, the child may be asked, "What do they (referring to the child figures) do now that the parents have gone?" A child's refusal to answer or avoidance of a story problem is considered a legitimate response, therefore a prompt to attend to a story problem will be used a maximum of only twice. If the child does not attend to the issue after two prompts, the response is taken as it is. The protocol is videotaped and the narrative response created by the child is coded for themes of interest (more on coding schemes in the following).

Selection of Story stems

The first version of the Narrative Story-Stem Technique was originally developed by Bretherton and colleagues. Their Attachment Story Completion Task (ASCT) (Bretherton, Ridgeway, and Cassidy 1990) consisted of five story stems portraying familiar problem situations that for most children would be likely to elicit attachment and/or care-giving behavior in child-parent relationships. (See Appendix 17.1 for a list of the story stems in the ASCT.)

Soon after this, Bretherton collaborated with other story-stem researchers who, with support from the MacArthur Foundation, created the MacArthur Story-Stem Battery (MSSB; Bretherton et al. 1990; Emde, Wolf, and Oppenheim 2003). The MSSB incorporated four of the five original stories of the ASCT, and added ten additional stories that represented diverse developmental themes such as moral decision-making, understanding of parental relationships, discipline, loss, and peer conflict (see Appendix 17.2). In recent years, researchers using this method have created additional story stems and modified the types of props to be more responsive to the specific experiences of their samples, including maltreated children (e.g., Hodges et al. 2003), children in middle childhood (Granot and Mayseless 2001), and children with internalizing disorders (Warren 2003a), while maintaining the essential features of the method. The stories that are selected for a protocol are chosen on the basis of the relevance of their themes to the research questions of interest. Bretherton and Oppenheim (2003) advise that any changes to existing narrative protocols should be described and pilot-tested carefully to maintain the integrity of the measure.

A Procedural Outline for the Administration of the NSST

As Bretherton and Oppenheim (2003) point out, the nature of rapport and interaction of examiner with child participant is the first major element in the successful administration of the NSST. It is very helpful if the examiner has some clinical experience working with children because the examiner role is very similar to therapeutic facilitation of the participant's personal expression. Story scripts should be memorized and delivered in as conversational a way as possible, using subtle encouragers, with moderate matching of affective response to the child's communication.

Prior to beginning the actual story protocol, the characters are introduced to the child individually, informing the child of the characters' names and relationships to the others. After this introduction, the examiner asks the child to repeat the names of each character in turn, reminding the child of any character's name that has not been remembered. This is followed by a general description of how the story protocol works (e.g., "I like to tell stories with my 'family', and the way this works is, I'll start a story and you get to finish it any way you want").

The story protocol begins with a warm-up story that is not coded. The purpose of this story is to introduce the method to the child, teaching the child how to manipulate the figures and create speech for them, and ensuring that the child in fact does this. Rarely, however, a child will be encountered who will not participate in the story protocol at all. A reasonable amount of time should be spent in teaching these children how to respond to the story stems, and encouraging them to do so, then moving on with the protocol. In a typical warm-up story stem, props consist of a table and a birthday cake that the mother has been baking. The mother invites the family to the table by saying, "C'mon everybody, let's have a birthday party!"

As the child tells his/her stories, the examiner can facilitate the process, and contribute to the accuracy of coding, by occasionally verbally noting the action (e.g., "He went high in a balloon!") or asking questions to clarify the action (e.g., "Now what's he doing?"). It is important to avoid providing interpretations of story responses, however; and that whenever comments are used to highlight a child's story enactments, they clearly reflect the child's intentions (see Bretherton and Oppenheim 2003).

Perhaps the most challenging aspect of administering the story stems is the judgment made about when the story has ended. Many children will end their stories very clearly and logically. Others, however, tell rambling and incoherent narratives, filled with unpredictable imagery. As a rule, the examiner pays attention to whether the central story problem has been addressed, and the point at which the child's story arrives at some sort of resolution. With experience, an examiner can help to bring a rambling story to a conclusion with the use of graduated responses, starting with "Is that the end of the story?" and moving to the more definite, "That was a good story, let me show you what I have for the next one."

The story protocol is typically concluded with a "wind-down" story that, like the initial warm-up story, is not coded. The purpose of this story is for the child to relax and disengage from the task. A typical wind-down story consists of saying that the family is going to "do something fun today" and asking the child to enact this, for which any of the props and figures may be used.

Overview of Coding the NSST

To date, there is no consensus about the most desirable coding system to use to interpret children's responses to the NSST. Three dimensions of coding, however, are commonly found among coding systems: Overall qualities of the characteristics of children's narratives, in terms of structure and process; specific types of content enacted within the stories; and qualities of the interactions between the child and the examiner (Page 2001a). Of course, some coding constructs will typically be applied a priori, particularly those that have been shown to be robust indicators of children's well-being and are consistent with the nature of the research questions. Others, however, will be derived after careful viewing of the children's story responses—fitting the coding system, to some extent, to the particular characteristics of the sample.

Robinson, Herot, Haynes, and Mantz-Simmons (2000) provide an example of how this process can occur. They studied the MSSB with a sample of African American children, a population that has been relatively overlooked in research with this method. One of their important methodological findings was that the children, especially boys, tended to portray much physical violence in their stories, and little reliance on help-seeking from adults to resolve conflict, characteristics in past research with mostly white participants that have been associated with less favorable adjustments (see Woolgar 1999; Page 2001a). They therefore modified their coding system to take these characteristics into account because they did not appear to be associated with the same social meaning as found in previously studied populations. At the same time, they also retained in their coding system several constructs that have been used widely in research with the NSST, such as "parent nurture."

In addition to culture, developmental considerations may also factor into the expected types and related meanings of story responses. Younger children tend to have parents intervene and solve problems more often, while older children tend to enact more autonomous solutions. Older children, of course, also demonstrate greater cognitive sophistication, as in understanding that the child's fear of a monster in the bedroom is imaginary (Bretherton and Oppenheim 2003). As Bretherton and Oppenheim point out, more research is needed with the NSST to further identify the ways in which children's story responses vary with developmental capacities.

Because the coding of the NSST is a flexible process that can allow for novel and idiosyncratic responses, researchers often collect a great many individual codes, at least in the first round of coding. The problem that this presents for data analysis is of course that any particular code must occur often enough, shared by a significant number of the children in the sample, if the intent of the research is to make meaningful comparisons among them. This means—inevitably—that no matter how much detail is observed that appears at face value to represent meaningful story responses, data reduction must be performed in some manner in order to derive variables that will be useful in quantitative analyses. This has been accomplished in some studies through simple conceptual groupings of codes (e.g., Page and Bretherton 2001), while others have used factor analysis (Woolgar et al. 2001; Steele, Hodges, Kaniuk, Hillman, and Henderson 2003).

The issue of the scale of coding units is also problematic with respect to the attempt to capture children's true intended meanings in their narratives. Page and Bretherton (2001) point out that the coding of narrative content themes should occur at a level that is small enough to capture discreet details of narrative compositions, yet large enough to reflect contextual meanings in narratives, so that the overall sense of the representation is captured. The meaning, for example, of a child's proximity-seeking to a parent is surely different, and of theoretical interest, when the parent subsequently rejects the child, compared to proximity-seeking that is followed by affection.

Representative Examples of NSST Coding Systems

The following discussion highlights representative coding systems with the NSST, but is not an exhaustive inventory of all systems. As noted previously, approaches to coding the NSST often vary with the specific research questions of interest. (A discussion of empirical findings discovered with these systems will follow here.) NSST coding may produce categorical or continuous variables. Because the NSST is an observational measure, inter-rater reliability of coding is an essential issue in its application, and most published coding systems report adequate, independent inter-rater reliabilities.

CATEGORICAL CLASSIFICATION SYSTEMS

The systems producing categorical variables are patterned to a great extent after the well-known attachment classifications discovered by Ainsworth and colleagues (1978) and Main and Solomon (1990) (i.e. secure, insecure-avoidant, insecure-ambivalent, and insecure-disorganized) (see coding systems by Cassidy 1988; Solomon, George, and DeJong 1995; Green, Stanley, Smith, and Goldwyn 2000; Granot and Mayseless 2001; and Gloger-Tippelt, Kappler, and Koenig 2010). A *secure/confident* classification was given by Cassidy (1988) to stories characterized by warm relationships, open negotiation, children's expression of attachment behavior toward the mother, and positive outcomes. *Avoidant* stories typically consisted of depictions of isolation and rejection of the children and minimization or denial of conflict or the need of help. Stories classified as *hostile/negative* typically contained portrayals of violent and/or bizarre imagery. Solomon, George, and DeJong

(1995) used a *confident* classification to represent narrative themes of danger and rescue that appeared along with representations of competent, autonomous child behavior. Their *busy* category of responses was typified by busy, happy moods, with abundant and irrelevant activity, with little sense of incorporation of any distress or direct acknowledgment of difficulty.

More recently, Granot and Mayseless (2001) integrated the three coding systems found in Bretherton, Ridgeway, and Cassidy (1990), Cassidy (1988), and Solomon, George, and DeJong (1995) to construct narrative-derived classifications that were patterned exactly to match attachment classifications based on infancy observational research: *Secure, avoidant, ambivalent,* and *disorganized.* Gloger-Tippelt and Koenig (2007) and Green, Stanley, and Peters (2007) also used the four-category attachment classification in their respective studies.

Continuous variables derived from the NSST have addressed a variety of developmental and social experience, including attachment organization. Bretherton, Ridgeway, and Cassidy (1990) coded children's responses to the five story stems of the ASCT protocol by first globally rating them on the basis of qualities such as directness and openness to the problem presented in the stem, benign problem resolution, portrayals of parents in caring roles, empathic concern, reasonable discipline, and child competence. These global ratings then provided the basis for a single "security score" rating on a four-point scale that was used in data analyses.

In a reanalysis of the Bretherton, Ridgeway, and Cassidy (1990) data, Waters, Rodrigues, and Ridgeway (1998) identified a priori standards for each story that represented optimal narrative resolutions (termed "ideal secure scripts") based on a theoretical model of secure attachment behavior and sensitive caregiving. Children's actual responses to the narratives were then sorted against these standard resolutions, and a numerical ranking was assigned on this basis for each child. This method accounted for unique variance in relation to a measure of children's attachment security.

The best known and most widely used of the NSST coding systems is the one developed by Robinson and associates for the MSSB (Robinson et al. 1992; 1995). Their coding system consists of themes related to the problems or conflicts presented in the MSSB stories, including interpersonal conflict, empathic relations, aggression, moral themes, and avoidant strategies. Each theme is counted as present or absent in each story and summed across stories, for a maximum possible score for each theme equal to the total number of coded stories. Additionally, performance codes are used that capture characteristics of the children's narratives such as intensity of affect, controlling behavior, degree of investment, and coherence (see Robinson and Mantz-Simmons 2003). Warren's Narrative Emotion Coding (NEC) (2003a) was introduced as a companion coding system to the Robinson et al. system, designed for their research on children's internalizing disorders. It focuses more on emotional expression portrayed in the narratives and on interactions with the examiner, recorded at specified points in each narrative.

Page and Bretherton (2001) used a theme-based approach similar to the Robinson et al. system, but included more specifically identified story protagonists, and summed frequencies of codes across stories, thus attempting to gain a greater level of precision.

This author summarized the existing NSST literature and synthesized coding systems based on continuous variables (Page 2001a). He noted that within the three major dimensions of coding found in studies with the NSST (narrative structure and process, narrative content, and interactive qualities between child and examiner), three commonly coded dimensions of narrative structure and process were apparent: Logic/coherence/benign resolution; moderate expression of emotion; and elaborateness of composition. At least six commonly coded narrative content themes were identified (each with positive and negative valences): Parent nurture; parent authoritative discipline; obedience to parent; openness of communication between child and parent; parent as source of protection/proximity seeking to parent; and competent/autonomous child. Three major interactive themes with the examiner were also identified: Engagement and directness of response to story; avoidance/non-engagement with story and/or digression; and the child's controlling behavior.

There are several examples of innovative coding systems developed more recently that reflect specific areas of research interest (e.g., Macfie, Cicchetti, and Toth 2001; Hill, Fonagy, Lancaster, and Broyden 2007; Davies, Woitach, Winter, and Cummings 2008; Page 2010). Macfie, Cicchetti, and Toth (2001) focused on dissociative processes of the child subject in the performance of story responses. Hill, Fonagy, Lancaster, and Broyden (2007) coded intentionality—the child's awareness of, and responsiveness to, the emotional and motivational experience of a relationship partner as communicated in the NSST. Davies, Woitach, Winter, and Cummings (2008) used three five-point scales to rate dimensions of children's representations of parental relationship qualities in their study of linkages among children's perceptions of parent conflict, attention problems, and school adjustment. Page (2010) created a coding system using three seven-point scales designed to conceptually match the attachment, exploratory, and caregiving behavioral systems identified by Bowlby (1982), in an attempt to achieve a parsimonious balance of conceptual breadth and brevity.

Summary of Empirical Findings: The NSST and Indices of Social Adjustment

Research with the NSST has been generally organized around two major foci: (1) Family characteristics and processes, including attachment organization and related constructs, and (2) social relationships outside the family. This body of research has demonstrated that, consistent with Bowlby's theory, NSST responses are predicted by the nature of attachment relationships and characteristics associated with the family caregiving environment; they are associated with a range of behavior in other social settings, particularly peer groups; and they represent intervening variables in pathways from family characteristics to children's social behavior.

Research with the NSST Addressing Attachment Organization and/or Characteristics of the Caregiving Environment

Among the first studies with the NSST that focused on linkages with measures of attachment, Bretherton, Ridgeway, and Cassidy (1990) found that children's story completions at 37 months were moderately correlated with attachment classifications at 18, 25, and 37 months (assessed at each time with different, validated attachment measures—the Strange Situation, Attachment Q-Sort, and Cassidy-Marvin Preschool Strange Situation Procedure, respectively; see Solomon and George [2008] for a discussion of these measures). Cassidy (1988) and Solomon, George, and DeJong (1995) found similar associations between attachment-derived classifications of children's responses to the NSST and a concurrent assessment of attachment in a laboratory separation-reunion procedure.

In a variation of the NSST that utilizes more dyadic parent-child interactions, a more limited number of story stems, more intense emotional expression in story stems, and props that include a dollhouse, the Manchester Child Attachment Story Task (MCAST; Green, Stanley, Smith, and Goldwyn 2000) codes children's narratives using four attachment classifications conceptually derived from observational attachment research with the Strange Situation. The authors found a distribution across attachment categories that closely mirrored distributions found for attachment classifications in community samples, and stability of these over approximately six months similar to stabilities of observed attachment classifications. Also using a four-category system for attachment classifications, Gloger-Tippelt, Kappler, and Koenig (2010) analyzed 19 samples from three European countries involving 803 children and showed, as predicted, that the distributions of the four attachment categories varied with children's risk level.

Associations between children's responses on the NSST and the attachment organization of their mothers (natural and adoptive) have been demonstrated. Steele, Steele et al. (2003) discovered longitudinal continuity between mothers' attachment organization assessed during pregnancy with the Adult Attachment Interview (AAI) and their children's NSST responses (specifically narrative representations of limit-setting by the mother figure) assessed when the children had attained the age of five. They also found children of insecure mothers tended to be more gender stereotypical in their NSST responses compared to children of secure mothers. Longitudinal associations have also been demonstrated for children's NSST representations, their parents' attachment security as assessed with the AAI one to two years earlier, and their attachment security assessed four to six years earlier in the Strange Situation (Gloger-Tippelt, Gomille, Koenig, and Vetter 2002).

In addition to the aforementioned studies of linkages between NSST enactments and measures of children's and/or their parents' attachment security, research has addressed attachment-related constructs assessed among children's caregivers. Given that attachment is conceptualized primarily as a relationship construct, attachment-promoting qualities associated with caregivers should be predictive of the qualities of children's internal working models of attachment relationships. Thus Oppenheim and colleagues (Oppenheim 2003) related MSSB responses to parental psychological distress, and Goodman, Aber, Berlin, and Brooks-Gunn (1998) related children's responses to the ASCT to maternal sensitive responding on a semistructured play task, observed in their homes. This study marked the first time that the central construct in attachment theory thought responsible for engendering secure attachments, caregiver sensitive responsiveness to children, was linked to a measure of children's internal working models of attachment relationships. This is also one of a small number of studies that has studied these questions among high-risk, urban, African American families.

Following related research paths investigating associations between NSST and the caregiving environment, Toth, Rogosch, Sturge-Apple, and Cicchetti (2009) reported that children's attachment security to their mothers, as assessed in the Strange Situation at 36 months, fully mediated the effect of maternal depression (assessed one year earlier) on increases in children's negative representations of parents, assessed at 48 months. Smeekens, Riksen-Walraven, Van Bakel, and de Weerth (2010) reported that ratings of insecurity of children's NSST responses were associated with higher levels of children's cortisol, but only for those who were observed to have displayed negative interactions with their parents during a structured discourse on emotions one week earlier.

Recently, research with the NSST has expanded to include direct, naturalistic observations of child-parent interactions in the home. Dubois-Comptois and Moss (2008) found that contemporaneous parent-child interactions observed in the home were better predictors of children's family representations in story completions than were mother-child interactions observed in the laboratory three years earlier. They found positive family interactions in the home to be associated with security indicators on the NSST, and certain problematic family interactions associated with indicators of attachment disorganization on the NSST.

Observations of caregiver interactions in home settings were also used by Poehlmann and colleagues (2008) in their study of children living with custodial grandmothers. They found that elevated depression in grandmothers was associated with children's NSST representations of family conflict, which in turn were associated with their behavior problems. Grandmothers' depression was not associated with children's behavior problems but behavior problems were associated with the quality of observed interactions in the home with grandmothers. This study thus suggests a possible pathway to behavior problems that includes custodial grandparent depression, poor interactions with grandparents, and children's representations of hostile caregiving environments.

CHILD MALTREATMENT

Of particular interest to social workers, perceptions of maltreated children have been assessed in several studies using the NSST. This work has also contributed significantly to the NSST literature by studying previously underrepresented families, particularly lower SES (socioeconomic status) and racial minorities. Several characteristics of the social perceptions of maltreated children have been illuminated by this research, among them: More aggression in their narratives (Buchsbaum et al. 1992); more negative and fewer positive representations of mothers and of children (Toth, Cicchetti, MacFie, and Emde 1997; Toth, et al. 2000); fewer representations of parents as authoritative disciplinarians (Toth et al. 2000); catastrophe and bizarrely frightening enactments (Hodges et al. 2003; Heller et al. 2006); parents responding less often to the distress of children (MacFie et al. 1999; Hodges et al. 2000); children responding less often to the distress of other children (MacFie et al. 1999); more grandiose representations of children (Toth et al. 2000; Hodges et al. 2003); and more frequent, sudden shifts of narrative character identity from good to bad and/or vice versa, suggesting confusion and conflict in integrating these internalized representations (Hodges et al. 2000; Toth et al. 2000). In addition to these differences in narrative content themes, maltreated children have been found to exhibit more controlling behavior and fewer pleasant interactions with NSST examiners (Toth, Cicchetti, MacFie, and Emde 1997; Toth et al. 2000).

Toth, Cicchetti, MacFie, and Emde (1997) were the first to examine qualities in children's NSST responses in relation to specific types of maltreatment. They found that physically abused children portrayed the mother and children in the NSST more negatively than other maltreated children and nonmaltreated controls; sexually abused children portrayed the child protagonist as positive more frequently than did neglected children; and physically and sexually abused children (but not neglected children) were more controlling and had fewer pleasant interactions with the examiner. In subsequent reports with these data, MacFie et al. (1999) found that abused children (physically and/or sexually) enacted more child-parent role-reversal in their stories, and Waldinger, Toth, and Gerber (2001) found that neglected children portrayed others as hurt, sad, or anxious more often than other maltreated and nonmaltreated groups.

In a longitudinal study with the NSST, Hodges et al. (2003) found that maltreated children in adoptive placements tended to portray adults more often as helpful and authoritative and more involved over the course of their one-year observation, yet as no less aggressive or rejecting and no more affectionate than at the time of their initial placement. Child figures were portrayed as more helpful and competent, and less grandiose over the course of the study. They suggest that changes in children's internal working models occur incrementally, not affecting perceptions equally or simultaneously.

Steele, Hodges, Kaniuk, Hillman, and Henderson (2003) assessed previously maltreated children and their adoptive mothers within the first three months of adoptive placement. They found that children of adoptive mothers with insecure attachment organizations, as assessed with the AAI, portrayed more enactments of aggression, inappropriate parental role behavior, child vulnerability, and bizarre content, and fewer enactments of child mastery and prosocial behavior toward siblings/peers on the NSST, compared to children whose adoptive mothers had secure attachment organizations. Regarded in the context of the wider literature on NSST representations among maltreated children, this study suggests that previously maltreated children adapt their internal working models of their caregiving environments rather rapidly as they encounter changes in their caregiving environments—in this case mothers' attachment organization.

Toth et al. (2002) moved this line of research further in a ground-breaking study of a randomized, controlled trial of an attachment-oriented intervention for maltreating parents. Following this 12-month intervention, co-occurring changes in parental caregiving and children's representations of caregiving were found as predicted. Children in the intervention condition created more positive representations of mother-child interactions on the NSST as their parents demonstrated improvement in sensitive understanding of their children, compared to two more skill-based intervention conditions and a control group. These findings are noteworthy for their potentially far-reaching implications for the assessment of family-based psychotherapy outcomes.

FAMILY VIOLENCE AND FAMILY CONFLICT

In one of few reported studies that has examined responses on the NSST enacted by children exposed to domestic violence, Grych, Wachsmuth-Schlaefer, and Klockow (2002) found that these children were more likely to enact stories with interparental conflict and fewer representations of positive mothers and children compared to controls. Children exposed to interparental violence were also more likely to enact incoherent stories and were more avoidant in their interactions with examiners. More recently, Minze, McDonald, Rosentraub, and Jouriles (2010) found that children's NSST responses, coded for story coherence, mediated a pathway from interparental violence to children's externalizing behavior problems, controlling for parent-child aggression.

Following the research thread of family conflict, Gloger-Tippelt and Koenig (2007) studied children living in postdivorce families in Germany and found that, in comparison to children in intact families, these children tended to create more NSST narratives classified as insecure versus secure. In contrast, Winter, Davies, Hightower, and Meyer (2006), utilizing a community sample, found no direct association between family discord and a security rating based on children's NSST responses. They did find, however, a mediated path between family discord, parent-child communication qualities such as affect and responsiveness, and children's NSST security ratings. Children who were exposed to family discord and whose parents (almost all were mothers) displayed high quality communication were the most likely to be rated as insecure on the NSST. They suggest that a deleterious effect of family discord on children's internal working models of families depends on whether or not parental communication style is congruent with children's experience with respect to exposure to family discord.

Correlates with Social Behavior in Relationships External to the Family

The utility of the NSST as a predictor of children's social behavior, as seen in some of the studies mentioned earlier, is another major area of inquiry. Much of this research focuses specifically on children's social adjustment in schools, as reported by their teachers. The assessment of social behavior problems in studies with the NSST has been conducted for the most part with survey measures such as the Child Behavior Checklist (CBCL; Achenbach and Edelbrock 1983). Several studies have identified linkages between children's narrative enactments with the NSST, particularly aggression, bizarre themes, and structural incoherence, and externalizing behavior on the CBCL (Solomon, George, and DeJong 1995; Ramos-Marcuse and Arsenio 2001). Von Klitzing et al. (2000) found similar associations over the course of two years, from children ages five to seven. They also found that NSST representations of aggression occurred more frequently in boys, consistent with gender stereotypes. Warren, Oppenheim, and Emde (1996) found that distress displayed in NSST responses (in representations of children or by the participant child) and destructive themes enacted in narratives were related to externalizing CBCL scores. These findings were more consistent for older (four- and five-year-old) children than three-year-olds.

Granot and Mayseless (2001) found associations between their NSST attachment classifications and teacher-reported externalizing and internalizing scores on the CBCL. Furthermore, they reported significant associations of NSST classifications and a measure of adjustment (scholastic, emotional, and social) to the school environment.

Warren (2003b) also reported linkages between some types of NSST responses and parent and teacher CBCL internalizing scores. This study used an aggregate variable composed of portrayals of child incompetence, absence of attachment behavior, role reversal, difficulty with separations with denial of negative affect, and negative story endings.

In the first study of the NSST with children in postdivorce families living in the custody of mothers, Page and Bretherton (2001) found that representations of the mother as nurturing, children's attachment behavior toward the mother, the mother as endangered, and the father as providing authoritative discipline were associated in predicted directions with social behavior with peers in preschool settings, as rated by teachers on inventories of social competence and behavior problems. This study also found that child gender moderated some relationships between NSST responses and social competence. Additional analyses (Page and Bretherton 2003) suggest that behavior represented in narratives typically associated with gender stereotypes (e.g., aggression and boys, empathic responsiveness and girls) may have particular significance for social adjustment when these representations are expressed by the *opposite* gender. More study of these questions is clearly needed, however.

In a longitudinal study of 154 primarily Swiss-German children, Stadelmann, Perren, Groeben, and von Klitzing (2010) investigated the role played by children's internal representations, as measured with the NSST, in the development of behavior problems (aggregated child, parent, and teacher reports). Children living in single-parent homes as a result of separation or divorce were compared to children in intact, two-parent homes. The sample represented a mix of community and clinic-referred children. They found an important interaction effect, where conduct problems were highest and increased the most between ages five and six for children living with separated parents *and* who demonstrated more negative parental representations on the NSST. They suggest that the effect of circumstances associated with parental separation on the development of conduct problems are moderated by children's internal representations of parental caregiving.

Green, Stanley, and Peters (2007) investigated cross-sectional associations between narrative representations, using the MCAST, and children's attention problems in schools. They found that children classified as insecure-disorganized on the MCAST were more likely to also be clinically diagnosed with ADHD. Further, NSST disorganization was also found to be associated with mothers' high Expressed Emotion (EE; hostile, critical comments, and emotional overinvolvement), which itself was associated with mothers' depression. Finally, NSST disorganization, mothers' depression, and ADHD diagnosis were each associated with children's behavioral problems as reported by mothers.

Following a similar line of research, Davies, Woitach, Winter, and Cummings (2008) used an adapted version of the NSST of only three story stems, each depicting some sort of interparental conflict, to explore the role of children's representations of parental relationship qualities in the emergence of attention problems. Their model showed that over the course of two years, children's attention problems partially mediated the influence of NSST representations of parent interactions on behavior with peers and teachers in school settings. They conclude that "attention problems may develop from elevated concerns about security in the interparental relationship and, in turn, undermine children's functioning in the face of challenges arising in other settings" (1578).

Recently, considerable attention has been brought to the question of the utility of narrative story-stem methods for clinical assessment and intervention. A 2007 issue of *Attachment and Human Development* was a response to this interest, where several original contributions documented the utility of NSST protocols for assessments of social problems indicative of adjustment problems and potential mental health risk, including mood disorders (Belden, Sullivan, and Luby 2007; Beresford, Robinson, Holmberg, and Ross 2007) and conduct disorders (Hill, Fonagy, Lancaster, and Broyden 2007). Beresford and colleagues (2007) provided a rare level of detail in their analyses by examining specific story effects. They found NSST associations with reported manic symptoms in preschool children for what they referred to as "high-challenge" story stems (with relatively intense portrayed distress) compared to "lower-challenge stories."

In a smaller body of research, the NSST has also been used to demonstrate that children as young as three are capable of understanding and resolving moral dilemmas, contradicting beliefs based in psychoanalytic and Piagetian theories that posited the emergence of such capacities at later ages (Oppenheim, Emde, Hasson, and Warren 1997). Additionally, Woolgar et al. (2001) found that NSST representations of maternal nonphysical punishment related to accurate emotion attributions in a story task involving a child stealing candy and confessing to their mother, suggesting that such narrative representations reflect children's moral understandings in other contexts.

Taken together, this body of research has begun to illuminate the place of children's representational processes, through which children interpret and organize their relational experiences, as an important dimension of their development within an interpersonal regulatory system that includes caregiver well-being, qualities of care provided, interparental conflict, children's physiological stress response, developing emotional security, and social adjustment. While a surprising amount has been discovered about these developmental linkages and the prominent place of children's representational experience within them, much remains to be discovered about the perceptions of qualities of close relationships that the NSST can reliably and validly assess. An important part of this research includes new studies with diverse story-stem content. To reiterate, the NSST refers to a global method within which diverse protocols composed of different story stems exist. Learning more about the differential, specific correlates of these diverse protocols remains an important direction for future work.

Qualitative Analyses

Beyond the quantitative analyses used for group-level comparisons, the NSST provides rich opportunities to directly examine children's social perceptions at the qualitative level. All studies with the NSST are enriched by the inclusion of this type of data, examples of which are provided here.

Page (2001b) compared the narrative content of three consecutive stories created by four children, each of whom enacted a high level of attachment behavior toward the mother in their narratives (this type of enactment was previously associated with prosocial behavior with peers; Page and

Bretherton 2001). The children were distinguished on the basis of social competence ratings, on which one boy and one girl were rated very high, and one boy and one girl were rated very low. From this analysis, a typology of narrative themes was derived that was identified with the high competence children, including: Simplicity, predictability, and positive resolution; parents as nurturers and role models; mutuality across relationships and reliable surrogate caregivers; responsiveness of parents toward children's activated attachment behavior; moderate expression of unpleasant emotion; and problem resolution through competence-building and repetition. Characteristics of the low-competence children's narratives included ambivalence toward attachment figures and parental isolation and exclusion.

The following is an example of the use of raw data collected with the NSST (reported previously in Heller et al. 2006) that shows the power of this instrument to illuminate the personal perceptions of children, inviting us to wonder about how experience has shaped this child's beliefs and emotions about her relational world. "Mary" is an eight-year-old, white female. The excerpt is a verbatim transcription of her response to the second section of the Bathroom Shelf story from the MSSB (see Appendix 17.2) (E = Examiner, S = Subject).

E: And the mom comes back. Here's mom back from the neighbor's.

S: And she goes in the bathroom and she said, "Why did you get a towel off the cabinet? I told you they have them in the laundry."

S: (Jane, younger child, replying) She said, "I don't know."

S: (mother) "Now clean the towel up." (Jane complies by putting the imaginary towel back on the shelf.)

S: Dad said, "I'm gonna use the bathroom." (S sets father on the toilet) Flushes the toilet, then it starts to flood.

E: It starts to flood.

S: Everybody gets out . . .

E: (per standard prompt for this part of the story) And mom asks Jane, "Jane, how did you get a bandaid on your finger?"

S: (Jane replies) "Dad went to the store and bought me one, 'cause I cut my finger."

S: Then (S takes Susan, the older sister, in hand) the sister was smoking and she left the cigarette on the ground and the house burned down. (S moves all off to the side)

E: She was smoking a cigarette, left it on the ground, and the house burned down.

Assessing Young Children's Perceptions of Family Relationships

s: (mother appears to ask) "What happened, y'all?"

s: (Jane appears to reply) "Oh, I don't know, but sister was smoking."

s: (mother) "Daughter, what have you been doing (unintell.)?"

s: (Jane complains to mother) "Now mommy, she made my toys get on fire. Mommy, could you buy me a new toy?"

s: (mother) "Yes, sweetie, at the toy store." (S moves all on table)

s: She, um, fireman (unintell.)

E: What did the firemen do?

s: Came and put the fire out.

E: Oh, I see.

s: She went to buy her a toy (moves all across the table), a Barbie, and she (refers to Susan) didn't get nothing.

E: Who got nothing?

s: She (holds Susan) didn't.

s: And for smoking, she died. (lays Susan down)

E: Oh, she died because she was smoking.

s: Yes. And they're at the funeral. (holds father, mother, Jane in front of Susan)

s: (moves father, mother, Jane across table) And they got a new house.

E: Got a new house.

s: And they had another daughter (stands Susan up with the rest, now apparently as "new" daughter).

s: So she died (takes Jane and sets her apart from the others) but she wasn't smoking. Then they had another daughter (now sets Jane back with the rest, apparently as another "new" daughter) and that would be her.

E: But she (pointing to Jane) died too?

s: (nods and smiles) She had another daughter, she had two more daughters.

E: Two more daughters.

s: Now they have a happy family (holds all in hand) . . . happy ever after.

Mary's history included severe maltreatment as an infant and multiple foster home placements, until finally settling in the home of an aunt and uncle. In infancy, Mary and her parents received intensive therapeutic services. At eighteen months, she was determined to have a dissociative disorder and disorganized attachment. At the time of the NSST assessment, her aunt and uncle were going through a divorce. Mary was also assessed at this time in the clinical range of the delinquent behavior sub-scale of the CBCL.

We see several important characteristics of Mary's narrative excerpt that illustrate many of the coding issues discussed previously. First, there are numerous frightening images that appear seemingly out of context, in an incoherent way. Other incoherent events appear, such as the father using the toilet and it flooding. Children's deviant behavior in the form of smoking is presented, and this leads to the destruction of the home and the death of the children. The mother's sweet response to buying more toys, and the focus on a new Barbie, is out of place with the other events, as is of course the reported happy ending. The transformation of the children is curious. While this is a positive resolution of sorts, it is far from a realistic solution to an everyday problem. The problem she creates (recall that the original story only poses the problem of how to address the child's cut finger) is no less than the death of the children, through the misdeeds of the older child. The replacement of the children suggests that new lives have been created (one cannot help but wonder about this as a metaphor for her own past caregiving history), yet she is clearly telling us that catastrophe is a constant and real possibility.

Implications for Social Work Practice and Research

Social work practitioners and researchers who work with young children should familiarize themselves with the NSST as a method that can assess children's perceptions of their relational worlds. As increasing numbers of social workers use attachment theory and its research for assessment and intervention, the value of NSST for social work researchers and practitioners should be evident. It should be clear from the review presented here that the NSST can contribute vital information about the issues involving vulnerable children about which social workers are most concerned, including the formation of attachment security, maltreatment, interparental violence, social behavior, school adjustment, psychopathology, and moral awareness. Assessment instruments for young children that are conducted from the child's point of view are rare. The NSST has taken this field into new directions, becoming an essential part of these efforts. As more social workers learn about and use this technology with their client populations, many more discoveries concerning the meaning of children's perceptions of their relational worlds are bound to occur.

Appendix 17.1

The Attachment Story Completion Task

1. Spilled Juice	The younger child accidentally spills juice at the dinner table.
2. Hurt Knee	The children and the parents go to the park; the younger child hurts his/her knee trying to climb a high rock.
3. Monster in the Bedroom	The mother tells the younger child to go to bed. The child goes to the bedroom, and then calls out that there is a monster in the bedroom.
4. Departure	The parents leave for an overnight trip; the grandmother babysits.
5. Reunion	The parents return from their overnight trip.

Source: Bretherton, Ridgeway, and Cassidy 1990

Appendix 17.2

The MacArthur Story-Stem Battery

1. Spilled Juice	The younger child accidentally spills juice at the dinner table.
2. Family Dog Lost/Reunion	The child goes outside to play with the family dog and discovers it is missing; then the dog returns.
3. Mom's Headache	The mother asks for quiet because of her headache; a friend comes to visit and asks to watch television.
4. Gift to Mom/Dad	The child brings home a beautiful picture made in preschool; to whom, Mom or Dad, will he/she give it?
5. Three's a Crowd	The two siblings play in their wagon; a friend arrives and demands that the younger child be excluded.
6. Hot Gravy	The mother warns the child not to get close to the stove; the child, impatient, reaches for the cooking food and burns his/her hand.
7. Lost Keys	The parents argue about missing car keys as the child watches.
8. Stealing Candy	The child, at the store with the mother, secretly steals candy.
9. Departure	The parents leave for an overnight trip; the grandmother babysits.

The parents return from their overnight trip.

10. Reunion	The parents return from their overnight trip.
11. Bathroom Shelf	The mother leaves the children alone, warning them not to touch the bathroom shelf; in her brief absence one cuts his/her finger; the mother returns.
12. Hurt Knee	The children and the parents go to the park; the younger child hurts his/her knee trying to climb a high rock.
13. Exclusion	The parents ask the child to go to his/her room so they can have "some time alone."
14. Cookie Jar	The child takes a cookie, despite the mother's prohibition, and asks the sibling not to tell.

Source: Emde, Wolf, and Oppenheim 2003

References

Achenbach T. M. and C. Edelbrock. 1983. *Manual for the Child Behavior Checklist and Revised Child Behavior Profile.* Burlington: University of Vermont.

Ainsworth, M. D. S., M. C. Blehar, E. Waters, and S. Wall. 1978. *Patterns of attachment: A psychological study of the strange situation.* Hillsdale, NJ: Erlbaum.

Anastas, J. W. 1999. *Research design for social work and the human services,* 2nd ed. New York: Columbia UP.

Ashford, J. B., C. W. LeCroy, and K. L. Lortie. 2001. *Human behavior in the social environment: A multidimensional perspective.* Belmont CA: Wadsworth/Thompson.

Belden, A., J. Sullivan, and J. Luby. 2007. Depressed and healthy preschoolers' internal representations of their mothers' caregiving: Associations with observed caregiving behaviors one year later. *Attachment* and *Human Development,* 9:239–254.

Beresford, C., J. L. Robinson, J. Holmberg, and R. G. Ross. 2007. Story stem responses of preschoolers with mood disturbances. *Attachment and Human Development,* 9:255–270.

Bowlby, J. 1973. *Attachment and loss,* Vol. II: *Separation: Anxiety and anger.* New York: Basic.

——. 1982. *Attachment and loss,* Vol. I: *Attachment,* 2nd ed. New York: Basic.

Bretherton, I., and K. A. Munholland. 2008. Internal working models in attachment relationships: Elaborating a central construct in attachment theory. In *Handbook of attachment: Theory, research, and clinical applications,* 2nd ed., J. Cassidy and P.R. Shaver, eds. 102–127. New York: Guilford.

Bretherton, I. and D. Oppenheim. 2003. The MacArthur Story Stem Battery: Development, administration, reliability, validity and reflections about meaning. In *Revealing the inner worlds of young children: The MacArthur Story Stem Battery and parent-child narratives*, R. N. Emde, D. P. Wolf, and D. Oppenheim, eds. 55–80. New York: Oxford UP.

Bretherton, I., D. Oppenheim, H. Buchsbaum, R. Emde, and the MacArthur Narrative Group. (1990). "The MacArthur story-stem battery." Unpublished manual, University of Wisconsin-Madison.

Bretherton, I., D. Ridgeway, and J. Cassidy. 1990. Assessing the internal working models of the attachment relationship: An attachment story completion task for 3-year-olds. In *Attachment in the preschool years: Theory, research, and intervention*, M.T. Greenberg, D. Cicchetti, and E.M. Cummings, eds. 273–308. Chicago: University of Chicago.

Buchsbaum, H. K., S. L. Toth, R. B. Clyman, D. Cicchetti, and R. N. Emde. 1992. The use of a narrative story stem technique with maltreated children: Implications for theory and practice. *Development and Psychopathology*, 4:603–625.

Cassidy, J. 1988. Child-mother attachment and the self in six-year-olds. *Child Development*, 59:121–134.

——. 2008. The nature of the child's ties. In *Handbook of attachment: Theory, research, and clinical applications*, 2nd ed., J. Cassidy and P.R. Shaver, eds. 3–22. New York: Guilford.

Davies, P. T., M. J. Woitach, M. A. Winter, and E. M. Cummings. 2008. Children's insecure representations of the interparental relationship and their school adjustment: The mediating role of attention difficulties. *Child Development*, 79:1570–1582.

Dubois-Comtois, K. and E. Moss. 2008. Beyond the dyad: Do family interactions influence children's attachment representations in middle childhood? *Attachment and Human Development*, 10:415–431.

Emde, R. N., D. P. Wolf, and D. Oppenheim, eds. 2003. *Revealing the inner worlds of young children: The MacArthur Story Stem Battery and parent-child narratives*. New York: Oxford UP.

Farmer-Dougan, V. and T. Kaszuba. 1999. Reliability and validity of play-based observations: Relationships between the PLAY behavior observation system and standardized measures of cognitive and social skills. *Educational Psychology*, 19:429–440.

Farnfield, S. December 5, 2002. Personal communication.

Fivush, R. 1993. Emotional content of parent-child conversations about the past. In *Memory and affect in development*, C.A. Nelson, ed. 39–77. Hillsdale, NJ: Lawrence Erlbaum.

Gloger-Tippelt, G., B. Gomille, L. Koenig, and J. Vetter, J. 2002. Attachment representations in 6-year-olds: Related longitudinally to the quality of attachment in infancy and mothers' attachment representations. *Attachment and Human Development*, 4:318–339.

Gloger-Tippelt, G., G. Kappler, and L. Koenig. (2010). "Narratives of attachment in children from clinical and non-clinical samples: Distributions of attachment groups and gender-specific effects." Poster presentation at the 12th biannual conference of the World Association of Infant Mental Health. Leipzig.

Gloger-Tippelt, G. and L. Koenig. 2007. Attachment representations in 6-year-old children from one and two parent families in Germany. *School Psychology International*, 28:313–330.

Goodman, G., J. L. Aber, L. Berlin, and J. Brooks-Gunn. 1998. The relations between maternal behaviors and urban preschool children's internal working models of attachment security. *Infant Mental Health Journal*, 19:378–393.

Granot, D. and O. Mayseless. 2001. Attachment security and adjustment to school in middle childhood. *International Journal of Behavioural Development*, 25:530–541.

Green, J., C. Stanley, and S. Peters. 2007. Disorganized attachment representations and atypical parenting in young school age children with externalizing disorder. *Attachment and Human Development*, 9:207–222.

Green, J., C. Stanley, V. Smith, and R. Goldwyn. 2000. A new method of evaluating attachment representations in young school-age children: The Manchester Child Attachment Story Task. *Attachment and Human Development*, 2:48–70.

Grych, J. H., T. Wachsmuth-Schlaefer, and L. L. Klockow. 2002. Interparental aggression and young children's representations of family relationships. *Journal of Family Psychology*, 16:259–272.

Heller, S. S., N.W. Boris, S. Hinshaw-Fuselier, T. Page, N. Koren-Karie, and D. Miron. 2006. Reactive attachment disorder in maltreated twins follow-up: From 18 months to 8 years. *Attachment and Human Development*, 8:63–86.

Hill, J., P. Fonagy, G. Lancaster, and N. Broyden. 2007. Aggression and intentionality in narrative responses to conflict and distress story stems: An investigation of boys with disruptive behaviour problems. *Attachment and Human Development*, 9:223–237.

Hodges, J., M. Steele, S. Hillman, K. Henderson, and J. Kaniuk. 2003. Changes in attachment representations over the first year of adoptive placement: Narratives of maltreated children. *Clinical Child Psychology and Psychiatry*, 8:347–363.

Hodges, J., M. Steele, S. Hillman, K. Henderson, and M. Neil. 2000. Effects of abuse on attachment representations: Narrative assessments of abused children. *Journal of Child Psychotherapy*, 26:433–455.

Macfie, J., D. Cicchetti, and S. L. Toth. 2001. The development of dissociation in maltreated preschool-aged children. *Development and Psychopathology*, 13:233–254.

MacFie, J., S. L. Toth, F. A. Rogosch, J. Robinson, R. N. Emde, and D. Cicchetti. 1999. Effect of maltreatment on preschoolers' narrative representations of responses to relieve distress and of role reversal. *Developmental Psychology*, 35:460–465.

Main, M., N. Kaplan, and J. Cassidy. 1985. Security in infancy, childhood, and adulthood: A move to the level of representation. In "Growing points of attachment theory and research," I. Bretherton and E. Waters, eds. *Monographs of the Society for Research in Child Development*, 50(1–2, Serial No. 209):66–104.

Main, M. and J. Solomon. 1990. Procedures for identifying infants as disorganized/disoriented during the Ainsworth Strange Situation. In *Attachment in the preschool years: Theory, research, and intervention*, M.T. Greenberg, D. Cicchetti, and E.M. Cummings, eds. 121–160. Chicago: University of Chicago.

Minze, L.C., R. McDonald, E. L. Rosentraub, and E. N. Jouriles. 2010. Making sense of family conflict: Intimate partner violence and preschoolers' externalizing problems. *Journal of Family Psychology*, 24:5–11.

Mize, J. and G.W. Ladd. 1988. Predicting preschoolers' peer behavior and status from their interpersonal strategies: A comparison of verbal and enactive responses to hypothetical social dilemmas. *Developmental Psychology*, 24:782–788.

Morris, R. J. and T. R. Kratochwill. 1998. Childhood fears and phobias. In *The practice of child therapy*, 3rd ed., R.J. Morris and T.R. Kratochwill, eds. 91–131. Needham Heights, MA: Allyn and Bacon.

Murray, L., M. Woolgar, S. Briers, and A. Hipwell. 1999. Children's social representations in dolls' house play and theory of mind tasks, and their relation to family adversity and child disturbance. *Social Development*, 8:179–200.

Oppenheim, D. 2003. Children's emotional resolution of MSSB narratives: Relations with child behavior problems and parental psychological distress. In *Revealing the inner worlds of young children: The MacArthur Story Stem Battery and parent-child narratives*, R. N. Emde, D. P. Wolf, and D. Oppenheim, eds. 147–162. New York: Oxford UP.

Oppenheim, D., R. N. Emde, M. Hasson, and S. Warren. 1997. Preschoolers face moral dilemmas: A longitudinal study of acknowledging and resolving internal conflict. *International Journal of Psychoanalysis*, 78:943–957.

Page, T. 2001a. The social meaning of children's narratives: A review of the attachment-based narrative story stem technique. *Child and Adolescent Social Work Journal*, 18:171–187.

——. 2001b. Attachment themes in the family narratives of preschool children: A qualitative analysis. *Child and Adolescent Social Work Journal*, 18:353–375.

——. (2010). "Attachment-related narrative representations enacted by high-risk children: Associations with their social-emotional adjustments." Paper presented in the symposium Play Narratives of Young Children from Different Cultures and Diverse Backgrounds, at the 12th biannual conference of the World Association of Infant Mental Health, Leipzig.

Page, T. and I. Bretherton. 2001. Mother- and father-child attachment themes in the story completions of preschoolers from postdivorce families: Do they predict relationships with peers and teachers? *Attachment and Human Development,* 3:1–29.

——. 2003. Gender differences in stories of violence and caring by preschool children in postdivorce families: Implications for social competence. *Child and Adolescent Social Work Journal,* 20:485–508.

Poehlmann, J., J. Park, L. Bouffiou, J. Abrahams, R. Shlafer, and E. Hahn. 2008. Representations of family relationships in children living with custodial grandparents. *Attachment and Human Development,* 10:165–188.

Ramos-Marcuse, F. and W. F. Arsenio. 2001. Young children's emotionally-charged moral narratives: Relations with attachment and behavior problems. *Early Education and Development,* 12:165–184.

Robinson, J., C. Herot, P. Haynes, and L. Mantz-Simmons. 2000. Children's story stem responses: A measure of program impact on developmental risks associated with dysfunctional parenting. *Child Abuse and Neglect,* 24:99–110.

Robinson J. and L. Mantz-Simmons. 2003. The MacArthur Narrative Coding System: One approach to highlighting affective meaning making in the MacArthur Story Stem Battery. In *Revealing the inner worlds of young children: The MacArthur Story Stem Battery and parent-child narratives,* R. N. Emde, D. P. Wolf, and D. Oppenheim, eds. 81–91. New York: Oxford UP.

Robinson, J., L. Mantz-Simmons, J. MacFie, and the MacArthur Narrative Working Group. (1992, 1995). "Narrative coding manual." Unpublished scoring system. Denver, CO: University of Colorado Health Sciences Center.

Schaefer, C. and K. O'Connor, eds. 1983. *Handbook of play therapy.* New York: John Wiley.

Smeekens, S., J. M. Riksen-Walraven, H. J. A. Van Bakel, and C. de Weerth. 2010. Five-year-olds' cortisol reactions to an attachment story completion task. *Psychoneuroendocrinology,* 35:858—865.

Solomon, J. and C. George. 2008. The measurement of attachment security and related constructs in infancy and childhood. In *Handbook of attachment: Theory, research, and clinical applications,* 2nd ed. J. Cassidy and P. Shaver, eds. 383–416. New York: Guilford.

Solomon, J., C. George, and A. DeJong. 1995. Children classified as controlling at age six: Evidence of disorganized representational strategies and aggression at home and school. *Development and Psychopathology,* 7:447–463.

Sroufe, L. A. and J. Fleeson. 1986. Attachment and the construction of relationships. In *Relationships and development,* W. Hartup and Z. Rubin, eds. 51–71. Hillsdale, NJ: Lawrence Erlbaum.

Stadelmann, S., S. Perren, M. Groeben, and K. von Klitzing. 2010. Parental separation and children's behavioral/emotional problems: The impact of parental representations and family conflict. *Family Process,* 49:92–108.

Steele, M., J. Hodges, J. Kaniuk, S. Hillman, and K. Henderson. 2003. Attachment representations and adoption: Associations between maternal states of mind and emotion narratives in previously maltreated children. *Journal of Child Psychotherapy*, 29:187–205.

Steele, M., H. Steele, M. Woolgar, S. Yabsley, P. Fonagy, D. Johnson, and C. Croft. 2003. An attachment perspective on children's emotion narratives: Links across generations. In *Revealing the inner worlds of young children: The MacArthur Story Stem Battery and parent-child narratives*, R. N. Emde, D. P. Wolf, and D. Oppenheim, eds. 163–181. New York: Oxford UP.

Toth, S.L., D. Cicchetti, J. MacFie, and R. N. Emde. 1997. Representations of self and other in the narratives of neglected, physically abused, and sexually abused preschoolers. *Development and Psychopathology*, 9:781–796.

Toth, S. L., D. Cicchetti, J. MacFie, A. Maughan, and K. VanMeenen. 2000. Narrative representations of caregivers and self in maltreated pre-schoolers. *Attachment and Human Development*, 2:271–305.

Toth, S. L., A. Maughan, J. Todd-Manly, M. Spagnola, and D. Cicchetti. 2002. The relative efficacy of two interventions in altering maltreated preschool children's representational models: Implications for attachment theory. *Development and Psychopathology*, 14:877–908.

Toth, S. L., F. A. Rogosch, M. Sturge-Apple, and D. Cicchetti. 2009. Maternal depression, children's attachment security, and representational development: An organizational perspective. *Child Development*, 80:192–208.

von Klitzing, K., K. Kelsay, R. N. Emde, J. Robinson, and S. Schmitz. 2000. Gender-specific characteristics of 5-year-olds' play narratives and associations with behavior ratings. *Journal of the American Academy of Child and Adolescent Psychiatry*, 39:1017–1023.

Waldinger, R. J., S. L. Toth, and A. Gerber. 2001. Maltreatment and internal representations of relationships: Core relationship themes in the narratives of abused and neglected preschoolers. *Social Development*, 10:41–58.

Warren, S. L. 2003a. Narrative Emotion Coding System (NEC). In *Revealing the inner worlds of young children: The MacArthur Story Stem Battery and parent-child narratives*, R. N. Emde, D. P. Wolf, and D. Oppenheim, eds. 92–105. New York: Oxford UP.

——. 2003b. Narratives in risk and clinical populations. In *Revealing the inner worlds of young children: The MacArthur Story Stem Battery and parent-child narratives*, R. N. Emde, D. P. Wolf, and D. Oppenheim, eds. 222–239. New York: Oxford UP.

Warren, S. L., D. Oppenheim, and R. N. Emde. 1996. Can emotions and themes in children's play predict behavior problems? *American Academy of Child and Adolescent Psychiatry*, 34:1331–1337.

Waters, H. S., L. M. Rodrigues, and D. Ridgeway. 1998. Cognitive underpinnings of narrative attachment assessment. *Journal of Experimental Child Psychology,* 71:211–234.

Winter, M. A., P. T. Davies, A. D. Hightower, and S. C. Meyer. 2006. Relations among family discord, caregiver communication, and children's family representations. *Journal of Family Psychology,* 20:348–351.

Woolgar, M. 1999. Projective doll play methodologies for preschool children. *Child Psychology and Psychiatry Review,* 4:126–134.

Woolgar, M., H. Steele, M. Steele, S. Yabsley, and P. Fonagy. 2001. Children's play narrative responses to hypothetical dilemmas and their awareness of moral emotions. *British Journal of Developmental Psychology,* 19:115–128.

18

Parenting and Child Neglect Among Families in Urban Poverty

A Qualitative Approach

LAURA FRAME

Much of qualitative research relies on a researcher's ability to balance flexibility and adaptiveness with organization and clarity of purpose. Each of these skills is likely to be challenged in the process of conducting an in-depth qualitative study. This chapter describes the methods used to collect and analyze qualitative data for a study of parenting in very low-income families. It focuses on the relationship between data collection and analysis, and illustrates in detail the process used to answer some of the key research questions.

The larger study of which this research is a part had two separate but related purposes. The primary purpose of the study, the findings of which are discussed in this chapter, was to develop a conceptual model that would account for the role of poverty in the problem of child neglect, in ways that existing theoretical models do not (Frame 2001). The second purpose of the research was to understand the experience of families' simultaneous involvement in the welfare and child welfare systems, during the early years of welfare reform, and was intended to describe some pathways between welfare and child welfare involvement, identifying key mediating factors between them. These findings are reported elsewhere (Frame and Berrick 2003). In the analysis process, the findings related to each question informed the other—and the study became a more seamless whole.

Qualitative methods were used to answer the research questions, and the data collection and analysis process was a decidedly nonlinear one.

It involved defining my questions, spending time with study subjects, reviewing the data I had collected along with the literature and then refining my questions, and returning to the field with a more focused lens with which to capture my topics of interest. Several key moments of "aha!" during data collection inspired me and led to an integration of ideas; these, along with a set of sensitizing concepts from the literature, generated new and more focused questions. Many long hours of painstaking review of the interview transcripts tested my method as it developed, and conversations with colleagues clarified my thinking over time. Ultimately, the data analysis integrated an inductively-derived description of urban poverty and its effects—a microanalytic study of parent-child interaction, and a process- and content-based analysis of parental narratives related to parenting. It took two-and-a-half years to collect and analyze the data for this study and to write it up. This chapter describes key parts of that process.

Parenting in Conditions of Urban Poverty Study

In the literature on child maltreatment, poverty is consistently noted for its strong link to child neglect (Nelson, Saunders and Landsman 1993; Gelles 1999), but this relationship has not been adequately explained (Vondra 1993; Crittenden 1999; Slack, Holl, McDaniel, Yoo, and Bolger 2004). Theory and research focused on explaining child neglect have generally fallen into three categories: psychological, sociological, and ecological. Parental mental health has long occupied a central focus of attention in the child maltreatment field (e.g., Polansky, Chalmers, Buttenweiser, and Williams 1981), but explanatory models of neglect that emphasize parental psychopathology have not sufficiently accounted for the role of contextual factors such as poverty. Some more recent models usefully focus on the role of parental information processing (Crittenden 1993, 1999) and deficits in parental empathy (DePaul and Guibert 2008), but again do not specifically incorporate this apparently central risk factor. Explanatory models of neglect that emphasize the role of socioeconomic conditions (e.g., Pelton 1981) are useful in their attention to the real constraints of poverty status, but have limited power to explain the considerable variability in parenting quality among poor families. The more complex ecological/transactional models of parenting and child maltreatment (e.g., Belsky and Vondra 1989) incorporate both psychological and contextual factors but do more to describe the association between economic hardship and neglectful parenting than to explain their co-occurrence. These conceptual limitations influence the design of interventions with neglecting families, and new approaches to understanding child neglect and child poverty are needed. In this study, I sought to develop an integrative explanatory model of child neglect that would propose some pathways between poverty conditions and neglectful parenting, and allow for variability among poor families and neglecting families. In particular, this study asked the question: In the context of urban poverty, how does a parent's subjective experience of their socioeconomic conditions affect their capacity to provide care and protection to an infant or toddler?

Methodology

This was a longitudinal, qualitative study conducted soon after the implementation of welfare reform in one California county. The research was designed to intensively study multiple families over a one- to two-year period, using a theoretical (Strauss and Corbin 1990) or purposive (Padgett 1998, 2008) sampling strategy that would represent a range of parenting quality and experiences with the child welfare system. The study population included families with very young children who participated in Temporary Assistance for Needy Families (TANF) or California's welfare-to-work program (CalWORKs); who lived in the predominantly urban areas of Alameda County, California, during the years 1999–2000; and who were identified as likely to be living an economically and/or socially precarious existence. Precariousness was considered likely if the parent had a long history of welfare receipt (defined as welfare receipt beginning in 1993), and/or involvement with the child welfare system because of child neglect.

Sampling

Because of the study's two purposes, and in order to ensure there would be a range of parenting quality and experiences with the welfare and child welfare systems, two sources were used to generate the sample. The first source included families who were part of a survey of long-term welfare recipients that was conducted by the University of California, Berkeley's Survey Research Center (SRC). These families had at least one child under age three and had received welfare (cash aid) during the year prior to study entry. The second source was the Alameda County Social Services Agency, Children and Family Services Division (the local public child welfare agency). In addition to the criteria listed here, families were recruited who had become involved with child welfare services because of child neglect, caretaker absence, or abandonment. A total of 20 individuals were identified and contacted by telephone and letter. Four of the seven SRC families agreed to participate, and six of the 13 child welfare families met the criteria and agreed to further contact.

Sample Description

In this resulting sample of 10 families, the primary caregivers ranged in age from 28 to 40, with the majority in their thirties during the study. All had at least one child age three or younger at study entry, and the total number of living children per family ranged from one to five. These children ranged in age from newborn to 23 years old. In a number of cases, the youngest children lived with the primary caregiver while older children lived outside of the home in arrangements that included relatives, foster care, and group homes. The majority of the sample (seven primary caregivers) was African American, two were Mexican American, and one primary caregiver was Caucasian. Nearly all children in the sample were of the same racial identity as their parents; one set of siblings was biracial. The primary caregiver was the biological mother in nine cases; the biological father headed one single-parent family. Four mothers lived with partners, one was legally married but separated, and at least four of the remaining five caregivers had partners for varying periods of time during their involvement in the study.

The educational level in the group ranged from eighth grade to some community college. Some had job experience (through a series of low-wage jobs), while others had minimal or no experience working in the legal economy. Most had received welfare, either intermittently or relatively consistently, for between 10 and 20 years.

All families in the sample lived in relative poverty, although their level of material well-being varied, depending upon a number of factors including availability of housing, family or partner support, work or other income sources, and the capacity to manage funds. Alternatives to both legal employment and public assistance had—to a large or small degree—supplemented the income of a number of families (in the past and in some cases, during study involvement). These means included selling food stamps, prostitution, panhandling, and drug-related transactions, and also included employment paid "under the table" such as housecleaning, yard work, and light construction.

All six child welfare-involved parents were in recovery from drug addiction (primarily crack cocaine and heroin), and many had been involved with drugs for more than 10 years, in and out of jail and prison. Four of the six parents had been involved with the child welfare system for more than a decade each, and three had experienced termination of their parental rights with older children. During the first year of data collection, three families' child welfare cases were considered successful reunifications and closed, while three families received continued child welfare services and monitoring. By the end of the follow-up period (two years after the study began), the youngest children in three families had reentered foster care.

Data Collection

Data collection consisted of multiple in-person and telephone contacts with families, using methods of participant observation. This included unstructured and semistructured interviewing in naturalistic or everyday environments (Atkinson and Hammersley 1998). On a continuum of involvement between researchers and study subjects, ranging from full participation of the researcher in the subject's life to detached observation (Padgett 1998; 2008), the approach used here could be considered "observer-participant." This was a conscious and ongoing decision that was under constant negotiation, and my[1] stance shifted toward greater participation as time went on.

Depending upon the family, the quality of our relationships, the context, and the circumstances, my level of actual participation or involvement in family life varied. My role as researcher was overt at the outset (Jorgensen 1989) and my outsider status apparent. At the same time, I sought to minimize the interpersonal distance between myself and the families by cultivating a role diffuse enough that each family could find their own place for me in their world. Some began to consider me "like a friend" while others seemed to think of me as "like a therapist" or "someone who does studies and writes books." My stance as observer-participant undoubtedly influenced the nature and quality of the data. I never fully entered these families' worlds; I merely visited for a few hours a month. Had I asked to move in with them and sleep on the couch, the depth and complexity of my knowledge would have increased in many ways. But the study was not a laboratory experiment. In my presence, dinner was eaten, the phone was answered, and children and neighbors were contended with in their backyards. The contextualized nature of the data thus rests on a balance between proximity to family life, and distance from it.

In-person contacts most often occurred in the families' homes, where they were most comfortable, although some interviews were conducted while walking in the park, watching children on the playground, over a milkshake in Burger King, or at the parent's workplace. In-person meetings were prearranged and tended to last between one and two hours. On a few occasions, I suggested an alternative meeting place, in order to increase the chances of observing the parent-child relationship in a new light (given, for example, obstacles to negotiate in a grocery store), or for the sake of privacy. Sometimes a parent's impromptu need for transportation resulted in a car trip to the youth activity center, the day care facility, or the therapist's office. The majority of the direct contact involved conversations with the parent, but no efforts were made to control the presence or absence of children during the interviews, since an essential part of data collection involved naturalistic observation of spontaneous parent-child interaction, while the parent was facing conflicting demands: to attend to me, as well as their child.

The original study design called for interviews on at least a monthly basis, and I attempted to follow this plan. Scheduling difficulties and concerns about retention led to uneven interview patterns in some cases, however. Some individuals were interviewed on a regular monthly basis, while others had multiple-month gaps, and a few (who entered the study late) were interviewed weekly. Increased frequency of the interviews resulted in a more rapidly intensifying relationship with me, and a different pacing of the interview content. It also led to some ethical considerations regarding the role of remuneration, given that more frequent contact led to a rather dramatically increased income, in some cases. Parents were paid $25 cash per interview for their participation, an arrangement that was discussed during the initial phone call, at the first meeting, and in an ongoing way. Each was assured that I would not report their income to the welfare department or anywhere else. The remuneration itself unexpectedly became a tool for data collection, because each individual had different feelings about the cash itself—the fact that I provided these funds and what it meant about the nature of our relationship, and the impact of study involvement on their lives.

General interview/observation topics are listed in box 18.1. As data collection was ongoing, general topic areas were identified for exploration based upon the literature and the ongoing analysis of data. A timeline was developed for data collection and a plan for addressing certain topics at certain points in time (e.g., welfare-to-work status, employment history, and "making ends meet" were assessed within the first three meetings). Before each set of monthly interviews, an interview guide was developed: While some were deliberately worded and offered a fair amount of structure (e.g., questions about experiences of parenting) others simply acted as a list of topic-related prompts. Over the entire data collection period, regular meetings with my research team (an advisor and a colleague) served as a means for examining the data collected up to that point, identifying gaps, focusing and reformulating the topics to be addressed in future interviews, as well as problem-solving ethical and practical dilemmas involving families.

Box 18.1 Interview/Observation Themes

- Welfare-to-work status
- Knowledge of and feelings about welfare reform
- Sources of income
- Budgeting
- Job history
- Educational history
- Child welfare services history and status of current involvement
- Experience of community—neighborhood safety and quality
- Social support and extended family support
- Child care resources
- Housing issues
- Role of formal agency assistance, both concrete help and psychosocial
- Partner relationships
- State of the home environment, regarding safety, child-friendliness, availability of cognitively stimulating toys and materials
- Presence and nature of any daily routines for self and/or children
- Parents' physical and mental health
- The subjective experience of parenting in conditions of poverty
- Adult's childhood experience of being parented, and influence on current parenting style, capacity
- Observations of child-parent relationship quality
- Child well-being and developmental status
- Impact of race and class on perception and experience of opportunity

---

I took a self-conscious approach in which I considered myself, the researcher/interviewer, to be the primary instrument of data collection (Miles and Huberman 1994; Padgett 1998, 2008). In general, my style of interviewing was a minimalist one, in that I tended to provide few direct observations, comments, or questions and tried to encourage people to continue through nonverbal means, and with as little verbal intervention as I could sustain. This was intended to increase the likelihood that a participant's responses would emerge as spontaneously as possible. I did, however, ask direct questions, seek clarification, and redirect conversations when necessary. Seldom did I ask people to explain why they did what they did; rather, I asked them to describe their experience, tell me what happened, and how they thought and felt about it. This approach assumes there is a web of meaning lying somewhere in between behavior, thoughts, and feelings, and that the reasons for actions (or inactions) are not always consciously accessible. It also assumes that not all accessible knowledge will be shared with a researcher (or anyone in particular), since even the most open informants have reasons to preciously guard their internal and relational life experience. Parenting, especially, is an arena of personal life about which many people are understandably sensitive and protective.

Initially, it was difficult to observe the parent-child relationship in detail and to simultaneously interview the parent, although my ability to split my attention and make mental notes improved. Efforts were made to compose verbal notes (into the tape recorder) immediately following the meeting on descriptive factors such as how people appeared that day (dress, demeanor, hair, makeup); the state of the home environment or neighborhood (particularly clean or messy, dangerous in some way); specific descriptions of microinteractions between the child and the parent (e.g., "he climbed in her lap requesting a bottle, and she did not look at him") as well as between myself and the parent (e.g., "she flipped the pages of the magazine while 'talking' to me, for the first 20 minutes") and myself and the child (e.g., "she immediately hugged me, which struck me as inappropriate since she had only met me once before, two months ago"). In these observations, I tried to note affective tone of the dyad, developmental progress of the child as reflected in the relationship or the interaction, parental responsiveness to the child, and any factors that seemed related to a cultural dimension of parenting or family life. I also made notes about the logistics of the meeting and how I simply felt being with the family or in the environment, that particular day.

Nearly all field contacts and in-person interviews were audiotaped with the consent of the parent. After the first several interviews, I began turning the recorder on prior to entering the home so that initial interactions with the family could be captured on tape. At the conclusion of most interviews, while driving from the field site, I entered verbal notes and observations into the recorder. When I was unable to audiotape, I made extensive written notes immediately following the interview.

At the end of the data collection period, the raw data consisted of audiotapes (more than 120) of in-person meetings; field notes made on the content and process of in-person meetings as well as telephone contacts; field notes made on the observation of parent-child relationships, the home environment, and reflection on our interactions; select documents or notes about the family (e.g., court reports given to me by a parent); and written documents created to facilitate some of the interviews (e.g., source of income grids for understanding budgeting, timelines to gather welfare history, genograms to clarify extended family relationships). All the audiotapes were professionally transcribed, as verbatim as possible, into written documents.

The Role of Theory in Data Collection and Analysis

I began the study with a question about the role of parents' subjective experience of poverty in parenting, something that I felt had not been explored in previous efforts to understand child neglect. In addition to my knowledge of social work and child welfare, I was informed early on by my work in the field of infant mental health and development, which draws upon relational psychodynamic and attachment theories, emphasizing the role of parents' internal, subjective experiences in the quality of parent-child relationships. But it was many months before the relationship between my research question, data collection process, and analytic method fully crystallized. In the first several months of visiting with families, we talked about welfare and income, parenting, child welfare, and various aspects of daily living. I kept asking myself: How do I focus on the relationship between poverty and parenting? Where, if at all, does poverty show up in the relationship between parents and children? For a time, I was in a constant state of focusing and refocusing, questioning where to place the weight of my attention: the parent-child interaction, the way a parent talks about her life, the children's development, or the state of the home or neighborhood, for example. With so many intense stimuli, holding my research question in mind was difficult, as was trusting that a pattern or set of ideas would emerge.

To help answer this question during the data collection process, I expanded my theoretical knowledge base by consulting the literature in cultural psychology, cultural anthropology, and developmental/clinical psychology. Each offered an important new perspective on the issue of poverty and parent-child relationships. First, the cultural psychology and anthropology literature drew attention to the construction of psychological meaning as interactively, reciprocally created between people in everyday life, while simultaneously placing people in a larger environmental context (e.g., LeVine 1990; Shweder 1990; LeVine et al. 1994; Cole 1996). The work of anthropologist Nancy Scheper-Hughes (1987, 1993, 1), conducted in a poor Brazilian community, contributed the important concept of a "political economy of the emotions." In this Brazilian context characterized by conditions of extreme poverty, high fertility, and infant mortality, certain infant deaths were influenced by what Scheper-Hughes called "mortal neglect." Constructing shared understandings of the meanings of infant illness and death, mothers practiced forms of selective neglect or passive infanticide with infants deemed hopeless cases: too sickly, disabled, "unprepared for life," or wanting to die. These children were let go without intervention, and Scheper-Hughes (1993:369) reports there to be "no expressed guilt or blame for those who aid such deaths." Scheper-Hughes' work illustrates ways in which deprivation and dangerous environmental conditions can influence the thinking, feeling, and behavior of parents; it also suggests that poverty influences the meaning of both childhood and parenting, at the existential and concrete levels of experience.

Next, ideas were drawn from the work of psychologists Crittenden (1993, 1999) and George and Solomon (George and Solomon 1996, 1999; Solomon and George 1996, 2000). Although they have differences, these writers share a general theory base that draws upon attachment and psychoanalytic learning and information-processing theories with roots in developmental psychology and ethology. Solomon and George (1996; George and Solomon 1996) have proposed a "theory of caregiving" that conceptualizes caregiving (parenting) as an organized behavioral system designed to provide care and protection for the child. The caregiving system is guided at the representational (psychological) level by both content (thoughts and feelings about self, other, and relationship) and process (the capacity to process information and affect relevant to the relationship, with or without relying on various psychological defenses). Theoretically, the caregiving system is activated in response to a perception of a situation as dangerous, frightening, or stressful. Caregiving behavior is determined by conscious and unconscious evaluation of sources of information, including the child's signals, and the caregiver's own perception of danger or threat to the child (Solomon and George 1999).

Writing specifically on the topic of child neglect and parental psychology, Crittenden (1993, 1999) has made the unique proposal that a link between poverty and neglect involves parental information processing and defensive processes. Crittenden (1993) has pointed out that omissions in child care can result from a parent's failure to perceive a child's signals or contextual indicators of need, inaccurate interpretation of a signal (believing a signal has no meaning, or overestimating a child's abilities), failure to select a response (understanding and correctly interpreting a signal but not knowing what to do), or knowing what to do, but being unable to implement a response. Together these writers suggest that sources of interference with information processing may include psychological defenses against important caregiving-related information (affective or cognitive) (Crittenden 1993; George and Solomon 1996), or the absence of any psychological defense against overwhelming information, which may be experienced as a profound sense of helplessness (George and Solomon 1999; Solomon and George 1996). Solomon and George (2000) also propose the concept of assaults to the caregiving system—events or conditions that overwhelm coping capacities in such a way that caregiving becomes disabled, and care is abdicated. Under such an assault, the parent is rendered helpless to effectively respond on behalf of the child, and neglect may be the result.

Thus through crossing disciplinary boundaries and examining alternative conceptualizations of parenting, a set of sensitizing concepts (Padgett 2008) began to emerge that would ultimately shape both data collection and analysis. The literature drawing on both the cultural/anthropological and psychological traditions spoke to ways in which the external world is internalized, subjectively experienced, and ultimately expressed in the behaviors that make up parents' daily lives—in the microinteractions and more readily observable behaviors that can be identified as parenting. Specific sensitizing concepts were identified for the study including: the concept of a political economy of the emotions; the notion of a caregiving system and its basis in parents' internal representations; a model of parental information processing as responses to signals from the child or contextual indicators of need; and the roles of psychological defenses and assaults to the caregiving system in parenting. Over time, these ideas helped to shape and refine my method for focusing on poverty, as I gathered data and examined it for patterns and meanings.

The Analysis Process

The early process of analysis included listening to audiotapes of prior interviews, and making notes and observations. Computer software designed specifically for the management of qualitative data, ATLAS.ti, was used to manage the data and the analysis process. I chose ATLAS.ti for its suitability in formulating theory "as a connected network of links among entities" rather than theory development through hierarchical coding, as in the case of some other software programs (Huberman and Miles 1998:191). The transcribed, edited interviews and field notes were entered into the software package along with demographic data and case identifiers. In this way, large amounts of data from a variety of sources could be integrated and examined for conceptual regularities and irregularities; units of text could be coded as signifying certain ideas; and relationships between larger conceptual units could be identified and examined in a process of constant comparison (Strauss and Corbin 1990).

Each interview transcript was first reviewed and edited while listening to the audiotape, but ultimately reviewed multiple times. Portions of transcripts were then marked, or coded, in two ways. The first was an open coding process (Strauss and Corbin 1990) wherein all content or process-oriented themes that appeared relevant were assigned a code. These themes included, for example, issues of financial strain, histories of drug use and recovery, a parent's employment aspirations, experiences of racism, availability of social support, and the parent's relationship with me. The second major coding step involved theory-guided coding, where a set of developing ideas from the literature (and the data itself) was sought in the text and coded (this process is described in greater detail here).

The data set ultimately included 143 separate documents (including transcribed interviews and written notes) coded into more than 4,800 narrative segments or quotations, with approximately 200 memos, 400 comments, and 400 quote segments that were hyperlinked together. The coded data were then studied for similarities and idiosyncrasies across families, and over time (Strauss and Corbin 1990). As themes began to emerge, the data were examined for discrepant or disconfirming evidence (Strauss and Corbin 1990; Padgett 1998, 2008). In other words, there was a deliberate search for data that would contradict an emerging idea. Analytic memos created during this process documented my reflections on the meaning of the data (Huberman and Miles 1998; Padgett 1998, 2008). Conceptual patterns that emerged were then considered in light of the research questions, and the preliminary hypotheses that were developing out of the literature and early analysis. The data were studied further for their fit with the conceptual patterns—thus moving from an inductive to a more deductive approach, and back again.

Twice during the first year, I wrote case summaries, or profiles, of the families that synthesized the information gathered to date, and described people in terms that brought them alive to others. These profiles served as background materials for discussion with my research team, with whom I met regularly to develop and refine my method. In these meetings, I described participants to the team, and together we reflected on what I did and did not yet know, what questions needed to be asked, and how I might better target my data collection efforts at the research questions. Between months four to eight of data collection, open coding was done to identify emergent themes warranting further study, as well as reflecting on my interview style. I created Excel spreadsheets to be used as data matrices (Miles and Huberman 1994), which facilitated within- and cross-case comparisons along multiple variables and conceptual domains (e.g., comparing all participants in terms of their welfare history, educational history, subjective experience of financial strain, and parenting stress). This helped to identify gaps in knowledge about a given family as well as to highlight the need for exploration of a new domain (e.g., children's developmental status, parental mental health) when I returned to the field. Then at 10 to 11 months into data collection, I conducted a more formal preliminary analysis, in which I tested some emerging ideas against a portion of the data and formulated some rough hypotheses for later study. The emerging ideas were generated in-the-moment, through the process of data collection described as follows.

It was in the eighth month of data collection that I had an important "aha" moment, in which my research question, sensitizing concepts, and analytic process suddenly came together. This moment occurred during the eighth interview with a mother, Leticia, and her three-year-old son, Dashon (the names are pseudonyms). The family was very low-income and under chronic financial strain. In the previous interview, we had discussed Leticia's waiting for her landlord to fix various problems in her apartment so that it might pass the inspection required for her housing voucher application. The landlord was not responding to her requests, and Leticia had noted that

> He . . . needs to paint in my room an' in Dashon's room. He gotta patch up holes 'cause there's some holes in there an' fix it where . . . the paint is chippin' at. He needs to fix that because it's a danger to Dashon, you know.

I followed up with her about the inspection and the landlord's cooperation. "He's really holding me up," she said, "Because they'll only give you a certain amount of time . . . on the housing certificate to find housing." We again discussed her view that the apartment would not pass inspection, given the need for certain repairs. She worried about fire, and noted the absence of working smoke alarms (for which batteries were needed), and a fire extinguisher (which she had borrowed from friends, but had to return). Saying "I would never leave [Dashon] in the house by himself," and noting that she makes efforts to prevent fire: "before I go to bed, I always check and make sure everything's . . . off" she added that "you just can't say that fire won't start anyway," and even that "somebody [might] throw something through my window, a bomb or something." Leticia had experienced many violent, traumatic events and lived in a relatively unsafe neighborhood, so her fear of such disasters was consistent with her life experience. But she equally emphasized her concern about danger to Dashon and the need to protect him. This was followed by a discussion of the broken toilet ("I ain't got the money to call Roto-Rooter or nobody, you know") and a broken heater: "I put extra blankets on my bed, Dashon's and my bed, and . . . I just make sure he [is] dressed warm when he go to bed so he won't be cold." Leticia indicated she had considered the cost of the apartment's repairs but felt helpless to make them herself given her limited means. Consequently she was waiting for the landlord to "do his job."

Analyzing Caregiving Moments

With this "smoke alarm moment" and others that followed, one method for studying the intersection between poverty and parent-child interaction came to life. Leticia demonstrated to me the link between poverty conditions, dangers to her child (as well as herself), her affect about the situation, and her sense of herself as a parent. Drawing upon sensitizing concepts discussed earlier, I developed a set of core ideas, including the caregiving moment and its component parts. Caregiving moments include brief, ordinary interactions between a parent and child, or parent and environment, in which the parent's actions can be understood as the result of a complex psychological process. A child, for instance, awakens in the morning and calls out to the parent. The parent responds by approaching, lifting the child out of her crib, and then holding her close. This caregiving moment involves the child's signal, calling out to be retrieved from the crib, and the parent's response in picking up the child. A caregiving moment may also include an interaction between the parent and the environment, as it pertains to child care and protection issues. In the "smoke alarm moment" with Leticia, environmental hazards threatened her child's safety. These hazards were directly related to living in poverty. Her ability to mitigate those hazards was also impacted by her poverty status, as well the feelings that were evoked in her, and her psychological process for managing those feelings.

At that point, to further define the concept of caregiving moments, I delineated 16 types of signals from children and the environment that mirrored Zuravin's (1991) well-accepted definition of "subtypes of neglect" (see table 18.1). These 16 signals were an explicit adaptation and elaboration of some of Crittenden's (1993) and Solomon and George's (1996) work and were thought to incorporate the essential aspects of care and protection that are absent in cases of physical neglect. I also hypothesized that conditions of poverty, when present, may be embedded in the parent-child relationship within these 16 signals. Living in poverty may increase the likelihood of encountering pernicious environmental signals as well as limiting conditions for children (e.g., poverty-related influences on children's capacity to signal their parents).

With the interview transcripts and observational data, I developed a coding method for identifying caregiving moments in the data, and then coding the separate components of each caregiving moment. These components included types of signals from the child and/or the environment,

Table 18.1 Child Signals and Environmental Signals Relevant to Care and Protection*

Child signals about the following basic needs and the associated physical, emotional distress if unmet	Environmental signals corresponding to conditions that may represent a need, danger, or threat
Hunger	Limited food/milk/formula
Illness	Limited access to medical care
Injury	Dangerous environmental conditions increasing likelihood of injury (e.g., objects on floor, unmanaged sewage, exposed wiring, unregulated water heaters, etc.)
Thermoregulation (extreme heat or cold)	Extreme environmental conditions (e.g., extreme heat/cold without ability to manage through heat/air conditioning, homelessness, problems paying utilities)
Wetness and soiling	Lack of diapers, the means to cleanse child, and keep dry
Sleep	Crowded, noisy conditions with many interruptions preventing adequate sleep
Bids for attention, affection	Competing demands that prevent caregiver from providing attention, affection
Physical and felt safety via proximity and its counterpart, exploration away from caregiver	Potentially unsafe conditions for exploration and/or situations where physical or felt safety compromised

Note: For further details see Frame (2001).

and responses from the parent along an information-processing sequence (whether they adequately perceived and interpreted the signal, selected a caregiving response, and implemented that caregiving response). Subsequently each caregiving moment that occurred—across every interview—was painstakingly coded in this way. Ultimately, 430 caregiving moments, a subset of the (clearest, most reliable) data, were used in the analysis to identify the types of child/environmental signals each parent experienced, the influence of poverty conditions on those signals, and their patterns of responses to those signals. Some parents, for example, were frequently confronted with extreme environmental conditions that threatened their children's safety, and certain parents tended to misinterpret their children's signals about hunger, injury, exploration, or attention.

Analyzing Representations of Caregiving

In addition to analyzing caregiving moments in this way, I coded the data regarding parents' representations of caregiving—their thoughts, feelings, and psychological processes regarding their children, their relationships with their children, and themselves as parents. Some of these data were collected specifically for this purpose, through using a particular semistructured interview that had been designed and implemented in the eleventh and twelfth months of data collection, drawing on the work of Solomon and George, as well as George, Kaplan, and Main (1984/1986). Other relevant data were identified throughout the interview transcripts, having spontaneously emerged in discussions between the parent and myself. The analytic approach used with these data followed the general approach of Solomon and George (1996) about the nature and quality of parents' narratives about caregiving. These features were identified through repeated reading of the transcripts and listening to the tapes. Important features included, for example, the parents' fluidity and organization of thought; the availability of detail and relative complexity of their elaboration on ideas; the relevance of detail they provided and overall consistency of their portrayals of themselves, their children, and their relationships with them; the evidence (verbal and nonverbal) of affect while discussing these topics; and the relative balance of negative and positive aspects of their representations. Additionally, the overall coherence of these narratives about caregiving was compared to each parent's dialogue with me regarding other topics. All of these factors were thought to shed light on the parents' capacity to think and feel about issues relevant to caregiving, and their apparent reliance on defensive processes (adaptive or maladaptive) to manage their experience of parenting.

Analyzing Poverty's Role

Next, I examined the ways in which poverty appeared to impact parents' sense of themselves, their children, and their relationships with their children. I did this by using an open coding process to first examine the general nature of parents' representations of themselves, their children, and their relationships. I coded the quality of parents' representations and their apparent reliance on adaptive or maladaptive defenses in relation to thinking and feeling about parenting. I then examined the ways in which poverty-related topics emerged in the content of parents' narratives about caregiving and socioeconomic conditions and also played a role in their psychological process. For example, every parent spoke of the difficulty providing necessities for their children (food, clothing, shelter), and all referred to ways in which their economic circumstances made parenting a difficult, limiting, and emotionally taxing experience. The emotional impact ranged from basic worry to full-blown anxiety, and from tiredness to utter depletion. But I found variation in the ways that parents coped. Some coped adequately with these feelings; however, for others these feelings appeared to negatively impact their sense of themselves as parents, and/or the quality of their relationship with their child. For a few, the impact of poverty conditions on their representational system was to engender fundamental feelings of helplessness or inadequacy, feelings that ultimately interfered with their capacity to think and feel about their children and their basic needs.

To integrate all these major analytic categories, I then used diagrams to visually examine the relationships between (a) each parent's information processing in caregiving moments, (b) the role of poverty conditions in those caregiving moments, and (c) the parent's representations of caregiving (in general, and as related to poverty). Patterns emerged that suggested that poverty conditions did, in fact, have a relationship to the realities of parenting, the ways that parents thought and felt about themselves as parents, and their individual capacities to respond to their children's needs.

Findings

The findings, which can be summarized as a relational contextual model of child protection, care, and neglect, are outlined in figure 18.1. Parents in this study subjectively experienced many poverty conditions not just as generic stressors, but as threats to their capacities to provide for, protect, and simply be with their children. Poverty conditions were present in the concrete, moment-to-moment realities of caregiving, influencing the demands placed on parents and the threats to their children. These material realities included the strains of low income and limited resources with which to meet their children's immediate needs; the dangerous realities of urban neighborhoods; restricted access to opportunity and increased competing demands in parenting; and the various persisting effects of deprivation over the parent's lifetime. To a lesser extent, poverty influenced the nature of caregiving

Parenting and Child Neglect Among Families in Urban Poverty

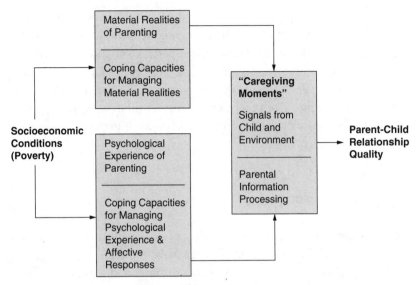

Figure 18.1 A relational contextual model of child protection, care, and neglect

moments related to child behavior, development, and health issues. Parents have differing capacities to cope with these material realities—for example, through having a greater or lesser ability to succeed in the labor market, or to access family support to feed their children.

Urban poverty also shaped the psychological experience of parents, by inserting itself into parents' sense of themselves as caregivers, and their beliefs about their relationships with their children. Poverty-related representational themes included the difficulty providing the necessities of life for children; the limited time and emotional availability to offer children due to the intense, competing demands parents face; the limited educational, cultural, and material opportunities that can be provided; the challenge of protecting children from environmental harm; and the related problem of a limited or foreshortened sense of children's futures. Each of these poverty-related caregiving themes had an emotional impact, to which some parents responded adaptively, and others less so. The emotional impact of poverty and the capacity to manage those emotions appear to be significant components of care and protection.

Out of the findings of this study, a conceptual model for understanding child neglect is proposed. In this relational contextual model of child neglect, a parent's capacity to care for and protect their child—in the immediate caregiving moment and in arranging the environment to prevent future risk—is related to their subjective experience of poverty conditions, the affective experience that is generated, and the coping mechanisms that can be marshaled by the parent to manage that experience effectively. Through describing these processes, the model illuminates how poverty conditions can be mediated by parents in ways that lead to inadequate care and protection of children.

Comments on the Methodology

The purpose of this detailed description of data collection and analysis has been to illustrate a process of progressive refinement central to an in-depth qualitative study. I began with a purpose and a question, along with the general outlines of a method. But I did not really know where I might locate poverty in parent-child relationships, until a parent participant unwittingly pointed me there—by talking about her landlord, her smoke alarm, and her child. I might not have "heard" this parent's point had I not already listened carefully to each parent's experience of daily life in poverty, and observed its pervasive impact on his/her family. When the "smoke alarm moment" occurred, I was sensitized to these realities. I had also been actively thinking about several major sensitizing concepts and their potential roles in relation to poverty: the construction of psychological meaning through interpersonal interactions; a political economy of the emotions; the caregiving system and the links between thinking, feeling, and behavior; the nature of signals related to children's fundamental needs; and the nature of parental information processing. Thus it was a dynamic, overlapping process of data collection, analysis, and theoretical formulation that led to the crystallization of a method, and the development of the findings.

Both flexibility of thought, and adaptiveness in my approach to data collection, were absolutely necessary in this process. I allowed for the exploration of newly emerging ideas, and for the method itself to unfold (e.g., I developed a specific interview to tap parental representations of caregiving, in the last few months of data collection). But this creative process was neither uncontained nor unfocused. I maintained organization through a general plan for data collection and the use of a careful data management system, and clarity of purpose through regular discussions with my research team. It was in these meetings that emerging ideas were spelled out, my thinking was challenged, and I was aided in remaining focused on the central research questions.

This study may offer an example of how combining somewhat disparate approaches can generate useful dynamic tensions. The combination of a broadly contextualized examination of family life with a micro-level analysis of parent-child interactions created an important balance of perspective. In this way, the participants' social and cultural meanings of parenting informed my understanding of moment-to-moment interactions, and the emotionally immediate nature of parent-child interaction brought those meanings to life. Similarly, a useful balance was made possible through the combination of inductive and more deductive approaches. The inductively-derived description of poverty and its effects was essential to articulating the lived experience of parents and children. By actively drawing on existing theory, I was able to integrate these findings with a method for understanding—in detail, the capacity of parents to meet their children's basic needs.

Note

1. References to "the researcher" are in first-person to acknowledge that my subjectivity was a part of the data collection and analysis process.

References

Atkinson, P. and M. Hammersley. 1998. Ethnography and participant observation. In *Strategies of qualitative inquiry*, N. K. Denzin and Y. S. Lincoln, eds. 110–136. Newbury Park: Sage.

Belsky, J., and J. Vondra. 1989. Lessons from child abuse: The determinants of parenting. In *Child maltreatment: Theory and research on the causes and consequences of child abuse and neglect*, D. Cicchetti and V. Carlson, eds. 153–202. Cambridge, UK: Cambridge UP.

Cole, M. 1996. *Cultural psychology: A once and future discipline*. Cambridge, MA: The Belknap Press of Harvard UP.

Crittenden, P. M. 1993. An information-processing perspective on the behavior of neglectful parents. *Criminal Justice and Behavior*, 20(1):27–48.

———. 1999. Child neglect: Causes and contributors. In *Neglected children: Research, practice, and policy,* H. Dubowitz, ed. 47–68. Thousand Oaks, CA: Sage.

DePaul, J. and M. Guibert. 2008. Empathy and child neglect: A theoretical model. *Child Abuse and Neglect,* 32:1063–1071.

Frame, L. (2001). "Parent-child relationships in conditions of urban poverty: Protection, care, and neglect of infants and toddlers." Doctoral dissertation, University of California, Berkeley, School of Social Welfare.

Frame, L. and J. D. Berrick. 2003. The effects of welfare reform on families involved with public child welfare services: Results from a qualitative study. *Children and Youth Services Review,* 25(1/2):113–138.

Gelles, R. 1999. Policy issues in child neglect. In *Neglected children: Research, practice, and policy,* H. Dubowitz, ed. 278–298. Thousand Oaks, CA: Sage.

George, C., N. Kaplan, and M. Main. (1984/1996). "Adult attachment interview," 3rd ed. Unpublished manuscript, Department of Psychology, University of California, Berkeley.

George, C. and J. Solomon. 1996. Representational models of relationships: Links between caregiving and attachment. *Infant Mental Health Journal,* 17(3):198–216.

———. 1999. Attachment and caregiving: The caregiving behavioral system. In *Handbook of attachment: Theory, research, and clinical applications,* J. Cassidy and P. Shaver, eds. 649–670. New York: Guilford.

Huberman, A. M. and M. B. Miles. 1998. Data management and analysis methods. In *Collecting and interpreting qualitative materials,* N. K. Denzin and Y. S. Lincoln, eds. 179–210. Thousand Oaks, CA: Sage.

Jorgensen, D. L. 1989. *Participant observation: A methodology for human studies.* Newbury Park: Sage.

LeVine, R. 1990. Infant environments in psychoanalysis: A cross-cultural view. In *Cultural psychology: Essays on comparative human development,* J. W. Stigler and R. A. Shweder, eds. 542–565. New York: Cambridge UP.

LeVine, R. A., S. Dixon, S. LeVine, A. Richman, P. H. Leiderman, C. H. Keefer, and T. B. Brazelton. 1994. *Child care and culture: Lessons from Africa.* New York: Cambridge UP.

Miles, M. B. and A. M. Huberman. 1994. *Qualitative data analysis: An expanded sourcebook,* 2nd ed. Thousand Oaks, CA: Sage.

Nelson, K. E., E. J. Saunders, and M. J. Landsman. 1993. Chronic child neglect in perspective. *Social Work,* 38(6):661–671.

Padgett, D. K. 1998. *Qualitative methods in social work research: Challenges and rewards.* Thousand Oaks, CA: Sage.

———. 2008. *Qualitative methods in social work research,* 2nd ed. Thousand Oaks, CA: Sage.

Pelton, L., ed. 1981. *The social context of child abuse and neglect.* New York: Human Services.

Polansky, N. A., M. Chalmers, E. Buttenweiser, and D. Williams. 1981. *Damaged parents: An anatomy of child neglect.* Chicago: U of Chicago P.

Scheper-Hughes, N., ed. 1987. *Child survival: Anthropological perspectives on the treatment and maltreatment of children.* Boston: D. Reidel.

Scheper-Hughes, N. 1993. *Death without weeping: The violence of everyday life in Brazil.* Berkeley, CA: University of California Press.

Shweder, R. A. 1990. Cultural psychology: What is it? In *Cultural psychology: Essays on comparative human development,* J. W. Stigler, R. A. Shweder, and G. Herdt, eds. 1–43. New York: Cambridge UP.

Slack, K. S., J. L. Holl, M. McDaniel, J. Yoo, and K. Bolger. 2004. Understanding the risks of child neglect: An exploration of poverty and parenting characteristics. *Child maltreatment,* 9(4):395–408.

Solomon, J. and C. George. 1996. Defining the caregiving system: Toward a theory of caregiving. *Infant Mental Health Journal,* 17(3):183–197.

——. 2000. Toward an integrated theory of maternal caregiving. In *WAIMH handbook of infant mental health.* Volume III: *Parenting and child care,* J. D. Osofsky and H. E. Fitzgerald, eds. 323–368. New York: Wiley.

Strauss, A. and J. Corbin. 1990. *Basics of qualitative research: Grounded theory procedures and techniques.* Newbury Park: Sage.

Vondra, J. 1993. Child poverty and child maltreatment. In *Child poverty and public policy,* J. Chafe, ed. 127–166. Washington, DC: The Urban Institute.

Zuravin, S. 1991. Research definitions of abuse and neglect. In *The effects of child abuse and neglect: Issues and research,* R. H. Starr and D. A. Wolfe, eds. 100–128. New York: Guilford.

19

Doing the Best You Can?

The Relationship Between Caseworker and Parent: A Case Study

JULANNE COLVIN

It is the context that fixes the nature of things.

Bateson, *Mind and Nature*

A parent says she is doing the best that she can: This said after more than a decade of involvement with the child welfare system and two children still in placements out of the home. Would society agree with the parent's assessment? Would the caseworker who worked with the parent and her family for the last 12 years agree? Who gets to decide? Does the assessment of "doing the best that she can" grow from the narrative of the parent and caseworker's relationship and the meaning they make from being a part of one another's lives? The investigation of this relationship may allow for greater understanding of the conditions that function to move neglecting behavior from a discrete event in the life of a family to an enduring behavior pattern. At present, this is not a pattern that is well understood.

Literature Review

In the child maltreatment literature, neglect has not been researched to the extent of abuse, even though neglect occurs with greater frequency, and may, in fact, have greater long-term consequences for the development of children (Wolock and Horowitz 1984; Schumacker, Slep, and Heyman 2001; Glaser 2002). The National Incidence Study of Child Abuse and Neglect shows not only a greater number of children neglected than abused, but the number is increasing at a greater rate (Sedlak and Broadhurst 1996). According to the third National Incidence Study of Child Abuse and Neglect (Sedlak and Broadhurst 1996), not only is there a greater number of children described as being neglected than abused, but this number is also increasing at a greater percentage. The most recent National Incidence Study documents that the estimated number of emotionally neglected children rose from 584,100 in 1993 to 1,173,800 in 2005–2006—a 101 percent increase in number, and an 83 percent increase in the rate (Sedlak et al. 2010).

Wolock and Horowitz (1984) suggest that U.S. culture is obsessed with violence, and that acts of physical aggression consume more attention than the acts of omission brought about by neglect. Perhaps it is because the bruises or scars endured from abusive behavior are easier to see than those left by the lack of supervision or inattentiveness to a child's emotional needs. They believe that marks or bruises are likely to elicit action on the child's behalf, while the scars of neglect are hidden behind poor school performance or marked social withdrawal (Wolock and Horowitz 1984).

Others suggest that the neglect of neglect can be attributed to the link between neglect and poverty (Drake and Pandey 1996; Garbarino and Collins 1999). Because of a lack of interest in poverty—except as an indicator of moral failures of poor people—there is a lack of interest in neglect. Twenty years ago, Wolock and Horowitz (1984) concluded that neglect is discussed from a psychological perspective, rather than as a social problem. Seeing neglect only as a deficit in parenting is short-sighted; neglect must be viewed in the larger social context, with poverty being central. The isolation and social distancing of neglecting families may also contribute to the relative silence in the literature regarding them (Polansky, Ammons, and Gaudin 1985; Gaudin 1993)—the "out of sight, out of mind" phenomenon.

Not only are there differences in how maltreatment may reveal itself, but the child protective issues between abuse and neglect differ (Garbarino and Collins 1999). In abuse, the child protective task is conceptualized as an act of protection—stopping the caregiver from assaulting the child. In neglect, the child protective issues require the worker to participate in a process of creating or restoring an appropriate ongoing pattern of caregiving behavior. The process of stopping child neglect is seen as labor intensive. The act of stopping child abuse is not.

To stop child neglect, child welfare professionals must "establish nurturant relationships with neglectful parents . . . [which are essential to] enable them to establish such relationships with their children" (Critten-den (1999:66). Changing the way that parents interact with their children requires a long-term relationship with the parents. What meaning does this relationship have for child welfare caseworkers and parents? How does the meaning evolve as these individuals remain engaged with each other over time? This qualitative research project was undertaken to explore the characteristics in the relationship between child welfare caseworkers and parents who display chronic patterns of engagement with services over a long time. More specifically, this research addressed the following questions:

- What kind of relationship emerges between child welfare case-workers and parents who have neglected their children?
- Does the relationship change over time?
- Does the relationship affect the length of engagement with child welfare services?

The changing relationship is explored through interviews with a parent and her child welfare caseworker, through observing the interaction of the caseworker and parent during a home visit, and discussing with the case-worker the family's case file.

Methodology

Definitions

Along with the neglect of child neglect is the problem of defining child maltreat-ment. There have been no clear definitions for child maltreatment (Hutchison 1990). Different groups and professions use different definitions for their own purposes. Thus the developers of social policies may have very different defini-tions of what is child maltreatment than those who are investigating, interven-ing, or researching this issue. The way a social problem is defined determines the range of possible solutions as well as the specific strategies that might be used. In child welfare, the choice of definitions governs important decisions such as which families become eligible for services, what kinds of services are provided, and whether those services are considered voluntary or mandated.

For child welfare workers, these decisions are guided by statutory defini-tions. The definitional dilemma poses ethical and technological problems for the child welfare worker, who cannot ethically engage in coercive interventions into the life of a family without a clear sense that they represent the social standards, rather than their own agenda or some other institutional or administrative agenda (Hutchison 1990). The ambiguity of defining neglect provides insufficient guidance to allow child welfare workers to do their job.

Thus it is important to understand what definitions guided the action taken by the child welfare caseworker; both from the actual written policy as well as from the study participants' perspectives. In New York State, a neglected child is one whose physical, mental, or emotional condition has been impaired, or placed in imminent danger of impairment by the parent or legal guardian's failure to exercise a minimum degree·of care (New York State Office of Children and Family Services 2002). Given the definitional dilemma, the statutory definition of child neglect is contrasted with that provided by the caseworker and the parent. Such a contrast is important because the definition guides a family's initial engagement with the child welfare system and provides the structure for the ongoing involvement between caseworker and parent.

The process of investigating suspected neglect presents choices of definitions of child neglect at various stages. The process—and choice of definitions—begins with whether there is "reasonable cause" to suspect abuse or maltreatment (New York State Office of Children and Family Services 2002). Allegations of maltreatment trigger a report to child protective authorities. Once a report is made, someone determines if there is enough evidence presented to link reasonable cause to an imminent risk of danger now or in the future (an indicated case). Such a determination warrants an investigation by a local child welfare agency. Once an investigation commences, then another determination is made as to whether there is enough evidence to substantiate a claim (substantiated case) and then, beyond that, whether there is evidence that points to an imminent risk of harm, which requires action that might include the removal of a child from their home or a mandate for services while the child remains in the parents' custody.

Selection Criteria for the Study

In this study, parents were considered eligible as participants if their engagement with the child welfare agency occurred as a result of being investigated for allegations of neglect. Whether these allegations were initially substantiated was not necessary for inclusion in the study. In addition to these allegations, parents needed to have been involved with a child welfare caseworker for 36 months or more. The average length of involvement for a family with child welfare services is 12 months (U.S. General Accounting Office 2002). Thus the 36-month criterion for participation is longer than average and suggests a family that could be considered as having a pattern of chronically neglecting behavior.

Recruitment of Participant

To select a participating family, I enlisted the aid of personnel at the department of social services (DSS). The county commissioner in the county chosen for the study reviewed all child welfare cases and found 17 that matched the criteria of having allegations of neglect and being involved with child welfare services for more than 36 months. The county commissioner then matched these cases to caseworkers. He met with the child welfare caseworkers for those families to review consent and study questions. Caseworkers who consented to participate were asked to contact the principle investigator. After a meeting with the researcher, the caseworkers sent parents recruitment letters, consent forms, and lists of questions. The caseworkers followed up with phone contact to review consents and answer questions. Given the sensitive nature of this project, they also reassured the parents that their participation would have no impact on their current status with the DSS. Once a parent consented to participate, he or she was asked to phone the principal investigator. The first family and caseworker to complete this complex recruitment procedure—which was designed to meet institutional review board (IRB) requirements for protection of human subjects—became the focus of the intensive single-case study.

Cases

The cases were from a county located in central New York State. Trend data for New York State counties from 1999 through 2009 (New York State Office of Children and Family Services 2010) indicated this county had an average of 610 reports of child maltreatment in 1999 but increased to more than 1,000 ten years later.

Caseworker: The caseworker who agreed to participate in the study had worked for her county's DSS for 14 years, 9 years investigating reports of child maltreatment, and 5 years as a foster care/preventive casework. In this role, her duties included monitoring the safety of children and families and providing or finding services that would prevent further maltreatment. She was also responsible for assisting parents in gaining parenting skills that were responsive to their children's developmental needs, their emotional safety, and their physical well-being. The caseworker had worked with the participating parent since the family was initially investigated for allegations of neglect approximately 12 years ago.

Parent: The parent selected for this study was a single mother. She had two previous marriages that ended in divorces and one relationship that resulted in a separation. From these relationships, she had four children, ranging in age from 7 to 19 years. The oldest child lived outside of the home. Two of the children were in the custody of the DSS and were placed out of the home at the time of the research. The youngest child remained in the custody of his mother.

Methods

The research included three semistructured, open-ended phenomenological interviews with both the caseworker and the parent. Because of the limited understanding of the relationship between child welfare caseworkers and parents with chronically neglecting behavior, I used a phenomenological approach described by Seidman (1998). Seidman recommends a series of three separate interviews with each participant. According to Seidman and consistent with Bateson (1979), people's behavior becomes meaningful when "placed in the context of their lives and the lives of those around them" (Seidman 1998:11). The first interview is used to put the participant's experience into context by asking them about themselves in light of the present topic. The second interview is used to gain details of the participant's present experience. The third interview is used to reflect on the meaning of their experience, both in terms of the topic and in terms of the interview process itself. In this study, the meaning of the caseworker and parent relationship was described from the point of view of the caseworker and the parent.

During the first interview with the caseworker, she was asked to discuss the role and function of casework in terms of the laws of New York State and then specifically how the regulations guided her behavior with the participating parent. The first interview also explored the caseworker's understanding of the definition of maltreatment and the caseworker's present relationship with the parent. During the second interview, the caseworker was asked to review the family's case file. She developed a timeline of important events that occurred over the course of the involvement with the family (for example, the date of the admission for services, prior allegations of abuse or neglect, subsequent allegations of neglect, and any court appearances). The caseworker was then asked to describe these events in hopes that the description would provide clues as to the nature of the relationship as it developed over time. The final interview was used to talk about the research process and how being interviewed might impact the caseworker as she continued to work with the parent in this and similar cases.

The first of the three interviews with the parent provided a context for their initial involvement with child welfare services. The parent talked about her family, how they first became involved with the child welfare services, and the response to the initial involvement with child protective services. As the interview process progressed, any changes in the meaning of the initial engagement were explored. During the second interview, the parent's relationship with the caseworker and how it had changed over time was discussed. In the last interview, the parent was also asked to describe what the research process might mean for her as she continued to work with the caseworker.

In addition to these interviews and the review of the family's case file, an observation was conducted with the caseworker and the family. The observation took place in the parent's home during a normal, scheduled visit that would have taken place regardless of the research investigation. The observation was used to gain a better understanding of the dynamics that occur in the relationship as it was happening in a naturalistic environment. The researcher's recorded impressions were then compared with how the caseworker and the parent described their relationship.

Analytic Procedure

Transcribed interviews were analyzed for recurrent regularities in themes and patterns. Data from the interviews were triangulated with the data in the family's case file and with the observations recorded during the home visit. Careful attention was given to how the caseworker and parent described the relationship, and how this was or was not congruent with the case file or the observation in the parent's home. Attention also focused on the meaning that each participant gave to the relationship and their theories about how the relationship may have contributed to the length of involvement with each other. As patterns and themes were identified, categories were developed and described for coding purposes. I used a natural systems approach to understand the possible relationship between these interpretive categories and to explain the patterns and connections in the data. In a natural systems perspective, individuals are seen as part of networks of relationships, embedded in larger networks (Capra 1996, 2002). Here, the network within which the caseworker and the parent are embedded is child welfare services. Federal regulations and state statutes dictate the initial engagement between the caseworker and the family and serve to frame the subsequent boundaries as they develop their relationship. Without these rules and statutes, there would be no relationship between the caseworker and parent. At the same time, they experience a relationship that is unique for each of them. To this relationship, each brings her own history, experiences, and beliefs. I hoped to capture the layers of this phenomenon.

Simultaneously, the structure of Seidman's interviewing approach (1998) was used to explore how these individuals relate to each other and to me within the context of the child welfare system and this research project. The connection between these individuals that was being explored is what Bateson (1979:7) describes as the "pattern which connects."

The information in the next section (Findings) is presented in the sequence in which the information was gathered, as recommended by Seidman (1998). The passages allow readers to gain their own perspectives, realizing that this is a snapshot of the many years the caseworker and parent spent working together. As a researcher, I simultaneously share the story of the caseworker and parent and at the same time tell the reader how I chose to tell the story. Telling stories is a major way that people make sense of themselves (Mishler 1986). The researcher's role was to look at how the story of this relationship might shed light on the type of relationship, the changes over time, and influences on the length of engagement.

The portions of text that follow emerged as representative of the relationship. They provide important information about how each participant felt about each other and the origins of these feelings. In analyzing more than 100 pages of interviews and observations, I initially highlighted passages that seemed important in answering the research questions about the nature of the caseworker and parent relationship and what that might tell me about the nature of chronic neglect. From those passages, I selected brief sections that offered a clear portrayal of the relationship. I then put them together in the order that they were provided to me as a way of presenting a coherent narrative in the participants' own words.

Findings

PARENT INTERVIEW #1

The first interview with the parent began with developing a genogram of the family. The parent described having her first of four children at age 16. She described her mother's reaction to the news that she was pregnant: "At first she was like really upset. She tried to have me get an abortion. I refused. Then she actually told me I was having a child for her, so she could raise it and have somebody to take care of." The parent says that her mother gained legal custody of her child shortly after he was born. She lived at home trying to raise her son with what she describes as her mother interfering by telling her, "I had him in the wrong clothes. I didn't change him enough. I changed him too often. I didn't feed him enough." The parent moved out of her mother's home when her son was a year and a half. Her son remained with his grandmother. When the grandmother died five years later, the child returned to live with his mother. By this time, the parent had two more children. She describes what it was like parenting her oldest child once he returned to live with her.

PRINCIPAL INVESTIGATOR (PI): When you finally got to raise him again as your son what was that like?

MOTHER (M): He was ruined.

PI: Tell me what you mean?

M: He was a brat. I had already had his sister and brother by then, and as far as he was concerned, he could do no wrong. He could do whatever he wanted, when he wanted. You know. The whole nine yards. Didn't have to listen to me or anybody else for that matter.

PI: So did your husband at the time help with him?

M: He tried. He did things the wrong way with all my kids. All except the one I had with him (the last of her four children). He would punish. He never flat out beat them, but he would spank 'em or he would call 'em stupid or dummy. Say a lot of nasty and mean things to them. He tried to make them mind. It never worked.

We then talked about her second child—her only daughter. She contrasted how she raised her daughter with how her first son was raised by his grandmother. She said, "I totally raised her . . . myself. I thought we would be like best friends." It did not turn out the way she planned. "Not even close," she said.

PI: When did things change?
M: I don't know actually what happened. I know that shortly after she started school—maybe her second year of school—things just went totally different. She was put into special education. She went to counseling and she is a drama queen and an attention-getter. She wants to be the center of attention at all times.
PI: Was she always that way or did it start when she went to school?
M: She started after she went to school. If she got grounded to her room, she would go to school and blow things up and I'd get turned in.
PI: And is that when you started to become involved with DSS [the Department of Social Services]?
M: Yeah.
PI: Her going to school and saying, mom did this, mom did that?
M: Yeah. Right.
PI: What would happen when they came out to your house?
M: Well, they always talked to the kids, and looked at the kids, and told me what was goin' on, what the charges were, and I mean there was so many times. You know, they'd come in and I'd say okay, and I'd open all my cupboards and my doors [to demonstrate that adequate food and supplies were in the home]. You know, show them their rooms. There was one time when I was turned in for unlawful imprisonment, I think it was, 'cause I grounded one of my children to their room for a week. They didn't have a door on their room, how was it unlawful imprisonment? They just weren't allowed out of their room.

Later in the interview, the parent is asked if she feels judged from all the investigations and the fact that several of her children have ended up in placement. I asked her how she has dealt with feeling judged. She responds, "What I say is they're clueless. They have no idea the crap that I've been through. They have no idea what I've been through. You know, they're clueless."

CASEWORKER INTERVIEW #1

In the first interview with the caseworker, I asked about her work with the DSS and the parameters around the expectations of being a caseworker. In addition, we discussed her relationship with the parent and family, with whom she has worked for over ten years. She worked for the DSS for 14 years, nine as a child protective investigator and the last five as a foster care/ preventive case worker. The caseworker described her function in foster care: "After children have been placed in foster care for x number of years . . . there's a number . . . 15 out of 22 months . . . the ASFA [Adoption and Safe Families Act] laws, then we file a petition against the parents to terminate their parental rights." The caseworker contrasted it to juvenile delinquent/ person in need of supervision (JD/PINS) cases where her work focused on the behaviors of the child rather than their parents, "What happens is we get a referral from court or from probation and I either am assigned that case after probation does their report or court gives their order to monitor the kids to make sure they're doing what the court is requesting them to do." The caseworker then described her goal in working with foster families, biological families, and children in placement:

PI: When you go and visit them, what do you want to get from that visit?
CW: From the foster parents, I want to make sure that everything is smooth with that child in their home. With parents, I like their cooperation: They're visiting with their children. If there is something that the judge might have asked them to do on the court order, I try to encourage them to let them know it is for the benefit of their child.
PI: What if you've got a child in an institution, then what's your goal there when you meet with the child or with the parents?
CW: I strive to get their relationship to a point where both are comfortable with the child returning home. If it's a school issue, the parents are either on board or not on board with the school with the PINS. But,

if it's a PINS filed by the parent, such as several of the cases I have
are, I want the parent to feel comfortable enough that the child has
completed the services they should be undergoing in order to get
them home.

PI: So, how do you want the parents to see you?

CW: I guess as a helper. Not necessarily as a friend, because there's that
line I don't want to go over when it comes to professionalism. But,
I want them to trust me enough . . . hopefully trust me enough to
have me in the position of making sure that child has whatever they
need to get home. Whether it be the counseling. Whether it be the
drug and alcohol inpatient program.

PI: How do you want the kids to see you?

CW: That's a little different. I guess I want them to know that the court
has given me a job to do, but I want them to not see me as an authority figure—if it's possible—because a lot of them don't like authority
figures. I guess kind of as a friend, but to know there are boundaries
in our relationship.

The caseworker is asked what motivates her to do this type of work:

CW: I didn't expect to quote unquote, save the world. But, I thought if
I could make a difference in at least 10 percent of the families I
worked with that would be making a difference for society.

PI: And what tells you that you're making a difference?

CW: When I was still in child protective, what I still related to is the subsequent recidivism of child protective reports. Some families, there's
a cycle. It's ongoing. It's generational. But, in other situations, they
were either unfounded reports or maybe isolated incidents, which
when you're going over the allegations, even if they are disciplining
their children with corporeal punishment, just explaining to them
the seriousness of what happens if it's excessive.

PI: So do you think that you've made a difference with 10 percent or one
out of ten families?

CW: I'd probably say more. And that, for me, has value . . . seventeen
years in the field . . .

Once the function and motivation were established for the caseworker,
the first interview established how the caseworker and the parent first met

and how that relationship evolved over the years as the caseworker went from investigating the family as a child protective investigator to placing two of the four children as a foster care/preventive case worker. The caseworker described her first impression as being "pretty average." She said, "I certainly didn't expect them to still be around now—eleven, thirteen years later."

PI: If you could think of maybe one or two reasons why they are still involved: Why they had the initial report, dealt with whatever was going on, and you never saw them again. Why didn't that happen with this family?

CW: It's the mother: Clear and simple. She probably should have had an evaluation, a mental health evaluation. There was never a court order to do so. There was court order to counseling, but never an evaluation, years ago with the neglect case.

PI: And what would the evaluation have told you that would have changed the case?

CW: Mom has been in some DV (domestic violence) situations with her first—her only real husband—as well as her second quote, unquote husband. I think she's very co-dependent. I think she's got a lot of self-esteem issues.

PI: You think those things were never dealt with?

CW: Never. Never.

PI: And if they had been dealt with, what do you think would be different?

CW: I think Mom could have pulled herself up by the bootstraps years ago, gotten out of the situations. I think a lot of what the kids have seen over the years has caused them to be very angry. Their PINS-able behaviors have been violent tendencies towards peers, toward school staff, and at home. Though this mother deals with their behaviors more now than she had before, they're angry toward her.

Later in the interview, the caseworker is asked if she thinks that by moving the family from a child protective case to a PINS case that somehow the system was no longer holding the parents in this case accountable. This is because in PINS cases the court focuses specifically on whether the child is following the judge's orders rather than what the parent is doing to manage the child's behaviors. The person in need of supervision is the child, not the parent. But, in child protective cases, the parents' behaviors are the ones that are monitored. The caseworker said, "Absolutely. Absolutely. Even with the neglect case, we got an adjudication of neglect based on domestic violence, the father's drug and alcohol misuse. Even when they did not complete services. They did not get the children the counseling they needed. Legal did not want to file a violation. They let the case close. It was never extended. This system has failed the family." Ultimately, the caseworker believed that the agency had an opportunity to cite the parents for not completing court-ordered services as a way to force them to get the counseling they needed. From the caseworker's perspective, this was an opportunity lost.

PI: It will have been fifteen years that she's been involved with this system. What do you think that says about the system and about her and about you?

CW: I see a big "F" stamped on the top of the page. Really. I feel bad that it's gone so long. And I feel bad that these kids are probably going to grow up to be very dysfunctional adults, specifically the daughter . . . She does not have the tools to be out there.

PI: What do you think will happen to her?

CW: I give her six months and she'll be pregnant. I foresee the baby being removed. I just see a whole terrible flood of events for her.

When asked about the relationship between the caseworker and the parent at this point, the caseworker remarked, "When it came to the child protective stuff, at least the initial investigation stages, that she didn't like me very much . . . At this point, because the pressure is not on her, she'll tell you she likes me, I have no doubt."

PARENT INTERVIEW #2

The second interview with the parent discussed the nature of her relationship with the caseworker as it evolved from child protective investigations to preventive services. The interview began with the parent recalling the first time that she and the caseworker met. During the previous interview with this parent, she described initially being turned in to child protective services when her daughter told school officials stories about her mother. But, during the first caseworker interview, the caseworker described their first meeting being related to an investigation involving the parent's third child. During the second parent interview, the parent describes the same event involving her third child:

M: Somebody had called and reported that he fell and hit his head on the coffee table and ended up with a bump and bruises on him.

PI: So, your first contact with her was a result of somebody calling and saying you haven't been watching your child?

M: Right. Right. It was all a farce. The caller was totally lying.

PI: Can you recall what the experience was like . . . having someone knock on your door?

M: It scared the heck out of me. I didn't like it one bit.

PI: And how did she act toward you? Do you remember?

M: Well, he had just gone down for a nap. I was moving that day and he had just gone down for a nap. I asked her, "I guess you need to see the child. I just got him to sleep." And she said, "Yeah, actually I do." So, I woke him up and brought him out in just his diaper. It was hot out. And she goes, "Oh my goodness." And there's not a mark on the kid. And she going, "Oh my God, look at this . . ." He was a pudge. He was a fat baby. She [the caseworker] says sarcastically, "Oh my goodness. Look at this poor neglected baby. Look at all the bruises on him." There was nothing wrong with him. It is the caseworker who is being sarcastic—I think by the addition of [the caseworker] that might be enough.

PI: So, how did that feel when she was pretty positive?

M: Oh, it made me feel better. I knew that there was nothing wrong with him. I, I, I wasn't scared. I just didn't like the fact that someone was knocking on my door. You know.

PI: Did you sense that she was trying to make it easier for you?

M: Yeah.

Later in the interview, the parent is asked how it feels to be a parent who is being investigated by child protective services. She said, "I didn't like it. I mean it made me . . . it didn't make me feel like a bad parent. But, then again, it did." When asked what she did with those feelings, the parent responded, "There is really nothing that I could do . . . There was no way to stop it." By contrast, she described how she now works with the caseworker more collegially, given the change in the caseworker's role with the family.

PI: Why do you still have a caseworker?

M: Oh because my daughter is in placement and my son was removed from the home and is in placement.

PI: So what are your expectations of her now?

M: When there a meeting, she . . . if I can't get a ride, she brings me. She will come and get me and bring me to the meeting. If there's something new, she calls me and tells me. If I have a problem, I call her and tell her.

The parent then talks about the fact that she will never allow her daughter to return home to live with the family. She is asked how she feels about that decision and if she feels that the caseworker supports her:

M: She knows that my daughter is too far gone to be home. She understands my feelings of—it's a safety issue with the children and the family. She knows. And for my daughter too.

PI: So, you don't feel judged about that?

M: No. No. I don't.

PI: Because that is a hard decision to come to.

M: I don't. But, you know what? I don't care what people think because they aren't where I am. They're not afraid of her. The people that are dealing with her are trained to deal with people like my daughter. I'm not.

The parent said she talks with her caseworker, her new boyfriend, and her sister about what it is like to come to the decision not to let her daughter return to live with her. They all tell her it is not her fault:

PI: Do you believe them or do you have doubts?

M: Not all the time. No. I think some of it is my fault being with a jerk for so long. But, I also know that there's mental problems in her father's side of the family. You know. And that may be a factor. She had meningitis when she was a baby. That may be a factor come to find out. I did some research on that. There's a lot of different factors. Then I feel alone. It's like, it's like I feel like I'm the only person who goes through this. I know I'm not. But, it's a very alone feeling when you're going through this with a child. You know. And there's really nothing that I can do to help. There really isn't. I brought the kid home. I wanted to make her life better. She had the opportunity to be with me as a family and have a good life. And obviously she wasn't ready for it.

In the last part of the interview, the parent is asked if there was a way that she could have ended the relationship with the caseworker and the DSS:

M: I would love for them to be out of my life now. You know. But, I know it's not, it's not an option. As long as I have children in placement . . .

PI: They have to be here?

M: They have to be here. Any parent would love for DSS—would want to do it themselves and love for DSS not to be involved. But, as long as you have a child in placement, it's not an option.

PI: Was there a time before the kids went into placement that they were working with you that you just wished . . .

M: They weren't working with me. I was being turned in and investigated.

PI: So, it sounds like there's two different phases?

M: Right.

The parent describes how things have changed and how she is happier since her relationship with a new boyfriend. She says she believes that her caseworker is "rooting for her" to be happy. She says, "I've noticed, they're rooting. Everybody. And it's an amazing feeling. You know . . . that to know that I actually have all these people who care about me. I was clueless."

CASEWORKER INTERVIEW #2

During the second interview with the caseworker, a review of the family's case file was completed. Due to the confidential nature of these records, with the parent's permission, the caseworker was asked to review the records and develop a timeline; the researcher and the caseworker then reviewed the timeline. We began with the neglect petition:

CW: In our neglect petition, which is contained in this brown folder, there are three specific allegations for three different reports. One being where the middle boy was slapped across the face was an indicated report (an investigation was completed and there was evidence to substantiate the allegations). One where the daughter was spanked on the butt by Mom's boyfriend at the time. That was an indicated report. Then the domestic violence situation where he was drunk and she was chasing him with a butcher knife.

PI: Now the ones that you've just mentioned sound to me like abuse rather than neglect. So how do you tell the difference?

CW: Actually, abuse is broken bones, severe physical abuse where the bruising is so bad it warrants police activity, or sex abuse. Just the hand print across the face would be seen as neglect or maltreatment, or a hand print on the buttock. It depends on the severity to warrant abuse.

PI: What do you do normally when you see that type of a pattern? When you see that there are a number of things like that are happening?

CW: That's when we would bring it to legal's attention. Actually, we'd bring anything, whether it be a single isolated incident, we'd bring it to legal's attention. Then legal would determine whether or not we would file a neglect petition or abuse petition against a family. And, I don't have the files, but I can only assume for those individual incidents broken down, legal didn't feel we have enough to file a petition. But, when we brought three incidents together, they felt there was enough because it was a pattern of behavior.

The caseworker went on to describe the complex nature of working with this family and the first time the daughter was removed from the home. At that point in time, the caseworker had transitioned from being a child protective investigator to a preventive caseworker:

CW: There was a report that I did not investigate. I was already in the foster care/preventive unit. A child protective report came out against the mother in this family, and it alleged physical abuse of the daughter. When the child protective worker went to the home to speak to the mother about that, she said, "Get her out of my home. I'm having problems with her." I was in the process of filing a PINS petition against the daughter. So, she was removed. Was Mom feeling guilty because she had, in fact, struck her daughter and wanted her out of there in case her explosive behavior would cause her to hit her again? Or was it just anger because, here we go, child protective is back here? Or was [it] her daughter's behavior and she had just had enough, and felt she might hurt her (meaning mom). I can't tell you.

The caseworker then talked about her discovery when she was putting together the neglect petition that the family had been involved with social services in a different county prior to their involvement with the caseworker's county. The caseworker reported that there were similar behaviors and investigations before she got involved with the family, when the daughter was less than a year old. Other than the parent talking about a previous history of domestic violence, the parent and caseworker had never talked about the previous child protective investigations. When asked if she thought talking about the previous investigations would have made any difference, the caseworker told a story from a recent meeting with the parent and a number of professionals talking about serious issues regarding the daughter: "The mother laughed and did not take the meeting seriously." The caseworker described not confronting the parent during this meeting because she thinks confrontation would have never made a difference with this case.

OBSERVATION OF MOTHER AND CASEWORKER

After completing the first two interviews with the mother and caseworker, the researcher observed a meeting between them. I did not speak during this observation. During the one-hour observation, I recorded the process of the meeting and, at least every five minutes, my impressions of the process (see table 19.1).

During the observation, the caseworker and parent continued to talk about the daughter while the youngest boy continuously interrupted their discussion. Parent and caseworker gave the child some choices and got him to stop after 30 minutes of interruptions. Eventually, the conversation turned to the mother's new boyfriend. The mother became animated in talking about her boyfriend and her boyfriend's mother. She was also animated in talking about her middle son coming home from placement. Each time the caseworker brought it back to the daughter, the parent either changed the subject or engaged with her young son's interrupting behaviors.

PARENT INTERVIEW #3

The third interview with the parent was used to talk about what it was like for her to be interviewed for the research. The parent talked about being

Table 19.1

Time	Caseworker Activity	Parent Activity	Research Note
3:45	When principal investigator (PI) comes to the home, the caseworker is already there waiting for me.	Parent's youngest son is on the phone with his principal who is questioning him about being hit by the bus driver. When he is finished the mother talks on the phone with the principal.	
	While the mother is on the phone, the caseworker talks with the child.		
		When mother is finished on the phone she talks with caseworker about what has happened.	
	Caseworker makes recommendations to mother about what she should do.		*Seems like CW (caseworker) is telling M (mother) what she should do, rather than having M decide a plan of action. It seems very natural for the CW to give recommendation to the M and seems to expect M to follow her advice.*
		Seems like the parent is trying to explain herself.	

(continued)

Table 19.1 (Continued)

Time	Caseworker Activity	Parent Activity	Research Note
	Caseworker provides more information.	Child goes out of the room and then brings his fish for the caseworker to see. Parent talks about his first fish. Parent tries to ask child to leave.	
	Caseworker reinforced Mom's directive.	Child slowly leaves.	*CW reinforcing what M says. Does not wait for M to say it again or say it and mean it.*
3:50	Caseworker begins telling parent about incidents with her daughter in placement, providing information. Caseworker helps Mom get rid of child.	Child returns. Interrupts parent and caseworker.	*CW providing information to M, but it's unclear what she wants M to do with this information.*
		Child interrupts, directing his attention to Mom.	*Is M wanting child to interrupt for some reason?*
	Caseworker continues to talk. Her affect is flat. CW tells M that public assistance is available for her daughter.		*Remember CW doesn't think M will take daughter back.*
		Parent discusses worry about her own safety if her daughter were to come home.	
	Caseworker continues to share more information.		
3:55		Child interrupts.	

questioned, in general, rather than specifically talking about me questioning her. She responded, "I guess any parent always has somebody questioning them. I just had New York State questioning me. You know, as opposed to my mom or my sister or whoever." I asked her to contrast what it felt like for her mom to question her parenting versus DSS:

M: I knew it was because my mother wanted my child.
PI: So, you knew there was a motive?
M: Yeah.
PI: What about DSS?
M: With DSS it was always the school questioning everything. It was mostly the school because my daughter would go to school and say I looked at her cross-eyed and I get turned in for some of the dumbest things.
PI: Given that you knew the motive your mom had, what did you start to feel or think the school's motive was?
M: I think it was my daughter's motive. I don't know what her motive was. But, she had one. I still don't know. I'm clueless.

We talked about her relationship with her daughter. I asked her what it felt like to see her friends interact with their daughters. She talked about feeling envious. She said, "I see other moms and daughters out shopping and doing regular mom and daughter stuff. I have nothing but ever wanted that for me and my daughter. And I know it's something that I'll never have. I know it's something we'll never have."

I then ask her what she thinks her caseworker might have said about their relationship. She believed that her caseworker would say that she knows she has had it rough, "Probably that I've had a rough 12 years and you know, me staying was being stupid. You know, and I could have done better." She is asked to describe herself as a parent:

M: I do the best I can . . . with what I've got. It's like, right now, I'm doin' the best I can. You know, that's all that any parent can really do. You know, kids these days want everything under the sun. It's just not a possibility.

CASEWORKER INTERVIEW #3

The third and final interview with the caseworker was used to talk about the process of being interviewed. I asked if the caseworker believes that she and the parent in this case are representative of other caseworker/parent relationships.

> cw: I think because we've gone through such a gamut of cases within this one case . . . the child protective reports with the neglect case, with two PINS cases on the boy who is in placement right now, the PINS cases on the girl who is down in Pennsylvania now. The oldest boy coming back into the home, trying to help him with housing, trying to help him with getting food after the mother moved out to be with her boyfriend. Being 18 and on his own. I don't think every case has that whole spectrum of things going on.
>
> pi: So, tell me what you would say is more of a typical case?
>
> cw: From my 17 years as a caseworker, 14 here. I think we typically get cases that might be just child protective related or just PINS or JD related. My belief is that a lot of the kids that come in as PINS or JD kids, there may have been oversights when they were younger with neglect or abuse issues. I would say probably a good portion of that. I don't know if there are statistics or what they'd be.

I asked if talking about this case had somehow changed how she views the case. She says, "Definitely. Hearing myself talk about things I wouldn't typically talk about regarding casework has made me try to fine tune things a little better."

> pi: How so?
>
> cw: I guess holding people more accountable. I think there were times that Mom frustrated me so much that it was just easier for me to do her work for her with her kids . . . And I am one to confront people, so I'm not sure at what point I stopped making her accountable and confronting her about things she should have been doing.
>
> pi: Do you think that will change your relationship with her in the future?
>
> cw: Not with the two kids that are in placement right now.
>
> pi: What about with the youngest one?
>
> cw: Definitely will.
>
> pi: How will it change?
>
> cw: Just seeing his behavior in the home. I've seen his behavior in the home more than I saw the other two, prior to them becoming PINS cases. She is the primary reason he has the behaviors he has.

We then discussed what might happen with the youngest child and if there is an unspoken message that if the child does not behave, he will be placed. The caseworker believed that to be the case. "She does love her kids. I believe that. But, I believe when they become too hard for her to handle, give them to somebody else to deal with so she doesn't have to."

PI: Do you think that one of those people who handled it was you?
CW: Absolutely. Sure. I guess I perpetuated her behavior.

In looking at this case, the caseworker was clear that she had behaved differently with this parent than she had with other parents. She believed she grew frustrated with the lack of follow-through. "The only way to do it was to do it myself." She said, "I think now, other than with her daughter, I think she's trying the best she can."

Data Analysis

Initial Engagement with the Child Welfare System

How the child welfare regulations guided the caseworker's decision-making provided an understanding of the context for how the caseworker put the regulations into action. The child welfare rules and regulations structured the relationship between the caseworker and the parent. As a child protective investigator, the caseworker's job was to go to the parent's home to determine if it was a safe environment and whether the parent had the capacity to care for her children and provide a minimum degree of care (New York State Office of Children and Family Services 2002). The caseworker had the authority of law to make decisions in the life of the family that affected the children's physical and emotional safety. Despite her clear authority, the caseworker talked about not wanting to be seen as an authority in the first interview, but as a helper. The caseworker acknowledged her authority, but she described not confronting the parent. "And I am one to confront people, so I'm not sure at what point I stopped making her accountable and confronting her about things she should have been doing."

Similarly, the parent recalled that in the first meeting 10 years earlier, the caseworker tried to make their first meeting one in which the parent did not feel the heavy hand of state authority. The caseworker stressed the size of the baby and how it was impossible that a baby that big could be neglected. She recalled the caseworker's laughing sarcasm: "Oh my goodness. Look at this poor neglected baby." In short, both caseworker and mother characterized the initial encounter as clearly difficult, but with much effort put into making the formal investigation process as painless as possible.

Shift in Roles, Shift in Relationship

As the caseworker changed her role within the child welfare agency from a child protective investigator to a foster care/preventive caseworker, she continued to work with this family. Why? The parent's daughter was placed out of the home. This event marked a shift in the relationship between the caseworker and parent. The parent made a clear distinction between the two phases. During the second interview, the parent was asked about the time before the kids went into placement: "Was there a time before the kids went into placement that they (social services) were working with you and you just wished. . . ." Before I finished the question, the parent corrected me by stating, "They weren't *working* with me. I was being turned in and investigated."

But, did the daughter get placed because her mother hit her and she was unsafe, or because there was a PINS being filed on the child? If the child was placed as a result of being hit this would mean that the mother's behavior was the source of the placement decision, rather than because of the daughter's ungovernable behavior as the PINS would indicate. The caseworker described the ambiguity of the placement: "There was a report that I did not investigate. I was already in the foster care/preventive unit. A child protective report came out against the mother in this family, and it alleged physical abuse of the daughter. When the child protective worker went to the home to speak to the mother about that, she (the mother) said, 'Get her (daughter) out of my home. I'm having problems with her.' I was in the process of filing a PINS (person in need of supervision) petition against the daughter. So, she was removed." The ambivalence from this event, especially for the caseworker, served as a covert source of ambivalence in the relationship. For the parent, the shift in the role of the caseworker from investigator to preventive worker was a relief. No longer was the caseworker coming to the home to question her parenting. Instead, she was there because the children were in placement because of the behavior *they* were exhibiting. There was a shift in responsibility for the caseworker's presence—from faulty parental behavior to the children's incorrigibility, a shift that is welcome to the parent.

Doing the Best You Can?

What Does This Tell Us About the Nature of Chronic Neglect?

In the last research interview, the caseworker described the nature of the children whom she saw as becoming PINS cases. For her, they were children who experienced neglect or abuse in their childhoods and consequently grew up into PINS cases. This view of the children provides a clue to the caseworker's perception of the chronicity of neglect. The caseworker said, "My belief is that a lot of the kids that come in as PINS or JD kids, there may have been oversights when they were younger with neglect or abuse issues. I would say probably a good portion of that." For the caseworker, this is the circumstance with this family: She began as an investigator of child maltreatment, but over time when the children became difficult to manage, their behaviors became the reason for placement.

In this case, the parent was planning for her son who is in placement to return home, but she was not going allow her daughter to return home. During the second parent interview, the parent described struggling with this decision. She described her doubts, the explanations she had considered and the loneliness she felt. ". . . it's like I feel like I'm the only person who goes through this. I know I'm not. But, it's a very alone feeling when you're going through this with a child." The caseworker characterized the circumstances as the failure of the system, the failure of the agency's legal department, and her own failure. The caseworker also described refusing to take the daughter back as the one exception to the parent doing the best she can.

Further Explanation from Systems Theory

As communications recur in multiple feedback loops, they produce a shared system of beliefs, explanations, and values—a common context for meaning—that is sustained by further communications. Through this shared context of meaning individuals acquire identities as members of the social network, and in this way the network generates its own boundary. It is not a physical boundary but a boundary of expectations, of confidentiality and loyalty, which is continually maintained and renegotiated by the network itself (Capra 2002:83).

Following Capra (2002), in this case, the rules governing child welfare set the boundaries for the initial meeting and for the lengthy connection between the caseworker and parent. However, each person's choices to act in that relationship were set by the expectations, values, and beliefs each brought to the relationship and were reinforced though their ongoing communication with one another. The caseworker described how unusual it was for her to not confront the parent about certain decisions or actions as she did in other cases. At one point, the caseworker felt that the parent had gotten her to take care of her children. Yet, the caseworker felt she had failed these children. She had not helped them—which is how she defined herself.

The parent had regrets as well. She regretted staying in previous relationships with men who were abusive. But the pattern for the mother doubting her ability to parent was present before she ever became involved with child protective services. The parent described her own mother questioning her parenting; and, in fact, her mother took over the parenting of the first child in this family. New York State was second in line to question the parent's child caring abilities. And then the parent, herself, was next in line to doubt her parenting abilities. Yet in spite of all the years of questioning, the parent described feeling like her caseworker wanted her to succeed. In the parent's words, the caseworker was "rooting" for her. And the parent believed the caseworker thought she was doing the best she can. The caseworker did feel that way, with one important exception: the parenting of the daughter. It is an exception that seemed to fill this caseworker with her own sense of doubt. Despite evidence that the parenting skills were deficient, the nature of the relationship changed between caseworker and parent and served to prevent either of them from confronting these deficiencies, leaving both with vague regrets the cause of which they did not recognize.

Limitations of the Study

This study is an intensive, single-case study using interviews, records, and observation and then analysis of what the data suggest about the relationship between caseworker and mother, about changes in the relationship, and inferences about the relationship and length of service. Of necessity, because data were collected long after service began, the narrative probably does not represent actual interaction but is instead the caseworker's and mother's "story."

Even given this limitation, I had hoped to get a broader picture of the interaction by interviewing the children and reviewing the case records. However, the IRB refused permission to interview the children. They reasoned that because this was an exploratory study and it was not clear what might emerge from the interviews, the parents might have strong feelings about the child welfare system that would generate uncomfortable emotions for the children to witness. Similarly, the IRB did not give permission for me to review the case records because there might be information about someone other than family members, and their privacy needed to be protected. Reviewing the case file might better have captured the changes in relationship because notes in the case file were written when events occurred. In place of my own review, I asked the caseworker to review and reflect on the record. These three limitations—participants' recollections, not interviewing the children, and reviewing the case record only through the caseworker's lens—means that the accounts are more "story" than reality. This story, real or not, guided the mother's and the caseworker's actions and interpretations about entering and staying entangled in child protective services.

Discussion and Implications

The relationship, in theory, is the mode through which parenting behavior is changed (Crittenden 1999). In this case, however, the parental behavior did not change. One reason may be the nature of the relationship. The relationship started with the caseworker in an authoritative, investigatory role but with the caseworker attempting to be viewed as a benevolent helper—thus creating an ambiguous situation for both herself and the parent. When the case was moved to foster care/preventive and the caseworker's role shifted to pure assistance, the pressure for the parent to change her behavior disappeared. This left the caseworker and the mother more comfortable with each other. Perhaps because of the previous ambiguity and dilemmas of the relationship during the investigatory phrase, the caseworker chose not to confront the mother's inadequate parenting behavior. Instead, together they created a new story to sustain the relationship: That the issue was not the parent's behavior but the children's behavior that lead to their removal from the home. Thus the mother perceived the caseworker as "rooting for her," and the caseworker could genuinely say "she's doing the best she can." But with no tension or pressure to change the situation, nothing changed. The mother resisted the potential return of the daughter, while the caseworker was left having uneasy regrets about the case.

. Neglect has a unique feature that complicates its definition, consequence, and intervention (Gelles 1999). With abuse, the key question is whether injury was inflicted on purpose or by accident; thus making intent the center of the consequence and intervention. With neglect, the question is could this (act of omission or inattention) have been prevented. Thus it is not always clear whether the neglect is due only to a parent's omission or to an absence of social, economic, or psychological resources. Could this parent have met her child's needs given the available resources?

Child welfare caseworkers are seen as resources made available to parents in order to change the neglecting behaviors. Yet, it is not clear that the caseworker did or could address the broader systemic causes and lack of resources in this case. For example, in addition to the interaction of the family conditions with inadequate resources, social isolation, or depression, there are many possible reasons for a child's needs not being met (Polansky, Ammons, and Gaudin 1985; DiLeonardi 1993; Drake and Pandey 1996).

According to DePanfilis (1999), to be effective, interventions have to be directed at the individual, microsystem, and exosystem, with changes to the macrosystem being the long-term goal. However, caseworkers may not have the leverage to change the conditions. In short, the context of the child welfare system constrained the caseworker's and parent's choice around intervention.

DePanfilis (1999) emphasizes the importance of developing a partnership with families. Intervention with neglect requires a process over time of assisting parents to meet the needs of their children. This requires the development of an alliance between service provider and family. Such an alliance may be particularly difficult with parents who have a difficult time asking for help or who do not expect to receive it when it is offered (Crittenden and Ainsworth 1989), as this case demonstrates. Nevertheless, over time, the goal of the partnership needs to be a relationship that allows parents to solve their own problems. An empowerment model (Fraser and Galinsky 1997), and a strength-based perspective (Saleeby 1996) are useful concepts; practitioners work with the family to build on their existing competencies. Instead of working on problems, they build solutions—a far cry from the psychological model of blaming parents. Yet, as the caseworker in this study recognized, the mother expected the caseworker to take care of the children. Inadvertently, between reluctance to confront the mother and difficulty establishing an empowering relationship, the caseworker and the child welfare system seem to have reinforced the family's pattern of neglecting behavior.

The goal of this research was to look at the nature of the relationship between a caseworker and a parent over time and in the context of the child welfare system. It provided some insight as to the nature of neglect and what might contribute to the chronicity of this phenomenon in some families.

This research offers: (1) A methodology for a way to explore the nature of relationships—in this case between caseworkers and parents, and (2) a closer look at a phenomenon that is not well understood. The voices and insights of individuals who have experienced chronic neglect begin to counter assumptions that policymakers, practitioners, and other service providers act on. If we listen closely, they may be able to tell us why neglect might occur, what contributes to its enduring nature, and what might be necessary in order to change the patterns.

References

Bateson, G. 1979. *Mind and nature: A necessary unity*. New York: Dutton.

Capra, F. 1996. *The web of life*. New York: Random House.

——. 2002. *The hidden connections*. New York: Doubleday.

Crittenden, P. M. 1999. Child neglect: Cause and contributors. In *Neglected children: Research, practice and theory*, H. Dubowitz, ed. 47–68. Thousand Oaks, CA: Sage.

Crittenden, P. M. and M. D. Ainsworth. 1989. Child maltreatment and attachment theory. In *Child Maltreatment*, D. Cicchetti and V. Carlson, eds. 432–464. Cambridge: Cambridge UP.

DePanfilis, D. 1999. Intervening with families when children are neglected. In *Neglected children: Research, practice and theory*, H. Dubowitz, ed. 211–236. Thousand Oaks, CA: Sage.

DiLeonardi, J. W. 1993. Families in poverty and chronic neglect of children. *Families in Society*, 74:557–562.

Drake, B. and S. Pandey. 1996. Understanding the relationship between neighborhood poverty and specific types of child maltreatment. *Child Abuse and Neglect*, 20(11):1003–1018.

Fraser, M. W. and M. J. Galinsky. 1997. Toward a resilience-based model of practice. In *Risk and resilience in childhood: An ecological perspective*, M. W. Fraser, ed. 265–275. Washington, DC: NASW.

Garbarino, J. and C. C. Collins. 1999. Child neglect: The family with the hole in the middle. In *Neglected children: Research, practice and policy*, H. Dubowitz, ed. 1–23. Thousand Oaks, CA: Sage.

Gaudin, J. 1993. *Child neglect: A guide for intervention.* Washington, DC: U.S. Department of Health and Human Services, National Center on Child Abuse and Neglect.

Gelles, R. J. 1999. Policy issues in child neglect. In *Neglected children: Research, practice and policy*, H. Dubowitz, ed. 278–298. Thousand Oaks, CA: Sage.

Glaser, D. 2002. Emotional abuse and neglect: A conceptual framework. *Child Abuse and Neglect*, 26:697–714.

Hutchison, E. D. 1990. Child maltreatment: Can it be defined? *Social Service Review*, 64(1):60–78.

Mishler, E. G. 1986. *Research interviewing.* Cambridge, MA: Harvard UP.

——. 2002. *Summary guide for mandated reporters in New York State.* New York: Office of Children and Family Services.

——. 2010. *Child Protective Services Reports 2009.* New York: Office of Children and Family Services.

Polansky, N. A., P. W. Ammons, and J. M. Gaudin. 1985. Loneliness and isolation in child neglect. *Social Casework*, 66:38–47.

Saleebey, D. 1996. The strengths perspective in social work practice: Extensions and cautions. *Social Work*, 41:296–305.

Schumacher, J. A., A. M. S. Slep, and R. E. Heyman. 2001. Risk factors for child neglect. *Aggression and Violent Behavior*, 6:231–254.

Sedlak, A. J. and D. D. Broadhurst. 1996. Executive Summary of the Third National Incidence Study of Child Abuse and Neglect. Washington, DC: U.S. Department of Health and Human Services, National Center on Child Abuse and Neglect.

Sedlak, A. J., J. Mettenburg, M. Basena, I. Petta, K. McPherson, A. Green, and S. Li. 2010. Fourth National Incidence Study of Child Abuse and Neglect (NIS-4): Report to Congress, Executive Summary. Washington, DC: U.S. Department of Health and Human Services, Administration for Children and Families.

Seidman, I. 1998. *Interviewing as qualitative research: A guide for researchers in education and the social services.* New York: Teachers College.

United States General Accounting Office. 2002. "Foster care: Recent legislation helps states focus on finding permanent homes for children, but long-standing barriers remain." GAO-02-585, Adoption and Safe Families Act. Washington, DC.

Wolock, I. and B. H. Horowitz. 1984. Child maltreatment as a social problem: The neglect of neglect. *American Journal of Orthopsychiatry*, 54(4):530–543.

20

Scholarships and Support Available to Foster Youth

A Qualitative Approach to Understanding Service Delivery*

TONI NACCARATO AND LILIANA HERNANDEZ

Qualitative research methods are instrumental in determining the imprint of particular interventions on specific client populations. For example, qualitative research can provide thick descriptions, a client's or service provider's in-depth perspective regarding a particular phenomenon and its meaning, and can be instrumental in program evaluations (Padgett 2004; Creswell 2007). In social work, there are important and vulnerable populations whose voices have not been heard or whose stories have not been told using qualitative methodology. Two such populations are older foster youth—both in the system and those who have aged out (alumni)—and the service providers delivering support to these youth as they face the transition to adulthood.

This chapter will discuss one possible qualitative research method as a useful mode of inquiry for this distinct child welfare population. More specifically, the chapter will focus on a qualitative study that used content analysis to explore support services currently available to foster care youth and alumni (hereafter referred to as foster youth). These scholarship and support services were selected based on their being part of the federally mandated independent living program (ILP) charged with serving older foster youth transitioning to adulthood. The content analysis approach was chosen due to its ability as a methodology to explore the common themes of a population's experiences in an in-depth manner (Creswell 2007). This qualitative study interviewed foster youth service providers in depth. Two research questions guided the study: (1) What is the greatest obstacle to increasing college retention rates among former or current foster youth? (2) What are successes in implementing your scholarship and support services programs at your university, college, or nonprofit? This chapter is a revision of Hernandez and Naccarato (2010), with special emphasis on the process of conducting the research.

The chapter describes the population and intervention characteristics. It also discusses the importance of studying this population and intervention qualitatively, outlines the special research considerations when studying this population, and describes the current study's format for the purposes of informing the readers about a vulnerable and understudied population that greatly benefits from qualitative research. Finally, the methodological steps needed to undertake the qualitative research process are described.

A Knowledge Gap

The lack of qualitative methods in addressing policy research has taken its toll. It appears that even with the use of complex statistical models, not much has been learned regarding social programs. Instead, a more complex, complicated, and partial view of the challenges and solutions has emerged (Rist 2001). There are many unanswered questions in child welfare research that qualitative research is poised to answer regarding certain interventions, personal experiences, and phenomena, especially in the area of how clients and service providers view a program's impact. This has led to a gap in knowledge among clients, researchers, practitioners, and policymakers. This gap has not only existed over time, but has continued to widen. It must be addressed in order to improve service delivery, which can only benefit the clients in a positive way. Many argue that if a program does not work then it should be eliminated or at least the client should be told that the program is not effective. Social work professionals hope to increase the knowledge base of child welfare using both qualitative and quantitative methods. By doing so, all four groups will be better informed and services to foster youth and the overall child welfare system can improve.

Older Foster Youth: A Special Population

Although foster youth are not the largest number of children in foster care, they are increasing in number and little is known about them either qualitatively or quantitatively. Even less is known about these youth after they are discharged from the system. Further, there are negative outcomes such as incarceration, homelessness, and mental health challenges associated with former foster youth (Courtney and Piliavin 1998; Courtney, Piliavin, Grogan-Kaylor, and Nesmith 2001; Courtney, Terao, and Bost 2004; Naccarato and DeLorenzo 2008). Foster youth are different from foster children due to age. Foster youth are typically defined in the literature as youth ages sixteen to eighteen or older who are in a state's custody. Several reporters and child advocates have looked at this population to inform the general public and policymakers about the plights of foster youth. For example, Shirk and Stangler (2004) interviewed former foster youth and presented their particular stories regarding their in-care experiences in *On Their Own: What Happens to Kids When They Age Out of the Foster Care System*. Although not a formal qualitative research study, the information is useful in educating the public. A second important media representation of former foster youth is a documentary entitled *Aging Out* (2005). Based on interviews of foster youth and their families—interviewing and filming them, the documentary describes the youth's family situations, their experiences while in-care, and their personal experiences after discharge from foster care. Again, *Aging Out* is not a formal, qualitative study performed by an academic researcher, but its information is useful to inform the public. However, these studies do not tell us whether the youth received any life-skills training or interventions prior to being discharged and what, if anything, helped shape their goals for the future. A systematic, formal, qualitative evaluation could provide important aids to successful transitions from foster care to postsecondary education.

Methodology

Qualitative methods require a large commitment to studying a problem and can often be laborious in terms of time and resources. A study that uses a mixed-methods approach is thought to be preferred because qualitative methods do not replace quantitative methods (Creswell 2007). The first step in the journey of qualitative research is thinking about what preliminary research questions will guide the study, followed by a thorough review of the literature, and then determining what theory will guide one's study.

In the current study, human capital theory guided the research questions related to education and support services needed to help foster youth succeed in postsecondary institutions. Human capital refers to the education, employment skills, and health-related stock that a person has obtained. Human capital is an economic theory that has been empirically tested. The results indicate that the more human capital a person possesses, the more ability one has to contribute to the labor market and thus be considered a more productive citizen (Becker 1993).

The qualitative researcher must also think about the uniqueness that the study will bring to the literature and to social work practice. It is important that the researcher gain a certain level of expertise and background in the importance of the research and its implications for practice and policy. For example, the researchers in this study completed a careful and thorough review of the literature in order to determine what other information existed related to former or current foster youth and education attainment and supports needed for academic success.

Collection of data may not begin until all necessary internal review board and human subject protocols have been followed. It is necessary to investigate all protocols that affect the research process because academic institutions may be quite different from an agency, particularly if minors in public care are involved. For this current study, human subject clearance was obtained through the University at Albany's institutional review board (IRB).

The volume of data in a qualitative study is determined by whether the researcher has sufficient information to generate themes. Thus if the sample is more alike than different, a smaller sample size is accepted (Crabtree and Miller 1999). The notion is that saturation should occur. That is, the researcher must get to the point where the collection of additional data is not adding new data or perspectives from the informants (Drisko 2005). The current study was conducted with program coordinators/service providers from around the United States to better understand the needs and types of support services available to foster youth. Very little has been studied with respect to program attributes from service providers that include preparing foster youth for the complexities of transitioning to adult life.

Study Design

The next step in the research process is to describe the purpose and clearly state the research questions. The purpose of the current study was to use content analysis to explore the personal experiences of service providers from postsecondary institutions that are providing foster youth scholarship and support services. The following two research questions guided the study:

1. What is the greatest obstacle to increasing college retention rates among former or current foster youth?
2. What are successes in implementing your scholarship and support services programs at your university, college, or nonprofit?

Sample

Next, the researchers chose a sample. The convenience sample consisted of program coordinators from different university, college, or nonprofit organizations that provided either scholarship or support services to foster youth in postsecondary education institutions. Interview participants were recruited by one researcher who analyzed the Internet and solicited recommendations from service providers. Twenty-one participants were recruited. Twelve participants agreed to participate.

Data Collection and Analysis

Telephone interviews of an average of 60 minutes were audiotaped. The semistructured interview protocol consisted of both closed and open-ended questions. The questions addressed which foster youth qualify for these programs and what types of services are available to them, such as mentoring, networking, or internship opportunities. The open-ended questions permitted the participants to describe in detail the valuable aspects of their program and the successes in implementation.

Next, the interviews were transcribed verbatim in order to extract significant statements. The researchers carefully read all of the program coordinators' responses in order to gain an understanding of them. They then hand-coded the statements by question and participant responses. Redundant statements and outlying information were eliminated. Both researchers conducted content and thematic analysis. Formulating meanings out of each significant statement was a difficult and time-consuming task. However, it was beneficial because more than one person reviewed each statement. The purpose of these reviews and formulations of meanings was to uncover those meanings that are hidden within the context of the phenomena under study. The researchers separately organized the two open-ended questions so that common themes across the study participants could be ascertained by clustering the responses. The purpose of developing these clusters was to permit the emergence of themes from participants' descriptions. Each researcher coded the same two open-ended questions to check for inter-rater reliability. Major themes were then assigned by hand coding. The themes were chosen by the researchers based on the use of key words by the participants. The major themes were then organized into a list and, in this case, a data file. When cases of disagreement occurred, the two researchers reexamined the quotes pertaining to a particular topic, and themes were defined that best illustrated what the participants intended.

Key terms related to this content and theme analysis process include: (1) *responses*: the raw transcript responses; (2) *abstract code*: a short summary phrase that represents the response; (3) *major category*: cluster of abstract codes; and, (4) *content areas*: arrangement of major categories into overall areas. This process moves from the most specific to the abstract and is considered an inductive reasoning process. The following steps guided the content and thematic analysis process: (1) consolidate responses from service providers for each question; (2) simplify responses into short phrases that represent the key theme (abstract codes) and combine abstract codes across questions; (3) look for similarities in key themes (major categories); (4) regroup the major categories into new content areas; and (5) presentation.

STEP 1: CONSOLIDATE RESPONSES FROM SERVICE PROVIDERS FOR EACH QUESTION

First, the researchers used the cut-and-paste function in the word processing program to move and separate out the participants' verbatim responses for questions 1 and 2. We then created two independent word processing files from the transcription files.

STEP 2: ABSTRACT CODES

Second, the researchers broke each participant's responses for question 1 into short phrases that represented the key theme or abstract code of each passage. Next, we followed the same process for question 2—again creating two independent word processing files for these two questions. In our initial generation of abstract codes, we erred on the side of caution with respect to empirical detail rather than vagueness or abstraction. In each abstract code, we also included a reference to the actor, because it must be clear in the abstract code who is doing what. We also included the subject's code for each participant's response so that data could be identified by who stated what. For example, we used the code 01JP to represent the first subject's code (see step 2 as follows). Thus first we used our transcription file to cut and paste abstract codes from each participant into two separate files based on questions 1 and 2; this is considered our response file. Next, we noted that many responses were strongly related to one another, so we combined the abstract codes of the strongly related responses into clusters. In step 2, the participants' responses are grouped by subject and, as previously stated, are assigned a subject code (01JP, 02MP), which is subject number and first and last initial. For example, here are some responses from questions 1 and 2:

STEP 2: RESPONSE ANALYSIS FILE

What do you believe is the greatest obstacle to increasing college retention rates among former or current foster youth?

Making sure that they have the education prior to leaving foster care 01JP
Just because they get a diploma or GED doesn't mean that you have the study skills or knowledge for college 01JP

Housing, lack of accessible and affordable housing 02MP

Mental health 03LP
Housing which goes in hand with financial stability 03LP
They don't know how to budget so they end up working 03LP
Youth not used to seeking help 03LP

Keeping connected with the students 04GJ
Once family members know they have a scholarship and that they have

money, a lot feel guilty and their biological family is struggling 04GJ
Self sabotage 04GJ
Giving their money to family 04GJ

Preparation for college 05JE
Students start out in community college and are unprepared for independent living 05JE
They don't have an advocate 05JE
Independent living responsibilities, housing, transportation, child care, food. How to function during school breaks, transportation 05JE
All colleges should be able to answer two questions. How are your students who are from foster care doing? And the second question is: What supports do you have in place that are effectively retaining them and getting them through their programs? 05JE

We don't start early enough talking with youth about going to college 06KN
Many don't know why they are going 06KN
Youth do not succeed because there is too much freedom on the college campus or in the SILP (supervised independent living program) 06KN

Emotional issues 07NW
Not academically prepared for college 07NW
Housing 07NW
Money 07NW
Youth don't know how to problem solve well 07NW
Foster care agencies tend to ignore them 07NW

They can get the money until 23, they start college later, they often don't take full workloads 08RF
They stop receiving money and they may not be able to afford school 08RF
Drug and alcohol 09SD

STEP 2: RESPONSE ANALYSIS FILE:
Describe some of the successes in implementing this program at your university/college/nonprofit.

Support system 01JP
Youth are homesick 01JP

More people succeeding at our associates program 01JP
More to do with the individual than the support system 01JP

Program growth 02MP
Phenomenal growth mainly due to our networking and collaborating with community partners. We are building a referral network 02MP
Advocating with some of the service providers 02MP
Youth see us as a referral source 02MP
Our program is client driven on a drop-in basis 02MP
Networking with the various city providers having an advocacy model 02MP

Advocacy work with the schools 03LP
We're one of the only programs in Washington State that provided funding for college 03LP
These students have access to so many resources 03LP
What we provide them is almost not necessary anymore 03LP

Support and drop-in center 04GJ
Lack of communication and problem-solving skills 04JG
Youth miss rites of passages of a traditional family 04JG
Digital storytelling 04JG
First time they are traveling 04JG
Learning to use public transportation 04JG
Bonding 04JG
Similar themes that their parents experience with alcohol, drugs, and jail 04JG

Mentoring 05JE
Support systems 05JE

Career assessment and career planning 06KN
Self sabotage 06KN
Panel of former foster youth 06KN
Challenges with families with mental illness 06KN

Graduating 07NW
Youth struggle but still in school 07NW

The relationship with OFA (Orphan Foundation of America, which offers a virtual mentor program and scholarship program) OFA 08RF
Manage, disperse the money 08RF
Handholding with the kids 08RF
Some youth don't receive money because they don't follow through 08RF

Modeled after the Cal State Fullerton program, and their success rate is 75 percent 09SD
They may slip, but they will succeed 09SD
They have the opportunity to attend community college and make their way back up 09SD

The data sharing 10DC
The incentive grant 10DC

STEP 3: LOOK FOR SIMILARITIES IN KEY THEMES (MAJOR CATEGORIES)

Once again we created new and separate word processing files for step 3. After our initial coding was completed, we had a long and detailed list of responses from each participant. We looked for codes that were related, repeated, or were minor word variations for question 1; this is referred to as axial coding. We followed the same process for question 2. We then clustered the axial codes into more generalized and abstract codes and again included the participants' codes. For example, here are the six major themes for question 1, about obstacles to college retention:

ACADEMIC PREPARATION (8)

Making sure that they have the education prior to leaving foster care 01JP
Just because they get a diploma or GED doesn't mean that you have the study skills or knowledge for college 01JP
Preparation for college 05JE
We don't start early enough talking with youth about going to college 06KN
Many don't know why they are going 06KN
Not academically prepared for college 07NW

HOUSING (6)

Housing, lack of accessible and affordable housing 02MP
Housing, which goes in hand with financial stability 03LP

Housing 07NW
Independent living responsibilities, housing, transportation, child care, food. How to function during school breaks, transportation 05JE
Housing 10DC
One of the issues is definitely housing for the youth 10DC

MENTAL HEALTH AND SUBSTANCE ABUSE (4)

Mental health 03LP
Emotional Issues 07NW
Self sabotage 04GJ
Drugs and alcohol 09SD

FINANCIAL STABILITY (6)

They don't know how to budget so they end up working 03LP
Once family members know they have a scholarship and that they have money, a lot feel guilty and their biological family is struggling 04GJ
Giving money to their family 04GJ
Money 07NW
They stop receiving money and they may not be able to afford school 08RF
Financial aid 10DC
Of course financial aid so that you can make sure they have what they need 10DC)

COMMUNITY CONNECTIONS (7)

Keeping connected with the students 04GJ
They don't have an advocate 05JE
All colleges should be able to answer two questions. How are your students that are from foster care doing? And the second question is: What supports do you have in place that are effectively retaining them and getting them through their programs? 05JE
Foster care agencies tend to ignore them because they feel that they are successful 07NW
I think mentors would make the most difference. I know that in terms of youth employment probably the most important factor or thing that can be done for youth to stay in jobs is having an adult on the job who serves as a mentor for them and I think that is true for youth in college 11JM

LACK OF INDEPENDENT LIVING SKILLS (5)

Youth not used to seeking help 03LP

Students start out in community college and are unprepared for independent living 05JE

Independent living responsibilities, housing, transportation, child care, food. How to function during school breaks, transportation 05JE

Youth do not succeed because there is too much freedom on the college campus or in the SILP program 06KN

Youth don't know how to problem solve well 07NW

Here are examples of major themes that emerged from question 2, about implementing retention programs:

STUDENT SUCCESS (4)

Youth have been in school for at least one year better chance of being employed 01JP

Graduating 07NW

Youth struggle but still in school 07NW

Guidance to students, they may slip, but they will succeed 09SD

YOUTH ADVOCACY (5)

Networking with the various city providers, having an advocacy model 02MP

Advocacy work with the schools 03LP

Support we give in the drop-in center 04GJ

Mentoring 05JE

Support systems 05JE

YOUTH ACCESS TO RESOURCES (15)

Youth see us as a as a real resource 02MP

Our program is client-driven on a drop-in basis 02MP

Now these students have access to so many resources 03LP

Apply for the scholarship 04GJ

Support we give in the drop-in center 04GJ

Take 10 students every winter called digital storytelling 04GJ

Students develop digital stories about who they are 04GJ

First time they are traveling, learning to use public transportation 04GJ

Mentoring 05JE

Selecting scholarship recipients using a holistic method 05JE
Support systems 05JE
Continual communication 05JE
Work upfront with career assessment and career planning 06KN
Panel of former foster youth 06KN
The relationship with OFA 08RF
Increase in number of youth attending schools 11JM

PROGRAM GROWTH AND INFRASTRUCTURE (6)

Program growth 02MP
Now there are more programs working directly with foster youth in college 03LP
The relationship with OFA 08RF
There is a viable plan with the colleges that has four aspects. A full financial aid package, so the college agrees to look at the student's financial aid package to make sure that they are funded to the full extent. The college leadership buys into the program and supports it on campus, they designate a campus support person kind of an air traffic controller on campus for foster care youth and the foster care youth can go directly to them if they have any issues or any questions or need any kind of support, that person agrees to help that youth get what they need. Um, and the fourth thing is that the college agrees to connect youth with social services within their community 10DC
The data sharing 10DC
The incentive grant 10DC
Getting our IT 10DC

STEP 4: REGROUP THE MAJOR CATEGORIES INTO NEW CONTENT AREAS

Once again, in step 4, we created new and independent word processing files for each question. After step 4 was completed, we wanted to ensure that we could logically reorganize the major response categories. Some responses may be out of place and more appropriate for other major response categories. These out of place responses were moved to the more appropriate major category. Again, we checked that the major categories were members of the same logical set. We also cross-checked to ensure that both researchers agreed with the major categories and subsequent content areas within the clusters. In cases where we did not agree, we went through the previous four steps again and engaged in dialogue until consensus about the content areas was established. This process of reaching consensus is considered checking inter-rater reliability. Again, we kept the subject codes. For example, content areas that emerged for questions 1 and 2 included academic preparation, housing, financial assistance, emergency assistance, youth's personal challenges, and the need for advocacy.

STEP 5: PRESENTATION

Finally, we met to discuss and present the abstract codes arranged into our new logical order, or content areas, and grouped these into our major categories. Once again, we kept our subjects' codes attached to the content areas. We used inductive reasoning in our content analyses as we moved from the more specific to the more abstract. The final action was writing up the steps of the study and dissemination including publication in a peer-reviewed journal.

Results

The results from the current qualitative study were as follows (further details are in Hernandez and Naccarato [2010]). When the program coordinators were asked to describe the greatest obstacle to increasing college retention rates among foster youth (question 1), six major themes emerged. The six greatest obstacles to youth's unmet needs were academic preparation; housing; financial assistance; the need for emergency assistance; youth's personal challenges; and the need for advocacy. The services that the program coordinators reported to address these needs were academic supports such as mentoring and tutoring; assistance in locating housing that included guaranteed college housing; scholarships; emergency financial aid such as providing debit cards for the college cafeteria; referrals and access to mental health and health services; and staff who provided advocacy for the youth.

Four themes emerged for question 2 that focused on how the program coordinators described the successes of their programs. These themes were student success; youth advocacy; youth access to resources; and program growth and infrastructure. One key finding that emerged related to both questions was a priority for the programs and ensuring that the foster youth who are in college receive needed support services. Most youth in the general population receive this support from their birth families and with foster youth it is provided by the agencies such as those in this study.

One unexpected finding was that four program coordinators described how these youths' financial stability and mental health well-being were hindered by their relationships to their biological families and monetary assistance. This highlights the unique relationships that some foster youth face with their biological families.

Discussion and Implications for Social Work

The current qualitative study examined twelve nationwide scholarship or supportive programs. Practice implications include the need for emotional support to foster youth who are attending college. Program coordinators spoke of the importance of foster youth attending student panels or peer activities in order to share their experiences with foster youth who are still attending high school. One recommendation is to connect foster youth with successful student role models and make these youth aware of the many supportive services on campus. This could include making students aware of the many multicultural colleges, associations, and ethnic fraternities or sororities that could act as a support.

A policy implication is that state foster care systems and postsecondary institutions must track educational outcomes of these foster youth. It is vitally important that postsecondary institutions maintain their own records because most of the programs for former foster youth are voluntary. Many youth may discontinue participating in the program, but may still be enrolled in the postsecondary institution.

Another policy implication is that housing is a major obstacle to academic success. Financial aid does not pay for housing during the summer months unless the student is attending summer classes. Program coordinators reported that many foster youth work throughout the school year to save up money for summer housing. The rate of homelessness of foster youth is high. One possibility is to incorporate tuition waivers that include year-round housing until the youth completes the bachelor's degree. Many foster youth are worried about their housing and this preoccupation hinders their academic success.

Further exploration of these support programs is needed. This exploration should include the gathering of data. Information/data on program effectiveness on the college retention and graduation rates of foster youth is currently limited or nonexistent. There are little data even on the number of foster youth in these programs who have graduated from college.

Another area for research is how foster parents or kinship placements provide supports, including emotional assistance for the college process.

Limitations

We acknowledge several limitations that affect recommendations from the current study. To begin, the study had a small sample size. Second, because a convenience sample was used, the participants may have similar perspectives and be close in geographic proximity. Third, the study had an overrepresentation of programs from Washington State, California, and New York. There was no representation at all from any southern states. This limits generalizability. Fourth, the participants volunteered for the study so results may be a result of selection bias (i.e., other program managers might have very different views). Fifth, because the interview protocol used was a self-designed semistructured questionnaire, the protocol's reliability and validity are unknown. There is the potential for interviewer bias regarding the phrasing of questions or in asking additional probes (this is, of course, a potential drawback of all qualitative research). Sixth, it was difficult to meld the analysis to the theory based on the exploratory nature of the study. We were attempting to use human capital to guide the study, but what we ended up exploring was what interfered with the human capital accumulation of the foster youth. The findings did indicate the actual obstacles that the program coordinators saw as interfering with these youths' human capital accumulation such as housing, lack of college preparation, mental health and substance abuse, financial stability, lack of community resources, and independent living skills.

Due to time constraints and the researchers' unfamiliarity with qualitative software such as ATLAS.ti, it was not used in this study. Any researcher should become familiar with qualitative software before engaging in the project. If there had been more time, the researcher would have expanded the study to include more participants. It is important that researchers take into account the challenges involved in recruiting a sample of participants that will complete the project; and therefore, should begin to reach out to participants as early as possible. To limit interviewer bias, it is recommended that at least two researchers conduct the interviews. The researcher could have engaged in a more in-depth review of standardized interview survey questionnaires in order to have the interview questions be similar to a standardized assessment tool.

Conclusions

It has been argued that qualitative methods are a useful mechanism for studying foster youth and social service interventions in general. This chapter outlines the importance of studying this population, as well as offering one strategy to enable the voices of program coordinators to be heard. The qualitative method highlighted here is the use of content analysis. This is important at all levels of social work: practice, policymaking, research, and client well-being. Foster youth and the independent living skills interventions should be studied using qualitative methods in order to explore both the youth's and service provider's perspectives. If the foster youth and service providers do not find the independent living skills intervention helpful in its current form, then perhaps the youth will not buy in and ultimately not accept these services. Foster youth are already at a disadvantage, as compared to their youth counterparts in the general population. Thus, if the voices of foster youth and service providers are heard, this can directly impact the quality of services and policy development with a target population that deserves effective and useful interventions. The results of this study did in fact yield some interesting findings. For example, the uniqueness of the relationship of these foster youth and their biological families in terms of money was of particular interest. Many of the biological families are in poverty. Thus the foster youth in some cases feel the need to give their scholarship and financial aid funds to their families. Other problems in the areas of housing stability appear easier to solve. For example, many postsecondary institutions have dormitories and it would seem that providing summer and holiday housing in these units would not be difficult. Social workers, policymakers, and researchers have typically not lived in the child welfare environment nor do they share similar backgrounds with the youth served. Thus it is argued that the voices of these clients are crucial in shaping clinical care, policy development, and quality of service.

Note

* This chapter is based on a previously published study. Citation is as follows: Hernandez, L. and T. Naccarato. 2010. Scholarship and supports available to foster care alumni: A study of 12 programs across the US. *Children and Youth Services Review*, 32(5):758–766.

References

Aging out [documentary]. R. Weisberg, writer/producer/director, and V. Roth, co-producer. New York: Filmmaker's Library, 2005.

Becker, G. S. 1993. *Human capital: A theoretical and empirical analysis with special reference to education,* 3rd ed. Chicago: U of Chicago P.

Courtney, M. E. and I. Piliavin. 1998. *Foster youth transitions to adulthood: Outcomes 12 to 18 months after leaving care.* Madison: Wisconsin School of Social Work and Institute for Research on Poverty.

Courtney, M. E., I. Piliavin, A. Grogan-Taylor, and A. Nesmith. 2001. Foster youth transitions to adulthood: A longitudinal view of youth leaving care. *Child Welfare,* 6:685–717.

Courtney, M. E., S. Terao, and N. Bost. (2004). "Midwest evaluation of the adult functioning of former foster youth: Conditions of youth preparing to leave state care." Unpublished manuscript, Chapin Hall Center for Children, University of Chicago.

Crabtree, B. F. and W. L. Miller. 1999. *Doing qualitative research,* 2nd ed. Thousand Oaks, CA: Sage.

Creswell, J. W. 2007. *Qualitative inquiry and research design: Choosing among the five approaches,* 2nd ed. Thousand Oaks, CA: Sage.

Denzin, N. K. and Y. S. Lincoln. 2003. The discipline and practice of qualitative research. In *Strategies of qualitative inquiry,* 2nd ed., N. K. Denzin and Y. S. Lincoln, eds. 1–45. Thousand Oaks, CA: Sage.

Drisko, J. W. 2005. Writing up qualitative research. *Families in Society,* 86(4):589–593.

Hernandez, L. and T. Naccarato. 2010. Scholarships and supports available to foster care alumni: A study of 12 programs across the US. *Children & Youth Services Review,* 32(5):758–766.

Naccarato, T. and E. DeLorenzo. 2008. Transitional youth services: Practice implications from a systematic review. *Child and Adolescent Social Work Journal,* 25(4):287–308.

Padgett, D. K. 2004. Introduction: Finding a middle ground in qualitative research. In *The qualitative research experience,* D. K. Padgett, ed. 1–18. Belmont, CA: Wadsworth/Thomson.

Rist, R. C. 2001. On the application of qualitative research to the policy process: An emergent link. In *The American tradition in qualitative research: Volume 4,* N. K. Denzin and Y. S. Lincoln, eds. 250–263. Thousand Oaks, CA: Sage.

Shirk, M. and G. J. Stangler. 2004. *On their own: What happens to kids when they age out of the foster care system?* Boulder, CO: Westview.

Collaboration Between Social Workers and Physicians

Development and Application of a Typology

JULIE S. ABRAMSON AND TERRY MIZRAHI

This updated chapter, first published in 1994 (Mizrahi and Abramson 1994), describes the process of discovering a typology of physician/social worker collaboration using grounded theory methodology. Because our typology was developed from our study of collaboration between social workers and physicians, we will include findings from that study in the literature review and show how those analyses contributed to its development. Those data are reported in two articles, one on both professions' comparative views of collaboration on a shared case (Mizrahi and Abramson 2000) and the other on each profession's perspectives on their most positive and negative experiences in collaborating with the other profession (Abramson and Mizrahi 1996). An updated literature review will allow us to examine the impact of more recent research and literature on our original view of the typology and to evaluate its utility in today's health care environment. In addition, we will share findings from our subsequent application of the typology back to our sample of social workers and physicians (Abramson and Mizrahi 2003) to demonstrate further how the development of a theoretical framework (in our case, the typology) can be used to deepen understanding of the issues being studied.

Since the methodology of the study and the essential steps in developing the typology remain the same, they will be re-presented here. In this edition, however, we will emphasize the thinking underlying some of the decisions we made in building the typology, using one of the five dimensions of the typology as an exemplar. Finally, we will reflect on the intellectual underpinnings of the typology as well as the evolution of our perspectives on collaboration. In sharing the various processes involved in developing the typology of collaboration between physicians and social workers, we expect to bring the application of grounded theory to life.

Interdisciplinary teamwork and collaboration are assuming greater importance in health care as changes in social and economic conditions, demographics, and medical care converge to focus attention on models of health care delivery (Hinton Walker and Elberson 2005; Harr, Souza, and Fairchild 2008). Social workers and other health care practitioners are providing care to patients in a health care environment that has undergone extensive changes since we began to examine physician-social work relationships in 1985 (Mizrahi and Abramson 1985; Abramson and Mizrahi 1986; Dranove 2000; Nauert 2000; Boswell and Cannon 2005).

Our original chapter on the development of the typology (Mizrahi and Abramson 1994) was published just as President Clinton's proposal for national health care reform failed (Mizrahi 1997). This event propelled the shift to a corporate model of health care that included the dominance of managed care, re-engineering, downsizing, cross-training, and other market-based, profit-driven approaches to cut costs and limit access (Lee and Alexander 1999; Coddington, Fischer, Moore, and Clarke 2000; Lown 2000; Redmond 2001; Vandiver 2008). Managed care companies and utilization review processes now dictate the scope of care, the length of hospital stay, and the number of patient visits they will cover (Barlett and Steele 2004; Kongstvedt 2007).

At the same time, collaboration and interdisciplinary teams have become central to many of these endeavors such as the development of continua of care and horizontal integration of services (Dunevitz 1997; Raiwet, Halliwell, Andruski, and Wilson 1997; Proenca 2000; Zimmerman and Dabelko 2007; Harr, Souza, and Fairchild 2008). In particular, collaboration has become a key element of expansions of comprehensive prevention, primary care, and community health initiatives (Resnick and Tighe 1997; Rock and Cooper 2000; Steele 2000; Keefe, Geron, and Enguidanos 2009). In addition, models that are more inclusive of patients and families as core members of the team are beginning to be practiced, if still relatively rare (Opie 2000; Abramson and Bronstein 2004; Zimmerman and Dabelko 2007; Aronoff 2008). These various efforts are more likely to emphasize shared solutions and multiple perspectives based on the recognition that effective prevention and treatment approaches require resources and competencies that go beyond the knowledge and expertise of any one profession or organization (Welton, Kantner, and Katz 1997; Lasker, Weiss, and Miller 2001; Minkler 2005; Korazim-Korosy, Mizrahi, Katz, Karmon, Bayne-Smith, and Garcia 2007).

The implementation of the omnibus health care reform legislation passed by Congress and signed into law by President Obama in the spring of 2010 (Relman 2007; Lawrence, Jacobs, and Skocpol 2010) will also have a major impact on the delivery of health care. The act emphasizes prevention, education, and integration of services in many of its elements. These transformative shifts have resulted in increased opportunities and even mandates for enhanced collaborative practice at the clinical and community levels (Rizzo, Mizrahi, and Kirkland 2005; Bayne-Smith, Mizrahi, and Garcia 2008; Ivery 2008); policymakers, funders, and health providers increasingly recognize the need to coordinate, if not integrate, services and collectively collaborate to solve myriad complex medical and psychosocial problems (Lasker and Weiss 2003; Mizrahi and Gorin 2008; Aldred-Crouch, Hickman, Kent, and Randall 2010).

These trends also have significantly influenced the structure, roles, and relationships within and between health care provider groups (Abdellah 1997; Callister 2001; Mizrahi and Berger 2001; Berger, Robbins, Lewis, Mizrahi, and Fleit 2003). More precisely, the demands of both public (government) and private (corporate) third-party payers have had a profound effect on the autonomy of professionals; physicians have significantly less freedom to make independent clinical medical decisions than in the past (Stevens 2001; Hafferty 2003), while social workers and nurses have sought greater input into shaping patient care (Lindeke and Sieckert 2005; Keefe, Geron, and Enguidanos 2009; Robertson 2010). Given this shift toward collaborative models, it is essential to understand the complexities of creating effective interdisciplinary relationships (Irvine, Kerridge, McPhee, and Freeman 2002; Leipzig et al. 2002; Reuben et al. 2004).

Literature Review

The theoretical, practice-based, and empirical literature on interprofessional relationships focuses on: (1) communication and teamwork among health professions (Leipzig et al. 2002; Reuben et al. 2004; D'Amour, Ferrada-Videla, San Martin-Rodriguez, and Beaulieu 2005); (2) social work roles in health care and their value to the physician (Cowles and Lefcowitz 1992, 1995; Keigher 1997; Fort Cowles 2003; Kitchen and Brook 2005; Mizrahi and Rizzo 2008; Kerson and McCoyd 2010); and (3) the importance of psychosocial factors in case collaboration (Cowles and Lefcowitz 1995; Egan and Kadushin 1997).

Communication was identified by Sargaent, Loney, and Murphy (2008) as a leading factor in effective collaboration based on research that analyzed data from nine focus groups of health professionals that included physicians, social workers, and nurses, among others. Our study of collaboration between physicians and social workers also found that the quality and amount of communication were among the top five determinants of successful collaboration identified by both physicians and social workers. This was true in cases shared by social worker and physician collaborators (Mizrahi and Abramson 2000) and in their descriptions of positive and negative collaborative experiences with the other professions (Abramson and Mizrahi 1996). Others (Couturier, Gagnon, Carrier, and Ethridge 2008) deepen this concept and name it the "relational" aspect of collaboration—meaning affective engagement that goes beyond the sharing of practical information. While the social workers in our study highly valued interaction and relationship-building, physicians more frequently emphasized the competence of social workers as an essential factor in positive collaboration (Abramson and Mizrahi 1996).

Such distinct preferences regarding what is valued in a collaborator are likely to affect interprofessional collaboration and teamwork. In fact, when we reviewed the medical literature for sources on collaboration or teamwork, the few that discussed teams referred to physician teams rather than interdisciplinary teams (Murray, Wartman, and Swanson 1992; Skochelak and Jackson 1992; Molleman, Broekhuis, Stoffels, and Jaspers 2010). In fact, most physicians are not socialized to or trained in a teamwork model (Mizrahi 1986; Gleason, Farness, Schneider, Wilson, and Fay 1998) so it is not surprising that novice physicians appear to be less satisfied with teams than their social work or nursing colleagues (Leipzig et al. 2002; Reuben et al. 2004). In addition, status inequalities among the professions persist, although these are diminished in some settings (Gair and Hartery 2001); thus when physicians are team leaders or team members, continuing physician dominance of patient care decision-making remains an important factor (Coombs and Ersser 2004; Chesluk and Holmboe 2010). Our findings related to control over decision-making are discussed at the end of this literature review.

Studies that began in the 1960s have repeatedly compared social work and physician perceptions of the social work role (Olsen and Olsen 1967; Carrigan 1978; Lister 1980). These findings have been consistent; namely, that physicians did not recognize or accept the breadth of roles that social workers claimed for themselves, particularly in relation to providing counseling and mental health services. In other studies, however, increasing numbers of physicians have acknowledged the social work role in counseling patients and families and in coordinating resources; although these are not always identified as roles exclusive to social work (Cowles and Lefcowitz 1992, 1995; Netting and Williams 1996, 1998; Badger, Ackerson, Buttell, and Rand 1997; Egan and Kadushin 1997). In fact, role confusion and role blurring among different health professionals can affect the integration of social work into health care teams (Davis, Milosevic, Baldry, and Walsh 2005; Keefe, Geron, and Enguidanos 2009; Shor 2010).

Our study also confirmed past findings about differences between social workers and physicians in relation to perspectives on the counseling function of social work. Social workers identified this role more often than physicians in their shared case, particularly where there were issues related to adjustment to illness; however, it is important to note that almost half of the physicians did identify a counseling role for social work, a substantial increase from past studies, and they recognized the importance of addressing patients' psychosocial problems with social workers as well (Abramson and Mizrahi 1996). Physicians in our study also understood and accepted the social work role in linking patients to services, as reported elsewhere (Lister 1980; Netting and Williams 1998); surprisingly, however, many in our cohort did not acknowledge the common social work role in negotiating the hospital system or advocating for and coordinating resources (Abramson and Mizrahi 1996).

Past research findings also document that physicians have been less interested in or less willing to address the psychosocial aspects of patient care (Eisenthal, Stoeckle, and Erlich 1994; Robinson and Roter 1999; Franks, Williams, Zwanziger, Mooney, and Sorbero 2000). Physician inattention to these factors is due in part to socialization during training that includes "mixed messages" from faculty regarding the importance of giving their time to broader issues in their patients' lives (Mizrahi 1986; Irvine et al.

2002; Reuben et al. 2004; Barker and Oandasan 2005). However, Decoster and Egan (2001) found that physicians did respond to patient anxiety and fear to some extent, but they were less responsive to anger and sadness. There is some indication from our research and others that physicians who had been in practice longer were more likely to attend to psychosocial issues, especially those in private practice with long-term patients (Franks et al. 2000). Some already were, or would be, interested in integrating psychosocial services into their practices (Badger et al. 1997; Wesson 1997).

However, control over patient care decision-making is still an area of contention between physicians and other team members. On shared cases in our study, very few of the physicians identified the social worker as case coordinator, while they laid claim to this role in a majority of the cases. On the other hand, social workers mostly saw themselves as case coordinators, a role that Dubus (2010) supports for social workers, and rarely identified the doctor as coordinator (Mizrahi and Abramson 2000). While there still appeared to be reluctance on the part of many physicians to relinquish control over decision-making, upon additional scrutiny of our narrative text, we found—unexpectedly—that a subset of physicians expressed an egalitarian and interdependent orientation to interdisciplinary practice. Markers of this more collaborative model included emphasis by some physicians on shared responsibility and active communication with social workers and use of the terms "we" and "our" (patient) instead of "I" and "my" (Abramson and Mizrahi 2003).

Hence, the variations of social work-physician collaborative relationships found in more recent literature, including in our own study, increased our awareness of a range of collaborative types and thus contributed to the shaping of the typology of physician/social worker collaborators discussed in the rest of this chapter. Because of their importance in the literature and in our findings, the various aspects of collaboration discussed in this literature review became the dimensions of our typology: communication, teamwork, psychosocial perspectives, views of the social work role, and control over decision-making.

In summary, available evidence continues to suggest that collaboration between social workers and physicians (and physicians and other health professionals as well), is not necessarily a smooth process, nor is it always grounded in shared perspectives and mutual appreciation (Barnes, Carpenter, and Dickinson 2000; Irvine et al. 2002; Cochrane Review 2003; San Martin-Rodriguez, Beaulieu, D'Amour, and Perrada-Videla 2005; Xyrichis and Lowton 2008). In addition, numerous structural and organizational aspects of the health care system add other constraints to successful collaborations for both professions. Yet, there are indications that physicians and social workers are developing more effective approaches to collaboration as a key part of better care for patients.

Methodology for the Whole Study

Methodological Rationale

In light of the lack of systematic and comprehensive research on physician/social work collaboration, our study is exploratory and descriptive. We drew on the classic work of Glaser and Straus (1967) and subsequent others (Strauss 1987; Charmaz 1990; Strauss and Corbin 1990; Corbin and Strauss 2008) on grounded theory methodology in our effort to construct a model of collaborative relationships. We were seeking the richness, diversity, accuracy, and contextual depth that qualitative data can provide (Shaw 2003; Padgett 2008).

Grounded theory methodology seemed best suited to develop and enrich knowledge in an area where past research has rarely examined the actual experiences and perspectives of the two professions. We decided on in-person interviews in order to collect data that would capture the participants' points of view in their own words. Analyzing data from intensive interviews can be used to characterize a group or process, uncover the analytic ordering of the world being studied, develop categories for rendering the flux of raw reality explicable, and locate structure, order, and patterns as well as variations (Lofland and Lofland 1995). Our study adhered to grounded theory methodology in asking open-ended questions, in the use of informants and comparative settings, by analyzing data from preliminary interviews, in overall data analysis processes, and in developing theory inductively.

The methodology of grounded theory assumes that data collection and analysis will be tightly interwoven processes and must occur alternately because preliminary analysis directs the amount and type of further sampling (Strauss and Corbin 1990; Oktay 2004). After reviewing early interviews, we: (1) modified questions and added new ones, such as what advice would respondents give to their own and the other profession;

(2) directed additional sampling to less represented groups (surgeons); and (3) improved interview techniques. In particular, we noted and addressed the difficulty the practitioner members of our research team encountered in transitioning from a clinical to a research interview format; for example, to refrain from commenting on a response given either in the affirmative or negative or asking "leading" questions (Padgett 1998).

Our methodological choices were also grounded in certain assumptions that were based on our clinical and research experiences and in the literature. We assumed that physicians would not share a common language with social workers about collaboration or about the role of social workers; nor given the nature of physician socialization, would they be reflective about collaboration (Mizrahi 1986). We anticipated that social workers would be more familiar with the issues but would be variable in their capacities to conceptualize elements of collaboration (Abramson and Mizrahi 1994).

Although we primarily employed qualitative methodology (grounded theory), we also used quantitative methods where we had better understanding of the issues addressed. In this way, we attempted to triangulate the data to achieve validity and trustworthiness by comparison of responses obtained through mixed methodologies (Padgett 2008; Humble 2009). For example, we used precoded lists from which we asked respondents to select attributes and behaviors of their collaborators in describing their most positive and negative collaborative experiences; in addition, we typed each respondent and then compared doctors and social workers by type on a number of variables using chi-square statistics in order to evaluate the impact of respondents' "type" of collaborative approach. We will discuss this analysis and findings later in the section on applying the typology to the sample to demonstrate how we used a typology to develop additional results and deeper understanding.

The Setting and the Subjects

We attempted to achieve a balance of breadth and depth in the sample selected. We wanted it to be large enough to provide comparisons within and across groups of subjects, make some limited generalizations, and identify patterns. At the same time, it needed to be small enough to allow us to probe deeply and begin to understand the context and meaning of the respondents' reported perceptions and experiences.

Our purposeful sample of 50 physicians and 54 social workers worked in internal medicine or surgery and their related subspecialties in twelve hospitals in the New York City area; Albany, NY; and western Massachusetts. We chose internal medicine and surgery because they are the largest and most influential branches of medicine and had been largely neglected in past studies of collaboration. We selected hospitals to achieve diversity of size and location (urban, suburban, rural). We obtained the sample by first securing participation from social workers with medical/surgical assignments in the various hospital departments. Each social worker was asked to identify a complex case where extensive collaboration (defined as three or more substantive in-person contacts) with a physician took place. We then recruited 50 of the 54 physicians on those cases, thus limiting our analysis to 50 pairs of collaborators.

Almost all of the social work subjects held masters of social work (MSW)' degrees except for nine bachelor of social work (BSW) or bachelor of arts-level workers, located in hospitals outside of New York City. The physician sample was comprised primarily of internists; a little over 25 percent were surgeons. Social workers and physicians in the sample were predominantly white. The social work sample was overwhelmingly female and the physician sample was primarily male. As we noted early patterns in the data indicating that some physicians collaborated with social workers in unanticipated ways, we added more social workers who worked with surgeons to our sample to see if specialty was a factor.

The Interviews

We interviewed respondents for one to one-and-one-half hours; all interviews were taped with permission and transcribed. In the beginning of the interview, we collected demographic data about the subjects as well as information about their current and past professional and personal experiences with the other profession. These variables provided a context for understanding the patterns of collaboration that emerged, since past experiences with the other profession in other settings or involving other services are crucial in shaping current perspectives on collaboration; therefore, respondents were asked to make comparisons of the current setting with past settings on several items. Padgett (2008) identifies this as diachronic reporting (telling the story through time). Commenting on our research, she notes

Mizrahi and Abramson (1994) developed a typology. . . . Taken at face value, this typology is an informative, but static, description of the working relationships of physicians and social workers. But Mizrahi and Abramson took a step toward diachronic reporting by pointing out the dynamic nature of these collaborative styles, how physicians and social workers can adopt differing approaches over time in response to new exigencies. This makes sense, particularly given the rapid pace of change in hospital staffing and management under managed care (Padgett 2008:202).

In the second section of the interview schedule, we asked respondents to describe the actual case on which they had worked together. By using the case as a control, comparisons between the collaborative views of the respondents were based in a common reality. Perceptions were sought with respect to the psychosocial aspects of the case and related interventions by the social worker. Data about case outcome were also obtained. Finally, information about satisfaction with the outcome and with the collaborator, as well as comparisons with other cases and collaborators, was collected.

Respondents were asked in the third section to discuss their most positive and negative collaborative experience with the other profession. These data provided information about approximately 200 additional collaborators and cases. We first asked respondents to briefly describe the case and the reasons for its choice as most positive or negative. We then asked them to select items that applied to their examples from a precoded list that we had developed of factors that contribute to positive and negative collaborative interaction. This section of the interview was more quantitative in derivation in that we structured the responses of the study participants (Abramson and Mizrahi 1996).

In both the shared case and in the positive and negative case descriptions, we deliberately skewed case selection toward atypical cases to obtain richer data regarding collaboration. These cases were not expected to reflect normative collaborative experiences. Rather, we assumed that cases involving extensive interaction, complex decision-making, or strong feelings regarding the case or collaborator are highly influential in shaping interprofessional perspectives. By using extreme examples, we felt we would be better able to tease out the most salient features and dynamics of collaboration.

The final section of the interview schedule asked the subjects to discuss their general collaborative strategies and to provide hypothetical advice to both social workers and physicians about the ingredients for successful collaboration. They were asked to compare their current and past points of view and experiences and also to compare themselves with others in their profession. In this section, we explored their conception of collaboration and also gained an understanding of how they would teach others to collaborate effectively.

Application of Grounded Theory

The first step in our data analysis was to devise a strategy to convert the mass of qualitative data into a systematic schema for examining its meaning, discovering themes and patterns, and making connections among concepts. We used the constant comparative method proposed by Glaser and Strauss (1967) and further developed by Strauss and Corbin (1990) to develop codes for specific variables and to gain understanding of broader conceptual issues and themes. The constant comparative method is a process of developing categories, concepts, and broader themes or theory inductively from the data and testing them out at each step by returning to the data to evaluate their fit and appropriateness.

Applying the constant comparative method to an initial sample of 10 transcripts, we scrutinized the responses to produce provisional concepts that fitted the data. In the mode of open coding suggested by grounded theory (Strauss 1987), the essential meaning of each response and related responses was compared with those already reviewed until the properties or characteristics of the concept became apparent and no new ideas were emerging. We then tried to put the data derived through open coding back together in new ways by making connections between and among categories; this process is identified in grounded theory as axial coding (Strauss and Corbin 1990). (Note that in subsequent work Corbin and Strauss [2008] state that they now combine the processes of open and axial coding). We continued to test the utility and relevance of our coding process by applying the codes to approximately 25 percent of the sample of 100. The transcripts reviewed were distributed equally between social workers and physicians. At that point, we had confidence in the codes and used them to code the entire sample. We used two coders for each transcript, a third when there was a discrepancy between the first two.

Clues to reframing a question or reinterpreting a response came as we found ourselves commenting on "surprises," that is, unexpected findings that exposed our taken-for-granted assumptions. As social workers, for example, we presumed to know more about the world of social workers in contrast to that of physicians'. Early on, however, we discovered more variability within disciplines and a greater overlapping of perspectives than anticipated. Among our surprises, a number of physicians expressed strong interest in psychosocial aspects of patient care and appreciation of the counseling social workers provide. For example, one of the first physicians we interviewed complained that his social work collaborator did not want to "talk psychosocial" with him. Consequently, we developed questions for both professions regarding the sharing of psychosocial information and assessments; our coding decisions changed as we saw how physicians acknowledged, assumed, or delegated psychosocial issues. We recognized that our assumption that physicians had superficial relationships with patients and families was based on observations of physicians-in-training, while community-based physicians in the sample often knew patients and families longer and better than social workers (Abramson and Mizrahi 1994).

In addition, we began to recognize certain patterns in the data. As a result, we systematically recorded our post-interview summary observations of the subjects with respect to: (1) their degree of involvement in the interview; (2) their general view of the other profession; (3) their attitudes toward collaboration; (4) their definition of the social work role and function as narrow versus broad; and (5) the degree of importance they gave to psychosocial issues. In addition, we characterized physician respondents on a process/outcome continuum, from those who understood the process by which social workers bring about particular outcomes to those whose only concern was the outcome of a social work intervention. We expected that social workers and doctors would give different emphasis to process over outcome in their work with patients due to differential socialization experiences.

We focused on these aspects of collaboration for various reasons. Social workers have long been frustrated by the limited role assigned them by doctors, particularly regarding the counseling function as discussed previously in the literature review section of this chapter. Therefore, it was critical to examine views of the social work role to see if physicians now identified a broader role for social work than in the past as well as to understand how each profession viewed the other and their collaboration together. We also wished to understand if physicians' interest in psychosocial aspects of care had shifted from the time of Mizrahi's study in 1980 (Mizrahi 1986).

Our "interviewer impressions guide" was similar to what Lofland and Lofland (1995) refer to as "reaction sheets." We also used it to note quotes that captured key issues. These notations became an integral part of data collection and data analysis and enhanced its rigor (Padgett, Mathew, and Conte 2004).

Following are two typical notes from an interviewer summary

A surgeon was characterized by the interviewer as someone who "saw the social work role as placement of patients . . . He demonstrated a good understanding of patients' psychosocial problems but was less clear about how social workers counseled patients . . . He left the social worker to do her job but felt badly for her in this difficult case . . . he even wished that she could have talked more about her frustrations but felt that she was too reserved for that and that he was too reserved to reach out . . . He was an interesting mix of rather impoverished responses and limited interest in social work while having an unusually good sense of the patient and the structural obstacles faced by social workers in solving problems . . . Yet he was primarily interested in outcome."

A family practitioner was described as viewing "other professionals with respect" although he may not understand how they get done what they do. He identified himself as coordinator of the case which he saw as appropriate for a family practitioner. The most important thing to him is what a social worker can do for the patient and what they can help him do with his patient. He values social work and is interested in sharing perceptions about patients and in having mutual goals.

Development of Dimensions from the Data

As we continued coding all of the transcripts, the notes we made on the back of transcripts about our overall impressions of the interviews began to coalesce into concepts at higher levels of abstraction. Gradually, we began to identify various dimensions of collaboration. Here, we will share the process involved in the development of one dimension—"control over" decision-making—to illustrate how these conceptual constructs emerged from the data.

Prior to doing the study, we had shared the commonly held assumption that physicians traditionally desired and achieved control over decisions with respect to patient care. That assumption informed our early work about differences between social workers and physicians (Mizrahi and Abramson 1985; Abramson and Mizrahi 1986) and led us then to propose collaborative strategies for social workers that took the power differential between the two professions into account. We asked questions of study respondents about their perspectives on control over decision-making in their shared cases based on our awareness of the long-standing authority and status of physicians (Freidson 1984, 2001; Stevens 2001). We wondered about how many social workers had moved from "handmaiden" status in their collaborations with physicians to a role with greater autonomy. We assumed that such autonomy would be achieved through a negotiated resource model in which social workers still placed the central concerns of physicians first but acted independently in attempting to meet the broader psychosocial needs of patients and families. We did not expect to find evidence of substantive equality in collaborative relationships or in decision-making.

However, early on in reading transcripts, we discovered that physician expectations about control over decision-making ranged from a strong emphasis on ultimate physician authority to significant support for shared responsibility; this unexpected finding sensitized us to look for other evidence of such a changed dynamic in our data. And by delving into the data, we uncovered a subset of physicians who used terms such as "we" and "us" in characterizing their decision-making processes with the social worker; over time, this became a marker of a shift toward more collegial relationships. As one physician noted, "we all bring our perspective to a family situation and discuss how we can help each other to help the families."

Gradually, it became apparent that control over decision-making was a critical dimension to better understanding the range of collaborative interactions between the two professions. In fact, it was the first dimension that emerged from the data. Reflection on this also led us to a more conceptual level of analysis and the beginning of a tripartite typology as the respondents' views of control over decision-making seemed to cluster in groups of like properties; Quinn Patton (1987) would call this an indigenous or emic typology since it is based on the participants' views. We labeled the three emerging models of collaboration as traditional, transitional, and transformational and began to examine other aspects of collaboration to see if these fit into similar configurations. The following quotes are illustrative of the views of the three types of physician collaborators about control over decision-making. One traditional physician commented: "We have the ultimate responsibility for the patient's care . . . sometimes the social worker may not appreciate that," while a transitional physician asserted: "My primary function in this case is captain of the ship. You guide the patients, you guide the family, you administer medication and call in consultants . . . you work with social services and everybody in the totality of patient care . . . but you are the captain." In contrast, a transformational physician said, "I think that the interrelationship here is one of shared responsibility . . . to get families through times of stress . . . "

While the dimension of control over decision-making first emerged from our examination of physician responses, we were unclear about whether this aspect of collaboration applied equally to social workers. However, upon returning to the data, we found that social workers as well as physicians could be classified as traditional, transitional, or transformational in relation to control over decision-making; they ranged from emphasis on ultimate physician authority to strong support for shared decision-making. The following quotes are illustrative of the views of the three types of social work collaborators about control over decision-making.

A traditional social worker reflected her deference to physician authority when she commented: "I tend to listen to physicians when they're giving me orders . . . I'll kind of agree with them. It's hard at times because I haven't really completed my assessment, so I go by what the doctor is telling me." Commenting on her collaborative strategy, a transitional social worker said, "A lot of time, it helps if you approach them [physicians] in such a way that they feel that they're the ones who are making the decisions. You can tell them, this is my impression, and ask, what are your suggestions? Making them feel like they are in control helps . . . A lot of doctors have that need." A transformational social worker demonstrated her respect for her physician colleague's psychosocial assessment. "This particular doctor has been working with this patient for many years, so he really knows this family intimately, knows all the psychosocial problems . . . so he was helpful to me in making an assessment of this family and their dynamics, how this patient could be best cared for."

As we began to articulate other dimensions, we found that both social workers and physicians could be described as traditional, transitional, or transformational for each dimension, although the elements of the dimension were defined somewhat differently for each profession. These dimensions included: (1) perspectives on psychosocial issues of care—ranging from a limited focus on concrete needs for discharge to strong emphasis on a breadth of psychosocial concerns; (2) definition of the role of the social worker—ranging from one that is limited to provision of services to one that incorporates counseling and adjustment to illness; (3) emphasis on teamwork—ranging from avoidance of team participation to strong appreciation of the contributions of other team members; and (4) attitudes about communication—ranging from minimal interest and little contact, or even avoidance, to strong interest and an active role. At a subsequent point, we recognized that the dimensions had coherence as components of a typology to characterize collaborators; namely, that they made up a traditional, transitional, or transformational perspective on collaboration, equally applicable to social workers and physicians. Patton (1987) notes that it can be helpful to cross-classify different dimensions to create new insights; in so doing, we saw that our related concepts had developed into a theoretical whole (Morse 2004). The elements of all the dimensions as they vary by type of collaborator are spelled out in the three grids in appendix 21.1; here, we present a composite description of each type of physician or social worker, including representative quotes from our interviews, to illustrate the typology.

Description and Illustration of the Typology

Traditional physicians demonstrated little understanding of psychosocial issues, saw social workers primarily as providers of concrete services, did not understand or accept a counseling role for social work, kept communication and teamwork to a minimum, and emphasized control over patient care. A traditional physician seemed to discount social work: "There are certain tasks that need to be done . . . that is a kind of drudgery to me [such as] . . . sorting out where somebody is going to go and what is going to happen to them. So that is what gets delegated [to the social worker]."

Traditional social workers also defined a limited psychosocial role that emphasized service provision and did not include counseling. They adhered to administrative and physician priorities and limited their independent assessment. They communicated minimally with physicians, although they did communicate actively with other health care professionals. One noted, "The bulk of what we do here is nursing home placement . . . We got rid of a lot of people last month."

Transitional physicians were characterized by their readiness to use the social worker as discharge planner and provider of resources but they also demonstrated little understanding of the counseling role. They were more appreciative of the contributions of other professionals in the care of their patients but saw themselves as team leaders who chose to delegate some responsibilities to the social worker or others. These physicians wanted information from the social worker and would share their own knowledge of the patient; however, they preferred focused communication related to physician priorities. A transitional physician articulated that "The social worker is a tremendous asset to the physician . . . I feel comfortable when I have a social worker in the case because there's a lot of work otherwise I would have to do which is para-medical . . . It takes part of my burden away which is great." Another reflected that "Social workers need to understand the time constraints doctors are under, just keep the lines of communication open and try to anticipate problems rather than to react to them."

Transitional social workers identified and often addressed a range of psychosocial issues; however, in conceptualizing their roles, they tended to separate service provision activities from counseling. They participated fully in teams, and communicated actively and often strategically with physicians and other professionals. Some seemed to "work around" or even evade direct communication with physicians as they sought autonomy or simply avoided those physicians they saw as difficult collaborators. They accepted the physician's primary responsibility for decision-making, but often attempted to influence outcomes through their assessments of patient/family circumstances.

One such social worker lamented, "One frustrating part of the job is that so much of it is discharge planning . . . a lot of it is not therapy . . . more concrete than clinical, by far." Another said, "I'd contact them [doctors] to explain that this is what we're dealing with . . . This is why she [the patient] can't go home without help." A third commented, "I would avoid them and speak with the nurse. Doctors are always . . . on the run . . . It's infuriating and frustrating so I learned other ways to get information."

Transformational physicians and social workers were more alike in their characteristics than either traditional or transitional respondents. Both had a broad view of the social work role, emphasizing integration of service provision with counseling. Both viewed the psychosocial aspects of care as central to medical outcomes. Many transformational physicians attended directly to the psychosocial aspects of patients' lives rather than delegating that role completely to social workers. Both were active team members and sought communication with the other profession. Hierarchy was less important to these practitioners; they functioned interdependently, shared responsibility for patient care decision-making, and often used the pronoun "we" in describing their collaborative activities. They seem to have given up or never acquired the norm of self-reliance so common in medical settings (Mizrahi 1986). For these transformational professionals, the whole (of patient care) is greater than the sum of its many parts (isolated professional perspectives).

A transformational physician noted, "Everyone looks at the problem differently . . . The social worker is coordinating things plus all the psychodynamic things that go on with the family. Everyone sees a different angle to the same problem. I think the social worker puts it together and addresses things on longer term." A transformational social worker described her role: "It was to work with the family as a support system . . . supporting their view and helping them work through the stages of denial, doing some concrete services for them, and negotiations and advocacy. We moved through the system and got what we wanted." Another social worker commented that she "helps the patient adjust to the illness, work with the family, and does a lot of counseling as well as making concrete arrangements."

Applying the Typology to the Whole Sample

A key tenet of grounded theory involves examining the degree of fit between theory and the data (Corbin and Strauss 2008). That led us to evaluate all 100 respondents for type. First, we characterized respondents within dimensions as traditional, transitional, or transformational; we did this by reading the entire transcript for evidence of collaborative attitude and behavior as it related to each dimension. We made notes on a blank grid that laid out the dimensions down the page and the types across the page. Two coders independently typed each respondent on each of the dimensions. Then, using the information from all the dimensions, coders assigned each respondent to one of the three types. Differences between the two coders in their assessment of type were resolved through peer discussion of criteria and the meaning of various statements by respondents. Occasionally, we used a third coder to add another perspective where there were differences that remained after discussion by the two primary coders. We found that the sample was primarily transitional (N = 28 or 56 percent of the social workers and N = 29 or 58 percent of the doctors); there were nine traditional social workers (18 percent) and 11 traditional physicians (22 percent) with similar numbers of transformational social workers (11 or 22 percent) and transformational physicians (12 or 24 percent) (Abramson and Mizrahi 2003).

Once we classified our respondents by type, we did quantitative analyses using chi-square tests to identify the variables that might be associated with type of collaborator for each profession. Since this is an exploratory and qualitative study, we selected a significance level of less than 0.10 to capture trends in the data. Background of the participants (gender, education, specialty, level of experience) was not a significant factor as related to type with the critical exception that most BSW social workers in the sample were classified as traditional. Type did have a major impact on the ratings of satisfaction with collaborators; both traditional doctors and traditional social workers were the least satisfied with their collaborator, while social workers were less satisfied with their collaborator than doctors, no matter their type. Perhaps most significantly, both groups were least transformational in regard to the dimension of control over decision-making (see Abramson and Mizrahi 2003 for complete findings).

Since all typologies are gross means of classifying complex data, we soon discovered that about 20 of the 100 respondents were not consistent by type across all five dimensions; we labeled them "straddlers." Harris (2006:145) comments that a dimension—in our case, a typology—is a "framework to guide and inform rather than determine or force." However, we felt that it was legitimate to assign straddlers to one of the three types for purposes of analysis by giving extra weight to the dimensions of teamwork and control over decision-making, based on their importance to the collaborative process.

The Intellectual and Professional Underpinnings of the Typology

As we began our research, we realized that we had specific but not fully articulated assumptions about the roles and relationships of physicians

and social workers. One critical influence on our thinking was the literature on professional socialization processes (Fox 1957; Bucher and Stelling
1977; Huntington 1981; Clark 1997), in particular, Mizrahi's ethnographic
study (1986) of the ways in which neophyte physicians in internal medicine
learned their attitudes and behaviors toward patients and other professionals. Based on this literature, and on Abramson's extensive clinical experience in collaborating with physicians in hospital settings, we presumed
that physicians had limited interest in the psychosocial needs of patients
(Eisenthal, Stoeckle, and Ehrlich 1994), minimal understanding of the contributions of social workers, and an aversion to teamwork. We attributed
these views to the norm of self-reliance and professional autonomy found
in the structure and culture of medical training (Freidson 1984; Mizrahi
1986; Abbott 1988).

This understanding of the experiences and socialization of physicians
led us in our early work to articulate the different perspectives between the
two professions as sources of strain (Mizrahi and Abramson 1985); we subsequently developed collaboration strategies for social workers based on an
understanding of these differences, particularly with regard to power. We
conceptualized the collaborative relationship as one where social workers
served as a resource to the physicians, negotiating their influence based
on their contribution of resources and other valued competencies, while
accepting (grudgingly or not) greater physician power and professional authority over patient care (Abramson and Mizrahi 1986).

It was only as the typology began to emerge from our data that we recognized, with hindsight, our assumption that a typical collaborative relationship involved a traditional physician and a transitional social worker.
Given this configuration, it then makes sense that strains would be evident
between them (Mizrahi and Abramson 1985). Therefore, the development
of the typology helped us to locate our prior work on a continuum of social
work/physician relationships.

Given our prior assumptions, we did not anticipate the range of social work responses we encountered; for example, in developing the dimensions, we began to realize that, based on their narrowly defined role
and their deferential interaction with physicians, there was a group of
"traditional" social workers. We were also surprised to discover some social workers who were "transformational" in that they assumed and often
achieved equal status with their physician partners. Grounded theory in-
sists that researchers be open to all possibilities, so we cast aside our prior

assumptions to explore the meaning of our findings. We had expected that professional "autonomy"—being able to act independently of the physician—was the sought after goal and "the highest" achievement for a social worker. The literature and practitioners had portrayed social workers in health care as being engaged in a struggle for autonomy (Livingston, Davidson, and Marshak 1989). Instead, we uncovered transformational social workers who seemed to value interdependence and reciprocity with their physician collaborators (or the team) as they jointly cared for patients. We also found that most physicians in the sample were or had become transitional rather than traditional, as we had anticipated, particularly as they described their positive collaborative experiences (Abramson and Mizrahi 1996). And even more surprising was the emergence of the transformational physician and a model of a transformational collaborative relationship with a social worker.

Trustworthiness and Credibility

Concerns about the trustworthiness of qualitative data often relate to bias that can arise from characteristics of the respondents and the sample or methodological choices; assumptions brought to the research by the investigator(s) can also be a significant source of bias (Padgett 2008). Since all subjects knew we were social work professors, we assume that some respondents may have reacted to our status with distortion or bias in their responses. They may have omitted or minimized negative feelings or interactions, as evidenced by the large number of physicians who spontaneously expressed their views that social workers should be treated as equals. Some physicians may not have wanted to offend us; conversely, some social workers may have wanted to impress us with a greater sense of their competence or their success as collaborators than actually existed. Because social workers selected the physicians in the sample, it is possible they had a selection bias toward those with whom the collaboration was positive.

We think bias was mitigated in several ways. Social workers were asked to select the case rather than the collaborator; in discussions with them regarding selection of cases, we both concluded that case complexity rather than quality of collaboration was the major factor in selecting cases and thus the physicians. The cases were so memorable that neither busy social workers nor physicians had any difficulty recalling details. Conscious bias or distortion on the part of physicians may have been moderated by the fact that they knew we had already received information from the social worker about them, their collaborative relationship with the social worker, and their performance. Moreover, several cases provided by the social workers were examples of negative collaboration, at least from their perspective, and indeed in many instances, the physicians concurred. Additionally, we asked both groups to provide negative as well as positive examples of collaborative experiences which they did (Abramson and Mizrahi 1996); Padgett (2008) refers to this as enhancing rigor. In this instance, reviewing these negative cases allowed us to refine and expand our concepts and have a measure of confidence in them, increasing trustworthiness of our data (Padgett 2008). They were also asked to be reflective about what they as well as their collaborator could have done differently, and almost all were able to be self-critical. As a result of this careful review, we do not believe that the subjects tried to make themselves or their collaborators more acceptable in our eyes.

Although inductive theory building appropriately begins with a "few assumptions and broad orienting concepts" (Kreuger and Newman 2006:64), theory is built directly from what the study participants have to say (Morse 2004); such an approach is grounded in their reality and therefore is less likely to be undermined by researcher bias. In fact, we discussed earlier some of the ways that encountering aspects of the data made us examine our prior or sometimes unacknowledged assumptions.

Nevertheless, while the collaborative typology did emerge from the perceptions of both social workers and doctors, it is important to recognize that we brought a social work perspective to its discovery and interpretation. Physician researchers might have perceived other dimensions of, or differently interpreted, the data. There certainly were instances during the early interview stage as well as in peer debriefings (Padgett, Mathew, and Conte 2004) when one of the researchers confessed a dislike for or disbelief in the statement a physician was making, or expressed disappointment in the paucity of a social worker's response. Conversely, admiration was expressed for those physicians who were more positively disposed toward social workers as well as for social workers who stood their ground with highly experienced and high status physicians. The concept of reflexivity (Padgett 2008)—that is, how much we recognized and articulated these feelings—helped minimize the imposition of our bias going forward in the interview process. Thus our efforts at self-awareness and our process of peer accountably allow some measure of confidence that personal feelings were effectively managed in the interpretation of the data. Yet, there is no doubt that our status as social workers, social work educators, and social work researchers had an impact on our study design and analysis of data.

Reflections on Constructing and Utilizing a Typology

We built our typology inductively—what Patton (1980:309) calls an "analyst constructed typology"—in that we looked for patterns and themes in the data that were not necessarily in the participants' vocabulary, yet were generated from their comments. A typology is innately an artificial and static construct that cannot completely reflect the range of individual responses (Szasz and Hollender 1956; Kvist 2006). For this reason, and because of the rapidly changing world of health care, we wondered about the usefulness and relevance of the typology. However, we realized that this typology/all typologies need to be viewed as dynamic and possibly directional constructs. Certainly the complexities we uncovered with respect to "straddlers" who varied by type across different dimensions, and the fact that some social workers and physicians reported collaborative behavior representative of different types at different times in their careers or in different situations raises questions. We began to see an evolutional aspect to the typology, for both professions as a whole and for individual physicians and social workers. Reflecting back on our preresearch assumptions of a traditional doctor and transitional social worker, it may be that the model of physician-social worker collaboration has fundamentally shifted to the transitional type. And at the individual level, physicians and social workers might "progress" from one type to another across the continuum unidirectionally toward the transformative type, although not necessarily in linear or consistent progression across all dimensions uniformly.

We also realized that we presumed a "preferred" direction or continuum (Smith and Sparkes 2008) from traditional to transformational as beneficial for both the health care system as a whole and for the professionals engaged in collaboration. This presumption was, in fact, supported by our finding that traditional collaborators were least satisfied with collaboration (Mizrahi and Abramson 2000). We anticipate that many physicians will evolve toward more transformational attitudes and behavior as the pressures of the practice environment and the nature of the management of a patient population with increasing chronic diseases moves them in that direction (Callister 2001). We did find many physicians who described themselves as changing over time in their collaborative behavior and attitudes, as they increasingly recognized the personal and patient benefits of shared responsibility for complex patient care situations. However, we expect that the dimension of control over decision-making will be the last dimension to shift from traditional to transitional and ultimately transformational.

The shift for social workers is even more complex. We question whether or not it is possible for social workers to be transformational collaborators, given the power and status differential between themselves and physicians, unless they are collaborating with a transformational physician (Abramson and Mizrahi 2003). At this point in time, social workers (at least in hospitals) are likely to continue to work with all types of physicians and so must retain the capacity to respond differentially and strategically to various settings and collaborators. When social workers are confronting pressures to function in more "traditional" ways, conceptual clarity about the professional aspects of their role will also assist them to more effectively assert their professional perspective. And if they are inherently collaborators in the transformational mode, they will need the confidence and competence to teach physicians who are traditional and transitional to learn a transformational collaborative style, at least with them.

Since this original chapter was written in the mid-1990s, both authors have had multiple opportunities to present the typology and related findings to social work and interdisciplinary audiences of health care professionals in hospital settings, a less direct form of member checking (i.e., going back to the subjects and inviting their responses and interpretation of the findings; Padgett 2008). The framework has overwhelmingly resonated with them; indeed, they were able to type themselves and to identify physicians who fit each of the three types. As we reflect on these encounters and on our findings, it is clear that the social work community has moved in conceptualization, if not always in behavior, toward an expectation of a transformative relationship. However, we need to test out the typology with physician groups as well to see if their practice reality also includes evidence of a shift toward a transformational collaborative stance. Such contacts can help us to determine if our concern about our social work bias is borne out.

Conclusion

We have presented the background, methodology, and theoretical findings of a grounded theory-based data analysis that led to the development of a tripartite typology of physician-social worker collaboration. This typology characterizes collaborative styles as traditional, transitional, or transformational. It can provide a conceptual framework for understanding collaboration between social workers and physicians. It can also assist practitioners in developing collaborative strategies based on assessment of their own and others' collaborative style or type. Additionally, it can increase awareness of the importance of collaborative skill development to successful practice in health care settings and thus influence curricula in schools of social work and medicine. Finally, it provides a useful mechanism for educating students about the collaborative process within each profession and in interprofessional education programs.

Further research is needed to see if the typology is applicable to other physician specialties as well as to physicians and social workers in nonhospital settings. Studying specialties such as family medicine and pediatrics that stress psychosocial factors to a greater extent may reveal more extensive transformational collaborative behavior. In a more recent study of social work roles in neighborhood health centers (Rizzo, Mizrahi, and Kirkland 2005), most physicians—as well as center administrators—provided rich descriptions of a broad and complex social work role, which seems to validate our belief that transformational social workers may be becoming more the norm, at least in those settings. The impact of professional status differences could be further explored by examining collaboration between social workers and professionals closer in status such as teachers or nurses (Campbell-Heider and Pollack 1987; Schmitt 1994).

We have tried to reflect on the evolution of our typology as "self-consciously" and deliberately as possible. However, we acknowledge the ultimate subjectivity of any such process. We recognize that many interactive elements have contributed to the development of the typology and thus cannot be adequately communicated in the linear fashion necessary for a written analysis. The typology has proved useful to both social workers and physicians and can be adapted easily to changing circumstances in health care. Ultimately, the measure of its value as the sum of our grounded theory analysis is the extent to which knowledge acquired about effective social work/physician collaboration improves patient care by strengthening team functioning and interdisciplinary decision-making.

Appendix 21.1 Traditional, Transitional, and Transformational Models of Social Work/Physician Collaboration

Type: Traditional Perspectives

Dimensions	Physicians	Social Workers
Psychosocial (PS) Aspects of Care	• Sees PS as optional or a necessary evil • Views PS as outside MD jurisdiction • Limits understanding of total patient • Gives priority to hospital's administrative and financial concerns	• Recognizes importance but not addressed • Accepts or alternatively is frustrated with MD's limited focus • Gives priority to hospital's administrative and financial concerns
Definition of the Social Work Role	• Limits to discharge/disposition • Blames SW for system obstacles • Does not understand or accept SW counseling role • Emphasizes outcome over process	• Limits to discharge planning/disposition; does not include clinical aspects • Minimizes patient/family involvement • Emphasizes outcome over process
Communication	• Keeps to minimum • Resents requests for on-going communication • Avoids or limits to one way from (MD to SW) • Resists meeting with patient, family, and SW	• Keeps to minimum • Stays with MD agenda • Communicates narrow SW role • Limits chart notes
Teamwork	• Views contact with other professions as a necessary evil • Functions independently • Resists participation in meetings • Views non-MDs in a hierarchical/nonreciprocal manner	• Uses information from other professionals for assessment • Participates in team • Views role as subordinate to MD's • May provide limited leadership
Control over Decision-Making	• Owns patient and controls decisions • Resents regulatory or other intrusions into MD autonomy • Rejects independent SW case finding • Grants SW autonomy or responsibility in areas where	• Accepts MD control of patient care • Limits independent assessment • Accepts MD definition of problems • Functions independently in those areas where

Dimensions	Physicians	Social Workers
Psychosocial (PS) Aspects of Care	• Recognizes but rarely addresses PS issues • Appreciates that SW handles PS aspects of care	• Gives priority to hospital's administrative and financial concerns • Assesses psychosocial complexities, but limits counseling intervention
Definition of the Social Work Role	• Emphasizes discharge planning as primary • Refers for SW assessment • Emphasizes counseling more if part of team • Blames SW for system obstacles	• Emphasizes discharge planning, but may vary role depending on service • Separates counseling and provision of concrete services • Reframes role for MD priorities
Communication	• Makes referrals • Requests information • May share psychosocial information to assist SW assessment • Focuses communication on MD concerns • Attends meetings with patients, family, and SW, sometimes reluctantly	• Communicates about discharge planning on chart or in person • Shares some psychosocial information • Omits information on process of activities • Educates actively or withholds information, depending on MD receptivity
Teamwork	• Views MD as team leader • Values others' contribution to care • Has hierarchical view of relationships with other professionals • Respects skills of other professionals • Cooperates in interest of efficiency and outcome	• Actively participates as team member • May provide situational leadership • Communicates with other professions (e.g., RN) in addition to or in lieu of MD
Control of Decision-Making	• Assumes role of team leader • Makes decisions with consultation from others • May delegate decision when others are viewed as expert and competent	• Accepts MD authority • Practices independently in areas of SW expertise • Provides consultation to MD and other professions

Type: Transformational Perspectives

Dimensions	Physicians	Social Workers
Psychosocial (PS) Aspects of Care	• Integrates PS aspects into own role and view of patient care • Views PS as pivotal to medical care • Shares responsibility with SW • Seeks and shares PS information with SW • Sees therapeutic value of PS component	• Emphasizes clinical aspects of patient care • Educates and involves MD on PS issues • Actively involves patient/family in decision making • Shares PS responsibility with MD
Definition of Social Work Role	• Involves SW for broad range of psychosocial tasks with patients and families • Accepts SW role in dealing with adjustment to illness and mental health assessment • Refers private patients for SW treatment • Does not blame social worker for system obstacles • Understands complexities of SW assessment and intervention	• Defines discharge planning role broadly • Integrates clinical and concrete service provision functions • Emphasizes adjustment to illness in working with patients and families
Communication	• Actively communicates • Seeks psychosocial information and SW assessment • Initiates and willingly attends meetings with social worker, patient, and family	• Actively communicates • Regularly provides PS information and assessment • Actively educates MDs and others
Teamwork	• Contributes actively to team • Sees team as responsible for patient care • Shares responsibilities • Functions interdependently • Assumes egalitarian, non-hierarchical/reciprocal relationships	• Contributes actively to team • Provides leadership on patient care and team process • Shares responsibilities • Functions interdependently • Assumes egalitarian, non-hierarchical/reciprocal relationships
Control of Decision-Making	• Shares ownership of patient with other professionals • Makes decisions jointly	• Shares responsibility • Stresses competence • Makes decisions jointly

References

Abbott, A. 1988. *The system of professions: An essay on the division of expert labor.* Chicago: U of Chicago P.

Abdellah, F. G. 1997. Managing the challenges of role diversification in an interdisciplinary environment. *Military Medicine, 162*(7):453–458.

Abramson, J. S. and L. Bronstein. 2004. Group process dynamics and skills in interdisciplinary Teamwork. In *Group work handbook*, C. Garvin, L. Gutierrez and M. Galinsky, eds. 384–399. NY: Guilford.

Abramson, J. S. and T. Mizrahi. 1986. Strategies for enhancing collaboration between social workers and physicians. *Social Work in Health Care, 12*(1):1–21.

——. 1994. Examining social work/physician collaboration: An application of grounded theory methods. In *Qualitative studies in social work research*, C. Riessman, ed. 28–47. Thousand Oaks, CA: Sage.

——. 1996. When social workers and physicians collaborate: Positive and negative interdisciplinary experiences. *Social Work, 41*:270–283.

——. 2003. Understanding collaboration between social workers and physicians: Application of a typology. *Social Work in Health Care, 37*(2):71–100.

Aldred-Crouch, M., S. Hickman, B. Kent, and E. Randall. 2010. The health-mental health connection: Integrated behavioral health collaborative care. *NASW Health Section Connection, 1*:3–5.

Aronoff, N. 2008. Interprofessional partnered practice. In *Encyclopedia of social work*, 20th ed., T. Mizrahi and L. David, eds. 533–536. Washington, DC: NASW.

Badger, L.W., B. Ackerson, F. Buttell, and E. H. Rand. 1997. The case for integration of social work psychosocial services into rural primary care practice. *Health and Social Work, 22*(1):20–29.

Barker, K. K. and I. Oandasan. 2005. Interprofessional care review with medical residents: Lessons learned, tensions aired—A pilot study. *Journal of Interprofessional Care, 19*(3):207–214.

Barlett, D. L. and J. B. Steele. 2004. *How health care in America became big business and bad medicine.* New York: Doubleday.

Barnes, D., J. Carpenter, and C. Dickinson. 2000. Interprofessional education for community mental health: Attitudes to community care and professional stereotypes. *Journal of Social Work Education, 19*(6):565–583.

Bayne-Smith, M., T. Mizrahi, and M. L. Garcia. 2008. Interdisciplinary community collaboration (ICC): Perspectives of community practitioners on successful strategies. *Journal of Community Practice, 16*(3):249–269.

Berger, C. S., C. Robbins, M. Lewis, T. Mizrahi, and S. Fleit. 2003. The impact of organizational change on social work staffing in a hospital setting: A national longitudinal study of social work in hospitals. *Social Work in Health Care,* 37(1):1–18.

Boswell, C. and S. Cannon. 2005. New horizons for collaborative partnerships. *Online Journal of Issues in Nursing,* 10(1):75–80.

Bucher, R. and J. Stelling. 1977. *Becoming professional.* Beverly Hills CA: Sage.

Callister, R. R. 2001. Conflict across organizational boundaries: Managed care organizations versus health care providers. *Journal of Applied Psychology,* 86(4): 754–755.

Campbell-Heider, N. and D. Pollack. 1987. Barriers to physician/nurse collegiality: An anthropological perspective. *Social Science and Medicine,* 25(5):421–425.

Carrigan, Z. 1978. Social workers in medical settings: Who defines us? *Social Work in Health Care,* 4(2):149–164.

Charmaz, K. 1990. Discovering chronic illness: Using grounded theory. *Social Science and Medicine,* 30(11):1161–1172.

Chesluk, B. and E. S. Holmboe. 2010. How teams work—or don't—in primary care: A field study on internal medicine practices. *Health Affairs,* 29(5):874–879.

Clark, P. G. 1997. Values in health care professional socialization: Implications for geriatric education in interdisciplinary teams. *The Gerontologist,* 37,441–451.

Cochrane Review. 2003. Interprofessional education: Effects on professional practice and health care outcomes. *Journal of Continuing Education in the Health Professions,* 23(2):124–125.

Coddington, D. C., E. A.Fischer, K. D. Moore, and R. L. Clarke. 2000. *Beyond managed care: How consumers and technology are changing the future of health care.* San Francisco: Jossey-Bass.

Coombs, M. and J. Ersser. 2004. Medical hegemony in decision-making—A barrier to interdisciplinary working in intensive care. *Journal of Advanced Nursing,* 46(3):245–252.

Couturier, Y., D. Gagnon, S. Carrier, and F. Ethridge. 2008. The interdisciplinary condition of work in relational professions of the health and social care field: A theoretical standpoint. *Journal of Interprofessional Care,* 22(4):341–351.

Corbin, J. M. and A. L. Strauss. 2008. *Basics of qualitative research: Techniques and procedures for developing grounded theory,* 3rd ed. Thousand Oaks, CA: Sage.

Cowles, L. and M. Lefcowitz. 1992. Interdisciplinary expectations of the medical social worker in the hospital setting. *Health and Social Work,* 17(1):58–65.

——. 1995. Interdisciplinary expectations of the medical social worker in the hospital setting: Part 2. *Health and Social Work,* 20(4):279–287.

D'Amour, D., M. Ferrada-Videla, L. San Martin-Rodriguez, and M. D. Beaulieu. 2005. The conceptual basis for interprofessional collaboration: Core concepts and theoretical frameworks. *Journal of Interprofessional Care. Supplement 1,* 19:116–131.

Davis, C., B. Milosevic, E. Baldry, and A. Walsh. 2005. Defining the role of the hospital social worker in Australia: Part 2. A qualitative approach. *International Social Work, 48*(3):289– 299.

Decoster, V. A. and M. Egan. 2001. Physicians' perceptions and responses to patient emotion: Implications for social work practice in health care. *Social Work in Health Care, 32*(3):21–40.

Dranove, D. 2000. *The economic evolution of American health care: From Marcus Welby to managed care.* Princeton, NJ: Princeton University.

Dubus, N. 2010. Who cares for the caregivers? Why medical social workers belong on end-of-life care teams. *Social Work in Health Care, 49*(7):603–617.

Dunevitz, B. 1997. Collaboration in a variety of ways creates health care value. *Nursing Economics, 15*(4):218–19.

Egan, M. and G. Kadushin. 1997. Rural social work: Views of physicians and social workers. *Social Work and Health Care, 26*(1):1–24.

Eisenthal, S., J. D. Stoeckle, and C. M. Ehrlich. 1994. Orientation of medical residents to the psychosocial aspects of primary care: Influence of training program. *Academic Medicine, 69*(1):48–54.

Fort Cowles, L. A. 2003. *Social work in the health field: A care perspective*, 2nd ed. Binghamton, NY: Haworth.

Fox, R. C. 1957. Training for uncertainty. In *The Student Physician*, R. Merton, G. G. Reader, and P. L. Kendal, eds. 207–243. Cambridge, MA: Harvard UP.

Franks, P., G. C. Williams, J. Zwanziger, C. Mooney, and M. Sorbero. 2000. Why do physicians vary so widely in their referral rates? *Journal of General Internal Medicine, 15*(3):163–168.

Freidson, E. 1984. The changing nature of professional control. *Annual Review of Sociology, 10*:1–20.

——. 2001. *Professionalism: The third logic.* Chicago: University of Chicago.

Gair, G. and T. Hartery. 2001. Medical dominance in multidisciplinary teamwork: A case study of discharge decision-making in a geriatric assessment unit. *Journal of Nursing Management, 9*(1):3–11.

Glaser, B. and A. Strauss. 1967. *The discovery of grounded theory.* Chicago: Aldine.

Gleason, M. S., J. Farness, A. Schneider, N. L. Wilson, and V. Fay. 1998. Structuring the GITT clinical experience. In *Geriatric interdisciplinary team training*, E. L. Siegler, K. Hyer, T. Fulmer, and M. Mezey, eds. 99–114. New York: Springer.

Hafferty, F. 2003. Review symposium on Eliot Freidson's *Professionalism: The third logic. Journal of Health Politics, Policy and Law, 28*(1):133–158.

Harr, C., L. Souza, and S. Fairchild. 2008. International models of hospital interdisciplinary teams for the identification, assessment and treatment of child abuse. *Social Work in Health Care, 46*(4):1–16.

Harris, E. L. 2006. Mary Douglas's typology of grid and group. In *Theoretical frameworks in qualitative research*, V. A. Anafra and N. T. Mertz, eds 129–154. Thousand Oaks, CA: Sage.

Hinton Walker, P. and K. Elberson. 2005. Collaboration: Leadership in a global technological environment. *Online Journal of Issues in Nursing, 10*(1):103–112.

Humble, A. M. 2009. Technique triangulation for validation in directed content analysis. *International Journal of Qualitative Methods, 8*(3):34–51.

Huntington, J. 1981. *Social work and general medical practice: Collaboration or conflict.* London: George Allen UP.

Irvine, R., I. Kerridge, J. McPhee, and S. Freeman. 2002. Interprofessionalism and ethics: Consensus or class of cultures? *Journal of Interprofessional Care, 16*(3):199–210.

Ivery, J. 2008. Policy mandated collaboration. *Journal of Sociology and Social Welfare, 35*(4):53–70.

Keefe, B., S. M. Geron, and S. Enguidanos. 2009. Integrating social workers into primary care: Physician and nurse perceptions of roles, benefits, and challenges. *Social Work in Health Care, 48*(6):579–596.

Keigher, S. M. 1997. What role for social work in the new health care practice paradigm? *Health and Social Work, 22*(4):479–484.

Kerson, T. S. and J. L. M. McCoyd and Associates 2010. *Social work in health settings: Practice in context,* 4th ed. New York: Routledge.

Kitchen, A. and J. Brook. 2005. Social work at the heart of the medical team. *Social Work in Health Care, 40*(4):1–18.

Kvist, J. 2006. Diversity, ideal types and fuzzy sets in comparative welfare states. In *Innovative comparative methods for policy analysis: Beyond the quantitative qualitative divide,* B. Rihoux and H. Grimm, eds.167–184. New York: Springer Science.

Kongstvedt, P. R. 2007. *Essentials of managed health care,* 5th ed. Ontario: Jones and Bartlett.

Korazim-Korosy, Y., T. Mizrahi, C. Katz, A. Karmon, M. Bayne-Smith, and M. L. Garcia. 2007. Toward interdisciplinarity in community development: Comparing knowledge and experience from Israel and the USA. *Journal of Community Practice, 15*(1/2):13–44.

Kreuger, L.W. and Newman, W. L. 2006. *Social work research methods: Qualitative and quantitative applications.* Boston: Allyn and Bacon.

Lasker, R.D. and E.S. Weiss. 2003. Creating partnership synergy: The critical role of community stakeholders. *Journal of Health and Human Services Administration* 26(1):119–139

Lasker, R. D., E. S. Weiss, and R. Miller. 2001. Partnership synergy: A practical framework for studying and strengthening the collaborative advantage. *The Milbank Quarterly, 79*(2):179–205.

Lawrence R., L. R. Jacobs, and T. Skocpol. 2010. *Health care reform and American politics: What everyone needs to know.* New York: Oxford UP.

Lee, S. D. and J. A. Alexander. 1999. Managing hospitals in turbulent times: Do organizational changes improve hospital survival? *Health Services Research,* 34(4):923–924.

Leipzig, R. M., K. Hyer, K. Ek, S. Wallenstein, M. L. Vezina, S. Fairchild, C. K. Cassel, and J. L. Howe. 2002. Attitudes toward working on interdisciplinary healthcare teams: A comparison by discipline. *Journal of the American Gerontological Society,* 50:1141–1148.

Lindeke, L. and A. Sieckert. 2005. Nurse-physician workplace collaboration. *Online Journal of Issues in Nursing,* 10(1):92–102.

Lister, L. 1980. Role expectations for social workers and other health care professionals. *Health and Social Work,* 5(2):41–49.

Livingston, D., K. Davidson, and E. Marshak. 1989. Education for autonomous practice: A challenge for field instructors. *Journal of Independent Social Work,* 4(1):69–82.

Lofland, J. and L. Lofland. 1995. *Analysing social settings.* Belmont, CA: Wadsworth.

Lown, N. 2000. Market health care: The commodification of health care. *Philosophy and Social Action,* 26(1–2):57–71.

Minkler, M., ed. 2005. *Community organizing and community building for health,* 2nd ed. New Brunswick, NJ: Rutgers UP.

Mizrahi, T. 1986. *Getting rid of patients: Contradictions in the socialization of physicians.* New Brunswick, NJ: Rutgers UP.

——. 1997. Health care: Policy development. In *Encyclopedia of social work,* 19th ed., *Supplement,* R. E. Edwards, ed. 133–142. Washington, DC: NASW.

Mizrahi, T. and J. S. Abramson. 1985. Sources of strain between physicians and social workers: Implications for social workers in health care settings. *Social Work in Health Care,* 10(3):33–51.

——. 1994. Collaboration between social workers and physicians: An emerging typology. In *Qualitative research in social work,* W. J. Reid and E. Sherman, eds. 135–151. New York: Columbia UP.

——. 2000. Social work and physician collaboration: Perspectives on a shared case. *Social Work in Health Care,* 31(3):1–24.

Mizrahi, T. and C. S. Berger. 2001. Leadership among social workers in health care: A longitudinal study of hospital social work directors over time. *Health and Social Work,* 30(2):155–165.

Mizrahi, T. and S. Gorin. 2008. Health care reform. In *Encyclopedia of social work,* 20th ed., T. Mizrahi and L. Davis, eds. 340–348. New York: NASW.

Mizrahi, T. and V. M. Rizzo. 2008. Perspectives on the roles and values of social work practice in neighborhood health centers. *Social Work in Public Health,* 23(6):99–125.

Molleman, E., M. Broekhuis, R. Stoffels, and F. Jaspers. 2010. Consequences of participating in multidisciplinary medical team meetings for surgical, nonsurgical and supporting specialties. *Medical Care Research and Review,* 67(2):173–193.

Morse, J. M. 2004. Constructing qualitatively derived theory: Concept construction and concept typologies. *Qualitative Health Research,* 14:1387–1395.

Murray, J. L., S. A. Wortman, and A. G. Swanson. 1992. A national interdisciplinary consortium of primary care organizations to promote the education of generalist specialists. *Academic Medicine,* 67:8–11.

Nauert, R. C. 2000. The new millennium: Health care evolution in the 21st century. *Journal of Health Care Finance,* 26(3):1–13.

Netting, E. F. and F. G. Williams. 1996. Case manager-physician collaboration: Implications for professional identity, roles and relationships. *Health and Social Work,* 21(3):216–224.

——. 1998. Can we prepare geriatric social workers to collaborate in primary care practices? *Journal of Social Work Education,* 34(2):195–209.

Oktay, J. S. 2004. Grounded theory. In *The qualitative research experience,* D. K. Padgett, ed. 23–47. Belmont, CA: Wadsworth Thomson.

Olsen, K. and M. Olsen. 1967. Role expectations and perceptions for social workers in medical settings. *Social Work,* 12:70–78.

Opie, A. 2000. *Thinking teams/thinking clients: Knowledge-based teamwork.* NY: Columbia UP.

Padgett, D. K. 1998. *Qualitative methods in social work research: Challenges and rewards.* Thousand Oaks, CA: Sage.

——. 2008. *Qualitative methods in social work research,* 2nd ed. Thousand Oaks, CA: Sage.

Padgett, D. K., R. Mathew, and S. Conte. 2004. Peer debriefing and support groups: Formation, care and maintenance. In *The qualitative research experience,* D. K. Padgett, ed. 229–239. Belmont, CA: Wadsworth Thomson.

Patton, M.Q. 1980. *Qualitative evaluation methods.* Newbury Park, CA: Sage.

Proenca, E. J. 2000. Community orientation in hospitals: An institutional and resource dependence perspective. *Health Services Research,* 35(5):210–218.

Raiwet, C., G. Halliwell, L. Andruski, and D. Wilson. 1997. Care maps across the continuum. *Canadian Nurse,* 93(1):26–30.

Redmond, H. 2001. The health care crisis in the United States: A call in action. *Health and Social Work,* 26(1):54–57.

Relman, A. S. 2007. Medical professionalism in a commercialized health care market. *JAMA,* 298:2668–2670.

Resnick, C. and E. G. Tighe. 1997. The role of multidisciplinary community clinics in managed care systems. *Social Work,* 42(1):91–98.

Reuben, D., L. Levy-Storms, M. N. Yee, M. Lee, K. Cole, M. Waite, L. Nichols, and J. C. Frank. 2004. Disciplinary split: A threat to geriatrics interdisciplinary team training. *Journal of the American Geriatrics Society, 52*(6):1000–1006.

Rizzo, V. M., T. Mizrahi, and K. Kirkland. 2005. Psychosocial problems in neighborhood health centers: Perspectives from health care providers. *Journal of Community Health, 30*(2):125–140.

Robertson, D. 2010. Multidisciplinary teams: Physician, nurse, social worker collaboration in primary care. Jrank medical encyclopedia. Accessed April 8, 2010. http://medicine.jrank.org/pages/1191/Multidisciplinary-Team.html.

Robinson, J. W. and D. L. Roter. 1999. Counseling by primary care physicians of patients who disclose psychosocial problems. *Journal of Family Practice, 48* (9):698–705.

Rock, B. and M. Cooper. 2000. Social work in primary care: A demonstration student unit utilizing practice research. *Social Work in Health Care, 31*(1):1–17.

San Martin-Rodriguez, L., M. D. Beaulieu, D. D'Amour, and M. Perrada-Videla. 2005. The determinants of successful collaboration: A review of theoretical and empirical studies. *Journal of Interprofessional Care, Supplement 1*:132–147.

Sargaent, J., E. Loney, and G. Murphy. 2008. Effective interprofessional teams: "Contact is not enough" to build a team. *Journal of Continuing Education in the Health Professions, 28*(4):228–234.

Schmitt, M. H. 1994. Focus on interprofessional practice, education, and research. *Journal of Interprofessional Care, 8*:9–18.

Shaw, I. 2003. Qualitative research and outcomes in health, social work and education. *Qualitative Research, 3*(1):57–77.

Shor, R. 2010. Interdisciplinary collaboration between social workers and dieticians in nutrition education programs for children-at-risk. *Social Work in Health Care, 49*:345–361.

Skochelak, S. and T. Jackson. 1992. An interdisciplinary clerkship model for teaching primary care. *Academic Medicine, 67*(10):639–641.

Smith, B. and A. C. Sparkes. 2008. Contrasting perspectives on narrating selves and identities: An invitation to dialogue. *Qualitative Research, 8*(1):5–35.

Steele, J. 2000. Leading the way with community health partnerships. *Healthcare Executive, 15*(2):20–25.

Stevens, R. A. 2001. Public roles for the medical profession in the United States: Beyond theories of decline and fall. *The Milbank Quarterly, 79*(3):327–353.

Strauss, A. 1987. *Qualitative analysis for social scientists.* Cambridge, UK: Cambridge UP.

Strauss, A. and J. Corbin. 1990. *Basics of qualitative research: Grounded theory procedures and techniques.* Newbury Park, CA: Sage.

Szasz, T. and M. Hollender. 1956. A contribution to the philosophy of medicine. *Archives of Internal Medicine*, 97:585–592.

Vandiver, V. L. 2008. Managed care. In *Encyclopedia of social work*, 20th ed., T. Mizrahi and L. Davis, eds. 144–148. New York: NASW.

Welton, W. E., T. A. Kantner, and S. M. Katz. 1997. Developing tomorrow's integrated community health systems: A leadership challenge for public health and primary care. *The Milbank Quarterly*, 75(2):261–288.

Wesson, J. S. 1997. Meeting the informational, psychosocial and emotional needs of each ICU patient and family. *Intensive Critical Care Nursing*, 13(2):111–118.

Xyrichis, A. and K. Lowton. 2008. What fosters or prevents interprofessional teamworking in primary and community care? A literature review. *International Journal of Nursing Studies*, 45:140–153.

Zimmerman, J. and H. Dabelko. 2007. Collaborative models of patient care: New opportunities for hospital social workers. *Social Work in Health Care*, 44(4):33–47.

Index

social globalization, 234n1
social groups, 83–84
Social justice value, NASW Code of Ethics, 39
social positioning, personal narratives, 177
social structures, situation, 198
social support, of parents with psychiatric disability, 406–407
social welfare evaluations. *See* qualitative program evaluation
social work and research: as advocacy function, 65; deconstructing epistemology, 65–68; ethics, explicitly maintaining, 14–15; overview, 64–65; reconsidering epistemology, 68–69
social workers. *See* physician/social worker collaboration study
social work knowledge, classifying, 329–333
Society for Social Work and Research (SSWR), 3, 349
socioeconomic status, 461–462. *See also* poverty
sociological research, explaining child neglect, 446
software, data analysis: ATLAS.ti program, 294, 296–297, 300; audio files, 291; Boolean queries, 295; choosing, 298–301; coding images with, 290–291; coding process, 293–294; Computer Assisted Qualitative Data Analysis project, 299; creating subsets of materials to focus analysis, 295; "drag and drop" coding, 294; getting started, 292–293; HyperRESEARCH, 300; identifying and visually portraying relationships within data, 295–296;

learning to use, 297–298; manuals, 300; MAXQDA, 300; memos and annotations, 293; multimedia analytic tools, 297; multimedia data, 289–291; multisite team qualitative research, 288–289; NVivo, 300; online resources, 301; organizing and analyzing text-based research, 286–287; output options and backing up work, 294; overview, 284–285; queries within coded materials, 295; raw data files, 292; search functions, 294; segmenting images with, 290–291; software-based qualitative analysis project, 292; video files, 291; Weitzman and Miles sourcebook, 299; what computer software does not do, 287–288; word counts and statistical functions, 296
South Africa (Women on Farms Project), 226
spiral process, action research, 217–220
spirituality, compared to religion, 74–75
SPMI (serious and persistent mental illness), 394
SSTA (Summer Study Tour to Africa), 223–225, 234n3
Stake, R., 342, 344, 349
stakeholders: identifying, situation analysis, 201; involving stakeholder groups in evaluation methods, 309; stakeholder-focused evaluability assessment, 335
standardized (structured) interviews, 244, 254, 316–317
standards, qualitative research, 26–28